Programming
Massively Parallel
Processors

Programming Massively Parallel Processors
A Hands-on Approach

Third Edition

David B. Kirk

Wen-mei W. Hwu

AMSTERDAM • BOSTON • HEIDELBERG • LONDON
NEW YORK • OXFORD • PARIS • SAN DIEGO
SAN FRANCISCO • SINGAPORE • SYDNEY • TOKYO

Morgan Kaufmann is an imprint of Elsevier

Morgan Kaufmann is an imprint of Elsevier
50 Hampshire Street, 5th Floor, Cambridge, MA 02139, United States

Notices
Knowledge and best practice in this field are constantly changing. As new research and
experience broaden our understanding, changes in research methods, professional practices,
or medical treatment may become necessary.

Practitioners and researchers must always rely on their own experience and knowledge
in evaluating and using any information, methods, compounds, or experiments described
herein. In using such information or methods they should be mindful of their own safety and
the safety of others, including parties for whom they have a professional responsibility.

To the fullest extent of the law, neither the Publisher nor the authors, contributors, or editors,
assume any liability for any injury and/or damage to persons or property as a matter of
products liability, negligence or otherwise, or from any use or operation of any methods,
products, instructions, or ideas contained in the material herein.

British Library Cataloguing-in-Publication Data
A catalogue record for this book is available from the British Library.

Library of Congress Cataloging-in-Publication Data
A catalog record for this book is available from the Library of Congress.

ISBN: 978-0-12-811986-0

For Information on all Morgan Kaufmann publications
visit our website at https://www.elsevier.com/

  Working together
to grow libraries in
developing countries

www.elsevier.com • www.bookaid.org

Publisher: Katey Birtcher
Acquisition Editor: Stephen Merken
Developmental Editor: Nate McFadden
Production Project Manager: Sujatha Thirugnana Sambandam
Cover Designer: Greg Harris

Typeset by MPS Limited, Chennai, India

To Caroline, Rose, Leo, Sabrina, Amanda, Bryan, and Carissa
For enduring our absence while working on the course and the book—once again!

Contents

Preface

We are proud to introduce to you the third edition of *Programming Massively Parallel Processors: A Hands-on Approach.*

Mass-market computing systems that combine multi-core CPUs and many-thread GPUs have brought terascale computing to laptops and petascale computing to clusters. Armed with such computing power, we are at the dawn of pervasive use of computational experiments for science, engineering, health, and business disciplines. Many will be able to achieve breakthroughs in their disciplines using computational experiments that are of unprecedented level of scale, accuracy, controllability and observability. This book provides a critical ingredient for the vision: teaching parallel programming to millions of graduate and undergraduate students so that computational thinking and parallel programming skills will be as pervasive as calculus.

Since the second edition came out in 2012, we have received numerous comments from our readers and instructors. Many told us about the existing features they value. Others gave us ideas about how we should expand its contents to make the book even more valuable. Furthermore, the hardware and software technology for heterogeneous parallel computing has advanced tremendously since then. In the hardware arena, two more generations of GPU computing architectures, Maxwell and Pascal, have been introduced since the first edition. In the software domain, CUDA 6.0 through CUDA 8.0 have allowed programmers to access the new hardware features of Maxwell and Pascal. New algorithms have also been developed. Accordingly, we added five new chapters and completely rewrote more than half of the existing chapters.

Broadly speaking, we aim for three major improvements in the third edition while preserving the most valued features of the first two editions. The improvements are (1) adding new Chapter 9, Parallel patterns—parallel histogram computation (histogram); Chapter 11, Parallel patterns: merge sort (merge sort); and Chapter 12, Parallel patterns: graph search (graph search) that introduce frequently used parallel algorithm patterns; (2) adding new Chapter 16, Application case study—machine learning on deep learning as an application case study; and (3) adding a chapter to clarify the evolution of advanced features of CUDA. These additions are designed to further enrich the learning experience of our readers.

As we made these improvements, we preserved the features of the previous editions that contributed to the book's popularity. First, we've kept the book as concise as possible. While it is tempting to keep adding material, we wanted to minimize the number of pages a reader needs to go through in order to learn all the key concepts. We accomplished this by moving some of the second edition chapters into appendices. Second, we have kept our explanations as intuitive as possible. While it is tempting to formalize some of the concepts, especially when we cover basic parallel algorithms, we have strived to keep all our explanations intuitive and practical.

TARGET AUDIENCE

The target audience of this book are the many graduate and undergraduate students from all science and engineering disciplines where computational thinking and parallel programming skills are needed to achieve breakthroughs. We assume that the reader has at least some basic C programming experience. We especially target computational scientists in fields such as computational financing, data analytics, cognitive computing, mechanical engineering, civil engineering, electrical engineering, bio-engineering, physics, chemistry, astronomy, and geography, all of whom use computation to further their field of research. As such, these scientists are both experts in their domain as well as programmers. The book takes the approach of teaching parallel programming by building up an intuitive understanding of the techniques. We use CUDA C, a parallel programming environment that is supported on NVIDIA GPUs. There are nearly 1 billion of these processors in the hands of consumers and professionals, and more than 4,00,000 programmers actively using CUDA. The applications that you develop as part of the learning experience will be used and run by a very large user community.

HOW TO USE THE BOOK

We would like to offer some of our experience in teaching courses with this book. Since 2006, we have taught multiple types of courses: in one-semester format and in one-week intensive format. The original ECE498AL course has become a permanent course known as ECE408 or CS483 of the University of Illinois at Urbana-Champaign. We started to write up some early chapters of this book when we offered ECE498AL the second time. The first four chapters were also tested in an MIT class taught by Nicolas Pinto in spring 2009. Since then, we have used the book for numerous offerings of ECE408 as well as the Coursera Heterogeneous Parallel Programming course, and the VSCSE and PUMPS summer schools.

A THREE-PHASED APPROACH

In ECE408, the lectures and programming assignments are balanced with each other and organized into three phases:

Phase 1: One lecture based on Chapter 2, Data parallel computing is dedicated to teaching the basic CUDA memory/threading model, the CUDA extensions to the C language, and the basic programming/debugging tools. After the lecture, students can write a simple vector addition code in a couple of hours. This is followed by a series of four-to-six lectures that give students the *conceptual* understanding of the CUDA memory model, the CUDA thread execution model, GPU hardware performance features, and modern computer system architecture. These lectures are based on Chapter 3, Scalable parallel execution; Chapter 4,

Memory and data locality; and Chapter 5, Performance considerations. The performance of their matrix multiplication codes increases by about 10 times through this period.

Phase 2: A series of lectures cover floating-point considerations in parallel computing and common data-parallel programming patterns needed to develop a high-performance parallel application. These lectures are based on Chapter 7, Parallel patterns: convolution; Chapter 8, Parallel patterns: prefix sum; Chapter 9, Parallel patterns—parallel histogram computation; Chapter 10, Parallel patterns: sparse matrix computation; Chapter 11, Parallel patterns: merge sort; and Chapter 12, Parallel patterns: graph search. The students complete assignments on convolution, vector reduction, prefix-sum, histogram, sparse matrix-vector multiplication, merge sort, and graph search through this period. We typically leave two or three of the more advanced patterns for a graduate level course.

Phase 3: Once the students have established solid CUDA programming skills, the remaining lectures cover application case studies, computational thinking, a broader range of parallel execution models, and parallel programming principles. These lectures are based on Chapter 13, CUDA dynamic parallelism; Chapter 14, Application case study—non-Cartesian magnetic resonance imaging; Chapter 15, Application case study—molecular visualization and analysis; Chapter 16, Application case study—machine learning; Chapter 17, Parallel programming and computational thinking; Chapter 18, Programming a heterogeneous computing cluster; Chapter 19, Parallel programing with OpenACC; and Chapter 20, More on CUDA and graphics processing unit computing. (The voice and video recordings of these lectures are available as part of the Illinois–NVIDIA GPU Teaching Kit.)

TYING IT ALL TOGETHER: THE FINAL PROJECT

While the lectures, labs, and chapters of this book help lay the intellectual foundation for the students, what brings the learning experience together is the final project, which is so important to the full-semester course that it is prominently positioned in the course and commands nearly 2 months' focus. It incorporates five innovative aspects: mentoring, workshop, clinic, final report, and symposium. (While much of the information about the final project is available in the Illinois–NVIDIA GPU Teaching Kit, we would like to offer the thinking that was behind the design of these aspects.)

Students are encouraged to base their final projects on problems that represent current challenges in the research community. To seed the process, the instructors should recruit several computational science research groups to propose problems and serve as mentors. The mentors are asked to contribute a one-to-two-page project specification sheet that briefly describes the significance of the application, what the mentor would like to accomplish with the student teams on the application, the technical skills (particular type of math, physics, and chemistry courses) required to understand and work on the application, and a list of Web and traditional resources that students can draw upon for technical background, general information, and building blocks, along with specific URLs or ftp paths to particular implementations and coding examples. These project specification sheets also provide students with learning experiences in defining their own research projects later in their careers. (Several examples are available in the Illinois–NVIDIA GPU Teaching Kit.)

Students are also encouraged to contact their potential mentors during their project selection process. Once the students and the mentors agree on a project, they enter into a collaborative relationship, featuring frequent consultation and project reporting. We, the instructors, attempt to facilitate the collaborative relationship between students and their mentors, making it a very valuable experience for both mentors and students.

The project workshop

The project workshop is the primary vehicle that enables the entire class to contribute to each other's final project ideas. We usually dedicate six of the lecture slots to project workshops. The workshops are designed for students' benefit. For example, if a student has identified a project, the workshop serves as a venue to present preliminary thinking, get feedback, and recruit teammates. If a student has not identified a project, he/she can simply attend the presentations, participate in the discussions, and join one of the project teams. Students are not graded during the workshops in order to keep the atmosphere nonthreatening and to enable them to focus on a meaningful dialog with the instructor(s), teaching assistants, and the rest of the class.

The workshop schedule is designed for the instructor(s) and teaching assistants to take some time to provide feedback to the project teams so that students can ask questions. Presentations are limited to 10 minutes to provide time for feedback and questions during the class period. This limits the class size to about 24 presenters, assuming 90-minute lecture slots. All presentations are pre-loaded into a PC in order to control the schedule strictly and maximize feedback time. Since not all students present at the workshop, we have been able to accommodate up to 50 students in each class, with extra workshop time available as needed. At the University of Illinois, the high demand for ECE408 has propelled the size of the classes significantly beyond the ideal size for project workshops. We will comment on this issue at the end of the section.

The instructor(s) and TAs must make a commitment to attend all the presentations and to give useful feedback. Students typically need most help in answering the following questions. First, are the projects too big or too small for the amount of time available? Second, is there existing work in the field that the project can benefit from? Third, are the computations being targeted for parallel execution appropriate for the CUDA programming model?

The design document

Once the students decide on a project and form a team, they are required to submit a design document for the project. This helps them to think through the project steps before they jump into it. The ability to do such planning will be important to their later career success. The design document should discuss the background and motivation for the project, application-level objectives and potential impact, main features of the end application, an overview of their design, an implementation plan, their performance goals, a verification plan and acceptance test, and a project schedule.

The teaching assistants hold a project clinic for final project teams during the week before the class symposium. This clinic helps ensure that students are on track and that they have identified the potential roadblocks early in the process. Student teams are asked to come to the clinic with an initial draft of the following three versions of their application: (1) The best CPU sequential code in terms of performance, preferably with AVX and other optimizations that establish a strong serial base of the code for their speedup comparisons and (2) The best CDUA parallel code in terms of performance. This version is the main output of the project. This version is used by the students to characterize the parallel algorithm overhead in terms of extra computations involved.

Student teams are asked to be prepared to discuss the key ideas used in each version of the code, any numerical stability issues, any comparison against previous results on the application, and the potential impact on the field if they achieve tremendous speedup. From our experience, the optimal schedule for the clinic is 1 week before the class symposium. An earlier time typically results in less mature projects and less meaningful sessions. A later time will not give students sufficient time to revise their projects according to the feedback.

The project report

Students are required to submit a project report on their team's key findings. We recommend a whole-day class symposium. During the symposium, students use presentation slots proportional to the size of the teams. During the presentation, the students highlight the best parts of their project report for the benefit of the whole class. The presentation accounts for a significant part of students' grades. Each student must answer questions directed to him/her as individuals so that different grades can be assigned to individuals in the same team. The symposium is an opportunity for students to learn to produce a concise presentation that motivates their peers to read a full paper. After their presentation, the students also submit a full report on their final project.

CLASS COMPETITION

In 2016, the enrollment level of ECE408 far exceeded the level that can be accommodated by the final project process. As a result, we moved from the final project to class competition. At the middle of the semester, we announce a competition challenge problem. We use one lecture to explain the competition challenge problem and the rules that will be used for ranking the teams. The students work in teams to solve the competition with their parallel solution. The final ranking of each team is determined by the execution time, correctness, and clarity of their parallel code. The students do a demo of their solution at the end of the semester and submit a final report. This is a compromise that preserves some of the benefits of final projects when the class size makes final projects infeasible.

ILLINOIS–NVIDIA GPU TEACHING KIT

The Illinois–NVIDIA GPU Teaching Kit is a publicly available resource that contains lecture, lab assignments, final project guidelines, and sample project specifications for instructors who use this book for their classes. While this book provides the intellectual contents for these classes, the additional material will be crucial in achieving the overall education goals. It can be accessed at http://syllabus.gputeachingkit.com/.

Finally, we encourage you to submit your feedback. We would like to hear from you if you have any ideas for improving this book. We would like to know how we can improve the supplementary on-line material. Finally, we would like to know what you liked about the book. We look forward to hearing from you.

ONLINE SUPPLEMENTS

The lab assignments, final project guidelines, and sample project specifications are available to instructors who use this book for their classes. While this book provides the intellectual contents for these classes, the additional material will be crucial in achieving the overall education goals. We would like to invite you to take advantage of the online material that accompanies this book, which is available at http://text-books.elsevier.com/9780128119860.

David B. Kirk and Wen-mei W. Hwu

Acknowledgements

There are so many people who have made special contributions to this third edition. First of all, we would like to thank the contributing authors of the new chapters: David Luebke, Mark Ebersole, Liwen Chang, Juan Gomez-Luna, Jie Lv, Izzat El Hajj, John Stone, Boris Ginsburg, Isaac Gelado, Jeff Larkin, and Mark Harris. Their names are listed in the chapters to which they made special contributions. Their expertise made a tremendous difference in the technical contents of this new edition. Without the contribution of these individuals, we would not have been able to cover the topics with the level of insight that we wanted to provide to our readers.

We would like to give special thanks to Izzat El Hajj, who tirelessly helped to verify the code examples and improved the quality of illustrations and exercises.

We would like to especially acknowledge Ian Buck, the father of CUDA and John Nickolls, the lead architect of Tesla GPU Computing Architecture. Their teams laid an excellent infrastructure for this course. John passed away while we were working on the second edition. We miss him dearly.

We would like to thank the NVIDIA reviewers Barton Fiske, Isaac Gelado, Javier Cabezas, Luke Durant, Boris Ginsburg, Branislav Kisacanin, Kartik Mankad, Alison Lowndes, Michael Wolfe, Jeff Larkin, Cliff Woolley, Joe Bungo, B. Bill Bean, Simon Green, Mark Harris, Nadeem Mohammad, Brent Oster, Peter Shirley, Eric Young, Urs Muller, and Cyril Zeller, all of whom provided valuable comments and corrections to the manuscript.

Our external reviewers spent numerous hours of their precious time to give us insightful feedback on the third edition: Bedrich Benes (Purdue University, West Lafayette, IN, United States); Kevin Farrell (Institute of Technology Blanchardstown, Dublin, Ireland); Lahouari Ghouti (King Fahd University of Petroleum and Minerals, Saudi Arabia); Marisa Gil, (Universitat Politecnica de Catalunya, Barcelona, Spain); Greg Peterson (The University of Tennessee-Knoxville, Knoxville, TN, United States); José L. Sánchez (University of Castilla-La Mancha, Real, Spain); and Jan Verschelde (University of Illinois at Chicago, Chicago, IL, United States). Their comments helped us to significantly improve the readability of the book.

Todd Green, Nate McFadden, and their staff at Elsevier worked tirelessly on this project.

We would like to especially thank Jensen Huang for providing a great amount of financial and human resources for developing the course that laid the foundation for this book.

We would like to acknowledge Dick Blahut, who challenged us to embark on the project. Beth Katsinas arranged a meeting between Dick Blahut and NVIDIA Vice President Dan Vivoli. Through that gathering, Blahut was introduced to David and challenged David to come to Illinois and create the original ECE498AL course with Wen-mei.

We would like to especially thank our colleagues who have taken the time to share their insight with us over the years: Kurt Akeley, Al Aho, Arvind, Dick Blahut, Randy Bryant, Bob Colwell, Bill Dally, Ed Davidson, Mike Flynn, John Hennessy, Pat Hanrahan, Nick Holonyak, Dick Karp, Kurt Keutzer, Dave Liu, Dave Kuck, Nacho Navarro, Yale Patt, David Patterson, Bob Rao, Burton Smith, Jim Smith, and Mateo Valero.

We are humbled by the generosity and enthusiasm of all the great people who contributed to the course and the book.

David B. Kirk and Wen-mei W. Hwu

Introduction

CHAPTER OUTLINE

Microprocessors based on a single central processing unit (CPU), such as those in the Intel Pentium family and the AMD Opteron family, drove rapid performance increases and cost reductions in computer applications for more than two decades. These microprocessors brought giga floating-point operations per second (GFLOPS, or Giga (10^9) Floating-Point Operations per Second), to the desktop and tera floating-point operations per second (TFLOPS, or Tera (10^{12}) Floating-Point Operations per Second) to datacenters. This relentless drive for performance improvement has allowed application software to provide more functionality, have better user interfaces, and generate more useful results. The users, in turn, demand even more improvements once they become accustomed to these improvements, creating a positive (virtuous) cycle for the computer industry.

This drive, however, has slowed since 2003 due to energy consumption and heat dissipation issues that limited the increase of the clock frequency and the level of productive activities that can be performed in each clock period within a single CPU. Since then, virtually all microprocessor vendors have switched to models where multiple processing units, referred to as processor cores, are used in each chip to increase the processing power. This switch has exerted a tremendous impact on the software developer community [Sutter 2005].

Traditionally, the vast majority of software applications are written as sequential programs that are executed by processors whose design was envisioned by von Neumann in his seminal report in 1945 [vonNeumann 1945]. The execution of these

Programming Massively Parallel Processors. DOI: http://dx.doi.org/10.1016/B978-0-12-811986-0.00001-7

programs can be understood by a human sequentially stepping through the code. Historically, most software developers have relied on the advances in hardware to increase the speed of their sequential applications under the hood; the same software simply runs faster as each new processor generation is introduced. Computer users have also become accustomed to the expectation that these programs run faster with each new generation of microprocessors. Such expectation is no longer valid from this day onward. A sequential program will only run on one of the processor cores, which will not become significantly faster from generation to generation. Without performance improvement, application developers will no longer be able to introduce new features and capabilities into their software as new microprocessors are introduced, reducing the growth opportunities of the entire computer industry.

Rather, the applications software that will continue to enjoy significant performance improvement with each new generation of microprocessors will be parallel programs, in which multiple threads of execution cooperate to complete the work faster. This new, dramatically escalated incentive for parallel program development has been referred to as the concurrency revolution [Sutter 2005]. The practice of parallel programming is by no means new. The high-performance computing community has been developing parallel programs for decades. These programs typically ran on large scale, expensive computers. Only a few elite applications could justify the use of these expensive computers, thus limiting the practice of parallel programming to a small number of application developers. Now that all new microprocessors are parallel computers, the number of applications that need to be developed as parallel programs has increased dramatically. There is now a great need for software developers to learn about parallel programming, which is the focus of this book.

1.1 HETEROGENEOUS PARALLEL COMPUTING

Since 2003, the semiconductor industry has settled on two main trajectories for designing microprocessors [Hwu 2008]. The *multicore* trajectory seeks to maintain the execution speed of sequential programs while moving into multiple cores. The multicores began with two-core processors with the number of cores increasing with each semiconductor process generation. A current exemplar is a recent *Intel* multicore microprocessor with up to 12 processor cores, each of which is an out-of-order, multiple instruction issue processor implementing the full X86 instruction set, supporting hyper-threading with two hardware threads, designed to maximize the execution speed of sequential programs. For more discussion of CPUs, see https://en.wikipedia.org/wiki/Central_processing_unit.

In contrast, the *many-thread* trajectory focuses more on the execution throughput of parallel applications. The many-threads began with a large number of threads and once again, the number of threads increases with each generation. A current exemplar is the NVIDIA Tesla P100 graphics processing unit (GPU) with 10s of 1000s of threads, executing in a large number of simple, in order pipelines. Many-thread processors, especially the GPUs, have led the race of floating-point performance since 2003. As of 2016, the ratio of peak floating-point calculation throughput between many-thread GPUs and multicore CPUs is about 10, and this ratio has been roughly constant for the past several years. These are not necessarily application speeds, but are merely the raw speed that the execution resources can potentially support in these chips. For more discussion of GPUs, see https://en.wikipedia.org/wiki/Graphics_processing_unit.

Such a large performance gap between parallel and sequential execution has amounted to a significant "electrical potential" build-up, and at some point, something will have to give. We have reached that point. To date, this large performance gap has already motivated many applications developers to move the computationally intensive parts of their software to GPU for execution. Not surprisingly, these computationally intensive parts are also the prime target of parallel programming—when there is more work to do, there is more opportunity to divide the work among cooperating parallel workers.

One might ask why there is such a large peak throughput gap between many-threaded GPUs and general-purpose multicore CPUs. The answer lies in the differences in the fundamental design philosophies between the two types of processors, as illustrated in Fig. 1.1. The design of a CPU is optimized for sequential code performance. It makes use of sophisticated control logic to allow instructions from a single thread to execute in parallel or even out of their sequential order while maintaining the appearance of sequential execution. More importantly, large cache memories are provided to reduce the instruction and data access latencies of large complex applications. Neither control logic nor cache memories contribute to the peak calculation throughput. As of 2016, the high-end general-purpose multicore microprocessors typically have eight or more large processor cores and many megabytes of on-chip cache memories designed to deliver strong sequential code performance.

Memory bandwidth is another important issue. The speed of many applications is limited by the rate at which data can be delivered from the memory system into the processors. Graphics chips have been operating at approximately 10x the memory bandwidth of contemporaneously available CPU chips. A GPU must be capable of moving extremely large amounts of data in and out of its main Dynamic Random

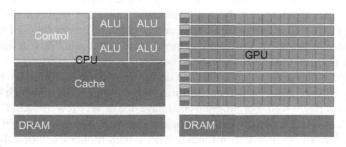

FIGURE 1.1

CPUs and GPUs have fundamentally different design philosophies.

Access Memory (DRAM) because of graphics frame buffer requirements. In contrast, general-purpose processors have to satisfy requirements from legacy operating systems, applications, and I/O devices that make memory bandwidth more difficult to increase. As a result, we expect that CPUs will continue to be at a disadvantage in terms of memory bandwidth for some time.

The design philosophy of the GPUs has been shaped by the fast growing video game industry that exerts tremendous economic pressure for the ability to perform a massive number of floating-point calculations per video frame in advanced games. This demand motivates GPU vendors to look for ways to maximize the chip area and power budget dedicated to floating-point calculations. An important observation is that reducing latency is much more expensive than increasing throughput in terms of power and chip area. Therefore, the prevailing solution is to optimize for the execution throughput of massive numbers of threads. The design saves chip area and power by allowing pipelined memory channels and arithmetic operations to have long-latency. The reduced area and power of the memory access hardware and arithmetic units allows the designers to have more of them on a chip and thus increase the total execution throughput.

The application software for these GPUs is expected to be written with a large number of parallel threads. The hardware takes advantage of the large number of threads to find work to do when some of them are waiting for long-latency memory accesses or arithmetic operations. Small cache memories are provided to help control the bandwidth requirements of these applications so that multiple threads that access the same memory data do not need to all go to the DRAM. This design style is commonly referred to as throughput-oriented design as it strives to maximize the total execution throughput of a large number of threads while allowing individual threads to take a potentially much longer time to execute.

The CPUs, on the other hand, are designed to minimize the execution latency of a single thread. Large last-level on-chip caches are designed to capture frequently accessed data and convert some of the long-latency memory accesses into short-latency cache accesses. The arithmetic units and operand data delivery logic are also designed to minimize the effective latency of operation at the cost of increased use of chip area and power. By reducing the latency of operations within the same thread, the CPU hardware reduces the execution latency of each individual thread. However, the large cache memory, low-latency arithmetic units, and sophisticated operand delivery logic consume chip area and power that could be otherwise used to provide more arithmetic execution units and memory access channels. This design style is commonly referred to as latency-oriented design.

It should be clear now that GPUs are designed as parallel, throughput-oriented computing engines and they will not perform well on some tasks on which CPUs are designed to perform well. For programs that have one or very few threads, CPUs with lower operation latencies can achieve much higher performance than GPUs. When a program has a large number of threads, GPUs with higher execution throughput can achieve much higher performance than CPUs. Therefore, one should expect that many applications use both CPUs and GPUs, executing the sequential parts on the

CPU and numerically intensive parts on the GPUs. This is why the CUDA programming model, introduced by NVIDIA in 2007, is designed to support joint CPU–GPU execution of an application.[1] The demand for supporting joint CPU–GPU execution is further reflected in more recent programming models such as OpenCL (Appendix A), OpenACC (see chapter: Parallel programming with OpenACC), and C++AMP (Appendix D).

It is also important to note that speed is not the only decision factor when application developers choose the processors for running their applications. Several other factors can be even more important. First and foremost, the processors of choice must have a very large presence in the market place, referred to as the *installed base* of the processor. The reason is very simple. The cost of software development is best justified by a very large customer population. Applications that run on a processor with a small market presence will not have a large customer base. This has been a major problem with traditional parallel computing systems that have negligible market presence compared to general-purpose microprocessors. Only a few elite applications funded by government and large corporations have been successfully developed on these traditional parallel computing systems. This has changed with many-thread GPUs. Due to their popularity in the PC market, GPUs have been sold by the hundreds of millions. Virtually all PCs have GPUs in them. There are nearly 1 billion CUDA enabled GPUs in use to date. Such a large market presence has made these GPUs economically attractive targets for application developers.

Another important decision factor is practical form factors and easy accessibility. Until 2006, parallel software applications usually ran on data center servers or departmental clusters. But such execution environments tend to limit the use of these applications. For example, in an application such as medical imaging, it is fine to publish a paper based on a 64-node cluster machine. However, real-world clinical applications on MRI machines utilize some combination of a PC and special hardware accelerators. The simple reason is that manufacturers such as GE and Siemens cannot sell MRIs with racks of computer server boxes into clinical settings, while this is common in academic departmental settings. In fact, NIH refused to fund parallel programming projects for some time; they felt that the impact of parallel software would be limited because huge cluster-based machines would not work in the clinical setting. Today, many companies ship MRI products with GPUs, and NIH funds research using GPU computing.

Yet another important consideration in selecting a processor for executing numeric computing applications is the level of support for IEEE Floating-Point Standard. The standard enables predictable results across processors from different vendors. While the support for the IEEE Floating-Point Standard was not strong in early GPUs, this has also changed for new generations of GPUs since 2006. As we will discuss in Chapter 6, Numerical considerations, GPU support for the IEEE Floating-Point Standard has become comparable with that of the CPUs. As a result, one can expect

---

[1] See Appendix A for more background on the evolution of GPU computing and the creation of CUDA.

that more numerical applications will be ported to GPUs and yield comparable result values as the CPUs. Up to 2009, a major barrier was that the GPU floating-point arithmetic units were primarily single precision. Applications that truly require double precision floating-point were not suitable for GPU execution. However, this has changed with the recent GPUs whose double precision execution speed approaches about half that of single precision, a level that only high-end CPU cores achieve. This makes the GPUs suitable for even more numerical applications. In addition, GPUs support Fused Multiply-Add, which reduces errors due to multiple rounding operations.

Until 2006, graphics chips were very difficult to use because programmers had to use the equivalent of graphics application programming interface (API) functions to access the processing units, meaning that OpenGL or Direct3D techniques were needed to program these chips. Stated more simply, a computation must be expressed as a function that paints a pixel in some way in order to execute on these early GPUs. This technique was called GPGPU, for General-Purpose Programming using a GPU. Even with a higher level programming environment, the underlying code still needs to fit into the APIs that are designed to paint pixels. These APIs limit the kinds of applications that one can actually write for early GPUs. Consequently, it did not become a widespread programming phenomenon. Nonetheless, this technology was sufficiently exciting to inspire some heroic efforts and excellent research results.

But everything changed in 2007 with the release of CUDA [NVIDIA 2007]. NVIDIA actually devoted silicon area to facilitate the ease of parallel programming, so this did not represent software changes alone; additional hardware was added to the chip. In the G80 and its successor chips for parallel computing, CUDA programs no longer go through the graphics interface at all. Instead, a new general-purpose parallel programming interface on the silicon chip serves the requests of CUDA programs. The general-purpose programming interface greatly expands the types of applications that one can easily develop for GPUs. Moreover, all the other software layers were redone as well, so that the programmers can use the familiar C/C++ programming tools. Some of our students tried to do their lab assignments using the old OpenGL-based programming interface, and their experience helped them to greatly appreciate the improvements that eliminated the need for using the graphics APIs for general-purpose computing applications.

1.2 ARCHITECTURE OF A MODERN GPU

Fig. 1.2 shows a high level view of the architecture of a typical CUDA-capable GPU. It is organized into an array of highly threaded streaming multiprocessors (SMs). In Fig. 1.2, two SMs form a building block. However, the number of SMs in a building block can vary from one generation to another. Also, in Fig. 1.2, each SM has a number of streaming processors (SPs) that share control logic and instruction cache. Each GPU currently comes with gigabytes of Graphics Double Data Rate (GDDR), Synchronous DRAM (SDRAM), referred to as Global Memory in Fig. 1.2. These

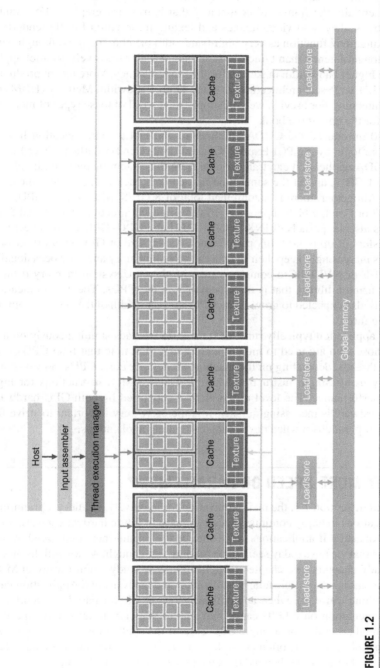

FIGURE 1.2

Architecture of a CUDA-capable GPU.

GDDR SDRAMs differ from the system DRAMs on the CPU motherboard in that they are essentially the frame buffer memory that is used for graphics. For graphics applications, they hold video images and texture information for 3D rendering. For computing, they function as very high-bandwidth off-chip memory, though with somewhat longer latency than typical system memory. For massively parallel applications, the higher bandwidth makes up for the longer latency. More recent products, such as NVIDIA's Pascal architecture, may use High-Bandwidth Memory (HBM) or HBM2 architecture. For brevity, we will simply refer to all of these types of memory as DRAM for the rest of the book.

The G80 introduced the CUDA architecture and had a communication link to the CPU core logic over a PCI-Express Generation 2 (Gen2) interface. Over PCI-E Gen2, a CUDA application can transfer data from the system memory to the global memory at 4 GB/S, and at the same time upload data back to the system memory at 4 GB/S. Altogether, there is a combined total of 8 GB/S. More recent GPUs use PCI-E Gen3 or Gen4, which supports 8–16 GB/s in each direction. The Pascal family of GPUs also supports NVLINK, a CPU–GPU and GPU–GPU interconnect that allows transfers of up to 40 GB/s per channel. As the size of GPU memory grows, applications increasingly keep their data in the global memory and only occasionally use the PCI-E or NVLINK to communicate with the CPU system memory if there is need for using a library that is only available on the CPUs. The communication bandwidth is also expected to grow as the CPU bus bandwidth of the system memory grows in the future.

A good application typically runs 5000 to 12,000 threads simultaneously on this chip. For those who are used to multithreading in CPUs, note that Intel CPUs support 2 or 4 threads, depending on the machine model, per core. CPUs, however, are increasingly using Single Instruction Multiple Data (SIMD) instructions for high numerical performance. The level of parallelism supported by both GPU hardware and CPU hardware is increasing quickly. It is therefore very important to strive for high levels of parallelism when developing computing applications.

1.3 WHY MORE SPEED OR PARALLELISM?

As we stated in Section 1.1, the main motivation for massively parallel programming is for applications to enjoy continued speed increase in future hardware generations. One might question if applications will continue to demand increased speed. Many applications that we have today seem to be running fast enough. As we will discuss in the case study chapters (see chapters: Application case study—non-Cartesian MRI, Application case study—molecular visualization and analysis, and Application case study—machine learning), when an application is suitable for parallel execution, a good implementation on a GPU can achieve more than 100 times (100x) speedup over sequential execution on a single CPU core. If the application contains what we call "data parallelism," it is often possible to achieve a 10x speedup with just a few hours of work. For anything beyond that, we invite you to keep reading!

Despite the myriad of computing applications in today's world, many exciting mass market applications of the future are what we previously consider "supercomputing applications," or super-applications. For example, the biology research community is moving more and more into the molecular-level. Microscopes, arguably the most important instrument in molecular biology, used to rely on optics or electronic instrumentation. But there are limitations to the molecular-level observations that we can make with these instruments. These limitations can be effectively addressed by incorporating a computational model to simulate the underlying molecular activities with boundary conditions set by traditional instrumentation. With simulation we can measure even more details and test more hypotheses than can ever be imagined with traditional instrumentation alone. These simulations will continue to benefit from the increasing computing speed in the foreseeable future in terms of the size of the biological system that can be modeled and the length of reaction time that can be simulated within a tolerable response time. These enhancements will have tremendous implications for science and medicine.

For applications such as video and audio coding and manipulation, consider our satisfaction with digital high-definition (HD) TV vs. older NTSC TV. Once we experience the level of details in an HDTV, it is very hard to go back to older technology. But consider all the processing needed for that HDTV. It is a very parallel process, as are 3D imaging and visualization. In the future, new functionalities such as view synthesis and high-resolution display of low resolution videos will demand more computing power in the TV. At the consumer level, we will begin to have an increasing number of video and image processing applications that improve the focus, lighting, and other key aspects of the pictures and videos.

User interfaces can also be improved by improved computing speeds. Modern smart phone users enjoy a more natural interface with high-resolution touch screens that rival that of large-screen televisions. Undoubtedly future versions of these devices will incorporate sensors and displays with three-dimensional perspectives, applications that combine virtual and physical space information for enhanced usability, and voice and computer vision-based interfaces, requiring even more computing speed.

Similar developments are underway in consumer electronic gaming. In the past, driving a car in a game was in fact simply a prearranged set of scenes. If the player's car collided with obstacles, the behavior of the car did not change to reflect the damage. Only the game score changes—and the score determines the winner. The car would drive the same—despite the fact that the wheels should be bent or damaged. With increased computing speed, the races can actually proceed according to simulation instead of approximate scores and scripted sequences. We can expect to see more of these realistic effects in the future: collisions will damage your wheels and the player's driving experience will be much more realistic. Realistic modeling and simulation of physics effects are known to demand very large amounts of computing power.

All the new applications that we mentioned involve simulating a physical, concurrent world in different ways and at different levels, with tremendous amounts of data being processed. In fact, the problem of handling massive amounts of data is so prevalent that the term "Big Data" has become a household phrase. And with this huge quantity of data, much of the computation can be done on different parts of the data in parallel, although they will have to be reconciled at some point. In most cases, effective management of data delivery can have a major impact on the achievable speed of a parallel application. While techniques for doing so are often well known to a few experts who work with such applications on a daily basis, the vast majority of application developers can benefit from more intuitive understanding and practical working knowledge of these techniques.

We aim to present the data management techniques in an intuitive way to application developers whose formal education may not be in computer science or computer engineering. We also aim to provide many practical code examples and hands-on exercises that help the reader to acquire working knowledge, which requires a practical programming model that facilitates parallel implementation and supports proper management of data delivery. CUDA offers such a programming model and has been well tested by a large developer community.

1.4 SPEEDING UP REAL APPLICATIONS

What kind of speedup can we expect from parallelizing an application? It depends on the portion of the application that can be parallelized. If the percentage of time spent in the part that can be parallelized is 30%, a 100X speedup of the parallel portion will reduce the execution time by no more than 29.7%. The speedup for the entire application will be only about 1.4X. In fact, even infinite amount of speedup in the parallel portion can only slash 30% off execution time, achieving no more than 1.43X speedup. The fact that the level of speedup one can achieve through parallel execution can be severely limited by the parallelizable portion of the application is referred to as Amdahl's Law. On the other hand, if 99% of the execution time is in the parallel portion, a 100X speedup of the parallel portion will reduce the application execution to 1.99% of the original time. This gives the entire application a 50X speedup. Therefore, it is very important that an application has the vast majority of its execution in the parallel portion for a massively parallel processor to effectively speed up its execution.

Researchers have achieved speedups of more than 100X for some applications. However, this is typically achieved only after extensive optimization and tuning after the algorithms have been enhanced so that more than 99.9% of the application execution time is in parallel execution. In practice, straightforward parallelization of applications often saturates the memory (DRAM) bandwidth, resulting in only about a 10X speedup. The trick is to figure out how to get around memory bandwidth limitations, which involves doing one of many transformations to utilize specialized GPU on-chip memories to drastically reduce the number of accesses to the DRAM. One must, however, further optimize the code to get around limitations such as limited on-chip memory capacity. An important goal of this book is to help the reader to fully understand these optimizations and become skilled in them.

Keep in mind that the level of speedup achieved over single core CPU execution can also reflect the suitability of the CPU to the application: in some applications, CPUs perform very well, making it harder to speed up performance using a GPU. Most applications have portions that can be much better executed by the CPU. Thus, one must give the CPU a fair chance to perform and make sure that code is written so that GPUs *complement* CPU execution, thus properly exploiting the heterogeneous parallel computing capabilities of the combined CPU/GPU system.

Fig. 1.3 illustrates the main parts of a typical application. Much of a real application's code tends to be sequential. These sequential parts are illustrated as the "pit" area of the peach: trying to apply parallel computing techniques to these portions is like biting into the peach pit—not a good feeling! These portions are very hard to parallelize. CPUs are pretty good with these portions. The good news is that these portions, although they can take up a large portion of the code, tend to account for only a small portion of the execution time of super-applications.

The rest is what we call the "peach meat" portions. These portions are easy to parallelize, as are some early graphics applications. Parallel programming in heterogeneous computing systems can drastically improve the speed of these applications. As illustrated in Fig. 1.3 early GPGPUs cover only a small portion of the meat section, which is analogous to a small portion of the most exciting applications. As we will see, the CUDA programming model is designed to cover a much larger section of the peach meat portions of exciting applications. In fact, as we will discuss in Chapter 20, More on CUDA and GPU computing, these programming models and their underlying hardware are still evolving at a fast pace in order to enable efficient parallelization of even larger sections of applications.

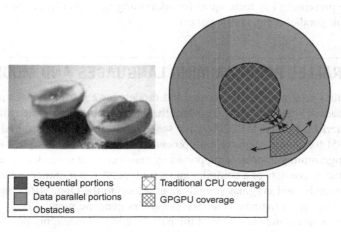

■ Sequential portions	⊠ Traditional CPU coverage	
■ Data parallel portions	▨ GPGPU coverage	
— Obstacles		

FIGURE 1.3

Coverage of sequential and parallel application portions.

1.5 CHALLENGES IN PARALLEL PROGRAMMING

What makes parallel programming hard? Someone once said that if you don't care about performance, parallel programming is very easy. You can literally write a parallel program in an hour. But then why bother to write a parallel program if you do not care about performance?

This book addresses several challenges in achieving high-performance in parallel programming. First and foremost, it can be challenging to design parallel algorithms with the same level of algorithmic (computational) complexity as sequential algorithms. Some parallel algorithms can add large overheads over their sequential counter parts so much that they can even end up running slower for larger input data sets.

Second, the execution speed of many applications is limited by memory access speed. We refer to these applications as memory-bound, as opposed to compute bound, which are limited by the number of instructions performed per byte of data. Achieving high-performance parallel execution in memory-bound applications often requires novel methods for improving memory access speed.

Third, the execution speed of parallel programs is often more sensitive to the input data characteristics than their sequential counter parts. Many real world applications need to deal with inputs with widely varying characteristics, such as erratic or unpredictable data rates, and very high data rates. The performance of parallel programs can sometimes vary dramatically with these characteristics.

Fourth, many real world problems are most naturally described with mathematical recurrences. Parallelizing these problems often requires nonintuitive ways of thinking about the problem and may require redundant work during execution.

Fortunately, most of these challenges have been addressed by researchers in the past. There are also common patterns across application domains that allow us to apply solutions derived from one domain to others. This is the primary reason why we will be presenting key techniques for addressing these challenges in the context of important parallel computation patterns.

1.6 PARALLEL PROGRAMMING LANGUAGES AND MODELS

Many parallel programming languages and models have been proposed in the past several decades [Mattson, 2004]. The ones that are the most widely used are message passing interface (MPI) [MPI 2009] for scalable cluster computing, and OpenMP [Open 2005] for shared memory multiprocessor systems. Both have become standardized programming interfaces supported by major computer vendors. An OpenMP implementation consists of a compiler and a runtime. A programmer specifies directives (commands) and pragmas (hints) about a loop to the OpenMP compiler. With these directives and pragmas, OpenMP compilers generate parallel code. The runtime system supports the execution of the parallel code by managing parallel threads and resources. OpenMP was originally designed for CPU execution. More recently, a variation called OpenACC (see chapter: Parallel programming with OpenACC) has been proposed and supported by multiple computer vendors for programming heterogeneous computing systems.

The major advantage of OpenACC is that it provides compiler automation and runtime support for abstracting away many parallel programming details from programmers. Such automation and abstraction can help make the application code more portable across systems produced by different vendors, as well as different generations of systems from the same vendor. We can refer to this property as "performance portability." This is why we teach OpenACC programming in Chapter 19, Parallel programming with OpenACC. However, effective programming in OpenACC still requires the programmers to understand all the detailed parallel programming concepts involved. Because CUDA gives programmers explicit control of these parallel programming details, it is an excellent learning vehicle even for someone who would like to use OpenMP and OpenACC as their primary programming interface. Furthermore, from our experience, OpenACC compilers are still evolving and improving. Many programmers will likely need to use CUDA style interfaces for parts where OpenACC compilers fall short.

MPI is a model where computing nodes in a cluster do not share memory [MPI 2009]. All data sharing and interaction must be done through explicit message passing. MPI has been successful in high-performance computing (HPC). Applications written in MPI have run successfully on cluster computing systems with more than 100,000 nodes. Today, many HPC clusters employ heterogeneous CPU/GPU nodes. While CUDA is an effective interface with each node, most application developers need to use MPI to program at the cluster level. It is therefore important that a parallel programmer in HPC understands how to do joint MPI/CUDA programming, which is presented in Chapter 18, Programming a Heterogeneous Computing Cluster.

The amount of effort needed to port an application into MPI, however, can be quite high due to lack of shared memory across computing nodes. The programmer needs to perform domain decomposition to partition the input and output data into cluster nodes. Based on the domain decomposition, the programmer also needs to call message sending and receiving functions to manage the data exchange between nodes. CUDA, on the other hand, provides shared memory for parallel execution in the GPU to address this difficulty. As for CPU and GPU communication, CUDA previously provided very limited shared memory capability between the CPU and the GPU. The programmers needed to manage the data transfer between CPU and GPU in a manner similar to the "one-sided" message passing. New runtime support for global address space and automated data transfer in heterogeneous computing systems, such as GMAC [GCN 2010], are now available. With such support, a CUDA programmer can declare variables and data structures as shared between CPU and GPU. The runtime hardware and software transparently maintains coherence by automatically performing optimized data transfer operations on behalf of the programmer as needed. Such support significantly reduces the programming complexity involved in overlapping data transfer with computation and I/O activities. As will be discussed later in Chapter 20, More on CUDA and GPU Computing, the Pascal architecture supports both a unified global address space and memory.

In 2009, several major industry players, including Apple, Intel, AMD/ATI, NVIDIA jointly developed a standardized programming model called Open Computing Language (OpenCL) [Khronos 2009]. Similar to CUDA, the OpenCL programming model defines language extensions and runtime APIs to allow programmers to manage parallelism and data delivery in massively parallel processors. In comparison to CUDA, OpenCL relies more on APIs and less on language extensions. This allows vendors to quickly adapt their existing compilers and tools to handle OpenCL programs. OpenCL is a standardized programming model in that applications developed in OpenCL can run correctly without modification on all processors that support the OpenCL language extensions and API. However, one will likely need to modify the applications in order to achieve high-performance for a new processor.

Those who are familiar with both OpenCL and CUDA know that there is a remarkable similarity between the key concepts and features of OpenCL and those of CUDA. That is, a CUDA programmer can learn OpenCL programming with minimal effort. More importantly, virtually all techniques learned using CUDA can be easily applied to OpenCL programming. Therefore, we introduce OpenCL in Appendix A and explain how one can apply the key concepts in this book to OpenCL programming.

1.7 OVERARCHING GOALS

Our primary goal is to teach you, the reader, how to program massively parallel processors to achieve high-performance, and our approach will not require a great deal of hardware expertise. Therefore, we are going to dedicate many pages to techniques for developing *high-performance* parallel programs. And, we believe that it will become easy once you develop the right insight and go about it the right way. In particular, we will focus on *computational thinking* [Wing 2006] techniques that will enable you to think about problems in ways that are amenable to high-performance parallel computing.

Note that hardware architecture features still have constraints and limitations. High-performance parallel programming on most processors will require some knowledge of how the hardware works. It will probably take ten or more years before we can build tools and machines so that most programmers can work without this knowledge. Even if we have such tools, we suspect that programmers with more knowledge of the hardware will be able to use the tools in a much more effective way than those who do not. However, we will not be teaching computer architecture as a separate topic. Instead, we will teach the essential computer architecture knowledge as part of our discussions on high-performance parallel programming techniques.

Our second goal is to teach parallel programming for correct functionality and reliability, which constitutes a subtle issue in parallel computing. Those who have worked on parallel systems in the past know that achieving initial performance is not enough. The challenge is to achieve it in such a way that you can debug the code and support users. The CUDA programming model encourages the use of simple forms of barrier synchronization, memory consistency, and atomicity for managing parallelism. In addition, it provides an array of powerful tools that allow one to debug not only the functional aspects but also the performance bottlenecks. We will show that by focusing on data parallelism, one can achieve high performance without sacrificing the reliability of their applications.

Our third goal is scalability across future hardware generations by exploring approaches to parallel programming such that future machines, which will be more and more parallel, can run your code faster than today's machines. We want to help you to master parallel programming so that your programs can scale up to the level of performance of new generations of machines. The key to such scalability is to regularize and localize memory data accesses to minimize consumption of critical resources and conflicts in accessing and updating data structures.

Still, much technical knowledge will be required to achieve these goals, so we will cover quite a few principles and patterns [Mattson 2004] of parallel programming in this book. We will not be teaching these principles and patterns in a vacuum. We will teach them in the context of parallelizing useful applications. We cannot cover all of them, however, we have selected what we found to be the most useful and well-proven techniques to cover in detail. To complement your knowledge and expertise, we include a list of recommended literature. We are now ready to give you a quick overview of the rest of the book.

1.8 ORGANIZATION OF THE BOOK

Chapter 2, Data parallel computing, introduces data parallelism and CUDA C programming. This chapter expects the reader to have had previous experience with C programming. It first introduces CUDA C as a simple, small extension to C that supports heterogeneous CPU/GPU joint computing and the widely used single program multiple data (SPMD) parallel programming model. It then covers the thought process involved in (1) identifying the part of application programs to be parallelized, (2) isolating the data to be used by the parallelized code, using an API function to allocate memory on the parallel computing device, (3) using an API function to transfer data to the parallel computing device, (4) developing a kernel function that will be executed by threads in the parallelized part, (5) launching a kernel function for execution by parallel threads, and (6) eventually transferring the data back to the host processor with an API function call.

While the objective of Chapter 2, Data parallel computing, is to teach enough concepts of the CUDA C programming model so that the students can write a simple parallel CUDA C program, it actually covers several basic skills needed to develop a parallel application based on any parallel programming model. We use a running example of vector addition to illustrate these concepts. In the later part of the book, we also compare CUDA with other parallel programming models including OpenMP, OpenACC, and OpenCL.

Chapter 3, Scalable parallel execution, presents more details of the parallel execution model of CUDA. It gives enough insight into the creation, organization, resource binding, data binding, and scheduling of threads to enable the reader to implement sophisticated computation using CUDA C and reason about the performance behavior of their CUDA code.

Chapter 4, Memory and data locality, is dedicated to the special memories that can be used to hold CUDA variables for managing data delivery and improving program execution speed. We introduce the CUDA language features that allocate and use these memories. Appropriate use of these memories can drastically improve the data access throughput and help to alleviate the traffic congestion in the memory system.

Chapter 5, Performance considerations, presents several important performance considerations in current CUDA hardware. In particular, it gives more details in desirable patterns of thread execution, memory data accesses, and resource allocation. These details form the conceptual basis for programmers to reason about the consequence of their decisions on organizing their computation and data.

Chapter 6, Numerical considerations, introduces the concepts of IEEE-754 floating-point number format, precision, and accuracy. It shows why different parallel execution arrangements can result in different output values. It also teaches the concept of numerical stability and practical techniques for maintaining numerical stability in parallel algorithms.

Chapters 7, Parallel patterns: convolution, Chapter 8, Parallel patterns: prefix sum, Chapter 9, Parallel patterns—parallel histogram computation, Chapter 10, Parallel patterns: sparse matrix computation, Chapter 11, Parallel patterns: merge sort, Chapter 12, Parallel patterns: graph search, present six important parallel computation patterns that give the readers more insight into parallel programming techniques and parallel execution mechanisms. Chapter 7, Parallel patterns: convolution, presents convolution and stencil, frequently used parallel computing patterns that require careful management of data access locality. We also use this pattern to introduce constant memory and caching in modern GPUs. Chapter 8, Parallel patterns: prefix sum, presents reduction tree and prefix sum, or scan, an important parallel computing pattern that converts sequential computation into parallel computation. We also use this pattern to introduce the concept of work-efficiency in parallel algorithms. Chapter 9, Parallel patterns—parallel histogram computation, covers histogram, a pattern widely used in pattern recognition in large data sets. We also cover merge operation, a widely used pattern in divide-and-concur work partitioning strategies. Chapter 10, Parallel patterns: sparse matrix computation, presents sparse matrix computation, a pattern used for processing very large data sets. This chapter introduces the reader to the concepts of rearranging data for more efficient parallel access: data compression, padding, sorting, transposition, and regularization. Chapter 11, Parallel patterns: merge sort, introduces merge sort, and dynamic input data identification and organization. Chapter 12, Parallel patterns: graph search, introduces graph algorithms and how graph search can be efficiently implemented in GPU programming.

While these chapters are based on CUDA, they help the readers build-up the foundation for parallel programming in general. We believe that humans understand best when they learn from concrete examples. That is, we must first learn the concepts in the context of a particular programming model, which provides us with solid footing to allow applying our knowledge to other programming models. As we do so, we can draw on our concrete experience from the CUDA model. An in-depth experience with the CUDA model also enables us to gain maturity, which will help us learn concepts that may not even be pertinent to the CUDA model.

Chapter 13, CUDA dynamic parallelism, covers dynamic parallelism. This is the ability of the GPU to dynamically create work for itself based on the data or program structure, rather than waiting for the CPU to launch kernels exclusively.

Chapters 14, Application case study—non-Cartesian MRI, Chapter 15, Application case study—molecular visualization and analysis, Chapter 16, Application case study—machine learning, are case studies of three real applications, which take the readers through the thought process of parallelizing and optimizing their applications for significant speedups. For each application, we start by identifying alternative ways of formulating the basic structure of the parallel execution and follow up with reasoning about the advantages and disadvantages of each alternative. We then go through the steps of code transformation needed to achieve high-performance. These three chapters help the readers put all the materials from the previous chapters together and prepare for their own application development projects. Chapter 14, Application case study—non-Cartesian MRI, covers non-Cartesian MRI reconstruction, and how the irregular data affects the program. Chapter 15, Application case study—molecular visualization and analysis, covers molecular visualization and analysis. Chapter 16, Application case study—machine learning, covers Deep Learning, which is becoming an extremely important area for GPU computing. We provide an introduction, and leave more in-depth discussion to other sources.

Chapter 17, Parallel programming and computational thinking, introduces computational thinking. It does so by covering the concept of organizing the computation tasks of a program so that they can be done in parallel. We start by discussing the translational process of organizing abstract scientific concepts into computational tasks, which is an important first step in producing quality application software, serial or parallel. It then discusses parallel algorithm structures and their effects on application performance, which is grounded in the performance tuning experience with CUDA. Although we do not go into these alternative parallel programming styles, we expect that the readers will be able to learn to program in any of them with the foundation they gain in this book. We also present a high level case study to show the opportunities that can be seen through creative computational thinking.

Chapter 18, Programming a heterogeneous computing cluster, covers CUDA programming on heterogeneous clusters where each compute node consists of both CPU and GPU. We discuss the use of MPI alongside CUDA to integrate both inter-node computing and intra-node computing, and the resulting communication issues and practices.

Chapter 19, Parallel programming with OpenACC, covers Parallel Programming with OpenACC. OpenACC is a directive-based high level programming approach which allows the programmer to identify and specify areas of code that can be subsequently parallelized by the compiler and/or other tools. OpenACC is an easy way for a parallel programmer to get started.

Chapter 20, More on CUDA and GPU computing and Chapter 21, Conclusion and outlook, offer concluding remarks and an outlook for the future of massively parallel programming. We first revisit our goals and summarize how the chapters fit together to help achieve the goals. We then present a brief survey of the major trends in the architecture of massively parallel processors and how these trends will likely impact parallel programming in the future. We conclude with a prediction that these fast advances in massively parallel computing will make it one of the most exciting areas in the coming decade.

REFERENCES

Gelado, I., Cabezas, J., Navarro, N., Stone, J.E., Patel, S.J., Hwu, W.W. (2010). An asynchronous distributed shared memory model for heterogeneous parallel systems. *International conference on architectural support for programming languages and operating systems.*

Hwu, W. W., Keutzer, K., & Mattson, T. (2008). The concurrency challenge. *IEEE Design and Test of Computers*, 25, 312–320.

Mattson, T. G., Sanders, B. A., & Massingill, B. L. (2004). *Patterns of parallel programming.* Boston, MA: Addison-Wesley Professional.

Message Passing Interface Forum. MPI – A Message Passing Interface Standard Version 2.2. http://www.mpi-forum.org/docs/mpi-2.2/mpi22-report.pdf, September 4, 2009.

NVIDIA Corporation. CUDA Programming Guide. February 2007.

OpenMP Architecture Review Board, "OpenMP application program interface," May 2005.

Sutter, H., & Larus, J. (September 2005). Software and the concurrency revolution. *ACM Queue*, 3(7), 54–62.

The Khronos Group. The OpenCL Specification version 1.0. http://www.khronos.org/registry/cl/specs/opencl-1.0.29.pdf.

von Neumann, J. (1972). First draft of a report on the EDVAC. In H. H. Goldstine (Ed.), *The computer: from Pascal to von Neumann*. Princeton, NJ: Princeton University Press. ISBN 0-691-02367-0.

Wing, J. (March 2006). Computational thinking. *Communications of the ACM*, 49(3), 33–35.

Data parallel computing

2

David Luebke

CHAPTER OUTLINE

Many code examples will be used to illustrate the key concepts in writing scalable parallel programs. For this we need a simple language that supports massive parallelism and heterogeneous computing, and we have chosen CUDA C for our code examples and exercises. CUDA C extends the popular C programming language with minimal new syntax and interfaces to let programmers target heterogeneous computing systems containing both CPU cores and massively parallel GPUs. As the name implies, CUDA C is built on NVIDIA's CUDA platform. CUDA is currently the most mature framework for massively parallel computing. It is broadly used in the high performance computing industry, with sophisticated tools such as compilers, debuggers, and profilers available on the most common operating systems.

An important point: while our examples will mostly use CUDA C for its simplicity and ubiquity, the CUDA platform supports many languages and application programming interfaces (APIs) including C++, Python, Fortran, OpenCL, OpenACC, OpenMP, and more. CUDA is really an architecture that supports a set of concepts for organizing and expressing massively parallel computation. It is those concepts that we teach. For the benefit of developers working in other languages (C++, FORTRAN, Python, OpenCL, etc.) we provide appendices that show how the concepts can be applied to these languages.

2.1 DATA PARALLELISM

When modern software applications run slowly, the problem is usually having too much data to be processed. Consumer applications manipulate images or videos, with millions to trillions of pixels. Scientific applications model fluid dynamics using billions of grid cells. Molecular dynamics applications must simulate interactions between thousands to millions of atoms. Airline scheduling deals with thousands of flights, crews, and airport gates. Importantly, most of these pixels, particles, cells, interactions, flights, and so on can be dealt with largely independently. Converting a color pixel to a greyscale requires only the data of that pixel. Blurring an image averages each pixel's color with the colors of nearby pixels, requiring only the data of that small neighborhood of pixels. Even a seemingly global operation, such as finding the average brightness of all pixels in an image, can be broken down into many smaller computations that can be executed independently. Such independent evaluation is the basis of *data parallelism*: (re)organize the computation around the data, such that we can execute the resulting independent computations in parallel to complete the overall job faster, often much faster.

TASK PARALLELISM VS. DATA PARALLELISM

Data parallelism is not the only type of parallelism used in parallel programming. Task parallelism has also been used extensively in parallel programming. Task parallelism is typically exposed through task decomposition of applications. For example, a simple application may need to do a vector addition and a matrix-vector multiplication. Each of these would be a task. Task parallelism exists if the two tasks can be done independently. I/O and data transfers are also common sources of tasks.

In large applications, there are usually a larger number of independent tasks and therefore larger amount of task parallelism. For example, in a molecular dynamics simulator, the list of natural tasks include vibrational forces, rotational forces, neighbor identification for nonbonding forces, nonbonding forces, velocity and position, and other physical properties based on velocity and position.

In general, data parallelism is the main source of scalability for parallel programs. With large data sets, one can often find abundant data parallelism to be able to utilize massively parallel processors and allow application performance to grow with each generation of hardware that has more execution resources. Nevertheless, task parallelism can also play an important role in achieving performance goals. We will be covering task parallelism later when we introduce streams.

FIGURE 2.1

Conversion of a color image to a greyscale image.

We will use image processing as a source of running examples in the next chapters. Let us illustrate the concept of data parallelism with the color-to-greyscale conversion example mentioned above. Fig. 2.1 shows a color image (left side) consisting of many pixels, each containing a red, green, and blue fractional value (r, g, b) varying from 0 (black) to 1 (full intensity).

RGB COLOR IMAGE REPRESENTATION

In an RGB representation, each pixel in an image is stored as a tuple of (r, g, b) values. The format of an image's row is (r g b) (r g b) ... (r g b), as illustrated in the following conceptual picture. Each tuple specifies a mixture of red (R), green (G) and blue (B). That is, for each pixel, the r, g, and b values represent the intensity (0 being dark and 1 being full intensity) of the red, green, and blue light sources when the pixel is rendered.

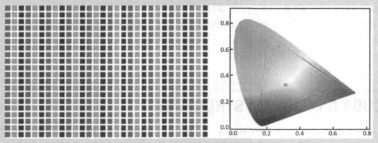

The actual allowable mixtures of these three colors vary across industry-specified color spaces. Here, the valid combinations of the three colors in the AdobeRGB color space are shown as the interior of the triangle. The vertical coordinate (y value) and horizontal coordinate (x value) of each mixture show the fraction of the pixel intensity that should be G and R. The remaining fraction ($1 - y - x$) of the pixel intensity that should be assigned to B. To render an image, the r, g, b values of each pixel are used to calculate both the total intensity (luminance) of the pixel as well as the mixture coefficients (x, y, $1 - y - x$).

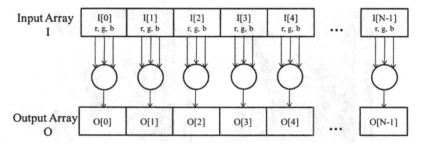

FIGURE 2.2

The pixels can be calculated independently of each other during color to greyscale conversion.

To convert the color image (left side of Fig. 2.1) to greyscale (right side) we compute the luminance value L for each pixel by applying the following weighted sum formula:

$$L = r * 0.21 + g * 0.72 + b * 0.07$$

If we consider the input to be an image organized as an array I of RGB values and the output to be a corresponding array O of luminance values, we get the simple computation structure shown in Fig. 2.2. For example, $O[0]$ is generated by calculating the weighted sum of the RGB values in $I[0]$ according to the formula above; $O[1]$ by calculating the weighted sum of the RGB values in $I[1]$, $O[2]$ by calculating the weighted sum of the RGB values in $I[2]$, and so on. None of these per-pixel computations depends on each other; all of them can be performed independently. Clearly the color-to-greyscale conversion exhibits a rich amount of data parallelism. Of course, data parallelism in complete applications can be more complex and much of this book is devoted to teaching the "parallel thinking" necessary to find and exploit data parallelism.

2.2 CUDA C PROGRAM STRUCTURE

We are now ready to learn to write a CUDA C program to exploit data parallelism for faster execution. The structure of a CUDA C program reflects the coexistence of a *host* (CPU) and one or more *devices* (GPUs) in the computer. Each CUDA source file can have a mixture of both host and device code. By default, any traditional C program is a CUDA program that contains only host code. One can add device functions and data declarations into any source file. The functions or data declarations for device are clearly marked with special CUDA C keywords. These are typically functions that exhibit rich amount of data parallelism.

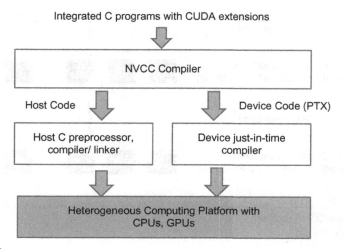

FIGURE 2.3

Overview of the compilation process of a CUDA C Program.

Once device functions and data declarations are added to a source file, it is no longer acceptable to a traditional C compiler. The code needs to be compiled by a compiler that recognizes and understands these additional declarations. We will be using a CUDA C compiler called NVCC (NVIDIA C Compiler). As shown at the top of Fig. 2.3, the NVCC compiler processes a CUDA C program, using the CUDA keywords to separate the host code and device code. The host code is straight ANSI C code, which is further compiled with the host's standard C/C++ compilers and is run as a traditional CPU process. The device code is marked with CUDA keywords for data parallel functions, called *kernels*, and their associated helper functions and data structures. The device code is further compiled by a run-time component of NVCC and executed on a GPU device. In situations where there is no hardware device available or a kernel can be appropriately executed on a CPU, one can also choose to execute the kernel on a CPU using tools like MCUDA [SSH 2008].

The execution of a CUDA program is illustrated in Fig. 2.4. The execution starts with host code (CPU serial code). When a kernel function (parallel device code) is called, or launched, it is executed by a large number of threads on a device. All the threads that are generated by a kernel launch are collectively called a *grid*. These threads are the primary vehicle of parallel execution in a CUDA platform. Fig. 2.4 shows the execution of two grids of threads. We will discuss how these grids are organized soon. When all threads of a kernel complete their execution, the corresponding grid terminates, the execution continues on the host until another kernel is launched. Note that Fig. 2.4 shows a simplified model where the CPU execution and the GPU execution do not overlap. Many heterogeneous computing applications actually manage overlapped CPU and GPU execution to take advantage of both CPUs and GPUs.

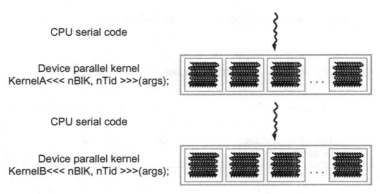

CPU serial code

Device parallel kernel
KernelA<<< nBIK, nTid >>>(args);

CPU serial code

Device parallel kernel
KernelB<<< nBIK, nTid >>>(args);

FIGURE 2.4

Execution of a CUDA program.

Launching a kernel typically generates a large number of threads to exploit data parallelism. In the color-to-greyscale conversion example, each thread could be used to compute one pixel of the output array O. In this case, the number of threads that will be generated by the kernel is equal to the number of pixels in the image. For large images, a large number of threads will be generated. In practice, each thread may process multiple pixels for efficiency. CUDA programmers can assume that these threads take very few clock cycles to generate and schedule due to efficient hardware support. This is in contrast with traditional CPU threads that typically take thousands of clock cycles to generate and schedule.

THREADS

A thread is a simplified view of how a processor executes a sequential program in modern computers. A thread consists of the code of the program, the particular point in the code that is being executed, and the values of its variables and data structures. The execution of a thread is sequential as far as a user is concerned. One can use a source-level debugger to monitor the progress of a thread by executing one statement at a time, looking at the statement that will be executed next and checking the values of the variables and data structures as the execution progresses.

Threads have been used in programming for many years. If a programmer wants to start parallel execution in an application, he/she creates and manages multiple threads using thread libraries or special languages. In CUDA, the execution of each thread is sequential as well. A CUDA program initiates parallel execution by launching kernel functions, which causes the underlying run-time mechanisms to create many threads that process different parts of the data in parallel.

2.3 A VECTOR ADDITION KERNEL

We now use vector addition to illustrate the CUDA C program structure. Vector addition is arguably the simplest possible data parallel computation, the parallel equivalent of "Hello World" from sequential programming. Before we show the kernel code for vector addition, it is helpful to first review how a conventional vector addition (host code) function works. Fig. 2.5 shows a simple traditional C program that consists of a main function and a vector addition function. In all our examples, whenever there is a need to distinguish between host and device data, we will prefix the names of variables that are processed by the host with "*h_*" and those of variables that are processed by a device "*d_*" to remind ourselves the intended usage of these variables. Since we only have host code in Fig. 2.5, we see only "*h_*" variables.

Assume that the vectors to be added are stored in arrays A and B that are allocated and initialized in the main program. The output vector is in array C, which is also allocated in the main program. For brevity, we do not show the details of how A, B, and C are allocated or initialized in the main function. The pointers (see sidebar below) to these arrays are passed to the vecAdd function, along with the variable N that contains the length of the vectors. Note that the formal parameters of the vectorAdd function are prefixed with "*h_*" to emphasize that these are processed by the host. This naming convention will be helpful when we introduce device code in the next few steps.

The vecAdd function in Fig. 2.5 uses a for-loop to iterate through the vector elements. In the *i*th iteration, output element $h\_C[i]$ receives the sum of $h\_A[i]$ and $h\_B[i]$. The vector length parameter n is used to control the loop so that the number of iterations matches the length of the vectors. The formal parameters h_A, h_B and h_C are passed by reference so the function reads the elements of h_A, h_B and writes the elements of h_C through the argument pointers A, B, and C. When the

```
// Compute vector sum h_C = h_A+h_B
void vecAdd(float* h_A, float* h_B, float* h_C, int n)
{
    for (int i = 0; i < n; i++) h_C[i] = h_A[i] + h_B[i];
}

int main()
{
    // Memory allocation for h_A, h_B, and h_C
    // I/O to read h_A and h_B, N elements each
    ...
    vecAdd(h_A, h_B, h_C, N);
}
```

FIGURE 2.5

A simple traditional vector addition C code example.

```
#include <cuda.h>
...
void vecAdd(float* A, float* B, float* C, int n)
{
    int  size = n* sizeof(float);
    float  *d_A *d_B, *d_C;
    ...
1. // Allocate device memory for A, B, and C
   // copy A and B to device memory

2. // Kernel launch code – to have the device
   // to perform the actual vector addition

3. // copy C from the device memory
   // Free device vectors
}
```

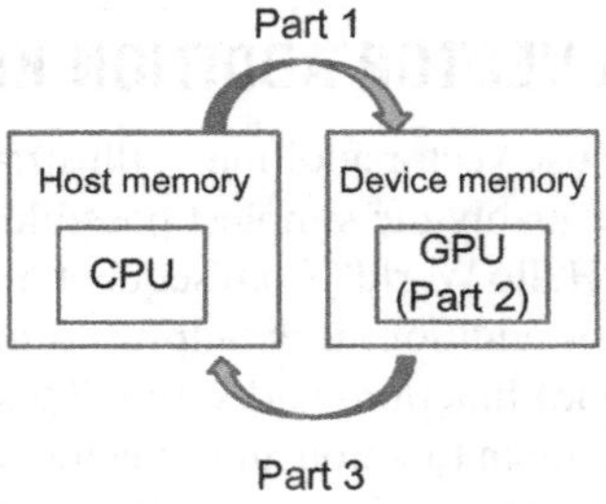

Part 1

Host memory | Device memory
CPU | GPU (Part 2)

Part 3

FIGURE 2.6

Outline of a revised vecAdd function that moves the work to a device.

vecAdd function returns, the subsequent statements in the main function can access the new contents of C.

A straightforward way to execute vector addition in parallel is to modify the vecAdd function and move its calculations to a device. The structure of such a modified vecAdd function is shown in Fig. 2.6. At the beginning of the file, we need to add a C preprocessor directive to include the cuda.h header file. This file defines the CUDA API functions and built-in variables (see sidebar below) that we will be introducing soon. Part 1 of the function allocates space in the device (GPU) memory to hold copies of the A, B, and C vectors and copies the vectors from the host memory to the device memory. Part 2 launches parallel execution of the actual vector addition kernel on the device. Part 3 copies the sum vector C from the device memory back to the host memory and frees the vectors in device memory.

POINTERS IN THE C LANGUAGE

The function arguments A, B, and C in Fig. 2.4 are pointers. In the C language, a pointer can be used to access variables and data structures. While a floating-point variable V can be declared with:

```
float V;
```

a pointer variable P can be declared with:

```
float *P;
```

By assigning the address of V to P with the statement P=&V, we make P "point to" V. *P becomes a synonym for V. For example U=*P assigns the value of V to U. For another example, *P=3 changes the value of V to 3.

> An array in a C program can be accessed through a pointer that points to its 0th element. For example, the statement `P=&(A[0])` makes `P` point to the 0th element of array `A`. `P[i]` becomes a synonym for `A[i]`. In fact, the array name `A` is in itself a pointer to its 0th element.
>
> In Fig. 2.5, passing an array name `A` as the first argument to function call to `vecAdd` makes the function's first parameter `h_A` point to the 0th element of `A`. We say that `A` is passed by reference to `vecAdd`. As a result, `h_A[i]` in the function body can be used to access `A[i]`.
>
> See Patt&Patel [Patt] for an easy-to-follow explanation of the detailed usage of pointers in C.

Note that the revised `vecAdd` function is essentially an outsourcing agent that ships input data to a device, activates the calculation on the device, and collects the results from the device. The agent does so in such a way that the main program does not need to even be aware that the vector addition is now actually done on a device. In practice, such "transparent" outsourcing model can be very inefficient because of all the copying of data back and forth. One would often keep important bulk data structures on the device and simply invocate device functions on them from the host code. For now, we will stay with the simplified transparent model for the purpose of introducing the basic CUDA C program structure. The details of the revised function, as well as the way to compose the kernel function, will be shown in the rest of this chapter.

2.4 DEVICE GLOBAL MEMORY AND DATA TRANSFER

In current CUDA systems, devices are often hardware cards that come with their own dynamic random access memory (DRAM). For example, the NVIDIA GTX1080 comes with up to 8 GB[1] of DRAM, called global memory. We will use the terms global memory and device memory interchangeably. In order to execute a kernel on a device, the programmer needs to allocate global memory on the device and transfer pertinent data from the host memory to the allocated device memory. This corresponds to Part 1 of Fig. 2.6. Similarly, after device execution, the programmer needs to transfer result data from the device memory back to the host memory and free up the device memory that is no longer needed. This corresponds to Part 3 of Fig. 2.6. The CUDA run-time system provides API functions to perform these activities on behalf of the programmer. From this point on, we will simply say that

---

[1] There is a trend to integrate the address space of CPUs and GPUs into a unified memory space (Chapter 20). There are new programming frameworks such as GMAC that take advantage of the unified memory space and eliminate data copying cost.

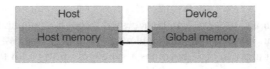

FIGURE 2.7

Host memory and device global memory.

a piece of data is transferred from host to device as shorthand for saying that the data is copied from the host memory to the device memory. The same holds for the opposite direction.

Fig. 2.7 shows a high level picture of the CUDA host memory and device memory model for programmers to reason about the allocation of device memory and movement of data between host and device. The device global memory can be accessed by the host to transfer data to and from the device, as illustrated by the bidirectional arrows between these memories and the host in Fig. 2.7. There are more device memory types than shown in Fig. 2.7. Constant memory can be accessed in a read-only manner by device functions, which will be described in Chapter 7, Parallel patterns: convolution. We will also discuss the use of registers and shared memory in Chapter 4, Memory and data locality. Interested readers can also see the CUDA programming guide for the functionality of texture memory. For now, we will focus on the use of global memory.

BUILT-IN VARIABLES

Many programming languages have built-in variables. These variables have special meaning and purpose. The values of these variables are often preinitialized by the run-time system and are typically read-only in the program. The programmers should refrain from using these variables for any other purposes.

In Fig. 2.6, Part 1 and Part 3 of the vecAdd function need to use the CUDA API functions to allocate device memory for A, B, and C, transfer A and B from host memory to device memory, transfer C from device memory to host memory at the end of the vector addition, and free the device memory for A, B, and C. We will explain the memory allocation and free functions first.

Fig. 2.8 shows two API functions for allocating and freeing device global memory. The cudaMalloc function can be called from the host code to allocate a piece of device global memory for an object. The reader should notice the striking similarity between cudaMalloc and the standard C run-time library malloc function. This is intentional; CUDA is C with minimal extensions. CUDA uses the standard C

cudaMalloc()
- Allocates object in the device global memory
- Two parameters
    ◦ **Address of a pointer** to the allocated object
    ◦ **Size** of allocated object in terms of bytes
cudaFree()
- Frees object from device global memory
    ◦ **Pointer** to freed object

FIGURE 2.8

CUDA API functions for managing device global memory.

run-time library malloc function to manage the host memory and adds cudaMalloc as an extension to the C run-time library. By keeping the interface as close to the original C run-time libraries as possible, CUDA minimizes the time that a C programmer spends to relearn the use of these extensions.

The first parameter to the cudaMalloc function is the **address** of a pointer variable that will be set to point to the allocated object. The address of the pointer variable should be cast to (void **) because the function expects a generic pointer; the memory allocation function is a generic function that is not restricted to any particular type of objects.[2] This parameter allows the cudaMalloc function to write the address of the allocated memory into the pointer variable.[3] The host code to launch kernels passes this pointer value to the kernels that need to access the allocated memory object. The second parameter to the cudaMalloc function gives the size of the data to be allocated, in number of bytes. The usage of this second parameter is consistent with the size parameter to the C malloc function.

We now use a simple code example to illustrate the use of cudaMalloc. This is a continuation of the example in Fig. 2.6. For clarity, we will start a pointer variable with letter "$d\_$" to indicate that it points to an object in the device memory. The program passes the *address* of pointer d_A (i.e., $\&d\_A$) as the first parameter after casting it to a void pointer. That is, d_A will point to the device memory region allocated for the A vector. The size of the allocated region will be n times the size of a single-precision floating number, which is 4 bytes in most computers today. After the computation, cudaFree is called with pointer d_A as input to free the storage space for the A vector from the device global memory. Note that cudaFree does not need to

---

[2] The fact that cudaMalloc returns a generic object makes the use of dynamically allocated multidimensional arrays more complex. We will address this issue in Section 3.2.

[3] Note that cudaMalloc has a different format from the C malloc function. The C malloc function returns a pointer to the allocated object. It takes only one parameter that specifies the size of the allocated object. The cudaMalloc function writes to the pointer variable whose address is given as the first parameter. As a result, the cudaMalloc function takes two parameters. The two-parameter format of cudaMalloc allows it to use the return value to report any errors in the same way as other CUDA API functions.

change the content of pointer variable d_A; it only needs to use the value of d_A to enter the allocated memory back into the available pool. Thus only the value, not the address of d_A, is passed as the argument.

```
float *d_A;
int size=n * sizeof(float);
cudaMalloc((void**)&d_A, size);
...
cudaFree(d_A);
```

The addresses in d_A, d_B, and d_C are addresses in the device memory. These addresses should not be dereferenced in the host code for computation. They should be mostly used in calling API functions and kernel functions. Dereferencing a device memory point in host code can cause exceptions or other types of run-time errors during execution.

The reader should complete Part 1 of the vecAdd example in Fig. 2.6 with similar declarations of d_B and d_C pointer variables as well as their corresponding cuda-Malloc calls. Furthermore, Part 3 in Fig. 2.6 can be completed with the cudaFree calls for d_B and d_C.

Once the host code has allocated device memory for the data objects, it can request that data be transferred from host to device. This is accomplished by calling one of the CUDA API functions. Fig. 2.9 shows such an API function, cudaMemcpy. The cudaMemcpy function takes four parameters. The first parameter is a pointer to the destination location for the data object to be copied. The second parameter points to the source location. The third parameter specifies the number of bytes to be copied. The fourth parameter indicates the types of memory involved in the copy: from host memory to host memory, from host memory to device memory, from device memory to host memory, and from device memory to device memory. For example, the memory copy function can be used to copy data from one location of the device memory to another location of the device memory.[4]

cudaMemcpy()
- Memory data transfer
- Requires four parameters
    o Pointer to destination
    o Pointer to source
    o Number of bytes copied
    o Type/Direction of transfer

FIGURE 2.9

CUDA API function for data transfer between host and device.

[4] Please note cudaMemcpy currently cannot be used to copy between different GPU's in multi-GPU systems.

The vecAdd function calls the cudaMemcpy function to copy h_A and h_B vectors from host to device before adding them and to copy the h_C vector from the device to host after the addition is done. Assume that the values of h_A, h_B, d_A, d_B and size have already been set as we discussed before, the three cudaMemcpy calls are shown below. The two symbolic constants, cudaMemcpyHostToDevice and cudaMemcpyDeviceToHost, are recognized, predefined constants of the CUDA programming environment. Note that the same function can be used to transfer data in both directions by properly ordering the source and destination pointers and using the appropriate constant for the transfer type.

```
cudaMemcpy(d_A, A, size, cudaMemcpyHostToDevice);
cudaMemcpy(d_B, B, size, cudaMemcpyHostToDevice);
cudaMemcpy(C, d_C, size, cudaMemcpyDeviceToHost);
```

To summarize, the main program in Fig. 2.5 calls vecAdd, which is also executed on the host. The vecAdd function, outlined in Fig. 2.6, allocates device memory, requests data transfers, and launches the kernel that performs the actual vector addition. We often refer to this type of host code as a *stub function* for launching a kernel. After the kernel finishes execution, vecAdd also copies result data from device to the host. We show a more complete version of the vecAdd function in Fig. 2.10.

```
void vecAdd(float* h_A, float* h_B, float* h_C, int n)
{
    int size = n * sizeof(float);
    float *d_A, *d_B, *d_C;

    cudaMalloc((void **) &d_A, size);
    cudaMemcpy(d_A, h_A, size, cudaMemcpyHostToDevice);
    cudaMalloc((void **) &d_B, size);
    cudaMemcpy(d_B, h_B, size, cudaMemcpyHostToDevice);

    cudaMalloc((void **) &d_C, size);

    // Kernel invocation code - to be shown later
    ...

    cudaMemcpy(h_C, d_C, size, cudaMemcpyDeviceToHost);

    // Free device memory for A, B, C
    cudaFree(d_A); cudaFree(d_B); cudaFree (d_C);
}
```

FIGURE 2.10

A more complete version of `vecAdd()`.

ERROR CHECKING AND HANDLING IN CUDA

In general, it is very important for a program to check and handle errors. CUDA API functions return flags that indicate whether an error has occurred when they served the request. Most errors are due to inappropriate argument values used in the call.

For brevity, we will not show error checking code in our examples. For example, Fig. 2.10 shows a call to cudaMalloc:

```
cudaMalloc((void **) &d_A, size);
```

In practice, we should surround the call with code that test for error condition and print out error messages so that the user can be aware of the fact that an error has occurred. A simple version of such checking code is as follows:

```
cudaError_t err=cudaMalloc((void **) &d_A, size);
if (error !=cudaSuccess) {
   printf("%s in %s at line %d\n", cudaGetErrorString(err),__
   FILE__,__LINE__);
   exit(EXIT_FAILURE);
}
```

This way, if the system is out of device memory, the user will be informed about the situation. This can save many hours of debugging time.

One could define a C macro to make the checking code more concise in the source.

Compared to Fig. 2.6, the vecAdd function in Fig. 2.10 is complete for Part 1 and Part 3. Part 1 allocates device memory for d_A, d_B, and d_C and transfer h_A to d_A and h_B to d_B. This is done by calling the cudaMalloc and cudaMemcpy functions. The readers are encouraged to write their own function calls with the appropriate parameter values and compare their code with that shown in Fig. 2.10. Part 2 invokes the kernel and will be described in the following subsection. Part 3 copies the sum data from device memory to host memory so that their values will be available in the main function. This is accomplished with a call to the cudaMemcpy function. It then frees the memory for d_A, d_B, and d_C from the device memory, which is done by calls to the cudaFree function.

2.5 KERNEL FUNCTIONS AND THREADING

We are now ready to discuss more about the CUDA kernel functions and the effect of launching these kernel functions. In CUDA, a kernel function specifies the code to be executed by all threads during a parallel phase. Since all these threads execute the same code, CUDA programming is an instance of the well-known Single-Program

Multiple-Data (SPMD) [Ata 1998] parallel programming style, a popular programming style for massively parallel computing systems.[5]

When a program's host code launches a kernel, the CUDA run-time system generates a grid of threads that are organized into a two-level hierarchy. Each grid is organized as an array of thread blocks, which will be referred to as blocks for brevity. All blocks of a grid are of the same size; each block can contain up to 1024 threads. [6] Fig. 2.11 shows an example where each block consists of 256 threads. Each thread is represented by a curly arrow stemming from a box that is labeled with a number. The total number of threads in each thread block is specified by the host code when a kernel is launched. The same kernel can be launched with different numbers of threads at different parts of the host code. For a given grid, the number of threads in a block is available in a built-in blockDim variable.

The blockDim variable is of struct type with three unsigned integer fields: x, y, and z, which help a programmer to organize the threads into a one-, two-, or three-dimensional array. For a one-dimensional organization, only the x field will be used. For a two-dimensional organization, x and y fields will be used. For a three-dimensional structure, all three fields will be used. The choice of dimensionality for organizing threads usually reflects the dimensionality of the data. This makes sense since the threads are created to process data in parallel. It is only natural that the organization of the threads reflects the organization of the data. In Fig. 2.11, each thread block is organized as a one-dimensional array of threads because the data are one-dimensional vectors. The value of the blockDim.x variable specifies the total number of threads in each block, which is 256 in Fig. 2.11. In general, the number of

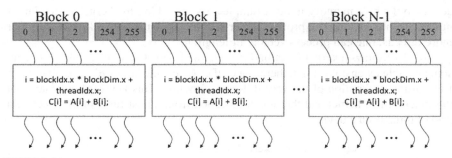

FIGURE 2.11

All threads in a grid execute the same kernel code.

---

[5] Note that SPMD is not the same as SIMD (Single Instruction Multiple-Data) [Flynn 1972]. In an SPMD system, the parallel processing units execute the same program on multiple parts of the data. However, these processing units do not need to be executing the same instruction at the same time. In an SIMD system, all processing units are executing the same instruction at any instant.

[6] Each thread block can have up to 1024 threads in CUDA 3.0 and beyond. Some earlier CUDA versions allow only up to 512 threads in a block.

threads in each dimension of thread blocks should be multiples of 32 due to hardware efficiency reasons. We will revisit this later.

CUDA kernels have access to two more built-in variables (threadIdx, blockIdx) that allow threads to distinguish among themselves and to determine the area of data each thread is to work on. Variable threadIdx gives each thread a unique coordinate within a block. For example, in Fig. 2.11, since we are using a one-dimensional thread organization, only threadIdx.x will be used. The threadIdx.x value for each thread is shown in the small shaded box of each thread in Fig. 2.11. The first thread in each block has value 0 in its threadIdx.x variable, the second thread has value 1, the third thread has value 2, etc.

The blockIdx variable gives all threads in a block a common block coordinate. In Fig. 2.11, all threads in the first block have value 0 in their blockIdx.x variables, those in the second thread block value 1, and so on. Using an analogy with the telephone system, one can think of threadIdx.x as local phone number and blockIdx.x as area code. The two together gives each telephone line a unique phone number in the whole country. Similarly, each thread can combine its threadIdx and blockIdx values to create a unique global index for itself within the entire grid.

In Fig. 2.11, a unique global index i is calculated as i = blockIdx.x*blockDim.x + threadIdx.x. Recall that blockDim is 256 in our example. The i values of threads in block 0 range from 0 to 255. The i values of threads in block 1 range from 256 to 511. The i values of threads in block 2 range from 512 to 767. That is, the i values of the threads in these three blocks form a continuous coverage of the values from 0 to 767. Since each thread uses i to access A, B, and C, these threads cover the first 768 iterations of the original loop. Note that we do not use the "$h\_$" and "$d\_$" convention in kernels since there is no potential confusion. We will not have any access to the host memory in our examples. By launching the kernel with a larger number of blocks, one can process larger vectors. By launching a kernel with n or more threads, one can process vectors of length n.

Fig. 2.12 shows a kernel function for vector addition. The syntax is ANSI C with some notable extensions. First, there is a CUDA C specific keyword "__global__" in front of the declaration of the vecAddKernel function. This keyword indicates that the function is a kernel and that it can be called from a host function to generate a grid of threads on a device.

```
// Compute vector sum C = A+B
// Each thread performs one pair-wise addition
__global__
void vecAddKernel(float* A, float* B, float* C, int n)
{
    int i = blockDim.x*blockIdx.x + threadIdx.x;
    if(i<n) C[i] = A[i] + B[i];
}
```

FIGURE 2.12

A vector addition kernel function.

	Executed on the:	Only callable from the:
`__device__` `float DeviceFunc()`	device	device
`__global__` `void KernelFunc()`	device	host
`__host__` `float HostFunc()`	host	host

FIGURE 2.13

CUDA C keywords for function declaration.

In general, CUDA C extends the C language with three qualifier keywords that can be used in function declarations. The meaning of these keywords is summarized in Fig. 2.13 The "__global__" keyword indicates that the function being declared is a CUDA C kernel function. Note that there are two underscore characters on each side of the word "global." Such kernel function is to be executed on the device and can only be called from the host code except in CUDA systems that support *dynamic parallelism*, as we will explain in Chapter 13, CUDA dynamic parallelism. The "__device__" keyword indicates that the function being declared is a CUDA device function. A device function executes on a CUDA device and can only be called from a kernel function or another device function.[7]

The "__host__" keyword indicates that the function being declared is a CUDA host function. A host function is simply a traditional C function that executes on host and can only be called from another host function. By default, all functions in a CUDA program are host functions if they do not have any of the CUDA keywords in their declaration. This makes sense since many CUDA applications are ported from CPU-only execution environments. The programmer would add kernel functions and device functions during porting process. The original functions remain as host functions. Having all functions to default into host functions spares the programmer the tedious work to change all original function declarations.

Note that one can use both "__host__" and "__device__" in a function declaration. This combination tells the compilation system to generate two versions of object files for the same function. One is executed on the host and can only be called from a host function. The other is executed on the device and can only be called from a device or kernel function. This supports a common use case when the same function source code can be recompiled to generate a device version. Many user library functions will likely fall into this category.

The second notable extension to ANSI C, in Fig. 2.12, are the built-in variables "threadIdx.x" "blockIdx.x" and "blockDim.x". Recall that all threads execute the same kernel code. There needs to be a way for them to distinguish among themselves and direct each thread towards a particular part of the data. These built-in variables

---

[7]We will explain the rules for using indirect function calls and recursions in different generations of CUDA later. In general, one should avoid the use of recursion and indirect function calls in their device functions and kernel functions to allow maximal portability.

are the means for threads to access hardware registers that provide the identifying coordinates to threads. Different threads will see different values in their threadIdx.x, blockIdx.x and blockDim.x variables. For simplicity, we will refer to a thread as thread$_{blockIdx.x, threadIdx.x}$. Note that the ".x" implies that there should be ".y" and ".z". We will come back to this point soon.

There is an automatic (local) variable i in Fig. 2.12. In a CUDA kernel function, automatic variables are private to each thread. That is, a version of i will be generated for every thread. If the kernel is launched with 10,000 threads, there will be 10,000 versions of i, one for each thread. The value assigned by a thread to its i variable is not visible to other threads. We will discuss these automatic variables in more details in Chapter 4, Memory and data locality.

A quick comparison between Figs. 2.5 and 2.12 reveals an important insight for CUDA kernels and CUDA kernel launch. The kernel function in Fig. 2.12 does not have a loop that corresponds to the one in Fig. 2.5. The readers should ask where the loop went. The answer is that the loop is now replaced with the grid of threads. The entire grid forms the equivalent of the loop. Each thread in the grid corresponds to one iteration of the original loop. This type of data parallelism is sometimes also referred to as *loop parallelism*, where iterations of the original sequential code are executed by threads in parallel.

Note that there is an if $(i < n)$ statement in addVecKernel in Fig. 2.12. This is because not all vector lengths can be expressed as multiples of the block size. For example, let's assume that the vector length is 100. The smallest efficient thread block dimension is 32. Assume that we picked 32 as block size. One would need to launch four thread blocks to process all the 100 vector elements. However, the four thread blocks would have 128 threads. We need to disable the last 28 threads in thread block 3 from doing work not expected by the original program. Since all threads are to execute the same code, all will test their i values against n, which is 100. With the if $(i < n)$ statement, the first 100 threads will perform the addition whereas the last 28 will not. This allows the kernel to process vectors of arbitrary lengths.

When the host code launches a kernel, it sets the grid and thread block dimensions via *execution configuration parameters*. This is illustrated in Fig. 2.14. The configuration parameters are given between the " <<<" and ">>>" before the traditional C function arguments. The first configuration parameter gives the number of thread blocks in the grid. The second specifies the number of threads in each thread block. In this example, there are 256 threads in each block. In order to ensure that we

```
int vectAdd(float* A, float* B, float* C, int n)
{
//  d_A, d_B, d_C allocations and copies omitted
// Run ceil(n/256) blocks of 256 threads each
    vecAddKernel<<<ceil(n/256.0), 256>>>(d_A, d_B, d_C, n);
}
```

FIGURE 2.14

A vector addition kernel launch statement.

have enough threads to cover all the vector elements, we apply the C ceiling function to *n*/256.0. Using floating-point value 256.0 ensures that we generate a floating value for the division so that the ceiling function can round it up correctly. For example, if we have 1000 threads, we would launch ceil(1000/256.0) = 4 thread blocks. As a result, the statement will launch 4*256 = 1024 threads. With the if ($i < n$) statement in the kernel as shown in Fig. 2.12, the first 1000 threads will perform addition on the 1000 vector elements. The remaining 24 will not.

2.6 KERNEL LAUNCH

Fig. 2.15 shows the final host code in the vecAdd function. This source code completes the skeleton in Fig. 2.6. Figs. 2.12 and 2.15 jointly illustrate a simple CUDA program that consists of both host code and a device kernel. The code is hardwired to use thread blocks of 256 threads each. The number of thread blocks used, however, depends on the length of the vectors (*n*). If *n* is 750, three thread blocks will be used. If *n* is 4000, 16 thread blocks will be used. If *n* is 2,000,000, 7813 blocks will be used. Note that all the thread blocks operate on different parts of the vectors. They can be executed in any arbitrary order. Programmers must not make any assumptions regarding execution order. A small GPU with a small amount of execution resources may execute only one or two of these thread blocks in parallel. A larger GPU may execute 64 or 128 blocks in parallel. This gives CUDA kernels scalability in execution speed with hardware, that is, same code runs at lower speed on small GPUs and

```
void vecAdd(float* A, float* B, float* C, int n)
{

  int size = n * sizeof(float);
  float *d_A, *d_B, *d_C;

  cudaMalloc((void **) &d_A, size);
  cudaMemcpy(d_A, A, size, cudaMemcpyHostToDevice);
  cudaMalloc((void **) &d_B, size);
  cudaMemcpy(d_B, B, size, cudaMemcpyHostToDevice);

  cudaMalloc((void **) &d_C, size);

  vecAddKernel<<<ceil(n/256.0), 256>>>(d_A, d_B, d_C, n);

  cudaMemcpy(C, d_C, size, cudaMemcpyDeviceToHost);

      // Free device memory for A, B, C
  cudaFree(d_A); cudaFree(d_B); cudaFree (d_C);
}
```

FIGURE 2.15

A complete version of the host code in the vecAdd.function.

higher speed on larger GPUs. We will revisit this point later in Chapter 3, Scalable parallel execution.

It is important to point out again that the vector addition example is used for its simplicity. In practice, the overhead of allocating device memory, input data transfer from host to device, output data transfer from device to host, and de-allocating device memory will likely make the resulting code slower than the original sequential code in Fig. 2.5. This is because the amount of calculation done by the kernel is small relative to the amount of data processed. Only one addition is performed for two floating-point input operands and one floating-point output operand. Real applications typically have kernels where much more work is needed relative to the amount of data processed, which makes the additional overhead worthwhile. They also tend to keep the data in the device memory across multiple kernel invocations so that the overhead can be amortized. We will present several examples of such applications.

2.7 SUMMARY

This chapter provided a quick, simplified overview of the CUDA C programming model. CUDA C extends the C language to support parallel computing. We discussed an essential subset of these extensions in this chapter. For your convenience, we summarize the extensions that we have discussed in this chapter as follows:

FUNCTION DECLARATIONS

CUDA C extends the C function declaration syntax to support heterogeneous parallel computing. The extensions are summarized in Fig. 2.13. Using one of "__global__", "__device__", or "__host__", a CUDA C programmer can instruct the compiler to generate a kernel function, a device function, or a host function. All function declarations without any of these keywords default to host functions. If both "__host__" and "__device__" are used in a function declaration, the compiler generates two versions of the function, one for the device and one for the host. If a function declaration does not have any CUDA C extension keyword, the function defaults into a host function.

KERNEL LAUNCH

CUDA C extends C function call syntax with kernel execution configuration parameters surrounded by <<< and >>>. These execution configuration parameters are only used during a call to a kernel function, or a kernel launch. We discussed the execution configuration parameters that define the dimensions of the grid and the dimensions of each block. The reader should refer to the CUDA Programming Guide [NVIDIA 2016] for more details of the kernel launch extensions as well as other types of execution configuration parameters.

BUILT-IN (PREDEFINED) VARIABLES

CUDA kernels can access a set of built-in, predefined read-only variables that allow each thread to distinguish among themselves and to determine the area of data each thread is to work on. We discussed the threadIdx, blockDim, and blockIdx variables in this chapter. In Chapter 3, Scalable parallel execution, we will discuss more details of using these variables.

RUN-TIME API

CUDA supports a set of API functions to provide services to CUDA C programs. The services that we discussed in this chapter are cudaMalloc(), cudaFree(), and cudaMemcpy() functions. These functions allocate device memory and transfer data between host and device on behalf of the calling program respectively. The reader is referred to the CUDA C Programming Guide for other CUDA API functions.

Our goal for this chapter is to introduce the core concepts of CUDA C and the essential CUDA C extensions to C for writing a simple CUDA C program. The chapter is by no means a comprehensive account of all CUDA features. Some of these features will be covered in the remainder of the book. However, our emphasis will be on the key parallel computing concepts supported by these features. We will only introduce enough CUDA C features that are needed in our code examples for parallel programming techniques. In general, we would like to encourage the reader to always consult the CUDA C Programming Guide for more details of the CUDA C features.

2.8 EXERCISES

1. If we want to use each thread to calculate one output element of a vector addition, what would be the expression for mapping the thread/block indices to data index?

    A. `i=threadIdx.x + threadIdx.y;`
    B. `i=blockIdx.x + threadIdx.x;`
    C. `i=blockIdx.x*blockDim.x + threadIdx.x;`
    D. `i=blockIdx.x * threadIdx.x;`

2. Assume that we want to use each thread to calculate two (adjacent) elements of a vector addition. What would be the expression for mapping the thread/block indices to i, the data index of the first element to be processed by a thread?

    A. `i=blockIdx.x*blockDim.x + threadIdx.x +2;`
    B. `i=blockIdx.x*threadIdx.x*2;`
    C. `i=(blockIdx.x*blockDim.x + threadIdx.x)*2;`
    D. `i=blockIdx.x*blockDim.x*2 + threadIdx.x;`

3. We want to use each thread to calculate two elements of a vector addition. Each thread block processes 2*blockDim.x consecutive elements that form two sections. All threads in each block will first process a section first, each processing one element. They will then all move to the next section, each processing one element. Assume that variable *i* should be the index for the first element to be processed by a thread. What would be the expression for mapping the thread/block indices to data index of the first element?

   A. `i=blockIdx.x*blockDim.x + threadIdx.x +2;`
   B. `i=blockIdx.x*threadIdx.x*2;`
   C. `i=(blockIdx.x*blockDim.x + threadIdx.x)*2;`
   D. `i=blockIdx.x*blockDim.x*2 + threadIdx.x;`

4. For a vector addition, assume that the vector length is 8000, each thread calculates one output element, and the thread block size is 1024 threads. The programmer configures the kernel launch to have a minimal number of thread blocks to cover all output elements. How many threads will be in the grid?

   A. 8000
   B. 8196
   C. 8192
   D. 8200

5. If we want to allocate an array of *v* integer elements in CUDA device global memory, what would be an appropriate expression for the second argument of the cudaMalloc call?

   A. n
   B. v
   C. `n * sizeof(int)`
   D. `v * sizeof(int)`

6. If we want to allocate an array of *n* floating-point elements and have a floating-point pointer variable *d_A* to point to the allocated memory, what would be an appropriate expression for the first argument of the cudaMalloc() call?

   A. n
   B. `(void *) d_A`
   C. `*d_A`
   D. `(void **) &d_A`

7. If we want to copy 3000 bytes of data from host array *h_A* (*h_A* is a pointer to element 0 of the source array) to device array *d_A* (*d_A* is a pointer to element 0 of the destination array), what would be an appropriate API call for this data copy in CUDA?

   A. `cudaMemcpy(3000, h_A, d_A, cudaMemcpyHostToDevice);`
   B. `cudaMemcpy(h_A, d_A, 3000, cudaMemcpyDeviceTHost);`
   C. `cudaMemcpy(d_A, h_A, 3000, cudaMemcpyHostToDevice);`
   D. `cudaMemcpy(3000, d_A, h_A, cudaMemcpyHostToDevice);`

8.   How would one declare a variable err that can appropriately receive returned value of a CUDA API call?

A.   `int err;`

B.   `cudaError err;`

C.   `cudaError_t err;`

D.   `cudaSuccess_t err;`

9.   A new summer intern was frustrated with CUDA. He has been complaining that CUDA is very tedious: he had to declare many functions that he plans to execute on both the host and the device twice, once as a host function and once as a device function. What is your response?

REFERENCES

Atallah, M. J. (Ed.). (1998). *Algorithms and theory of computation handbook.* Boca Raton: CRC Press.

Flynn, M. (1972). Some computer organizations and their effectiveness. *IEEE Transactions on Computers, C-21*, 948--960.

NVIDIA Corporation. (2016). NVIDIA CUDA C Programming Guide, version 7.

Patt, Y. N., & Patel, S. J. (2003). *Introduction to computing systems: from bits and gates to C and beyond.* McGraw Hill Publisher.

Stratton, J. A., Stone, S. S., & Hwu, W. W. (2008). MCUDA: an Efficient Implementation of CUDA Kernels for Multi-Core CPUs. *The 21st international workshop on languages and compilers for parallel computing*, July 30–31, Canada, 2008. Also available as Lecture Notes in Computer Science.

CHAPTER

Scalable parallel execution

3

Mark Ebersole

CHAPTER OUTLINE

In Chapter 2, Data parallel computing, we learned to write a simple CUDA C program that launches a kernel and a grid of threads to operate on elements in one-dimensional arrays. The kernel specifies the C statements executed by each thread. As we unleash such a massive execution activity, we need to control these activities to achieve desired results, efficiency, and speed. In this chapter, we will study important concepts involved in the control of parallel execution. We will start by learning how thread index and block index can facilitate processing multidimensional arrays. Subsequently, we will explore the concept of flexible resource assignment and the concept of occupancy. We will then advance into thread scheduling, latency tolerance, and synchronization. A CUDA programmer who masters these concepts is well-equipped to write and understand high-performance parallel applications.

3.1 CUDA THREAD ORGANIZATION

All CUDA threads in a grid execute the same kernel function; they rely on coordinates to distinguish themselves from one another and identify the appropriate portion of data to process. These threads are organized into a two-level hierarchy: a grid consists of one or more blocks, and each block consists of one or more threads. All threads in a block share the same block index, which is the value of the `blockIdx` variable in a kernel. Each thread has a thread index, which can be accessed as the value of the `threadIdx` variable in a kernel. When a thread executes a kernel function, references to the `blockIdx` and `threadIdx` variables return the coordinates of the thread. The execution configuration parameters in a kernel launch statement specify the dimensions of the grid and the dimensions of each block. These dimensions are the values of the variables `gridDim` and `blockDim` in kernel functions.

HIERARCHICAL ORGANIZATIONS

Similar to CUDA threads, many real-world systems are organized hierarchically. The United States telephone system is a good example. At the top level, the telephone system consists of "areas," each of which corresponds to a geographical area. All telephone lines within the same area have the same 3-digit "area code". A telephone area can be larger than a city; e.g., many counties and cities in Central Illinois are within the same telephone area and share the same area code 217. Within an area, each phone line has a seven-digit local phone number, which allows each area to have a maximum of about ten million numbers.

Each phone line can be considered as a CUDA thread, the area code as the value of `blockIdx`, and the seven-digit local number as the value of `threadIdx`. This hierarchical organization allows the system to accommodate a considerably large number of phone lines while preserving "locality" for calling the same area. When dialing a phone line in the same area, a caller only needs to dial the local number. As long as we make most of our calls within the local area, we seldom need to dial the area code. If we occasionally need to call a phone line in another area, we dial "1" and the area code, followed by the local number. (This is the reason why no local number in any area should start with "1.") The hierarchical organization of CUDA threads also offers a form of locality, which will be examined here.

In general, a grid is a three-dimensional array of blocks[1], and each block is a three-dimensional array of threads. When launching a kernel, the program needs to specify the size of the grid and blocks in each dimension. The programmer can use fewer than three dimensions *by setting the size of the unused dimensions to 1*. The exact organization of a grid is determined by the execution configuration parameters (within <<< >>>) of the kernel launch statement. The first execution configuration parameter specifies the dimensions of the grid in the number of blocks. The second specifies the dimensions of each block in the number of threads. Each such parameter is of the `dim3` type, which is a C `struct` with three unsigned integer fields: x, y, and z. These three fields specify the sizes of the three dimensions.

---

[1] Devices with compute capability less than 2.0 support grids with up to two-dimensional arrays of blocks.

To illustrate, the following host code can be used to launch the `vecAddkernel()` kernel function and generate a 1D grid that consists of 32 blocks, each of which consists of 128 threads. The total number of threads in the grid is 128*32 = 4096.

```
dim3 dimGrid(32, 1, 1);
dim3 dimBlock(128, 1, 1);
vecAddKernel<<<dimGrid, dimBlock>>>(…);
```

Note that `dimBlock` and `dimGrid` are host code variables defined by the programmer. These variables can have any legal C variable names as long as they are of the `dim3` type and the kernel launch uses the appropriate names. For instance, the following statements accomplish the same as the statements above:

```
dim3 dog(32, 1, 1);
dim3 cat(128, 1, 1);
vecAddKernel<<<dog, cat>>>(…);
```

The grid and block dimensions can also be calculated from other variables. The kernel launch in Fig. 2.15 can be written as follows:

```
dim3 dimGrid(ceil(n/256.0), 1, 1);
dim3 dimBlock(256, 1, 1);
vecAddKernel<<<dimGrid, dimBlock>>>(…);
```

The number of blocks may vary with the size of the vectors for the grid to have sufficient threads to cover all vector elements. In this example, the programmer chose to fix the block size at 256. The value of variable n at kernel launch time will determine the dimension of the grid. If n is equal to 1000, the grid will consist of four blocks. If n is equal to 4000, the grid will have 16 blocks. In each case, there will be enough threads to cover all of the vector elements. Once `vecAddKernel` is launched, the grid and block dimensions will remain the same until the entire grid finishes execution.

For convenience, CUDA C provides a special shortcut for launching a kernel with one-dimensional grids and blocks. Instead of `dim3` variables, arithmetic expressions can be used to specify the configuration of 1D grids and blocks. In this case, the CUDA C compiler simply takes the arithmetic expression as the x dimensions and assumes that the y and z dimensions are 1. Thus, the kernel launch statement is as shown in Fig. 2.15:

```
vecAddKernel<<<ceil(n/256.0), 256>>>(…);
```

Readers familiar with the use of structures in C would realize that this "shorthand" convention for 1D configurations takes advantage of the fact that the x field is the first field of the `dim3` structures `gridDim(x, y, z)` and `blockDim{x, y, z)`. This shortcut allows the compiler to conveniently initialize the x fields of `gridDim` and `blockDim` with the values provided in the execution configuration parameters.

Within the kernel function, the x field of the variables `gridDim` and `blockDim` are pre-initialized according to the values of the execution configuration parameters.

If n is equal to 4000, references to `gridDim.x` and `blockDim.x` in the `vectAddkernel` kernel will obtain 16 and 256, respectively. Unlike the `dim3` variables in the host code, the names of these variables within the kernel functions are part of the CUDA C specification and cannot be changed—i.e., `gridDim` and `blockDim` in a kernel always reflect the dimensions of the grid and the blocks.

In CUDA C, the allowed values of `gridDim.x`, `gridDim.y` and `gridDim.z` range from 1 to 65,536. All threads in a block share the same `blockIdx.x`, `blockIdx.y`, and `blockIdx.z` values. Among blocks, the `blockIdx.x` value ranges from 0 to `gridDim.x-1`, the `blockIdx.y` value from 0 to `gridDim.y-1`, and the `blockIdx.z` value from 0 to `gridDim.z-1`.

Regarding the configuration of blocks, each block is organized into a three-dimensional array of threads. Two-dimensional blocks can be created by setting `blockDim.z` to 1. One-dimensional blocks can be created by setting both `blockDim.y` and `blockDim.z` to 1, as was the case in the `vectorAddkernel` example. As previously mentioned, all blocks in a grid have the same dimensions and sizes. The number of threads in each dimension of a block is specified by the second execution configuration parameter at the kernel launch. Within the kernel, this configuration parameter can be accessed as the x, y, and z fields of blockDim.

The total size of a block is limited to 1024 threads, with flexibility in distributing these elements into the three dimensions as long as the total number of threads does not exceed 1024. For instance, `blockDim(512, 1, 1)`, `blockDim(8, 16, 4)`, and `blockDim(32, 16, 2)` are allowable blockDim values, but `blockDim(32, 32, 2)` is not allowable because the total number of threads would exceed 1024.[2]

The grid can have higher dimensionality than its blocks and vice versa. For instance, Fig. 3.1 shows a small toy grid example of `gridDim(2, 2, 1)` with `blockDim(4, 2, 2)`. The grid can be generated with the following host code:

```
dim3 dimGrid(2, 2, 1);
dim3 dimBlock(4, 2, 2);
KernelFunction<<<dimGrid, dimBlock>>>(…);
```

The grid consists of four blocks organized into a 2 × 2 array. Each block in Fig. 3.1 is labeled with (`blockIdx.y`, `blockIdx.x`), e.g., Block(1,0) has `blockIdx.y=1` and `blockIdx.x=0`. The labels are ordered such that the highest dimension comes first. *Note that this block labeling notation is the reversed ordering of that used in the C statements for setting configuration parameters where the lowest dimension comes first.* This reversed ordering for labeling blocks works more effectively when we illustrate the mapping of thread coordinates into data indexes in accessing multidimensional data.

Each `threadIdx` also consists of three fields: the x coordinate `threadId.x`, the y coordinate `threadIdx.y`, and the z coordinate `threadIdx.z`. Fig. 3.1 illustrates the organization of threads within a block. In this example, each block is organized into 4 × 2 × 2 arrays of threads. All blocks within a grid have the same dimensions; thus, we

---

[2] Devices with capability less than 2.0 allow blocks with up to 512 threads.

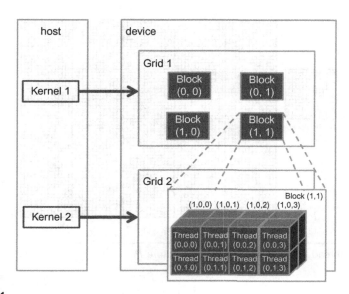

FIGURE 3.1

A multidimensional example of CUDA grid organization.

only need to show one of them. Fig. 3.1 expands Block(1,1) to show its 16 threads. For instance, Thread(1,0,2) has `threadIdx.z=1`, `threadIdx.y=0`, and `threadIdx.x=2`. This example shows 4 blocks of 16 threads each, with a total of 64 threads in the grid. We use these small numbers to keep the illustration simple. Typical CUDA grids contain thousands to millions of threads.

3.2 MAPPING THREADS TO MULTIDIMENSIONAL DATA

The choice of 1D, 2D, or 3D thread organizations is usually based on the nature of the data. Pictures are 2D array of pixels. Using a 2D grid that consists of 2D blocks is often convenient for processing the pixels in a picture. Fig. 3.2 shows such an arrangement for processing a 76 × 62 picture P (76 pixels in the horizontal or x direction and 62 pixels in the vertical or y direction). Assume that we decided to use a 16 × 16 block, with 16 threads in the x direction and 16 threads in the y direction. We will need 5 blocks in the x direction and 4 blocks in the y direction, resulting in 5 × 4 = 20 blocks, as shown in Fig. 3.2. The heavy lines mark the block boundaries. The shaded area depicts the threads that cover pixels. It is easy to verify that one can identify the Pin element processed by thread(0,0) of block(1,0) with the formula:

$$P_{\text{blockIdx.y*blockDim.y+threadIdx.y,blockIdx.x*blockDim.x+threadIdx.x}} = P_{1*16+0,0*16+0} = P_{16,0}.$$

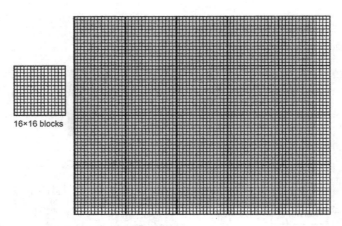

FIGURE 3.2

Using a 2D thread grid to process a 76 × 62 picture *P*.

Note that we have 4 extra threads in the *x* direction and 2 extra threads in the *y* direction—i.e., we will generate 80 × 64 threads to process 76 × 62 pixels. This case is similar to the situation in which a 1000-element vector is processed by the 1D kernel vecAddKernel in Fig. 2.11 by using four 256-thread blocks. Recall that an if statement is needed to prevent the extra 24 threads from taking effect. Analogously, we should expect that the picture processing kernel function will have if statements to test whether the thread indexes threadIdx.x and threadIdx.y fall within the valid range of pixels.

Assume that the host code uses an integer variable m to track the number of pixels in the *x* direction and another integer variable n to track the number of pixels in the *y* direction. We further assume that the input picture data have been copied to the device memory and can be accessed through a pointer variable d_Pin. The output picture has been allocated in the device memory and can be accessed through a pointer variable d_Pout. The following host code can be used to launch a 2D kernel colorToGreyscaleConversion to process the picture, as follows:

```
dim3 dimGrid(ceil(m/16.0), ceil(n/16.0), 1);
dim3 dimBlock(16, 16, 1);
colorToGreyscaleConversion<<<dimGrid,dimBlock>>>(d_Pin,d_Pout,m,n);
```

In this example, we assume, for simplicity, that the dimensions of the blocks are fixed at 16 × 16. Meanwhile, the dimensions of the grid depend on the dimensions of the picture. To process a 2000 × 1500 (3-million-pixel) picture, we will generate 11,750 blocks—125 in the *x* direction and 94 in the *y* direction. Within the kernel function, references to gridDim.x, gridDim.y, blockDim.x, and blockDim.y will result in 125, 94, 16, and 16, respectively.

MEMORY SPACE

Memory space is a simplified view of how a processor accesses its memory in modern computers. It is usually associated with each running application. The data to be processed by an application and instructions executed for the application are stored in locations in its memory space. Typically, each location can accommodate a byte and has an address. Variables that require multiple bytes—4 bytes for float and 8 bytes for double—are stored in consecutive byte locations. The processor generates the starting address (address of the starting byte location) and the number of bytes needed when accessing a data value from the memory space.

The locations in a memory space are similar to phones in a telephone system where everyone has a unique phone number. Most modern computers have at least 4G byte-sized locations, where each G is 1,073,741,824 (2^{30}). All locations are labeled with an address ranging from 0 to the largest number. Every location has only one address; thus, we say that the memory space has a "flat" organization. As a result, all multidimensional arrays are ultimately "flattened" into equivalent one-dimensional arrays. Whereas a C programmer can use a multidimensional syntax to access an element of a multidimensional array, the compiler translates these accesses into a base pointer that points to the initial element of the array, along with an offset calculated from these multidimensional indexes.

Before we show the kernel code, we need to first understand how C statements access elements of dynamically allocated multidimensional arrays. Ideally, we would like to access d_Pin as a two-dimensional array where an element at row *j* and column *i* can be accessed as d_Pin[j][i]. However, the ANSI C standard on which the development of CUDA C was based requires that the number of columns in d_Pin be known at compile time for d_Pin to be accessed as a 2D array. Unfortunately, this information is not known at compiler time for dynamically allocated arrays. In fact, part of the reason dynamically allocated arrays are used is to allow the sizes and dimensions of these arrays to vary according to data size at run time. Thus, the information on the number of columns in a dynamically allocated two-dimensional array is unknown at compile time by design. Consequently, programmers need to explicitly linearize or "flatten" a dynamically allocated two-dimensional array into an equivalent one-dimensional array in the current CUDA C. The newer C99 standard allows multidimensional syntax for dynamically allocated arrays. Future CUDA C versions may support multidimensional syntax for dynamically allocated arrays.

In reality, all multidimensional arrays in C are linearized because of the use of a "flat" memory space in modern computers (see "Memory Space" sidebar). In statically allocated arrays, the compilers allow the programmers to use higher-dimensional indexing syntax such as d_Pin[j][i] to access their elements. Under the hood, the

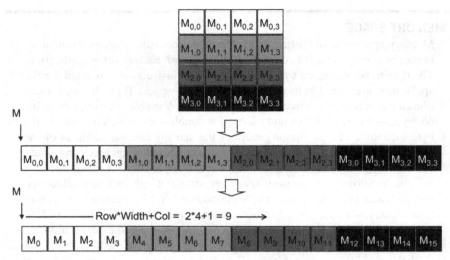

FIGURE 3.3

Row-major layout for a 2D C array. The result is an equivalent 1D array accessed by an index expression $j*$Width$+$ i for an element that is in the j th row and i th column of an array of Width elements in each row.

compiler linearizes them into an equivalent one-dimensional array and translates the multidimensional indexing syntax into a one-dimensional offset. In dynamically allocated arrays, the current CUDA C compiler leaves the work of such translation to the programmers because of the lack of dimensional information at compile time.

A two-dimensional array can be linearized in at least two ways. One way is to place all elements of the same row into consecutive locations. The rows are then placed one after another into the memory space. This arrangement, called *row-major layout*, is depicted in Fig. 3.3. To improve readability, we will use $M_{j,i}$ to denote the M element at the jth row and the ith column. $P_{j,i}$ is equivalent to the C expression $M[j][i]$ but is slightly more readable. Fig. 3.3 illustrates how a 4×4 matrix M is linearized into a 16-element one-dimensional array, with all elements of row 0 first, followed by the four elements of row 1, and so on. Therefore, the one-dimensional equivalent index for M in row j and column i is $j*4 + i$. The $j*4$ term skips all elements of the rows before row j. The i term then selects the right element within the section for row j. The one-dimensional index for $M_{2,1}$ is $2*4 + 1 = 9$, as shown in Fig. 3.3, where M_9 is the one-dimensional equivalent to $M_{2,1}$. This process shows the way C compilers linearize two-dimensional arrays.

Another method to linearize a two-dimensional array is to place all elements of the same column into consecutive locations. The columns are then placed one after another into the memory space. This arrangement, called the *column-major layout* is used by FORTRAN compilers. The column-major layout of a two-dimensional array is equivalent to the row-major layout of its transposed form. Readers whose primary previous programming experience were with FORTRAN should be aware that CUDA C uses the row-major layout rather than the column-major layout. In addition, numerous C libraries that are designed for FORTRAN programs use the column-major layout to match the FORTRAN compiler layout. Consequently, the manual pages for these libraries, such as Basic Linear Algebra Subprograms (BLAS) (see "Linear Algebra Functions" sidebar), usually instruct the users to transpose the input arrays if they call these libraries from C programs.

LINEAR ALGEBRA FUNCTIONS

Linear algebra operations are widely used in science and engineering applications. BLAS, a de facto standard for publishing libraries that perform basic algebraic operations, includes three levels of linear algebra functions. As the level increases, the number of operations performed by the function increases as well. Level-1 functions perform vector operations of the form $\mathbf{y} = \alpha\mathbf{x} + \mathbf{y}$, where $\mathbf{x}$ and $\mathbf{y}$ are vectors and α is a scalar. Our vector addition example is a special case of a level-1 function with $\alpha=1$. Level-2 functions perform matrix–vector operations of the form $\mathbf{y} = \alpha\mathbf{A}\mathbf{x} + \beta\mathbf{y}$, where $\mathbf{A}$ is a matrix, $\mathbf{x}$ and $\mathbf{y}$ are vectors, and α, β are scalars. We will be examining a form of level-2 function in sparse linear algebra. Level-3 functions perform matrix–matrix operations of the form $\mathbf{C} = \alpha\mathbf{A}\mathbf{B} + \beta\mathbf{C}$, where $\mathbf{A}$, $\mathbf{B}$, $\mathbf{C}$ are matrices and α, β are scalars. Our matrix–matrix multiplication example is a special case of a level-3 function, where $\alpha=1$ and $\beta=0$. These BLAS functions are used as basic building blocks of higher-level algebraic functions such as linear system solvers and eigenvalue analysis. As we will discuss later, the performance of different implementations of BLAS functions can vary by orders of magnitude in both sequential and parallel computers.

We are now ready to study the source code of `colorToGreyscaleConversion` shown in Fig. 3.4. The kernel code uses the formula

$$L = r * 0.21 + g * 0.72 + b * 0.07$$

to convert each color pixel to its greyscale counterpart.

A total of `blockDim.x*gridDim.x` threads can be found in the horizontal direction. As in the `vecAddKernel` example, the expression

`Col=blockIdx.x*blockDim.x+threadIdx.x` generates every integer value from 0 to `blockDim.x*gridDim.x-1`. We know that `gridDim.x*blockDim.x` is greater than or equal to `width` (m value passed in from the host code). We have at least as many threads as the number of pixels in the horizontal direction. Similarly, we know that

```
// we have 3 channels corresponding to RGB
// The input image is encoded as unsigned characters [0, 255]
__global__
void colorToGreyscaleConversion(unsigned char * Pout, unsigned
                   char * Pin, int width, int height) {,
int Col = threadIdx.x + blockIdx.x * blockDim.x;
int Row = threadIdx.y + blockIdx.y * blockDim.y;
if (Col < width && Row < height) {
   // get 1D coordinate for the grayscale image
   int greyOffset = Row*width + Col;
   // one can think of the RGB image having
   // CHANNEL times columns than the grayscale image
   int rgbOffset = greyOffset*CHANNELS;
   unsigned char r = Pin[rgbOffset    ]; // red value for pixel
   unsigned char g = Pin[rgbOffset + 2]; // green value for pixel
   unsigned char b = Pin[rgbOffset + 3]; // blue value for pixel
   // perform the rescaling and store it
   // We multiply by floating point constants
   Pout[grayOffset] = 0.21f*r + 0.71f*g + 0.07f*b;
 }
 }
```

FIGURE 3.4

Source code of colorToGreyscaleConversion showing 2D thread mapping to data.

at least as many threads as the number of pixels in the vertical direction are present. Therefore, as long as we test and make sure only the threads with both Row and Col values are within range—i.e., (Col<width) && (Row<height)—we can cover every pixel in the picture.

Given that each row has width pixels, we can thus generate the one-dimensional index for the pixel at row Row and column Col as Row*width+Col. This one-dimensional index greyOffset is the pixel index for Pout as each pixel in the output greyscale image is one byte (unsigned char). By using our 76 × 62 image example, the linearized one-dimensional index of the Pout pixel is calculated by thread(0,0) of block(1,0) with the formula:

$$Pout_{blockIdx.y*blockDim.y+threadIdx.y,\ blockIdx.x*blockDim.x+threadIdx.x} = Pout_{1*16+0,0*16+0}$$
$$= Pout_{16,0} = Pout[16 * 76 + 0] = Pout[1216]$$

As for Pin, we multiply the gray pixel index by 3 because each pixel is stored as (r, g, b), with each equal to one byte. The resulting rgbOffset gives the starting location of the color pixel in the Pin array. We read the r, g, and b values from the three consecutive byte locations of the Pin array, perform the calculation of the greyscale pixel value, and write that value into the Pout array by using greyOffset. With our 76 × 62 image example, the linearized one-dimensional index of the Pin pixel is calculated by thread(0,0) of block(1,0) with the following formula:

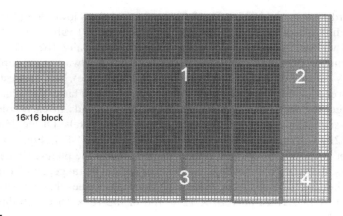

16×16 block

FIGURE 3.5

Covering a 76 × 62 picture with 16 × 16 blocks.

$$Pin_{blockIdx.y*blockDim.y+threadIdx.y,blockIdx.x*blockDim.x+threadIdx.x} = Pin_{1*16+0,0*16+0}$$
$$= Pin_{16,0} = Pin[16 * 76 * 3 + 0] = Pin[3648]$$

The data being accessed are the three bytes, starting at byte index 3648.

Fig. 3.5 illustrates the execution of colorToGreyscaleConversion when processing our 76 × 62 example. Assuming that we use 16 × 16 blocks, launching color-ToGreyscaleConvertion generates 80 × 64 threads. The grid will have 20 blocks—5 in the horizontal direction and 4 in the vertical direction. The execution behavior of blocks will fall into one of four different cases, depicted as four shaded areas in Fig. 3.5.

The first area, marked as "1" in Fig. 3.5, consists of threads that belong to the 12 blocks covering the majority of pixels in the picture. Both the Col and Row values of these threads are within range; all these threads will pass the if-statement test and process pixels in the heavily shaded area of the picture—i.e., all 16 × 16 = 256 threads in each block will process pixels. The second area, marked as "2" in Fig. 3.5, contains the threads that belong to the three blocks in the medium-shaded area covering the upper right pixels of the picture. Although the Row values of these threads are always within range, some Col values exceed the m value (76). The reason is that the number of threads in the horizontal direction is always a multiple of the blockDim.x value chosen by the programmer (16 in this case). The smallest multiple of 16 needed to cover 76 pixels is 80. Thus, 12 threads in each row will have Col values that are within range and will process pixels. Meanwhile, 4 threads in each row will have Col values that are out of range and thus fail the if-statement condition. These threads will not process any pixels. Overall, 12 × 16 = 192 of the 16 × 16 = 256 threads in each of these blocks will process pixels.

The third area, marked "3" in Fig. 3.5, accounts for the 3 lower left blocks covering the medium-shaded area in the picture. Although the Col values of these threads are always within range, some Row values exceed the m value (62). The reason is that the number of threads in the vertical direction is always a multiple of the blockDim.y value chosen by the programmer (16 in this case). The smallest multiple of 16 to cover 62 is 64. Thus, 14 threads in each column will have Row values that are within range and will process pixels. Meanwhile, 2 threads in each column will fail the if-statement of area 2 and will not process any pixels. Of the 256 threads, $16 \times 14 = 224$ will process pixels. The fourth area, marked "4" in Fig. 3.5, contains threads that cover the lower right, lightly shaded area of the picture. In each of the top 14 rows, 4 threads will have Col values that are out of range, similar to Area 2. The entire bottom two rows of this block will have Row values that are out of range, similar to area "3". Thus, only $14 \times 12 = 168$ of the $16 \times 16 = 256$ threads will process pixels.

We can easily extend our discussion of 2D arrays to 3D arrays by including another dimension when we linearize arrays. This is accomplished by placing each "plane" of the array one after another into the address space. The assumption is that the programmer uses variables m and n to track the number of columns and rows in a 3D array. The programmer also needs to determine the values of blockDim.z and gridDim.z when launching a kernel. In the kernel, the array index will involve another global index:

```
int Plane = blockIdx.z*blockDim.z + threadIdx.z
```

The linearized access to a three-dimensional array P will be of the form P[Plane*m*n+Row*m+Col]. A kernel processing the 3D P array needs to check whether all the three global indexes—Plane, Row, and Col—fall within the valid range of the array.

3.3 IMAGE BLUR: A MORE COMPLEX KERNEL

We have studied vecAddkernel and colorToGreyscaleConversion in which each thread performs only a small number of arithmetic operations on one array element. These kernels serve their purposes well: to illustrate the basic CUDA C program structure and data parallel execution concepts. At this point, the reader should ask the obvious question—do all CUDA threads perform only such simple, trivial amount of operation independently of each other? The answer is no. In real CUDA C programs, threads often perform complex algorithms on their data and need to cooperate with one another. For the next few chapters, we are going to work on increasingly more complex examples that exhibit these characteristics. We will start with an image blurring function.

Image blurring smooths out the abrupt variation of pixel values while preserving the edges that are essential for recognizing the key features of the image. Fig. 3.6 illustrates the effect of image blurring. Simply stated, we make the image appear blurry. To the human eye, a blurred image tends to obscure the fine details and present

FIGURE 3.6

An original image and a blurred version.

the "big picture" impression or the major thematic objects in the picture. In computer image processing algorithms, a common use case of image blurring is to reduce the impact of noise and granular rendering effects in an image by correcting problematic pixel values with the clean surrounding pixel values. In computer vision, image blurring can be used to allow edge detection and object recognition algorithms to focus on thematic objects rather than being impeded by a massive quantity of fine-grained objects. In displays, image blurring is sometimes used to highlight a particular part of the image by blurring the rest of the image.

Mathematically, an image blurring function calculates the value of an output image pixel as a weighted sum of a patch of pixels encompassing the pixel in the input image. As we will learn in Chapter 7, Parallel pattern: convolution, the computation of such weighted sums belongs to the *convolution* pattern. We will be using a simplified approach in this chapter by taking a simple average value of the N×N patch of pixels surrounding, and including, our target pixel. To keep the algorithm simple, we will not place a weight on the value of any pixels based on its distance from the target pixel, which is common in a convolution blurring approach such as Gaussian blur.

Fig. 3.7 shows an example using a 3 × 3 patch. When calculating an output pixel value at the (Row, Col) position, we see that the patch is centered at the input pixel located at the (Row, Col) position. The 3 × 3 patch spans three rows (Row-1, Row, Row+1) and three columns (Col-1, Col, Col+1). To illustrate, the coordinates of the nine pixels for calculating the output pixel at (25, 50) are (24, 49), (24, 50), (24, 51), (25, 49), (25, 50), (25, 51), (26, 49), (26, 50), and (26, 51).

Fig. 3.8 shows an image blur kernel. Similar to that in colorToGreyscaleConversion, we use each thread to calculate an output pixel. That is, the thread to output data mapping remains the same. Thus, at the beginning of the kernel, we see the familiar calculation of the Col and Row indexes. We also see the familiar if-statement that verifies whether both Col and Row are within the valid range according to the height and width of the image. Only the threads whose Col and Row indexes are within the value ranges will be allowed to participate in the execution.

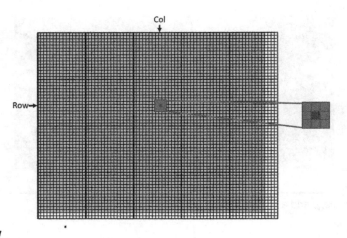

FIGURE 3.7

Each output pixel is the average of a patch of pixels in the input image.

```
    __global__
    void blurKernel(unsigned char * in, unsigned char * out, int w, int h)
       {
       int Col  = blockIdx.x * blockDim.x + threadIdx.x;
       int Row  = blockIdx.y * blockDim.y + threadIdx.y;

       if (Col < w && Row < h) {
1.        int pixVal = 0;
2.        int pixels = 0;

          // Get the average of the surrounding BLUR_SIZE x BLUR_SIZE box
3.        for(int blurRow = -BLUR_SIZE; blurRow < BLUR_SIZE+1; ++blurRow) {
4.          for(int blurCol = -BLUR_SIZE; blurCol < BLUR_SIZE+1; ++blurCol)
          {

5.             int curRow = Row + blurRow;
6.             int curCol = Col + blurCol;
             // Verify we have a valid image pixel
7.             if(curRow > -1 && curRow < h && curCol > -1 && curCol < w) {

8.                 pixVal += in[curRow * w + curCol];
9.                 pixels++; // Keep track of number of pixels in the avg
                }
             }
          }

          // Write our new pixel value out
10.       out[Row * w + Col] = (unsigned char)(pixVal / pixels);
       }
    }
```

FIGURE 3.8

An image blur kernel.

As shown in Fig. 3.7, the Col and Row values also generate the central pixel location of the patch used to calculate the output pixel for the thread. The nested for-loop Lines 3 and 4 of Fig. 3.8 iterate through all pixels in the patch. We assume that the program has a defined constant, BLUR_SIZE. The value of BLUR_SIZE is set such that 2*BLUR_SIZE gives the number of pixels on each side of the patch. For a 3 × 3 patch, BLUR_SIZE is set to 1, whereas for a 7 × 7 patch, BLUR_SIZE is set to 3. The outer loop iterates through the rows of the patch. For each row, the inner loop iterates through the columns of the patch.

In our 3 × 3 patch example, the BLUR_SIZE is 1. For the thread that calculates the output pixel (25, 50), during the first iteration of the outer loop, the curRow variable is Row-BLUR_SIZE = (25 − 1) = 24. Thus, during the first iteration of the outer loop, the inner loop iterates through the patch pixels in row 24. The inner loop iterates from the column Col-BLUR_SIZE = 50 − 1 = 49 to Col+BLUR_SIZE = 51 by using the curCol variable. Therefore, the pixels processed in the first iteration of the outer loop are (24, 49), (24, 50), and (24, 51). The reader should verify that in the second iteration of the outer loop, the inner loop iterates through pixels (25, 49), (25, 50), and (25, 51). Finally, in the third iteration of the outer loop, the inner loop iterates through pixels (26, 49), (26, 50), and (26, 51).

Line 8 uses the linearized index of curRow and curCol to access the value of the input pixel visited in the current iteration. It accumulates the pixel value into a running sum variable pixVal. Line 9 records the addition of one more pixel value into the running sum by incrementing the pixels variable. After all pixels in the patch are processed, Line 10 calculates the average value of the pixels in the patch by dividing the pixVal value by the pixels value. It uses the linearized index of Row and Col to write the result into its output pixel.

Line 7 contains a conditional statement that guards the execution of Lines 9 and 10. For output pixels near the edge of the image, the patch may extend beyond the valid range of the picture. This is illustrated in Fig. 3.9 assuming 3 × 3 patches. In Case 1, the pixel at the upper left corner is being blurred. Five of the nine pixels in the intended patch do not exist in the input image. In this case, the Row and Col values of the output pixel are 0 and 0. During the execution of the nested loop, the CurRow and CurCol values for the nine iterations are (−1,−1), (−1,0), (−1,1), (0,−1), (0,0), (0,1), (1,−1), (1,0), and (1,1). Note that for the five pixels outside the image, at least one of the values is less than 0. The curRow<0 and curCol<0 conditions of the if-statement capture these values and skip the execution of Lines 8 and 9. As a result, only the values of the four valid pixels are accumulated into the running sum variable. The pixels value is also correctly incremented four times so that the average can be calculated properly at Line 10.

The readers should work through the other cases in Fig. 3.9 and analyze the execution behavior of the nested loop in the blurKernel. Note that most of the threads will find all pixels in their assigned 3 × 3 patch within the input image. They will accumulate all the nine pixels in the nested loop. However, for the pixels on the four corners, the responsible threads will accumulate only 4 pixels. For other pixels on the four edges, the responsible threads will accumulate 6 pixels in the nested loop.

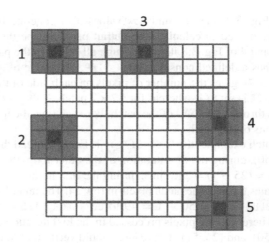

FIGURE 3.9

Handling boundary conditions for pixels near the edges of the image.

These variations necessitate keeping track of the actual number of pixels accumulated with variable `pixels`.

3.4 SYNCHRONIZATION AND TRANSPARENT SCALABILITY

We have discussed thus far how to launch a kernel for execution by a grid of threads and how to map threads to parts of the data structure. However, we have not yet presented any means to coordinate the execution of multiple threads. We will now study a basic coordination mechanism. CUDA allows threads in the same block to coordinate their activities by using a barrier synchronization function `__syncthreads()`. Note that "`__`" consists of two "`_`" characters. When a thread calls `__syncthreads()`, it will be held at the calling location until every thread in the block reaches the location. This process ensures that all threads in a block have completed a phase of their execution of the kernel before any of them can proceed to the next phase.

Barrier synchronization is a simple and popular method for coordinating parallel activities. In real life, we often use barrier synchronization to coordinate parallel activities of multiple persons. To illustrate, assume that four friends go to a shopping mall in a car. They can all go to different stores to shop for their own clothes. This is a parallel activity and is much more efficient than if they all remain as a group and sequentially visit all stores of interest. However, barrier synchronization is needed before they leave the mall. They have to wait until all four friends have returned to the car before they can leave. The ones who finish ahead of others need to wait for those who finish later. Without the barrier synchronization, one or more persons can be left behind in the mall when the car leaves, which can seriously damage their friendship!

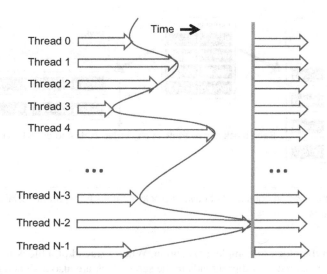

FIGURE 3.10

An example execution timing of barrier synchronization.

Fig. 3.10 illustrates the execution of barrier synchronization. There are N threads in the block. Time goes from left to right. Some of the threads reach the barrier synchronization statement early and some of them much later. The ones who reach the barrier early will wait for those who arrive late. When the latest one arrives at the barrier, everyone can continue their execution. With barrier synchronization, "No one is left behind."

In CUDA, a __syncthreads() statement, if present, must be executed by all threads in a block. When a __syncthread() statement is placed in an if-statement, either all or none of the threads in a block execute the path that includes the __syncthreads(). For an if-then-else statement, if each path has a __syncthreads() statement, either all threads in a block execute the then-path or all of them execute the else-path. The two __syncthreads() are different barrier synchronization points. If a thread in a block executes the then-path and another executes the else-path, they would be waiting at different barrier synchronization points. They would end up waiting for each other forever. It is the responsibility of the programmers to write their code so that these requirements are satisfied.

The ability to synchronize also imposes execution constraints on threads within a block. These threads should execute in close temporal proximity with each other to avoid excessively long waiting times. In fact, one needs to make sure that all threads involved in the barrier synchronization have access to the necessary resources to eventually arrive at the barrier. Otherwise, a thread that never arrives at the barrier synchronization point can cause everyone else to wait forever. CUDA runtime systems satisfy this constraint by assigning execution resources to all threads in a block as a unit. A block can begin execution only when the runtime system has secured all resources needed for

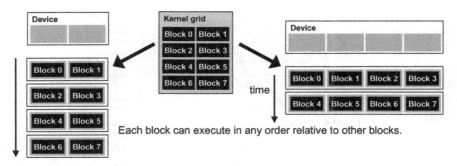

Each block can execute in any order relative to other blocks.

FIGURE 3.11

Lack of synchronization constraints between blocks enables transparent scalability for CUDA programs.

all threads in the block to complete execution. When a thread of a block is assigned to an execution resource, all other threads in the same block are also assigned to the same resource. This condition ensures the temporal proximity of all threads in a block and prevents excessive or indefinite waiting time during barrier synchronization.

This leads us to an important tradeoff in the design of CUDA barrier synchronization. By not allowing threads in different blocks to perform barrier synchronization with each other, the CUDA runtime system can execute blocks in any order relative to each other because none of them need to wait for each other. This flexibility enables scalable implementations as shown in Fig. 3.11, where time progresses from top to bottom. In a low-cost system with only a few execution resources, one can execute a small number of blocks simultaneously, portrayed as executing two blocks at a time on the left hand side of Fig. 3.11. In a high-end implementation with more execution resources, one can execute a large number of blocks simultaneously, shown as four blocks at a time on the right hand side of Fig. 3.11.

The ability to execute the same application code within a wide range of speeds allows the production of a wide range of implementations in accordance with the cost, power, and performance requirements of particular market segments. For instance, a mobile processor may execute an application slowly but at extremely low power consumption, and a desktop processor may execute the same application at a higher speed but at increased power consumption. Both execute exactly the same application program with no change to the code. The ability to execute the same application code on hardware with different numbers of execution resources is referred to as *transparent scalability*. This characteristic reduces the burden on application developers and improves the usability of applications.

3.5 RESOURCE ASSIGNMENT

Once a kernel is launched, the CUDA runtime system generates the corresponding grid of threads. As discussed in the previous section, these threads are assigned to

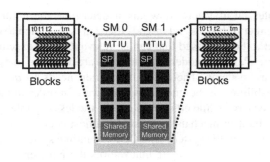

FIGURE 3.12

Thread block assignment to Streaming Multiprocessors (SMs).

execution resources on a block-by-block basis. In the current generation of hardware, the execution resources are organized into Streaming Multiprocessors (SMs). Fig. 3.12 illustrates that multiple thread blocks can be assigned to each SM. Each device sets a limit on the number of blocks that can be assigned to each SM. For instance, let us consider a CUDA device that may allow up to 8 blocks to be assigned to each SM. In situations where there is shortage of one or more types of resources needed for the simultaneous execution of 8 blocks, the CUDA runtime automatically reduces the number of blocks assigned to each SM until their combined resource usage falls below the limit. With limited numbers of SMs and limited numbers of blocks that can be assigned to each SM, the number of blocks that can be actively executing in a CUDA device is limited as well. Most grids contain many more blocks than this number. The runtime system maintains a list of blocks that need to execute and assigns new blocks to SMs as previously assigned blocks complete execution.

Fig. 3.12 shows an example in which three thread blocks are assigned to each SM. One of the SM resource limitations is the number of threads that can be simultaneously tracked and scheduled. It takes hardware resources (built-in registers) for SMs to maintain the thread and block indexes and track their execution status. Therefore, each generation of hardware sets a limit on the number of blocks and number of threads that can be assigned to an SM. For instance in the Fermi architecture, up to 8 blocks and 1536 threads can be assigned to each SM. This could be in the form of 6 blocks of 256 threads each, 3 blocks of 512 threads each, and so on. If the device only allows up to 8 blocks in an SM, it should be obvious that 12 blocks of 128 threads each is not a viable option. If a CUDA device has 30 SMs, and each SM can accommodate up to 1536 threads, the device can have up to 46,080 threads simultaneously residing in the CUDA device for execution.

3.6 QUERYING DEVICE PROPERTIES

Our discussions on assigning execution resources to blocks raise an important question. How do we find out the amount of resources available? When a CUDA application executes on a system, how can it determine the number of SMs in a device and the number of blocks and threads that can be assigned to each SM? Other resources have yet to be discussed that can be relevant to the execution of a CUDA application. In general, many modern applications are designed to execute on a wide variety of hardware systems. The application often needs to *query* the available resources and capabilities of the underlying hardware in order to take advantage of the more capable systems while compensating for the less capable systems.

In CUDA C, a built-in mechanism exists for a host code to query the properties of the devices available in the system. The CUDA runtime system (device driver) has an API function cudaGetDeviceCount that returns the number of available CUDA devices in the system. The host code can determine the number of available CUDA devices by using the following statements:

```
int dev_count;
cudaGetDeviceCount(&dev_count);
```

RESOURCE AND CAPABILITY QUERIES

In everyday life, we often query the resources and capabilities available in an environment. When we make a hotel reservation, we can check the amenities that come with a hotel room. If the room comes with a hair dryer, we do not need to bring one. Most American hotel rooms come with hair dryers; many hotels in other regions do not.

Some Asian and European hotels provide toothpastes and even toothbrushes, whereas most American hotels do not. Many American hotels provide both shampoo and conditioner, whereas hotels in other continents often only provide shampoo.

If the room comes with a microwave oven and a refrigerator, we can take the leftover from dinner and expect to eat it the following day. If the hotel has a pool, we can bring swimsuits and take a dip after business meetings. If the hotel does not have a pool but has an exercise room, we can bring running shoes and exercise clothes. Some high-end Asian hotels even provide exercise clothing!

These hotel amenities are part of the properties, or resources and capabilities, of the hotels. Veteran travelers check these properties at hotel web sites, choose the hotels that better match their needs, and pack more efficiently and effectively given these details.

While it may not be obvious, a modern PC system often has two or more CUDA devices. The reason is that many PC systems come with one or more "integrated" GPUs. These GPUs are the default graphics units and provide rudimentary capabilities and hardware resources to perform minimal graphics functionalities for modern Windows-based user interfaces. Most CUDA applications will not perform very well on these integrated devices. This weakness would be a reason for the host code to iterate through all the available devices, query their resources and capabilities, and choose the ones with adequate resources to execute the application satisfactorily.

The CUDA runtime numbers all available devices in the system from 0 to dev_count-1. It provides an API function cudaGetDeviceProperties that returns the properties of the device whose number is given as an argument. We can use the following statements in the host code to iterate through the available devices and query their properties:

```
cudaDeviceProp dev_prop;
for (int i = 0; i < dev_count; i++) {
    cudaGetDeviceProperties(&dev_prop, i);
   //decide if device has sufficient resources and capabilities
 }
```

The built-in type cudaDeviceProp is a C struct type with fields representing the properties of a CUDA device. The reader is referred to the CUDA C Programming Guide for all fields of the type. We will discuss a few of these fields that are particularly relevant to the assignment of execution resources to threads. We assume that the properties are returned in the dev_prop variable whose fields are set by the cudaGetDeviceProperties function. If the reader chooses to name the variable differently, the appropriate variable name will obviously need to be substituted in the following discussion.

As the name suggests, the field dev_prop.maxThreadsPerBlock indicates the maximal number of threads allowed in a block in the queried device. Some devices allow up to 1024 threads in each block and other devices allow fewer. Future devices may even allow more than 1024 threads per block. Therefore, the available devices should be queried, and the ones that will allow a sufficient number of threads in each block should be determined.

The number of SMs in the device is given in dev_prop.multiProcessorCount. As we discussed earlier, some devices have only a small number of SMs (e.g., two) and some have a much larger number of SMs (e.g., 30). If the application requires a large number of SMs in order to achieve satisfactory performance, it should definitely check this property of the prospective device. Furthermore, the clock frequency of the device is in dev_prop.clockRate. The combination of the clock rate and the number of SMs provides a good indication of the hardware execution capacity of the device.

The host code can find the maximal number of threads allowed along each dimension of a block in fields dev_prop.maxThreadsDim[0], dev_prop.maxThreadsDim[1], and dev_prop.maxThreadsDim[2] (for the *x*, *y*, and *z* dimensions). Such information can be used for an automated tuning system to set the range of block dimensions when evaluating the best performing block dimensions for the underlying hardware. Similarly, it can determine the maximal number of blocks allowed along each dimension of a grid in `dev_prop.maxGridSize[0]`, `dev_prop.maxGridSize[1]`, and `dev_prop.maxGridSize[2]` (for the x, y, and z dimensions). This information is typically used to determine whether a grid can have sufficient threads to handle the entire data set or whether some iteration is needed.

The `cudaDeviceProp` type has many more fields. We will discuss them as we introduce the concepts and features that they are designed to reflect.

3.7 THREAD SCHEDULING AND LATENCY TOLERANCE

Thread scheduling is strictly an implementation concept. Thus, it must be discussed in the context of specific hardware implementations. In the majority of implementations to date, a block assigned to an SM is further divided into 32 thread units called *warps*. The size of warps is implementation-specific. Warps are not part of the CUDA specification; however, knowledge of warps can be helpful in understanding and optimizing the performance of CUDA applications on particular generations of CUDA devices. The size of warps is a property of a CUDA device, which is in the `warpSize` field of the device query variable (`dev_prop` in this case).

The warp is the unit of thread scheduling in SMs. Fig. 3.13 shows the division of blocks into warps in an implementation. Each warp consists of 32 threads of consecutive `threadIdx` values: thread 0 through 31 form the first warp, 32 through 63 the

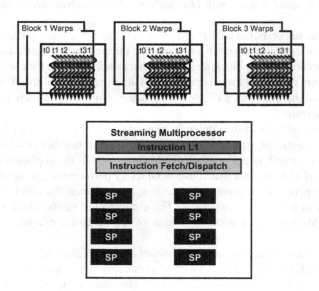

FIGURE 3.13

Blocks are partitioned into warps for thread scheduling.

second warp, and so on. In this example, three blocks—Block 1, Block 2, and Block 3—are assigned to an SM. Each of the three blocks is further divided into warps for scheduling purposes.

We can calculate the number of warps that reside in an SM for a given block size and a given number of blocks assigned to each SM. In Fig. 3.13, if each block has 256 threads, we can determine that each block has 256/32 or 8 warps. With three blocks in each SM, we have $8 \times 3 = 24$ warps in each SM.

An SM is designed to execute all threads in a warp following the Single Instruction, Multiple Data (SIMD) model—i.e., at any instant in time, one instruction is fetched and executed for all threads in the warp. This situation is illustrated in Fig. 3.13 with a single instruction fetch/dispatch shared among execution units (SPs) in the SM. These threads will apply the same instruction to different portions of the data. Consequently, all threads in a warp will always have the same execution timing.

Fig. 3.13 also shows a number of hardware Streaming Processors (SPs) that actually execute instructions. In general, there are fewer SPs than the threads assigned to each SM; i.e., each SM has only enough hardware to execute instructions from a small subset of all threads assigned to the SM at any point in time. In early GPU designs, each SM can execute only one instruction for a single warp at any given instant. In recent designs, each SM can execute instructions for a small number of warps at any point in time. In either case, the hardware can execute instructions for a small subset of all warps in the SM. A legitimate question is why we need to have so many warps in an SM if it can only execute a small subset of them at any instant. The answer is that this is how CUDA processors efficiently execute long-latency operations, such as global memory accesses.

When an instruction to be executed by a warp needs to wait for the result of a previously initiated long-latency operation, the warp is not selected for execution. Instead, another resident warp that is no longer waiting for results will be selected for execution. If more than one warp is ready for execution, a priority mechanism is used to select one for execution. This mechanism of filling the latency time of operations with work from other threads is often called "latency tolerance" or "latency hiding" (see "Latency Tolerance" sidebar).

Warp scheduling is also used for tolerating other types of operation latencies, such as pipelined floating-point arithmetic and branch instructions. Given a sufficient number of warps, the hardware will likely find a warp to execute at any point in time, thus making full use of the execution hardware in spite of these long-latency operations. The selection of ready warps for execution avoids introducing idle or wasted time into the execution timeline, which is referred to as zero-overhead thread scheduling. With warp scheduling, the long waiting time of warp instructions is "hidden" by executing instructions from other warps. This ability to tolerate long-latency operations is the main reason GPUs do not dedicate nearly as much chip area to cache memories and branch prediction mechanisms as do CPUs. Thus, GPUs can dedicate more of its chip area to floating-point execution resources.

LATENCY TOLERANCE

Latency tolerance is also needed in various everyday situations. For instance, in post offices, each person trying to ship a package should ideally have filled out all necessary forms and labels before going to the service counter. Instead, some people wait for the service desk clerk to tell them which form to fill out and how to fill out the form.

When there is a long line in front of the service desk, the productivity of the service clerks has to be maximized. Letting a person fill out the form in front of the clerk while everyone waits is not an efficient approach. The clerk should be assisting the other customers who are waiting in line while the person fills out the form. These other customers are "ready to go" and should not be blocked by the customer who needs more time to fill out a form.

Thus, a good clerk would politely ask the first customer to step aside to fill out the form while he/she can serve other customers. In the majority of cases, the first customer will be served as soon as that customer accomplishes the form and the clerk finishes serving the current customer, instead of that customer going to the end of the line.

We can think of these post office customers as warps and the clerk as a hardware execution unit. The customer that needs to fill out the form corresponds to a warp whose continued execution is dependent on a long-latency operation.

We are now ready for a simple exercise.[3] Assume that a CUDA device allows up to 8 blocks and 1024 threads per SM, whichever becomes a limitation first. Furthermore, it allows up to 512 threads in each block. For image blur, should we use 8×8, 16×16, or 32×32 thread blocks? To answer the question, we can analyze the pros and cons of each choice. If we use 8×8 blocks, each block would have only 64 threads. We will need 1024/64 = 12 blocks to fully occupy an SM. However, each SM can only allow up to 8 blocks; thus, we will end up with only $64 \times 8 = 512$ threads in each SM. This limited number implies that the SM execution resources will likely be underutilized because fewer warps will be available to schedule around long-latency operations.

The 16×16 blocks result in 256 threads per block, implying that each SM can take 1024/256 = 4 blocks. This number is within the 8-block limitation and is a good configuration as it will allow us a full thread capacity in each SM and a maximal number of warps for scheduling around the long-latency operations. The 32×32 blocks would give 1024 threads in each block, which exceeds the 512 threads per block limitation of this device. Only 16×16 blocks allow a maximal number of threads assigned to each SM.

---

[3] Note that this is an over-simplified exercise. As we will explain in Chapter 4, Memory and data locality, the usage of other resources such as registers and shared memory must also be considered when determining the most appropriate block dimensions. This exercise highlights the interactions between the limit on number of blocks and the limit on the number of threads that can be assigned to each SM.

3.8 SUMMARY

The kernel execution configuration parameters define the dimensions of a grid and its blocks. Unique coordinates in `blockIdx` and `threadIdx` allow threads of a grid to identify themselves and their domains of data. It is the responsibility of the programmer to use these variables in kernel functions so that the threads can properly identify the portion of the data to process. This model of programming compels the programmer to organize threads and their data into hierarchical and multidimensional organizations.

Once a grid is launched, its blocks can be assigned to SMs in an arbitrary order, resulting in the transparent scalability of CUDA applications. The transparent scalability comes with a limitation: threads in different blocks cannot synchronize with one another. To allow a kernel to maintain transparent scalability, the simple method for threads in different blocks to synchronize with each other is to terminate the kernel and start a new kernel for the activities after the synchronization point.

Threads are assigned to SMs for execution on a block-by-block basis. Each CUDA device imposes a potentially different limitation on the amount of resources available in each SM. Each CUDA device sets a limit on the number of blocks and the number of threads each of its SMs can accommodate, whichever becomes a limitation first. For each kernel, one or more of these resource limitations can become the limiting factor for the number of threads that simultaneously reside in a CUDA device.

Once a block is assigned to an SM, it is further partitioned into warps. All threads in a warp have identical execution timing. At any time, the SM executes instructions of only a small subset of its resident warps. This condition allows the other warps to wait for long-latency operations without slowing down the overall execution throughput of the massive number of execution units.

3.9 EXERCISES

1. A matrix addition takes two input matrices A and B and produces one output matrix C. Each element of the output matrix C is the sum of the corresponding elements of the input matrices A and B, i.e., $C[i][j] = A[i][j] + B[i][j]$. For simplicity, we will only handle square matrices whose elements are single-precision floating-point numbers. Write a matrix addition kernel and the host stub function that can be called with four parameters: pointer-to-the-output matrix, pointer-to-the-first-input matrix, pointer-to-the-second-input matrix, and the number of elements in each dimension. Follow the instructions below:

    A. Write the host stub function by allocating memory for the input and output matrices, transferring input data to device; launch the kernel, transferring the output data to host and freeing the device memory for the input and output data. Leave the execution configuration parameters open for this step.

B. Write a kernel that has each thread to produce one output matrix element. Fill in the execution configuration parameters for this design.

C. Write a kernel that has each thread to produce one output matrix row. Fill in the execution configuration parameters for the design.

D. Write a kernel that has each thread to produce one output matrix column. Fill in the execution configuration parameters for the design.

E. Analyze the pros and cons of each kernel design above.

2. A matrix–vector multiplication takes an input matrix B and a vector C and produces one output vector A. Each element of the output vector A is the dot product of one row of the input matrix B and C, i.e., $A[i] = \sum^j B[i][j] + C[j]$. For simplicity, we will only handle square matrices whose elements are single-precision floating-point numbers. Write a matrix–vector multiplication kernel and a host stub function that can be called with four parameters: pointer-to-the-output matrix, pointer-to-the-input matrix, pointer-to-the-input vector, and the number of elements in each dimension. Use one thread to calculate an output vector element.

3. If the SM of a CUDA device can take up to 1536 threads and up to 4 thread blocks. Which of the following block configuration would result in the largest number of threads in the SM?

A. 128 threads per block
B. 256 threads per block
C. 512 threads per block
D. 1024 threads per block

4. For a vector addition, assume that the vector length is 2000, each thread calculates one output element, and the thread block size is 512 threads. How many threads will be in the grid?

A. 2000
B. 2024
D. 2048
D. 2096

5. With reference to the previous question, how many warps do you expect to have divergence due to the boundary check on vector length?

A. 1
B. 2
C. 3
D. 6

6. You need to write a kernel that operates on an image of size 400 × 900 pixels. You would like to assign one thread to each pixel. You would like your thread blocks to be square and to use the maximum number of threads per block possible on the device (your device has compute capability 3.0). How would you select the grid dimensions and block dimensions of your kernel?

7. With reference to the previous question, how many idle threads do you expect to have?

8. Consider a hypothetical block with 8 threads executing a section of code before reaching a barrier. The threads require the following amount of time (in microseconds) to execute the sections: 2.0, 2.3, 3.0, 2.8, 2.4, 1.9, 2.6, and 2.9 and to spend the rest of their time waiting for the barrier. What percentage of the total execution time of the thread is spent waiting for the barrier?

9. Indicate which of the following assignments per multiprocessor is possible. In the case where it is not possible, indicate the limiting factor(s).
    A. 8 blocks with 128 threads each on a device with compute capability 1.0
    B. 8 blocks with 128 threads each on a device with compute capability 1.2
    C. 8 blocks with 128 threads each on a device with compute capability 3.0
    D. 16 blocks with 64 threads each on a device with compute capability 1.0
    E. 16 blocks with 64 threads each on a device with compute capability 1.2
    F. 16 blocks with 64 threads each on a device with compute capability 3.0

10. A CUDA programmer says that if they launch a kernel with only 32 threads in each block, they can leave out the __syncthreads() instruction wherever barrier synchronization is needed. Do you think this is a good idea? Explain.

11. A student mentioned that he was able to multiply two 1024 × 1024 matrices by using a tiled matrix multiplication code with 32 × 32 thread blocks. He is using a CUDA device that allows up to 512 threads per block and up to 8 blocks per SM. He further mentioned that each thread in a thread block calculates one element of the result matrix. What would be your reaction and why?

Memory and data locality

4

CHAPTER OUTLINE

So far, we have learned how to write a CUDA kernel function and how to configure and coordinate its execution by a massive number of threads. In this chapter, we will study how one can organize and position the data for efficient access by a massive number of threads. We discussed in Chapter 2, Data parallel computing that the data are first transferred from the host memory to the device global memory. In Chapter 3, Scalable parallel execution we determined how to direct the threads to access their portions of the data from the global memory by using their block indexes and thread indexes. We have also explored resource assignment and thread scheduling. Although the scope we have covered is a very good start, the CUDA kernels that we have learned thus far will likely achieve only a tiny fraction of the potential speed of the underlying hardware. The poor performance is attributable to the long access latencies (hundreds of clock cycles) and finite access bandwidth of global memory, which is typically implemented with Dynamic Random Access Memory. While having numerous threads available for execution can theoretically tolerate long memory access latencies, one can easily run into a situation where traffic congestion in the global memory access paths prevents all but very few threads from making progress, thus rendering some of the Streaming Multiprocessors (SMs) idle. To circumvent such congestion, CUDA provides a number of additional resources and methods for accessing memory that can remove the majority of traffic to and from the global memory. In this chapter, you will learn to use different memory types to boost the execution efficiency of CUDA kernels.

Programming Massively Parallel Processors. DOI: http://dx.doi.org/10.1016/B978-0-12-811986-0.00004-2

4.1 IMPORTANCE OF MEMORY ACCESS EFFICIENCY

We can illustrate the effect of memory access efficiency by calculating the expected performance level of the most executed portion of the image blur kernel code in Fig. 3.8, which is replicated in Fig. 4.1. The most important part of the kernel in terms of execution time is the nested for-loop that performs pixel value accumulation with the blurring patch.

In every iteration of the inner loop, one global memory access is performed for one floating-point addition. The global memory access fetches an in[] array element. The floating-point add operation accumulates the value of the in[] array element into pixVal. Thus, the ratio of floating-point calculation to global memory access operation is 1 to 1, or 1.0. We will refer to this ratio as the *compute-to-global-memory-access ratio*, defined as the number of floating-point calculation performed for each access to the global memory within a region of a program.

The compute-to-global-memory-access ratio has major implications on the performance of a CUDA kernel. In a high-end device today, the global memory bandwidth is around 1,000 GB/s, or 1 TB/s. With four bytes in each single-precision floating-point value, no more than $1000/4 = 250$ giga single-precision operands per second can be expected to load. With a compute-to-global-memory ratio of 1.0, the execution of the image blur kernel will be limited by the rate at which the operands (e.g., the elements of in[]) can be delivered to the GPU. We will refer to programs whose execution speed is limited by memory access throughput as *memory-bound* programs. In our example, the kernel will achieve no more than 250 giga floating-point operations per second (GFLOPS).

While 250 GFLOPS is a respectable number, it is only a tiny fraction (2%) of the peak single-precision performance of 12 TFLOPS or higher for these high-end devices. In order to achieve a higher level of performance for the kernel, we need to increase the ratio by reducing the number of global memory accesses. To achieve the peak 12 TFLOPS rating of the processor, we need a ratio of 48 or higher. In general, the desired ratio has been increasing in the past few generations of devices as

```
        for(int blurRow = -BLUR_SIZE; blurRow < BLUR_SIZE+1; ++blurRow) {
4.          for(int blurCol = -BLUR_SIZE; blurCol < BLUR_SIZE+1; ++blurCol) {

5.              int curRow = Row + blurRow;
6.              int curCol = Col + blurCol;
                // Verify we have a valid image pixel
7.              if(curRow > -1 && curRow < h && curCol > -1 && curCol < w) {
8.                  pixVal += in[curRow * w + curCol];
9.                  pixels++; // Keep track of number of pixels in the avg
                }
            }
        }
```

FIGURE 4.1

The most executed part of the image blurring kernel in Fig. 3.8.

computational throughput has been increasing faster than memory bandwidth. The rest of this chapter introduces a commonly used technique for reducing the number of global memory accesses.

4.2 MATRIX MULTIPLICATION

Matrix–matrix multiplication, or matrix multiplication for short, between an $i \times j$ (i rows by j columns) matrix M and a $j \times k$ matrix N produces an $i \times k$ matrix P. Matrix multiplication is an important component of the Basic Linear Algebra Subprograms (BLAS) standard (see the "Linear Algebra Functions" sidebar in Chapter 3: Scalable Parallel Execution). This function is the basis of many linear algebra solvers such as LU decomposition. As we will see, matrix multiplication presents opportunities for reduction of global memory accesses that can be captured with relatively simple techniques. The execution speed of matrix multiplication functions can vary by orders of magnitude, depending on the level of reduction of global memory accesses. Therefore, matrix multiplication provides an excellent initial example for such techniques.

When performing a matrix multiplication, each element of the output matrix P is an inner product of a row of *M* and a column of *N*. We will continue to use the convention where $P_{\text{Row,Col}}$ is the element at Row^{th} position in the vertical direction and Col^{th} position in the horizontal direction. As shown in Fig. 4.2, $P_{\text{Row,Col}}$ (the small square in *P*) is the inner product of the vector formed from the Row^{th} row of M (shown as a horizontal strip in *M*) and the vector formed from the Col^{th} column of N (shown as a vertical strip in *N*). The inner product, also called the dot product, of two vectors is the sum of products of the individual vector elements, i.e., $P_{\text{Row,Col}} = \sum_{} M_{\text{Row},k} * N_{k,\text{Col}}$, for $k = 0,1,\ldots\text{Width} - 1$. For instance,

$$P_{1,5} = M_{1,0} * N_{0,5} + M_{1,1} * N_{1,5} + M_{1,2} * N_{2,5} + \cdots + M_{1,\text{Width}-1} * N_{\text{Width}-1,5}$$

In our initial matrix multiplication implementation, we map threads to elements of P with the same approach that we used for `colorToGreyscaleConversion`; i.e., each thread is responsible for calculating one P element. The row and column indexes for the P element to be calculated by each thread are as follows:

```
    Row=blockIdx.y*blockDim.y+threadIdx.y
and
    Col=blockIdx.x*blockDim.x+threadIdx.x.
```

With this one-to-one mapping, the `Row` and `Col` thread indexes are also the row and column indexes for output array. Fig. 4.3 shows the source code of the kernel based on this thread-to-data mapping. The reader should immediately see the familiar pattern of calculating `Row`, `Col` and the if statement testing if both `Row` and `Col` are within range. These statements are almost identical to their counterparts in `colorToGreyscale Conversion`. The only significant difference is that we are assuming square matrices for `matrixMulKernel`, thus replacing both `width` and `height` with `Width`.

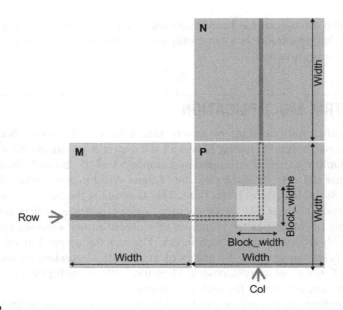

FIGURE 4.2

Matrix multiplication using multiple blocks by tiling P.

The thread-to-data mapping effectively divides P into tiles, one of which is shown as a large square in Fig. 4.2. Each block is responsible for calculating one of these tiles.

We now turn our attention to the work done by each thread. Recall that $P_{Row, Col}$ is the inner product of the Row^{th} row of M and the Col^{th} column of N. In Fig. 4.3, we use a for-loop to perform this inner product operation. Before entering the loop, we initialize a local variable Pvalue to 0. Each iteration of the loop accesses an element from the Row^{th} row of M and one from the Col^{th} column of N, multiplies the two elements together, and accumulates the product into Pvalue.

First, we focus on accessing the M element within the for-loop. Recall that M is linearized into an equivalent 1D array where the rows of M are placed one after another in the memory space, starting with the 0th row. Therefore, the beginning element of the 1st row is M[1*Width] because we need to account for all elements of the 0th row. In general, the beginning element of the Row^{th} row is M[Row*Width]. Since all elements of a row is placed in consecutive locations, the kth element of the Row^{th} row is at M[Row*Width+k]. This method was applied in Fig. 4.3.

We now turn our attention to N. As shown in Fig. 4.3, the beginning element of the Col^{th} column is the Col^{th} element of the 0th row, which is N[Col]. Accessing each additional element in Col^{th} column requires skipping over entire rows. The reason is that the next element of the same column is actually the same element in the next row. Therefore, the kth element of the Col^{th} column is N[k*Width+Col].

```
__global__ void MatrixMulKernel(float* M, float* N, float* P,
  int Width) {
  // Calculate the row index of the P element and M
  int Row = blockIdx.y*blockDim.y+threadIdx.y;
  // Calculate the column index of P and N
  int Col = blockIdx.x*blockDim.x+threadIdx.x;
  if ((Row < Width) && (Col < Width)) {
    float Pvalue = 0;
    // each thread computes one element of the block sub-matrix
    for (int k = 0; k < Width; ++k) {
      Pvalue += M[Row*Width+k]*N[k*Width+Col];
    }
    P[Row*Width+Col] = Pvalue;
  }

}
```

FIGURE 4.3

A simple matrix multiplication kernel using one thread to compute one P element.

After the execution exits the `for-loop`, all threads have their P element values in the `Pvalue` variables. Each thread then uses the one-dimensional equivalent index expression `Row*Width+Col` to write its P element. Again, this index pattern is similar to that used in the `colorToGreyscaleConversion` kernel.

We now use a small example to illustrate the execution of the matrix multiplication kernel. Fig. 4.4 shows a 4×4 P with `BLOCK_WIDTH=2`. The small sizes allow us to fit the entire example in one picture. The P matrix is now divided into four tiles, and each block calculates one tile. We do so by creating blocks that are 2×2 arrays of threads, with each thread calculating one P element. In the example, thread(0,0) of block(0,0) calculates $P_{0,0}$, whereas thread(0,0) of block(1,0) calculates $P_{2,0}$.

`Row` and `Col` in the `matrixMulKernel` identify the P element to be calculated by a thread. `Row` also identifies the row of M, whereas `Col` identifies the column of N as input values for the thread. Fig. 4.5 illustrates the multiplication operations in each thread block. For the small matrix multiplication example, threads in block (0,0) produce four dot products. The `Row` and `Col` variables of thread(1,0) in block(0,0) are $0*0 + 1= 1$ and $0*0 + 0= 0$. It maps to $P_{1,0}$ and calculates the dot product of row 1 of M and column 0 of N.

We walk through the execution of the `for-loop` in Fig. 4.3 for thread(0,0) in block(0,0). During the 0th iteration (`k=0`), `Row*Width+k`=$0*4 + 0 = 0$ and `k*Width+Col`=$0*4 + 0= 0$. Therefore, we are accessing M[0] and N[0], which are the 1D equivalent of $M_{0,0}$ and $N_{0,0}$, according to Fig. 3.3. Note that these are indeed the 0th elements of row 0 of M and column 0 of N. During the 1st iteration (`k=1`), `Row*Width+k`=$0*4+1=1$ and `k*Width+Col`=$1*4+0=4$. We are accessing M[1] and N[4], which are the 1D equivalent of $M_{0,1}$ and $N_{1,0}$, according to Fig. 3.3. These are the 1st elements of row 0 of M and column 0 of N.

During the 2nd iteration ($k=2$), `Row*Width+k`=$0*4+2=2$ and `k*Width+Col`=8, which results in M[2] and N[8]. Therefore, the elements accessed are the 1D equivalent of $M_{0,2}$ and d_$N_{2,0}$. Finally, during the 3rd iteration ($k=3$), `Row*Width+ k`=$0*4+ 3$ and

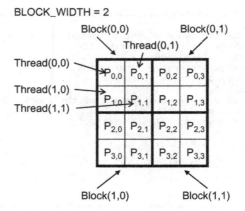

FIGURE 4.4

A small execution example of matrixMulKernel.

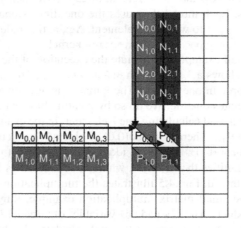

FIGURE 4.5

Matrix multiplication actions of one thread block.

k*Width+ Col= 12, which results in M[3] and N[12], the 1D equivalent of $M_{0,3}$ and $N_{3,0}$. We now have verified that the for-loop performs inner product between the 0th row of M and the 0th column of N. After the loop, the thread writes P[Row*Width+Col], which is P[0], the 1D equivalent of $P_{0,0}$. Thus, thread(0,0) in block(0,0) successfully calculated the inner product between the 0th row of M and the 0th column of N and deposited the result in $P_{0,0}$.

We will leave it as an exercise for the reader to hand-execute and verify the for-loop for other threads in block(0,0) or in other blocks.

Note that matrixMulKernel can handle matrices of up to 16 × 65,535 elements in each dimension. In a situation where matrices larger than this limit are to be multiplied, one can divide the P matrix into submatrices with sizes that can be covered by a grid. We can then use the host code to iteratively launch kernels and complete the P matrix. Alternatively, we can change the kernel code so that each thread calculates more P elements.

We can estimate the effect of memory access efficiency by calculating the expected performance level of the matrix multiplication kernel code in Fig. 4.3. The dominating part of the kernel in terms of execution time is the for-loop that performs inner product calculation:

```
for(int k = 0;k < Width;+ + k)Pvalue +
    = M[Row * Width + k] * N[k * Width + Col];
```

In every iteration of this loop, two global memory accesses are performed for one floating-point multiplication and one floating-point addition. One global memory access fetches an M element, and the other fetches an N element. One floating-point operation multiplies the M and N elements fetched, and the other accumulates the product into Pvalue. Thus, the compute-to-global-memory-access ratio of the loop is 1.0. From our discussion in Chapter 3, Scalable parallel execution, this ratio will likely result in less than 2% utilization of the peak execution speed of the modern GPUs. We need to increase the ratio by at least an order of magnitude for the computation throughput of modern devices to achieve good utilization. In the next section, we will show that we can use special memory types in CUDA devices to accomplish this goal.

4.3 CUDA MEMORY TYPES

A CUDA device contains several types of memory that can help programmers improve compute-to-global-memory-access ratio and thus achieve high execution speed. Fig. 4.6 shows these CUDA device memories. Global memory and constant memory appear at the bottom of the picture. These types of memory can be written (W) and read (R) by the host by calling API functions.[1] We have already introduced global memory in Chapter 2, Data parallel computing. The global memory can be written and read by the device. The constant memory supports short-latency, high-bandwidth *read-only access* by the device.

Registers and shared memory, as shown in Fig. 4.6, are on-chip memories. Variables that reside in these types of memory can be accessed at very high-speed in a highly parallel manner. Registers are allocated to individual threads; each thread can only access its own registers. A kernel function typically uses registers to hold frequently accessed variables that are private to each thread. Shared memory locations are allocated to thread blocks; all threads in a block can access shared memory variables allocated to the block. Shared memory is an efficient means for threads to

---

[1] See CUDA Programming Guide for zero-copy access to the global memory.

Device code can:

- – R/W per-thread registers
- – R/W per-thread local memory
- – R/W per-block shared memory
- – R/W per-grid global memory
- – Read only per-grid constant memory

Host code can

- – Transfer data to/from per grid global and constant memories

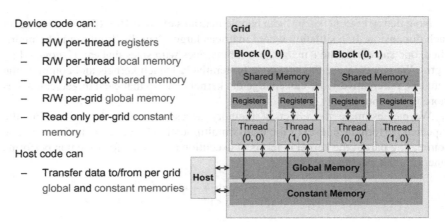

FIGURE 4.6

Overview of the CUDA device memory model.

cooperate by sharing their input data and intermediate results. By declaring a CUDA variable in one of the CUDA memory types, a CUDA programmer dictates the visibility and access speed of the variable.

In order to fully appreciate the difference between registers, shared memory, and global memory, we need to go into a little more detail of how these different memory types are realized and used in modern processors. Virtually all modern processors find their root in the model proposed by John von Neumann in 1945, which is shown in Fig. 4.7. The CUDA devices are no exception. The Global Memory in a CUDA device maps to the Memory box in Fig. 4.7. The processor box corresponds to the processor chip boundary that we typically see today. The Global Memory is off the processor chip and is implemented with DRAM technology, which implies long access latencies and relatively low access bandwidths. The Registers correspond to the Register File of the von Neumann model. The Register File is on the processor chip, which implies very short access latency and drastically higher access bandwidth compared with the global memory. In a typical device, the aggregated access bandwidth of the register files is at least two orders of magnitude higher than that of the global memory. Furthermore, when a variable is stored in a register, its accesses no longer consume off-chip global memory bandwidth. This reduced bandwidth consumption will be reflected as an increased compute-to-global-memory-access ratio.

A subtler point is that each access to registers involves fewer instructions than an access to the global memory. Arithmetic instructions in most modern processors have "built-in" register operands. For example, a floating-point addition instruction might be of the form

```
fadd r1, r2, r3
```

where r2 and r3 are the register numbers that specify the location in the register file where the input operand values can be found. The location for storing the

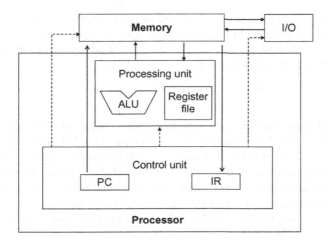

FIGURE 4.7

Memory vs. registers in a modern computer based on the von Neumann model.

floating-point addition result value is specified by r1. Therefore, when an operand of an arithmetic instruction is in a register, no additional instruction is required to make the operand value available to the arithmetic and logic unit (ALU), where the arithmetic calculation is performed.

THE VON NEUMANN MODEL

In his seminal 1945 report, John von Neumann described a model for building electronic computers, which is based on the design of the pioneering Electronic Discrete Variable Automatic Computer (EDVAC) computer. This model, now commonly referred to as the von Neumann Model, has been the foundational blueprint for virtually all modern computers.

The von Neumann Model is illustrated in Fig. 4.7. The computer has an input/output function that allows both programs and data to be provided to and generated from the system. To execute a program, the computer first inputs the program and its data into the Memory.

The program consists of a collection of instructions. The Control Unit maintains a Program Counter (PC), which contains the memory address of the next instruction to be executed. In each "instruction cycle," the Control Unit uses the PC to fetch an instruction into the Instruction Register (IR). The instruction bits are then used to determine the action to be taken by all components of the computer, which is why the model is also called the "stored program" model. The term implies that a user can change the behavior of a computer by storing a different program into its memory.

Meanwhile, if an operand value is in the global memory, the processor needs to perform a memory load operation to make the operand value available to the ALU. For example, if the first operand of a floating-point addition instruction is in the global memory, the instructions involved will likely be

```
load r2, r4, offset
fadd r1, r2, r3
```

where the load instruction adds an offset value to the contents of r4 to form an address for the operand value. It then accesses the global memory and places the value into register r2. Once the operand value is in r2, the fadd instruction performs the floating-point addition by using the values in r2 and r3 and then places the result into r1. Since the processor can only fetch and execute a limited number of instructions per clock cycle, the version with an additional load will likely take more time to process than the one without an additional load. Thus, placing the operands in registers can improve execution speed.

Finally, there is another subtle reason why placing an operand value in registers is preferable. In modern computers, the energy consumed for accessing a value from the register file is at least an order of magnitude lower than that for accessing a value from the global memory. We will examine the speed and energy difference in accessing these two hardware structures in modern computers. However, as we will soon learn, the number of registers available to each thread (see "Processing Units and Threads" sidebar) is quite limited in today's GPUs. We need to be careful not to oversubscribe to this limited resource.

Fig. 4.8 shows the shared memory and registers in a CUDA device. Although both are on-chip memories, they differ significantly in functionality and cost of access. Shared memory is designed as part of the memory space that resides on the processor chip. When the processor accesses data that reside in the shared memory,

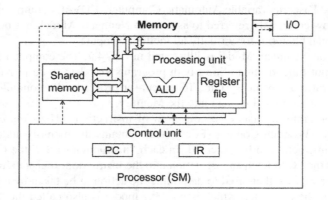

FIGURE 4.8

Shared memory vs. registers in a CUDA device SM.

it needs to perform a memory load operation, similar to accessing data in the global memory. However, because shared memory resides on-chip, it can be accessed with much lower latency and much higher throughput than the global memory. Shared memory has longer latency and lower bandwidth than registers because of the need to perform a load operation. In computer architecture terminology, the shared memory is a form of *scratchpad memory*.

One important difference between the shared memory and registers in CUDA is that the variables that reside in the shared memory are accessible by all threads in a block, whereas register data are private to a thread. Shared memory is designed to support efficient, high-bandwidth sharing of data among threads in a block. As shown in Fig. 4.8, a CUDA device SM typically employs multiple processing units, to allow multiple threads to make simultaneous progress (see Processing Units and Threads sidebar). Threads in a block can be spread across these processing units. Therefore, the hardware implementations of the shared memory in these CUDA devices are typically designed to allow multiple processing units to simultaneously access its contents to support efficient data sharing among threads in a block. We will be learning several important types of parallel algorithms that can greatly benefit from such efficient data sharing among threads.

PROCESSING UNITS AND THREADS

Now that we have introduced the von Neumann model, we are ready to discuss how threads are implemented. A thread in modern computers is the state of executing a program on a von Neumann Processor. Recall that a thread consists of the code of a program, the particular point in the code that is being executed, and value of its variables and data structures.

In a computer based on the von Neumann model, the code of the program is stored in the memory. The PC keeps track of the particular point of the program that is being executed. The IR holds the instruction that is fetched from the point execution. The register and memory hold the values of the variables and data structures.

Modern processors are designed to allow context-switching, where multiple threads can time-share a processor by taking turns to make progress. By carefully saving and restoring the PC value and the contents of registers and memory, we can suspend the execution of a thread and then correctly resume the execution of the thread later.

Some processors provide multiple processing units, which allow multiple threads to make simultaneous progress. Fig. 4.8 shows a Single-Instruction, Multiple-Data design style where multiple processing units share a PC and IR. Under this design, all threads make simultaneous progress by executing the same instruction in the program.

Table 4.1 CUDA Variable Type Qualifiers

Variable declaration	Memory	Scope	Lifetime
Automatic variables other than arrays	Register	Thread	Kernel
Automatic array variables	Local	Thread	Kernel
__device__ __shared__ int SharedVar;	Shared	Block	Kernel
__device__ int GlobalVar;	Global	Grid	Application
__device__ __constant__ int ConstVar;	Constant	Grid	Application

It should be clear by now that registers, shared memory, and global memory have different functionalities, latencies, and bandwidths. Therefore, the process of declaring a variable must be understood so that it will reside in the intended type of memory. Table 4.1 presents the CUDA syntax for declaring program variables into the various memory types. Each such declaration also gives its declared CUDA variable a scope and lifetime. Scope identifies the range of threads that can access the variable: a single thread only, all threads of a block, or all threads of all grids. If the scope of a variable is a single thread, a private version of the variable will be created for every thread; each thread can only access its private version of the variable. To illustrate, if a kernel declares a variable whose scope is a thread and it is launched with one million threads, one million versions of the variable will be created so that each thread initializes and uses its own version of the variable.

Lifetime indicates the portion of the program execution duration when the variable is available for use: either within a kernel execution or throughout the entire application. If the lifetime of a variable is within a kernel execution, it must be declared within the kernel function body and will be available for use only *by the kernel code. If the kernel is invoked several times, the value of the variable is not* maintained across these invocations. Each invocation must initialize the variable in order to use them. Meanwhile, if the lifetime of a variable continues throughout the entire application, it must be declared outside of any function body. The contents of these variables are maintained throughout the execution of the application and available to all kernels.

We refer to variables that are not arrays or matrices as *scalar* variables. As shown in Table 4.1, all automatic scalar variables declared in kernel and device functions are placed into registers. The scopes of these automatic variables are within individual threads. When a kernel function declares an automatic variable, a private copy of that variable is generated for every thread that executes the kernel function. When a thread terminates, all its automatic variables also cease to exist. In Fig. 4.1, variables blurRow, blurCol, curRow, curCol, pixels, and pixVal are automatic variables and fall into this category. Note that accessing these variables is extremely fast and parallel; however, one must be careful not to exceed the limited capacity of the register storage in hardware implementations. Using a large number of registers can negatively affect the number of active threads assigned to each SM. We will address this point in Chapter 5, Performance considerations.

Automatic array variables are not stored in registers.[2] Instead, they are stored into the global memory and may incur long access delays and potential access congestions. Similar to automatic scalar variables, the scope of these arrays is limited to individual threads; i.e., a private version of each automatic array is created for and used by every thread. Once a thread terminates its execution, the contents of its automatic array variables also cease to exist. From our experience, automatic array variables are rarely used in kernel functions and device functions.

If a variable declaration is preceded by the "__shared__" (each "__" consists of two "_" characters) keyword, it declares a shared variable in CUDA. An optional "__device__" in front of "__shared__" keyword may also be added in the declaration to achieve the same effect. Such declaration typically resides within a kernel function or a device function. Shared variables reside in the shared memory. The scope of a shared variable is within a thread block; i.e., all threads in a block see the same version of a shared variable. A private version of the shared variable is created for and used by each thread block during kernel execution. The lifetime of a shared variable is within the duration of the kernel. When a kernel terminates its execution, the contents of its shared variables cease to exist. As discussed earlier, shared variables are an efficient means for threads within a block to collaborate with one another. Accessing shared variables from the shared memory is extremely fast and highly parallel. CUDA programmers often use shared variables to hold the portion of global memory data that are heavily used in a kernel execution phase. The algorithms may need to be adjusted to create execution phases that heavily focus on small portions of the global memory data, as we will demonstrate with matrix multiplication in Section 4.4.

If a variable declaration is preceded by the keyword "__constant__" (each "__" consists of two "_" characters), it declares a constant variable in CUDA. An optional "__device__" keyword may also be added in front of "__constant__" to achieve the same effect. Declaration of constant variables must be outside any function body. The scope of a constant variable spans all grids, meaning that all threads in all grids see the same version of a constant variable. The lifetime of a constant variable is the entire application execution. Constant variables are often used for variables that provide input values to kernel functions. Constant variables are stored in the global memory but are cached for efficient access. With appropriate access patterns, accessing constant memory is extremely fast and parallel. Currently, the total size of constant variables in an application is limited to 65,536 bytes. The input data volume may need to be divided to fit within this limitation, as we will illustrate in Chapter 7, Parallel pattern: convolution.

A variable whose declaration is preceded only by the keyword "__device__" (each "__" consists of two "_" characters) is a global variable and will be placed in the global memory. Accesses to a global variable are slow. Latency and throughput of accessing global variables have been improved with caches in relatively recent

---

[2] There are some exceptions to this rule. The compiler may decide to store an automatic array into registers if all accesses are done with constant index values.

devices. One important advantage of global variables is that they are visible to all threads of all kernels. Their contents also persist throughout the entire execution. Thus, global variables can be used as a means for threads to collaborate across blocks. However, the only easy way to synchronize between threads from different thread blocks or to ensure data consistency across threads when accessing global memory is by terminating the current kernel execution.[3] Therefore, global variables are often used to pass information from one kernel invocation to another kernel invocation.

In CUDA, pointers are used to point to data objects in the global memory. Pointer usage arises in kernel and device functions in two ways: (1) if an object is allocated by a host function, the pointer to the object is initialized by cudaMalloc and can be passed to the kernel function as a parameter (e.g., the parameters M, N, and P in Fig. 4.3) and (2) the address of a variable declared in the global memory is assigned to a pointer variable. To illustrate, the statement {float* ptr= &GlobalVar;} in a kernel function assigns the address of GlobalVar into an automatic pointer variable ptr. The reader should refer to the CUDA Programming Guide for using pointers in other memory types.

4.4 TILING FOR REDUCED MEMORY TRAFFIC

We have an intrinsic tradeoff in the use of device memories in CUDA: the global memory is large but slow, whereas the shared memory is small but fast. A common strategy is to partition the data into subsets called *tiles* so that each tile fits into the shared memory. The term "tile" draws on the analogy that a large wall (i.e., the global memory data) can be covered by tiles (i.e., subsets that each can fit into the shared memory). An important criterion is that kernel computation on these tiles can be performed independently of each other. Note that not all data structures can be partitioned into tiles given an arbitrary kernel function.

The concept of tiling can be illustrated using the matrix multiplication example in Fig. 4.5, which corresponds to the kernel function in Fig. 4.3. We replicate the example in Fig. 4.9 for convenient reference by the reader. For brevity, we use Py,x, My,x, and Ny,x to represent P[y*Width+ x], M[y*Width+ x], and N[y*Width+ x], respectively. This example assumes that we use four 2× 2 blocks to compute the P matrix. Fig. 4.9 highlights the computation performed by the four threads of block(0,0). These four threads compute for $P_{0,0}$, $P_{0,1}$, $P_{1,0}$, and $P_{1,1}$. The accesses to the M and N elements by thread(0,0) and thread(0,1) of block(0,0) are highlighted with black arrows; e.g., thread(0,0) reads $M_{0,0}$ and $N_{0,0}$, followed by $M_{0,1}$ and $N_{1,0}$, followed by $M_{0,2}$ and $N_{2,0}$, followed by $M_{0,3}$ and $N_{3,0}$.

Fig. 4.10 shows the global memory accesses performed by all threads in block$_{0,0}$. The threads are listed in the vertical direction, with time of access increasing to the

[3] Note that one can use CUDA memory fencing to ensure data coherence between thread blocks if the number of thread blocks is smaller than the number of SMs in the CUDA device. See the CUDA programming guide for more details.

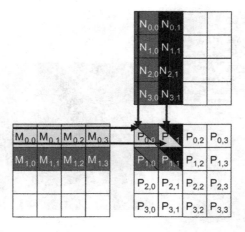

FIGURE 4.9

A small example of matrix multiplication. For brevity, we show $M[y*\text{Width}+ x]$, $N[y*\text{Width} + x]$, $P[y*\text{Width}+ x]$ as $M_{y,x}$, $N_{y,x}$ $P_{y,x}$.

	Access order			
$\text{thread}_{0,0}$	$M_{0,0} * N_{0,0}$	$M_{0,1} * N_{1,0}$	$M_{0,2} * N_{2,0}$	$M_{0,3} * N_{3,0}$
$\text{thread}_{0,1}$	$M_{0,0} * N_{0,1}$	$M_{0,1} * N_{1,1}$	$M_{0,2} * N_{2,1}$	$M_{0,3} * N_{3,1}$
$\text{thread}_{1,0}$	$M_{1,0} * N_{0,0}$	$M_{1,1} * N_{1,0}$	$M_{1,2} * N_{2,0}$	$M_{1,3} * N_{3,0}$
$\text{thread}_{1,1}$	$M_{1,0} * N_{0,1}$	$M_{1,1} * N_{1,1}$	$M_{1,2} * N_{2,1}$	$M_{1,3} * N_{3,1}$

FIGURE 4.10

Global memory accesses performed by threads in $\text{block}_{0,0}$.

right in the horizontal direction. Each thread accesses four elements of M and four elements of N during execution. Among the four threads highlighted, a significant overlap occurs in the M and N elements they access. For instance, both $\text{thread}_{0,0}$ and $\text{thread}_{0,1}$ access $M_{0,0}$ and the rest of row 0 of M. Similarly, both $\text{thread}_{0,1}$ and $\text{thread}_{1,1}$ access $N_{0,1}$ and the rest of column 1 of N.

The kernel in Fig. 4.3 is written so that both $\text{thread}_{0,0}$ and $\text{thread}_{0,1}$ access row 0 elements of M from the global memory. If $\text{thread}_{0,0}$ and $\text{thread}_{0,1}$ can be made to collaborate so that these M elements are only loaded from the global memory once, the total number of accesses to the global memory can be reduced by half. Every M and N element is accessed exactly twice during the execution of $\text{block}_{0,0}$. Therefore, if all four threads can be made to collaborate in their accesses to global memory, traffic to the global memory can be reduced by half.

Readers should verify that the potential reduction in global memory traffic in the matrix multiplication example is proportional to the dimension of the blocks used.

FIGURE 4.11

Reducing traffic congestion in highway systems.

With Width × Width blocks, the potential reduction of global memory traffic would be Width. Thus, if we use 16 × 16 blocks, the global memory traffic can be potentially reduced to 1/16 through collaboration between threads.

Traffic congestion arises not only in computing but in highway systems as well, as illustrated in Fig. 4.11. The root cause of highway traffic congestion is too many cars squeezing through a road that is designed for a much smaller number of vehicles. When congestion occurs, the travel time for each vehicle is greatly increased. Commute time to work can easily double or triple during traffic congestion.

Most solutions for reduced traffic congestion involve reduction of cars on the road. Assuming that the number of commuters is constant, people need to share rides in order to reduce the number of cars on the road. A common way to share rides in the US is carpooling, where a group of commuters take turns to drive the group to work in one vehicle. The government usually needs to create policies encouraging carpooling. In some countries, the government simply bans certain classes of cars from the road on a daily basis. For example, cars with odd license plates may not be allowed on the road on Monday, Wednesday, or Friday. This rule encourages people whose cars are allowed on different days to form a carpool group. In some countries, gasoline price is so high that people form carpools to save money. In other countries, the government may provide incentives for behaviors that reduce the number of cars on the road. In the US, some lanes of congested highways are designated as carpool lanes; only cars with more than two or three people are allowed to use these lanes. All of these measures for encouraging carpooling are designed to overcome the fact that carpooling requires extra effort, as shown in Fig. 4.12.

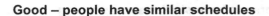

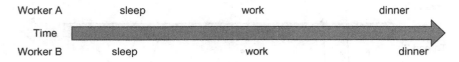

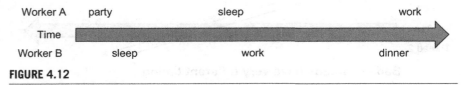

FIGURE 4.12

Carpooling requires synchronization among people.

Carpooling requires workers who wish to carpool to compromise and agree on a common commute schedule. The top half of Fig. 4.12 presents a good schedule pattern for carpooling. Time goes from left to right. Workers A and B share a similar schedule for sleep, work, and dinner. This schedule allows these two workers to conveniently go to work and return home in one car. Their similar schedules allow them to easily agree on common departure and return times. By contrast, the schedules in the bottom half of Fig. 4.12 show Workers A and B having different habits: Worker A parties until sunrise, sleeps during the day, and goes to work in the evening; Worker B sleeps at night, goes to work in the morning, and returns home for dinner at 6 p.m. The schedules are so different that these two workers cannot arrange a common time to drive to work and return home in one car. For these workers to form a carpool, they need to negotiate a common schedule similar to that in the top half of Fig. 4.12.

Tiled algorithms are highly similar to carpooling arrangements. We can consider threads accessing data values as commuters and DRAM access requests as vehicles. When the rate of DRAM requests exceeds the provisioned access bandwidth of the DRAM system, traffic congestion arises and the arithmetic units become idle. If multiple threads access data from the same DRAM location, they can potentially form a "carpool" and combine their accesses into one DRAM request. However, this process requires a similar execution schedule for the threads so that their data accesses can be combined. This scenario is shown in Fig. 4.13, where the cells at the center represent DRAM locations. An arrow from a DRAM location pointing to a thread represents an access by the thread to that location at the time marked by the head of the arrow. Note that the time goes from left to right. The top portion shows two threads that access the same data elements with similar timing. The bottom half shows two threads that access their common data at varying times; i.e., the accesses by Thread 2 lag significantly behind their corresponding accesses by Thread 1. The reason the

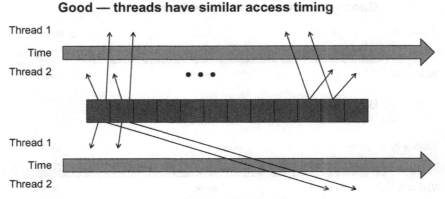

Good — threads have similar access timing

Bad — threads have very different timing

FIGURE 4.13

Tiled Algorithms require synchronization among threads.

bottom is an undesirable arrangement is that data elements that are brought back from the DRAM need to be stored in the on-chip memory for an extended time, waiting to be consumed by Thread 2. A large number of data elements will need to be stored, resulting in an excessive on-chip memory requirement.

In the context of parallel computing, tiling is a program transformation technique that localizes the memory locations accessed among threads and the timing of their accesses. It divides the long access sequences of each thread into phases and uses barrier synchronization to keep the timing of accesses to each section at close intervals. This technique controls the amount of on-chip memory required by localizing the accesses both in time and in space. In terms of our carpool analogy, we force the threads that form the "carpool" group to follow approximately the same execution timing.

We now present a tiled matrix multiplication algorithm. The basic idea is for the threads to collaboratively load subsets of the M and N elements into the shared memory before they individually use these elements in their dot product calculation. The size of the shared memory is quite small, and the capacity of the shared memory should not be exceeded when these M and N elements are loaded into the shared memory. This condition can be satisfied by dividing the M and N matrices into smaller tiles so that they can fit into the shared memory. In the simplest form, the tile dimensions equal those of the block, as illustrated in Fig. 4.11.

In Fig. 4.14, we divide M and N into 2 × 2 tiles, as delineated by the thick lines. The dot product calculations performed by each thread are now divided into phases. In each phase, all threads in a block collaborate to load a tile of M and a tile of N into the shared memory. This collaboration can be accomplished by having every thread in a block to load one M element and one N element into the shared memory,

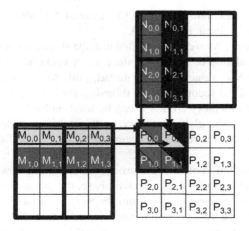

FIGURE 4.14

Tiling M and N to utilize shared memory.

	Phase 1			Phase 2		
thread$_{0,0}$	$M_{0,0}$ ↓ Mds$_{0,0}$	$N_{0,0}$ ↓ Nds$_{0,0}$	PValue$_{0,0}$ += Mds$_{0,0}$*Nds$_{0,0}$ + Mds$_{0,1}$*Nds$_{1,0}$	$M_{0,2}$ ↓ Mds$_{0,0}$	$N_{2,0}$ ↓ Nds$_{0,0}$	PValue$_{0,0}$ += Mds$_{0,0}$*Nds$_{0,0}$ + Mds$_{0,1}$*Nds$_{1,0}$
thread$_{0,1}$	$M_{0,1}$ ↓ Mds$_{0,1}$	$N_{0,1}$ ↓ Nds$_{1,0}$	PValue$_{0,1}$ += Mds$_{0,0}$*Nds$_{0,1}$ + Mds$_{0,1}$*Nds$_{1,1}$	$M_{0,3}$ ↓ Mds$_{0,1}$	$N_{2,1}$ ↓ Nds$_{0,1}$	PValue$_{0,1}$ += Mds$_{0,0}$*Nds$_{0,1}$ + Mds$_{0,1}$*Nds$_{1,1}$
thread$_{1,0}$	$M_{1,0}$ ↓ Mds$_{1,0}$	$N_{1,0}$ ↓ Nds$_{1,0}$	PValue$_{1,0}$ += Mds$_{1,0}$*Nds$_{0,0}$ + Mds$_{1,1}$*Nds$_{1,0}$	$M_{1,2}$ ↓ Mds$_{1,0}$	$N_{3,0}$ ↓ Nds$_{1,0}$	PValue$_{1,0}$ += Mds$_{1,0}$*Nds$_{0,0}$ + Mds$_{1,1}$*Nds$_{1,0}$
thread$_{1,1}$	$M_{1,1}$ ↓ Mds$_{1,1}$	$N_{1,1}$ ↓ Nds$_{1,1}$	PValue$_{1,1}$ += Mds$_{1,0}$*Nds$_{0,1}$ + Mds$_{1,1}$*Nds$_{1,1}$	$M_{1,3}$ ↓ Mds$_{1,1}$	$N_{3,1}$ ↓ Nds$_{1,1}$	PValue$_{1,1}$ += Mds$_{1,0}$*Nds$_{0,1}$ + Mds$_{1,1}$*Nds$_{1,1}$

time ⟶

FIGURE 4.15

Execution phases of a tiled matrix multiplication.

as illustrated in Fig. 4.15. Each row in Fig. 4.15 shows the execution activities of a thread. Note that time progresses from left to right. We only need to show the activities of threads in block$_{0,0}$; all of the other blocks have the same behavior. The shared memory array for the M elements is called Mds, and that for the N elements is called Nds. At the beginning of Phase 1, the four threads of block$_{0,0}$ collaboratively load a tile of M into a shared memory: thread$_{0,0}$ loads $M_{0,0}$ into Mds$_{0,0}$, thread$_{0,1}$ loads $M_{0,1}$ into Mds$_{0,1}$, thread$_{1,0}$ loads $M_{1,0}$ into Mds$_{1,0}$, and thread$_{1,1}$ loads $M_{1,1}$ into Mds$_{1,1}$, as shown in the second column in Fig. 4.15. A tile of N is also similarly loaded, as presented in the third column in Fig. 4.15.

After the two tiles of M and N are loaded into the shared memory, these elements are used in the calculation of the dot product. Each value in the shared memory is used twice; e.g., the $M_{1,1}$ value loaded by $thread_{1,1}$ into $Mds_{1,1}$ is used twice: the first time by $thread_{1,0}$ and the second time by $thread_{1,1}$. By loading each global memory value into the shared memory so that it can be used multiple times, we reduce the number of accesses to the global memory; in this case, we reduce it by half. The reader should verify that the reduction occurs by a factor of N if the tiles are N × N elements.

Note that the calculation of each dot product in Fig. 4.3 is now performed in two phases, Phases 1 and 2 in Fig. 4.15. In each phase, the products of two pairs of the input matrix elements are accumulated into the Pvalue variable. Pvalue is an automatic variable; a private version is generated for each thread. We added subscripts to indicate different instances of the Pvalue variable created for each thread. The first- and second-phase calculations are shown in the fourth and seventh columns in Fig. 4.15, respectively. In general, if an input matrix is of the dimension Width and the tile size is referred to as TILE_WIDTH, the dot product would be performed in Width/TILE_WIDTH phases. The creation of these phases is key to the reduction of accesses to the global memory. With each phase focusing on a small subset of the input matrix values, the threads can collaboratively load the subset into the shared memory and use the values in the shared memory to satisfy their overlapping input demands in the phase.

Note also that Mds and Nds are reused to hold the input values. In each phase, the same Mds and Nds are used to hold the subset of M and N elements in the phase, thereby allowing a much smaller shared memory to serve most of the accesses to global memory. This is due to the fact that each phase focuses on a small subset of the input matrix elements. Such focused access behavior is called locality. When an algorithm exhibits locality, an opportunity arises to use small, high-speed memories in order to serve most of the accesses and remove these accesses from the global memory. Locality is as important for achieving high-performance in multi-core CPUs as in many-thread GPUs. We will return to the concept of locality in Chapter 5, Performance considerations.

4.5 A TILED MATRIX MULTIPLICATION KERNEL

We are now ready to present a tiled matrix multiplication kernel that uses shared memory to reduce traffic to the global memory. The kernel presented in Fig. 4.16 implements the phases illustrated in Fig. 4.15. In Fig. 4.16, Lines 1 and 2 declare Mds and Nds as shared memory variables. Recall that the scope of shared memory variables is a block. Thus, one pair of Mds and Nds will be created for each block, and all threads of a block can access the same Mds and Nds. This is important since all threads in a block must have access to the M and N elements loaded

```
__global__ void MatrixMulKernel(float* d_M, float* d_N, float* d_P,
    int Width) {

1.    __shared__ float Mds[TILE_WIDTH][TILE_WIDTH];
2.    __shared__ float Nds[TILE_WIDTH][TILE_WIDTH];

3.    int bx = blockIdx.x;  int by = blockIdx.y;
4.    int tx = threadIdx.x; int ty = threadIdx.y;

      // Identify the row and column of the d_P element to work on
5.    int Row = by * TILE_WIDTH + ty;
6.    int Col = bx * TILE_WIDTH + tx;

7.    float Pvalue = 0;
      // Loop over the d_M and d_N tiles required to compute d_P element
8.    for (int ph = 0; ph < Width/TILE_WIDTH; ++ph) {

        // Collaborative loading of d_M and d_N tiles into shared memory
9.      Mds[ty][tx] = d_M[Row*Width + ph*TILE_WIDTH + tx];
10.     Nds[ty][tx] = d_N[(ph*TILE_WIDTH + ty)*Width + Col];
11.     __syncthreads();

12.     for (int k = 0; k < TILE_WIDTH; ++k) {
13.       Pvalue += Mds[ty][k] * Nds[k][tx];
        }
14.     __syncthreads();
      }
15.   d_P[Row*Width + Col] = Pvalue;
    }
```

FIGURE 4.16

A tiled Matrix Multiplication Kernel using shared memory.

into Mds and Nds by their peers so that they can use these values to satisfy their input needs.

Lines 3 and 4 save the threadIdx and blockIdx values into automatic variables and thus into registers for fast access. Recall that automatic scalar variables are placed into registers. Their scope is in each individual thread; i.e., one private version of tx, ty, bx, and by is created by the run-time system for each thread and will reside in registers that are accessible by the thread. They are initialized with the threadIdx and blockIdx values and used many times during the lifetime of the thread. Once the thread ends, the values of these variables cease to exist.

Lines 5 and 6 determine the row and column indexes of the P element to be produced by the thread. The code assumes that each thread is responsible for calculating one P element. As shown in Line 6, the horizontal (x) position, or the column index of the P element to be produced by a thread, can be calculated as bx*TILE_WIDTH+ tx because each block covers TILE_WIDTH elements in the horizontal dimension. A thread in block bx would have bx blocks of threads, or (bx*TILE_WIDTH) threads, before it; they cover bx*TILE_WIDTH elements of P. Another tx threads within the same block would cover another tx elements. Thus, the thread with bx and tx should be responsible for calculating the P element whose x index is bx*TILE_WIDTH+ tx.

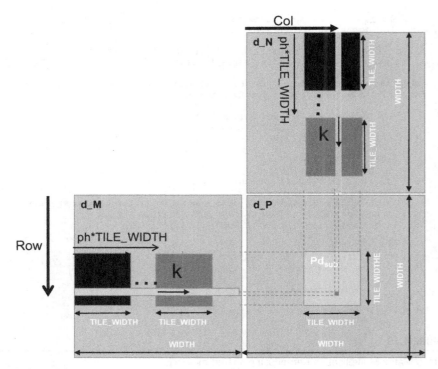

FIGURE 4.17

Calculation of the matrix indexes in tiled multiplication.

This horizontal index is saved in the variable Col for the thread and is also illustrated in Fig. 4.17.

In Fig. 4.14, the x index of the P element to be calculated by thread$_{0,1}$ of block$_{1,0}$ is 0*2+ 1= 1. Similarly, the y index can be calculated as by*TILE_WIDTH+ ty. This vertical index is saved in the variable Row for the thread. Thus, each thread calculates the P element at the Colth column and the Rowth row, as shown in Fig. 4.17. Recalling the example in Fig. 4.14, the y index of the P element to be calculated by thread$_{1,0}$ of block$_{0,1}$ is 1*2+ 0= 2. Thus, the P element to be calculated by this thread is P$_{2,1}$.

Line 8 in Fig. 4.16 marks the beginning of the loop that iterates through all the phases of calculating the P element. Each iteration of the loop corresponds to one phase of the calculation presented in Fig. 4.15. The ph variable indicates the number of phases that have already been done for the dot product. Recall that each phase uses one tile of M and one tile of N elements. Therefore, at the beginning of each phase, ph*TILE_WIDTH pairs of M and N elements have been processed by previous phases.

In each phase, Line 9 loads the appropriate M element into the shared memory. Since we already know the row of M and column of N to be processed by the thread, we now discuss the column index of M and row index of N. As shown in Fig. 4.17, each block has TILE_WIDTH^2 threads that will collaborate to load TILE_WIDTH^2 M elements into the shared memory. Thus, we only need to assign each thread to load one M element, which can be conveniently accomplished using `blockIdx` and `threadIdx`. The beginning column index of the section of M elements to be loaded is `ph*TILE_WIDTH`. Therefore, an easy approach is to have every thread load an element that is `tx` (the `threadIdx.x` value) positions away from that beginning point.

This case is represented by Line 9, where each thread loads M[Row*Width + ph*TILE_WIDTH + tx], where the linearized index is formed with the row index `Row` and column index `ph*TILE_WIDTH + tx`. Since the value of `Row` is a linear function of ty, each of the TILE_WIDTH^2 threads will load a unique M element into the shared memory. Together, these threads will load a dark square subset of M in Fig. 4.17. The reader should use the examples in Fig. 4.14 and Fig. 4.15 to verify that the address calculation works correctly for individual threads.

The barrier `__syncthreads()` in Line 11 ensures that all threads have finished loading the tiles of M and N into Mds and Nds before any of them can move forward. The loop in Line 12 then performs one phase of the dot product on the basis of these tile elements. The progression of the loop for thread$_{ty,tx}$ is shown in Fig. 4.17, with the access direction of the M and N elements along the arrow marked with k, the loop variable in Line 12. These elements will be accessed from Mds and Nds, the shared memory arrays holding these M and N elements. The barrier `__syncthreads()` in Line 14 ensures that all threads have finished using the M and N elements in the shared memory before any of them move on to the next iteration and load the elements from the next tiles. In this manner, none of the threads would load the elements too early and corrupt the input values for other threads.

The nested loop from Line 8 to Line 14 illustrates a technique called *strip-mining*, which takes a long-running loop and break it into phases. Each phase consists of an inner loop that executes a number of consecutive iterations of the original loop. The original loop becomes an outer loop whose role is to iteratively invoke the inner loop so that all the iterations of the original loop are executed in their original order. By adding barrier synchronizations before and after the inner loop, we force all threads in the same block to focus their work entirely on a section of their input data. Strip-mining can create the phases needed by tiling in data parallel programs.[4]

After all phases of the dot product are completed, the execution exits the loop of Line 8. All threads write to their P element by using the linearized index calculated from `Row` and `Col`.

The tiled algorithm provides a substantial benefit. For matrix multiplication, the global memory accesses are reduced by a factor of TILE_WIDTH. If one uses 16×16 tiles, we can reduce the global memory accesses by a factor of 16. This increases the compute-to-global-memory-access ratio from 1 to 16. This improvement

---

[4] Interested reader should note that strip-mining has long been used in programming CPUs. Strip-mining followed by loop interchange is often used to enable tiling for improved locality in sequential programs. Strip-mining is also the main vehicle for vectorizing compilers to generate vector or Single-Instruction, Multiple-Data instructions for CPU programs.

allows the memory bandwidth of a CUDA device to support a computation rate close to its peak performance; e.g. a device with 150 GB/s global memory bandwidth can approach ((150/4)*16) = 600 GFLOPS!

While the performance improvement of the tiled matrix multiplication kernel is impressive, it includes a few simplifying assumptions. First, the width of the matrices is assumed to be a multiple of the width of the thread blocks. This assumption prevents the kernel from correctly processing arbitrary-sized matrices. The second assumption is that the matrices are square matrices, which is not always true in real-life settings. In the next section, we will present a kernel with boundary checks that remove these assumptions.

4.6 BOUNDARY CHECKS

We now extend the tiled matrix multiplication kernel to handle matrices with arbitrary widths. The extensions will have to allow the kernel to correctly handle matrices whose width is not a multiple of the tile width. By changing the example in Fig. 4.14 to 3×3 M, N, and P matrices, Fig. 4.18 is created. The matrices have a width of 3, which is not a multiple of the tile width (2). Fig. 4.18 shows the memory access pattern during phase 1 of $block_{0,0}$. $Thread_{0,1}$ and $thread_{1,1}$ will attempt to load M elements that do not exist. Similarly, $thread_{1,0}$ and $thread_{1,1}$ will attempt to access N elements that do not exist.

Accessing nonexisting elements is problematic in two ways. Accessing a nonexisting elements past the end of a row (M accesses by $thread_{1,0}$ and $thread_{1,1}$ in Fig. 4.18) will be done to incorrect elements. In our example, the threads will attempt to access $M_{0,3}$ and $M_{1,3}$, both of which do not exist. In this case, what will happen to these

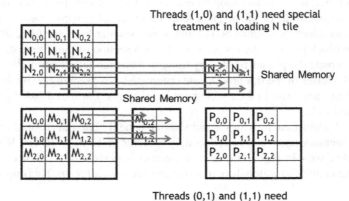

FIGURE 4.18

Loading input matrix elements that are close to the edge—phase 1 of $Block_{0,0}$.

memory loads? To answer this question, we need to go back to the linearized layout of 2D matrices. The element after $M_{0,2}$ in the linearized layout is $M_{1,0}$. Although $thread_{0,1}$ is attempting to access $M_{0,3}$, it will instead obtain $M_{1,0}$. The use of this value in the subsequent inner product calculation will certainly corrupt the output value.

A similar problem arises when accessing an element past the end of a column (N accesses by $thread_{1,0}$ and $thread_{1,1}$ in Fig. 4.18). These accesses are to memory locations outside the allocated area for the array. Some systems will return random values from other data structures, whereas others will reject these accesses and cause the program to abort. Either way, such accesses lead to undesirable outcomes.

From our discussion thus far, the problematic accesses only seem to arise in the last phase of execution of the threads. This observation suggests that the problem can be dealt with by taking special actions during the last phase of the tiled kernel execution. Unfortunately, problematic accesses can occur in all phases. Fig. 4.19 shows the memory access pattern of $block_{1,1}$ during phase 0. We see that $thread_{1,0}$ and $thread_{1,1}$ attempt to access nonexisting M elements $M_{3,0}$ and $M_{3,1}$, whereas $thread_{0,1}$ and $thread_{1,1}$ attempt to access $N_{0,3}$ and $N_{1,3}$, which do not exist.

Note that these problematic accesses cannot be prevented by excluding the threads that do not calculate valid P elements. For instance, $thread_{1,0}$ in $block_{1,1}$ does not calculate any valid P element. However, it needs to load $M_{2,1}$ during phase 0. Further, some threads that calculate valid P elements will attempt to access M or N elements that do not exist. As shown in Fig. 4.18, $thread_{0,1}$ of block 0,0 calculates a valid P element $P_{0,1}$. However, it attempts to access a nonexisting $M_{0,3}$ during phase 1. These observations indicate that different boundary condition tests need to be conducted for loading M tiles, loading N tiles, and calculating/storing P elements.

We start with the boundary test condition for loading input tiles. When a thread intends to load an input tile element, it should test that input element for validity,

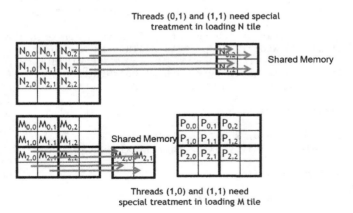

FIGURE 4.19

Loading input elements during phase 0 of $block_{1,0}$.

which is easily done by examining the y and x indexes. To illustrate, at Line 9 in Fig. 4.16, the linearized index is derived from a y index of Row and an x index of ph*TILE_WIDTH + tx. The boundary condition test would be that both indexes are smaller than Width: (Row<Width) && (ph*TILE_WIDTH+tx)<Width. If the condition is satisfied, the thread should load the M element. The reader should verify that the condition test for loading the N element is (ph*TILE_WIDTH+ty)<Width && Col<Width.

If the condition is not satisfied, the thread should not load the element, in which case, the question is what should be placed into the shared memory location. The answer is 0.0, a value that will not cause any harm if used in the inner product calculation. If any thread uses this 0.0 value in the calculation of its inner product, no change will be observed in the inner product value.

Finally, a thread should only store its final inner product value if it is responsible for calculating a valid P element. The test for this condition is (Row < Width) && (Col < Width). The kernel code with the additional boundary condition checks is shown in Fig. 4.20.

With the boundary condition checks, the tile matrix multiplication kernel is just one more step away from being a general matrix multiplication kernel. In general, matrix multiplication is defined for rectangular matrices: a j×k M matrix multiplied by a k×l N matrix results in a j×l P matrix. Currently, our kernel can only handle square matrices.

Fortunately, our kernel can be easily extended to a general matrix multiplication kernel by making simple modifications. First, the Width argument is replaced by three unsigned integer arguments j, k, and l. Where Width is used to refer to the height of M or height of P, it may be replaced with j. Where Width is used to refer to the width of M or height of N, it may be replaced with k. Where Width is used to refer to the width of N or width of P, it may be replaced with l. The revision of the kernel with these changes is left as an exercise.

```
// Loop over the M and N tiles required to compute P element
8.    for (int ph = 0; ph < ceil(Width/(float)TILE_WIDTH); ++ph) {

        // Collaborative loading of M and N tiles into shared memory
9.       if ((Row< Width) && (ph*TILE_WIDTH+tx)< Width)
            Mds[ty][tx] = M[Row*Width + ph*TILE_WIDTH + tx];
10.      if ((ph*TILE_WIDTH+ty)<Width && Col<Width)
            Nds[ty][tx] = N[(ph*TILE_WIDTH + ty)*Width + Col];

11.      __syncthreads();

12.      for (int k = 0; k < TILE_WIDTH; ++k) {
13.        Pvalue += Mds[ty][k] * Nds[k][tx];
         }
14.      __syncthreads();
      }
15.   if ((Row<Width) && (Col<Width)P[Row*Width + Col] = Pvalue;
```

FIGURE 4.20

Tiled matrix multiplication kernel with boundary condition checks.

4.7 MEMORY AS A LIMITING FACTOR TO PARALLELISM

While CUDA registers and shared memory can be extremely effective in reducing the number of accesses to global memory, one must be careful to stay within the capacity of these memories. These memories are forms of resources necessary for thread execution. Each CUDA device offers limited resources, thereby limiting the number of threads that can simultaneously reside in the SM for a given application. In general, the more resources each thread requires, the fewer the threads that can reside in each SM, and likewise, the fewer the threads that can run in parallel in the entire device.

To illustrate the interaction between register usage of a kernel and the level of parallelism that a device can support, assume that in a current-generation device D, each SM can accommodate up to 1536 threads and 16,384 registers. While 16,384 is a large number, each thread is only allowed to use a very limited number of registers, considering the number of threads that can reside in each SM. To support 1536 threads, each thread can use only $16,384/1536 = 10$ registers. If each thread uses 11 registers, the number of threads that can be executed concurrently in each SM will be reduced. Such reduction occurs at the block granularity; e.g., if each block contains 512 threads, the reduction of threads will be accomplished by reducing 512 threads at a time. Thus, the next smaller number of threads from 1536 will be 1024, indicating a 1/3 reduction of threads that can simultaneously reside in each SM. This procedure can substantially reduce the number of warps available for scheduling, thereby decreasing the ability of the processor to find useful work in the presence of long-latency operations.

The number of registers available to each SM varies from one device to another. An application can dynamically determine the number of registers available in each SM of the device used and choose a version of the kernel that uses the number of registers appropriate for the device. The number of registers can be determined by calling the `cudaGetDeviceProperties` function, which was discussed in Section 3.6. Assume that the variable `&dev_prop` is passed to the function for the device property and the field `dev_prop.regsPerBlock` generates the number of registers available in each SM. For device D, the returned value for this field should be 16,384. The application can then divide this number by the targeted number of threads to reside in each SM to determine the number of registers that can be used in the kernel.

Shared memory usage can also limit the number of threads assigned to each SM. We can assume that the same device D has 16,384 (16K) bytes of shared memory, is allocated to thread blocks, in each SM. We can also assume that each SM in D can accommodate up to 8 blocks. To reach this maximum, each block must not use more than 2K bytes of shared memory; otherwise, the number of blocks that can reside in each SM is reduced such that the total amount of shared memory used by these blocks does not exceed 16K bytes. For instance, if each block uses 5K bytes of shared memory, no more than three blocks can be assigned to each SM.

For the matrix multiplication example, shared memory can become a limiting factor. For a tile size of 16×16, each block needs $16 \times 16 \times 4 = 1K$ bytes of storage for `Mds`. (Note that each element is a float type, which is 4 bytes.) Another 1KB is needed for `Nds`. Thus, each block uses 2K bytes of shared memory. The 16K-byte shared memory allows

8 blocks to simultaneously reside in an SM. Since this is the same as the maximum allowed by the threading hardware, shared memory is not a limiting factor for this tile size. In this case, the real limitation is the threading hardware limitation that only allows 1536 threads in each SM. This constraint limits the number of blocks in each SM to six. Consequently, only 6*2KB= 12KB of the shared memory will be used. These limits change from one device to another but can be determined at runtime with device queries.

The size of shared memory in each SM can also vary depending on the device. Each generation or model of device can have different amounts of shared memory in each SM. It is often desirable for a kernel to be able to use different amount of shared memory according to the amount available in the hardware. We may want a host code to dynamically determine the size of the shared memory and adjust the amount of shared memory used by a kernel, which can be done by calling the `cuda-GetDeviceProperties` function. We make the assumption that variable &dev_prop is passed to the function and that field `dev_prop.sharedMemPerBlock` gives the number of registers available in each SM. The programmer can then determine the amount of shared memory that should be used by each block.

Unfortunately, the kernel in Fig. 4.16 does not support this. The declarations used in Fig. 4.16 hardwire the size of its shared memory usage to a compile-time constant:

```
__shared__ float Mds[TILE_WIDTH][TILE_WIDTH];
__shared__ float Nds[TILE_WIDTH][TILE_WIDTH];
```

That is, the size of `Mds` and `Nds` is set to be `TILE_WIDTH2` elements, regardless of the value of `TILE_WIDTH` at compile-time. To illustrate, assume that the file contains

```
#define TILE_WIDTH 16.
```

Both `Mds` and `Nds` will have 256 elements. If we want to change the size of `Mds` and `Nds`, we change the value of `TILE_WIDTH` and recompile the code. The kernel cannot easily adjust its shared memory usage at runtime without recompilation.

We can enable such an adjustment with a different style of declaration in CUDA. We can add a C "extern" keyword in front of the shared memory declaration and omit the size of the array in the declaration. In this manner, the declarations for `Mds` and `Nds` read as

```
extern __shared__ Mds[];
extern __shared__ Nds[];
```

Note that the arrays are now one-dimensional. We will need to use a linearized index based on the vertical and horizontal indexes.

At runtime when we launch the kernel, we can dynamically determine the amount of shared memory to be used according to the device query result and supply that as a **third** configuration parameter to the kernel launch. The revised kernel could be launched with the following statements:

```
size_t size=
  calculate_appropriate_SM_usage(dev_prop.sharedMemPerBlock,....);
matrixMulKernel<<<dimGrid, dimBlock, size>>>(Md, Nd, Pd, Width);
```

where size_t is a built-in type for declaring a variable to holds the size information for dynamically allocated data structures. The size is expressed in bytes. In our matrix multiplication example, for a 16 × 16 tile, we have a size of 16 × 16 × 4=1024 bytes. The details of the calculation for setting the value of size at run-time have been omitted.

4.8 SUMMARY

In summary, the execution speed of a program in modern processors can be severely limited by the speed of the memory. To achieve good utilization of the execution throughput of CUDA devices, a high compute-to-global-memory-access ratio in the kernel code should be obtained. If the ratio obtained is low, the kernel is memory-bound; i.e., its execution speed is limited by the rate at which its operands are accessed from memory.

CUDA defines registers, shared memory, and constant memory. These memories are much smaller than the global memory but can be accessed at much higher rates. Using these memories effectively requires a redesign of the algorithm. We use matrix multiplication to illustrate tiling, a widely used technique to enhance locality of data access and effectively use shared memory. In parallel programming, tiling forces multiple threads to jointly focus on a subset of the input data at each phase of execution so that the subset data can be placed into these special memory types, consequently increasing the access speed. We demonstrate that with 16 × 16 tiling, global memory accesses are no longer the major limiting factor for matrix multiplication performance.

However, CUDA programmers need to be aware of the limited sizes of these types of memory. Their capacities are implementation-dependent. Once their capacities are exceeded, they limit the number of threads that can simultaneously execute in each SM. The ability to reason about hardware limitations when developing an application is a key aspect of computational thinking.

Although we introduced tiled algorithms in the context of CUDA programming, the technique is an effective strategy for achieving high-performance in virtually all types of parallel computing systems. The reason is that an application must exhibit locality in data access in order to effectively use high-speed memories in these systems. In a multicore CPU system, data locality allows an application to effectively use on-chip data caches to reduce memory access latency and achieve high-performance. Therefore, the reader will find the tiled algorithm useful when he/she develops a parallel application for other types of parallel computing systems using other programming models.

Our goal for this chapter is to introduce the concept of locality, tiling, and different CUDA memory types. We introduced a tiled matrix multiplication kernel by using shared memory. The use of registers and constant memory in tiling has yet to be discussed. The use of these memory types in tiled algorithms will be explained when parallel algorithm patterns are discussed.

4.9 EXERCISES

1. Consider matrix addition. Can one use shared memory to reduce the global memory bandwidth consumption? Hint: Analyze the elements accessed by each thread and see if there is any commonality between threads.

2. Draw the equivalent of Fig. 4.14 for an 8× 8 matrix multiplication with 2× 2 tiling and 4× 4 tiling. Verify that the reduction in global memory bandwidth is indeed proportional to the dimensions of the tiles.

3. What type of incorrect execution behavior can happen if one or both __syncthreads() are omitted in the kernel of Fig. 4.16?

4. Assuming that capacity is not an issue for registers or shared memory, give one important reason why it would be valuable to use shared memory instead of registers to hold values fetched from global memory? Explain your answer.

5. For our tiled matrix–matrix multiplication kernel, if we use a 32x32 tile, what is the reduction of memory bandwidth usage for input matrices M and N?
    - **A.** 1/8 of the original usage
    - **B.** 1/16 of the original usage
    - **C.** 1/32 of the original usage
    - **D.** 1/64 of the original usage

6. Assume that a CUDA kernel is launched with 1,000 thread blocks, with each having 512 threads. If a variable is declared as a local variable in the kernel, how many versions of the variable will be created through the lifetime of the execution of the kernel?
    - **A.** 1
    - **B.** 1000
    - **C.** 512
    - **D.** 512000

7. In the previous question, if a variable is declared as a shared memory variable, how many versions of the variable will be created throughout the lifetime of the execution of the kernel?
    - **A.** 1
    - **B.** 1000
    - **C.** 512
    - **D.** 51200

8. Consider performing a matrix multiplication of two input matrices with dimensions N × N. How many times is each element in the input matrices requested from global memory in the following situations?
    - **A.** There is no tiling.
    - **B.** Tiles of size T × T are used.

9. A kernel performs 36 floating-point operations and 7 32-bit word global memory accesses per thread. For each of the following device properties, indicate whether this kernel is compute- or memory-bound.

    A. Peak FLOPS= 200 GFLOPS, Peak Memory Bandwidth= 100 GB/s

    B. Peak FLOPS= 300 GFLOPS, Peak Memory Bandwidth= 250 GB/s

10. To manipulate tiles, a new CUDA programmer has written the following device kernel, which will transpose each tile in a matrix. The tiles are of size BLOCK_WIDTH by BLOCK_WIDTH, and each of the dimensions of matrix A is known to be a multiple of BLOCK_WIDTH. The kernel invocation and code are shown below. BLOCK_WIDTH is known at compile time, but could be set anywhere from 1 to 20.

    ```
    dim3 blockDim(BLOCK_WIDTH,BLOCK_WIDTH);
    dim3 gridDim(A_width/blockDim.x,A_height/blockDim.y);
    BlockTranspose<<<gridDim, blockDim>>>(A, A_width, A_height);
    __global__ void
    BlockTranspose(float* A_elements, int A_width, int A_height)
    {
      __shared__ float blockA[BLOCK_WIDTH][BLOCK_WIDTH];
      int baseIdx=blockIdx.x * BLOCK_SIZE + threadIdx.x;
      baseIdx += (blockIdx.y * BLOCK_SIZE + threadIdx.y) * A_width;
      blockA[threadIdx.y][threadIdx.x]=A_elements[baseIdx];
      A_elements[baseIdx]=blockA[threadIdx.x][threadIdx.y];
    }
    ```

    A. Out of the possible range of values for BLOCK_SIZE, for what values of BLOCK_SIZE will this kernel function execute correctly on the device?

    B. If the code does not execute correctly for all BLOCK_SIZE values, suggest a fix to the code to make it work for all BLOCK_SIZE values.

Performance considerations 5

CHAPTER OUTLINE

The execution speed of a parallel program can vary greatly depending on the resource constraints of the computing hardware. While managing the interaction between parallel code and hardware resource constraints is important for achieving high performance in virtually all parallel programming models, it is a practical skill that is best learned with hands-on exercises in a parallel programming model designed for high performance. In this chapter, we will discuss the major types of resource constraints in a CUDA device and how they can affect the kernel execution performance [Ryoo 2008][CUDA C Best Practice]. In order to achieve his/her goals, a programmer often has to find ways to achieve a required level of performance that is higher than that of an initial version of the application. In different applications, different constraints may dominate and become the limiting factors, commonly referred to as *bottlenecks*. One can often dramatically improve the performance of an application on a particular CUDA device by trading one resource usage for another. This strategy works well if the resource constraint thus alleviated was actually the dominating constraint before the strategy was applied, and the one thus exacerbated does not have negative effects on parallel execution. Without such understanding, performance tuning would be guesswork; plausible strategies may or may not lead to performance enhancements. Beyond insights into these resource constraints, this chapter further offers principles and case studies designed to cultivate intuition about the type of algorithm patterns that can result in high performance execution. It also establishes idioms and ideas that will likely lead to good performance improvements during your performance tuning efforts.

Programming Massively Parallel Processors. DOI: http://dx.doi.org/10.1016/B978-0-12-811986-0.00005-4

5.1 GLOBAL MEMORY BANDWIDTH

One of the most important factors of CUDA kernel performance is accessing data in the global memory. CUDA applications exploit massive data parallelism. Naturally, CUDA applications tend to process a massive amount of data from the global memory within a short period of time. In Chapter 4, Memory and data locality, we studied tiling techniques that utilize shared memories to reduce the total amount of data that must be accessed from the global memory by a collection of threads in each thread block. In this chapter, we will further discuss memory coalescing techniques that can more effectively move data from the global memory into shared memories and registers. Memory coalescing techniques are often used in conjunction with tiling techniques to allow CUDA devices to reach their performance potential by more efficiently utilizing the global memory bandwidth.[1]

The global memory of a CUDA device is implemented with DRAMs. Data bits are stored in DRAM cells that are small capacitors, where the presence or absence of a tiny amount of electrical charge distinguishes between 0 and 1. Reading data from a DRAM cell requires the small capacitor to use its tiny electrical charge to drive a highly capacitive line leading to a sensor and set off its detection mechanism that determines whether a sufficient amount of charge is present in the capacitor to qualify as a "1" (see "Why is DRAM so slow?" sidebar). This process takes 10s of nanoseconds in modern DRAM chips. This is in sharp contrast with the sub-nanosecond clock cycle time of modern computing devices. Because this is a very slow process relative to the desired data access speed (sub-nanosecond access per byte), modern DRAMs use parallelism to increase their rate of data access, commonly referred to as memory access throughput.

WHY ARE DRAMS SO SLOW?

The following figure shows a DRAM cell and the path for accessing its content. The decoder is an electronic circuit that uses a transistor to drive a line connected to the outlet gates of thousands of cells. It can take a long time for the line to be fully charged or discharged to the desired level.

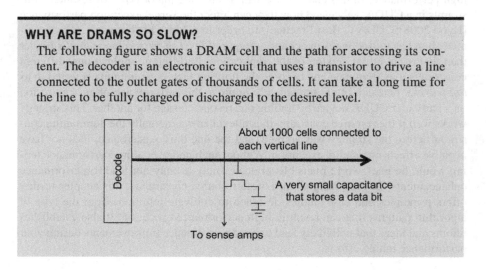

About 1000 cells connected to each vertical line

A very small capacitance that stores a data bit

Decode

To sense amps

[1] Recent CUDA devices use on-chip caches for global memory data. Such caches automatically coalesce more of the kernel access patterns and somewhat reduce the need for programmer to manually rearrange their access patterns. However, even with caches, coalescing techniques will continue to have significant effect on kernel execution performance in the foreseeable future.

A more formidable challenge is for the cell to drive the vertical line to the sense amplifiers and allow the sense amplifier to detect its content. This is based on electrical charge sharing. The gate lets out the tiny amount of electrical charge stored in the cell. If the cell content is "1", the tiny amount of charge must raise the electrical potential of the large capacitance of the long bit line to a sufficiently high level that can trigger the detection mechanism of the sense amplifier. A good analogy would be for someone to hold a small cup of coffee at one end of a long hallway for another person to smell the aroma propagated through the hallway to determine the flavor of the coffee.

One could speed up the process by using a larger, stronger capacitor in each cell. However, the DRAMs have been going in the opposite direction. The capacitors in each cell have been steadily reduced in size and thus reduced in their strength over time so that more bits can be stored in each chip. This is why the access latency of DRAMs has not decreased over time.

Each time a DRAM location is accessed, a range of consecutive locations that includes the requested location are actually accessed. Many sensors are provided in each DRAM chip and they work in parallel. Each senses the content of a bit within these consecutive locations. Once detected by the sensors, the data from all these consecutive locations can be transferred at very high-speed to the processor. These consecutive locations accessed and delivered are referred to as DRAM *bursts*. If an application makes focused use of data from these bursts, the DRAMs can supply the data at a much higher rate than if a truly random sequence of locations were accessed.

Recognizing the burst organization of modern DRAMs, current CUDA devices employ a technique that allows the programmers to achieve high global memory access efficiency by organizing memory accesses of threads into favorable patterns. This technique takes advantage of the fact that threads in a warp execute the same instruction at any given point in time. When all threads in a warp execute a load instruction, the hardware detects whether they access consecutive global memory locations. That is, the most favorable access pattern is achieved when all threads in a warp access consecutive global memory locations. In this case, the hardware combines, or *coalesces*, all these accesses into a consolidated access to consecutive DRAM locations. For example, for a given load instruction of a warp, if thread 0 accesses global memory location N[2], thread 1 location $N+1$, thread 2 location $N+2$, and so on, all these accesses will be coalesced, or combined into a single request for consecutive locations when accessing the DRAMs. Such coalesced access allows the DRAMs to deliver data as a burst.[3]

---

[2] Different CUDA devices may also impose alignment requirements on N. For example, in some CUDA devices, N is required to be aligned to 16-word boundaries. That is, the lower 6 bits of N should all be 0 bits. Such alignment requirements have been relaxed in recent CUDA devices due to the presence of 2nd-level caches.

[3] Note that modern CPUs also recognize the DRAM burst organization in their cache memory design. A CPU cache line typically maps to one or more DRAM bursts. Applications that make full use of bytes in each cache line they touch tend to achieve much higher performance than those that randomly access memory locations. The techniques presented in this chapter can be adapted to help CPU programs to achieve high performance.

In order to understand how to effectively use the coalescing hardware, we need to review how the memory addresses are formed in accessing C multidimensional array elements. Recall from Chapter 3, Scalable parallel execution (Fig. 3.3, replicated as Fig. 5.1 for convenience) that multidimensional array elements in C and CUDA are placed into the linearly addressed memory space according to the row-major convention. The term *row major* refers to the fact that the placement of data preserves the structure of rows: all adjacent elements in a row are placed into consecutive locations in the address space. In Fig. 5.1, the four elements of row 0 are first placed in their order of appearance in the row. Elements in row 1 are then placed, followed by elements of row 2, followed by elements of row 3. It should be clear that $M_{0,0}$ and $M_{1,0}$, though appear to be consecutive in the two-dimensional matrix, are placed four locations away in the linearly addressed memory.

Fig. 5.2 illustrates the favorable vs. unfavorable CUDA kernel 2D row-major array data access patterns for memory coalescing. Recall from Fig. 4.7 that in our simple matrix multiplication kernel, each thread accesses a row of the M array and

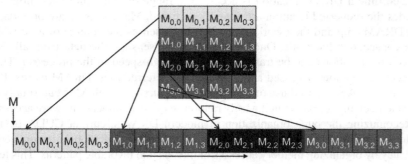

Linearized order in increasing address

FIGURE 5.1

Placing matrix elements into linear order.

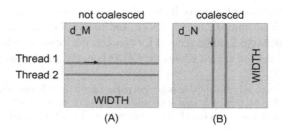

FIGURE 5.2

Memory access patterns in C 2D arrays for coalescing.

a column of the N array. The reader should review Section 4.3 before continuing. Figure 5.2(A) illustrates the data access pattern the M array, where threads in a warp read adjacent rows. That is, during iteration 0, threads in a warp read element 0 of rows 0 through 31. During iteration 1, these same threads read element 1 of rows 0 through 31. None of the accesses will be coalesced. A more favorable access pattern is shown in Fig. 5.2(B), where each thread reads a column of N. During iteration 0, threads in warp 0 read element 1 of columns 0 through 31. All these accesses will be coalesced.

In order to understand why the pattern in Fig. 5.2(B) is more favorable than that in Fig. 5.2(A), we need to review how these matrix elements are accessed in more detail. Fig. 5.3 shows a small example of the favorable access pattern in accessing a 4×4 matrix. The arrow in the top portion of Fig. 5.3 shows the access pattern of the kernel code. This access pattern is generated by the access to N in Fig. 4.3:

```
N[k*Width + Col]
```

Within a given iteration of the k loop, the k*Width value is the same across all threads. Recall that Col=blockIdx.x*blockDim.x+threadIdx.x. Since the value of blockIndx.x and blockDim.x are of the same value for all threads in the same block, the only part of k*Width+Col that varies across a thread block is threadIdx.x. Since adjacent threads have consecutive threadIdx.x values, their accessed elements will have consecutive addresses. For example, in Fig. 5.3, assume that we are using 4×4 blocks and that the warp size is 4. That is, for this toy example, we are using only 1 block to calculate the entire P matrix. The values of Width, blockDim.x,

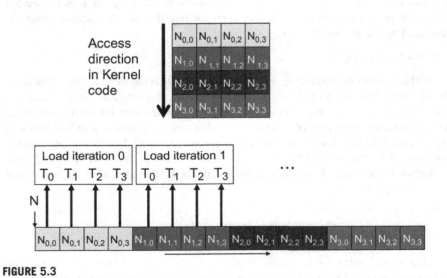

FIGURE 5.3

A coalesced access pattern.

`blockIdx.x` are 4, 4, and 0 for all threads in the block. In iteration 0, the `k` value is 0. The index used by each thread for accessing `N` is

```
N[k*Width+Col]=N[k*Width+blockIdx.x*blockDim.x+threadIdx.x]
             =N[0*4 + 0*4 + threadidx.x]
             =N[threadIdx.x]
```

That is, within this thread block, the index for accessing N is simply the value of `threadIdx.x`. The N elements accessed by T_0, T_1, T_2, T_3 are `N[0]`, `N[1]`, `N[2]`, and `N[3]`. This is illustrated with the "Load iteration 0" box of Fig. 5.3. These elements are in consecutive locations in the global memory. The hardware detects that these accesses are made by threads in a warp and to consecutive locations in the global memory. It coalesces these accesses into a consolidated access. This allows the DRAMs to supply data at a high rate.

During the next iteration, the `k` value is 1. The index used by each thread for accessing N becomes:

```
N[k*Width+Col]  =N[k*Width+blockIdx.x*blockDim.x+threadIdx.x]
                =N[1*4 + 0*4 + threadidx.x]
                =N[4+threadIdx.x]
```

The N elements accessed by T_0, T_1, T_2, T_3 in this iteration are `N[5]`, `N[6]`, `N[7]`, and `N[8]`, as shown with the "Load iteration 1" box in Fig. 5.3. All these accesses are again coalesced into a consolidated access for improved DRAM bandwidth utilization.

Fig. 5.4 shows an example of a matrix data access pattern that is not coalesced. The arrow in the top portion of the figure shows that the kernel code for each thread accesses elements of a row in sequence. The arrow in the top portion of Figure 5.4 shows the access pattern of the kernel code for one thread. This access pattern is generated by the access to `M` in Fig. 4.3:

```
M[Row*Width+k]
```

Within a given iteration of the `k` loop, `k*Width` value is the same across all threads. Recall from Fig. 4.3 that `Row=blockIdx.y*blockDim.y+threadIdx.y`. Since the value of `blockIndx.y` and `blockDim.y` are of the same value for all threads in the same block, the only part of `Row*Width+k` that can vary across a thread block is `threadIdx.y`. In Fig. 5.4, we assume again that we are using 4×4 blocks and that the warp size is 4. The values of `Width`, `blockDim.y`, `blockIdx.y` are 4, 4, and 0 for all threads in the block. In iteration 0, the `k` value is 0. The index used by each thread for accessing M is:

```
M[Row*Width+k]  =M[(blockIdx.y*blockDim.y+threadIdx.y)*Width+k]
                =M[((0*4+threadIdx.y)*4 + 0]
                =M[threadIdx.x*4]
```

That is, the index for accessing M is simply the value of `threadIdx.x*4`. The M elements accessed by T_0, T_1, T_2, T_3 are `M[0]`, `M[4]`, `M[8]`, and `M[12]`. This is illustrated with the "Load iteration 0" box of Fig. 5.4. These elements are not in

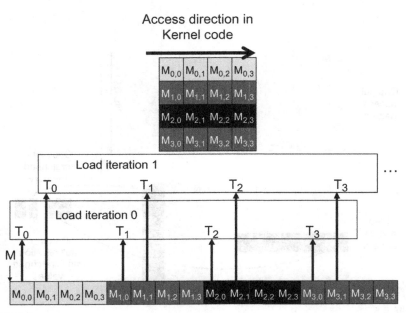

Access direction in
Kernel code

FIGURE 5.4

An un-coalesced access pattern.

consecutive locations in the global memory. The hardware cannot coalesce these accesses into a consolidated access.

During the next iteration, the k value is 1. The index used by each thread for accessing M becomes:

```
M[Row*Width+k]  =M[(blockIdx.y*blockDim.y+threadIdx.y)*Width+k]
                =M[(0*4+threadidx.x)*4+1]
                =M[threadIdx.x*4+1]
```

The M elements accessed by T_0, T_1, T_2, T_3 are M[1], M[5], M[9], and M[13], as shown with the "Load iteration 1" box in Fig. 5.4. Again, these accesses cannot be coalesced into a consolidated access.

For a realistic matrix, there are typically hundreds or even thousands of elements in each dimension. The M elements accessed in each iteration by neighboring threads can be hundreds or even thousands of elements apart. The "Load iteration 0" box in the bottom portion shows how the threads access these nonconsecutive locations in the 0th iteration. The hardware will determine that accesses to these elements are far away from each other and cannot be coalesced. As a result, when a kernel loop iterates through a row, the accesses to global memory are much less efficient than the case where a kernel iterates through a column.

If an algorithm intrinsically requires a kernel code to iterate through data along the row direction, one can use the shared memory to enable memory coalescing. The

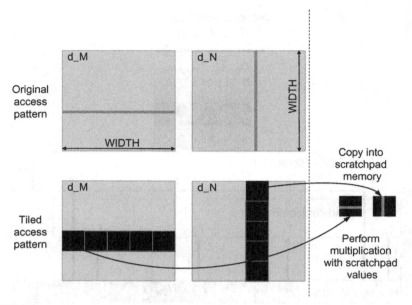

FIGURE 5.5

Using shared memory to enable coalescing.

technique, called *corner turning*, is illustrated in Fig. 5.5 for matrix multiplication. Each thread reads a row from M, a pattern that cannot be coalesced. Fortunately, a tiled algorithm can be used to enable coalescing. As we discussed in Chapter 4, Memory and data locality, threads of a block can first cooperatively load the tiles into the shared memory. *Care must be taken to ensure that these tiles are loaded in a coalesced pattern.* Once the data is in shared memory, they can be accessed either on a row basis or a column basis with much less performance variation because the shared memories are implemented as intrinsically high-speed on-chip memory that does not require coalescing to achieve high data access rate.

We replicate Fig. 4.16 here as Fig. 5.6, where the matrix multiplication kernel loads two tiles of matrix M and N into the shared memory. Recall that at the beginning of each phase (Lines 9–11) each thread in a thread block is responsible for loading one M element and one N element into Mds and Nds. Note that there are TILE_WIDTH² threads involved in each tile. The threads use threadIdx.y and threadIdx.y to determine the elements to load.

The M elements are loaded in line 9, where the index calculation for each thread uses ph to locate the left end of the tile. The linearized index calculation is equivalent to the two-dimensional array access expression M[Row][ph*TILE_SIZE+tx]. Note that the column index used by the threads only differs in terms of threadIdx. The row index is determined by blockIdx.y and threadIdx.y (Line 5), which means that threads in the same thread block with identical blockIdx.y/threadIdx.y and adjacent threadIdx.x values will access adjacent M elements. That is, each row of the tile

```
__global__ void MatrixMulKernel(float* M, float* N, float* P, int Width)
{
1.    __shared__ float Mds[TILE_WIDTH][TILE_WIDTH];
2.    __shared__ float Nds[TILE_WIDTH][TILE_WIDTH];

3.    int bx = blockIdx.x;  int by = blockIdx.y;
4.    int tx = threadIdx.x; int ty = threadIdx.y;

      // Identify the row and column of the P element to work on
5.    int Row = by * TILE_WIDTH + ty;
6.    int Col = bx * TILE_WIDTH + tx;

7.    float Pvalue = 0;
      // Loop over the M and N tiles required to compute the P element
8.    for (int ph = 0; ph < Width/TILE_WIDTH; ++ph) {

         // Collaborative loading of M and N tiles into shared memory
9.       Mds[ty][tx] = M[Row*Width + ph*TILE_WIDTH + tx];
10.      Nds[ty][tx] = N[(ph*TILE_WIDTH + ty)*Width + Col];
11.      __syncthreads();

12.         for (int k = 0; k < TILE_WIDTH; ++k) {
13.            Pvalue += Mds[ty][k] * Nds[k][tx];
            }
14.         __syncthreads();
         }
15.      P[Row*Width + Col] = Pvalue;
}
```

FIGURE 5.6

Tiled Matrix Multiplication Kernel using shared memory.

is loaded by TILE_WIDTH threads whose threadIdx are identical in the y dimension and consecutive in the x dimension. The hardware will coalesce these loads.

In the case of N, the row index ph*TILE_SIZE+ty has the same value for all threads with the same threadIdx.y value. The question is whether threads with adjacent threadIdx.x values access adjacent N elements of a row. Note the column index calculation for each thread, Col=bx*TILE_SIZE+tx (see line 6). The first term, bx*TILE_SIZE, is the same for all threads in the same block. The second term, tx, is simply the threadIdx.x value. Therefore, threads with adjacent threadIdx.x values access adjacent N elements in a row. The hardware will coalesce these loads.

Note that in the simple algorithm, threads with adjacent threadIdx.x values access vertically adjacent elements that are not physically adjacent in the row major layout. The tiled algorithm "transformed" this into a different access pattern where threads with adjacent threadIdx.x values access horizontally adjacent elements. That is, we turned a vertical access pattern into a horizontal access pattern, which is sometimes referred to as *corner turning*. Corner turning could be also used to turn a horizontal access pattern into a vertical access pattern, which is beneficial in languages such as FORTRAN where 2D arrays are laid out in column-major order.

In the tiled algorithm, loads to both the M and N elements are coalesced. Therefore, the tiled matrix multiplication algorithm has two advantages over the simple matrix multiplication. First, the number of memory loads is reduced due to the reuse of data in the shared memory. Second, the remaining memory loads are coalesced so the DRAM bandwidth utilization is further improved. These two improvements have multiplicative effect on each other and result in very significant increased execution speed of the kernel. On a current generation device, the tiled kernel can run more than 30x faster than the simple kernel.

Lines 5, 6, 9, 10 in Fig. 5.6 form a frequently used programming pattern for loading matrix elements into shared memory in tiled algorithms. We would also like to encourage the reader to analyze the data access pattern by the dot-product loop in lines 12 and 13. Note that the threads in a warp do not access consecutive locations of Mds. This is not a problem since Mds is in shared memory, which does not require coalescing to achieve high-speed data access.

5.2 MORE ON MEMORY PARALLELISM

As we explained in Section 5.1, DRAM bursting is a form of parallel organization: multiple locations around are accessed in the DRAM core array in parallel. However, bursting alone is not sufficient to realize the level of DRAM access bandwidth required by modern processors. DRAM systems typically employ two more forms of parallel organization – banks and channels. At the highest level, a processor contains one or more channels. Each channel is a memory controller with a bus that connects a set of DRAM banks to the processor. Fig. 5.7 illustrates a processor that contains four channels, each with a bus that connects four DRAM banks to the processor. In real systems, a processor typically has one to eight channels and each channel is connected to a large number of banks.

The data transfer bandwidth of a bus is defined by its width and clock frequency. Modern *double data rate* (DDR) busses perform two data transfers per clock cycle, one at the rising edge and one at the falling edge of each clock cycle. For example, a 64-bit DDR bus with a clock frequency of 1 GHz has a bandwidth of 8B*2*1 GHz = 16 GB/sec. This seems to be a large number but is often too small for modern CPUs

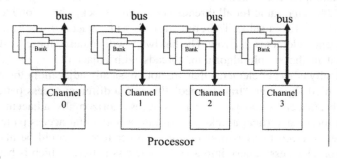

FIGURE 5.7

Channels and banks in DRAM systems.

and GPUs. A modern CPU might require a memory bandwidth of at least 32 GB/s, whereas a modern GPU might require 128 GB/s. For this example, the CPU would require 2 channels and the GPU would require 8 channels.

For each channel, the number of banks connected to it is determined by the number of banks required to fully utilize the data transfer bandwidth of the bus. This is illustrated in Fig. 5.8. Each bank contains an array of DRAM cells, the sensing amplifiers for accessing these cells, and the interface for delivering bursts of data to the bus (Section 5.1).

Fig. 5.8(A) illustrates the data transfer timing when a single bank is connected to a channel. It shows the timing of two consecutive memory read accesses to the DRAM cells in the bank. Recall from Section 5.1 that each access involves a long latency for the decoder to enable the cells and for the cells to share their stored charge with the sensing amplifier. This latency is shown as the light gray section at the left end of the time frame. Once the sensing amplifier completes its work, the burst data is delivered through the bus. The time for transferring the burst data through the bus is shown as the left dark section of the time frame in Fig. 5.8(A). The second memory read access will incur a similar long access latency (light section between the dark sections of the time frame) before its burst data can be transferred (right dark section).

In reality, the access latency (light sections) is much longer than the data transfer time (dark section). It should be apparent that the access-transfer timing of a one-bank organization would grossly underutilize the data transfer bandwidth of the channel bus. For example, if the ratio of DRAM cell array access latency to the data transfer time is 20:1, the maximal utilization of the channel bus would be $1/21 = 4.8\%$. That is a 16 GB/s channel would deliver data to the processor at a rate no more than 0.76 GB/s. This would be totally unacceptable. This problem is solved by connecting multiple banks to a channel bus.

When two banks are connected to a channel bus, an access can be initiated in the second bank while the first bank is serving another access. Therefore, one can overlap the latency for accessing the DRAM cell arrays. Fig. 5.8(B) shows the timing of a two-bank organization. We assume that the bank 0 started at a time earlier than the window shown in Fig. 5.8(B). Shortly after the first bank starts accessing its cell

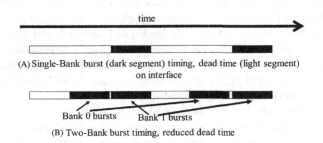

(A) Single-Bank burst (dark segment) timing, dead time (light segment) on interface

Bank 0 bursts   Bank 1 bursts

(B) Two-Bank burst timing, reduced dead time

FIGURE 5.8

Banking improves the utilization of data transfer bandwidth of a channel.

array, the second bank also starts accessing its cell array. When the access in bank 0 is complete, it transfers the burst data (leftmost dark section of the time frame). Once bank 0 completes its data transfer, bank 1 can transfer its burst data (second dark section). This pattern repeats for the next accesses.

From Fig. 5.8(B), we can see that by having two banks, we can potentially double the utilization of the data transfer bandwidth of the channel bus. In general, if the ratio of the cell array access latency and data transfer time is R, we need to have at least R+1 banks if we hope to fully utilize the data transfer bandwidth of the channel bus. For example, if the ratio is 20, we will need at least 21 banks connected to each channel bus. In reality, the number of banks connected to each channel bus needs to be larger than R for two reasons. One is that having more banks reduces the probability of multiple simultaneous accesses targeting the same bank, a phenomenon called bank conflict. Since each bank can serve only one access at a time, the cell array access latency can no longer be overlapped for these conflicting accesses. Having a larger number of banks increases the probability that these accesses will be spread out among multiple banks. The second reason is that the size of each cell array is set to achieve reasonable latency and manufacturability. This limits the number of cells that each bank can provide. One may need a large number of banks just to be able to support the memory size required.

There is an important connection between the parallel execution of threads and the parallel organization of the DRAM system. In order to achieve the memory access bandwidth specified for device, there must be a sufficient number of threads making simultaneous memory accesses. Furthermore, these memory accesses must be evenly distributed to the channels and banks. Of course, each access to a bank must also be a coalesced access, as we studied in Section 5.1.

Fig. 5.9 shows a toy example of distributing array M elements to channels and banks. We assume a small burst size of two elements (eight bytes). The distribution is done by hardware design. The addressing of the channels and banks is such that the first eight bytes of the array (M[0] and M[1]) are stored in bank 0 of channel 0, the next eight bytes (M[2] and M[3]) in bank 0 of Channel 1, the next eight bytes (M[4] and M[5]) in bank 0 of Channel 2, and the next eight bytes (M[6] and M[7]) in bank 0 of Channel 3.

At this point, the distribution wraps back to Channel 0 but will use bank 1 for the next eight bytes (M[8] and M[9]). This way, elements M[10] and M[11] will be in bank 1 of Channel 1, M[12] and M[13] in bank 1 of Channel 2, and M[14] and M[15] in bank 1 of Channel 3. Although not shown in the figure, any additional elements will be wrapped around and start with bank 0 of Channel 0. For example, if there are more elements, M[16] and M[17] will be stored in bank 0 of Channel 0, M[18] and M[19] will be in bank 0 of Channel 1, and so on.

The distribution scheme illustrated in Fig. 5.9, often referred to as *interleaved data distribution*, spreads the elements across the banks and channels in the system. This scheme ensures that even relatively small arrays are spread out nicely. That is, we only assign enough elements to fully utilize the DRAM burst of bank 0 of Channel 0 before moving on to bank 0 of Channel 1. In our toy example, as long as

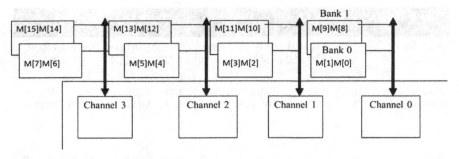

FIGURE 5.9

Distributing array elements into channels and banks.

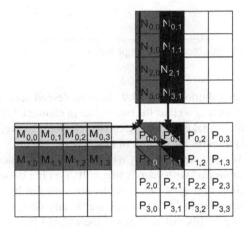

FIGURE 5.10

A small example of matrix multiplication (replicated from Fig. 4.9).

we have at least 16 elements, the distribution will involve all the channels and banks for storing the elements.

We now illustrate the interaction between parallel thread execution and the parallel memory organization. We will use the example in Fig. 4.9, replicated as Fig. 5.10. We assume that the multiplication will be performed with 2×2 thread blocks and 2×2 tiles.

During the phase 0 of the kernel's execution, all four thread blocks will be loading their first tile. The M elements involved in each tile are shown in Fig. 5.11. Row 2 shows the M elements accessed in Phase 0, with their 2D indices. Row 3 shows the same M elements with their linearized indices. Assume that all thread blocks are executed in parallel. We see that each block will make two coalesced accesses.

Tiles loaded by	Block 0,0	Block 0,1	Block 1,0	Block 1,1
Phase 0 (2D index)	M[0][0],M[0][1], M[1][0], M[1][1]	M[0][0], M[0][1], M[1][0], M[1][1]	M[2][0], M[2][1], M[3][0], M[3][1]	M[2][0], M[2][1], M[3][0], M[3][1]
Phase 0 (linearized index)	M[0], M[1], M[4], M[5]	M[0], M[1], M[4], M[5]	M[8], M[9], M[12], M[13]	M[8], M[9], M[12], M[13]
Phase 1 (2D index)	M[0][2],M[0][3], M[1][2], M[1][3]	M[0][2],M[0][3], M[1][2], M[1][3]	M[2][2], M[2][3], M[3][2], M[3][3]	M[2][2], M[2][3], M[3][2], M[3][3]
Phase 1 (linearized index)	M[2], M[3], M[6], M[7]	M[2], M[3], M[6], M[7]	M[10], M[11], M[14], M[15]	M[10], M[11], M[14], M[15]

FIGURE 5.11

M elements loaded by thread blocks in each phase.

According to the distribution in Fig. 5.9, these coalesced accesses will be made to the two banks in channel 0 as well as the two banks in channel 2. These four accesses will be done in parallel to take advantage of two channels as well as improving the utilization of the data transfer bandwidth of each channel.

We also see that Block$_{0,0}$ and Block$_{0,1}$ will load the same M elements. Most of the modern devices are equipped with caches that will combine these accesses into one as long as the execution timing of these blocks are sufficiently close to each other. In fact, the cache memories in GPU devices are mainly designed to combine such accesses and reduce the number of accesses to the DRAM system.

Rows 4 and 5 show the M elements loaded during phase 1 of the kernel execution. We see that the accesses are now done to the banks in channel 1 and channel 3. Once again, these accesses will be done in parallel. It should be clear to the reader that there is a symbiotic relationship between the parallel execution of the threads and the parallel structure of the DRAM system. On one hand, good utilization of the potential access bandwidth of the DRAM system requires that many threads simultaneously access data that reside in different banks and channels. On the other hand, the execution throughput of the device relies on good utilization of the parallel structure of the DRAM system. For example, if the simultaneously executing threads all access data in the same channel, the memory access throughput and the overall device execution speed will be greatly reduced.

The reader is invited to verify that multiplying two larger matrices, such as 8×8 with the same 2×2 thread block configuration, will make use of all the four channels in Fig. 5.9. Also, an increased DRAM burst size would require multiplication of even larger matrices to fully utilize the data transfer bandwidth of all the channels.

5.3 WARPS AND SIMD HARDWARE

We now turn our attention to aspects of the thread execution that can limit performance. Recall that launching a CUDA kernel generates a grid of threads that is organized as a two-level hierarchy. At the top level, a grid consists of a one-, two-, or three-dimensional array of blocks. At the bottom level, each block, in turn, consists of a one-, two-, or three-dimensional array of threads. In Chapter 3, Scalable parallel execution, we saw that blocks can execute in any order relative to each other, which allows for transparent scalability across different devices. However, we did not say much about the execution timing of threads within each block.

Conceptually, one should assume that threads in a block can execute in any order with respect to each other. In algorithms with phases, barrier synchronizations should be used whenever we want to ensure that all threads have completed a common phase of their execution before any of them start the next phase. We saw such an example in the tiled matrix multiplication kernel. The correctness of executing a kernel should not depend on the fact that certain threads will execute in synchrony with each other. Having said this, we also want to point out that due to various hardware cost considerations, current CUDA devices actually bundle multiple threads for execution. Such implementation strategy leads to performance limitations for certain types of kernel code constructs. It is advantageous for application developers to change these types of constructs to other equivalent forms that perform better.

As we discussed in Chapter 3, Scalable parallel execution, each thread block is partitioned into *warps*. The execution of warps is implemented by an SIMD hardware (see "Warps and SIMD Hardware" sidebar). This implementation technique helps to reduce hardware manufacturing cost, lower run-time operation electricity cost, and enable coalescing of memory accesses. In the foreseeable future, we expect that warp partitioning will remain as a popular implementation technique. However, the size of warps can easily vary from implementation to implementation. Up to this point in time, all CUDA devices have used similar warp configurations where each warp consists of 32 threads.

WARPS AND SIMD HARDWARE

The motivation for executing threads as warps is illustrated in the following picture (Same as Fig. 4.8). The processor has only one control unit that fetches and decodes instructions. The same control signal goes to multiple processing units, each of which executes one of the threads in a warp. Since all processing units are controlled by the same instruction, their execution differences are due to the different data operand values in the register files. This is called Single-Instruction-Multiple-Data (SIMD) in processor design. For example, although all processing units are controlled by an instruction:

add r1, r2, r3

the r2 and r3 values are different in different processing units.

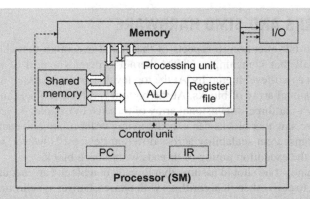

Control units in modern processors are quite complex, including sophisticated logic for fetching instructions and access ports to the instruction memory. They include on-chip instruction caches to reduce the latency of instruction fetch. Having multiple processing units to share a control unit can result in significant reduction in hardware manufacturing cost and power consumption.

As the processors are increasingly power-limited, new processors will likely use SIMD designs. In fact, we may see even more processing units sharing a control unit in the future.

Thread blocks are partitioned into warps based on thread indices. If a thread block is organized into a one-dimensional array, i.e., only threadIdx.x is used, the partition is straightforward. ThreadIdx.x values within a warp are consecutive and increasing. For warp size of 32, warp 0 starts with thread 0 and ends with thread 31, warp 1 starts with thread 32 and ends with thread 63. In general, warp n starts with thread 32*n and ends with thread $32(n+1) - 1$. For a block whose size is not a multiple of 32, the last warp will be padded with extra threads to fill up the 32-thread positions. For example, if a block has 48 threads, it will be partitioned into two warps, and its warp 1 will be padded with 16 extra threads.

For blocks that consist of multiple dimensions of threads, the dimensions will be projected into a linearized row-major order before partitioning into warps. The linear order is determined by placing the rows with larger y and z coordinates after those with lower ones. That is, if a block consists of two dimensions of threads, one would form the linear order by placing all threads whose threadIdx.y is 1 after those whose threadIdx.y is 0. Threads whose threadIdx.y is 2 will be placed after those whose threadIdx.y is 1, and so on.

Fig. 5.12 shows an example of placing threads of a two-dimensional block into linear order. The upper part shows the two-dimensional view of the block. The reader

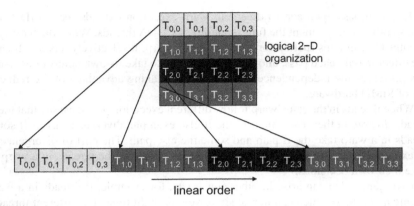

FIGURE 5.12

Placing 2D threads into linear order.

should recognize the similarity with the row-major layout of two-dimensional arrays. Each thread is shown as $T_{y,x}$, x being `threadIdx.x` and y being `threadIdx.y`. The lower part of Fig. 5.12 shows the linearized view of the block. The first four threads are those threads whose `threadIdx.y` value is 0; they are ordered with increasing `threadIdx.x` values. The next four threads are those threads whose `threadIdx.y` value is 1. They are also placed with increasing `threadIdx.x` values. For this example, all 16 threads form half a warp. The warp will be padded with another 16 threads to complete a 32-thread warp. Imagine a two-dimensional block with 8×8 threads. The 64 threads will form two warps. The first warp starts with $T_{0,0}$ and ends with $T_{3,7}$. The second warp starts with $T_{4,0}$ and ends with $T_{7,7}$. It would be a useful exercise to draw out the picture.

For a three-dimensional block, we first place all threads whose `threadIdx.z` value is 0 into the linear order. Among these threads, they are treated as a two-dimensional block as shown in Fig. 5.12. All threads whose `threadIdx.z` value is 1 will then be placed into the linear order, and so on. For a three-dimensional thread block of dimensions 2×8×4 (four in the x dimension, eight in the y dimension, and two in the z dimension), the 64 threads will be partitioned into two warps, with $T_{0,0,0}$ through $T_{0,7,3}$ in the first warp and $T_{1,0,0}$ through $T_{1,7,3}$ in the second warp.

The SIMD hardware executes all threads of a warp as a bundle. An instruction is run for all threads in the same warp. It works well when all threads within a warp follow the same execution path, or more formally referred to as control flow, when working their data. For example, for an if-else construct, the execution works well when either all threads execute the if part or all execute the else part. When threads within a warp take different control flow paths, the SIMD hardware will take multiple passes through these divergent paths. One pass executes those threads that follow the if part and another pass executes those that follow the else part. During each pass, the threads that follow the other path are not allowed to take effect. These passes are sequential to each other, thus will add to the execution time.

The multipass approach to divergent warp execution extends the SIMD hardware's ability to implement the full semantics of CUDA threads. While the hardware executes the same instruction for all threads in a warp, it selectively lets the threads take effect in only each pass, allowing every thread to take its own control flow path. This preserves the independence of threads while taking advantage of the reduced cost of SIMD hardware.

When threads in the same warp follow different execution paths, we say that these threads *diverge* in their execution. In the if-else example, divergence arises if some threads in a warp take the if path and some the else path. The cost of divergence is the extra pass the hardware needs to take in order to allow the threads in a warp to make their own decisions.

Divergence also can arise in other constructs, for example, if threads in a warp execute a `for`-loop which can iterate six, seven, or eight times for different threads. All threads will finish the first six iterations together. Two passes will be used to execute the 7th iteration, one for those that take the iteration and one for those that do not. Two passes will be used to execute the 8th iteration, one for those that take the iteration and one for those that do not.

One can determine if a control construct can result in thread divergence by inspecting its decision condition. If the decision condition is based on `threadIdx` values, the control statement can potentially cause thread divergence. For example, the statement `if(threadIdx.x > 2) {}` causes the threads to follow two divergent control flow paths. Threads 0, 1, and 2 follow a different path than threads 3, 4, 5, etc. Similarly, a loop can cause thread divergence if its loop condition is based on thread index values.

A prevalent reason for using a control construct with thread divergence is handling boundary conditions when mapping threads to data. This is usually because the total number of threads needs to be a multiple of the block size whereas the size of the data can be an arbitrary number. Starting with our vector addition kernel in Fig. 2.12, we had an `if (i<n)` statement in `addVecKernel`. This is because not all vector lengths can be expressed as multiples of the block size. For example, assume that the vector length is 1003. Assume that we picked 64 as block size. One would need to launch 16 thread blocks to process all the 1003 vector elements. However, the 16 thread blocks would have 1024 threads. We need to disable the last 21 threads in thread block 15 from doing work not expected/allowed by the original program. Keep in mind that these 16 blocks are partitioned into 32 warps. Only the last warp will have control divergence.

Note that the performance impact of control divergence decreases with the size of the vectors being processed. For a vector length of 100, one of the four warps will have control divergence, which can have significant impact on performance. For a vector size of 1000, only one out of the 32 warps will have control divergence. That is, control divergence will affect only about 3% of the execution time. Even if it doubles the execution time of the warp, the net impact to the total execution time will be about 3%. Obviously, if the vector length is 10,000 or more, only one of the 313 warps will have control divergence. The impact of control divergence will be much less than 1%!

For two-dimensional data, such as the color-to-greyscale conversion example, if-statements are also used to handle the boundary conditions for threads that operate at the edge of the data. In Fig. 3.2, to process the 76×62 picture, we used 20 = 5*4 two-dimensional blocks that consist of 16×16 threads each. Each block will be partitioned into 8 warps, each one consists of two rows of a block. There are a total 160 warps (8 warps per block) involved.

To analyze the impact of control divergence, refer to Fig. 3.5. None of the warps in the 12 blocks in region 1 will have control divergence. There are 12*8 = 96 warps in region 1. For region 2, all the 24 warps will have control divergence. For region 3, note that all the bottom warps are mapped to data that are completely outside the picture. As a result, none of them will pass the if-condition. The reader should verify that these warps would have had control divergence if the picture had an odd number of pixels in the vertical dimension. Since they all follow the same control flow path, none of these 32 warps will have control divergence! In region 4, the first seven warps will have control divergence but the last warp will not. All in all, 31 out of the 160 warps will have control divergence.

Once again, the performance impact of control divergence decreases as the number of pixels in the horizontal dimension increases. For example, if we process a 200×150 picture with 16×16 blocks, there will be a total 130 = 13*10 thread blocks or 1040 warps. The number of warps in regions 1 through 4 will be 864 (12*9*8), 72 (9*8), 96 (12*8), and 8 (1*8). Only 80 of these warps will have control divergence. Thus, the performance impact of control divergence will be less than 8%. Obviously, if we process a realistic picture with more than 1000 pixels in the horizontal dimension, the performance impact of control divergence will be less than 2%.

Control divergence also naturally arises in some important parallel algorithms where the number of threads participating in the computation varies over time. We will use a reduction algorithm to illustrate such behavior.

A reduction algorithm derives a single value from an array of values. The single value could be the sum, the maximal value, the minimal value, etc., among all elements. All these types of reductions share the same computation structure. A reduction can be easily done by sequentially going through every element of the array. When an element is visited, the action to take depends on the type of reduction being performed. For a sum reduction, the value of the element being visited at the current step, or the current value, is added to a running sum. For a maximal reduction, the current value is compared to a running maximal value of all the elements visited so far. If the current value is larger than the running maximal, the current element value becomes the running maximal value. For a minimal reduction, the value of the element currently being visited is compared to a running minimal. If the current value is smaller than the running minimal, the current element value becomes the running minimal. The sequential algorithm ends when all the elements are visited.

The sequential reduction algorithm is work efficient in that every element is only visited once and only a minimal amount of work is performed when each element is visited. Its execution time is proportional to the number of elements involved. That is, the computational complexity of the algorithm is $O(N)$, where N is the number of elements involved in the reduction.

The time needed to visit all elements of a large array motivates parallel execution. A parallel reduction algorithm typically resembles the structure of a soccer tournament. In fact, the elimination process of the World Cup is a reduction of "maximal" where the maximal is defined as the team that "beats" all other teams. The tournament "reduction" is done in multiple rounds. The teams are divided into pairs. During the first round, all pairs play in parallel. Winners of the first round advance to the second round, whose winners advance to the third round, etc. With 16 teams entering a tournament, eight winners will emerge from the first round, four from the second round, two from the third round, and one final winner from the fourth round.

It should be easy to see that even with 1024 teams, it takes only 10 rounds to determine the final winner. The trick is to have enough soccer fields to hold the 512 games in parallel during the first round, 256 games in the second round, 128 games in the third round, and so on. With enough fields, even with sixty thousand teams, we can determine the final winner in just 16 rounds. Of course, one would need to have enough soccer fields and enough officials to accommodate the thirty thousand games in the first round, etc.

Fig. 5.13 shows a kernel function that performs parallel sum reduction. The original array is in the global memory. Each thread block reduces a section of the array by loading the elements of the section into the shared memory and performing parallel reduction on these elements. The code loads the elements of the input array X from global memory into the shared memory. The reduction is done *in place*, which means some of the elements in the shared memory will be replaced by partial sums. Each iteration of the for-loop in the kernel function implements a round of reduction.

The __syncthreads() statement (Line 5) in the for-loop ensures that all partial sums for the previous iteration have been generated and before any one of the threads is allowed to begin the current iteration. This way, all threads that enter the second iteration will be using the values produced in the first iteration. After the first round, the even elements will be replaced by the partial sums generated in the first round. After the second round, the elements whose indices are multiples of four will be replaced with the partial sums. After the final round, the total sum of the entire section will be in partialSum[0].

```
1.  __shared__ float partialSum[SIZE];
    partialSum[threadIdx.x] = X[blockIdx.x*blockDim.x+threadIdx.x];
2.  unsigned int t = threadIdx.x;
3.  for (unsigned int stride = 1; stride < blockDim.x; stride *= 2)
4.  {
5.    __syncthreads();
6.    if (t % (2*stride) == 0)
7.      partialSum[t] += partialSum[t+stride];
8.  }
```

FIGURE 5.13

A simple sum reduction kernel.

In Fig. 5.13, Line 3 initializes the `stride` variable to 1. During the first iteration, the if-statement in Line 6 is used to select only the even threads to perform addition between two neighboring elements. The execution of the kernel is illustrated in Fig. 5.14. The threads and the array element values are shown in the horizontal direction. The iterations taken by the threads are shown in the vertical direction with time progressing from top to bottom. Each row of Fig. 5.14 shows the contents of the array elements after an iteration of the for-loop.

As shown in Fig. 5.16, the even elements of the array hold the pair-wise partial sums after iteration 1. Before the second iteration, the value of the `stride` variable is doubled to 2. During the second iteration, only those threads whose indices are multiples of four will execute the add-statement in Line 7. Each thread generates a partial sum of four elements, as shown in row 2. With 512 elements in each section, the kernel function will generate the sum of the entire section after 9 iterations. By using `blockDim.x` as the loop bound in Line 4, the kernel assumes that it is launched with the same number of threads as the number of elements in the section. That is, for section size of 512, the kernel needs to be launched with 512 threads.[4]

Let us analyze the total amount of work done by the kernel. Assume that the total number of elements to be reduced is N. The first round requires $N/2$ additions. The second round requires $N/4$ additions. The final round has only one addition. There are $\log_2(N)$ rounds. The total number of additions performed by the kernel is $N/2 + N/4 + N/8 + \ldots + 1 = N-1$. Therefore, the computational complexity of the reduction algorithm is $O(N)$. The algorithm is work efficient. However, we also need to make sure that the hardware is efficiently utilized while executing the kernel.

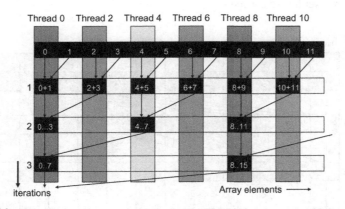

FIGURE 5.14

Execution of the sum reduction kernel.

[4] Note that using the same number of threads as the number of elements in a section is wasteful. Half of the threads in a block will never execute. The reader is encouraged to modify the kernel and the kernel launch execution configuration parameters to eliminate this waste (Exercise 5.1).

The kernel in Fig. 5.13 clearly has thread divergence. During the first iteration of the loop, only those threads whose threadIdx.x are even will execute the add-statement. One pass will be needed to execute these threads and one additional pass will be needed to execute those that do not execute Line 7. In each successive iteration, fewer threads will execute Line 7 but two passes will be still needed to execute all the threads during each iteration. This divergence can be reduced with a slight change to the algorithm.

Fig. 5.15 shows a modified kernel with a slightly different algorithm for sum reduction. Instead of adding neighbor elements in the first round, it adds elements that are half a section away from each other. It does so by initializing the stride to be half the size of the section. All pairs added during the first round are half the section size away from each other. After the first iteration, all the pair-wise sums are stored in the first half of the array, as shown in Fig. 5.16. The loop divides the stride by 2 before entering the next iteration. Thus for the second iteration, the stride variable

```
1.  __shared__ float partialSum[SIZE];
    partialSum[threadIdx.x] = X[blockIdx.x*blockDim.x+threadIdx.x];

2.  unsigned int t = threadIdx.x;
3.  for (unsigned int stride = blockDim.x/2; stride >= 1; stride = stride>>1)
4.  {
5.     __syncthreads();
6.     if (t < stride)
7.        partialSum[t] += partialSum[t+stride];
8.  }
```

FIGURE 5.15

A kernel with fewer thread divergence.

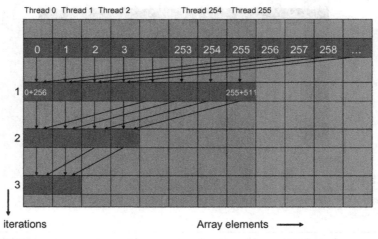

FIGURE 5.16

Execution of the revised algorithm.

value is one-quarter of the section size. That is, the threads add elements that are quarter a section away from each other during the second iteration.

Note that the kernel in Fig. 5.15 still has an if-statement (Line 6) in the loop. The number of threads that execute Line 7 in each iteration is the same as in Fig. 5.13. So, why should there be a performance difference between the two kernels? The answer lies in the positions of threads that execute Line 7 relative to those that do not.

Fig. 5.16 illustrates the execution of the revised kernel in Fig. 5.15. During the first iteration, all threads whose `threadIdx.x` values are less than half of the size of the section execute Line 7. For a section of 512 elements, Threads 0 through 255 execute the add-statement during the first iteration while threads 256 through 511 do not. The pair-wise sums are stored in elements 0 through 255 after the first iteration. Since the warps consists of 32 threads with consecutive `threadIdx.x` values, all threads in warp 0 through warp 7 execute the add-statement, whereas warp 8 through warp 15 all skip the add-statement. Since all threads in each warp take the same path, there is no thread divergence!

The kernel in Fig. 5.15 does not completely eliminate the divergence caused by the if-statement. The reader should verify that starting with the 5th iteration, the number of threads that execute Line 7 will fall below 32. That is, the final five iterations will have only 16, 8, 4, 2, and 1 thread(s) performing the addition. This means that the kernel execution will still have divergence in these iterations. However, the number of iterations of the loop that has divergence is reduced from ten to five.

The difference between Figs. 5.13 and 5.15 is small but has very significant performance impact. It requires someone with clear understanding of the execution of threads on the SIMD hardware of the device to be able to confidently make such adjustments.

5.4 DYNAMIC PARTITIONING OF RESOURCES

The execution resources in an SM include registers, shared memory, thread block slots, and thread slots. These resources are dynamically partitioned and assigned to threads to support their execution. In Chapter 3, Scalable parallel execution, we have seen that Fermi generation of devices have 1536 thread slots. These thread slots are partitioned and assigned to thread blocks during runtime. If each thread block consists of 512 threads, the 1536 thread slots are partitioned and assigned to three blocks. In this case, each SM can accommodate up to three thread blocks due to limitations on thread slots.

If each thread block contains 256 threads, the 1536 thread slots are partitioned and assigned to 6 thread blocks. The ability to dynamically partition the thread slots among thread blocks makes SMs versatile. They can either execute many thread blocks each having few threads, or execute few thread blocks each having many threads. This is in contrast to a fixed partitioning method where each block receives a fixed amount of resources regardless of their real needs. Fixed partitioning results in wasted thread slots when a block has few threads and fails to support blocks that require more thread slots than the fixed partition allows.

Dynamic partitioning of resources can lead to subtle interactions between resource limitations, which can cause underutilization of resources. Such interactions can occur between block slots and thread slots. For example, if each block has 128 threads, the 1536 thread slots can be partitioned and assigned to 12 blocks. However, since there are only 8 block slots in each SM, only 8 blocks will be allowed. This means that in the end, only 1024 of the thread slots will be utilized. Therefore, to fully utilize both the block slots and thread slots, one needs at least 256 threads in each block.

As we mentioned in Chapter 4, Memory and data locality, the automatic variables declared in a CUDA kernel are placed into registers. Some kernels may use lots of automatic variables and others may use few of them. Thus, one should expect that some kernels require many registers and some require fewer. By dynamically partitioning the registers among blocks, the SM can accommodate more blocks if they require few registers, and fewer blocks if they require more registers. One does, however, need to be aware of potential interactions between register limitations and other resource limitations.

In the matrix multiplication example, assume that each SM has 16,384 registers and the kernel code uses 10 registers per thread. If we have 16×16 thread blocks, how many threads can run on each SM? We can answer this question by first calculating the number of registers needed for each block, which is 10*16*16 = 2560. The number of registers required by six blocks is 15,360, which is under the 16,384 limit. Adding another block would require 17,920 registers, which exceeds the limit. Therefore, the register limitation allows six blocks that altogether have 1536 threads to run on each SM, which also fits within the limit of 8 block slots and 1536 thread slots.

Now assume that the programmer declares an additional two automatic variables in the kernel and bumps the number of registers used by each thread to 12. Assuming the same 16×16 blocks, each block now requires 12*16*16 = 3072 registers. The number of registers required by six blocks is now 18,432, which exceeds the register limitation for some CUDA hardware. The CUDA runtime system deals with this situation by reducing the number of blocks assigned to each SM by one, thus reducing the number of registers required to 15,360. This, however, reduces the number of threads running on an SM from 1536 to 1280. That is, by using two extra automatic variables, the program saw a 1/6 reduction in the warp parallelism in each SM. This is sometimes a referred to as a "performance cliff" where a slight increase in resource usage can result in significant reduction in parallelism and performance achieved [RRS 2008].

Shared memory is another resource that is dynamically partitioned at run-time. Tiled algorithms often require a large amount of shared memory to be effective. Unfortunately, large shared memory usage can reduce the number of thread blocks running on an SM. As we discussed in Section 5.3, reduced thread parallelism can negatively affect the utilization of the memory access bandwidth of the DRAM system. The reduced memory access throughput, in turn, can further reduce the thread execution throughput. This is a pitfall that can result in disappointing performance of tiled algorithms and should be carefully avoided.

It should be clear to the reader that the constraints of all the dynamically partitioned resources interact with each other in a complex manner. Accurate determination of the number of threads running in each SM can be difficult. The reader is referred to the CUDA Occupancy Calculator [NVIDIA], which is a downloadable Excel sheet that calculates the actual number of threads running on each SM for a particular device implementation given the usage of resources by a kernel.

5.5 THREAD GRANULARITY

An important algorithmic decision in performance tuning is the granularity of threads. It is sometimes advantageous to put more work into each thread and use fewer threads. Such advantage arises when some redundant work exists between threads. In the current generation of devices, each SM has limited instruction processing bandwidth. Every instruction consumes instruction processing bandwidth, whether it is a floating-point calculation instruction, a load instruction, or a branch instruction. Eliminating redundant work can ease the pressure on the instruction processing bandwidth and improve the overall execution speed of the kernel.

Fig. 5.17 illustrates such an opportunity in matrix multiplication. The tiled algorithm in Fig. 5.6 uses one thread to compute one element of the output P matrix. This requires a dot-product between one row of M and one column of N.

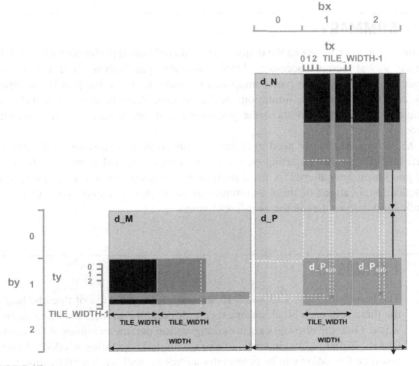

FIGURE 5.17

Increased thread granularity with rectangular tiles.

The opportunity of thread granularity adjustment comes from the fact that multiple blocks redundantly load each M tile. This was also demonstrated in Fig. 5.11. As shown in Fig. 5.17, the calculation of two P elements in adjacent tiles uses the same M row. With the original tiled algorithm, the same M row is redundantly loaded by the two blocks assigned to generate these two P tiles. One can eliminate this redundancy by merging the two thread blocks into one. Each thread in the new thread block now calculates two P elements. This is done by revising the kernel so that two dot-products are computed by the innermost loop of the kernel. Both dot-products use the same Mds row but different Nds columns. This reduces the global memory access by one-quarter. The reader is encouraged to write the new kernel as an exercise.

The potential downside is that the new kernel now uses even more registers and shared memory. As we discussed in the previous section, the number of blocks that can be running on each SM may decrease. For a given matrix size, this also reduces the total number of thread blocks by half, which may result in an insufficient amount of parallelism for matrices of smaller dimensions. In practice, combining up to four adjacent horizontal blocks to compute adjacent horizontal tiles significantly improves the performance of large (2048×2048 or more) matrix multiplication.

5.6 SUMMARY

In this chapter, we reviewed the major aspects of application performance on a CUDA device: global memory access coalescing, memory parallelism, control flow divergence, dynamic resource partitioning and instruction mixes. Each of these aspects is rooted in the hardware limitations of the devices. With these insights, the reader should be able to reason about the performance of any kernel code he/she comes across.

More importantly, we need to be able to convert poor performing code into well performing code. As a starting point, we presented practical techniques for creating good program patterns for these performance aspects. We will continue to study practical applications of these techniques in the parallel computation patterns and application case studies in the next few chapters.

5.7 EXERCISES

1. The kernels in Figs. 5.13 and 5.15 are wasteful in their use of threads; half of the threads in each block never execute. Modify the kernels to eliminate such waste. Give the relevant execute configuration parameter values at the kernel launch. Is there a cost in terms of extra arithmetic operation needed? Which resource limitation can be potentially addressed with such modification?

(Hint: (1) Line 2 and/or Line 3 can be adjusted in each case. (2) The number of elements in a section may need to increase.)

2. Compare the modified kernels you wrote for Exercise 5.1. Which kernel incurred fewer additional arithmetic operations from the modification?

3. Write a complete kernel based on Exercise 5.1 by (1) adding the statements that load a section of the input array from global memory to shared memory, (2) using `blockIdx.x` to allow multiple blocks to work on different sections of the input array, (3) writing the reduction value for the section to a location according to the `blockIdx.x` so that all blocks will deposit their section reduction value to the lower part of the input array in global memory.

4. Design a reduction program based on the kernel you wrote for Exercise 5.3. The host code should (1) transfer a large input array to the global memory, (2) use a loop to repeatedly invoke the kernel you wrote for Exercise 5.3 with adjusted execution configuration parameter values so that the reduction result for the input array will eventually be produced.

5. For the tiled matrix multiplication kernel in Fig. 5.6, draw the access patterns of threads in a warp of Lines 9 and 10 for a small 16×16 matrix size. Calculate the `tx` values and `ty` values for each thread in a warp and use these values in the M and N index calculations in Lines 9 and 10. Show that the threads indeed access consecutive M and N locations in global memory during each iteration.

6. For the simple matrix multiplication ($P = M*N$) based on row-major layout, which input matrix will have coalesced accesses?
   A. M
   B. N
   C. M, N
   D. Neither

7. For the tiled matrix–matrix multiplication ($M*N$) based on row-major layout, which input matrix will have coalesced accesses?
   A. M
   B. N
   C. M, N
   D. Neither

8. For the simple reduction kernel, if the block size is 1024 and warp size is 32, how many warps in a block will have divergence during the 5th iteration?
   A. 0
   B. 1
   C. 16
   D. 32

9. For the improved reduction kernel, if the block size is 1024 and warp size is 32, how many warps will have divergence during the 5th iteration?

   A. 0
   B. 1
   C. 16
   D. 32

10. Write a matrix multiplication kernel function that corresponds to the design illustrated in Figure 5.17.

11. For tiled matrix multiplication out of the possible range of values for BLOCK_SIZE, for what values of BLOCK_SIZE will the kernel completely avoid un-coalesced accesses to global memory? (You need to consider only square blocks.)

12. In an attempt to improve performance, a bright young engineer changed the reduction kernel into the following. (A) Do you believe that the performance will improve? Why or why not? (B) Should the engineer receive a reward or a lecture? Why?

```
__shared__ float partialSum[];
unsigned int tid=threadIdx.x;
for (unsigned int stride=n>>1; stride >= 32; stride >>= 1) {
        __syncthreads();
      if (tid < stride)
            shared[tid] += shared[tid + stride];
}
__syncthreads();
if (tid < 32) {    // unroll last 5 predicated steps
    shared[tid] += shared[tid + 16];
    shared[tid] += shared[tid + 8];
    shared[tid] += shared[tid + 4];
    shared[tid] += shared[tid + 2];
    shared[tid] += shared[tid + 1];
}
```

REFERENCES

CUDA C Best Practices Guide v. 4.2, January 2012.

CUDA Occupancy Calculator. Web search using keywords "CUDA Occupancy Calculator".

Ryoo, S., Rodrigues, C. I., Baghsorkhi, S. S., Stone, S. S., Kirk, D. B., and Hwu, W. W. February 2008. Optimization principles and application performance evaluation of a multithreaded GPU using CUDA. Proceedings of the 13th ACM SIGPLAN symposium on principles and practice of parallel programming.

Ryoo, S., Rodrigues, C., Stone, S., Baghsorkhi, S., Ueng, S., Stratton, J., Hwu, W. April 6–9, 2008. Program optimization space pruning for a multithreaded GPU. Proceedings of the 6th ACM/IEEE international symposium on code generation and optimization.

Numerical considerations

In the early days of computing, floating-point arithmetic capability was found only in mainframes and supercomputers. Although many microprocessors designed in the 1980's started to have floating-point coprocessors, their floating-point arithmetic speed was extremely slow, about three orders of magnitude slower than that of mainframes and supercomputers. With advances in microprocessor technology, many microprocessors designed in the 1990's, such as Intel Pentium III and AMD Athlon, started to have high performance floating-point capabilities that rival supercomputers. High speed floating-point arithmetic has become a standard feature for microprocessors and GPUs today. Floating-point representation allows for larger dynamic range of representable data values and more precise representation of tiny data values. These desirable properties make floating-point preferred data representative for modeling the physical and artificial phenomena, such as combustion, aerodynamics, light illumination, and financial risks. Large scale evaluation of these models has been driving the need for parallel computing. As a result, it is important for application programmers to understand the nature of floating-point arithmetic in developing their parallel applications. In particular, we will focus on the accuracy of floating-point arithmetic operations, the precision of floating-point number representation, the stability of numerical algorithms and how they should be taken into consideration in parallel programming.

Programming Massively Parallel Processors. DOI: http://dx.doi.org/10.1016/B978-0-12-811986-0.00006-6

6.1 FLOATING-POINT DATA REPRESENTATION

The IEEE-754 Floating-Point Standard is an effort for the computer manufacturers to conform to a common representation and arithmetic behavior for floating-point data [IEEE 2008]. Most, if not all, of the computer manufacturers in the world have accepted this standard. In particular, virtually all microprocessors designed in the future will either fully conform to or almost fully conform to the IEEE-754 Floating-Point Standard and its more recent IEEE-754 2008 revision [2008]. Therefore, it is important for application developers to understand the concepts and practical considerations of this standard.

A floating-point number system starts with the representation of a numerical value as bit patterns. In the IEEE Floating-Point Standard, a numerical value is represented in three groups of bits: sign (S), exponent (E), and mantissa (M). With some exceptions that will be detailed later, each (S, E, M) pattern uniquely identifies a numeric value according to the following formula:

$$\text{Value} = (-1)^S * 1.M * \{2^{E-\text{bias}}\} \tag{6.1}$$

The interpretation of S is simple: $S = 0$ means a positive number and $S = 1$ a negative number. Mathematically, any number, including -1, when raised to the power of 0, results in 1. Thus the value is positive. On the other hand, when -1 is raised to the power of 1, it is -1 itself. With a multiplication by -1, the value becomes negative. The interpretation of M and E bits are, however, much more complex. We will use the following example to help explain the interpretation of M and E bits.

Assume for the sake of simplicity that each floating-point number consists of a 1-bit sign, 3-bit exponent, and 2-bit mantissa. We will use this hypothetical 6-bit format to illustrate the challenges involved in encoding E and M. As we discuss numeric values, we will sometimes need to express a number either in decimal place value or in binary place value. Numbers expressed in decimal place value will have subscript $_D$ and those in binary place value will have subscript $_B$. For example, 0.5_D ($5*10^{-1}$ since the place to the right of the decimal point carries a weight of 10^{-1}) is the same as 0.1_B ($1*2^{-1}$ since the place to the right of the decimal point carries a weight of 2^{-1}).

NORMALIZED REPRESENTATION OF M

Formula (6.1) requires that all values are derived by treating the mantissa value as $1.M$, which makes the mantissa bit pattern for each floating-point number unique. For example, under this interpretation of the M bits, the only mantissa bit pattern allowed for 0.5_D is the one where all bits that represent M are 0s:

$$0.5_D = 1.0_B * 2^{-1}$$

Other potential candidates would be $0.1_B * 2^0$ and $10.0_B * 2^{-2}$, but neither fits the form of $1.M$. The numbers that satisfy this restriction will be referred to as normalized numbers. Because all mantissa values that satisfy the restriction are of the form 1.XX, we can omit the "1." part from the representation. Therefore, the mantissa value of 0.5 in a 2-bit mantissa representation is 00, which is derived by omitting "1." from 1.00. This makes a 2-bit mantissa effectively a 3-bit mantissa. In general, with IEEE format, an m-bit mantissa is effectively an $(m+1)$-bit mantissa.

EXCESS ENCODING OF E

The number of bits used to represent E determines the range of numbers that can be represented. Large positive E values result in very large floating-point absolute values. For example, if the value of E is 64, the floating-point number being represented is between 2^{64} ($>10^{18}$) and 2^{65}. You would be extremely happy if this was the balance of your savings account! Large negative E values result in very small floating values. For example, if E value is -64, the number being represented is between 2^{-64} ($<10^{-18}$) and 2^{-63}. This is a very tiny fractional number. The E field allows a floating-point number format to represent a wider range of numbers than integer number formats. We will come back to this point when we look at the representable numbers of a format.

The IEEE standard adopts an excess or biased encoding convention for E. If e bits are used to represent the exponent E, $(2^{e-1}-1)$ is added to the two's complement representation for the exponent to form its excess representation. A two's complement representation is a system where the negative value of a number can be derived by first complementing every bit of the value and adding one to the result. In our 3-bit exponent representation, there are three bits in the exponent ($e = 3$). Therefore, the value $2^{3-1}-1 = 011$ will be added to the 2's complement representation of the exponent value.

The advantage of excess representation is that an unsigned comparator can be used to compare signed numbers. As shown in Fig. 6.1, in our 3-bit exponent representation, the excess-3 bit patterns increase monotonically from -3 to 3 when viewed as unsigned numbers. We will refer to each of these bit patterns as the code for

2's complement	Decimal value	Excess-3
101	−3	000
110	−2	001
111	−1	010
000	0	011
001	1	100
010	2	101
011	3	110
100	Reserved pattern	111

FIGURE 6.1

Excess-3 encoding, sorted by excess-3 ordering.

the corresponding value. For example, the code for −3 is 000 and that for 3 is 110. Thus, if one uses an unsigned number comparator to compare excess-3 code for any number from −3 to 3, the comparator gives the correct comparison result in terms of which number is larger, smaller, etc. For another example, if one compares excess-3 codes 001 and 100 with an unsigned comparator, 001 is smaller than 100. This is the right conclusion since the values that they represent, −2 and 1, have exactly the same relation. This is a desirable property for hardware implementation since unsigned comparators are smaller and faster than signed comparators.

Fig. 6.1 also shows that the pattern of all 1's in the excess representation is a reserved pattern. Note that a 0 value and an equal number of positive and negative values result in an odd number of patterns. Having the pattern 111 as either an even number or odd number would result in an unbalanced number of positive and negative numbers. The IEEE standard uses this special bit pattern in special ways that will be discussed later.

Now we are ready to represent 0.5_D with our 6-bit format:

$$0.5_D = 001000, \quad \text{where } S = 0, E = 010, \text{ and } M = (1.)00$$

That is, the 6-bit representation for 0.5_D is 001000.

In general, with normalized mantissa and excess-coded exponent, the value of a number with an n-bit exponent is:

$$(-1)S * 1.M * 2^{(E - (2^{(n-1)} - 1))}$$

6.2 REPRESENTABLE NUMBERS

The representable numbers of a representation format are the numbers that can be exactly represented in the format. For example, if one uses a 3-bit unsigned integer format, the representable numbers are shown in Fig. 6.2.

Neither −1 nor 9 can be represented in the format given above. We can draw a number line to identify all the representable numbers, as shown in Fig. 6.3 where all representable numbers of the 3-bit unsigned integer format are marked with stars.

000	0
001	1
010	2
011	3
100	4
101	5
110	6
111	7

FIGURE 6.2

Representable numbers of a 3-bit unsigned integer format.

The representable numbers of a floating-point format can be visualized in a similar manner. In Fig. 6.4, we show all the representable numbers of what we have so far and two variations. We use a 5-bit format to keep the size of the table manageable. The format consists of 1-bit S, 2-bit E (excess-1 coded), and 2-bit M (with "1." part omitted). The no-zero column gives the representable numbers of the format we discussed thus far. The reader is encouraged to generate at least part of the no-zero column using the formula given in Section 6.1. Note that with this format, 0 is not one of the representable numbers.

A quick look at how these representable numbers populate the number line, as shown in Fig. 6.5, provides further insights about these representable numbers. In Fig. 6.5, we show only the positive representable numbers. The negative numbers are symmetric to their positive counterparts on the other side of 0.

We can make five observations. First, the exponent bits define the major intervals of representable numbers. In Fig. 6.5, there are three major intervals on each side of 0

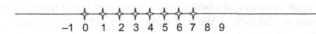

FIGURE 6.3

Representable numbers of a 3-bit unsigned integer format.

E	M	No-zero		Abrupt underflow		Denorm	
		S = 0	S = 1	S = 0	S = 1	S = 0	S = 1
00	00	2^{-1}	$-(2^{-1})$	0	0	0	0
	01	$2^{-1}+1*2^{-3}$	$-(2^{-1}+1*2^{-3})$	0	0	$1*2^{-2}$	$-1*2^{-2}$
	10	$2^{-1}+2*2^{-3}$	$-(2^{-1}+2*2^{-3})$	0	0	$2*2^{-2}$	$-2*2^{-2}$
	11	$2^{-1}+3*2^{-3}$	$-(2^{-1}+3*2^{-3})$	0	0	$3*2^{-2}$	$-3*2^{-2}$
01	00	2^0	$-(2^0)$	2^0	$-(2^0)$	2^0	$-(2^0)$
	01	2^0+1*2^{-2}	$-(2^0+1*2^{-2})$	2^0+1*2^{-2}	$-(2^0+1*2^{-2})$	2^0+1*2^{-2}	$-(2^0+1*2^{-2})$
	10	2^0+2*2^{-2}	$-(2^0+2*2^{-2})$	2^0+2*2^{-2}	$-(2^0+2*2^{-2})$	2^0+2*2^{-2}	$-(2^0+2*2^{-2})$
	11	2^0+3*2^{-2}	$-(2^0+3*2^{-2})$	2^0+3*2^{-2}	$-(2^0+3*2^{-2})$	2^0+3*2^{-2}	$-(2^0+3*2^{-2})$
10	00	2^1	$-(2^1)$	2^1	$-(2^1)$	2^1	$-(2^1)$
	01	2^1+1*2^{-1}	$-(2^1+1*2^{-1})$	2^1+1*2^{-1}	$-(2^1+1*2^{-1})$	2^1+1*2^{-1}	$-(2^1+1*2^{-1})$
	10	2^1+2*2^{-1}	$-(2^1+2*2^{-1})$	2^1+2*2^{-1}	$-(2^1+2*2^{-1})$	2^1+2*2^{-1}	$-(2^1+2*2^{-1})$
	11	2^1+3*2^{-1}	$-(2^1+3*2^{-1})$	2^1+3*2^{-1}	$-(2^1+3*2^{-1})$	2^1+3*2^{-1}	$-(2^1+3*2^{-1})$
11		Reserved pattern					

FIGURE 6.4

Representable numbers of no-zero, abrupt underflow, and denorm formats.

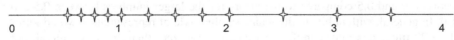

FIGURE 6.5

Representable numbers of the no-zero representation.

because there are two exponent bits. Basically, the major intervals are between powers of 2s. With two bits of exponents and one reserved bit pattern (11), there are three powers of two ($2^{-1} = 0.5_D$, $2^0 = 1.0_D$, $2^1 = 2.0_D$), each starts an interval of representable numbers. Keep in mind that there are also three powers of two ($-2^{-1} = -0.5_D$, $-2^0 = -1.0_D$, $-2^1 = -2.0_D$) on the left of zero, are not shown in Fig. 6.5.

The second observation is that the mantissa bits define the number of representable numbers in each interval. With two mantissa bits, we have four representable numbers in each interval. In general, with N mantissa bits, we have 2^N representable numbers in each interval. If a value to be represented falls within one of the intervals, it will be rounded to one of these representable numbers. Obviously, the larger the number of representable numbers in each interval, the more precisely we can represent a value in the region. Therefore, the number of mantissa bits determines the *precision* of the representation.

The third observation is that 0 is not representable in this format. It is missing from the representable numbers in the no-zero column of Fig. 6.5. Because 0 is one of the most important numbers, not being able to represent 0 in a number representation system is a serious deficiency. We will address this deficiency soon.

The fourth observation is that the representable numbers become closer to each other toward the neighborhood of 0. Each interval is half the size of the previous interval as we move toward zero. In Fig. 6.5, the rightmost interval is of width 2, the next one is of width 1, and the next one is of width 0.5. While not shown in Fig. 6.5, there are three intervals on the left of zero. They contain the representable negative numbers. The leftmost interval is of width 2, the next one is of width 1 and the next one is width 0.5. Since every interval has the same representable numbers, four in Fig. 6.5, the representable numbers become closer to each other as we move toward zero. In other words, the representative numbers become closer as their absolute values become smaller. This is a desirable trend because as the absolute value of these numbers become smaller, it is more important to represent them more precisely. The distance between representable numbers determines the maximal rounding error for a value that falls into the interval. For example, if you have 1 billion dollars in your bank account, you may not even notice that there is a 1 dollar rounding error in calculating your balance. However, if the total balance is 10 dollars, having a 1 dollar rounding error would be much more noticeable!

The fifth observation is that, unfortunately, the trend of increasing density of representable numbers, and thus increasing precision of representing numbers in the intervals as we move toward zero, does not hold for the very vicinity of 0. That is, there is a gap of representable numbers in the immediate vicinity of 0. This is because the range of normalized mantissa precludes 0. This is another serious deficiency. The representation introduces significantly larger (4×) errors when representing numbers between 0 and 0.5 compared to the errors for the larger numbers between 0.5 and 1.0. In general, with m bits in the mantissa, this style of representation would introduce 2^m times more error in the interval closest to zero than the next interval. For numerical methods that rely on accurate detection of convergence conditions based on very small data values, such deficiency can cause instability in execution time and accuracy of results. Furthermore, some algorithms generate small numbers and eventually use them as denominators. The errors in representing these small numbers can be greatly magnified in the division process and cause numerical instability in these algorithms.

One method that can accommodate 0 into a normalized floating-point number system is the *abrupt underflow* convention, which is illustrated in the second column of Fig. 6.4. Whenever E is 0, the number is interpreted as 0. In our 5-bit format, this method takes away eight representable numbers (four positive and four negative) in the vicinity of 0 (between −1.0 and +1.0) and makes them all 0. Due to its simplicity, some mini-computers in the 1980s used abrupt underflow. Even to this day, some arithmetic units that need to operate in high-speed still use abrupt underflow convention. Although this method makes 0 a representable number, it creates an even larger gap between representable numbers in 0's vicinity, as shown in Fig. 6.6. It is obvious, when compared with Fig. 6.5, that the gap of representable numbers has been enlarged significantly (by 2×) from 0.5 to 1.0. As we explained before, this is very problematic for many numerical algorithms whose correctness relies on accurate representation of small numbers near zero.

The actual method adopted by the IEEE standard is called denormalization. The method relaxes the normalization requirement for numbers very close to 0. As shown in Fig. 6.8, whenever $E = 0$, the mantissa is no longer assumed to be of the form 1.XX. Rather, it is assumed to be 0.XX. The value of the exponent is assumed to be the same as the previous interval. For example, in Fig. 6.4, the denormalized representation 00001 has exponent value 00 and mantissa value 01. The mantissa is assumed to be 0.01 and the exponent value is assumed to be the same as that of the previous interval: 0 rather than −1. That is, the value that 00001 represents is now $0.01*2^0$ $= 2^{-2}$. Fig. 6.7 shows the representable numbers for the denormalized format. The representation now has uniformly spaced representable numbers in the close vicinity of 0. Intuitively, the denormalized convention takes the four numbers in the last interval of representable numbers of a no-zero representation and spreads them out to cover the gap area. This eliminates the undesirable gap in the previous two methods.

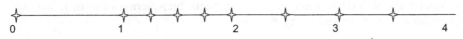

FIGURE 6.6

Representable numbers of the abrupt underflow format.

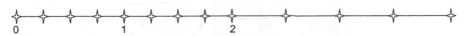

FIGURE 6.7

Representable numbers of a denormalization format.

Note that the distances between representable numbers in the last two intervals are actually identical. In general, if the n-bit exponent is 0, the value is:

$$0.M * 2^{-2^{(n-1)}+2}$$

As we can see, the denormalization formula is quite complex. The hardware also needs to be able to detect whether a number falls into the denormalized interval and choose the appropriate representation for that number. The amount of hardware required to implement denormalization in high speed is quite significant. Implementations that use a moderate amount of hardware often introduce thousands of clock cycles of delay whenever a denormalized number needs to be generated or used. This was the reason why early generations of CUDA devices did not support denormalization. However, virtually all recent generations of CUDA devices, thanks to the increasing number of available transistors of more recent fabrication processes, support denormalization. More specifically, all CUDA devices of compute capability 1.3 and up support denormalized double-precision operands, and all devices of compute capability 2.0 and up support denormalized single-precision operands.

In summary, the precision of a floating-point representation is measured by the maximal error that we can introduce to a floating-point number by representing that number as one of the representable numbers. The smaller the error is, the higher the precision. The precision of a floating-point representation can be improved by adding more bits to mantissa. Adding one bit to the representation of the mantissa improves the precision by reducing the maximal error by half. Thus, a number system has higher precision when it uses more bits for mantissa. This is reflected in double precision versus single precision numbers in the IEEE standard.

6.3 SPECIAL BIT PATTERNS AND PRECISION IN IEEE FORMAT

We now turn to more specific details of the actual IEEE format. When all exponent bits are 1s, the number represented is an infinity value if the mantissa is 0. It is a Not a Number (NaN) if the mantissa is not 0. All special bit patterns of the IEEE floating-point format are described in Fig. 6.8.

Exponent	Mantissa	Meaning
11...1	$\neq 0$	NaN
11...1	$= 0$	$(-1)^S * \infty$
00...0	$\neq 0$	denormalized
00...0	$= 0$	0

FIGURE 6.8

Special bit patterns in the IEEE standard format.

All other numbers are normalized floating-point numbers. Single precision numbers have 1-bit S, 8-bit E, and 23-bit M. Double precision numbers have 1-bit S, 11-bit E, and 52-bit M. Since a double precision number has 29 more bits for mantissa, the largest error for representing a number is reduced to $1/2^{29}$ of that of the single precision format! With the additional three bits of exponent, the double precision format also extends the number of intervals of representable numbers. This extends the range of representable numbers to very large as well as very small values.

All representable numbers fall between $-\infty$ (negative infinity) and $+\infty$ (positive infinity). An ∞ can be created by overflow, e.g., a large number divided by a very small number. Any representable number divided by $+\infty$ or $-\infty$ results in 0.

NaN is generated by operations whose input values do not make sense, for example, $0/0$, $0*\infty$, ∞/∞, $\infty-\infty$. They are also used for data that have not been properly initialized in a program. There are two types of NaN's in the IEEE standard: signaling and quiet. Signaling NaN's (SNaNs) should be represented with the most significant mantissa bit cleared, whereas Quiet NaN's are represented with most significant mantissa bit set.

Signaling NaN causes an exception when used as input to arithmetic operations. For example, the operation (1.0+ signaling NaN) raises an exception signal to the operating system. Signaling NaN's are used in situations where the programmer would like to make sure that the program execution be interrupted whenever any NaN values are used in floating-point computations. These situations usually mean that there is something wrong with the execution of the program. In mission critical applications, the execution cannot continue until the validity of the execution can be verified with a separate means. For example, software engineers often mark all the uninitialized data as signaling NaN. This practice ensures the detection of using uninitialized data during program execution. The current generation of GPU hardware does not support signaling NaN. This is due to the difficulty of supporting accurate signaling during massively parallel execution.

Quiet NaN generates another quiet NaN without causing an exception when used as input to arithmetic operations. For example, the operation (1.0+ quiet NaN) generates a quiet NaN. Quiet NaN's are typically used in applications where the user can review the output and decide if the application should be re-run with a different input for more valid results. When the results are printed, Quiet NaN's are printed as "NaN" so that the user can spot them in the output file easily.

6.4 ARITHMETIC ACCURACY AND ROUNDING

Now that we have a good understanding of the IEEE floating-point format, we are ready to discuss the concept of arithmetic accuracy. While the precision is determined by the number of mantissa bits used in a floating-point number format, the accuracy is determined by the operations performed on a floating number. The accuracy of a floating-point arithmetic operation is measured by the maximal error introduced by the operation. The smaller the error is, the higher the accuracy. The most common source of error in floating-point arithmetic is when the operation generates a result that cannot be exactly represented and thus requires rounding. Rounding occurs if the mantissa of the result value needs too many bits to be represented exactly. For example, a multiplication generates a product value that consists of twice the number of bits than either of the input values. For another example, adding two floating-point numbers can be done by adding their mantissa values together if the two floating-point values have identical exponents. When two input operands to a floating-point addition have different exponents, the mantissa of the one with the smaller exponent is repeatedly divided by 2 or right-shifted (i.e., all the mantissa bits are shifted to the right by one bit position) until the exponents are equal. As a result, the final result can have more bits than the format can accommodate.

Alignment shifting of operands can be illustrated with a simple example based on the 5-bit representation in Fig. 6.4. Assume that we need to add 1.00_B*2^{-2} (0, 00, 01) to $1.00*2^1{}_D$ (0, 10, 00), i.e., we need to perform $1.00_B*2^1 + 1.00_B*2^{-2}$. Due to the difference in exponent values, the mantissa value of the second number needs to be right-shifted by 3-bit positions before it is added to the first mantissa value. That is, the addition becomes $1.00_B*2^1 + 0.001_B*2^1$. The addition can now be performed by adding the mantissa values together. The ideal result would be 1.001_B*2^1. However, we can see that this ideal result is not a representable number in a 5-bit representation. It would have required three bits of mantissa and there are only two mantissa bits in the format. Thus, the best one can do is to generate one of the closest representable numbers, which is either 1.01_B*2^1 or 1.00_B*2^1. By doing so, we introduce an error, 0.001_B*2^1, which is half the place value of the least significant place. We refer to this as 0.5_D ULP (Units in the Last Place). If the hardware is designed to perform arithmetic and rounding operations perfectly, the most error that one should introduce should be no more than 0.5_D ULP. To our knowledge, this is the accuracy achieved by the addition and subtraction operations in all CUDA devices today.

In practice, some of the more complex arithmetic hardware units, such as division and transcendental functions, are typically implemented with polynomial approximation algorithms. If the hardware does not use a sufficient number of terms in the approximation, the result may have an error larger than 0.5_D ULP. For example, if the ideal result of an inversion operation is 1.00_B*2^1 but the hardware generates a 1.10_B*2^1 due to the use of an approximation algorithm, the error is 2_D ULP since the error ($1.10_B - 1.00_B = 0.10_B$) is two times bigger than the units in the last place (0.01_B). In practice, the hardware inversion operations in some early devices introduce an error that is twice the place value of the least place of the mantissa, or 2 ULP. Thanks to the more abundant transistors in more recent generations of CUDA devices, their hardware arithmetic operations are much more accurate.

6.5 ALGORITHM CONSIDERATIONS

Numerical algorithms often need to sum up a large number of values. For example, the dot product in matrix multiplication needs to sum up pair-wise products of input matrix elements. Ideally, the order of summing these values should not affect the final total since addition is an associative operation. However, with finite precision, the order of summing these values can affect the accuracy of the final result. For example, if we need to perform a sum reduction on four numbers in our 5-bit representation: $1.00_B*2^0+1.00_B*2^0+1.00_B*2^{-2}+1.00_B*2^{-2}$.

If we add up the numbers in strict sequential order, we have the following sequence of operations:

$$1.00_B*2^0 + 1.00_B*2^0 + 1.00_B*2^{-2} + 1.00_B*2^{-2} = 1.00_B*2^1 + 1.00_B*2^{-2} +$$
$$1.00_B*2^{-2} = 1.00_B*2^1 + 1.00_B*2^{-2} = 1.00_B*2^1$$

Note that in the second step and third step, the smaller operand simply disappears because it is too small compared to the larger operand.

Now, let us consider a parallel algorithm where the first two values are added and the second two operands are added in parallel. The algorithm then adds up the pair-wise sum:

$$(1.00_B*2^0 + 1.00_B*2^0) + (1.00_B*2^{-2} + 1.00_B*2^{-2}) = 1.00_B*2^1 + 1.00_B*2^{-1}$$
$$= 1.01_B*2^1$$

Note that the results are different from the sequential result! This is because the sum of the third and fourth values is large enough that it now affects the addition result. This discrepancy between sequential algorithms and parallel algorithms often surprises application developers who are not familiar with floating-point precision and accuracy considerations. Although we showed a scenario where a parallel algorithm produced a more accurate result than a sequential algorithm, the reader should be able to come up with a slightly different scenario where the parallel algorithm produces a less accurate result than a sequential algorithm. Experienced application developers either make sure that the variation in the final result can be tolerated, or ensure that the data is sorted or grouped in a way that the parallel algorithm results in the most accurate results.

A common technique to maximize floating-point arithmetic accuracy is to presort data before a reduction computation. In our sum reduction example, if we presort the data according to ascending numerical order, we will have the following:

$$1.00_B*2^{-2} + 1.00_B*2^{-2} + 1.00_B*2^0 + 1.00_B*2^0$$

When we divide up the numbers into groups in a parallel algorithm, say the first pair in one group and the second pair in another group, numbers with numerical values close to each other are in the same group. Obviously, the sign of the numbers needs to be taken into account during the presorting process. Therefore, when we perform addition in these groups, we will likely have accurate results. Furthermore, some parallel algorithms use each thread to sequentially reduce values within each group. Having the numbers sorted in ascending order allows a sequential addition to get higher accuracy. This is a reason why sorting is frequently used in massively parallel numerical algorithms. Interested readers should study more advanced techniques such as compensated summation algorithm, also known as Kahan's Summation Algorithm, for getting even a more robust approach to accurate summation of floating-point values [Kahan 1965].

6.6 LINEAR SOLVERS AND NUMERICAL STABILITY

While the order of operations may cause variation in the numerical outcome of reduction operations, it may have even more serious implications on some types of computation such as solvers for linear systems of equations. In these solvers, different numerical values of input may require different ordering of operations in order to find a solution. If an algorithm fails to follow a desired order of operations for an input, it may fail to find a solution even though the solution exists. Algorithms that can always find an appropriate operation order, thus finding a solution to the problem as long as it exists for any given input values, are called *numerically stable*. Algorithms that fall short are referred to as *numerically unstable*.

In some cases, numerical stability considerations can make it more difficult to find efficient parallel algorithms for a computational problem. We can illustrate this phenomenon with a solver that is based on Gaussian Elimination. Consider the following system of linear equations:

$$3X + 5Y + 2Z = 19 \qquad \text{(Equation 1)}$$

$$2X + 3Y + Z = 11 \qquad \text{(Equation 2)}$$

$$X + 2Y + 2Z = 11 \qquad \text{(Equation 3)}$$

As long as the three planes represented by these equations have an intersection point, we can use Gaussian elimination to derive the solution that gives the coordinate of the intersection point. We show the process of applying Gaussian elimination to this system in Fig. 6.9, where variables are systematically eliminated from lower positioned equations.

In the first step, all equations are divided by their coefficient for the X variable: 3 for Equation 1, 2 for Equation 2, and 1 for Equation 3. This makes the coefficients for X in all equations the same. In step two, Equation 1 is subtracted from Equation 2 and Equation 3. These subtractions eliminate variable X from Equation 2 and Equation 3, as shown in Fig. 6.9.

We can now treat Equation 2 and Equation 3 as a smaller system of equations with one fewer variable than the original equation. Since they do not have variable X, they can be solved independently from Equation 1. We can make more progress by eliminating variable Y from Equation 3. This is done in step 3 by dividing Equation 2 and Equation 3 by the coefficients for their Y variables: $-1/6$ for Equation 2 and $1/3$ for Equation 3. This makes the coefficients for Y in both Equation 2 and Equation 3

$$\begin{aligned} 3X + 5Y + 2Z &= 19 \\ 2X + 3Y + Z &= 11 \\ X + 2Y + 2Z &= 11 \end{aligned}$$

Original

$$\Rightarrow \begin{aligned} X + 5/3Y + 2/3Z &= 19/3 \\ X + 3/2Y + 1/2Z &= 11/2 \\ X + 2Y + 2Z &= 11 \end{aligned}$$

Step 1: divide Equation 1 by 3, Equation 2 by 2

$$\Rightarrow \begin{aligned} X + 5/3Y + 2/3Z &= 19/3 \\ -1/6Y - 1/6Z &= -5/6 \\ 1/3Y + 4/3Z &= 14/3 \end{aligned}$$

Step 2: subtract Equation 1 from Equation 2 and Equation 3

$$\Rightarrow \begin{aligned} X + 5/3Y + 2/3Z &= 19/3 \\ Y + Z &= 5 \\ Y + 4Z &= 14 \end{aligned}$$

Step 3: divide Equation 2 by -1/6 and Equation 3 by 1/3

$$\Rightarrow \begin{aligned} X + 5/3Y + 2/3Z &= 19/3 \\ Y + Z &= 5 \\ + 3Z &= 9 \end{aligned}$$

Step 4: subtract Equation 2 from Equation 3

$$\Rightarrow \begin{aligned} X + 5/3Y + 2/3Z &= 19/3 \\ Y + Z &= 5 \\ Z &= 3 \end{aligned}$$

Step5 : divide Equation 3 by 3 Solution for *Z*!

$$\Rightarrow \begin{aligned} X + 5/3Y + 2/3Z &= 19/3 \\ Y &= 2 \\ Z &= 3 \end{aligned}$$

Step 6: substitute Z solution into Equation 2. Solution for *Y*!

$$\Rightarrow \begin{aligned} X &= 1 \\ Y &= 2 \\ Z &= 3 \end{aligned}$$

Step 7: substitute *Y* and *Z* into Equation 1. Solution for *X*!

FIGURE 6.9

Gaussian elimination and backward substitution for solving systems of linear equations.

the same. In step four, Equation 2 is subtracted from Equation 3, which eliminates variable *Y* from Equation 3.

For systems with larger number of equations, the process would be repeated more. However, since we have only three variables in this example, the third equation has only the *Z* variable. We simply need to divide Equation 3 by the coefficient for variable *Z*. This conveniently gives us the solution $Z = 3$.

With the solution for *Z* variable in hand, we can substitute the *Z* value into Equation 2 to get the solution $Y = 2$. We can then substitute both $Z = 3$ and $Y = 2$ into Equation 1 to get the solution $X = 1$. We now have the complete solution for the original system. It should be obvious why step 6 and step 7 form the second phase of the method called backward substitution. We go backwards from the last equation to the first equation to get solutions for more and more variables.

In general, the equations are stored in matrix forms in computers. Since all calculations only involve the coefficients and the right-hand-side values, we can just store these coefficients and right-hand-side values in a matrix. Fig. 6.10 shows the matrix view of the Gaussian elimination and back substitution process. Each row of the matrix corresponds to an original equation. Operations on equations become operations on matrix rows.

3	5	2	19		1	5/3	2/3	19/3		1	5/3	2/3	19/3
2	3	1	11	⇨	1	3/2	1/2	11/2	⇨		−1/6	−1/6	−5/6
1	2	2	11		1	2	2	11			1/3	4/3	14/3

Original · Step 1: divide row 1 by 3, row 2 by 2 · Step 2: subtract row 1 from row 2 and row 3

	1	5/3	2/3	19/3			1	5/3	2/3	19/3
⇨		1	1	5				1	1	5
		1	4	14	⇨				3	9

Step 3: divide row 2 by -1/6 and row 3 by 1/3 · Step 4: subtract row 2 from row 3

	1	5/3	2/3	19/3			1	5/3	2/3	19/3
⇨		1	1	5	⇨			1		2
			1	3					1	3

Step 5: divide Equation 3 by 3 Solution for Z! · Step 6: substitute Z solution into Equation 2. Solution for Y!

	1			1
⇨		1		2
			1	3

Step 7: substitute Y and Z into Equation 1. Solution for X!

FIGURE 6.10

Gaussian elimination and backward substitution in matrix view.

After Gaussian elimination, the matrix becomes a triangular matrix. This is a very popular type of matrix for various physics and mathematics reasons. We see that the end goal is to make the coefficient part of the matrix into a diagonal form, where each row has only a value 1 on the diagonal line. This is called an identity matrix because the result of multiplying any matrix multiplied by an identity matrix is itself. This is also the reason why performing Gaussian elimination on a matrix is equivalent to multiplying the matrix by its inverse matrix.

In general, it is straightforward to design a parallel algorithm for the Gaussian elimination procedure that we described in Fig. 6.10. For example, we can write a CUDA kernel and designate each thread to perform all calculations to be done on a row of the matrix. For systems that can fit into shared memory, we can use a thread block to perform Gaussian elimination. All threads iterate through the steps. After each division step, all threads participate in barrier synchronization. They then all perform a subtraction step, after which one thread will stop its participation since its designated row has no more work to do until the backward substitution phase. After the subtraction step, all threads need to perform barrier synchronization again to ensure that the next step will be done with the updated information. With systems of equations with many variables, we can expect reasonable amount of speedup from the parallel execution.

Unfortunately, the simple Gaussian elimination algorithm we have been using can suffer from numerical instability. This can be illustrated with the example:

$$5Y + 2Z = 16 \qquad \text{(Equation 1)}$$

$$2X + 3Y + Z = 11 \qquad \text{(Equation 2)}$$

$$X + 2Y + 2Z = 11 \qquad \text{(Equation 3)}$$

We will encounter a problem when we perform step 1 of the algorithm. The coefficient for the X variable in Equation 1 is zero. We will not be able to divide Equation 1 by the coefficient for variable X and eliminate the X variable from Equation 2 and Equation 3 by subtracting Equation 1 from Equation 2 and Equation 3. The reader should verify that this system of equation is solvable and has the same solution $X = 1$, $Y = 2$, and $Z = 3$. Therefore, the algorithm is numerically unstable. It can fail to generate a solution for certain input values even though the solution exists.

This is a well-known problem with Gaussian elimination algorithms and can be addressed with a method commonly referred to as *pivoting*. The idea is to find one of the remaining equations whose coefficient for the lead variable is not zero. By swapping the current top equation with the identified equation, the algorithm can successfully eliminate the lead variable from the rest of the equations. If we apply pivoting to the three equations, we end up with the following set:

$$2X + 3Y + Z = 11 \qquad \text{(Equation 1', original Equation 2)}$$

$$5Y + 2Z = 16 \qquad \text{(Equation 2', original Equation 1)}$$

$$X + 2Y + 2Z = 11 \qquad \text{(Equation 3', original Equation 3)}$$

Note that the coefficient for X in Equation 1' is no longer zero. We can proceed with Gaussian elimination, as illustrated in Fig. 6.11.

The reader should follow the steps in Fig. 6.11. The most important additional insight is that some equations may not have the variable that the algorithm is eliminating at the current step (see row 2 of Step 1 in Fig. 6.11). The designated thread does not need to do the division on the equation.

In general, the pivoting step should choose the equation with the largest absolute coefficient value among all the lead variables and swap its equation (row) with the current top equation as well as swap the variable (column) with the current variable. While pivoting is conceptually simple, it can incur significant implementation complexity and performance overhead. In the case of our simple CUDA kernel implementation, recall that each thread is assigned a row. Pivoting requires an inspection and perhaps swapping of coefficient data spread across these threads. This is not a big problem if all coefficients are in the shared memory. We can run a parallel max reduction using threads in the block as long as we control the level of control flow divergence within warps.

However, if the system of linear equations is being solved by multiple thread blocks or even multiple nodes of a compute cluster, the idea of inspecting data spread

```
    5   2      16        2   3   1   11        1   3/2  1/2  11/2
2   3   1   11    ⇨      5   2       16   ⇨        5    2    16
1   2   2   11            1   2   2   11            1    2    2    11
        Original         Pivoting: Swap row 1 (Equation1)   Step 1: divide row 1 by 3, no
                         with row 2 (Equation 2)            need to divide row 2 or row 3

        1    3/2   1/2   11/2                1    3/2   1/2   11/2
             5     2     16                       1     2/5   16/5
   ⇨         1/2   3/2   11/2       ⇨             1     3     11
        Step 2: subtract row 1 from row 3        Step 3: divide row 2 by 5 and row
        (column 1 of row 2 is already 0)         3 by 1/2

        1    3/2   1/2   11/2                1    5/3   2/3   19/3
   ⇨         1     2/5   16/5       ⇨             1     2/5   16/5
                   13/5  39/5                           1     3
        Step 4: subtract row 2 from row 3        Step 5: divide row 3 by 13/5
                                                 Solution for Z!

        1    5/3   2/3   19/3                1                    1
   ⇨         1           2         ⇨              1               2
                   1     3                              1         3
        Step 6: substitute Z solution into        Step 7: substitute Y and Z into
        Equation 2. Solution for Y!               Equation 1. Solution for X!
```

FIGURE 6.11

Gaussian elimination with pivoting.

across multiple thread blocks or multiple compute cluster nodes can be an extremely expensive proposition. This is the main motivation for *communication avoiding algorithms* that avoids a global inspection of data such as pivoting [Ballard 2011]. In general, there are two approaches to this problem. Partial pivoting restricts the candidates of the swap operation to come from a localized set of equations so that the cost of global inspection is limited. This can, however, slightly reduce the numerical accuracy of the solution. Researchers have also demonstrated that randomization tends to maintain a high level of numerical accuracy for the solution.

6.7 SUMMARY

This chapter introduces the concepts of floating-point format and representable numbers that are foundational to the understanding of precision. Based on these concepts, we also explain the denormalized numbers and why they are important in many numerical applications. In early CUDA devices, denormalized numbers were not supported. However, later hardware generations support denormalized numbers. We have also explained the concept of arithmetic accuracy of floating-point operations. This is important for CUDA programmers to understand the potential lower accuracy of fast arithmetic operations implemented in the special function units. More importantly, the readers should now have a good understanding of why parallel algorithms often can affect the accuracy of calculation results and how one can potentially use sorting and other techniques to improve the accuracy of their computation.

6.8 EXERCISES

1. Draw the equivalent of Fig. 6.5 for a 6-bit format (1-bit sign, 3-bit mantissa, 2-bit exponent). Use your result to explain what each additional mantissa bit does to the set of representable numbers on the number line.

2. Draw the equivalent of Fig. 6.5 for another 6-bit format (1-bit sign, 2-bit mantissa, 3-bit exponent). Use your result to explain what each additional exponent bit does to the set of representable numbers on the number line.

3. Assume that in a new processor design, due to technical difficulty, the floating-point arithmetic unit that performs addition can only do "round to zero" (rounding by truncating the value toward 0). The hardware maintains sufficient number of bits that the only error introduced is due to rounding. What is the maximal ulp error value for add operations on this machine?

4. A graduate student wrote a CUDA kernel to reduce a large floating-point array to the sum of all its elements. The array will always be sorted with the smallest values to the largest values. To avoid branch divergence, he decided to implement the algorithm of Fig. 6.4. Explain why this can reduce the accuracy of his results.

5. Assume that in an arithmetic unit design, the hardware implements an iterative approximation algorithm that generates two additional accurate mantissa bits of the result for the sin() function in each clock cycle. The architect decided to allow the arithmetic function to iterate 9 clock cycles. Assume that the hardware fills in all remaining mantissa bits as 0's. What would be the maximal ulp error of the hardware implementation of the sin() function in this design for the IEEE single-precision numbers? Assume that the omitted "1." mantissa bit must also be generated by the arithmetic unit.

REFERENCES

Ballard, G., Demmel, J., Holtz, O., & Schwartz, O. (2011). Minimizing communication in numerical linear algebra. *SIAM Journal of Matrix Analysis Applications*, 32(3), 866–901. <http://developer.nvidia.com/content/precision-performance-floating-point-and-ieee-754-compliance-nvidia-gpus>.

IEEE Microprocessor Standards Committee, Draft Standard for Floating-Point Arithmetic P754, Most recent revision January 2008.

Kahan, W. (January 1965). Further remarks on reducing truncation errors. *Communications of the ACM*, 8(1), 40. http://dx.doi.org/10.1145/363707.363723.

Parallel patterns: convolution
An introduction to stencil computation

CHAPTER OUTLINE

In the next several chapters, we will discuss a set of important patterns of parallel computation. These patterns are the basis of a wide range of parallel algorithms that appear in many parallel applications. We will start with convolution, which is a popular array operation that is used in various forms in signal processing, digital recording, image processing, video processing, and computer vision. In these application areas, convolution is often performed as a filter that transforms signals and pixels into more desirable values. Our image blur kernel is such a filter that smooths out the signal values so that one can see the big-picture trend. For another example, Gaussian filters are convolution filters that can be used to sharpen boundaries and edges of objects in images.

In high-performance computing, the convolution pattern is often referred to as stencil computation, which appears widely in numerical methods for solving differential equations. It also forms the basis of many force calculation algorithms in simulation models. Convolution typically involves a significant number of arithmetic operations on each data element. For large data sets such as high-definition images and videos, the amount of computation can be very large. Each output data element can be calculated independently of each other, a desirable trait for parallel computing. On the other hand, there is substantial level of input data sharing among output data elements with somewhat challenging boundary conditions. This makes convolution an important use case of sophisticated tiling methods and input data staging methods.

Programming Massively Parallel Processors. DOI: http://dx.doi.org/10.1016/B978-0-12-811986-0.00007-8

7.1 BACKGROUND

Convolution is an array operation where each output data element is a weighted sum of a collection of neighboring input elements. The weights used in the weighted sum calculation are defined by an input mask array, commonly referred to as the *convolution kernel*. Since there is an unfortunate name conflict between the CUDA kernel functions and convolution kernels, we will refer to these mask arrays as *convolution masks* to avoid confusion. The same convolution mask is typically used for all elements of the array.

In audio digital signal processing, the input data are in 1D form and represent sampled signal volume as a function of time. Fig. 7.1 shows a convolution example for 1D data where a 5-element convolution mask array M is applied to a 7-element input array N. We will follow the C language convention where N and P elements are indexed from 0 to 6 and M elements are indexed from 0 to 4. The fact that we use a 5-element mask M means that each P element is generated by a weighted sum of the N element at the corresponding position, two N elements to the left and two N elements to the right.

For example, the value of P[2] is generated as the weighted sum of N[0] (i.e., N[2-2]) through N[4] (i.e., N[2+2]). In this example, we arbitrarily assume that the values of the N elements are 1, 2, 3, …,7. The M elements define the weights, whose values are 3, 4, 5, 4, 3 in this example. Each weight value is multiplied to the corresponding N element values before the products are summed together. As shown in Fig. 7.1, the calculation for P[2] is as follows:

```
P[2] = N[0]*M[0] + N[1]*M[1] + N[2]*M[2] + N[3]*M[3] + N[4]*M[4]
     = 1*3 + 2*4 + 3*5 + 4*4 + 5*3
     = 57
```

In general, the size of the mask tends to be an odd number, which makes the weighted sum calculation symmetric around the element being calculated. That is, an odd number of mask elements defines the weighted sum to include the same number of elements on each side of the element being calculated. In Fig. 7.1, the mask size is

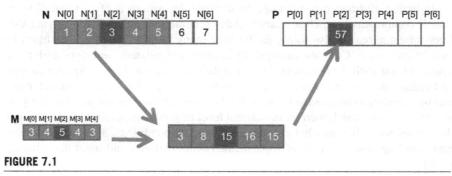

FIGURE 7.1

A 1D convolution example, inside elements.

5 elements. Each output element is calculated as the weighted sum of the corresponding input element, two elements on the left, and two elements on the right.

In Fig. 7.1, the calculation for P[i] can be viewed as an inner product between the subarray of N that starts at N[i-2] and the M array. Fig. 7.2 shows the calculation for P[3]. The calculation is shifted by one N element from that of Fig. 7.1. That is, the value of P[3] is the weighted sum of N[1] (i.e., N[3-2]), through N[5] (i.e., N[3 + 2]). We can think of the calculation for P[3] as follows:

```
P[3] = N[1]*M[0] + N[2]*M[1] + N[3]*M[2] + N[4]*M[3] + N[5]*M[4]
     = 2*3 + 3*4 + 4*5 + 5*4 + 6*3
     = 76
```

Because convolution is defined in terms of neighboring elements, boundary conditions naturally arise for output elements that are close to the ends of an array. As shown in Fig. 7.3, when we calculate P[1], there is only one N element to the left of N[1]. That is, there are not enough N elements to calculate P[1] according to our definition of convolution. A typical approach to handling such boundary condition is to define a default value to these missing N elements. For most applications, the

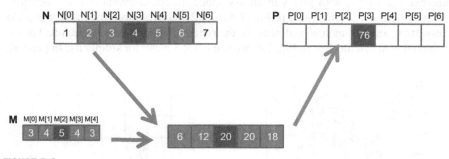

FIGURE 7.2

1D convolution, calculation of P[3].

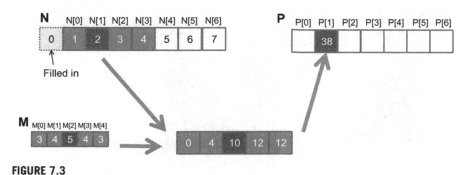

FIGURE 7.3

1D convolution boundary condition.

default value is 0, which is what we used in Fig. 7.3. For example, in audio signal processing, we can assume that the signal volume is 0 before the recording starts and after it ends. In this case, the calculation of P[1] is as follows:

```
P[1] = 0 * M[0] + N[0]*M[1] + N[1]*M[2] + N[2]*M[3] + N[3]*M[4]
     = 0 * 3 + 1*4 + 2*5 + 3*4 + 4*3
     = 38
```

The N element that does not exist in this calculation is illustrated as a dashed box in Fig. 7.3. It should be clear that the calculation of P[0] will involve two missing N elements, both will be assumed to be 0 for this example. We leave the calculation of P[0] as an exercise. These missing elements are typically referred to as "ghost cells" or "halo cells" in literature. There are also other types of ghost cells due to the use of tiling in parallel computation. These ghost cells can have significant impact on the effectiveness and/or efficiency of tiling. We will come back to this point soon.

Also, not all applications assume that the ghost cells contain 0. For example, some applications might assume that the ghost cells contain the same value as the closest valid data element.

For image processing and computer vision, input data are typically two-dimensional arrays, with pixels in an x-y space. Image convolutions are therefore 2D convolutions, as illustrated in Fig. 7.4. In a 2D convolution, the mask M is a 2D array. Its x- and y-dimensions determine the range of neighbors to be included in the weighted sum calculation. In Fig. 7.4, we use a 5 × 5 mask for simplicity. In general,

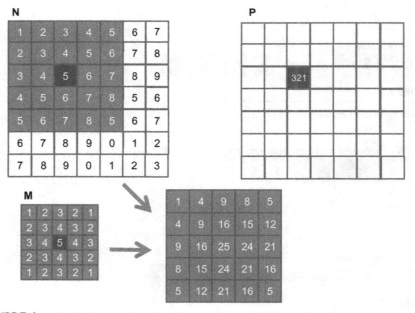

FIGURE 7.4

A 2D convolution example.

the mask does not have to be a square array. To generate an output element, we take the subarray whose center is at the corresponding location in the input array N. We then perform pairwise multiplication between elements of the mask array and those of the image array. For our example, the result is shown as the 5×5 product array below N and P in Fig. 7.4. The value of the output element is the sum of all elements of the product array.

The example in Fig. 7.4 shows the calculation of $P_{2,2}$. For brevity, we will use $N_{y,x}$ to denote N[y][x] in addressing a C array. Since N and P are most likely dynamically allocated arrays, we will be using linearized indices in our actual code examples. The subarray of N for calculating the value of $P_{2,2}$ spans from $N_{0,0}$ to $N_{0,4}$ in the x or horizontal direction and $N_{0,0}$ to $N_{4,0}$ in the y or vertical direction. The calculation is as follows:

$$
\begin{aligned}
P_{2,2} &= N_{0,0}*M_{0,0} + N_{0,1}*M_{0,1} + N_{0,2}*M_{0,2} + N_{0,3}*M_{0,3} + N_{0,4}*M_{0,4} \\
&+ N_{1,0}*M_{1,0} + N_{1,1}*M_{1,1} + N_{1,2}*M_{1,2} + N_{1,3}*M_{1,3} + N_{1,4}*M_{1,4} \\
&+ N_{2,0}*M_{2,0} + N_{2,1}*M_{1,1} + N_{2,2}*M_{2,2} + N_{2,3}*M_{2,3} + N_{2,4}*M_{2,4} \\
&+ N_{3,0}*M_{3,0} + N_{3,1}*M_{3,1} + N_{3,2}*M_{3,2} + N_{3,3}*M_{3,3} + N_{3,4}*M_{3,4} \\
&+ N_{4,0}*M_{4,0} + N_{4,1}*M_{4,1} + N_{4,2}*M_{4,2} + N_{4,3}*M_{4,3} + N_{4,4}*M_{4,4} \\
&= 1*1 + 2*2 + 3*3 + 4*2 + 5*1 \\
&+ 2*2 + 3*3 + 4*4 + 5*3 + 6*2 \\
&+ 3*3 + 4*4 + 5*5 + 6*4 + 7*3 \\
&+ 4*2 + 5*3 + 6*4 + 7*3 + 8*2 \\
&+ 5*1 + 6*2 + 7*3 + 8*2 + 5*1 \\
&= 1 + 4 + 9 + 8 + 5 \\
&+ 4 + 9 + 16 + 15 + 12 \\
&+ 9 + 16 + 25 + 24 + 21 \\
&+ 8 + 15 + 24 + 21 + 16 \\
&+ 5 + 12 + 21 + 16 + 5 \\
&= 321
\end{aligned}
$$

Like 1D convolution, 2D convolution must also deal with boundary conditions. With boundaries in both the x and y dimensions, there are more complex boundary conditions: the calculation of an output element may involve boundary conditions along a horizontal boundary, a vertical boundary, or both. Fig. 7.5 illustrates the calculation of a P element that involves both boundaries. From Fig. 7.5, the calculation of $P_{1,0}$ involves two missing columns and one missing horizontal row in the subarray of N. Like in 1D convolution, different applications assume different default values for these missing N elements. In our example, we assume that the default value is 0. These boundary conditions also affect the efficiency of tiling. We will come back to this point soon.

7.2 1D PARALLEL CONVOLUTION—A BASIC ALGORITHM

As we mentioned in Section 7.1, the calculation of all output (P) elements can be done in parallel in a convolution. This makes convolution an ideal problem for parallel computing. Based on our experience in matrix–matrix multiplication, we can

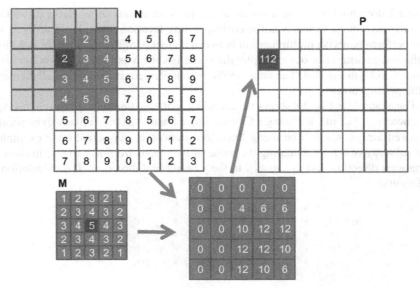

FIGURE 7.5

A 2D convolution boundary condition.

quickly write a simple parallel convolution kernel. For simplicity, we will start with 1D convolution.

The first step is to define the major input parameters for the kernel. We assume that the 1D convolution kernel receives five arguments: pointer to input array N, pointer to input mask M, pointer to output array P, size of the mask Mask_Width, and size of the input and output arrays Width. Thus, we have the following setup:

```
__global__ void convolution_1D_basic_kernel(float *N, float *M,
float *P,
    int Mask_Width, int Width) {
    // kernel body
}
```

The second step is to determine and implement the mapping of threads to output elements. Since the output array is 1D, a simple and good approach is to organize the threads into a 1D grid and have each thread in the grid to calculate one output element. The reader should recognize that this is the same arrangement as the vector addition example as far as output elements are concerned. Therefore, we can use the following statement to calculate an output element index from the block index, block dimension, and thread index for each thread:

```
int i = blockIdx.x*blockDim.x + threadIdx.x;
```

Once we determined the output element index, we can access the input N elements and the mask M elements using offsets to the output element index. For simplicity, we assume that Mask_Width is an odd number and the convolution is symmetric, i.e., Mask_Width is 2*n + 1 where n is an integer. The calculation of P[i] will use N[i-n], N[i-n+1],…, N[i-1], N[i], N[i+1], N[i+n-1], N[i+n]. We can use a simple loop to do this calculation in the kernel:

```
float Pvalue = 0;
int N_start_point = i - (Mask_Width/2);
for (int j = 0; j < Mask_Width; j++) {
    if (N_start_point + j >= 0 && N_start_point + j < Width) {
      Pvalue += N[N_start_point + j]*M[j];
    }
}
P[i] = Pvalue;
```

The variable Pvalue will allow all intermediate results to be accumulated in a register to save DRAM bandwidth. The for loop accumulates all the contributions from the neighboring elements to the output P element. The if statement in the loop tests if any of the input N elements used are ghost cells, either on the left side or the right side of the N array. Since we assume that 0 values will be used for ghost cells, we can simply skip the multiplication and accumulation of the ghost cell element and its corresponding N element. After the end of the loop, we release the Pvalue into the output P element. We now have a simple kernel in Fig. 7.6.

We can make two observations about the kernel in Fig. 7.6. First, there will be control flow divergence. The threads that calculate the output P elements near the left end or the right end of the P array will handle ghost cells. As we showed in Section 7.1, each of these neighboring threads will encounter a different number of ghost cells. Therefore, they will all be somewhat different decisions in the if statement. The thread that calculates P[0] will skip the multiply-accumulate statement about half of the time

```
__global__ void convolution_1D_basic_kernel(float *N, float *M, float *P,
  int Mask_Width, int Width) {

  int i = blockIdx.x*blockDim.x + threadIdx.x;

  float Pvalue = 0;
  int N_start_point = i - (Mask_Width/2);
  for (int j = 0; j < Mask_Width; j++) {
    if (N_start_point + j >= 0 && N_start_point + j < Width) {
      Pvalue += N[N_start_point + j]*M[j];
    }
  }
  P[i] = Pvalue;

}
```

FIGURE 7.6

A 1D convolution kernel with boundary condition handling.

whereas the one that calculates P[1] will skip one fewer times, and so on. The cost of control divergence will depend on Width the size of the input array and Mask_Width the size of the mask. For large input arrays and small masks, the control divergence only occurs in a small portion of the output elements, which will keep the effect of control divergence small. Since convolution is often applied to large images and spatial data, we typically expect that the effect of convergence to be modest or insignificant.

A more serious problem is memory bandwidth. The ratio of floating-point arithmetic calculation to global memory accesses is only about 1.0 in the kernel. As we have seen in the matrix–matrix multiplication example, this simple kernel can only be expected to run at a small fraction of the peak performance. We will discuss two key techniques for reducing the number of global memory accesses in the next two sections.

7.3 CONSTANT MEMORY AND CACHING

There are three interesting properties of the way the mask array M is used in convolution. First, the size of the M array is typically small. Most convolution masks are less than 10 elements in each dimension. Even in the case of a 3D convolution, the mask typically contains only less than 1000 elements. Second, the contents of M are not changed throughout the execution of the kernel. Third, all threads need to access the mask elements. Even better, all threads access the M elements in the same order, starting from M[0] and move by one element a time through the iterations of the for loop in Fig. 7.6. These two properties make the mask array an excellent candidate for constant memory and caching (Fig. 7.7).

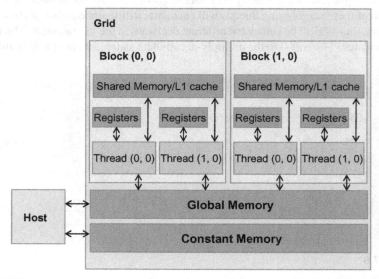

FIGURE 7.7

A review of the CUDA Memory Model.

As we discussed in Chapter 5, Performance Considerations, the CUDA programming model allows programmers to declare a variable in the constant memory. Like global memory variables, constant memory variables are also visible to all thread blocks. The main difference is that a constant memory variable cannot be changed by threads during kernel execution. Furthermore, the size of the constant memory is quite small, currently at 64KB.

In order to use constant memory, the host code needs to allocate and copy constant memory variables in a different way than global memory variables. To declare an M array in constant memory, the host code declares it as a global variable as follows:

```
#define MAX_MASK_WIDTH 10
__constant__ float M[MAX_MASK_WIDTH];
```

This is a global variable declaration and should be outside any function in the source file. The keyword __constant__ (two underscores on each side) tells the compiler that array M should be placed into the device constant memory.

Assume that the host code has already allocated and initialized the mask in a mask M_h array in the host memory with Mask_Width elements. The contents of the M_h can be transferred to M in the device constant memory as follows:

```
cudaMemcpyToSymbol(M, M_h, Mask_Width*sizeof(float));
```

Note that this is a special memory copy function that informs the CUDA runtime that the data being copied into the constant memory will not be changed during kernel execution. In general, the use of cudaMemcpyToSymble() function is as follows:

```
cudaMemcpyToSymbol(dest, src, size)
```

where dest is a pointer to the destination location in the constant memory, src is a pointer to the source data in the host memory, and size is the number of bytes to be copied.

Kernel functions access constant memory variables as global variables. Thus, their pointers do not need to be passed to the kernel as parameters. We can revise our kernel to use the constant memory as shown in Fig. 7.8. Note that the kernel looks almost identical to that in Fig. 7.6. The only difference is that M is no longer accessed through a pointer passed in as a parameter. It is now accessed as a global variable declared by the host code. Keep in mind that all the C language scoping rules for global variables apply here. If the host code and kernel code are in different files, the kernel code file must include the relevant external declaration information to ensure that the declaration of M is visible to the kernel.

Like global memory variables, constant memory variables are also located in DRAM. However, because the CUDA runtime knows that constant memory variables are not modified during kernel execution, it directs the hardware to aggressively cache the constant memory variables during kernel execution. In order to understand the benefit of constant memory usage, we need to first understand more about modern processor memory and cache hierarchies.

```
__global__ void convolution_1D_ba sic_kernel(float *N, float *P, int Mask_Width,
  int Width) {

  int i = blockIdx.x*blockDim.x + threadIdx.x;

  float Pvalue = 0;
  int N_start_point = i - (Mask_Width/2);
  for (int j = 0; j < Mask_Width; j++) {
    if (N start_point + j >= 0 && N_start_point + j < Width) {
      Pvalue += N[N_start_point + j]*M[j];
    }
  }
  P[i] = Pvalue;

}
```

FIGURE 7.8

A 1D convolution kernel using constant memory for M.

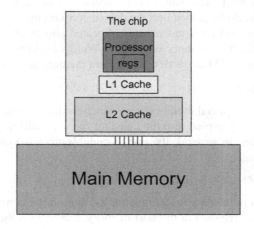

FIGURE 7.9

A simplified view of the cache hierarchy of modern processors.

As we discussed in Chapter 5, Performance considerations, the long latency and limited bandwidth of DRAM has been a major bottleneck in virtually all modern processors. In order to mitigate the effect of memory bottleneck, modern processors commonly employ on-chip cache memories, or caches, to reduce the number of variables that need to be accessed from the main memory (DRAM) as shown in Fig. 7.9.

Unlike CUDA shared memory, or scratch memories in general, caches are "transparent" to programs. That is, in order to use CUDA shared memory, a program needs to declare variables as __shared__ and explicitly move a global memory variable into a shared memory variable. On the other hand, when using caches, the program simply accesses the original variables. The processor hardware will automatically retain some of the most recently or frequently used variables in the cache and remember their original DRAM addresses. When one of the retained variables is used later, the hardware will detect from their addresses that a copy of the variable is available in cache. The value of the variable will then be provided from the cache, eliminating the need to access DRAM.

There is a tradeoff between the size of a memory and the speed of a memory. As a result, modern processors often employ multiple levels of caches. The numbering convention for these cache levels reflects the distance to the processor. The lowest level, L1 or Level 1, is the cache that is directly attached to a processor core. It runs at a speed very close to the processor in both latency and bandwidth. However, an L1 cache is small in size, typically between 16KB and 64KB. L2 caches are larger, in the range of 128KB to 1MB, but can take tens of cycles to access. They are typically shared among multiple processor cores, or SMs in a CUDA device. In some high-end processors today, there are even L3 caches that can be several MB in size.

A major design issue with using caches in a massively parallel processor is cache coherence, which arises when one or more processor cores modify cached data. Since L1 caches are typically directly attached to only one of the processor cores, changes in its contents are not easily observed by other processor cores. This causes a problem if the modified variable is shared among threads running on different processor cores. A *cache coherence mechanism* is needed to ensure that the contents of the caches of the other processor cores are updated. Cache coherence is difficult and expensive to provide in massively parallel processors. However, their presence typically simplifies parallel software development. Therefore, modern CPUs typically support cache coherence among processor cores. While modern GPUs provide two levels of caches, they typically do without cache coherence to maximize hardware resources available to increase the arithmetic throughput of the processor.

Constant memory variables play an interesting role in using caches in massively parallel processors. Since they are not changed during kernel execution, there is no cache coherence issue during the execution of a kernel. Therefore, the hardware can aggressively cache the constant variable values in L1 caches. Furthermore, the design of caches in these processors is typically optimized to broadcast a value to a large number of threads. As a result, when all threads in a warp access the same constant memory variable, as is the case of M, the caches can provide tremendous amount of bandwidth to satisfy the data needs of threads. Also, since the size of M is typically small, we can assume that all M elements are effectively always accessed from caches. Therefore, we can simply assume that no DRAM bandwidth is spent on M accesses. With the use of constant memory and caching, we have effectively doubled the ratio of floating-point arithmetic to memory access to 2.

As it turns out, the accesses to the input N array elements can also benefit from caching in more recent GPUs. We will come back to this point in Section 7.5.

7.4 TILED 1D CONVOLUTION WITH HALO CELLS

We will now address the memory bandwidth issue in accessing N array element with a tiled convolution algorithm. Recall that in a tiled algorithm, threads collaborate to load input elements into an on-chip memory and then access the on-chip memory for their subsequent use of these elements. For simplicity, we will continue to assume that each thread calculates one output P element. With up to 1024 threads in a block we can process up to 1024 data elements. We will refer to the collection of output elements processed by each block as an *output tile*. Fig. 7.10 shows a small example of 16-element 1D convolution using four thread blocks of four threads each. In this example, there are four output tiles. The first output tile covers N[0] through N[3], the second tile N[4] through N[7], the third tile N[8] through N[11], and the fourth tile N[12] through N[15]. Keep in mind that we use four threads per block to keep the example small. In practice, there should be at least 32 threads per block for the current generation of hardware. From this point on, we will assume that M elements are in the constant memory.

We will discuss two input data tiling strategies for reducing the total number of global memory accesses. The first one is the most intuitive and involves loading all input data elements needed for calculating all output elements of a thread block into the shared memory. The number of input elements to be loaded depends on the size of the mask. For simplicity, we will continue to assume that the mask size is an odd number equal to 2*n+1. That is each output element P[i] is a weighted sum of the input element at the corresponding input element N[i], the n input elements to the left (N[i-n], ... N[i-1]), and the n input elements to the right (N[i+1], ... N[i+n]). Fig. 7.10 shows an example where Mask_Width=5 and n=2.

Threads in the Block 0 calculate output elements P[0] through P[3]. They collectively require input elements N[0] through N[5]. Note that the calculation also

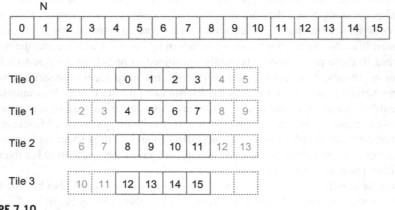

FIGURE 7.10

A 1D tiled convolution example.

requires two ghost cell elements to the left of N[0]. This is shown as two dashed empty elements on the left end of Tile 0 of Fig. 7.6. These ghost elements will be assumed have default value of 0. Tile 3 has a similar situation at the right end of input array N. In our discussions, we will refer to tiles like Tile 0 and Tile 3 as boundary tiles since they involve elements at or outside the boundary of the input array N.

Threads in Block 1 calculate output elements P[4] through P[7]. They collectively require input elements N[2] through N[9], also shown in Fig. 7.7. Note that elements N[2] and N[3] belong to two tiles and are loaded into the shared memory twice, once to the shared memory of Block 0 and once to the shared memory of Block 1. Since the contents of shared memory of a block are only visible to the threads of the block, these elements need to be loaded into the respective shared memories for all involved threads to access them. The elements that are involved in multiple tiles and loaded by multiple blocks are commonly referred to as *halo cells* or *skirt cells* since they "hang" from the side of the part that is used solely by a single block. We will refer to the center part of an input tile that is used solely by a single block the *internal cells* of that input tile. Tile 1 and Tile 2 are commonly referred to as *internal tiles* since they do not involve any ghost elements at our outside the boundaries of the input array N.

We now show the kernel code that loads the input tile into shared memory. We first declare a shared memory array N_ds to hold the N tile for each block. The size of the shared memory array must be large enough to hold the left halo cells, the center cells, and the right halo cells of an input tile. We assume that Mask_Width is an odd number. Assume that the constant MAX_MASK_WIDTH specifies the maximal possible value of Mask_Width. The maximal possible size of the shared memory array is TILE_SIZE + MAX_MASK_WIDTH - 1, which is used in the following declaration in the kernel:

```
__shared__ float N_ds[TILE_SIZE + MAX_MASK_WIDTH - 1];
```

We then load the left halo cells, which include the last n = Mask_Width/2 center elements of the previous tile. For example, in Fig. 7.6, the left halo cells of Tile 1 consist of the last 2 center elements of Tile 0. In C, assuming that Mask_Width is an odd number, the expression Mask_Width/2 will result in an integer value that is the same as (Mask_Wdith-1)/2. We will use the last (Mask_Width/2) threads of the block to load the left halo element. This is done with the following two statements:

```
    int halo_index_left = (blockIdx.x - 1)*blockDim.x +
threadIdx.x;
    if (threadIdx.x >= blockDim.x - n) {
      N_ds[threadIdx.x - (blockDim.x - n)] =
        (halo_index_left < 0) ? 0 : N[halo_index_left];
    }
```

In the first statement, we map the thread index to element index into the previous tile with the expression (blockIdx.x-1)*blockDim.x+threadIdx.x. We then pick only the last n threads to load the needed left halo elements using the condition in the if statement. For example, in Fig. 7.6, blockDim.x equals 4 and n equals 2; only thread 2 and thread 3 will be used. Thread 0 and thread 1 will not load anything due to the failed condition.

For the threads used, we also need to check if their halo cells are actually ghost cells. This can be checked by testing if the calculated `halo_index_left` value is negative. If so, the halo cells are actually ghost cells since their N indices are negative, outside the valid range of the N indices. The conditional C assignment will choose 0 for threads in this situation. Otherwise, the conditional statement will use the `halo_index_left` to load the appropriate N elements into the shared memory. The shared memory index calculation is such that left halo cells will be loaded into the shared memory array starting at element 0. For example, in Fig. 7.6, `blockDim.x-n` equals 2. So for block 1, thread 2 will load the left most halo element into `N_ds[0]` and thread 3 will load the next halo element into `N_ds[1]`. However, for block 0, both thread 2 and thread 3 will load value 0 into `N_ds[0]` and `N_ds[1]`.

The next step is to load the center cells of the input tile. This is done by mapping the `blockIdx.x` and `threadIdx.x` values into the appropriate N indices, as shown in the following statement. The reader should be familiar with the N index expression used:

```
N_ds[n + threadIdx.x] = N[blockIdx.x*blockDim.x +
threadIdx.x];
```

Since the first n elements of the `N_ds` array already contain the left halo cells, the center elements need to be loaded into the next section of `N_ds`. This is done by adding n to `threadIdx.x` as the index for each thread to write its loaded center element into `N_ds`.

We now load the right halo elements, which is quite similar to loading the left halo. We first map the `blockIdx.x` and `threadIdx.x` to the elements of next output tile. This is done by adding `(blockIdx.x+1)*blockDim.x` to the thread index to form the N index for the right halo cells. In this case, we are loading the beginning n elements of the next tile.

```
int halo_index_right = (blockIdx.x + 1)*blockDim.x +
threadIdx.x;
    if (threadIdx.x < n) {
        N_ds[n + blockDim.x + threadIdx.x] =
            (halo_index_right >= Width) ? 0 : N[halo_index_right];
    }
```

Now that all the input tile elements are in `N_ds`, each thread can calculate their output P element value using the `N_ds` elements. Each thread will use a different section of the `N_ds`. Thread 0 will use `N_ds[0]` through `N_ds[Mask_Width-1]`; thread 1 will use `N_ds[1]` through `N[Mask_Width]`. In general, each thread will use `N_ds[threadIdx.x]` through `N[threadIdx.x+Mask_Width-1]`. This is implemented in the following `for` loop to calculate the P element assigned to the thread:

```
float Pvalue = 0;
for(int j = 0; j < Mask_Width; j++) {
    Pvalue += N_ds[threadIdx.x + j]*M[j];
}
P[i] = Pvalue;
```

```
__global__ void convolution_1D_tiled_kernel(float *N, float *P, int Mask_Width,
int Width) {

int i = blockIdx.x*blockDim.x + threadIdx.x;
__shared__ float N_ds[TILE_SIZE + MAX_MASK_WIDTH - 1];

int n = Mask_Width/2;

int halo_index_left = (blockIdx.x - 1)*blockDim.x + threadIdx.x;
if (threadIdx.x >= blockDim.x - n) {
  N_ds[threadIdx.x - (blockDim.x - n)] =
    (halo_index_left < 0) ? 0 : N[halo_index_left];
}

N_ds[n + threadIdx.x] = N[blockIdx.x*blockDim.x + threadIdx.x];

int halo_index_right = (blockIdx.x + 1)*blockDim.x + threadIdx.x;
if (threadIdx.x < n) {
  N_ds[n + blockDim.x + threadIdx.x] =
    (halo_index_right >= Width) ? 0 : N[halo_index_right];
}

__syncthreads();

float Pvalue = 0;
for(int j = 0; j < Mask_Width; j++) {
  Pvalue += N_ds[threadIdx.x + j]*M[j];
}
P[i] = Pvalue;

}
```

FIGURE 7.11

A tiled 1D convolution kernel using constant memory for M.

However, one must not forget to do a barrier synchronization using __syncthreads() to make sure that all threads in the same block have completed loading their assigned N elements before anyone should start using them from the shared memory.

Note that the code for multiply and accumulate is simpler than the base algorithm. The conditional statements for loading the left and right halo cells have placed the 0 values into the appropriate N_ds elements for the first and last thread block.

The tiled 1D convolution kernel is significantly longer and more complex than the basic kernel. We introduced the additional complexity in order to reduce the number of DRAM accesses for the N elements. The goal is to improve the arithmetic to memory access ratio so that the achieved performance is not limited or less limited by the DRAM bandwidth. We will evaluate improvement by comparing the number of DRAM accesses performed by each thread block for the kernels in Figs. 7.8 and 7.11.

In Fig. 7.8, there are two cases. For thread blocks that do not handle ghost cells, the number of N elements accessed by each thread is Mask_Width. Thus, the total number of N elements accessed by each thread block is blockDim.x*Mask_Width or blockDim.x*(2n+1). For example, if Mask_Width is equal to 5 and each block contains 1024 threads, each block access a total of 5120 N elements.

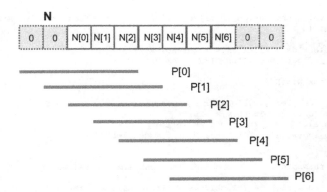

FIGURE 7.12

A small example of accessing N elements and ghost cells.

For the first and the last blocks, the threads that handle ghost cells do not perform memory access for the ghost cells. This reduces the number of memory accesses. We can calculate the reduced number of memory accesses by enumerating the number of threads that use each ghost cell. This is illustrated with a small example in Fig. 7.12. The leftmost ghost cell is used by one thread. The second left ghost cell is used by two threads. In general, the number of ghost cells is n and the number of threads that use each of these ghost cells, from left to right is 1, 2, ... n. This is a simple series with sum n(n+1)/2, which is the total number of accesses that were avoided due to ghost cells. For our simple example where Mask_Width is equal to 5 and n is equal to 2, the number of accesses avoided due to ghost cells is 2*3/2 = 3. A similar analysis gives the same results for the right ghost cells. It should be clear that for large thread blocks, the effect of ghost cells for small mask sizes will be insignificant.

We now calculate the total number of memory accesses for N elements by the tiled kernel in Fig. 7.11. All the memory accesses have been shifted to the code that loads the N elements into the shared memory. In the tiled kernel, each N element is only loaded by one thread. However, 2n halo cells will also be loaded, n from the left and n from the right, for blocks that do not handle ghost cells. Therefore, we have the blockDim.x+2n elements loaded by the internal thread blocks and blockDim+n by boundary thread blocks.

For internal thread blocks, the ratio of memory accesses between the basic and the tiled 1D convolution kernel is:

```
(blockDim.x*(2n+1)) / (blockDim.x+2n)
```

whereas the ratio for boundary blocks is:

```
(blockDim.x*(2n+1) - n(n+1)/2) / (blockDim.x+n)
```

For most situations, blockDim.x is much larger than n. Both ratios can be approximated by eliminating the small terms n(n+1)/2 and n:

```
(blockDim.x*(2n+1)/ blockDim.x = 2n+1 = Mask_Width
```

This should be quite an intuitive result. In the original algorithm, each N element is redundantly loaded by approximately Mask_Width threads. For example, in Fig. 7.12, N[2] is loaded by the 5 threads that calculate P[2], P[3], P[4], P[5], and P[6]. That is, the ratio of memory access reduction is approximately proportional to the mask size.

However, in practice, the effect of the smaller terms may be significant and cannot be ignored. For example, if blockDim.x is 128 and n is 5, the ratio for the internal blocks is:

```
(128*11 - 10) / (128 + 10) = 1398 / 138 = 10.13
```

whereas the approximate ratio would be 11. It should be clear that as the blockDim.x becomes smaller, the ratio also becomes smaller. For example, if block-Dim is 32 and n is 5, the ratio for the internal blocks becomes:

```
(32*11 - 10) / (32+10) = 8.14
```

The readers should always be careful when using smaller block and tile sizes. They may result in significantly less reduction in memory accesses than expected. In practice, smaller tile sizes are often used due to insufficient amount of on-chip memory, especially for 2D and 3D convolution where the amount of on-chip memory needed grows quickly with the dimension of the tile.

7.5 A SIMPLER TILED 1D CONVOLUTION— GENERAL CACHING

In Fig. 7.11, much of the complexity of the code has to do with loading the left and right halo cells in addition to the internal elements into the shared memory. More recent GPUs such as Fermi provide general L1 and L2 caches, where L1 is private to each streaming multiprocessor and L2 is shared among all streaming multiprocessors. This leads to an opportunity for the blocks to take advantage of the fact that their halo cells may be available in the L2 cache.

Recall that the halo cells of a block are also internal cells of a neighboring block. For example, in Fig. 7.10, the halo cells N[2] and N[3] of Tile 1 are also internal elements of Tile 0. There is a significant probability that by the time Block 1 needs to use these halo cells, they are already in L2 cache due to the accesses by Block 0. As a result, the memory accesses to these halo cells may be naturally served from L2 cache without causing additional DRAM traffic. That is, we can leave the accesses to these halo cells in the original N elements rather than loading them into the N_ds. We now present a simpler tiled 1D convolution algorithm that only loads the internal elements of each tile into the shared memory.

In the simpler tiled kernel, the shared memory N_ds array only needs to hold the internal elements of the tile. Thus, it is declared with the TILE_SIZE, rather than TILE_SIZE+Mask_Width-1.

```
__shared__ float N_ds[TILE_SIZE];
```

```
    __syncthreads();

    int This_tile_start_point = blockIdx.x * blockDim.x;
    int Next_tile_start_point = (blockIdx.x + 1) * blockDim.x;
    int N_start_point = i - (Mask_Width/2);
    float Pvalue = 0;
    for (int j = 0; j < Mask_Width; j++) {
      int N_index = N_start_point + j;
      if (N_index >= 0  && N_index < Width) {
        if ((N_index >= This_tile_start_point)
          && (N_index < Next_tile_start_point)) {
          Pvalue += N_ds[threadIdx.x+j-(Mask_Width/2)]*M[j];
        } else {
          Pvalue += N[N_index] * M[j];
        }
      }
    }
    P[i] = Pvalue;
```

FIGURE 7.13

Using general caching for halo cells.

Loading the tile becomes very simple with only one line of code:

```
N_ds[threadIdx.x] = N[blockIdx.x*blockDim.x+threadIdx.x];
```

We still need a barrier synchronization before using the elements in N_ds. The loop that calculates P elements, however, becomes more complex. It needs to add conditions to check for use of both halo cells and ghost cells. The handling of ghost cells is done with the same conditional statement as that in Fig. 7.6. The multiply-accumulate statement becomes more complex, shown in Fig. 7.13.

The variables This_tile_start_point and Next_tile_start_point hold the starting position index of the tile processed by the current block and that of the tile processed by the next in the next block. For example, in Fig. 7.10, the value of This_tile_start_point for Block 1 is 4 and the value of Next_tile_start_point is 8.

The new if statement tests if the current access to the N element falls within tile by testing it against This_tile_start_point and Next_tile_start_point. If the element falls within the tile, that is, it is an internal element for the current block, it is accessed from the N_ds array in the shared memory. Otherwise, it is accessed from the N array, which is hopefully in the L2 cache. The complete tiled kernel using general caching is shown in Fig. 7.14.

7.6 TILED 2D CONVOLUTION WITH HALO CELLS

Now that we have learned how to tile a parallel 1D convolution computation, we can extend our knowledge to 2D quite easily. For a little more fun, we will use an example based on a class of 2D image format that is frequently encountered in image libraries and applications.

As we have seen in Chapter 3, Scalable Parallel Execution, real-world images are represented as 2D matrices and come in all sizes and shapes. Image processing

```
__global__ void convolution_1D_tiled_caching_kernel(float *N, float *P, int
Mask_Width,int Width) {

    int i = blockIdx.x*blockDim.x + threadIdx.x;
    __shared__ float N_ds[TILE_SIZE];

    N_ds[threadIdx.x] = N[i];

    __syncthreads();

    int This_tile_start_point = blockIdx.x * blockDim.x;
    int Next_tile_start_point = (blockIdx.x + 1) * blockDim.x;
    int N_start_point = i - (Mask_Width/2);
    float Pvalue = 0;
    for (int j = 0; j < Mask_Width; j++) {
        int N_index = N_start_point + j;
        if (N_index >= 0  && N_index < Width) {
            if ((N_index >= This_tile_start_point)
                && (N_index < Next_tile_start_point)) {
                Pvalue += N_ds[threadIdx.x+j-(Mask_Width/2)]*M[j];
            } else {
                Pvalue += N[N_index] * M[j];
            }
        }
    }
    P[i] = Pvalue;

}
```

FIGURE 7.14

A simpler tiled 1D convolution kernel using constant memory and general caching.

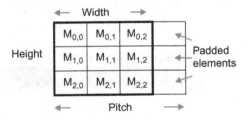

FIGURE 7.15

A padded image format and the concept of pitch.

libraries typically store these images in row-major layout when reading them from files into memory. If the width of the image in terms of bytes is not a multiple of the DRAM burst size, the starting point of row 1 and beyond can be misaligned from the DRAM burst boundaries. As we have seen in Chapter 5, Performance Considerations, such misalignment can result in poor utilization of DRAM bandwidth when we attempt to access data in one of the rows. As a result, image libraries often also convert images into a padded format when reading them from files into memory, as illustrated in Fig. 7.15.

In Fig. 7.15, we assume that the original image is 3x3. We further assume that each DRAM burst encompasses 4 pixels. Without padding, $M_{1,0}$ in row 1 would reside in one DRAM burst unit whereas $M_{1,1}$ and $M_{1,2}$ would reside in the next DRAM burst unit. Accessing row 1 would require two DRAM bursts and wasting half of the memory bandwidth. To address this inefficiency, the library pads one element at the end of each row. With the padded elements, each row occupies an entire DRAM burst size. When we access row 1 or row 2, the entire row can now be accessed in one DRAM burst. In general, the images are much larger; each row can encompass multiple DRAM bursts. The padded elements will be added such that each row ends at the DRAM burst boundaries.

With padding, the image matrix has been enlarged by the padded elements. However, during computation such as image blur (see Chapter: Scalable Parallel Execution), one should not process the padded elements. Therefore, the library data structure will indicate the original width and height of the image as shown in Fig. 7.15. However, the library also has to provide the users with the information about the padded elements so that the user code can properly find the actual starting position of all the rows. This information is conveyed as the *pitch* of the padded matrix.

Fig. 7.16 shows how the image pixel elements can be accessed in the row-major layout of the padded image matrix. The lower layout shows the linearized order. Note that the padded elements are at the end of each row. The top layout shows the linearized 1D index of pixel elements in the padded matrix. As before, the three original elements, $M_{0,1}$, $M_{0,2}$, $M_{0,3}$ of row 0 become M_0, M_1, and M_2 in the linearized 1D array. Note that the padded elements become "dummy" linearized elements M_3, M_7, and M_{11}. The original elements of row 1, $M_{1,1}$, $M_{1,2}$, $M_{1,3}$, have their linearized 1D index as M_4, M_5, and M_6. That is, as shown in the top of Fig. 7.16, to calculate

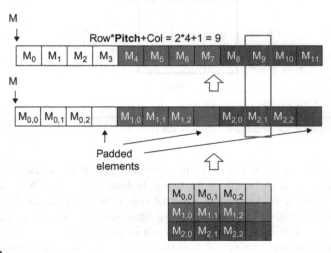

FIGURE 7.16

Row-major layout of a 2D image matrix with padded elements.

the linearized 1D index of the pixel elements, we will use `pitch` instead of `width` in the expression:

```
Linearized 1D index = row * pitch + column
```

However, when we iterate through a row, we will use `width` as the loop bound to ensure that we use only the original elements in a computation.

Fig. 7.17 shows the image type that we will be using for the kernel code example. Note the `channels` field indicates the number of channels in the pixel: 3 for an RGB color image and 1 for a greyscale image as we have seen in Chapter 2, Data parallel computing. We assume that the value of these fields will be used as arguments when we invoke the 2D convolution kernel.

We are now ready to work on the design of a tiled 2D convolution kernel. In general, we will find that the design of the 2D convolution kernel is a straightforward extension of the 1D convolution kernel presented in Section 7.5. We need to first design the input and output tiles to be processed by each thread block, as shown in Fig. 7.18. Note that the input tiles must include the halo cells and extend beyond their corresponding output tiles by the number of halo cells in each direction. Fig. 7.19 shows the first part of the kernel:

```
// Image Matrix Structure declaration
//
typedef struct {
    int width;
    int height;
    int pitch;
    int channels;
    float* data;
} * wbImage_t;
```

FIGURE 7.17

The C type structure definition of the image pixel element.

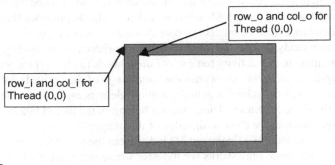

FIGURE 7.18

Starting element indices of the input tile versus output tile.

```
__global__ void convolution_2D_tiled_kernel(float *P, float *N, int height, int width,
                          int pitch, int channels, int Mask_Width,
                          const float __restrict__ *M)
{

  int tx = threadIdx.x;
  int ty = threadIdx.y;
  int row_o = blockIdx.y*O_TILE_WIDTH + ty;
  int col_o = blockIdx.x*O_TILE_WIDTH + tx;

  int row_i = row_o - Mask_Width/2;
  int col_i = col_o - Mask_Width/2;
```

FIGURE 7.19

Part 1 of a 2D convolution kernel.

```
      __shared__ float N_ds[TILE_SIZE+MAX_MASK_WIDTH-1]
                         [TILE_SIZE+MAX_MASK_HEIGHT-1];
      if((row_i >= 0) && (row_i < height) &&
        (col_i >= 0) && (col_i < width)) {
        N_ds[ty][tx] = data[row_i * pitch + col_i];
      } else{
        N_ds[ty][tx] = 0.0f;
      }
```

FIGURE 7.20

Part 2 of a 2D convolution kernel.

Each thread of the kernel first calculates the y and x indices of its output element. These are the `col_o` and `row_o` variables of the kernel. The index values for thread$_{0,0}$ of the thread block (which is responsible for the output element at the upper left corner) is shown in Fig. 7.18. Each thread then calculates the y and x indices of the input element it is to load into the shared memory by subtracting (`Mask_Width/2`) from `row_o` and `col_o` and assigning the results to `row_i` and `col_i`, also shown in Fig. 7.18. Note that the input tile element to be loaded by thread$_{0,0}$ is also shown in Fig. 7.18. To simply the tiling code over the kernel in Fig. 7.14, we will configure each thread block to be of the same size as the input tile. In this design, we can simply have each thread to load one input `N` element. We will turn off some of the threads when we calculate the output since there are more threads in each block than the number of data elements in each output tile.

We are now ready to load the input tiles into the shared memory (Fig. 7.20). All threads participate in this activity but each of them needs to check if the y and x indices of its input tile elements are within the valid range of the input. If not, the input element it is attempting to load is actually a ghost element and a 0.0 value should be placed into the shared memory. These threads belong in the thread blocks that calculate the image tiles that are close to the edge of the image. Note that we use the `pitch` value when we compute the linearized 1D index from the y and x index of the pixel. Also note that this code only works for the case where the number of channels is 1. In general, we should use a for-loop to load all the pixel channel values based on the number of channels present.

```
float output = 0.0f;
if(ty < O_TILE_WIDTH && tx < O_TILE_WIDTH){
    for(i = 0; i < MASK_WIDTH; i++) {
      for(j = 0; j < MASK_WIDTH; j++) {
        output += M[i][j] * N_ds[i+ty][j+tx];
      }
    }

    if(row_o < height && col_o < width){
        data[row_o*width + col_o] = output;
    }
}
```

FIGURE 7.21

Part 3 of a 2D convolution kernel.

The last part of the kernel, shown in Fig. 7.21, computes the output value using the input elements in the shared memory. Keep in mind that we have more threads in the thread block than the number of pixels in the output tile. The if-statement ensures that only the threads whose indices are both smaller than the O_TILE_WIDTH should participate in the calculation of output pixels. The doubly nested for-loop iterates through the mask array and performs the multiply and accumulate operation on the mask element values and input pixel values. Since the input tile in the shared memory N_ds includes all the halo elements, the index expressions N_ds[i+ty][j+tx] gives the N_ds element that should be multiplied with M[i][j]. The reader should notice that this is a straightforward extension of the index expression in corresponding for-loop in Fig. 7.11. Finally, all threads whose output elements are in the valid range write their result values into their respective output elements.

To assess the benefit of the 2D tiled kernel over a basic kernel, we can also extend the analysis from 1D convolution. In a basic kernel, every thread in a thread block will perform $(\text{Mask\_Width})^2$ accesses to the image array. Thus, each thread block performs a total of $(\text{Mask\_Width})^2 * (\text{O\_TILE\_WIDTH})^2$ accesses to the image array.

In the tiled kernel, all threads in a thread block collectively load one input tile. Therefore, the total number of accesses by a thread block to the image array is $(\text{O\_TILE\_WIDTH} + \text{Mask\_Width} - 1)^2$. That is, the ratio of image array accesses between the basic and the tiled 2D convolution kernel is:

$$(\text{Mask\_Width})^2 * (\text{O\_TILE\_WIDTH})^2 / (\text{O\_TILE\_WIDTH} + \text{Mask\_Width} - 1)^2$$

The larger the ratio, the more effective the tiled algorithm in reducing the number of memory accesses as compared to the basic algorithm.

Fig. 7.22 shows the trend of the image array access reduction ratio as we vary O_TILE_WIDTH, the output tile size. As O_TILE_WIDTH becomes very large, the size of the mask becomes negligible compared to tile size. Thus, each input element loaded will be used about $(\text{Mask\_Width})^2$ times. For Mask_Width value of 5, we expect that the ratio will approach 25 as the O_TILE_SIZE becomes much larger than 5. For example, for O_TILE_SIZE=64, the ratio is 22.1. This is significantly higher than the

TiILE_WIDTH	8	16	32	64
Reduction Mask_Width = 5	11.1	16	19.7	22.1
Reduction Mask_Width = 9	20.3	36	51.8	64

FIGURE 7.22

Image array access reduction ratio for different tile sizes.

ratio of 11.1 for O_TILE_WIDTH=8. The important takeaway point is that we must have a sufficiently large O_TILE_WIDTH in order for the tiled kernel to deliver its potential benefit. The cost of a large O_TILE_WIDTH is the amount of shared memory needed to hold the input tiles.

For a larger Mask_Width, such as 9 in the bottom row of Fig. 7.22, the ideal ratio should be 9^2=81. However, even with a large O_TILE_WIDTH such as 64, the ratio is only 64. Note that O_TILE_WIDTH=64 and Mask_Width=9 translate into input tile size of 72^2=5184 elements or 20,736 bytes assuming single precision data. This is more than the amount of available shared memory in each SM of the current generation of GPUs. Stencil computation that is derived from finite difference methods for solving differential equation often require a Mask_Width of 9 or above to achieve numerical stability. Such stencil computation can benefit from larger amount of shared memory in future generations of GPUs.

7.7 SUMMARY

In this chapter, we have studied convolution as an important parallel computation pattern. While convolution is used in many applications such as computer vision and video processing, it also represents a general pattern that forms the basis of many parallel algorithms. For example, one can view the stencil algorithms in partial differential equation solvers as a special case of convolution. For another example, one can also view the calculation of grid point force or potential value as a special case of convolution.

We have presented a basic parallel convolution algorithm whose implementations will be limited by DRAM bandwidth for accessing both the input N and mask M elements. We then introduced the constant memory and a simple modification to the kernel and host code to take advantage of constant caching and eliminate practically all DRAM accesses for the mask elements. We further introduced a tiled parallel convolution algorithm that reduces DRAM bandwidth consumption by introducing more control flow divergence and programming complexity. Finally we presented a simpler tiled parallel convolution algorithm that takes advantage of the L2 caches.

Although we have shown kernel examples for only 1D convolution, the techniques are directly applicable to 2D and 3D convolutions. In general, the index calculation for the N and M arrays are more complex due to higher dimensionality. Also, one will have more loop nesting for each thread since multiple dimensions need to be traversed when loading tiles and/or calculating output values. We encourage the reader to complete these higher dimension kernels as homework exercises.

7.8 EXERCISES

1. Calculate the P[0] value in Fig. 7.3.
2. Consider performing a 1D convolution on array N = {4,1,3,2,3} with mask M = {2,1,4}. What is the resulting output array?
3. What do you think the following 1D convolution masks are doing?
   a. [0 1 0]
   b. [0 0 1]
   c. [1 0 0]
   d. [−1/2 0 1/2]
   e. [1/3 1/3 1/3]
4. Consider performing a 1D convolution on an array of size n with a mask of size m:
   a. How many halo cells are there in total?
   b. How many multiplications are performed if halo cells are treated as multiplications (by 0)?
   c. How many multiplications are performed if halo cells are not treated as multiplications?
5. Consider performing a 2D convolution on a square matrix of size nxn with a square mask of size mxm:
   a. How many halo cells are there in total?
   b. How many multiplications are performed if halo cells are treated as multiplications (by 0)?
   c. How many multiplications are performed if halo cells are not treated as multiplications?
6. Consider performing a 2D convolution on a rectangular matrix of size n1xn2 with a rectangular mask of size m1xm2:
   a. How many halo cells are there in total?
   b. How many multiplications are performed if halo cells are treated as multiplications (by 0)?
   c. How many multiplications are performed if halo cells are not treated as multiplications?
7. Consider performing a 1D tiled convolution with the kernel shown in Fig. 7.11 on an array of size n with a mask of size m using a tiles of size t:
   a. How many blocks are needed?
   b. How many threads per block are needed?

      c. How much shared memory is needed in total?

      d. Repeat the same questions if you were using the kernel in Fig. 7.13.

8. Revise the 1D kernel in Fig. 7.6 to perform 2D convolution. Add more width parameters to the kernel declaration as needed.

9. Revise the tiled 1D kernel in Fig. 7.8 to perform 2D convolution. Keep in mind that the host code also needs to be changed to declare a 2D M array in the constant memory. Pay special attention to the increased usage of shared memory. Also, the N_ds needs to be declared as a 2D shared memory array.

10. Revise the tiled 1D kernel in Fig. 7.11 to perform 2D convolution. Keep in mind that the host code also needs to be changed to declare a 2D M array in the constant memory. Pay special attention to the increased usage of shared memory. Also, the N_ds needs to be declared as a 2D shared memory array.

Parallel patterns: prefix sum

An introduction to work efficiency in parallel algorithms

Li-Wen Chang and Juan Gómez-Luna

CHAPTER OUTLINE

Our next parallel pattern is prefix sum, also commonly known as scan. Parallel scan is frequently used to convert seemingly sequential operations into parallel operations. These operations include resource allocation, work assignment, and polynomial evaluation. In general, a computation that is naturally described as a mathematical recursion can likely be parallelized as a parallel scan operation. Parallel scan plays a key role in massive parallel computing for a simple reason: any sequential section of an application can drastically limit the overall performance of the application. Many such sequential sections can be converted into parallel computing with parallel scans. Another reason parallel scan is an important parallel pattern is that sequential scan algorithms are linear algorithms and are extremely work-efficient, which emphasizes the importance of controlling the work efficiency of parallel scan algorithms. A slight increase in algorithm complexity can make a parallel scan run slower than a sequential scan for large data sets. Therefore, a work-efficient parallel scan algorithm also represents an important class of parallel algorithms that can run effectively on parallel systems with a wide range of computing resources.

Programming Massively Parallel Processors. DOI: http://dx.doi.org/10.1016/B978-0-12-811986-0.00008-X

8.1 BACKGROUND

Mathematically, an *inclusive scan* operation takes a binary associative operator $\oplus$ and an input array of n elements $[x_0, x_1, \ldots, x_{n-1}]$ and returns the following output array:

$$[x_0, (x_0 \oplus x_1), \ldots, (x_0 \oplus x_1 \oplus \ldots \oplus x_{n-1})]$$

To illustrate, if $\oplus$ is an addition operation, then an inclusive scan operation on the input array [3 1 7 0 4 1 6 3] would return [3 4 11 11 15 16 22 25].

The applications for inclusive scan operations can be illustrated thus: Assume that we have a 40-inch sausage to serve to eight people. Each person orders different quantities of sausage: 3, 1, 7, 0, 4, 1, 6, and 3 inches. Person number 0 wants 3 inches of sausage, person number 1 wants 1 inch, and so on. The sausage can be cut either sequentially or in parallel. The sequential method is very straightforward. We first cut a 3-inch section for person number 0; the sausage is now 37 inches long. We then cut a 1-inch section for person number 1; the sausage becomes 36 inches long. We can continue to cut more sections until we serve the 3-inch section to person number 7. By then, we have served a total of 25 inches of sausage, with 15 inches remaining.

With an inclusive scan operation, we can calculate the locations of all cut points on the basis of the quantity each person orders; i.e., given an addition operation and an order input array [3 1 7 0 4 1 6 3], the inclusive scan operation returns [3 4 11 11 15 16 22 25]. The numbers in the return array are the cutting locations. With this information, we can simultaneously make all of the eight cuts, thereby generating the sections ordered by each person. The first cut point is at the 3-inch location so that the first section will be 3 inches long, as ordered by person number 0. The second cut point is at the 4-inch location so that the second section will be 1-inch long, as ordered by person number 1. The final cut point will be at the 25-inch location, which will produce a 3-inch long section since the previous cut point is at the 22-inch point. Person number 7 will eventually be given what she ordered. Note that since all the cut points are known from the scan operation, all cuts can be done in parallel.

In summary, an intuitive way of considering an inclusive scan operation is that the operation takes an order from a group of people and identifies all the cut points that allow the orders to be served all at once. The order could be for sausage, bread, camp ground space, or a contiguous chunk of memory in a computer. All orders can be served in parallel as long as we can quickly calculate all the cut points.

An exclusive scan operation is similar to an inclusive operation, except that the former returns the following output array:

$$[0, x_0, (x_0 \oplus x_1), \ldots, (x_0 \oplus x_1 \oplus \ldots \oplus x_{n-2})]$$

The first output element is 0, whereas the last output element only reflects the contribution of up to x_{n-2}.

The applications of an exclusive scan operation are rather similar to those of an inclusive scan operation. The inclusive scan provides a slightly different information.

In the sausage example, an exclusive scan would return [0 3 4 11 11 15 16 22], which are the beginning points of the cut sections. To illustrate, the section for person number 0 starts at the 0-inch point, and the section for person number 7 starts at the 22-inch point. The beginning point information is useful for applications such as memory allocation, where the allocated memory is returned to the requester via a pointer to its beginning point.

Converting between the inclusive scan output and the exclusive scan output can occur easily. We simply need to shift all elements and fill in an element. To convert from inclusive to exclusive, we can simply shift all elements to the right and fill in the value 0 for the 0th element. To convert from exclusive to inclusive, we only need to shift all elements to the left and fill in the last element with the previous last element and the last input element. It is just a matter of convenience that we can directly generate an inclusive or exclusive scan, whether we care about the cut points or the beginning points for the sections.

In practice, parallel scan is often used as a primitive operation in parallel algorithms that perform radix sort, quick sort, string comparison, polynomial evaluation, solving recurrences, tree operations, stream compaction, and histograms.

Before we present parallel scan algorithms and their implementations, we will first show a work-efficient sequential inclusive scan algorithm and its implementation, with the assumption that the operation involved is addition. The algorithm assumes that the input elements are in the x array and the output elements are to be written into the y array.

```
void sequential_scan(float *x, float *y, int Max_i) {
  int accumulator = x[0];
  y[0] = accumulator;
  for (int i = 1; i < Max_i; i++) {
      accumulator += x[i];
      y[i] = accumulator;
  }
}
```

The algorithm is work-efficient, performing only a small amount of work for each input or output element. With a reasonably good compiler, only one addition, one memory load, and one memory store are used in processing each input x element. This amount of work is pretty much the minimal that we will ever be able to do. As we will see, when the sequential algorithm of a computation is so "lean and mean," it is extremely challenging to develop a parallel algorithm that will consistently beat the sequential algorithm when the data set size becomes large.

8.2 A SIMPLE PARALLEL SCAN

We start with a simple parallel inclusive scan algorithm by performing a reduction operation for each output element. The main objective is to create each element quickly by calculating a reduction tree of the relevant input elements for each output

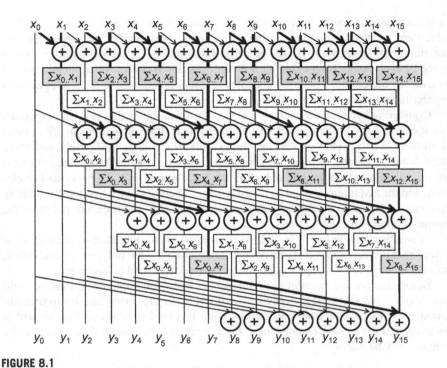

FIGURE 8.1

A parallel inclusive scan algorithm based on Kogge–Stone adder design.

element. The reduction tree for each output element may be designed in multiple ways. The first method we will present is based on the Kogge–Stone algorithm, which was originally invented for designing fast adder circuits in the 1970s [KS 1973]. This algorithm is currently being used in the design of high-speed computer arithmetic hardware.

The algorithm, shown is Fig. 8.1, is an in-place scan algorithm that operates on an array XY that originally contains input elements. Subsequently, it iteratively evolves the contents of the array into output elements. Before the algorithm begins, we assume that XY [i] contains the input element x_i. At the end of iteration n, XY[i] will contain the sum of up to 2^n input elements at and before the location; i.e., at the end of iteration 1, XY[i] will contain $x_{i-1}+x_i$, at the end of iteration 2, XY[i] will contain $x_{i-3}+x_{i-2}+x_{i-1}+x_i$, and so on.

Fig. 8.1 illustrates the steps of the algorithm with a 16-element input. Each vertical line represents an element of the XY array, with XY[0] in the leftmost position. The vertical direction shows the progress of iterations, starting from the top. For inclusive scan, by definition, y_0 is x_0; thus, XY[0] contains its final answer. In the first iteration, each position other than XY[0] receives the sum of its current content and that of its left neighbor, as indicated by the first row of addition operators in Fig. 8.1. XY[i] contains $x_{i-1}+x_i$, as reflected in the labeling boxes under the first row of addition operators in Fig. 8.1. To illustrate, after the first iteration, XY[3] contains x_2+x_3, shown as $\sum x_2...x_3$ and XY[1] is equal to x_0+x_1, which is the final answer for this position. Thus, no further changes to XY[1] should be made in subsequent iterations.

In the second iteration, each position other than XY[0] and XY[1] receives the sum of its current content and that of the position that is two elements away, as illustrated in the labeling boxes below the second row of addition operators. XY[i] now contains $x_{i-3}+x_{i-2}+x_{i-1}+x_i$. To illustrate, after the first iteration, XY[3] contains $x_0+x_1+x_2+x_3$, shown as $\sum x_0...x_3$. After the second iteration, XY[2] and XY[3] contain their final answers and need no changes in subsequent iterations.

The reader is encouraged to work through the rest of the iterations. We now work on the parallel implementation of the algorithm illustrated in Fig. 8.1. We assign each thread to evolve the contents of one XY element. We will write a kernel that performs scan on **one section** of the input that is small enough for a block to handle. The size of a section is defined as the compile-time constant SECTION_SIZE. We assume that the kernel launch will use SECTION_SIZE as the block size so that the number of threads is equal to the number of section elements. Each thread will be responsible for calculating one output element.

All results will be calculated as if the array only contains the elements in the section. **Later on, we will make final adjustments to these sectional scan results for large input arrays.** We also assume that input values were originally in a global memory array X, whose address is passed to the kernel as an argument. We will have all the threads in the block to collaboratively load the X array elements into a shared memory array XY . Such loading is accomplished by having each thread calculate its global data index `i = blockIdx.x*blockDim.x + threadIdx.x` for the output vector element position it is responsible for. Each thread loads the input element at that position into the shared memory at the beginning of the kernel. At the end of the kernel, each thread will write its result into the assigned output array Y.

```
__global__ void Kogge_Stone_scan_kernel(float *X, float *Y,
  int InputSize) {

  __shared__ float XY[SECTION_SIZE];
  int i = blockIdx.x*blockDim.x + threadIdx.x;
  if (i < InputSize) {
    XY[threadIdx.x] = X[i];
  }
  // the code below performs iterative scan on XY
    ...

  Y[i] = XY[threadIdx.x];
}
```

We now focus on the implementation of the iterative calculations for each XY element in Fig. 8.1 as a `for` loop:

```
for (unsigned int stride = 1; stride < blockDim.x; stride
    *= 2) {
    __syncthreads();
    if (threadIdx.x >= stride) XY[threadIdx.x] +=
XY[threadIdx.x-stride];
    }
```

The loop iterates through the reduction tree for the XY array position assigned to a thread. We use a barrier synchronization to ensure that all threads have finished their previous iteration of additions in the reduction tree before any of them starts the next iteration. This is the same use of __syncthreads() as in the reduction discussion in Chapter 5, Performance Considerations. When the stride value exceeds the threadIdx.x value of a thread, the assigned XY position of the thread is understood to have accumulated all required input values.

The execution behavior of the for-loop is consistent with the example in Fig. 8.1. The actions of the smaller positions of XY end earlier than those of the larger positions. This behavior will cause a certain degree of control divergence in the first warp when stride values are small. Adjacent threads will tend to execute the same number of iterations. The effect of divergence should be quite modest for large block sizes. The detailed analysis is left as an exercise. The final kernel is shown in Fig. 8.2.

We can easily convert an inclusive scan kernel to an exclusive scan kernel. Recall that an exclusive scan is equivalent to an inclusive scan with all elements shifted to the right by one position and the element 0 filled with the value 0, as illustrated in Fig. 8.3. The only real difference is the alignment of elements on top of the picture.

```
__global__ void Kogge-Stone_scan_kernel(float *X, float *Y,
  int InputSize) {

  __shared__ float XY[SECTION_SIZE];

  int i = blockIdx.x*blockDim.x + threadIdx.x;
  if (i < InputSize) {
    XY[threadIdx.x] = X[i];
  }

  // the code below performs iterative scan on XY
  for (unsigned int stride = 1; stride < blockDim.x; stride *= 2) {
    __syncthreads();
    if (threadIdx.x >= stride)XY[threadIdx.x] += XY[threadIdx.x-stride];
  }

  Y[i] = XY[threadIdx.x];

}
```

FIGURE 8.2

A Kogge–Stone kernel for inclusive scan.

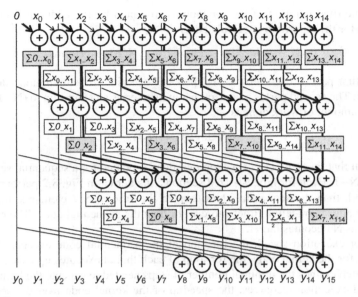

FIGURE 8.3

A parallel exclusive scan algorithm based on Kogge–Stone adder design.

All labeling boxes are updated to reflect the new alignment. All iterative operations remain the same.

We can now easily convert the kernel in Fig. 8.2 into an exclusive scan kernel. We only need to load 0 into XY[0] and X[i−1] into XY[threadIdx.x], as shown in the code below:

```
if (i < InputSize && threadIdx.x != 0) {
  XY[threadIdx.x] = X[i-1];
} else {
  XY[threadIdx.x] = 0;
}
```

Note that the XY positions whose associated input elements are outside the range are now also filled with 0, which causes no harm and yet simplifies the code slightly. We leave the rest of the steps to complete the exclusive scan kernel as an exercise.

8.3 SPEED AND WORK EFFICIENCY

We now analyze the speed and work efficiency of the kernel in Fig. 8.2. All threads will iterate up to $\log_2 N$ steps, where N is SECTION_SIZE. In each iteration, the number of inactive threads is equal to the stride size. Therefore, the amount of work done (one iteration of the for loop, represented by the addition operation in Fig. 8.1) for the algorithm is calculated as

$$\sum(N - stride), \text{for strides } 1, 2, 4, \ldots N/2 (\log_2 N \text{ terms})$$

The first part of each term is independent of stride; its summation adds up to $N*\log_2 N$. The second part is a familiar geometric series and sums up to $(N-1)$. Thus, the total amount of work done is

$$N*\log_2 N - (N-1)$$

Recall that the number of for-loop iterations executed for a sequential scan algorithm is $N-1$. Even for modest-sized sections, the kernel in Fig. 8.2 performs much more work than the sequential algorithm. In the case of 512 elements, the kernel performs approximately 8 times more work than the sequential code. The ratio will increase as N becomes larger.

As for execution speed, the for-loop of the sequential code executes N iterations. As for the kernel code, the for-loop of each thread executes up to $\log_2 N$ iterations, which defines the minimal number of steps needed to execute the kernel. With unlimited execution resources, the speedup of the kernel code over the sequential code would be approximately $N/\log_2 N$. For $N = 512$, the speedup would be about $512/9 = 56.9$.

In a real CUDA GPU device, the amount of work done by the Kogge–Stone kernel is more than the theoretical $N*\log_2 N-(N-1)$ because we are using N threads. While many of the threads stop participating in the execution of the for-loop, they still consume execution resources until the entire thread block completes execution. Realistically, the amount of execution resources consumed by the Kogge–Stone Stone is closer to $N*\log_2 N$.

The concept of time units will be used as an approximate indicator of execution time for comparing between scan algorithms. The sequential scan should take approximately N time units to process N input elements. For instance, the sequential scan should take approximately 1024 time units to process 1024 input elements. With P execution units (streaming processors) in the CUDA device, we can expect the Kogge–Stone kernel to execute for $(N*\log_2 N)/P$ time units. To illustrate, if we use 1024 threads and 32 execution units to process 1024 input elements, the kernel will likely take $(1024*10)/32 = 320$ time units. In this case, a speedup of $1024/320 = 3.2$ is expected.

The additional work done by the Kogge–Stone kernel over the sequential code is problematic in two ways. First, the use of hardware for executing the parallel kernel is much less efficient. A parallel machine requires at least 8 times more execution units than the sequential machine just to break even. If we execute the kernel on a parallel machine with four times the execution resources as a sequential machine, the parallel machine executing the parallel kernel can end up with only half the speed of the sequential machine executing the sequential code. Second, the extra work consumes additional energy. This additional demand makes the kernel less appropriate for power-constrained environments such as mobile applications.

The strength of the Kogge–Stone kernel lies in its satisfactory execution speed given sufficient hardware resource. The Kogge-Stone kernel is typically used to calculate the scan result for a section with a modest number of elements, such as 32 or 64. Its execution has very limited amount of control divergence. In newer GPU architecture generations, its computation can be efficiently performed with shuffle instructions within warps. We will see later in this chapter that the Kogge-Stone kernel is an important component of the modern high-speed parallel scan algorithms.

8.4 A MORE WORK-EFFICIENT PARALLEL SCAN

While the Kogge–Stone kernel in Fig. 8.2 is conceptually simple, its work efficiency is quite low for some practical applications. Mere inspection of Figs. 8.1 and 8.3 indicates potential opportunities presented by sharing several intermediate results to streamline the operations performed. However, we need to strategically calculate the intermediate results to be shared and then readily distribute them to different threads in order to allow more sharing across multiple threads.

As we know, the fastest parallel way to produce sum values for a set of values is a reduction tree. With sufficient execution units, a reduction tree can generate the sum for N values in $\log_2 N$ time units. The tree can also generate a number of sub-sums that can be used to calculate some scan output values. This observation forms the basis of the Brent–Kung adder design [BK 1979], which can also be used in a parallel scan algorithm.

In Fig. 8.4, we produce the sum of all 16 elements in four steps. We use the minimal number of operations needed to generate the sum. In the first step, only the odd element of XY[i] will be updated to XY[i-1]+XY[i]. In the second step, only the XY elements whose indexes are of the form 4*n−1 will be updated; these elements are

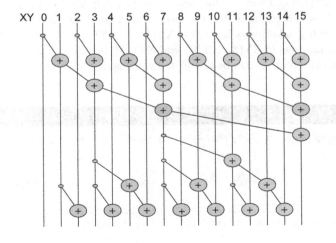

FIGURE 8.4

A parallel inclusive scan algorithm based on the Brent–Kung adder design.

3, 7, 11, 15 in Fig. 8.4. In the third step, only the XY elements whose indexes are of the form $8*n-1$ will be updated; these elements are 7 and 15. Finally, in the fourth step, only XY[15] is updated. The total number of operations performed is $8 + 4 + 2 + 1 = 15$. In general, for a scan section of N elements, we would do $(N/2) + (N/4) + \ldots + 2 + 1 = N-1$ operations for this reduction phase.

The second part of the algorithm is to use a reverse tree in order to distribute the partial sums to the positions that can use these values as quickly as possible, as illustrated in the bottom half of Fig. 8.4. At the end of the reduction phase, we have quite a few usable partial sums. The first row in Fig. 8.5 shows all the partial sums in XY right after the top reduction tree. An important observation is that XY[0], XY[7], and X[15] contain their final answers. Therefore, all remaining XY elements can obtain the partial sums they need from no farther than four positions away.

To illustrate, XY[14] can obtain all partial sums it needs from XY[7], XY[11], and XY[13]. To organize our second half of the addition operations, we will first show all operations that need partial sums from four positions away, then two positions away, and 1 position way. By inspection, XY[7] contains a critical value needed by many positions in the right half. A satisfactory method is to add XY[7] to XY[11], which brings XY[11] to the final answer. More importantly, XY[7] also becomes a good partial sum for XY[12], XY[13], and XY[14]. No other partial sums have so many uses. Therefore, only one addition XY[11] = XY[7] + XY[11] needs to occur at the four-position level in Fig. 8.4. The updated partial sum is shown in the second row in Fig. 8.5.

We now identify all additions by using partial sums that are two positions away. XY[2] only needs the partial sum adjacent to it in XY[1]. XY[4] likewise needs the partial sum next to it to be complete. The first XY element that can need a partial sum two positions away is XY[5]. Once we calculate XY[5] = XY[3] + XY[5], XY[5] contains the final answer. The same analysis indicates that XY[6] and XY[8] can become complete with the partial sums adjacent to them in XY[5] and XY[7].

The next two-position addition is XY[9] = XY[7] + XY[9], which makes XY[9] complete. XY[10] can wait for the next round to catch XY[9]. XY[12] only needs the XY[11], which contains its final answer after the four-position addition. The final two-position addition is XY[13] = XY[11] + XY[13]. The third row shows all updated partial sums in XY[5], XY[9], and XY[13]. It is clear that now, every position is either complete or can be completed when added by their left neighbor. This

0	1	2	3	4	5	6	7	8	9	10	11	12	13	14	15
x_0	$x_0..x_1$	x_2	$x_0..x_3$	x_4	$x_4..x_5$	x_6	$x_0..x_7$	x_8	$x_8..x_9$	x_{10}	$x_8..x_{11}$	x_{12}	$x_{12}..x_{13}$	x_{14}	$x_0..x_{15}$
											$x_0..x_{11}$				
					$x_0..x_5$				$x_0..x_9$				$x_0..x_{13}$		

FIGURE 8.5

Partial sums available in each XY element after the reduction tree phase.

leads to the final row of additions in Fig. 8.4, which completes the contents for all of the incomplete positions XY[2], XY[4], XY[6], XY[8], XY[10], and XY[12].

We could implement the reduction tree phase of the parallel scan by using the following loop:

```
for (unsigned int stride = 1; stride <= blockDim.x; stride *= 2) {
  __syncthreads();
  if ((threadIdx.x + 1)%(2*stride) == 0) {
    XY[threadIdx.x] += XY[threadIdx.x - stride];
  }
}
```

This loop is highly similar to the reduction in Fig. 5.2. The only difference is that we want the threads with a thread index in the form 2^n-1 rather than 2^n to perform addition in each iteration. This objective is the reason for adding 1 to threadIdx.x when we select the threads for performing addition in each iteration. However, this style of reduction involves control divergence problems. As seen in Chapter 5, Performance Considerations, a preferable technique is to use a decreasing number of contiguous threads to perform the additions as the loop advances:

```
for (unsigned int stride = 1; stride <= blockDim.x; stride *= 2) {
  __syncthreads();
  int index = (threadIdx.x+1) * 2* stride -1;
  if (index < SECTION_SIZE) {
    XY[index] += XY[index - stride];
  }
}
```

By using a more complex index calculation in each iteration of the for-loop, kernel execution has much fewer control divergence within warps. Fig. 8.4 shows 16 threads in a block. In the first iteration, a stride is equal to 1. The first eight consecutive threads in the block will satisfy the if condition. The index values calculated for these threads will be 1, 3, 5, 7, 9, 11, 13, and 15. These threads will perform the first row of additions in Fig. 8.4. In the second iteration, a stride is equal to 2. Only the first four threads in the block will satisfy the if condition. The index values calculated for these threads will be 3, 7, 11, 15. These threads will perform the second row of additions in Fig. 8.4. Since each iteration will always be using consecutive threads in each iteration, the control divergence problem does not arise until the number of active threads drops below the warp size.

The distribution tree is slightly more complex to implement. We observe that the stride value decreases from SECTION_SIZE/4 to 1. In each iteration, we need to "push" the value of the XY element from a position that is a multiple of the stride value minus 1 to a position that is a stride away. For example, in Fig. 8.4, the stride value decreases from 4 to 1. In the first iteration in Fig. 8.4, we aim to push the value of XY[7] to XY[11], where 7 is 2*4−1. Note that only one thread (thread 0) is needed for this iteration. In the second iteration, we intend to push the values of

186 CHAPTER 8 Parallel patterns: prefix sum

XY[3], XY[7], and XY[11] to XY[5], XY[9], and XY[13]. This plan can be implemented using the following loop:

```
for (int stride = SECTION_SIZE/4; stride > 0; stride /= 2) {
  __syncthreads();
  int index = (threadIdx.x+1)*stride*2 - 1;
  if(index + stride < SECTION_SIZE) {
    XY[index + stride] += XY[index];
  }
}
```

The calculation of the index is similar to that in the reduction tree phase. The final kernel code for a Brent–Kung parallel scan is presented in Fig. 8.6. The reader should notice that having more than SECTION_SIZE/2 threads is unnecessary for the reduction phase or the distribution phase. Thus, we could simply launch a kernel with SECTION_SIZE/2 threads in a block. Since we can have up to 1024 threads in a block, each scan section can have up to 2048 elements. However, each thread has to load two X elements at the beginning and store two Y elements at the end.

As in the case of the Kogge–Stone scan kernel, the Brent–Kung inclusive parallel scan kernel can be easily adapted into an exclusive scan kernel, with a minor adjustment to the statement that loads X elements into XY. [Harris 2007] presents an interesting natively exclusive scan kernel based on a different method of designing the distribution tree phase of the scan kernel.

```
__global__ void Brent_Kung_scan_kernel(float *X, float *Y,
  int InputSize) {

  __shared__ float XY[SECTION_SIZE];
  int i = 2*blockIdx.x*blockDim.x + threadIdx.x;
  if (i < InputSize) XY[threadIdx.x] = X[i];
  if (i+blockDim.x < InputSize) XY[threadIdx.x+blockDim.x] = X[i+blockDim.x];

  for (unsigned int stride = 1; stride <= blockDim.x; stride *= 2) {
    __syncthreads();
    int index = (threadIdx.x+1) * 2* stride -1;
    if (index < SECTION_SIZE) {
      XY[index] += XY[index - stride];
    }
  }

  for (int stride = SECTION_SIZE/4; stride > 0; stride /= 2) {
    __syncthreads();
    int index = (threadIdx.x+1)*stride*2 - 1;
    if(index + stride < SECTION_SIZE) {
      XY[index + stride] += XY[index];
    }
  }

  __syncthreads();
  if (i < InputSize) Y[i] = XY[threadIdx.x];
  if (i+blockDim.x < InputSize) Y[i+blockDim.x] = XY[threadIdx.x+blockDim.x];
}
```

FIGURE 8.6

A Brent–Kung kernel for inclusive scan.

We now turn our attention to the analysis of the number of operations in the distribution tree stage. The number of operations is $(2 - 1) + (4 - 1) + (16/2 - 1)$. In general, for N input elements, the total number of operations would be $(2 - 1) + (4 - 1) + ... + (N/4 - 1) + (N/2 - 1)$, which is $N\text{-}1\text{-}\log_2(N)$. This expression results in the total number of operations in the parallel scan, $2N\text{-}2\text{-}\log_2(N)$, including both the reduction tree $(N - 1$ operations) and the inverse reduction tree phases ($N\text{-}1\text{-}\log_2(N)$ operations). The number of operations is now proportional to N rather than $N*\log_2(N)$.

The advantage of the Brent–Kung algorithm is rather clear in the comparison. As the input section increases, the Brent–Kung algorithm never performs more than twice the number of operations performed by the sequential algorithm. In an energy-constrained execution environment, the Brent–Kung algorithm strikes a good balance between parallelism and efficiency.

While the Brent–Kung algorithm exhibits a considerably higher level of theoretical work-efficiency than the Kogge–Stone algorithm, its advantage in a CUDA kernel implementation is more limited. Recall that the Brent–Kung algorithm is using N/2 threads. The major difference is that the number of active threads drops much faster through the reduction tree than the Kogge–Stone algorithm. However, the inactive threads continue to consume execution resources in a CUDA device. Consequently, the amount of resources consumed by the Brent–Kung kernel is actually closer to $(N/2)*(2*\log_2(N)-1)$. This finding makes the work-efficiency of the Brent–Kung algorithm similar to that of Kogge–Stone in a CUDA device. In Section 8.4, if we process 1024 input elements with 32 execution units, the Brent–Kung kernel is expected to take approximately $512*(2*10-1)/32 = 304$ time units. This results in a speedup of $1024/304 = 3.4$.

8.5 AN EVEN MORE WORK-EFFICIENT PARALLEL SCAN

We can design a parallel scan algorithm that achieves a higher work efficiency than does the Brent–Kung algorithm by adding a phase of fully independent scans on the subsections of the input. At the beginning of the algorithm, we partition the input section into subsections. The number of subsections is the same as the number of threads in a thread block, one for each thread. During the first phase, each thread performs a scan on its subsection. In Fig. 8.7, we assume that a block contains four threads; we partition the input section into four subsections. During the first phase, thread 0 will perform a scan on its section (2, 1, 3, 1) and generate (2, 3, 6, 7). Thread 1 will perform a scan on its section (0, 4, 1, 2) and generate (0, 4, 5, 7), and so on.

Notably, if each thread directly performs a scan by accessing the input from global memory, their accesses would not be coalesced. For instance, in the first iteration, thread 0 would be accessing the input element 0, thread 1 input element 4, and so on. Therefore, we use the **corner turning** technique presented in Chapter 4, Memory and Data Locality, to improve memory coalescing. At the beginning of the phase, all threads collaborate to load the input into the shared memory iteratively. In each iteration, adjacent threads load adjacent elements to enable memory coalescing.

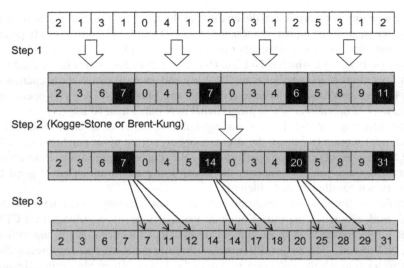

FIGURE 8.7

Three-phase parallel scan for higher work efficiency and speed.

In Fig. 8.7, all threads have to collaborate and load four elements in a coalesced manner: thread 0 to load element 0, thread 1 to load element 1, and so on. All threads move to load the next four elements: thread 0 to load element 4, thread 1 to load element 5, and so on.

Once all input elements are in the shared memory, the threads access their own subsection from the shared memory, as shown in Fig. 8.7 as Step 1. At the end of Step 1, the last element of each section (highlighted in black in the second row) contains the sum of all input elements in the section. The last element of section 0 contains the value 7, which is the sum of the input elements (2, 1, 3, 1) in the section.

During the second phase, all threads in each block collaborate and perform a scan operation on a logical array that consists of the last elements of all sections. This procedure can be performed using a Kogge–Stone or Brent–Kung algorithm since only a modest number (number of threads in a block) of elements are involved. In Step 3, each thread adds to its elements the new value of the last element of its predecessor's section. The last elements of each subsection need not be updated during this phase. In Fig. 8.7, thread 1 adds the value 7 to elements (0, 4, 5) in its section in order to produce (7, 11, 12). Note that the last element of the section is already the correct value 14 and requires no updating.

Using this three-phase approach, we can use a much smaller number of threads than the number of elements in a section. The maximal size of the section is no longer limited by the number of threads in the block but rather, the size of the shared memory; all elements in the section must fit into the shared memory. This limitation will be removed in the hierarchical methods, which will be discussed in the remainder of this chapter.

The major advantage of the three-phase approach is its efficiency use of execution resources. Assume that we use the Kogge–Stone algorithm for phase 2. For an input list of N elements, if we use T threads, the amount of work done is N−1 for phase 1, $T*\log_2 T$ for phase 2, and N−T for phase 3. If we use P execution units, the execution can be expected to take $(N−1+T*\log_2 T+N−T)/P$ time units.

To illustrate, if we use 64 threads and 32 execution units to process 1024 elements, the algorithm should take approximately (1024−1+ 64*6+ 1024−64)/32= 74 time units. This number results in a speedup of 1024/74= 13.8.

8.6 HIERARCHICAL PARALLEL SCAN FOR ARBITRARY-LENGTH INPUTS

For a number of applications, a scan operation can process elements in the millions or even billions. The three kernels presented thus far assume that the entire input can be loaded in the shared memory. Obviously, we cannot expect all input elements of these large scan applications to fit into the shared memory, which is why we say that these kernels process a section of the input. Furthermore, using only one thread block to process these large data sets would be a loss of parallelism opportunity.

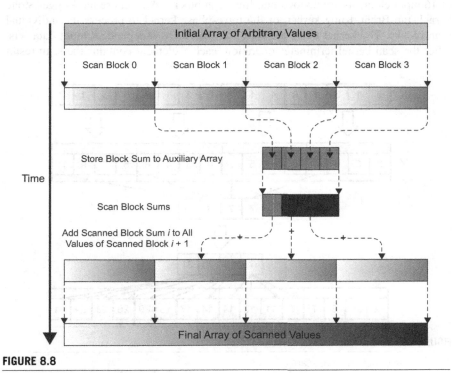

FIGURE 8.8

A hierarchical scan for arbitrary length inputs.

Fortunately, a hierarchical approach can extend the scan kernels that we have generated so far to handle inputs of arbitrary size. The approach is illustrated in Fig. 8.8.

For a large data set, we first partition the input into sections so that each of them can fit into the shared memory and be processed by a single block. For the current generation of CUDA devices, the Brent–Kung kernel in Fig. 8.8 can process up to 2048 elements in each section by using 1024 threads in each block. To illustrate, if the input data consist of 2,000,000 elements, we can use ceil (2,000,000/2048.0) = 977 thread blocks. With up to 65,536 thread blocks in the x-dimension of a grid, this approach can process up to 134,217,728 elements in the input set. If the input is larger than this number, additional levels of hierarchy can be used to handle a truly arbitrary number of input elements. However, for this chapter, we will restrict our discussion to a two-level hierarchy that can process up to 134,217,728 elements.

Assume that we launch one of the three kernels in Sections 8.2, 8.4, and 8.5 on a large input data set. At the end of the grid execution, the Y array will contain the scan results for individual sections, called *scan blocks*, in Fig. 8.8. Each result value in a scan block only contains the accumulated values of all preceding elements within the same scan block. These scan blocks need to be combined into the final result; i.e., we need to write and launch another kernel that adds the sum of all elements in preceding scan blocks to each element of a scan block.

Fig. 8.9 shows an example of the hierarchical scan approach in Fig. 8.8. A total of 16 input elements are divided into four scan blocks. We can use the Kogge–Stone kernel, the Brent–Kung kernel, or the three-phase kernel to process the individual scan blocks. The kernel treats the four scan blocks as independent input data sets. After the scan kernel terminates operation, each Y element contains the scan result

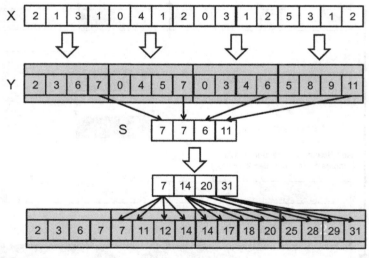

FIGURE 8.9

An example of hierarchical scan.

within its scan block. To illustrate, scan block 1 has inputs 0, 4, 1, 2. The scan kernel produces the scan result for this section: 0, 4, 5, 7. These results do not include contributions from any of the elements in scan block 0. In order to produce the final result for this scan block, the sum of all elements in scan block 0—i.e., 2+1+3+1 = 7–should be added to every result element of scan block 1.

Another illustration is as follows: The inputs in scan block 2 are 0, 3, 1, 2. The kernel produces the scan result for this scan block: 0, 3, 4, 6. To produce the final results for this scan block, the sum of all elements in both scan block 0 and scan block 1, 2+1+3+1+0+4+1+2 = 14, should be added to every result element of scan block 2.

The last output element of each scan block yields the sum of all input elements of the scan block. These values are 7, 7, 6, and 11 in Fig. 8.9. The second step of the hierarchical scan algorithm in Fig. 8.8 gathers the last result elements from each scan block into an array and performs a scan on these output elements. This step is also illustrated in Fig. 8.9, where the last scan output elements of all collected into a new array S.

This procedure can be carried out by changing the code at the end of the scan kernel so that the last thread of each block writes its result into an S array by using its blockIdx.x as index. A scan operation is then performed on S to produce the output values 7, 14, 20, 31. Each of these second-level scan output values is an accumulated sum from the starting location X[0] to the end of each scan block. The output value in S[0]=7 is the accumulated sum from X[0] to the end of scan block 0, which is X[3]. The output value in S[1]=14 is the accumulated sum, from X[0] to the end of scan block 1, which is X[7].[1]

Therefore, the output values in the S array yield the scan results at "strategic" locations of the original scan problem. In Fig. 8.9, the output values in S[0], S[1], S[2], and S[3] provide the final scan results for the original problem at positions X[3], X[7], X[11], and X[15]. These outcomes can be used to bring the partial results in each scan block to their final values. This brings us to the last step of the hierarchical scan algorithm in Fig. 8.8. The second-level scan output values are added to the values of their corresponding scan blocks.

To illustrate, in Fig. 8.9, the value of S[0] (value 7) will be added to Y[0], Y[1], Y[2], Y[3] of thread block 1, thereby completing the results in these positions. The final results in these positions are 7, 11, 12, 14 as S[0] contains the sum of the values of the original input X[0] through X[3]. These final results are 14, 17, 18, and 20. The value of S[1] (14) will be added to Y[8], Y[9], Y[10], Y[11], thereby completing the results in these positions. The value of S[2] (20) will be added to Y[12], Y[13], Y[14], Y[15]. Finally, the value of S[3] is the sum of all elements of the original input, which is also the final result in Y[15].

Readers who are familiar with computer arithmetic algorithms should recognize that the hierarchical scan algorithm is quite similar to the carry look-ahead in the

---

[1] While the second step of Figure 8.9 is logically the same as the second step of Figure 8.7. The main difference is that Figure 8.9 involves threads from different thread blocks. As a result, the last element of each section needs to be collected into a global memory array so that they can be visible across thread blocks.

hardware adders of modern processors. This similarity should be expected considering that the two parallel scan algorithms we have examined thus far are based on innovative hardware adder designs.

We can implement the hierarchical scan with three kernels. The first kernel is largely the same as the three-phase kernel. (We could just as easily use the Kogge–Stone kernel or the Brent–Kung kernel.) We need to add a parameter S, which has the dimension of InputSize/SECTION_SIZE. At the end of the kernel, we add a conditional statement. The last thread in the block writes the output value of the last XY element in the scan block to the blockIdx.x position of S:

```
__syncthreads();
if (threadIdx.x == blockDim.x-1) {
  S[blockIdx.x] = XY[SECTION_SIZE - 1];
}
```

The second kernel is simply one of the three parallel scan kernels, which takes S as input and writes S as output.

The third kernel takes the S and Y arrays as inputs and writes its output back into Y. Assuming that we launch the kernel with SECTION_SIZE threads in each block, each thread adds one of the S elements (selected by blockIdx.x-1) to one Y element:

```
int i = blockIdx.x * blockDim.x + threadIdx.x;
Y[i] += S[blockIdx.x-1];
```

The threads in a block add the sum of the previous scan block to the elements of their scan block. As an exercise, completing the details of each kernel and the host code is left to the reader.

8.7 SINGLE-PASS SCAN FOR MEMORY ACCESS EFFICIENCY

In the hierarchical scan mentioned in Section 8.6, the partially scanned results are stored into the global memory before the global scan kernel is launched and then reloaded back from the global memory by the third kernel. The latencies of these extra memory stores and loads do not overlap with the computation in the subsequent kernels. The latencies can also significantly influence the speed of the hierarchical scan algorithms. Multiple techniques [DGS 2008] [YLZ 2013] [MG 2016] have been proposed to avoid such a negative impact. A stream-based scan algorithm is discussed in this chapter. The reader is encouraged to read the references in order to understand the other techniques.

In the context of CUDA C programming, a stream-based scan algorithm (not to be confused with CUDA Streams, which will be introduced in chapter: Programming a Heterogeneous Computing Cluster) refers to a hierarchical scan algorithm where partial sum data are passed in one direction through the global memory between neighboring thread blocks. Stream-based scan builds on a key observation that the global scan step (middle part in Fig. 8.8) can be performed in a domino fashion. For example, in Fig. 8.9, Scan Block 0 can pass its partial sum value 7 to Scan Block 1 and then complete its job. Scan Block 1 receives the partial sum value 7 from Scan Block 0, sums up with its local partial sum value 7 to get 14, passes its partial sum value 14 to Scan Block 2, and then completes its final step.

In a stream-based scan, a single kernel can be written to perform all three steps of the hierarchical scan algorithm in Fig. 8.8. Thread block i first performs a scan on its scan block, using one of the three parallel algorithms in Sections 8.2–8.5. The block then waits for its left neighbor block i−1 to pass the sum value. Once the sum from block i−1 is received, the block generates and passes its sum value to its right neighbor block i+1. The block then moves on to add the sum value received from block i−1 in order to complete all the output values of the scan block.

During the first phase of the kernel, all blocks can execute in parallel. The blocks will be serialized during the data streaming phase. However, as soon as each block receives the sum value from its predecessor, the block can perform its final phase in parallel with all other blocks that have received the sum values from their predecessors. As long as the sum values can be passed through the blocks quickly, there can be ample parallelism among blocks.

To make this stream-based scan work, adjacent (block) synchronization has been proposed in [YLZ 2013]. Adjacent synchronization is a customized synchronization to allow the adjacent thread blocks to synchronize and/or exchange data. In a scan, data are passed from Scan Block i−1 to Scan Block i, similar to a producer–consumer chain. On the producer side (Scan Block i−1), the flag is set to a particular value after the partial sum is stored to the memory, whereas on the consumer side (Scan Block i), the flag is checked to determine whether it is that particular value before the passed partial sum is loaded. As previously mentioned, the loaded value is added to the local sum and is then passed to the next block (Scan Block i+1). Adjacent synchronization can be implemented using atomic operations. The following code segment illustrates the use of atomic operations to implement adjacent synchronization.

```
__shared__ float previous_sum;
if (threadIdx.x == 0){
  // Wait for previous flag
  while (atomicAdd(&flags[bid], 0) == 0){;}
  // Read previous partial sum
  previous_sum = scan_value[bid];
  // Propagate partial sum
  scan_value[bid + 1] = previous_sum + local_sum;
  // Memory fence
  __threadfence();
  // Set flag
  atomicAdd(&flags[bid + 1], 1);
}
__syncthreads();
```

This code section is only executed by one leader thread in each block (e.g., thread with index 0). The rest of the threads will wait in __syncthreads() in the last line. In block bid, the leader thread repeatedly checks flags[bid], a global memory array, until it is set. It then loads the partial sum from its predecessor by accessing the global memory array scan_value[bid] and stores the value into its local register variable, previous_sum. It sums up with its local partial sum local sum and stores the result into the global memory array `scan_value[bid+1]`. The memory fence function `__threadfence()` ensures that the partial sum is completely stored to memory before the flag is set with `atomicAdd()`. The array `scan_value` must be declared as volatile to prevent the compiler from optimizing, reordering, or register-allocating the accesses to scan_value elements.

The atomic operations on the flags array and the accesses to the `scan_value` array could appear to incur global memory traffic; however, these operations are mostly performed in the second-level caches of recent GPU architectures (more details in chapter: Parallel Patterns: Parallel Histogram Computation). Any stores and loads to the global memory will likely be overlapped with the phase 1 and phase 3 computational activities of other blocks. Meanwhile, when executing the three-kernel scan algorithm in Section 8.5, the stores to and loads from the S array elements in the global memory are in a separate kernel and cannot be overlapped with phase 1 and phase 3.

Stream-based algorithms have one subtle issue. In GPUs, thread blocks may not *always* be scheduled linearly in accordance with their blockIdx values; Scan Block i may be scheduled and performed after Scan Block i+1. In this situation, the execution order arranged by the scheduler may contradict the order assumed by the adjacent synchronization code and cause performance loss or even a dead lock. For instance, the scheduler may schedule Scan Block i through Scan Block i+N before it schedules Scan Block i−1. If Scan Block i through Scan Block i+N occupies all streaming multiprocessors, Scan Block i−1 would not be able to start execution until at least one of them finishes execution. However, all of them are waiting for the sum value from Scan Block i−1. This scenario causes the system to deadlock.

To resolve this issue, multiple techniques [YLZ 2013] [GSO 2012] have been proposed. Here, we only discuss one particular method, dynamic block index assignment; the rest is left as reference for readers. Dynamic block index assignment basically decouples the usage of the thread block index from the built-in blockIdx.x. In scan, the particular i of the Scan Block i is no longer tied to the value of blockIdx.x. Instead, it is calculated using the following code after the thread block is scheduled:

```
__shared__ int sbid;
if (threadIdx.x == 0)
  sbid = atomicAdd(DCounter, 1);
__syncthreads();
const int bid = sbid;
```

The leader thread increments atomically a global counter variable pointed by `DCounter`. The global counter stores the dynamic block index of the next block that is scheduled. The leader thread then stores the acquired dynamic block index value in a shared memory variable, `sbid`, so that it is accessible by all threads of the block after `__syncthreads()`. This process guarantees that all Scan Blocks are scheduled linearly and prevents a potential deadlock.

8.8 SUMMARY

In this chapter, we studied scan as an important parallel computing pattern. Scan enables parallel allocation of resources to parties whose needs are not uniform. The process converts a seemingly sequential recursive computation into a parallel computation, which helps reduce sequential bottlenecks in various applications. We show that a simple sequential scan algorithm performs only N additions for an input of N elements.

We first introduced a parallel Kogge–Stone scan algorithm that is fast and conceptually simple but not work-efficient. As the data set size increases, the number of execution units needed for a parallel algorithm to break even with the simple sequential algorithm also increases. For an input of 1024 elements, the parallel algorithm performs over nine times more additions than the sequential algorithm. The algorithm also requires at least nine times more execution resources to break even with the sequential algorithm. Thus, Kogge–Stone scan algorithms are typically used within modest-sized scan blocks.

We then presented a parallel Brent–Kung scan algorithm that is conceptually more complicated than the Kogge–Stone algorithm. Using a reduction tree phase and a distribution tree phase, the algorithm performs only $2*N-3$ additions regardless of the size of the input data set. With its number of operations increasing linearly with the size of the input set, thus work-efficient algorithm is often referred to as data-scalable algorithm. Unfortunately, due to the nature of threads in a CUDA device, the resource consumption of a Brent–Kung kernel ends up very similar to that of a Kogge–Stone kernel. A three-phase scan algorithm that employs corner turning and barrier synchronization proves to be effective in addressing the work-efficiency problem.

We also presented a hierarchical approach to extending the parallel scan algorithms in order to manage arbitrary-sized input sets. Unfortunately, a straightforward, three-kernel implementation of the hierarchical scan algorithm incurs redundant global memory accesses whose latencies are not overlapped with computation. We show that one can use a stream-based hierarchical scan algorithm to enable a single-pass, single kernel implementation and improve the global memory access efficiency of the hierarchical scan algorithm. However, this algorithm requires a carefully designed adjacent block synchronization using atomic operations, thread memory fence, and barrier synchronization. In addition, special care is needed to prevent deadlocks using dynamic block index assignment.

8.9 EXERCISES

1. Analyze the parallel scan kernel in Fig. 8.2. Show that control divergence only occurs in the first warp of each block for stride values up to half the warp size; i.e., for warp size 32, control divergence will occur to iterations for stride values 1, 2, 4, 8, and 16.

2. For the Brent–Kung scan kernel, assume that we have 2048 elements. How many additions will be performed in both the reduction tree phase and the inverse reduction tree phase?
   a. (2048−1)*2
   b. (1024−1)*2
   c. 1024*1024
   d. 10*1024

3. For the Kogge–Stone scan kernel based on reduction trees, assume that we have 2048 elements. Which of the following gives the closest approximation of the number of additions that will be performed?
   a. (2048−1)*2
   b. (1024−1)*2
   c. 1024*1024
   d. 10*1024

4. Use the algorithm in Fig. 8.3 to complete an exclusive scan kernel.

5. Complete the host code and all three kernels for the hierarchical parallel scan algorithm in Fig. 8.9.

6. Analyze the hierarchical parallel scan algorithm and show that it is work-efficient and the total number of additions is no more than 4*N−3.

7. Consider the following array: [4 6 7 1 2 8 5 2]. Perform a parallel inclusive prefix scan on the array by using the Kogge-Stone algorithm. Report the intermediate states of the array after each step.

8. Repeat the previous problem by using the work-efficient algorithm.

9. By using the two-level hierarchical scan discussed in Section 8.5, determine the largest possible dataset that can be handled if computing on a:
   a. GeForce GTX 280?
   b. Tesla C2050?
   c. GeForce GTX 690?

REFERENCES

Brent, R. P., & Kung, H. T. (1979). *"A regular layout for parallel adders,"* Technical Report. Computer Science Department, Carnegie-Mellon University.

Dotsenko, Y., Govindaraju, N. K., Sloan, P.-P., Boyd, C., & Manferdelli, J. (2008). Fast scan algorithms on graphics processors. In *Proceedings of the 22nd annual international conference on supercomputing* (pp. 205–213).

Gupta, K., Stuart, J.A. & Owens, J.D. (2012). A study of persistent threads style GPU programming for GPGPU Workloads. In *Innovative parallel computing (InPar)*, (pp. 1–14). IEEE.

Harris, M., Sengupta, S., & Owens, J.D. (2007). Parallel prefix sum with CUDA, GPU Gems
  3. <http://developer.download.nvidia.com/compute/cuda/1_1/Website/projects/scan/doc/
  scan.pdf>.
Kogge, P., & Stone, H. (1973). A parallel algorithm for the efficient solution of a general class
  of recurrence equations. *IEEE Transactions on Computers, C-22*, 783–791.
Merrill, D. & Garland, M. (March 2016). *Single-pass parallel prefix scan with decoupled look-
  back*. Technical Report NVR2016-001, NVIDIA Research.
Yan, S., Long, G., & Zhang, Y. (2013), StreamScan: fast scan algorithms for GPUs without global barrier synchronization, PPoPP. In *ACM SIGPLAN Notices* (Vol. 48, No. 8,
  pp. 229–238).

Parallel patterns—parallel histogram computation

An introduction to atomic operations and privatization

CHAPTER OUTLINE

The parallel computation patterns that we have presented so far all allow the task of computing each output element to be assigned to a thread. Therefore, these patterns are amenable to the owner-computes rule, where every thread can write into their designated output element(s) without concern about interference from other threads. This chapter introduces the parallel histogram computation pattern, a frequently encountered application computing pattern where each output element can potentially be updated by all threads. As such, one must take care to coordinate among threads as they update output elements and avoid any interference that corrupts the final results. In practice, there are many other important parallel computation patterns where output interference cannot be easily avoided. Therefore, the parallel histogram computation pattern provides an example with output interference in these patterns. We will first examine a baseline approach that uses *atomic operations* to serialize the updates to each element. This baseline approach is simple but inefficient, often resulting in disappointing execution speed. We will then present some widely used optimization techniques, most notably privatization, to significantly enhance execution speed while preserving correctness. The cost and benefit of these techniques depend on the underlying hardware as well as the characteristics of the input data. It is therefore important for a developer to understand the key ideas of these techniques in order to soundly reason about their applicability under different circumstances.

Programming Massively Parallel Processors. DOI: http://dx.doi.org/10.1016/B978-0-12-811986-0.00009-1

9.1 BACKGROUND

A histogram is a display of the frequency of data items in successive numerical intervals. In the most common form of histogram, the value intervals are plotted along the horizontal axis and the frequency of data items in each interval is represented as the height of a rectangle, or bar, rising from the horizontal axis. For example, a histogram can be used to show the frequency of alphabets in the phrase "programming massively parallel processors." For simplicity, we assume that the input phrase is in all lowercase. By inspection, we see that there are four "a" letters, zero 'b' letters, one "c" letter, and so on. We define each value interval as a continuous range of four alphabets. Thus, the first value interval is "a" through "d", the second "e" through "h", and so on. Fig. 9.1 shows the histogram that displays the frequency of letters in the phrase "programming massively parallel processors" according to our definition of value interval.

Histograms provide useful summaries of data sets. In our example, we can see that the phrase being represented consists of letters that are heavily concentrated in the middle intervals of the alphabet and very light in the later intervals. Such shape of the histogram is sometimes referred to as a *feature* of the data set, and provides a quick way to determine if there are significant phenomena in the data set. For example, the shape of a histogram of the purchase categories and locations of a credit card account can be used to detect fraudulent usage. When the shape of the histogram deviates significantly from the norm, the system raises a flag of potential concern.

Many other application domains rely on histograms to summarize data sets for data analysis. One such area is computer vision. Histograms of different types of object images, such as faces versus cars, tend to exhibit different shapes. By dividing an image into subareas and analyzing the histograms for these subareas, one can quickly identify the interesting subareas of an image that potentially contain the objects of interest. The process of computing histograms of image subareas is the basis of *feature extraction* in computer vision, where feature refers to patterns of interest in images. In practice, whenever there is a large volume of data that needs

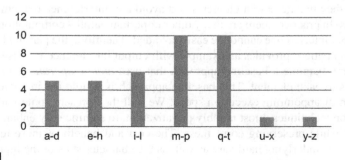

FIGURE 9.1

A histogram representation of "programming massively parallel processors."

to be analyzed to distill interesting events (i.e., "Big Data"), histograms are likely used as a foundational computation. Credit card fraudulence detection and computer vision obviously meet this description. Other application domains with such needs include speech recognition, website purchase recommendations, and scientific data analysis such as correlating heavenly object movements in astrophysics.

Histograms can be easily computed in a sequential manner, as shown in Fig. 9.2. For simplicity, the function is only required to recognize lowercase letters. The C code assumes that the input data set comes in a char array *data[]* and the histogram will be generated into the int array *histo[]* (Line 1). The number of data items is specified in function parameter *length*. The *for* loop (Line 2 through Line 4) sequentially traverses the array, identifies the particular alphabet index into the *index* variable, and increments the *histo[index/4]* element associated with that interval. The calculation of the alphabet index relies on the fact that the input string is based on the standard ASCII code representation where the alphabet characters "a" through "z" are encoded in consecutive values according to the alphabet order.

Although one may not know the exact encoded value of each letter, one can assume that the encoded value of a letter is the encoded value of "a" plus the alphabet position difference between that letter and "a". In the input, each character is stored in its encoded value. Thus, the expression *data[i] – "a"* (Line 3) derives the alphabet position of the letter with the position of "a" being 0. If the position value is greater than or equal to 0 and less than 26, the data character is indeed a lowercase alphabet letter (Line 4). Keep in mind that we defined the intervals such that each interval contains four alphabet letters. Therefore, the interval index for the letter is its alphabet position value divided by 4. We use the interval index to increment the appropriate *histo[]* array element (Line 4).

The C code in Fig. 9.2 is quite simple and efficient. The data array elements are accessed sequentially in the for loop so the CPU cache lines are well used whenever they are fetched from the system DRAM. The *histo[]* array is so small that it fits well in the level-one (L1) data cache of the CPU, which ensures very fast updates to the *histo[]* elements. For most modern CPUs, one can expect execution speed of this code to be memory bound, i.e., limited by the rate at which the *data[]* elements can be brought from DRAM into the CPU cache.

```
1.    sequential_Histogram(char *data, int length, int *histo) {
2.        for (int i = 0; i < length; i++) {
3.            int alphabet_position = data[i] - 'a';
4.            if (alphabet_position >= 0 && alphabet_position < 26) {
5.                histo[alphabet_position/4]++
6.            }
7.        }
8.    }
```

FIGURE 9.2

A simple C function for calculating histogram for an input text string.

9.2 USE OF ATOMIC OPERATIONS

A straightforward strategy for parallel histogram computation is dividing the input array into sections and having each thread process one of the sections. If we use P threads, each thread would be doing approximately 1/P of the original work. We will refer to this approach as "Strategy I" in our discussions. Using this strategy, we should be able to expect a speedup close to P. Fig. 9.3 illustrates this approach using our text example. To make the example fit in the picture, we reduce the input to the first 24 characters in the phrase. We assume that P = 4 and each thread processes a section of 6 characters. We show part of the workload of the four threads in Fig. 9.3.

Each thread iterates through its assigned section and increments the appropriate interval counter for each character. Fig. 9.3 shows the actions taken by the four threads in the first iteration. Observe that threads 0, 1, and 2 all need to update the same counter (m-p), which is a conflict referred to as output interference. One must understand the concepts of race conditions and atomic operations in order to safely handle such output interferences in his/her parallel code.

An increment to an interval counter in the *histo[]* array is an update, or read-modify-write, operation on a memory location. The operation involves reading the memory location (read), adding one to the read content (modify), and writing the new value back to the memory location (write). Read-modify-write is a common operation for safe coordination of collaborative activities across concurrent threads.

For example, when we make a flight reservation with an airline, we bring up the seat map and look for available seats (read), we pick a seat to reserve (modify), and change the seat status to unavailable in the seat map (write). A bad potential scenario can happen as follows:

- Two customers simultaneously bring up seat map of the same flight.
- Both customers pick the same seat, say 9C.
- Both customers change the status of seat 9C to unavailable in the seat map.

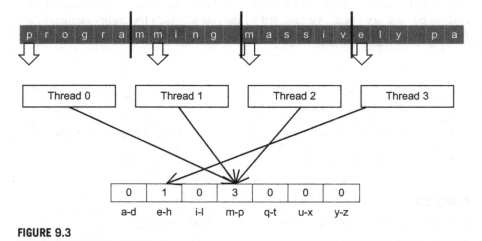

FIGURE 9.3

Strategy I for parallelizing histogram computation.

After the sequence, both customers logically conclude that they are now exclusive owners of seat 9C. We can imagine that they will have an unpleasant situation when they board the flight and find out that one of them cannot take the reserved seat! Believe it or not, such unpleasant situations indeed happen in real life due to flaws in airline reservation software.

For another example, some stores allow customers to wait for service without standing in line. They ask each customer to take a number from one of the kiosks. There is a display that shows the number that will be served next. When a service agent becomes available, he/she asks the customer to present the ticket that matches the number, verify the ticket, and update the display number to the next higher number. Ideally, all customers will be served in the order they enter the store. An undesirable outcome would be that two customers simultaneously sign in at two kiosks and both receive tickets with the same number. Once a service agent calls for that number, both customers will feel that they are the one who should receive service.

In both examples, undesirable outcomes are caused by a phenomenon called *race condition*, where the outcome of two or more simultaneous update operations varies depending on the relative timing of the operations involved. Some outcomes are correct and some are incorrect. Fig. 9.4 illustrates a race condition when two threads attempt to update the same *histo[]* element in our text histogram example. Each row in Fig. 9.4 shows the activity during a time period, with time progressing from top to bottom.

Fig. 9.4(A) depicts a scenario where Thread 1 completes all three parts of its read-modify-write sequence during time periods 1 through 3 before Thread 2 starts its sequence at time period 4. The value in the parenthesis in front of each operation shows the value being written into the destination, assuming the value of *histo[x]* was initially 0. With this interleaving, the value of *histo[x]* afterwards is 2, exactly as one would expect. That is, both threads successfully incremented the *histo[x]* element. The element value starts with 0 and ends at 2 after the operations complete.

In Fig. 9.4(B), the read-modify-write sequences of the two threads overlap. Note that Thread 1 writes the new value into *histo[x]* at time period 4. When Thread 2 reads *histo[x]* at time period 3, it still has the value 0. As a result, the new value it calculates and eventually writes to *histo[x]* is 1 rather than 2. The problem is that Thread 2 read *histo[x]* too early, before Thread 1 completes its update. The net outcome is that the value of *histo[x]* afterwards is 1, which is incorrect. The update by Thread 1 is lost.

During parallel execution, threads can run in any order relative to each other. In our example, Thread 2 can easily start its update sequence ahead of Thread 1.

Time	Thread 1	Thread 2	Time	Thread 1	Thread 2
1	(0) Old ← histo[x]		1	(0) Old ← histo[x]	
2	(1) New ← Old + 1		2	(1) New ← Old + 1	
3	(1) histo[x] ← New		3		(0) Old ← histo[x]
4		(1) Old ← histo[x]	4	(1) histo[x] ← New	
5		(2) New ← Old + 1	5		(1) New ← Old + 1
6		(2) histo[x] ← New	6		(1) histo[x] ← New
	(A)			(B)	

FIGURE 9.4

Race condition in updating a *histo[]* array element.

Fig. 9.5 shows two such scenarios. In Fig. 9.5(A), Thread 2 completes its update before Thread 1 starts its. In Fig. 9.5(B), Thread 1 starts its update before Thread 2 completes its. It should be obvious that the sequences in 9.5(A) result in correct outcome for histo[x] but those in 9.5(B) produce incorrect outcome.

The fact that the final value of *histo[x]* varies depending on the relative timing of the operations involved indicates that there is a race condition. We can eliminate such variations by preventing the interleaving of operation sequences of Thread 1 and Thread 2. That is, we would like to allow the timings shown in Figs. 9.4(A) and 9.5(A) while eliminating the possibilities shown in Figs. 9.4(B) and 9.5(B). Such timing constraints can be enforced with the use of *atomic operations*.

An atomic operation on a memory location is an operation that performs a read-modify-write sequence on the memory location in such a way that no other read-modify-write sequence to the location can overlap with it. That is, the read, modify, and write parts of the operation form an indivisible unit, hence the name atomic operation. In practice, atomic operations are realized with hardware support to lock out other threads from operating on the same location until the current operation is complete. In our example, such support eliminates the possibilities depicted in Figs. 9.4(B) and 9.5(B) since the trailing thread cannot start its update sequence until the leading thread completes its update.

It is important to remember that atomic operations do not force particular thread execution orderings. In our example, both orders shown in Fig. 9.4(A) and 9.5(B) are allowed by atomic operations. Thread 1 can run either ahead of or behind Thread 2. The rule being enforced is that if any one of the two threads begins an atomic operations to the same memory location, the trailing thread cannot perform any operations to the memory location until the leading thread completes its atomic operation. This effectively serializes the atomic operations being performed on a memory location.

Atomic operations are usually named according to the modification performed on the memory location. In our text histogram example, we are adding a value to the memory location so the atomic operation is called atomic add. Other types of atomic operations include subtraction, increment, decrement, minimum, maximum, logical and, logical or, etc.

A CUDA program can perform an atomic add operation on a memory location through a function call:

```
int atomicAdd(int* address, int val);
```

Time	Thread 1	Thread 2		Time	Thread 1	Thread 2
1		(0) Old ← histo[x]		1		(0) Old ← histo[x]
2		(1) New ← Old + 1		2		(1) New ← Old + 1
3		(1) histo[x] ← New		3	(0) Old ← histo[x]	
4	(1) Old ← histo[x]			4		(1) histo[x] ← New
5	(2) New ← Old + 1			5	(1) New ← Old + 1	
6	(2) histo[x] ← New			6	(1) histo[x] ← New	
	(A)				(B)	

FIGURE 9.5

Race condition scenarios where Thread 2 runs ahead of Thread 1.

INTRINSIC FUNCTIONS

Modern processors often offer special instructions that either perform critical functionality (such as the atomic operations) or substantial performance enhancement (such as vector instructions). These instructions are typically exposed to the programmers as intrinsic functions, or simply instrinsics. From the programmer's perspective, these are library functions. However, they are treated in a special way by compilers; each such call is translated into the corresponding special instruction. There is typically no function call in the final code, just the special instructions in line with the user code. All major modern compilers, such as Gnu C Compiler (gcc), Intel C Compiler and LLVM C Compiler support intrinsics.

The function is an intrinsic function that will be compiled into a hardware atomic operation instruction which reads the 32-bit word pointed to by the `address` argument in global or shared memory, adds `val` to the old content, and stores the result back to memory at the same address. The function returns the old value of the address.

Fig. 9.6 shows a CUDA kernel that performs parallel histogram computation based on Strategy I. Line 1 calculates a global thread index for each thread. Line 2 divides the total amount of data in the buffer by the total number of threads to determine the number of characters to be processed by each thread. The ceiling formula, introduced in Chapter 2, Data Parallel Computing, is used to ensure that all contents of the input buffer are processed. Note that the last few threads will likely process a section that is only partially filled. For example, if we have 1000 characters in the input buffer and 256 threads, we would assign sections of $(1000 - 1)/256 + 1 = 4$ elements to each of the first 250 threads. The last 6 threads will process empty sections.

Line 3 calculates the starting point of the section to be processed by each thread using the global thread index calculated in Line 1. In the example above, the starting point of the section to be processed by thread i would be i*4 since each section consists of 4 elements. That is, the starting point of thread 0 is 0, thread 8 is 32, and so on.

The `for` loop starting in line 4 is very similar to the one we have in Fig. 9.2. This is because each thread essentially executes the sequential histogram computation on its assigned section. There are two noteworthy differences. First, the calculation of the alphabet position is guarded by an if-condition. This test ensures that only the threads whose index into the buffer is within bounds will access the buffer. It is to prevent the threads that receive partially filled or empty sections from making out-of-bound memory accesses.

Finally, the increment expression (`histo[alphabet_position/4]++`) in Fig. 9.2 becomes an `atomicAdd()` function call in Line 6 of Fig. 9.6. The address of the location to be updated, `&(histo[alphabet_position/4])`, is the first argument. The value to be added to the location, 1, is the second argument. This ensures that any simultaneous updates to any `histo[]` array element by different threads are properly serialized.

```
__global__ void histo_kernel(unsigned char *buffer, long size, unsigned int *histo)
{
1.   int i = threadIdx.x + blockIdx.x * blockDim.x;
2.   int section_size = (size-1) / (blockDim.x * gridDim.x) +1;
3.   int start = i*section_size;

// All threads handle blockDim.x * gridDim.x
 // consecutive elements
4.   for (k = 0; k < section_size; k++) {
5.     if (start+k < size) {
6.       int alphabet_position = buffer[start+k] – 'a';
7.       if (alphabet_position >= 0 && alpha_position < 26) atomicAdd(&(histo[alphabet_position/4]), 1);
       }
     }
}
```

FIGURE 9.6

A CUDA kernel for calculation histogram based on Strategy I.

9.3 BLOCK VERSUS INTERLEAVED PARTITIONING

In Strategy I, we partition the elements of buffer[] into sections of continuous elements, or blocks, and assign each block to a thread. This partitioning strategy is often referred to as *block partitioning*. Partitioning data into continuous blocks is an intuitive and conceptually simple approach. On a CPU, where parallel execution typically involves a small number of threads, block partitioning is often the best performing strategy since the sequential access pattern by each thread makes good use of cache lines. Since each CPU cache typically supports only a small number of threads, there is little interference in cache usage by different threads. The data in cache lines, once brought in for a thread, can be expected to remain for the subsequent accesses.

As we learned in Chapter 5, Performance Considerations, the large number of simultaneously active threads in an SM typically cause too much interference in the caches that one cannot expect a data in a cache line to remain available for all the sequential accesses by a thread under Strategy I. Rather, we need to make sure that threads in a warp access consecutive locations to enable memory coalescing. This means that we need to adjust our strategy for partitioning buffer[].

Fig. 9.7 shows the desirable access pattern for memory coalescing for our text histogram example. During the first iteration, the four threads access characters 0 through 3 ("prog"), as shown in Fig. 11.7(A). With memory coalescing, all the elements will be fetched with only one DRAM access. During the second iteration, the four threads access characters "ramm" in one coalesced memory access. Obviously, this is a toy example. In reality, there will be many more threads. There is a subtle relationship between the number of characters processed by a thread in each iteration and performance. To fully utilize the bandwidth between the caches and SMs each thread should process four characters in each iteration.

Now that we understand the desired access pattern, we can derive the partitioning strategy to solve this problem. Instead of the block partitioning strategy, we will use

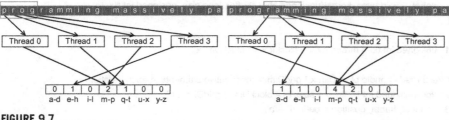

FIGURE 9.7

Desirable access pattern to the input buffer for memory coalescing—Strategy II.

an interleaved partitioning strategy where each thread will process elements that are separated by the elements processed by all threads during one iteration. In Fig. 9.7, the partition to be processed by thread 0 would be elements 0 ("p"), 4 ("r"), 8 ("i"), 12 ("m"), 16 ("i"), and 20 ("y"). Thread 1 would process elements 1 ("r"), 5 ("a"), 9 ("n"), and 13 ("a"), 17 ("v"), and 21 ("_"). It should be clear why this is called interleaved partitioning: the partition to be processed by different threads are interleaved with each other.

Fig. 9.8 shows a revised kernel based on Strategy II. It implements interleaved portioning in Line 2 by calculating a stride value, which is the total number threads launched during kernel invocation (`blockDim.x*gridDim.x`). In the first iteration of the `while` loop, each thread index the input buffer using its global thread index: Thread 0 accesses element 0, Thread 1 accesses element 1, Thread 2 accesses element 2, etc. Thus, all threads jointly process the first `blockDim.x*gridDim.x` elements of the input buffer. In the second iteration, all threads add `blockDim.x*gridDim.x` to their indices and jointly process the next section of `blockDim.x*gridDim.x` elements.

The `for-` loop controls the iterations for each thread. When the index of a thread exceeds the valid range of the input buffer (`i` is greater than or equal to `size`), the thread has completed processing its partition and will exit the loop. Since the size of the buffer may not be a multiple of the total number of threads, some of the threads may not participate in the processing of the last section. So some threads will execute one fewer `for-` loop iteration than others.

Thanks to the coalesced memory accesses, the version in Fig. 9.8 will likely execute several times faster than that in Fig. 9.6. However, there is still plenty of room for improvement, as we will show in the rest of this chapter. It is interesting that the code in Fig. 9.8 is actually simpler even though interleaved partitioning is conceptually more complicated than block partitioning. This is often true in performance optimization. While an optimization may be conceptually complicated, its implementation can be quite simple.

9.4 LATENCY VERSUS THROUGHPUT OF ATOMIC OPERATIONS

The atomic operation used in the kernels of Figs. 9.6 and 9.8 ensures the correctness of updates by serializing any simultaneous updates to a location. As we all know,

```
__global__ void histo_kernel(unsigned char *buffer, long size, unsigned int *histo)
{

1.  unsigned int tid = threadIdx.x + blockIdx.x * blockDim.x;

// All threads handle blockDim.x * gridDim.x consecutive elements in each iteration
2.  for (unsigned int i = tid;  i < size; i += blockDim.x*gridDim.x ) {
3.      int alphabet_position = buffer[i] – 'a';
4.      if (alphabet_position >= 0 && alpha_position < 26) atomicAdd(&(histo[alphabet_position/4]), 1);
    }

}
```

FIGURE 9.8

A CUDA kernel for calculating histogram based on Strategy II.

serializing any portion of a massively parallel program can drastically increase the execution time and reduce the execution speed of the program. Therefore, it is important that such serialized operations account for as little execution time as possible.

As we learned in Chapter 5, Performance Considerations, the access latency to data in DRAMs can take hundreds of clock cycles. In Chapter 3, Scalable Parallel Execution, we learned that GPUs use zero-cycle context switching to tolerate such latency. As long as we have many threads whose memory access latencies can overlap with each other, the execution speed is limited by the throughput of the memory system. Thus it is important that GPUs make full use of DRAM bursts, banks, and channels to achieve very high memory access throughput.

At this point, It should be clear to the reader that the key to high memory access throughput is the assumption that many DRAM accesses can be simultaneously in progress. Unfortunately, this assumption breaks down when many atomic operations update the same memory location. In this case, the read-modify-write sequence of a trailing thread cannot start until the read-modify-write sequence of a leading thread is complete. As shown in Fig. 9.9, the execution of atomic operations to the same memory location proceeds such that only one is in progress during any unit of time. The duration of each atomic operation is approximately the latency of a memory read (the left section of the atomic operation time) plus the latency of a memory write (the right section of the atomic operation time). The length of these time sections of each read-modify-write operation, usually hundreds of clock cycles, defines the minimal amount time hat must be dedicated to servicing each atomic operation and thus limits the throughput, or the rate at which atomic operations can be performed.

For example, assume a memory system with 64-bit Double Data Rate DRAM interface, 8 channels, 1 GHz clock frequency, and typical access latency of 200 cycles. The peak access throughput of the memory system is 8 (bytes/transfer)*2 (transfers

Atomic Operations on DRAM

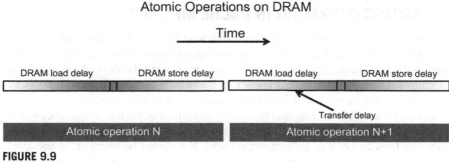

FIGURE 9.9

Throughput of atomic operation is determined by the memory access latency.

per clock per channel)*1G (clocks per second)*8 (Channels) = 128 GB/second. Assuming each data accessed is 4 bytes, the system has a peak access throughput of 32G data elements per second.

However, when performing atomic operations on a particular memory location, the highest throughput one can achieve is one atomic operation every 400 cycles (200 cycles for the read and 200 cycles for the write). This translates into a time-based throughput of 1/400 atomics/clock*1G (clocks/second) = 2.5 M atomics/second. This is dramatically lower than most users expect from a GPU memory system.

In practice, not all atomic operations will be performed on a single memory location. In our text histogram example, the histogram has 7 intervals. If the input characters are uniformly distributed in the alphabet, the atomic operations evenly distributed among the histo[] elements. This would boost the throughput to 7*2.5 M = 17.5 M atomic operations per second. In reality, the boost factor tends to be much lower than the number of intervals in the histogram because the characters tend to have biased distribution in the alphabet. For example, in Fig. 9.1, we see that characters in the example phrase are heavily biased towards the m-p and q-t intervals. The heavy contention traffic to update these intervals will likely reduce the achievable throughput to much less than 17.5 M atomic operations per second.

For the kernels of Figs. 9.6 and 9.8, low throughput of atomic operations will have significant negative impact on the execution speed. To put things into perspective, assume for simplicity that the achieved throughput of the atomic operations is 17.5 M atomic operations per second. We see that the kernel in Fig. 9.8 performs approximately six arithmetic operations ($-$, $>=$, $<$, $/$, $+$, $+$) with each atomic operation. Thus the maximal arithmetic execution throughput of the kernel will be 6*17.5 M = 105 M arithmetic operations per second. This is only a tiny fraction of the typical peak throughput of 1,000,000 M or more arithmetic operations per second on modern GPUs! This type of insight has motivated several categories of optimizations to improve the speed of parallel histogram computation as well as other types of computation using atomic operations.

9.5 ATOMIC OPERATION IN CACHE MEMORY

A key insight from the previous section is that long latency of memory access translates into low throughput in executing atomic operations on heavily contended locations. With this insight, an obvious approach to improving the throughput of atomic operations is to reduce the access latency to the heavily contended locations. Cache memories are the primary tool for reducing memory access latency.

Recent GPUs allow atomic operation to be performed in the last level cache, which is shared among all SMs. During an atomic operation, if the updated variable is found in the last level cache, it is updated in the cache. If it cannot be found in the last level cache, it triggers a cache miss and is brought into the cache where it is updated. Since the variables updated by atomic operations tend to be heavily accessed by many threads, these variables tend to remain in the cache once they are brought in from DRAM. Since the access time to the last level cache is in tens of cycles rather than hundreds of cycles, the throughput of atomic operations is improved by at least an order of magnitude by just allowing them to be performed in the last level cache. This was evident in the big throughput improvement of atomic operations from the Tesla generation to the Fermi generation, where the atomic operations are first supported in the last level (L2) cache. However, the improved throughput is still insufficient for many applications.

9.6 PRIVATIZATION

The latency for accessing memory can be dramatically reduced by placing data in the shared memory. Shared memory is private to each SM and has very short access latency (a few cycles). Recall that this reduced latency directly translates into increase throughput of atomic operations. The problem is that due to the private nature of shared memory, the updates by threads in one thread block are no longer visible to threads in other blocks. The programmer must explicitly deal with this lack of visibility of histogram updates across thread blocks.

In general, a technique referred to as *privatization* is commonly used to address the output interference problem in parallel computing. The idea is to replicate highly contended output data structures into private copies so that each thread (or each subset of threads) can update its private copy. The benefit is that the private copies can be accessed with much less contention and often at much lower latency. These private copies can dramatically increase the throughput for updating the data structures. The downside is that the private copies need to be merged into the original data structure after the computation completes. One must carefully balance between the level of contention and the merging cost. Therefore, in massively parallel systems, privatization is typically done for subsets of threads rather than individual threads.

In our text histogram example, we can create a private histogram for each thread block. Under this scheme, a few hundred threads would work on a copy of the histogram stored in short-latency shared memory, as opposed to tens of thousands of threads pounding on a histogram stored in medium latency second level cache or long latency DRAM. The combined effect of fewer contending threads and shorter access latency can result in orders of magnitude of increase in update throughput.

```
__global__ void histogram_privatized_kernel(unsigned char* input, unsigned int* bins,
    unsigned int num_elements, unsigned int num_bins) {

1.   unsigned int tid = blockIdx.x*blockDim.x + threadIdx.x;

     // Privatized bins
2.   extern __shared__ unsigned int histo_s[];
3.   for(unsigned int binIdx = threadIdx.x; binIdx < num_bins; binIdx +=blockDim.x) {
4.       histo_s[binIdx] = 0u;
     }
5.   __syncthreads();

     // Histogram
6.   For (unsigned int i = tid; i < num_elements; i += blockDim.x*gridDim.x) {
         int alphabet_position = buffer[i] – "a";
7.       if (alphabet_position >= 0 && alpha_position < 26) atomicAdd(&(histo_s[alphabet_position/4]), 1);
     }
8.   __syncthreads();

     // Commit to global memory
9.   for(unsigned int binIdx = threadIdx.x; binIdx < num_bins; binIdx += blockDim.x) {
10.      atomicAdd(&(histo[binIdx]), histo_s[binIdx]);
     }
}
```

FIGURE 9.10

A privatized text histogram kernel.

Fig. 9.10 shows a privatized histogram kernel. Line 2 allocates a shared memory array histo_s[] whose dimension is set during kernel launch. In the for - loop at Line 3, all threads in the thread block cooperatively initialize all the bins of their private copy of the histogram. The barrier synchronization in Line 5 ensures that all bins of the private histogram have been properly initialized before any thread starts to update them.

The for loop at Lines 6–7 is identical to that in Fig. 9.8, except that the atomic operation is performed on the shared memory histo_s[]. The barrier synchronization in Line 8 ensures that all threads in the thread block complete their updates before merging the private copy into the original histogram.

Finally, the for loop at Lines 9–10 cooperatively merges the private histogram values into the original version. Note that atomic add operation is used to update the original histogram elements. This is because multiple thread blocks can simultaneously update the same histogram elements and must be properly serialized with atomic operations. Note that both for loops in Fig. 9.10 are written so that the kernel can handle histograms of arbitrary number of bins.

9.7 AGGREGATION

Some data sets have a large concentration of identical data values in localized areas. For example, in pictures of the sky, there can be large patches of pixels of identical value. Such high concentration of identical values causes heavy contention and reduced throughput of parallel histogram computation.

For such data sets, a simple and yet effective optimization is for each thread to aggregate consecutive updates into a single update if they are updating the same element of the histogram [Merrill 2015]. Such aggregation reduces the number of atomic operations to the highly contended histogram elements, thus improving the effective throughput of the computation.

Fig. 9.11 shows an aggregated text histogram kernel. Each thread declares three additional register variables `curr_index`, `prev_index` and `accumulator`. The accumulator keeps track of the number of updates aggregated thus far and `prev_index` tracks the index of the histogram element whose updates has been aggregated. Each

```
__global__ void histogram_privatized_kernel(unsigned char* input, unsigned int* bins,
    unsigned int num_elements, unsigned int num_bins) {

1.    unsigned int tid = blockIdx.x*blockDim.x + threadIdx.x;

    // Privatized bins
2.    extern __shared__ unsigned int histo_s[];
3.    for(unsigned int binIdx = threadIdx.x; binIdx < num_bins; binIdx +=blockDim.x) {
4.        histo_s[binIdx] = 0u;
    }
5.    __syncthreads();

6.    unsigned int prev_index = -1;
7.    unsigned int accumulator = 0;

8.    for(unsigned int i = tid; i < num_elements; i += blockDim.x*gridDim.x) {
9.        int alphabet_position = buffer[i] – "a";
10.       if (alphabet_position >= 0 && alpha_position < 26) {
11.           unsigned int curr_index = alphabet_position/4;
12.           if (curr_index != prev_index) {
13.               if (accumulator >= 0) atomicAdd(&(histo_s[alphabet_position/4]), accumulator);
14.               accumulator = 1;
15.               prev_index = curr_index;
           }
16.       else {
17.           accumulator++;
           }
        }
    }
18.   __syncthreads();

    // Commit to global memory
19.   for(unsigned int binIdx = threadIdx.x; binIdx < num_bins; binIdx += blockDim.x) {
20.       atomicAdd(&(histo[binIdx]), histo_s[binIdx]);
    }
}
```

FIGURE 9.11

An aggregated text histogram kernel.

thread initializes the prev_index to −1 (Line 6) so that no alphabet input will match it. The accumulator is initialized to zero (Line 7), indicating that no updates have been aggregated.

When an alphabet data is found, the thread compares the index of the histogram element to be updated (curr_index) with the index of the one currently being aggregated (prev_index). If the index is different, the streak of aggregated updates to the histogram element has ended (Line 12). The thread uses atomic operation to add the accumulator value to the histogram element whose index is tracked by prev_index. This effectively flushes out the total contribution of the previous streak of aggregated updates. If the curr_index matches the prev_index, the thread simply adds one to the accumulator (Line 17), extending the streak of aggregated updates by one.

One thing to keep in mind is that the aggregated kernel requires more statements and variables. Thus, if the contention rate is low, an aggregated kernel may execute at lower speed than the simple kernel. However, if the data distribution leads to heavy contention in atomic operation execution, aggregation results in significant performance gains.

9.8 SUMMARY

Histogramming is a very important computation for analyzing large data sets. It also represents an important class of parallel computation patterns where the output location of each thread is data-dependent, which makes it infeasible to apply owner-computes rule. It is therefore a natural vehicle for introducing the practical use of atomic operations that ensure the integrity of read-modify-write operations to the same memory location by multiple threads. Unfortunately, as we explained in this chapter, atomic operations have much lower throughput than simpler memory read or write operations because their throughput is approximately the inverse of two times the memory latency. Thus, in the presence of heavy contention, histogram computation can have surprisingly low computation throughput. Privatization is introduced as an important optimization technique that systematically reduces contention and enables the use of local memory such as the shared memory, which supports low latency and thus improved throughput. In fact, supporting very fast atomic operations among threads in a block is an essential use case of the shared memory. For data sets that cause heavy contention, aggregation can also lead to significantly higher execution speed.

9.9 EXERCISES

1. Assume that each atomic operation in a DRAM system has a total latency of 100 ns. What is the maximal throughput we can get for atomic operations on the same global memory variable?
    a. 100 G atomic operations per second
    b. 1 G atomic operations per second

    c.   0.01 G atomic operations per second

    d.   0.0001 G atomic operations per second

2.   For a processor that supports atomic operations in L2 cache, assume that each atomic operation takes 4 ns to complete in L2 cache and 100 ns to complete in DRAM. Assume that 90% of the atomic operations hit in L2 cache. What is the approximate throughput for atomic operations on the same global memory variable?

    a.   0.225 G atomic operations per second

    b.   2.75 G atomic operations per second

    c.   0.0735 G atomic operations per second

    d.   100 G atomic operations per second

3.   In question 1, assume that a kernel performs 5 floating-point operations per atomic operation. What is the maximal floating-point throughput of the kernel execution as limited by the throughput of the atomic operations?

    a.   500 GFLOPS

    b.   5 GFLOPS

    c.   0.05 GFLOPS

    d.   0.0005 GFLOPS

4.   In Question 1, assume that we privatize the global memory variable into shared memory variables in the kernel and the shared memory access latency is 1 ns. All original global memory atomic operations are converted into shared memory atomic operation. For simplicity, assume that the additional global memory atomic operations for accumulating privatized variable into the global variable adds 10% to the total execution time. Assume that a kernel performs 5 floating-point operations per atomic operation. What is the maximal floating-point throughput of the kernel execution as limited by the throughput of the atomic operations?

    a.   4500 GFLOPS

    b.   45 GFLOPS

    c.   4.5 GFLOPS

    d.   0.45 GFLOPS

5.   To perform an atomic add operation to add the value of an integer variable Partial to a global memory integer variable Total, which one of the following statements should be used?

    a.   atomicAdd(Total, 1)

    b.   atomicAdd(&Total, &Partial)

    c.   atomicAdd(Total, &Partial)

    d.   atomicAdd(&Total, Partial)

REFERENCE

Merrill, D. (2015). Using compression to improve the performance response of parallel histogram computation, NVIDIA Research Technical Report.

Parallel patterns: sparse matrix computation

10

An introduction to data compression and regularization

CHAPTER OUTLINE

Our next parallel pattern is sparse matrix computation. In a sparse matrix, the majority of the elements are zeros. Many important real-world problems involve sparse matrix computation. Storing and processing these zero elements are wasteful in terms of memory capacity, memory bandwidth, time, and energy. To address these problems, several sparse matrix storage formats and their corresponding processing methods have been proposed and widely used in the field. These approaches employ a compaction technique to avoid storing or processing zero elements at the cost of introducing a certain degree of irregularity into the data representation. Unfortunately, such irregularity can lead to underutilization of memory bandwidth, control flow divergence, and load imbalance in parallel computing. Striking a good balance between compaction and regularization is important. Some storage formats achieve a high level of compaction at high levels of irregularity, whereas others attain a modest level of compaction while keeping the representation more regular. The parallel computation performance of their corresponding methods depends heavily on the distribution of nonzero elements in the sparse matrices. Understanding the wealth of work in sparse matrix storage formats and their corresponding parallel algorithms provides a parallel programmer an overview for addressing compaction and regularization challenges in solving related problems.

10.1 BACKGROUND

A sparse matrix is a matrix where the majority of the elements are zeros. Sparse matrices arise in many science, engineering, and financial modeling problems. As seen in Chapter 6, Numerical Considerations, matrices can be used to represent the coefficients in a linear system of equations. Each row of the matrix represents one equation of the linear system. In various science and engineering problems, the large number of variables and equations involved are sparsely coupled; i.e., each equation involves only a small number of variables. This point is illustrated in Fig. 10.1, where each column of the matrix corresponds to the coefficients for a variable: column 0 for x_0, column 1 for x_1, etc. For instance, the fact that row 0 has nonzero elements in columns 0 and 2 indicates that variables x_0 and x_2 are involved in equation 0. It should be clear that none of the variables are present in equation 1, variables x_1, x_2 and x_3 are present in equation 2, and finally variables x_0 and x_3 are present in equation 3.

Sparse matrices are typically stored in a format, or a representation, that avoids storing zero elements. We will start with the Compressed Sparse Row (CSR) storage format, which is illustrated in Fig. 10.2. CSR stores only nonzero values in a one-dimensional data storage, shown as data[] in Fig. 10.2. Array data[] stores all nonzero values in the sparse matrix in Fig. 10.1. The nonzero elements of Row 0 (3 and 1) are stored first, followed by the nonzero elements of Row 1 (none), the nonzero elements of Row 2 (2, 4, 1), and the nonzero elements of Row 3 (1, 1). The format compresses away all the zero elements.

With the compressed format, we need to input two sets of markers to preserve the structure of the original sparse matrix in the compressed representation. The first set of markers forms a column index array, col_index[], in Fig. 10.2. This array gives the column index of every nonzero value in the original sparse matrix. Since we have squeezed away the nonzero elements of each row, we need to use these markers to

Row 0	3	0	1	0
Row 1	0	0	0	0
Row 2	0	2	4	1
Row 3	1	0	0	1

FIGURE 10.1

A simple sparse matrix example.

		Row 0		Row 2			Row 3	
Nonzero values	data[7]	{ 3,	1,	2,	4,	1,	1,	1 }
Column indices	col_index[7]	{ 0,	2,	1,	2,	3,	0,	3 }
Row Pointers	row_ptr[5]	{ 0,	2,	2,	5,	7 }		

FIGURE 10.2

Example of Compressed Sparse Row (CSR) format.

remember the location of the remaining elements in the original rows of the sparse matrix; e.g., values 3 and 1 came from columns 0 and 2 of row 0 in the original sparse matrix. The `col_index[0]` and `col_index[1]` elements are assigned to store the column indices for these two elements. For another example, values 2, 4, and 1 came from columns 1, 2, and 3 of row 2 in the original sparse matrix. Therefore, `col_index[2]`, `col_index[3]`, and `col_index[4]` store indices 1, 2, and 3.

The second set of markers indicates the starting location of every row in the compressed format as the size of each row varies after the zero elements are removed. The starting location of each row in the compressed storage can no longer be identified using indexing based on the fixed row size. Fig. 10.2 shows a `row_ptr[]` array whose elements are the indices for the beginning locations of each row; `row_ptr[0]` indicates that Row 0 starts at location 0 of the `data[]` array, `row_ptr[1]` indicates that Row 1 starts at location 2, etc. Both `row_ptr[1]` and `row_ptr[2]` have a value of 2, implying that none of the elements of Row 1 is stored in the compressed format. This statement makes sense since Row 1 in Fig. 10.1 consists entirely of zero values. In addition, `row_ptr[4]` stores the starting location of a nonexistent "Row 4". This choice is for convenience, as some algorithms need to use the starting location of the next row to delineate the end of the current row. This extra marker provides a convenient way to locate the ending location of Row 3.

As discussed in Chapter 6, Numerical Considerations, matrices are often used in solving a linear system of N equations of N variables in the form `A*X+Y=0`, where A is an N × N matrix, X is a vector of N variables, and Y is a vector of N constant values. The objective is to solve for the X variable that will satisfy all the equations. An intuitive approach is to inverse the matrix such that `X=A⁻¹*(-Y)`. This technique can be used for matrices of moderate size through methods such as Gaussian elimination, as illustrated in Chapter 6, Numerical Considerations. While these methods can be used theoretically to solve equations represented in sparse matrices, the sheer size of numerous sparse matrices can overwhelm this intuitive approach. Furthermore, an inversed sparse matrix is often much larger than the original because the inversion process tends to generate a large number of additional nonzero elements called fill-ins. As a result, it is often impractical to compute and store the inversed matrix in solving real-world problems.

Instead, linear systems of equations represented in sparse matrices can be better solved with an iterative approach. When the sparse matrix A is positive—definite (i.e., $x^TAx > 0$ for all nonzero vectors x in R^n), the conjugate gradient method can be used to iteratively solve the corresponding linear system with guaranteed convergence to a solution [HS 1952]. The conjugate gradient methods predicts a solution for X and performs `A*X+Y`. If the result is not close to a 0 vector, a gradient vector formula can be used to refine the predicted X and another iteration of `A*X+Y` performed.

The most time-consuming aspect of such iterative approaches is the evaluation of `A*X+Y`, which is a sparse matrix–vector multiplication and accumulation. Fig. 10.3 illustrates matrix–vector multiplication and accumulation, where A is a sparse matrix. The dark squares in A represent nonzero elements. By contrast, both X and Y are typically dense vectors; i.e., most of the elements of X and Y hold nonzero values.

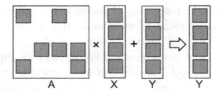

FIGURE 10.3

An example of matrix–vector multiplication and accumulation.

```
1.    for (int row = 0; row < num_rows; row++) {
2.        float dot = 0;
3.        int row_start = row_ptr[row];
4.        int row_end =   row_ptr[row+1];
5.        for (int elem = row_start; elem < row_end; elem++) {
6.            dot += data[elem] * x[col_index[elem]];
          }
7.        y[row] += dot;
      }
```

FIGURE 10.4

A sequential loop that implements SpMV based on the CSR format.

Owing to its importance, standardized library function interfaces have been created to perform this operation referred to as Sparse Matrix–Vector (SpMV) multiplication and accumulation. We will use SpMV to illustrate the important tradeoffs between different storage formats in parallel sparse matrix computation.

A sequential implementation of SpMV based on the CSR format is quite straightforward, as shown in Fig. 10.4. We assume that the code has access to (1) num_rows, a function argument that specifies the number of rows in the sparse matrix, (2) a floating point data array of A elements (via the data[] input parameter), two floating point x[] and y[] arrays of X and Y elements, and two integer row_ptr and col_index arrays, as described in Fig. 10.2. Only seven lines of code exist. Line 1 is a loop that iterates through all rows of the matrix, with each iteration calculating a dot product of the current row and the vector x.

In each row, Line 2 first initializes the dot product to zero. It then sets up the range of data[] array elements that belong to the current row. The starting and ending locations can be loaded from the row_ptr[] array, as illustrated in Fig. 10.5 for the small sparse matrix in Fig. 10.1. For row=0, row_ptr[row] is 0 and row_ptr[row+1] is 2. The two elements from Row 0 reside in data[0] and data[1]. That is, row_ptr[row] gives the starting position of the current row and row_ptr[row+1] gives the starting position of the next row, which is one after the ending position of the current row. This process is reflected in the loop in Line 5, where the loop index iterates from the position given by row_ptr[row] to the position given by row_ptr[row+1]-1.

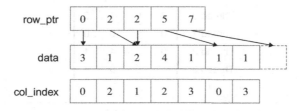

FIGURE 10.5

Illustration of the sequential SpMV loop when operating on the sparse matrix example in Fig. 10.1.

The loop body in Line 6 calculates the dot product for the current row. For each element, the loop body uses the loop index elem to access the matrix A element in data[elem]. The code also uses elem to retrieve the column index for the element from col_index[elem]. This column index is then used to access the appropriate x element for multiplication. To illustrate, the elements in data[0] and data[1] come from column 0 (col_index[0]=0) and column 2 (col_index[1]=2), respectively. Thus, the inner loop will perform the dot product for row 0 as data[0]*x[0]+data[1]*x[2]. The reader is encouraged to perform the dot product for other rows as an exercise.

CSR completely removes all zero elements from the storage. It incurs storage overhead by introducing the col_index and row_ptr arrays. In our example where the number of zero elements is not much larger than the number of nonzero elements, the storage overhead is greater than the space saved by not storing the zero elements. However, for sparse matrices where the vast majority of elements are zeros, the overhead introduced is far smaller than the space saved by not storing zeros. For instance, in a sparse matrix where only 1% of the elements are nonzero values, the total storage for the CSR representation, including the overhead, would be around 2% of the space required to store both zero and nonzero elements.

Removing all zero elements from the storage also eliminates the need to fetch these zero elements from memory or to perform useless multiplication operations on these zero elements. This method can significantly reduce the consumption of memory bandwidth and computational resources.

Any SpMV computation code will reflect the storage format assumed. Therefore, we will add the storage format to the name of a code to clarify the combination used. The SpMV code in Fig. 10.4 will be referred to as sequential SpMV/CSR. With a good understanding of sequential SpMV/CSR, we are now ready to discuss parallel sparse computation.

10.2 PARALLEL SPMV USING CSR

The dot product calculation for each row of the sparse matrix is independent of the dot product for other rows; i.e., all iterations of the outer loop (Line 1) in Fig. 10.4 are logically independent of each other. We can easily convert this sequential

Thread 0	3	0	1	0
Thread 1	0	0	0	0
Thread 2	0	2	4	1
Thread 3	1	0	0	1

FIGURE 10.6

Example of mapping threads to rows in parallel SpMV/CSR.

```
1.   __global__ void SpMV_CSR(int num_rows, float *data, int *col_index,
     int *row_ptr, float *x, float *y) {

2.     int row = blockIdx.x * blockDim.x + threadIdx.x;

3.     if (row < num_rows) {
4.       float dot = 0;
5.       int row_start = row_ptr[row];
6.       int row_end =   row_ptr[row+1];
7.       for (int elem = row_start; elem < row_end; elem++) {
8.         dot += data[elem] * x[col_index[elem]];
       }
9.       y[row] += dot;
     }

   }
```

FIGURE 10.7

A parallel SpMV/CSR kernel.

SpMV/CSR into a parallel CUDA kernel by assigning each iteration of the outer loop to a thread. Each thread calculates the inner product for a row of the matrix, which is illustrated in Fig. 10.6, where Thread 0 calculates the dot product for row 0, Thread 1 for row 1, and so on.

A real-world sparse matrix application usually consists of thousands to millions of rows, each of which contains tens to hundreds of nonzero elements. The mapping in Fig. 10.6 seems appropriate, showing multiple threads, with each of them having a substantial amount of work. We present a parallel SpMV/CSR in Fig. 10.7.

It should be clear that the kernel appears almost identical to the sequential SpMV/CSR loop. The outermost loop construct has been removed and is replaced by the thread grid. In Line 2, the row index assigned to a thread is calculated as the familiar expression `blockIdx.x*blockDim.x + threadIdx.x`. With the need to manage any arbitrary number of rows, Line 3 checks whether the row index of a thread exceeds the number of rows. This method handles the situation where the number of rows is not a multiple of the thread block size.

Despite its simplicity, the parallel SpMV/CSR kernel has two major shortcomings. First the kernel does not make coalesced memory accesses. As shown in

Fig. 10.5, adjacent threads will be making simultaneous nonadjacent memory accesses. In our example, threads 0, 1, 2, and 3 will access `data[0]`, none, `data[2]`, and `data[5]` in the first iteration of their dot product loop. The same threads will then access `data[1]`, none, `data[3]`, and `data[6]` in the second iteration, and so on. Thus, the parallel SpMV/CSR kernel in Fig. 10.7 fails to efficiently use the memory bandwidth.

The second shortcoming of the SpMV/CSR kernel is its potential to incur significant control flow divergence in all warps. The number of iterations performed by a thread in the dot product loop depends on the number of nonzero elements in the row assigned to the thread. Since the distribution of nonzero elements among rows can be random, adjacent rows can have varying numbers of nonzero elements. Consequently, a widespread control flow divergence can occur in most or even all warps.

Both the execution efficiency and memory bandwidth efficiency of the parallel SpMV kernel depends on the distribution of the input data matrix. This behavior somehow differs from those of most of the kernels we have thus far studied. However, such data-dependent performance behavior is commonly observed in real-world applications. Such occurrence justifies the importance of parallel SpMV as a parallel pattern. Although simple, parallel SpMV depicts an important behavior in many complex parallel applications. We will discuss three important techniques in the next sections to address the noncoalesced memory accesses and control flow divergence in the parallel SpMV/CSR kernel.

10.3 PADDING AND TRANSPOSITION

The problems of noncoalesced memory accesses and control divergence can be addressed by applying data padding and transposition on the sparse matrix data. These ideas were used in the ELL storage format, whose name came from the sparse matrix package in ELLPACK, a package for solving elliptic boundary value problems [RB 1984]. A simple way to understand the ELL format is to start with the CSR format, as is illustrated in Fig. 10.8.

From a CSR representation, we first determine the rows with the maximal number of nonzero elements. We then add **dummy** (zero) elements to all other rows after the nonzero elements for them to be of the same length as the maximal rows, thereby generating a rectangular matrix. For our small sparse matrix example, we determine that row 2 has the maximal number of elements. We then add one zero element to row 0, three zero elements to row 1, and one zero element to row 3 for the rows to be of equal lengths. These additional zero elements appear as squares with an * in Fig. 10.8, thereby generating a rectangular matrix. Note that the `col_index` array also needs to be padded the same way to preserve their correspondence to the data values.

We can now lay the padded matrix out in the column major order; i.e., we will place all elements of column 0 in consecutive memory locations, followed by all elements of column 1, and so on. This method is equivalent to **transposing** the rectangular matrix in the row major order used by the C language. In terms of our

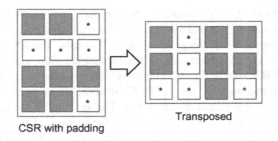

CSR with padding   Transposed

FIGURE 10.8

ELL storage format.

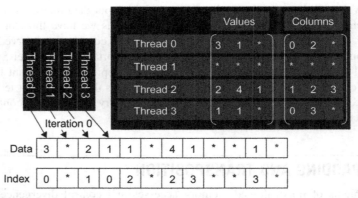

FIGURE 10.9

More details of our small example in ELL.

small example, after transposition, data[0] through data[3] contain 3, *, 2, 1, the 0th elements of all rows, as illustrated in Fig. 10.9, bottom portion. Similarly, col_index[0] through col_index[3] contain the column positions of the 0th elements of all rows. We no longer need row_ptr since the beginning of row i has been simplified to data[i]. With the padded elements, it is also very easy to move from the current element of row i to the next element by simply adding the number of rows in the original matrix to the index. To illustrate, the 0th element of row 2 is in data[2], and the next element is in data[2+4]=data[6], where 4 is the number of rows in the original matrix in our small example.

Using the ELL format, we show a parallel SpMV/ELL kernel in Fig. 10.10. The kernel receives slightly different arguments. The kernel no longer needs the row_ptr; instead, it needs an argument, num_elem, to determine the number of elements in each row after padding. Recall that num_elem is the maximal number of nonzero elements among all rows in the original sparse matrix.

```
1.   __global__ void SpMV_ELL(int num_rows, float *data, int *col_index,
     int num_elem, float *x, float *y) {
2.     int row = blockIdx.x * blockDim.x + threadIdx.x;
3.     if (row < num_rows) {
4.       float dot = 0;
5.       for (int i = 0; i < num_elem; i++) {
6.         dot += data[row+i*num_rows] * x[col_index[row+i*num_rows]];
       }
7.       y[row] += dot;
     }
   }
```

FIGURE 10.10

A parallel SpMV/ELL kernel.

A first observation is that the kernel code of SpMV/ELL kernel is simpler than that of SpMV/CSR. With padding, all rows are now of the same length. In the dot product loop in Line 5, all threads can simply loop through the number of elements given by num_elem. Consequently, control flow divergence no longer occurs in warps: all threads now iterate exactly the same number of times in the dot product loop. In the case where a dummy element is used in a multiplication and accumulation step, it will not affect the final result because its value is 0.

A second observation is that in the dot product loop body, each thread accesses its 0th element in data[row], and in general, its ith element in data[row+i*num_rows]. As we have seen in Fig. 10.9, by arranging the elements in the column major order, all adjacent threads are now accessing adjacent memory locations, enabling memory coalescing, thereby using memory bandwidth more efficiently.

By eliminating control flow divergence and enabling memory coalescing, SpMV/ELL should run faster than SPMV/CSR. Furthermore, SpMV/ELL is simpler, making SpMV/ELL an all-around winning approach. Unfortunately, SpMV/ELL has a potential downside. In situations where one or a small number of rows have an exceedingly large number of nonzero elements, the ELL format will result in excessive number of padded elements. These padded elements will require storage space, need to be fetched, and perform calculations despite their lack of influence on the final result. They consume memory storage, memory bandwidth, and execution cycles. Consider our sample matrix: in the ELL format, we have replaced a 4× 4 matrix with a 4× 3 matrix, and with the overhead from the column indices we are storing more data than contained in the original 4× 4 matrix.

To illustrate, a 1000× 1000 sparse matrix has 1% of its elements of nonzero value. On average, each row has 10 nonzero elements. With the overhead, the size of a CSR representation would be about 2% of the uncompressed total size. Assume that one of the rows has 200 nonzero values while all other rows have less than 10. Using the ELL format, we would pad all other rows to 200 elements. This method makes the ELL representation about 40% of the uncompressed total size and 20 times larger than the CSR representation. The excessively long row will extend the runtime of only one of the warps of the SpMV/CSR kernel, whereas the padding will extend the runtime of all warps of the SpMV/ELL kernel. With numerous padded dummy elements, an SpMV/ELL kernel can run more slowly compared with an SpMV/CSR kernel. This inadequacy requires a method to control the number of padded elements when we convert from the CSR format to the ELL format.

10.4 USING A HYBRID APPROACH TO REGULATE PADDING

The root of the problem with excessive padding in the ELL representation is that one or a small number of rows have an exceedingly large number of nonzero elements. If we have a mechanism to "take away" some elements from these rows, we can reduce the number of padded elements in ELL. The Coordinate (COO) format provides such a mechanism.

The COO format is illustrated in Fig. 10.11, where each nonzero element is stored with both its column index and row index. We have both the col_index and row_index arrays to accompany the data array. To illustrate, A[0,0] of our small example is now stored with both its column index (0 in col_index[0]) and its row index (0 in row_index[0]). With the COO format, one can look at any element in the storage and know where the element came from in the original sparse matrix. As in the case of the ELL format, row_ptr is unnecessary because each element self-identifies its column and row positions.

Although the COO format involves additional storage cost for the row_index array, it has the additional benefit of flexibility. The elements in a COO format can be arbitrarily reordered without losing any information provided that the data, col_index, and row_index arrays are reordered in the same manner, as illustrated in Fig. 10.12.

In Fig. 10.12, we have reordered the elements of data, col_index, and row_index. Currently, data[0] contains an element from row 3 and column 0 of the original sparse matrix. We have also shifted the row index and column index values along with the data value; thus, we can correctly identify the location of this element location in the original sparse matrix. The reader may ask why we would want to reorder these elements. Such reordering would disturb the locality and sequential patterns necessary for the efficient use of memory bandwidth.

The answer lies in an important use case for the COO format. It can be used to curb the length of rows in the CSR format or the ELL format. First, we make an important observation. In the COO format, we can process the elements in any desired order. For each element in data[i], we can simply perform a y[row_index[i]]+=data[i]*x[col_index[i]] operation. The correct y element identified by row_index[i] will receive the correct contribution from the product of data[i] and x[col_index]. If this operation is performed for all elements of data, the correct final answer will be obtained regardless of the order in which these elements are processed.

Before converting a sparse matrix from the CSR format to the ELL format, we can remove some elements from rows with exceedingly large numbers of nonzero

		Row 0		Row 2			Row 3		
Nonzero values	data[7]	{ 3,	1,	2,	4,	1,	1,	1	}
Column indices	col_index[7]	{ 0,	2,	1,	2,	3,	0,	3	}
Row indices	row_index[7]	{ 0,	0,	2,	2,	2,	3,	3	}

FIGURE 10.11

Example of Coordinate (COO) format.

Nonzero values	data[7]	{ 1	1,	2,	4,	3,	1	1 }
Column indices	col_index[7]	{ 0	2,	1,	2,	0,	3,	3 }
Row indices	row_index[7]	{ 3	0,	2,	2,	0,	2,	3 }

FIGURE 10.12

Reordering the Coordinate (COO) format.

elements and place them into a separate COO storage. We can use SpMV/ELL on the remaining elements. With excess elements removed from the extra-long rows, the number of padded elements for other rows can be significantly reduced. We can then use a SpMV/COO to finish the job. This approach of employing two formats to collaboratively complete a computation is often referred to as a hybrid method.

A hybrid ELL and COO method for SpMV using our small sparse matrix is shown in Fig. 10.13. Row 2 has the largest number of nonzero elements. We remove the last nonzero element of row 2 from the ELL representation and move it into a separate COO representation. By removing the last element of row 2, we reduce the maximal number of nonzero elements among all rows in the small sparse matrix from 3 to 2. As shown in Fig. 10.13, the number of padded elements is reduced from 5 to 2. More importantly, all of the threads only need to perform 2 rather than 3 iterations, which can accelerate the parallel execution of the SpMV/ELL kernel by 50%.

A typical way of using an ELL–COO hybrid method is for the host to convert the format from one similar to the CSR format into the ELL format. During conversion, the host removes some nonzero elements from the rows with exceedingly large number of nonzero elements. The host places these elements into a COO representation and then transfers the ELL representation of the data to a device. When the device completes the SpMV/ELL kernel, it transfers the resulting y values back to the host. These values are missing the contributions from the elements in the COO representation. The host performs a sequential SpMV/COO kernel on the COO elements and finishes their contributions to the y element values.

The user may question whether the additional work performed by the host to separate COO elements from an ELL format could incur excessive overhead. It depends. In situations where a sparse matrix is only used in one SpMV calculation, this extra work can indeed incur a significant large overhead. However, in a number of real-work applications, the SpMV is performed on the same sparse kernel repeatedly in an iterative solver. In each iteration of the solver, the x and y vectors vary; however,

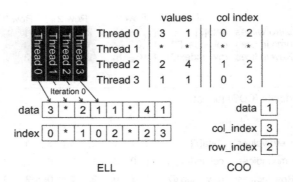

FIGURE 10.13

Our small example in ELL and COO hybrid.

```
1.    for (int i = 0; i < num_elem; row++)
2.        y[row_index[i]] += data[i] * x[col_index[i]];
```

FIGURE 10.14

A sequential loop that implements SpMV/COO.

the sparse matrix remains the same because its elements correspond to the coefficients of the linear system of equations being solved, and these coefficients remain
the same from iteration to iteration. Thus, the work done to produce both the hybrid
ELL and COO representations can be amortized across many iterations. We will
return to this point in the next section.

In our small example, the device finishes the SpMV/ELL kernel on the ELL portion of the data. The y values are then transferred back to the host, which then adds
the contribution of the COO element with the operation y[2]+=data[0]*x[col_
index[0]]=1*x[3]. Note that in general, the COO format includes multiple nonzero
elements. Thus, we expect the host code to be a loop, as shown in Fig. 10.14.

The loop is extremely simple. It iterates through all the data elements and performs the multiply-and-accumulate operation on the appropriate x and y elements by
using the accompanying col_index and row_index elements. We will not present a
parallel SpMV/COO kernel. It can be easily constructed using each thread to process
a portion of the data elements and to use an atomic operation in order to accumulate
the results into y elements. The reason is that the threads are no longer mapped to
a particular row. Many rows will likely be missing from the COO representation;
only the rows that have exceedingly large numbers of nonzero elements will have
elements in the COO representation. Therefore, it is better for each thread to take a
portion of the data element and use an atomic operation in order to ensure that none
of the threads will trample the contribution of other threads.

The hybrid SpMV/ELL–COO method illustrates a productive use of both CPUs
and GPUs in a heterogeneous computing system. The CPU can readily perform

SpMV/COO by using its large cache memory. The GPU can quickly perform SpMV/ ELL by using its coalesced memory accesses and large number of hardware execution units. The removal of some elements from the ELL format is a regularization technique: it reduces the disparity between long and short rows and improves the workload uniformity of all threads. Such enhanced uniformity provides certain benefits, including less control divergence in an SpMV/CSR kernel or less padding in an SpMV/ELL kernel.

10.5 SORTING AND PARTITIONING FOR REGULARIZATION

While COO helps regulate the amount of padding in an ELL representation, we can further reduce the padding overhead by sorting and partitioning the rows of a sparse matrix. The idea is to sort the rows according to their length, e.g., from the longest to the shortest, as illustrated in our small sparse matrix in Fig. 10.15. Since the sorted matrix looks largely like a triangular matrix, the format is often referred to as the Jagged Diagonal Storage (JDS) format. As we sort the rows, we typically maintain an additional jds_row_index array that preserves the original index of the row. For CSR, this array is similar to the row_ptr array in that both arrays have one element for each row of the matrix. Whenever we exchange two rows during sorting, we also exchange the corresponding elements of the jds_row_index array, thereby keeping track of the original position of all rows.

Once a sparse matrix is in the JDS format, we can partition the matrix into sections of rows. Since the rows have been sorted, all rows in a section will likely have similar numbers of nonzero elements. As shown in Fig. 10.15, the small matrix can be divided into three sections: the first section consists of one row with three elements, and the second section consists of two rows with two elements each. The third section consists of one row without any element. We can then generate an ELL representation for each section. Within each section, we only need to pad the rows to match the row with the maximal number of elements in that section. This method would reduce the number of padded elements. In our example, we do not even need to pad within any of the three sections. We can then transpose each section independently and launch a separate kernel on each section. In fact, we do not even need to launch a kernel for the section of rows with no nonzero elements.

Fig. 10.16 shows a JDS–ELL representation of our small sparse matrix, which assumes similar sorting and partitioning results found in Fig. 10.15. The first section has only one row so that the transposed layout is the same as the original one. The second section is a 2 × 2 matrix and has been transposed. The third section consists of Row 1, which has no nonzero element. This lack of nonzero elements is reflected in the fact that its starting location and the starting position of the next section are identical.

An SpMV/JDS kernel will not be presented in this chapter. Either an SpMV/CSR kernel on each section of the CSR or an SpMV/ELL kernel on each section of the ELL after padding may be used to represent the kernel. The host code required to create a JDS representation and to launch SpMV kernels on each section of the JDS representation is left as an exercise.

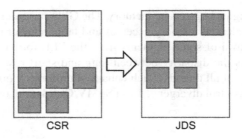

FIGURE 10.15

Sorting rows according to their length.

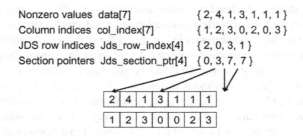

FIGURE 10.16

JDS format and sectioned ELL.

Note that we want each section to have a large number of rows so that its kernel launch will be worthwhile. In extreme cases where a very small number of rows have extremely large numbers of nonzero elements, the COO hybrid with JDS can still be used to allow more rows in each section.

Once again, the reader should ask whether sorting rows will lead to incorrect solutions to the linear system of equations. Recall that we can freely reorder equations of a linear system without changing the solution. Provided that the y elements are reordered along with the rows, we are effectively reordering the equations. Therefore, we will obtain the correct solution. The only extra step is to reorder the final solution back to the original order by using the jds_row_index array.

Whether sorting will incur a significant overhead, the answer is similar to what we saw in the hybrid method. Provided that the SpMV/JDS kernel is used in an iterative solver, such sorting and reordering of the final solution x elements can be performed, and the cost can be amortized among many iterations of the solver.

In relatively recent devices, the memory coalescing hardware has relaxed the address alignment requirement, allowing the simple transposition of a JDS-CSR representation. The jds_section_ptr array does not need to be adjusted after transposition. This further eliminates the need to pad rows in each section. As memory bandwidth becomes increasingly the limiting factor of performance, eliminating the need to store and fetch padded elements can be a significant advantage. Indeed, we have observed that while sectioned JDS–ELL tends to exhibit the best performance on older CUDA devices, transposed JDS-CSR tends to exhibit the best performance on Fermi and Kepler.

We would like to make an additional remark on the performance of sparse matrix computation compared with dense matrix computation. In general, the FLOPS achieved by either CPUs or GPUs is much lower for sparse matrix computation than for dense matrix computation. This finding is particularly true for SpMV, where there is no data reuse in the sparse matrix. The CGMA value (see Chapter 4: Memory and Data Locality) is essentially 1, limiting the attainable FLOPS to a small fraction of the peak performance. The various formats are important for CPUs and GPUs since both are limited by memory bandwidth when performing SpMV. Many have been surprised by the low FLOPS of this type of computation on both CPUs and GPUs. After reading this chapter, one should no longer be surprised.

10.6 SUMMARY

In this chapter, we presented sparse matrix computation as an important parallel pattern. Sparse matrices are important in a number of real-world applications that involve modeling complex phenomena. Furthermore, sparse matrix computation is a simple example demonstrating data-dependent performance behavior of many large real-world applications. Owing to the large number of zero elements, compaction techniques are used to reduce the amount of storage, memory accesses, and computation performed on these zero elements. Unlike most other kernels presented thus far in this book, the SpMV kernels are sensitive to the distribution of data, specifically the nonzero elements in sparse matrices. Not only can the performance of each kernel vary significantly across matrices; their relative merit can change significantly as well. Using this pattern, we introduce the concept of regularization applying hybrid methods and sorting/partitioning. These regularization techniques are used in many real-world applications. Interestingly, some of the regularization techniques re-introduce zero elements into the compacted representations. We use hybrid methods to mitigate the pathological cases where we could introduce too many zero elements. Readers are referred to [Bell 2009] and encouraged to experiment with different sparse data sets to gain additional insights into the data-dependent performance behavior of the various SpMV kernels presented in this chapter.

10.7 EXERCISES

1. Complete the host code to produce the hybrid ELL–COO format, launch the ELL kernel on the device, and complete the contributions of the COO elements.

2. Complete the host code for creating JDS–ELL and launch one kernel for each section of the representation.

3. Consider the following sparse matrix:

1 0 7 0
0 0 8 0
0 4 3 0
2 0 0 1

Represent the matrix in each of the following formats: (a) COO, (b) CSR, and (c) ELL.

4. Given a sparse matrix of integers with m rows, n columns, and z nonzeros, how many integers are needed to represent the matrix in (a) COO, (b) CSR, and (c) ELL. If the information provided is insufficient, indicate the missing information.

REFERENCES

Bell, N. & Garland, M. (2009). Implementing sparse matrix–vector multiplication on throughput-oriented processors. In *Proceedings of the ACM Conference on High-Performance Computing Networking Storage and Analysis (SC'09)*.

Hestenes, M. R., & Stiefel, E. (December, 1952). Methods of conjugate gradients for solving linear systems (PDF).. *Journal of Research of the National Bureau of Standards, 49*(6).

Rice, J. R., & Boisvert, R. F. (1984). *Solving Elliptic Problems Using, ELLPACK*. Springer Verlag. 497 pages.

Parallel patterns: merge sort

An introduction to tiling with dynamic input data identification

11

Li-Wen Chang and Jie Lv

CHAPTER OUTLINE

Our next parallel pattern is an ordered merge operation, which takes two ordered lists and generates a combined, ordered sort. Ordered merge operations can be used as a building block of sorting algorithms. Sorting is an important, classic problem in computer science with enormous number of applications. Ordered merge operations also form the basis of modern map-reduce frameworks. They are good examples for the divide-and-concur approach to parallelization. This chapter presents a parallel ordered merge algorithm where the input data for each thread are dynamically determined. The dynamic nature of the data accesses makes it challenging to exploit locality for improved memory access efficiency and performance. We present increasingly sophisticated buffer management schemes to achieving increasing levels of memory access efficiency.

11.1 BACKGROUND

An ordered merge function takes two sorted lists A and B and merges them into a single sorted list C. For the purpose of this chapter, we assume that the sorted lists are stored in arrays. We further assume that each element in such an array has a key. An order relation denoted by $\leq$ is defined on the keys. For example, the keys may be simply integer values and $\leq$ may be defined as the conventional *less than or equal to* relation between these integer values. In the simplest case, the keys are the elements.

Suppose that we have two elements e_1 and e_2 whose keys are k_1 and k_2 respectively. In a sorted list based on the relation $\leq$, if e_1 appears before e_2, then $k_1 \leq k_2$. Fig. 11.1 shows a simple example of a sorted list vs. an unsorted list. In this example, the elements are integer values, the keys are the elements and the elements are sorted according to the conventional mathematical $\leq$ relation between integers.

The upper array in Fig. 11.1 contains a sorted list because whenever an element appears before another element, the former always has a numerical value that is less than or equal to the latter. On the contrary, the lower list contains an unsorted list: element 0 (numerical value 12) appears before element 1 (numerical value 7) whereas the numerical value of element 0 is greater than (not less than or equal to) that of element 1.

We are now ready for a more detailed definition of the merge function. A merge function based on an ordering relation R takes two sorted input arrays A and B having m and n elements respectively, where m and n do not have be to equal. Both array A and array B are sorted based on the ordering relation R. The function produces an output sorted array C having m + n elements. Array C consists of all the input elements from arrays A and B, and is sorted by the ordering relation R.

Fig. 11.2 shows the operation of a simple merge function based on the conventional numerical ordering relation. A has five elements (m = 5) and B has four elements (n = 4). The merge function generates C with all its nine elements (m + n)

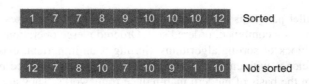

FIGURE 11.1

Examples of sorted versus unsorted lists.

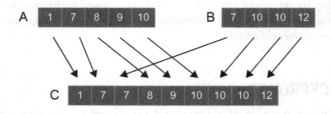

FIGURE 11.2

Example of a merge operation.

from A and B. These elements must be sorted. The arrows in Fig. 11.2 show how elements of A and B should be placed into C in order to complete the merge operation. Here we assume that whenever the numerical values are equal between an element of A and an element of B, the element of A should appear first in the output list C.

The merge operation is the core of merge sort, an important parallelizable sort algorithm. A parallel merge sort function divides up the input list into multiple sections and distributes them to parallel threads. The threads sort the individual section(s) and then cooperatively merge the sorted sections. Such divide-and-concur approach allows efficient parallelization of sorting.

In modern map-reduce distributed computing frameworks such as Hadoop, the computation is distributed to a massive number of compute nodes. The reduce process assembles the result of these compute nodes into the final result. Many applications require that the results be sorted according to an ordering relation. These results are typically assembled using the merge operation in a reduction tree pattern. As a result, efficient merge operations are critical to the efficiency of these frameworks.

11.2 A SEQUENTIAL MERGE ALGORITHM

The merge operation can be implemented with a fairly straightforward sequential algorithm. Fig. 11.3 shows a sequential merge function.

The sequential function in Fig. 11.3 consists of two main parts. The first part, on the left side, consists of a while-loop (line 5) that visits the A and B list elements in order. The loop starts with the first elements: A[0] and B[0]. Every iteration fills one position in the output array C; either one element of A or one element of B will

```
1  void merge_sequential(int *A, int m, int *B,      12  if (i == m) {
              int n, int *C) {                                //done with A[] handle remaining B[]
2     int i = 0; //index into A                      13      for (; j < n; j++) {
3     int j = 0; //index into B                      14          C[k++] = B[j];
4     int k = 0; //index into C                       15      }
                                                      16  } else {
       // handle the start of A[] and B[]                      //done with B[], handle remaining A[]
5     while ((i < m) && (j < n)) {                    17      for (; i < m; i++) {
6        if (A[i] <= B[j]) {                          18          C[k++] = A[i];
7           C[k++] = A[i++];                          19      }
8        } else {                                     20  }
9           C[k++] = B[j++];                          21  }
10       }
11    }
```

FIGURE 11.3

A sequential merge function.

be selected for the position (lines 6–10). The loop uses i and j to identify the A and B elements currently under consideration; i and j are both 0 when the execution first enters the loop. The loop further uses k to identify the current position to be filled in the output list array C. In each iteration, if element A[i] is less than or equal to B[j], the value of A[i] is assigned to C[k]. In this case, the execution increments both i and k before going to the next iteration. Otherwise, the value of B[j] is assigned to C[k]. In this case, the execution increments both j and k before going to the next iteration.

The execution exits the while-loop when it reaches either the end of array A or the end of array B. The execution moves on to the second part, which is on the right Fig. 11.3. If array A is the one that has been completely visited, as indicated by the fact that i is equal to m, then the code uses a for-loop to copy the remaining elements of array B to the remaining positions of array C (lines 13–15). Otherwise, array B is the one that was completely visited, as indicated by the fact that j is equal to n. In this case, a for-loop is used to copy the remaining elements of A to the remaining positions of C (lines 17-19).

We can illustrate the operation of the sequential merge function using the simple example from Fig. 11.2. During the first three (0 − 2) iterations of the while-loop, A[0], A[1], and B[0] are assigned to C[0], C[1], and C[2]. The execution continues until the end of iteration 5. At this point, list A is completely visited and the execution exits the while- loop. A total of six C positions have been filled by A[0] through A[4] and B[0]. The for-loop in the else part of the if-construct is used to copy the remaining B elements—B[1]-B[3] into the remaining C positions.

The sequential merge function visits every input element from both A and B once and writes into each C position once. Its algorithm complexity is O(m + n) and its execution time is linearly proportional to the total number of elements to be merged. Any work-efficient parallel algorithm will need to maintain this level of work-efficiency.

11.3 A PARALLELIZATION APPROACH

Siebert et al. [ST 2012] proposed an approach to parallelizing the merge operation. In their approach, each thread first calculates the range of output positions (output range) that it is going to produce, and uses that range as the input to a *co-rank function* to identify the corresponding input ranges that will be merged to produce the output range. Once the input and output ranges are determined, each thread can independently access its two input subarrays and one output subarray. Such independence allows each thread to perform the sequential merge function on their subarrays to do the merge in parallel. It should be clear that the key to the proposed parallelization approach is the co-rank function. We will now formulate the co-rank function.

Let A and B be two input arrays with m and n elements respectively. We assume that both input arrays are sorted according to an ordering relation. The index of each array starts from 0. Let C be the sorted output array generated by merging A and B. Obviously, C has m+n elements. We can make the following observation:

Observation 1: For any k such that 0≤k<m+n, there is either (case 1) an i such that 0 ≤ i<m and C[k] receives its value from A[i], or (case 2) a j such that 0≤j<n and C[k] receives its value from B[j] in the merge process.

Fig. 11.4 shows the two cases of observation (1). In the first case, the C element in question comes from array A. For example, in Fig. 11.4a, C[4] (value 9) receives its values from A[3]. In this case, k=4 and i=3. We can see that the prefix subarray C[0]-C[3] of C[4] (the subarray of 4 elements that precedes C[4]) is the result of merging the prefix subarray A[0]-A[2] of A[3] (the subarray of 3 elements that precedes A[3]) and the prefix subarray B[0] of B[1] (the subarray of 4 − 3 = 1 element that precedes B[1]). The general formula is that subarray C[0]-C[k-1] (k elements) is the result of merging A[0]-A[i-1] (of i elements) and B[0]-B[k-i-1] (k-i elements).

In the second case, the C element in question comes from array B. For example, in Fig. 11.4b, C[6] receives its value from B[1]. In this case, k=6 and j=1. The prefix subarray C[0]-C[5] of C[6] (the subarray of 6 elements that precedes C[6]) is the result of merging the prefix subarray A[0]-A[4] (the subarray of 5 elements preceding A[5]) and B[0] (the subarray of 1 element that precedes B[1]). The general formula for this case is that subarray C[0]-C[k-1] (k elements) is the results of merging A[0]-A[k-j-1] (k-j elements) and B[0]-B[j-1] (j elements).

In the first case, we find i and derive j as k-i. In the second case, we find j and derive i as k-j. We can take advantage of the symmetry and summarize the two cases into one observation:

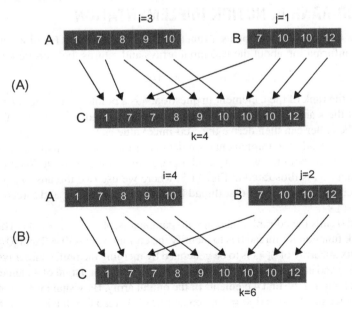

FIGURE 11.4

Examples of observation (1). (A) shows case 1 and (B) shows case 2.

Observation 2: For any k such that 0≤k<m+n, we can find i and j such that k=i+j, 0≤i<m and 0≤j<n and the subarray C[0]-C[k-1] is the result of merging subarray A[0]-A[i-1] and subarray B[0]-B[j-1].

Siebert et al. also proved that i and j, which define the prefix subarrays of A and B needed to produce the prefix subarray of C of length k, are unique. For an element C[k], the index k is referred to as its rank. The unique indices i and j are referred to as its co-ranks. For example, in Fig. 11.4a, the rank and co-rank of C[4] are 4, 3, and 1. For another example, the rank and co-rank of C[6] is 6, 5, and 1.

The concept of co-rank gives us a path to parallelizing the merge function. We can divide the work among threads by dividing the output array into subarrays and assign the generation of one subarray to each thread. Once the assignment is done, the rank of output elements to be generated by each thread is known. Each thread then uses the co-rank function to determine the subarrays of the input arrays that it needs to merge into its output subarray.

Note that the main difference between the parallelization of the merge function versus the parallelization of our previous patterns such as histogram is that the range of input to be used by each thread cannot be determined with a simple rule. *The range of input elements to be used by each thread is a function of the input values.* This makes the parallelized merge operation an interesting and challenging parallel computation pattern.

11.4 CO-RANK FUNCTION IMPLEMENTATION

We define the co-rank function as a function that takes the rank (k) of a C array element and information about the two input arrays and returns the i co-rank value:

```
int co_rank(int k, int * A, int m, int * B, int n)
```

where k is the rank of the C element in question, A is a pointer to the input A array, m is the size of the A array, B is a pointer to the input B array, and n is the size of the input B array. The caller can then derive the j co-rank value as k-i.

Before we study the implementation details of the co-rank function, it is beneficial to first learn about the ways a parallel merge function will use it. Such use of the co-rank function is illustrated in Fig. 11.5, where we use two threads to perform the merge operation. We assume that thread 0 generates C[0]-C[3] and thread 1 generates C[4]-C[8].

Thread 0 calls the co-rank function with parameters (4, A, 5, B, 4). The goal of the co-rank function for thread 0 is to identify the co-rank values i0 = 3 and j0 = 1. That is, the prefix subarray of C[4] is to be generated by merging the prefix subarrays of A[3] (A[0]-A[2]) and B[1] (B[0]). Intuitively, we are looking for a total of 4 elements from A and B that will fill the first 4 elements of the output array. By visual inspection, we see that the choice of i0 = 3 and j0 = 1 meets our need. Thread 0 will take A[0]-A[2] and B[0] to We leave out A[3] (value 9) and B[1] (value 10), which is correct since they are both larger than the four elements we include (1, 7, 8 from A and 7 from B).

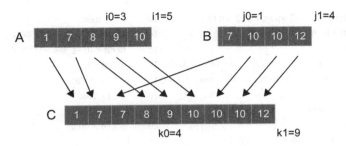

FIGURE 11.5

Example of co-rank function execution.

If we changed the value of i0 to 2, we need to set the j0 value to 2 so that we can still have a total of 4 elements. However, this means that we would include B[1] whose value is 10. This value is larger than A[2] (value 8) that would be left out for this choice. Such a change would make the resulting C array not properly sorted. On the other hand, if we changed the value of i0 to 4, we need to set the j0 value to 0 to keep the total number of elements at 4. However, this would mean that we include A[4] (value 10), which is larger than B[0] (value 7) that we would incorrectly leave out when generating the output subarray of thread 0. These two examples point to a search algorithm can quickly identify the value.

Thread 1 calls the co-rank function with parameters (9, A, 5, B, 4). From Fig. 11.4, we see that the co-rank function should produce co-rank values i1 = 5 and j1 = 4. Note that the input subarrays to be used by thread 1 are actually defined by the co-rank values of thread 0 and those of thread 1: A[3]-A[4] and B[1]-B[3]. That is, the starting index of the A subarray for thread 1 is actually thread 0's co-rank i value. The starting index of the B subarray for thread 1 is thread 0's co-rank j value. In general, the input subarrays to be used by thread t are defined by the co-rank values for thread (t − 1) and thread t: A[i_(t-1)]-A[i_t-1] and B[j_(t-1)]-B[j_t-1].

One important point is that the amount of search work can vary dramatically among threads for large input arrays. The threads that generate the beginning sections of the output array may need to search through only a small number of A and B elements. On the other hand, the high-numbered threads may need to search through a large number of A or B elements. It is therefore very important to minimize the latency for searching through a large number of elements. Since both input arrays are sorted, we can use a binary search or even a higher radix search to reduce the computational complexity from $O(N)$ to $O(log(N))$. Fig. 11.5 shows a co-rank function based on binary search.

The co-rank function uses two pairs of marker variables to delineate the range of A array indices and the range of B array indices being considered for the co-rank values. Variables i_low and j_low are the smallest possible co-rank values that could be generated by the function. Variables i and j are the candidate co-rank return values

```
1  int co_rank(int k, int* A, int m, int* B, int n) {      13      i = i - delta;
2    int i= k<m ? k : m;  //i = min(k,m)                     14    } else if (j > 0 && i < m && B[j-1] >= A[i]) {
3    int j = k- i;                                           15      delta = ((j - j_low +1) >> 1);
4    int i_low = 0>(k-n) ? 0 : k-n;  //i_low = max(0, k-n)   16      i_low = i;
5    int j_low = 0>(k-m) ? 0 : k-m;  //i_low = max(0, k-m)   17      i = i + delta;
6    int delta;                                              18      j = j - delta;
7    bool active = true;                                     19    } else {
8    while(active)  {                                        20      active = false;
9      if (i > 0 && j < n && A[i-1] > B[j]) {                21    }
10        delta = ((i - i_low +1) >> 1);  // ceil(i-i_low)/2 22  }
11        j_low = j;                                         23  return i;
12        j = j + delta;                                     24 }
```

FIGURE 11.6

A co-rank function based on binary search.

being considered in the current iteration. Line 2 initializes i to its largest possible value. If the k value is greater than m, line 2 initializes i to m, since the co-rank i value cannot be larger than the size of the A array. Otherwise, line 2 initializes i to k, since i cannot be larger than k. The co-rank j value is initialized as k - i (line 3). Throughout the execution, the co-rank function maintains this important invariant relation. The sum of the i and j variable is always equal to the value of the input variable k (the rank value).

The initialization of the i_low and j_low variables (lines 4 and 5) requires a little more explanation. These variables allow us to limit the scope of the search and make it faster. Functionally, we could set both values to zero and let the rest of the execution elevate them to more accurate values. This indeed makes sense when the k value is smaller than m and n. However, when k is larger than n, we know that the i value cannot be less than k - n. The reason is that the most number of C[k] prefix subarray elements that can come from the B array is n. Therefore, a minimal of k − n elements must come from A. Therefore, the i value can never be smaller than k − n; we may as well set i_low to k − n.

The same argument shows that the j_low value cannot be less than k - m, which is the least number of elements of B that must be used in the merge process and thus the lower bound of the final co-rank j value.

We will use the example in Fig. 11.7 to illustrate the operation of the co-rank function in Fig. 11.6. The example assumes that three threads are used to merge arrays A and B into C. Each thread is responsible for generating an output subarray of three elements. We will first trace through the binary search steps of the co-rank function for thread 0 which is responsible for generating C[0]-C[2]. The reader should be able to determine that thread 0 calls the co-rank function with parameters (3, A, 5, B, 4).

As shown in Fig. 11.6, line 2 of the co-rank function initializes i to 3, which is the k value since k is smaller than m (value 5) in this example. Also, i_low is set 0. The i and i_low values define the section of A array that is currently being searched to determine the final co-rank i value. Thus, only 0, 1, 2, and 3 are being considered for the co-rank i value. Similarly, the j and j_low values are set to 0 and 0.

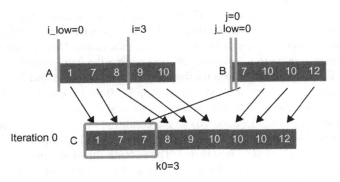

FIGURE 11.7

Iteration 0 of the co-rank function operation example for thread 0.

The main body of the co-rank function is a while-loop (line 8) that iteratively zooms into the final co-rank i and j values. The goal is to find a pair of i and j that result in A[i-1] ≤ B[j] and B[j-1] < A[i]. The intuition is that we choose the i and j values so none of the values in the A subarray used for generating a output subarray (referred to as the current A subarray) should be greater than any elements in the B subarray used for generating the next output subarray (referred to as the next B subarray). Note that the largest A element in the current subarray could be equal to the smallest element in the next B subarray since the A elements take precedence in placement into the output array whenever a tie occurs between an A element and a B element in our definition of the merge process.

In Fig. 11.6, the first if-construction in the while-loop (line 9) tests if the current i value is too high. If so, it will adjust the marker values so that it reduces the search range for i by about half toward the smaller end. This is done by reducing the i value by about half the difference between i and i_low. In Fig. 11.7, for iteration 0 of the while-loop, the if-construct finds that the i value (3) is too high since A[i − 1], whose value is 8, is greater than B[j], whose value is 7. The next few statements proceed to reduce the search range for i by reducing its value by delta = (3-0+1)>>1 = 2 (lines 10 and 13) while keeping the i_low value unchanged. Therefore, the i_low and i values for the next iteration will be 0 and 1.

The code also makes the search range for j to be comparable to that of i and shifts it to above the current j location. This is done by assigning the current j value to j_low (line 11) and adding the delta value to j (line 12). In our example, the j_low and j values for the next iteration will be 0 and 2 (Fig. 11.8).

During iteration 1 of the while-loop, the i and j values are 1 and 2. The if-construct (line 9) finds the i value to be acceptable since A[i − 1] is A[0], whose value is 1 while B[j] is B[2] whose value is 10, so A[i − 1] is less than B[j]. Thus, the condition of the first if-construct fails and the body of the if-construct is skipped. However, the j value is found to be too high during this iteration since B[j − 1] is B[1] (line 14), whose value is 10 while A[i] is A[1], whose value is 7. So the second if-construct will adjust the markers for the next iteration so that the search range for j will be reduced by about half toward the lower values. This is done by subtracting delta= (j-j_low+1)>>1=1 from j (lines 15 and 18). As a result, the j_low and j values for the next iteration will be 0 and 1. It also makes the next search range for i the same size as that for j but shifts it up by delta locations. This is done by assigning the current i value to i_low (line 16) and adding the delta value to i (line 17). Therefore, the i_low and i values for the next iteration will be 1 and 2.

During iteration 2, the i and j values are 2 and 1. Both if -constructs (lines 9 and 14) will find both i and j values acceptable. For the first if-construct, A[i − 1] is A[1] (value 7) and B[j] is B[1] (value 10) so the condition A[i-1] ≤ B[j] is satisfied. For the second if-construct, B[j − 1] is B[0] (value 7) and A[i] is A[2] (value 8) so the condition B[j-1] < A[i] is satisfied. The co-rank function exits the while-loop (lines 20 and 8) and returns the final i value 2 as the co-rank i value (line 23). The caller thread can derive the final co-rank j value as k-i=3 − 2 = 1. An inspection of Fig. 11.9 confirms that co-rank values of 2 and 1 indeed identify the correct A and B input subarrays for thread 0.

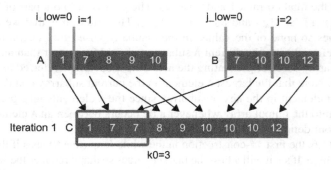

FIGURE 11.8

Iteration 1 of the co-rank function operation example for thread 0.

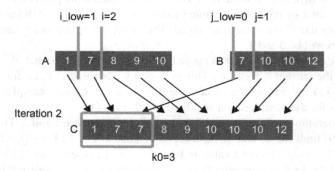

FIGURE 11.9

Iteration 2 of the co-rank function operation example for thread 0.

The reader should repeat the same process for thread 2 as an exercise. Also, note that if the input streams are much longer, the delta values will be reduced by half in each step so the algorithm is of $\log_2(N)$ complexity where N is the maximal of the two input array sizes.

11.5 A BASIC PARALLEL MERGE KERNEL

For the rest of this chapter, we assume that the input A and B arrays reside in the global memory. Further assume that a kernel is launched to merge the two input arrays to produce an output array C in the global memory. Fig. 11.10 shows a basic kernel that is a straightforward implementation of the parallel merge function described in Section 11.3.

As we can see, the kernel is fairly simple. It first divides the work among threads by calculating the starting point of the output subarray to be produced by the current thread (k_curr) and of the next thread (k_next). Keep in mind that the total number of output elements may not be a multiple of the number of threads. Each thread then makes two calls to the co-rank function. The first call uses k_curr as the rank parameter to get the co-rank values of the first (lowest-indexed) element of the output subarray that the current thread is to generate. These returned co-rank values give the lowest-indexed input A and B array elements that belong in the input subarray to be used by the thread. That is, the i_curr and j_curr values mark the beginning of the input subarrays for the thread. Therefore, &A[i_curr] and &B[j_curr] are the pointers to the beginning of the input subarrays to be used by the current thread.

The second call uses k_next as the rank parameter to get the co-rank values for the next thread. These co-rank values mark the positions of the lowest-indexed input

```
__global__ void merge_basic_kernel(int* A, int m, int* B, int n, int* C)


{
    int tid= blockIdx.x*blockDim.x + threadIdx.x;
    int k_curr = tid*ceil((m+n)/(blockDim.x*gridDim.x));                  // start index of output
    int k_next = min((tid+1) * ceil((m+n)/(blockDim.x*gridDim.x)), m+n);  // end index of output
    int i_curr= co_rank(k_curr, A, m, B, n);
    int i_next = co_rank(k_next, A, m, B, n);
    int j_curr = k_curr -i_curr;
    int j_next = k_next-i_next;
        /* All threads call the sequential merge function */
    merge_sequential(&A[i_curr], i_next-i_curr, &B[j_curr], j_next-j_curr, &C[k_curr] );
}
```

FIGURE 11.10

A basic merge kernel.

array elements to be used by the next thread. Therefore, i_next-i_curr and j_next-j_curr give m and n, the sizes of the subarrays of A and B to be used by the current thread. The pointer to the beginning of the output subarray to be produced by the current thread is &C[k_curr]. The final step of the kernel is to call the merge_sequential function (Fig. 11.3) with these parameters.

The execution of the basic merge kernel can be illustrated with the example in Fig. 11.9. The k_curr values for the three threads (threads 0, 1, and 2) will be 0, 3, and 6. We will focus on the execution of thread 1 whose k_curr value will be 3. The i_curr and j_curr values returned from the two co-rank function calls are 2 and 1. The k_next value for thread 1 will be 6. The call to the co-rank function gives the i_next and j_next values of 5 and 1. Thread 1 then calls the merge function with parameters (&A[2], 3, &B[1], 0, &C[3]). Note that the 0 value for parameter n indicates that none of the three elements of the output subarray for thread 1 should come from array B. This is indeed the case in Fig. 11.9: output elements C[3]-C[5] come from A[2]-A[4].

While the basic merge kernel is quite simple and elegant, it falls short in memory access efficiency. First, it is clear that when executing the merge_sequential function, adjacent threads in a warp are not accessing adjacent memory locations when they read and write the input and output subarray elements. For the example in Fig. 11.9, during the first iteration of the merge_sequential function execution, the three adjacent threads would read A[0], A[2], and B[0]. They will then write to C[0], C[3], and C[6]. Thus, their memory accesses are not coalesced, resulting in poor utilization of memory bandwidth.

Second, the threads also need to access A and B elements from the global memory when they execute the co-rank function. Since we are doing a binary search, the access patterns are somewhat irregular and will unlikely be coalesced. As a result, these accesses can further reduce the efficiency of utilizing the memory bandwidth. It would be helpful if we can reduce the number accesses to the global memory by the co-rank function.

11.6 A TILED MERGE KERNEL

As we have seen in Chapter 4, Memory and data locality, we can use shared memory to change the memory access patterns of the merge kernel into ones that can be coalesced. The key observation is that the input A and B subarrays to be used by the adjacent threads are adjacent to each other in memory. Essentially, all threads in a block will collectively use larger, block-level subarrays of A and B to generate a larger, block-level subarray of C. We can call the co-rank function for the entire block to get the starting and ending locations for the block-level A and B subarrays. Using these block-level co-rank values, all threads in the block can cooperatively load the elements of the block-level A and B subarrays into the shared memory in a coalesced pattern.

Fig. 11.11 shows the block-level design of a tiled merge kernel. In this example, we assume that three blocks will be used for the merge operation. At the bottom of the figure, we show that C is partitioned into three block-level subarrays. We delineate these partitions with gray vertical bars. Based on the partition, each block calls the co-rank functions to partition the input array into subarrays to be used for each block. We also delineate the input partitions with gray vertical bars. Note that the input partitions can vary significantly in size according to the actual data element values in the input arrays. For example, input A subarray is significantly larger than input B subarray for thread 0. On the other hand, input subarray A is significantly smaller than input B subarray for thread 1. Obviously, the combined size of the two input subarrays must always be equal to the size of the output subarray for each thread.

We will declare two shared memory arrays A_S and B_S for each block. Due to the limited shared memory size, A_S and B_S may not be able to cover the entire input subarrays for the block. Therefore, we will take an iterative approach. Assume that the A_S and B_S arrays can each hold x elements while each output subarray contains y elements. Each thread block will perform its operation in y/x iterations. During iteration, all threads in a block will cooperatively load x elements from the block's input A subarray and x elements from its input B subarray.

The first iteration of each thread is illustrated in Fig. 11.11. We show that for each block, a light gray section of input A subarray is loaded into A_S. A light gray section of the input B subarray is loaded into B_S. With x A elements and x B elements in the shared memory, the thread block has enough input elements to generate at least x output array elements. All threads are guaranteed to have all the input subarray elements they need for the iteration. One might ask why loading a total of 2x input elements can only guarantee the generation of x output elements. The reason is that in the worst case, all elements of the current output section may all come from one of the input sections. *This uncertainty of input usage makes the tiling design for the merge kernel much more challenging than the previous patterns.*

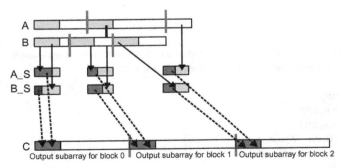

FIGURE 11.11

Design of a tiled merge kernel

Fig. 11.11 also shows that threads in each block will use a portion of the A_S and a portion of the B_S in each iteration, shown as dark gray sections, to generate a section of x elements in their output C subarray. This process is illustrated with the *dotted arrows* going from the A_S and B_S dark gray sections to the C dark sections. Note that each thread block may well use a different portion of its A_S versus B_S sections. Some blocks may use more elements from A_S and others may use more from B_S. The actual portions used by each block depend on the input data element values.

Fig. 11.12 shows the first part of a tiled merge kernel. A comparison against Fig. 11.10 shows remarkable similarity. This part is essentially the block-level version of the setup code for the thread-level basic merge kernel. Only one thread in the block needs to calculate the co-rank values for the rank values of the beginning output index of current block and that of the beginning output index of the next block. The values are placed into the shared memory so that they can be visible to all threads in the block. Having only one thread to call the co-rank function reduces the number of global memory accesses by the co-rank function and should improve the efficiency of the global memory. A barrier synchronization is used to ensure all threads wait until the block-level co-rank values are available in the shared memory A_S[0] and A_S[1] locations before they proceed to use the values.

```
_global_ void merge_tiled_kernel(int* A, int m, int* B, int n, int* C, int tile_size)



{
  /* shared memory allocation */
  extern _shared_ int shareAB[];
  int * A_S = &shareAB[0];              //shareA is first half of shareAB
  int * B_S = &shareAB[tile_size];      //ShareB is second half of ShareAB
  int C_curr = blockIdx.x * ceil((m+n)/gridDim.x) ;       // starting point of the C subarray for current block
  int C_next = min((blockIdx.x+1) * ceil((m+n)/gridDim.x), (m+n));   // starting point for next block

  if (threadIdx.x ==0)
  {
    A_S[0] = co_rank(C_curr, A, m, B, n);    // Make the block-level co-rank values visible to
    A_S[1] = co_rank(C_next, A, m, B, n);    // other threads in the block
  }
  _syncthreads();
  int A_curr = A_S[0];
  int A_next = A_S[1];
  int B_curr = C_curr - A_curr;
  int B_next = C_next - A_next;
  _syncthreads();
```

FIGURE 11.12

Part 1—identifying block-level output and input subarrays.

Recall that since the input subarrays may be too large to fit into the shared memory, the kernel takes an iterative approach. The kernel receives a `tile_size` argument that specifies the number of A elements and B elements to be accommodated in the shared memory. For example, `tile_size` value 1024 means that 1024 A array elements and 1024 B array elements are to be accommodated in the shared memory. This means that each block will dedicate (1024 + 1024)*4 = 8192 bytes of shared memory to hold the A and B array elements.

As a simple example, assume that we would like to merge an A array of 33,000 elements (m = 33,000) with a B array of 31,000 elements (n = 31,000). The total number of output C elements is 64,000. Further assume that we will use 16 blocks (`gridDim.x` = 16) and 128 threads in each block (`blockDim.x` = 128). Each block will generate 64,000/16 = 4,000 output C array elements.

If we assume that the `tile_size` value is 1024, the while-loop in Fig. 11.13 will need to take four iterations for each block to complete the generation of its 4000 output elements.

During iteration 0 of the `while`-loop, the threads in each block will cooperatively load 1024 elements of A and 1024 elements of B into the shared memory. Since there are 128 threads in a block, they can collectively load 128 elements in each iteration. So, the first `for`-loop in Fig. 11.13 will iterate eight times for all threads in a block to complete

```
int counter = 0;                                //iteration counter
int C_length = C_next – C_curr;
int A_length = A_next – A_curr;
int B_length = B_next – B_curr;
int total_iteration = ceil((C_length)/tile_size);    //total iteration
int C_completed = 0;
int A_consumed = 0;

int B_consumed = 0;
while(counter < total_iteration)
{
    /* loading tile-size A and B elements into shared memory */
    for(int i=0; i<tile_size; i+=blockDim.x)
    {
        if( i + threadIdx.x < A_length – A_consumed)
        {
            A_S[i + threadIdx.x] = A[A_curr + A_consumed + i + threadIdx.x ];
        }
    }
    for(int i=0; i<tile_size; i+=blockDim.x)
    {
        if(i + threadIdx.x  < B_length – B_consumed)
        {
            B_S[i + threadIdx.x] = B[B_curr + B_consumed + i + threadIdx.x];
        }
    }
    __syncthreads();
```

FIGURE 11.13

Part 2—loading A and B elements into the shared memory.

the loading of the 1024 A elements. The second `for`-loop will also iterate eight times to complete the loading of the 1024 B elements. Note that threads use their `threadIdx.x` values to select the element to load, so consecutive threads load consecutive elements. The memory accesses are coalesced. We will come back later and explain the `if`-conditions and how the index expressions for loading the A and B elements are formulated.

Once the input tiles are in the shared memory, individual threads can divide up the input tiles and merge their portions in parallel. This is done by assigning a section of the output to each thread and running the co-rank function to determine the sections of shared memory data that should be used for generating that output section. The code in Fig. 11.14 completes this step. Keep in mind that this is a continuation of the `while`-loop that started in Fig. 11.13. During each iteration of the `while`-loop, threads in a block will generate a total of `tile_size` C elements using the data we loaded into shared memory. (The exception is the last iteration, which will be addressed later.) The co-rank function is run on the data in shared memory for individual threads. Each thread first calculates the starting position of its output range and that of the next thread, and then uses these starting positions as the inputs to the co-rank function to identify its input ranges.

Let us resume our running example. In each iteration of the while-loop, all threads in a block will be collectively generating 1024 output elements using the two input tiles of A and B elements in the shared memory. (Once again, we will deal with the

```
int c_curr = threadIdx.x  * (tile_size/blockDim.x);
int c_next = (threadIdx.x+1) * (tile_size/blockDim.x);
c_curr  = (c_curr <= C_length − C_completed) ? c_curr : C_length − C_completed;
c_next = (c_next <= C_length − C_completed) ? c_next : C_length − C_completed;
/* find co-rank for c_curr and c_next */
int a_curr = co_rank(c_curr, A_S, min(tile_size, A_length-A_consumed),
                                    B_S, min(tile_size, B_length-B_consumed));
int b_curr = c_curr − a_curr;
int a_next = co_rank(c_next, A_S, min(tile_size, A_length-A_consumed),
                                    B_S, min(tile_size, B_length-B_consumed));
int b_next = c_next − a_next;

/* All threads call the sequential merge function */
merge_sequential (A_S+a_curr, a_next-a_curr, B_S+b_curr, b_next-b_curr,
            C+C_curr+C_completed+c_curr);
/* Update the A and B elements that have been consumed thus far */
counter ++;
C_completed += tile_size;
A_consumed += co_rank(tile_size,  A_S, tile_size, B_S, tile_size);
B_consumed = C_completed − A_consumed;
 _syncthreads();
   }
 }
```

FIGURE 11.14

Part 3—all threads merge their individual subarrays in parallel last iteration of the while-loop later.) The work is divided among 128 threads so each thread will be generating 8 output elements. While we know that each thread will consume a total of 8 input elements in the shared memory, we need to call the co-rank function to find out the exact number of A elements versus B elements that each thread will consume. Some threads may use 3 A elements and 5 B elements. Others may use 6 A elements and 2 B elements, and so on.

Collectively, the total number of A elements and B elements used by all threads in a block for the iteration will add up to 1024 for our example. For example, if all threads in a block used 476 A elements, we know that they also used 1024 − 476 = 548 B elements. It may even be possible that all threads end up using 1024 A elements and 0 B elements. Keep in mind that a total of 2048 elements are loaded in the shared memory. Therefore, in each iteration of the while-loop, only half of the A and B elements that were loaded into the shared memory will be used by all the threads in the block.

Each thread will then call the sequential merge function to merge its portions of A and B elements (identified by the co-rank values) from the shared memory into its designated range of C elements.

We are now ready to examine more details of the kernel function. Recall that we skipped the explanation of the index expressions for loading the A and B elements from global memory into the shared memory. For each iteration of the while-loop, the starting point for loading the current tile in the A and B array depends on the total number of A and B elements that have been consumed by all threads of the block during the previous iterations of the while-loop. Assume that we keep track of the total number of A elements consumed by all the previous iterations of the while-loop in variable A_consumed. We initialize A_consumed to 0 before entering the while-loop. During iteration 0, all blocks start their tiles from A[A_curr] since A_consumed is 0 at the beginning of iteration 0. During each subsequent iteration of the while-loop, the tile of A elements will start at A[A_curr+A_consumed].

Figs. 11.11 and 11.15 illustrate the index calculation for iteration 1 of the while-loop. In our running example in Fig. 11.11, we show the A_S elements that are consumed by the block of threads during iteration 0 as the dark gray portion of the tile in A_S. During iteration 1, the tile to be loaded from the global memory for block 0 should start at the location right after the section that contains the A elements consumed in iteration 0. In Fig. 11.15, for each block, the section of A elements consumed in iteration 0 is shown as the small white section at the beginning of the A subarray assigned to the block. Since the length of the small section is given by the value of A_consumed, the tile to be loaded for iteration 1 of the while-loop starts at A[A_curr+A_consumed]. Similarly, the tile to be loaded for iteration 1 of the while-loop starts at B[B_curr+B_consumed].

Note in Fig. 11.14 that A_consumed and B_consumed are accumulated through the while-loop iterations. Therefore, at the beginning of each iteration, the tiles to be loaded for the iteration always start with A[A_curr+A_consumed] and B[B_curr+B_consumed].

During the last iterations of the while-loop, there may not be enough input A or B elements to fill the input tiles in the shared memory for some of the thread blocks.

For example, in Fig. 11.15, for thread block 2, the number of remaining A elements for iteration 1 is less than the tile size. An if-statement should be used to prevent the threads from attempting to load elements that are outside the input subarrays for the block. The first if-statement in Fig. 11.13 detects such attempts by checking if the index of the A_S element that a thread is trying to load exceeds the number of remaining A elements given by the value of the expression A_length-A_consumed. The if-statement ensures that the threads only load the elements that are within the remaining section of the A subarray. The same is done for the B elements.

With the if-statements and the index expressions, the tile loading process should work well as long as A_consumed and B_consumed give the total number of A and B elements consumed by the thread block in previous iterations of the while-loop. This brings us to the code at the end of the while-loop in Fig. 11.14. These statements update the total number of C elements generated by the while-loop iterations thus far. For all but the last iteration, each iteration generates additional tile_size C elements.

The next two statements update the total number of A and B elements consumed by the threads in the block. For all but the last iteration, the number of additional A elements consumed by the thread block is the returned value of

```
co_rank(tile_size, A_S, tile_size, B_S, tile_size)
```

As we mentioned before, the calculation of the number of elements consumed may not be correct at the end of the last iteration of the while-loop. There may not be a full tile of elements left for the final iteration. However, since the while-loop will not iterate any further, the A_consumed, B_consumed, and C_completed values will not be used so the incorrect results will not cause any harm. However, one should remember that if for any reason these values are needed after exiting the while-loop, the three variables will not have the correct values. The values of A_length, B_length, and C_length should be used instead since all the elements in the designated subarrays to the thread block will have been consumed at the exit of the while-loop.

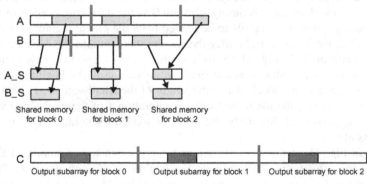

FIGURE 11.15

Iteration 1 of the running example.

The tiled kernel achieves substantial reduction in global memory accesses by the co-rank function and makes the global memory accesses coalesced. However, as is, the kernel has a significant deficiency. It only makes use of half of the data that is loaded into the shared memory. The unused data in the shared memory are simply reloaded in the next iteration. This wastes half of the memory bandwidth. In the next section, we will present a circular buffer scheme for managing the tiles of data elements in the shared memory, which allows the kernel to fully utilize all the A and B elements loaded into the shared memory. As we will see, this increased efficiency comes with a substantial increase in code complexity.

11.7 A CIRCULAR-BUFFER MERGE KERNEL

The design of the circular-buffer merge kernel, which will be referred to as `merge_circular_buffer_kernel`, is largely the same as the `merge_tiled_kernel` kernel in the previous section. The main difference lies in the management of A and B elements in the shared memory to enable full utilization of all the elements loaded from the global memory. The overall structure of the `merge_tiled_kernel` is the same as that shown in Figs. 11.12–11.14, which assumes that the tiles of A and B elements always start at A_S[0] and B_S[0]. After each while-loop iteration, the kernel loads the next tile starting from A_S[0] and B_S[0]. The inefficiency of `merge_tiled_kernel` comes from the fact that part of the next tiles of elements are in the shared memory but we reload the entire tile from the global memory and write over these remaining elements from the previous iteration.

Fig. 11.16 shows the main idea of the circular-buffer merge kernel, called `merge_circular_buffer_kernel`. We will continue to use the example from Figs. 11.11 and 11.15. Two additional variables A_S_start and B_S_start are added to allow each iteration of the while-loop in Fig. 11.13 to start its A and B tiles at dynamically determined positions inside A_S[0] and B_S[0]. This added tracking allows each iteration of the while-loop to start the tiles with the remaining A and B elements from the previous iteration. Since there is no previous iteration when we first enter the while-loop, these two variables are initialized to 0 before entering the while-loop.

During iteration 0, since the values of A_S_start and B_S_start are both 0, the tiles will start with A_S[0] and B_S[0]. This is illustrated in Fig. 11.16A, where we show the tiles that will be loaded from the global memory (A and B) into the shared memory (A_S and B_S) as light gray sections. Once these tiles are loaded into the shared memory, `merge_circular_buffer_kernel` will proceed with the merge operation in the same way as the `merge_tile` kernel.

We also need to update the A_S_start and B_S_start variables for use in the next iteration by advancing the value of these variables by the number of A and B elements consumed from the shared memory during the current iteration. Keep in mind that the size each buffer is limited to `tile_size`. At some point, we will need to reuse the buffer locations at the beginning part of the A_S and B_S arrays. This is done by

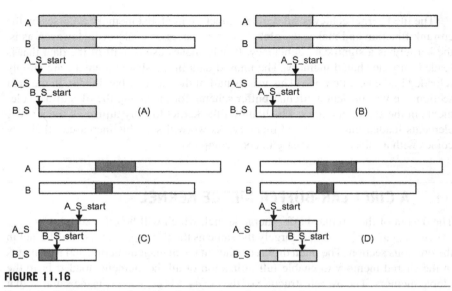

FIGURE 11.16

A circular buffer scheme for managing the shared memory tiles.

checking if the new A_S_start and B_S_start values exceed the tile_size. If so, we subtract tile_size from them as shown in the if-statement below:

```
A_S_start = A_S_start + A_S_consumed;
if (A_S_start >= tile_size) A_S_start = A_S_start - tile_size;
B_S_start = B_S_start + B_S_consumed;
if (B_S_start >= tile_size) B_S_start = B_S_start - tile_size;
```

Fig. 11.16B illustrates the update of the A_S_start and B_S_start variables. At the end of iteration 0, a portion of the A tile and a portion of the B tile have been consumed. The consumed portions are shown as white sections in A_S and B_S in Fig. 11.16B. We update the A_S_start and B_S_start values to the position immediately after the consumed sections in the shared memory.

Fig. 11.16C illustrates the operations for filling the A and B tiles at the beginning of iteration 1 of the while-loop. A_S_consumed is a variable added to track the number of A elements used in the current iteration for use in filling the tile in the next iteration. At the beginning of each iteration, we need to load a section of up to A_S_consumed elements to fill up the A tile in the shared memory. Similarly, we need to load a section of up to B_S_consumed elements to fill up the B tile in the shared memory. The two sections loaded are shown as dark gray sections in Fig. 11.16C. Note that the tiles effectively "wrap around" in the A_S and B_S arrays since we are reusing the space of the A and B elements that were consumed during iteration 0.

Fig. 11.16D illustrates the updates to A_S_start and B_S_start at the end of iteration 1. The sections of elements consumed during iteration 1 are shown as the white sections. Note that in A_S, the consumed section wraps around to beginning part of A_S. The value of the A_S_start variable is also wrapped around in the if-statement.

It should be clear that we will need to adjust the code for loading and using the tiled elements to support this circular usage of the A_S and B_S arrays.

Part 1 of `merge_circular_buffer_kernel` is identical to that of `merge_tiled_kernel` in Fig. 11.12 so we will not present it. Fig. 11.17 shows Part 2 of the circular buffer kernel. Refer to Fig. 11.13 for variable declarations that remain the same. New variables A_S_start, B_S_start, A_S_consumed, and B_S_consumed are initialized to 0 before we enter the while-loop.

Note that the exit conditions of the two for-loops have been adjusted. Instead of always loading a full tile, as was the case in the merge kernel in Fig. 11.13, each for-loop in Fig. 11.13 is set up to only load the number of elements needed to refill the tiles, given by A_S_consumed. The section of the A elements to be loaded by a thread block in the ith for-loop iteration starts at global memory location A[A_curr + A_consumed + i]. Thus, the A element to be loaded by a thread in the ith for-loop iteration is A[A_curr + A_consumed + i+ threadIdx.x]. The index for each thread to place its A element into the A_S array is A_S_start+(tile_size-A_S_consumed)+ i+threadIdx since the tile starts at A_S[A_S_start] and there are (tile_size-A_S_consumed) elements remaining in the buffer from the previous iteration of the while-loop. The if-statement checks if the index value is greater than or equal to tile_size. If so, it is wrapped back into the beginning part of the array by subtracting tile_size

```
int A_S_start = 0;
int B_S_start = 0;
int A_S_consumed = tile_size;   //in the first iteration, fill the tile_size
int B_S_consumed = tile_size;   //in the first iteration, fill the tile_size
while(counter < total_iteration)
{
        /* loading A_S_consumed elements into A_S */
        for(int i=0; i<A_S_consumed; i+=blockDim.x)
        {
                if( i + threadIdx.x < A_length – A_consumed && i + threadIdx.x < A_S_consumed)
                {
                        A_S[(A_S_start + i + threadIdx.x)%tile_size] =
                                A[A_curr + A_consumed + i + threadIdx.x ];
                }
        }
        /* loading B_S_consumed elements into B_S */
        for(int i=0; i<B_S_consumed; i+=blockDim.x)
        {
                if(i + threadIdx.x  < B_length – B_consumed && i + threadIdx.x < B_S_consumed)
                {
                        B_S[(B_S_start + i + threadIdx.x)%tile_size] =
                                B[B_curr + B_consumed + i + threadIdx.x];

                }
        }
```

FIGURE 11.17

Part 2 of a circular-buffer merge kernel.

from the index value. The same analysis applies to the for-loop for loading the B tile and is left as an exercise.

Using the A_S and B_S arrays as circular buffers also incurs additional complexity in the implementation of the co-rank and merge functions. Part of the additional complexity could be reflected in the thread-level code that calls these functions. However, in general, it is better if one can efficiently handle the complexities inside the library functions to minimize the increased level of complexity in the user code. We show such an approach in Fig. 11.18. Fig. 11.18A shows the implementation of the circular buffer. A_S_start and B_S_start mark the beginning of the tile in the circular buffer. The tiles wrap around in the A_S and B_S arrays, shown as the light gray section to the left of A_S_start and B_S_start.

Keep in mind that the co-rank values are used for threads to identify the starting position, ending position, and length of the input subarrays that they are to use. When we employ circular buffers, we could provide the co-rank values as the actual indices in the circular buffer. However, this would incur quite a bit of complexity in the merge_circular_buffer_kernel code. For example, the a_next value could be smaller than the a_curr value since the tile is wrapped around in the A_S array. Thus, one would need to test for the case and calculate the length of the section as a_next- a_curr+tile_size. However, in other cases when a_next is larger than a_curr, the length of the section is simply a_next-a_curr.

Fig. 11.18B shows a simplified model for defining, deriving, and using the co-rank values with the circular buffer. In this model, the tiles appear to be in continuous sections starting at A_S_start and B_S_start. In the case of the B_S tile in Fig. 11.18A, b_next is wrapped around and would be smaller than b_curr in the circular buffer. However, as shown in Fig. 11.18B, the simplified model provides the illusion that all elements are in a continuous section of up to tile_size elements and thus

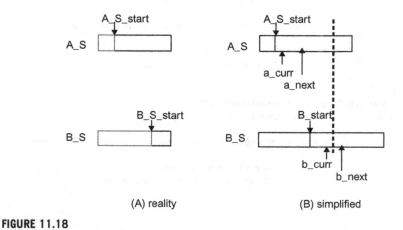

(A) reality   (B) simplified

FIGURE 11.18

A simplified model for the co-rank values when using a circular buffer.

a_next is always larger than or equal to a_curr and b_next is always larger than or equal to b_curr. It is up to the implementation of the co_rank_circular and merge_ sequential_circular functions to map this simplified view of the co-rank values into the actual circular buffer indices so that they can carry out their functionalities correctly and efficiently.

The co_rank_circular and merge_sequential_circular functions have the same set of parameters as the original co_rank and merge functions except for three additional ones: A_S_start, B_S_start, and tile_size. These three additional parameters inform the functions where the current starting points of the buffers are and how big the buffers are. Fig. 11.19 shows the revised thread-level code based on the simplified model for the co-rank value using circular buffers. The only change to the code is that co_rank_circular and merge_sequential_circular functions are called instead of the co_rank and merge functions. This demonstrates that a well-designed library interface can reduce the impact on the user code when employing sophisticated data structures.

Fig. 11.20 shows an implementation of the co-rank function that provides the simplified model for the co-rank values while correctly operated on circular buffers. It treats i, j, i_low, and j_low values in exactly the same way as the co-rank function in Fig. 11.6. The only change is that i, i-1, j, and j-1 are no longer used directly as indices when accessing the A_S and B_S arrays. They are used as offsets that are to be added to the values of A_S_start and B_S_start to form the index values i_cir, i_m_1_cir, j_cir, and j_m_1_cir. In each case, we need to test if the actual index values need to be wrapped around to the beginning part of the buffer. Note that we cannot simply use i_cir-1 to replace i-1, we need to form the final index value and check for the need to wrap it around. It should be clear that the simplified model also helps to keep the co-rank function code simple: all the manipulations of the i, j, i_low, j_low values remain the same; they do not need to deal with the circular nature of the buffers.

Fig. 11.21 shows an implementation of the merge_sequential_circular function. Similar to the co_rank_circular function, the logic of the code remains essentially unchanged from the original merge function. The only change is in the way i and j are used to access the A and B elements. Since the merge_sequential_circular function will only be called by the thread-level code of merge_circular_buffer_kernel, the A and B elements accessed will be in the A_S and B_S arrays. In all four places where i or j is used to access the A or B elements, we need to form the i_cir or j_cir and test if the index value needs to be wrapped around to the beginning part of the array. Otherwise, the code is the same as the merge function in Fig. 11.3.

Although we did not list all parts of merge_circular_buffer_kernel, the reader should be able to put it all together based on the parts that we discussed. The use of tiling and circular buffers adds quite a bit of complexity. In particular, each thread uses quite a few more registers to keep track of the starting point and remaining number of elements in the buffers. All these additional usages can potentially reduce the occupancy, or the number of thread-blocks that can be assigned to each of the

```
int c_curr = threadIdx.x  * (tile_size/blockDim.x);
int c_next = (threadIdx.x+1) * (tile_size/blockDim.x);

c_curr = (c_curr <= C_length-C_completed) ? c_curr : C_length-C_completed;
c_next = (c_next <= C_length-C_completed) ? c_next : C_length-C_completed;
        /* find co-rank for c_curr and c_next */
int a_curr = co_rank_circular(c_curr,
        A_S, min(tile_size, A_length-A_consumed),
        B_S, min(tile_size, B_length-B_consumed),
        A_S_start, B_S_start, tile_size);
int b_curr = c_curr -a_curr;
int a_next = co_rank_circular(c_next,
        A_S, min(tile_size, A_length-A_consumed),
        B_S, min(tile_size, B_length-B_consumed),
        A_S_start, B_S_start, tile_size);

int b_next = c_next -a_next;
        /* All threads call the circular-buffer version of the sequential merge function */
merge_seqetial_circular( A_S, a_next-a_curr,
        B_S, b_next-b_curr, C+C_curr+C_completed+c_curr,
                A_S_start+a_curr, B_S_start+b_curr, tile_size);

        /* Figure out the work has been done */
counter ++;
A_S_consumed = co_rank_circular(min(tile_size,C_length-C_completed),
        A_S, min(tile_size, A_length-A_consumed),
        B_S, min(tile_size, B_length-B_consumed),
        A_S_start, B_S_start, tile_size);
B_S_consumed = min(tile_size, C_length-C_completed) -A_S_consumed;
A_consumed+= A_S_consumed;
C_completed += min(tile_size, C_length-C_completed);
B_consumed = C_completed -A_consumed;

A_S_start = A_S_start + A_S_consumed;
if (A_S_start >= tile_size) A_S_start = A_S_start -tile_size;
B_S_start = B_S_start + B_S_consumed;
if (B_S_start >= tile_size) B_S_start = B_S_start -tile_size;

__syncthreads();
        }
    }
```

FIGURE 11.19

Part 3 of a circular-buffer merge kernel.

streaming multiprocessors when the kernel is executed. However, since the merge operation is memory bandwidth bound, the computational and register resources are likely underutilized. Thus, increasing the number of registers used and address calculations to conserve memory bandwidth are a reasonable tradeoff.

```
int co_rank_circular(int k, int* A, intm, int* B, int n,
int A_S_start, int B_S_start, inttile_size)
{
    inti= k<m ? k : m;  //i = min (k,m)
    int j = k-i;
    int i_low = 0>(k-n) ? 0 : k-n;  //i_low = max(0, k-n)
    int j_low = 0>(k-m) ? 0: k-m;  //j_low = max(0,k-m)
    int delta;
    bool active = true;
    while(active)
    {
        int i_cir = (A_S_start+i> = tile_size) ?
            A_S_start+i-tile_size : A_S_start+i;

        int i_m_1_cir = (A_S_start+i-1 > = tile_size)?
            A_S_start+i-1-tile_size: A_S_start+i-1;

        int j_cir = (B_S_start+j> = tile_size) ?
            B_S_start+j-tile_size : B_S_start+j;

        int j_m_1_cir = (B_S_start+i-1 >= tile_size)?
            B_S_start+j-1-tile_size: B_S_start+j-1;

        if (i > 0 && j < n && A[i_m_1_cir] > B[j_cir]) {
            delta = ((i-i_low +1) >> 1) ; // ceil(i-i_low)/2)
            j_low = j;
            i = i - delta;
            j = j + delta;
        } else if (j > 0 && i < m && B[j_m_1_cir] >= A[i_cir]) {
            delta = ((j - j_low +1) >> 1) ;
            i_low = i;
            i = i + delta;
            j = j - delta;
        } else {
            active = false;
        }
    }
    return i;
}
```

FIGURE 11.20

A co_rank_circular function that operates on circular buffers.

```
void merge_sequential_circular(int*A, intm,
            int*B, intn, int*C, intA_S_start,
            intB_S_start, inttile_size)
{
    int i = 0; //virtual index into A
    int j = 0; //virtual index into B
    int k = 0; //virtual index into C

    while ((i < m) && (j < n)) {
        int i_cir= (A_S_start+ i>= tile_size)?
            A_S_start+i-tile_size; A_S_start+i;
        int j_cir= (B_S_start+ j>= tile_size)?
            B_S_start+j-tile_size; B_S_start+j;
        if (A[i_cir] <= B[j_cir]) {
            C[k++] = A[i_cir]; i++;
        } else {
            C[k++] = B[j_cir]; j++;
        }
    }
    if (i == m) { //done with A[] handle remaining B[]
        for (; j < n; j++) {
            int j_cir = (B_S_start + j>= tile_size)?
                B_S_start+j-tile_size; B_S_start+j;
            C[k++] = B[j_cir];
        }
    } else { //done with B[], handle remaining A[]
        for (; i <m; i++) {
            int i_cir = (A_S_start + i>= tile_size)?
                A_S_start+i-tile_size; A_S_start+i;
            C[k++] = A[i_cir];
        }
    }
}
```

FIGURE 11.21

Implementation of the merge_sequential_circular function.

11.8 SUMMARY

In this chapter, we introduced the merge sort pattern whose parallelization requires each thread to dynamically identify its input ranges. The fact that the input ranges are data dependent also creates extra challenges when we use tiling technique to conserve memory bandwidth. As a result, we introduce the use of circular buffers to allow us to make full use of the memory data loaded. We showed that introducing a more complex data structure such as circular buffers can significantly increase the complexity of the code that uses these data structures. Thus, we introduce a simplified buffer access model for the code that manipulates and uses the indices to remain largely unchanged. The actual circular nature of the buffers is only exposed when these indices are used to access the elements in the buffer.

11.9 EXERCISES

1. Assume that we need to merge lists A and B. A = (1, 7, 8, 9, 10) and B = (7, 10, 10, 12). What are the co-rank values for C[8]?

2. Complete the calculation of co-rank functions for Thread 1 and Thread 2 in the example shown in Fig. 11.7 through Fig. 11.9.

REFERENCE

Siebert, C., & Traff, J. L. (2012). Efficient MPI implementation of a parallel, stable merge algorithm: *Proceedings of the 19th European conference on recent advances in the Message Passing Interface (EuroMPI'12)*. Heidelberg: Springer-Verlag Berlin, pp. 204–213.

Parallel patterns: graph search

12

Juan Gómez-Luna and Izzat El Hajj

CHAPTER OUTLINE

Our final parallel pattern is graph search. A graph is a data structure that represents the relations between entities. The entities involved are represented as vertices and the relations are represented as edges. Many important real-world problems are naturally formulated as large-scale graph problems and can benefit from massively parallel computation. Prominent examples include social networks and driving direction services. Graphs are intrinsically related to sparse matrices. In fact, graph computation can be formulated in terms of sparse matrix operations. However, one can often improve the efficiency of graph computation by exploiting properties that are specific to the type of graph computation being performed. In this chapter, we will focus on graph search, a graph computation that underlies many real-world applications. Since graph search computation is about examining the vertex values, there is very little computation on these values once they are loaded from memory. As a result, the speed of graph search is typically limited by memory bandwidth. We will discuss graph data formats that help minimize the consumption of memory bandwidth. We will then introduce work queues, an important class of parallel data structures that supports work-efficient iterative algorithms that require dynamic discovery and collection of the data to be processed. We will show that the privatization technique can be productively used to minimize serialization when collecting data into the work queues.

12.1 BACKGROUND

A graph data structure represents the relation between entities. For example, in social media, the entities are users and the relations are connections between users. For another example, in map driving direction applications, the entities are locations and the relations are the roadways between them. Some relations are bi-directional, such as friend connections in a social network. Other relations are directional. For example, roads may be one-way streets. We will focus on directional relations; bi-directional relations can be represented with two directional relations, one in each direction. A directional relation is represented as an arrowed edge going from a source vertex to a destination vertex.

Fig. 12.1 shows a simple graph with directional edges. We assign a unique number to each vertex. There is one edge going from vertex 0 to vertex 1 and one going from vertex 0 to vertex 2. For a driving direction application, we may need to find all the alternative routes that we could take going from the location represented by vertex 0 to that represented by vertex 5. By visual inspection, we see that there are three possible paths: 0→1→3→4→5, 0→1→4→5, and 0→2→5.

An intuitive representation of a graph is an *adjacency matrix*. We assign a unique number to each vertex. When there is an edge going from vertex i to vertex j, the value of element A[i][j] of the adjacency matrix is 1. Otherwise, it is 0. Fig. 12.2 shows the adjacency matrix for the simple graph in Fig. 12.1. We see that A[1][3] and A[4][5] are 1 since there are edges going from vertex 1 to vertex 3. For clarity, we leave the 0 values out of the adjacency matrix. That is, if an element is empty, its value is 0.

If a graph with N vertices is fully connected, each vertex should have (N-1) outgoing edges. There should be a total of N(N-1) edges, since there is no edge going from a vertex to itself. For example, if our 9-vertex graph were fully connected, there

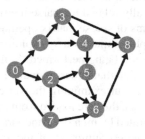

FIGURE 12.1

A simple graph with directional edges.

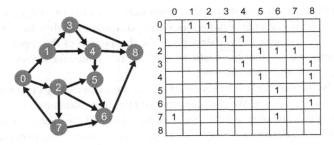

FIGURE 12.2

Adjacency matrix representation of the simple graph example.

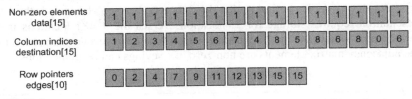

FIGURE 12.3

Sparse matrix (CSR) representation of adjacency matrix.

should be eight edges going out of each vertex. There should be a total of 72 edges. Obviously, our graph is much less connected; each vertex has three or fewer outgoing edges. Such graph is referred to as being *sparsely connected*. That is, the average number of outgoing edges from each vertex is much smaller than N-1.

At this point, the reader has most likely made the correct observation that sparsely connected graphs can probably benefit from a sparse matrix representation. Indeed, many real-world graphs are sparsely connected. For example, in a social network such as Facebook, Twitter, or LinkedIn, the average number of connections for each user is much smaller than the total number of users. This makes the number of non-zero elements in the adjacency matrix much smaller than the total number of elements. As we have seen in Chapter 10, Parallel patterns: sparse matrix computation, using a compressed representation such as Compressed Sparse Row (CSR) can drastically reduce the amount of storage for and the number of wasted operations on the zero elements.

Fig. 12.3 shows a CSR representation of our simple graph example. We will refer to the row pointer array as the edges array. Recall that each row pointer gives the starting location for the non-zero elements in a row. For example, edges[3] = 7 gives the starting location of the non-zero elements in row 3 of the original adjacency matrix. Also, edges[4] = 9 gives the starting location of the non-zero elements in row 4 of the original matrix. Thus, we expect to find the non-zero data for row 3 in data[7] and data[8] and the column indices for these elements in destination[7] and destination[8]. These are the data and column indices for the two edges leaving vertex 3. The reason we call the column index array destination is that the column index of an element in the adjacency matrix gives the destination of the represented edge. In our example, we see that the destination of the two edges for source vertex 3 are destination[7] = 4 and destination[8] = 8.

Obviously, the data array is unnecessary. Since the value of all its elements is 1, we really don't need to store it. We can make the data implicit—whenever one of the non-zero element values is used, we can just assume it is 1. That is, the existence of each column index in the destination array implies that an edge does exist. However, in some applications, the adjacency matrix may store additional information about the relationship, such the distance between two locations or the date when two social network users became connected. In those applications, the data array will need to be used.

Sparse representation can lead to significant savings in storing the adjacency matrix. For our example, assuming that the data array can be eliminated, the CSR representation requires storage for 25 locations versus the $9^2=81$ locations if we stored the entire adjacency matrix. For real-life problems where a very small fraction of the adjacency matrix elements are non-zero, the savings can be tremendous.

12.2 BREADTH-FIRST SEARCH

An important graph computation is breadth-first search (BFS). BFS is often used to discover the shortest number of edges that one needs to take in order to go from one vertex to another vertex of the graph. There are several forms of BFS. Each form derives a different type of result but one can typically derive the result of one form from that of another.

A simple form of BFS, given a vertex referred to as the source, label each vertex with the smallest number of edges that one needs to traverse in order to go from the source to the vertex.

Fig. 12.4(A) shows the desired BFS result with vertex 0 as the source. Through one edge, we can get to vertices 1 and 2. Thus, we mark these vertices as level 1. By

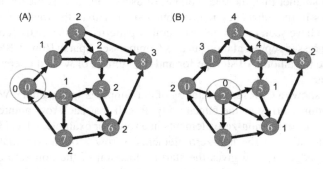

FIGURE 12.4

Breadth-first search results. (A) Vertex 0 is source, (B) vertex 2 is source.

traversing another edge, we can get to vertices 3 (through vertex 1), 4 (through vertex 1), 5 (through vertex 2), 6 (through vertex 2) and 7 (through vertex 2). Thus we mark these vertices as level 2. Finally, by traversing one more edge, we can get to vertex 8 (through any of vertices 3, 4, or 6). Obviously, the BFS result with another vertex as the source, say vertex 2, would be quite different.

Fig. 12.4(B) shows the desired result of BFS with vertex 2 as the source. The level 1 vertices are 5, 6, and 7. The level 2 vertices are 8 (through vertex 6) and 0 (through vertex 7). Only vertex 1 is at level 3 (through vertex 0). Finally, the level 4 vertices are 3 and 4 (both through vertex 1). It is interesting to note that the outcome is quite different for each vertex even though we moved the source to a vertex that is only one edge away from the original source.

Once we have all the vertices labeled, we can easily find a path from the source to any of the vertices in terms of the number of edges traveled. For example, in Fig. 12.4(B), we see that vertex 1 is labeled as level 3. So we know that the smallest number of edges between the source (vertex 2) and vertex 1 is 3. If we need to find the path, we can simply start from the destination vertex and trace back to the source. At each step, we select the predecessor whose level is one less than the current vertex. If there are multiple predecessors with the same level, we can randomly pick one. Any one thus selected would give a sound solution. The fact that there are multiple predecessors to choose from means that there are multiple equally good solutions to the problem. In our example, we can find a shortest path from vertex 2 to vertex 1 by starting from vertex 1, choosing vertex 0, then vertex 7, and then vertex 2. Therefore a solution path is 2→7→0→1. This of course assumes that each vertex has a list of pointers to the source vertices of all the incoming edges so that one can find the predecessors of a given vertex.

Fig. 12.5 shows an important application of BFS in computer-aided design (CAD). When designing an integrated circuit chip, there are many electronic components that need to be connected to complete the design. The connectors of these components are called net terminals. Fig. 12.5(A) shows two such net terminals as red dots, one belongs to a component in the upper left part and the other belongs to another component in the lower right part of the chip. Assume that the design

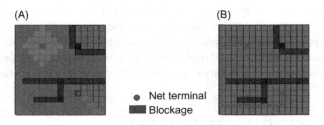

(A)   (B)

● Net terminal
▬ Blockage

FIGURE 12.5

Maze routing in integrated circuits—an application for breadth-first search. (A) Breadth-first search, (B) identifying a routing path.

requires that these two net terminals be connected. This is done by running, or routing, a wire of a given width from the first net terminal to the second net terminal.

The routing software represents the chip as a grid of wiring blocks where each block can potentially serve as a piece of a wire. A wire can be formed by extending in either the horizontal or the vertical direction. For example, the black J-shape in the lower half of the chip consists of 21 wiring blocks and connects three net terminals. Once a wiring block is used as part of a wire, it can no longer be used as part of any other wires. Furthermore, it forms a blockage for wiring blocks around it. No wires can be extended from a used block's lower neighbor to its upper neighbor, or from its left neighbor to its right neighbor, etc. Once a wire is formed, all other wires must be routed around it. Routing blocks can also be occupied by circuit components, which impose the same blockage constraint as when they are used as part of a wire. This is why the problem is called a maze routing problem. The previously formed circuit components and wires form a maze for the wires that are yet to be formed. The maze routing software finds a route for each additional wire given all the constraints from the previously formed components and wires.

The maze routing application represents the chip as a graph. The routing blocks are vertices. An edge from vertex i to vertex j indicates that one can extend a wire from block i to block j. Once a block is occupied by a wire or a component, it is either marked as a blockage vertex or taken away from the graph, depending on the design of the application. Fig. 12.5 shows that the application solves the maze routing problem with a BFS from the source net terminal to the destination net terminal. This is done by starting with the source vertex and labeling the vertices into levels. The immediate vertical or horizontal neighbors (a total of four) that are not blockages are marked as level 1. We see that all four neighbors of the source are reachable and will be marked as level 1. The neighbors of level 1 vertices that are neither blockages nor visited by the current search will be marked as level 2. The reader should verify that there are 4 level-1 vertices, 8 level-2 vertices, and 12 level-3 vertices, etc. in Fig. 12.5(A). As we can see, the BFS essentially forms a wave front of vertices for each level. These wave fronts start small for level 1 but can grow very large very quickly in a few levels.

Fig. 12.5(B) shows that once the BFS is complete, we can form a wire by finding a shortest path from the source to the destination. As we explained earlier in this chapter, this can be done by starting with the destination vertex and tracing back to the predecessors whose levels are one lower than the current vertex. Whenever there are multiple predecessors that have equivalent levels, there are multiple routes that are of the same length. One could design heuristics to choose the predecessor in such a way that minimizes the difficulty of constraints for wires that are yet to be formed.

12.3 A SEQUENTIAL BFS FUNCTION

We are now ready to write a sequential breadth-first function. We assume that the graph is represented in the CSR format shown in Fig. 12.3. The function receives the index of the source vertex, the edges (edges) array, and the destination (dest) array for the graph. Furthermore, it receives a label array whose elements will be used to store the visit status information for the vertices.

Before the search, the label element for the source is initialized to 0, indicating that it is a level 0 vertex. All other label elements are initialized to -1, indicating that their associated vertices have not been visited. At the end of the search, all label array elements corresponding to vertices reachable from the source should be set to a positive level number. If the label array element of any vertex remains -1 after the search, it means that the vertex is unreachable from the source.

Fig. 12.6 shows a sequential implementation of the BFS function. It maintains two frontier arrays: one stores the frontier vertices discovered in the previous iteration (previous frontier), and one stores the frontier vertices that are being discovered in the current iteration (current frontier). These arrays are declared as frontier[0] [MAX_FRONTIER_SIZE] and frontier[1][MAX_FRONTIER_SIZE]. The roles of these two arrays alternate. During the first iteration, frontier[0] stores the current frontier and frontier[1] stores the previous frontier, the source vertex. During the second iteration, the two arrays exchange their roles: frontier[0] stores the previous frontier and frontier[1] stores the current frontier. That is, what is being assembled as the current in one iteration becomes the previous frontier in the next iteration. This way, one of the arrays holds the stable frontier formed during the previous iteration while the other one's contents are being assembled. By switching the roles of these two arrays, we avoid the need for copying the contents from a current frontier array to a previous frontier array when we move to the next iteration. This technique is commonly called *ping-pong buffering*.

The function assumes that all label array elements are initialized to -1 by the caller. At the beginning of the function, the label[source] element is initialized

```
void BFS_sequential(int source, int *edges, int *dest, int *label)
{
    int frontier[2][MAX_FRONTIER_SIZE];
    int *c_frontier = &frontier[0];
    int c_frontier_tail = 0;
    int *p_frontier = &frontier[1];
    int p_frontier_tail = 0;

    insert_frontier(source, p_frontier, &p_frontier_tail);
    label[source] = 0;

    while (p_frontier_tail > 0) {
        for (int f=0; f < p_frontier_tail; f++) {   // visit all previous frontier vertices
            c_vertex = p_frontier[f];                      // Pick up one of the previous frontier vertex
            for  (int i = edges[c_vertex]; i < edges[c_vertex+1]; i++) { //for all its edges
                if (label[dest[i]] == -1) {           // The dest vertex has not been visited
                    insert_frontier(dest[i], c_frontier, &c_frontier_tail); // overflow check omitted for brevity
                    label[dest[i]] = label[c_vertex]+1;
                }
            }
        }
        int temp = c_frontier;   c_frontier = p_frontier; p_frontier = temp; //swap previous and current
        p_frontier_tail = c_frontier_tail;   c_frontier_tail = 0; //
    }
}
```

FIGURE 12.6

A sequential breadth-first search function.

to 0, indicating that the source is the level 0 vertex for the search. It maintains a pointer variable c_frontier to point to the beginning of the current frontier array and another pointer variable p_frontier to point to the beginning of the previous frontier array. At the beginning of the function, c_frontier is initialized so that it points to frontier[0] and p_frontier to frontier[1]. The function also maintains two tail indices. The p_frontier_tail variable indicates the number of elements that have been inserted into the previous frontier array. The c_frontier_tail variable stores the index of position at which a newly discovered frontier vertex can be accommodated in the current frontier array. It also indicates the number of frontier vertices that have been inserted into the current frontier array thus far.

Before the first iteration, the source vertex is inserted into the previous frontier. The insert_frontier function will place the source into p_frontier[0] and increment the p_frontier_tail variable to 1. This makes the source the only vertex in the previous frontier array for processing in the first iteration.

Note that there is no easy way to determine the number of iterations that the while-loop will take before entering the while-loop. Even with the same number of vertices and edges, some graphs will have more levels and others will have fewer. In fact, some of the vertices are even unreachable from the source, making it inappropriate to try to use a test such as "all vertices have been visited" as a termination condition. So, the only reliable way to detect that all levels have been discovered is when there is no new current frontier vertex being discovered in the current iteration. This condition is available as p_frontier_tail > 0 before entering the next iteration.

We will use the example in Fig. 12.4(B) to illustrate the design of the while-loop, which implements the iterative process for labeling the vertices. The outer for-loop iterates through all the vertices in the previous frontier array. For the first iteration, there is only one vertex in the previous frontier array, the source. In our example, it is vertex 2. This means that the outer for-loop will only iterate once for the first iteration of the while-loop. During this only iteration of the outer for-loop, we first assign the value of p_frontier[0] (which is 2) to c_vertex.

We will then identify all the edges that go from c_vertex to its neighbors. As we have shown in Fig. 12.3, these edges are in a dest array section that starts at index edges[c_vertex] and ends at the location edges[c_vertex+1]-1. In our example edges[2] has value 4 and edges[3]-1 has value 6. This means that the edges for vertex 2 can be found in dest[4], dest[5], and dest[6]. The inner for-loop will iterate through these three edges.

For each edge, the if-statement checks if the destination of the edge has been visited. If the label value of the destination is still -1, it has not been visited before and a new vertex has been discovered for the current frontier. The code inside the if-statement inserts the destination into the current frontier array. It marks the destination as one level higher than the c_vertex. For our example, since vertex 2 is at level 0, the destination vertices dest[4] (vertex 5), dest[5] (vertex 6), and dest[6] (vertex 7) will all be labeled as level 1 at the end of the inner for-loop. This is indeed the correct result for these three vertices according to Fig. 12.4(B).

In our example, since vertex 2 is the only one in the p_frontier array during the first iteration of the while-loop, the outer for-loop will not iterate beyond the first iteration, we are at the end of the first iteration of the while-loop. The c_frontier array contains the three new frontier vertices 5, 6, and 7. The code at the end of the while-loop swaps the roles of the two frontier arrays. It copies the value of c_frontier_tail value (3) to p_frontier_tail, indicating that there are three vertices in the p_frontier array for the next iteration of the while-loop. It then resets the c_frontier_tail to 0, effectively empties the c_frontier array for use by the next while-loop iteration.

During the next iteration of the while-loop, the outer for-loop will iterate three iterations, one for each of the previous frontier vertices 5, 6, and 7. The inner for-loop instance for each of these three vertices are more interesting. The if-statement of the inner-loop iteration for vertex 5 will discover that the destination of the only edge leaving vertex 5, vertex 6, has been visited in the previous while-loop iteration; its label is 1. Thus, no further action will be taken for this edge. The reader should verify that one of the edges from vertex 7 requires action (to vertex 0) and the other one does not (to vertex 6).

12.4 A PARALLEL BFS FUNCTION

When it comes to parallelizing BFS, there are a few options. For example, Harish and Narayanan propose a parallelization where each thread is assigned to a vertex. During each iteration, all vertices are visited [HN 2007]. If any of the sources of the incoming edges of a vertex just become visited in the previous iteration, the vertex will be marked as visited in the current iteration. The amount of work done is proportional to V*L where V is the total number of vertices in the graph and L is the number of levels of the search results. For large graphs, the number of levels can be quite high and the work efficiency of the algorithm can be very low, causing the parallel code to run slower than sequential code.

One can design a parallel BFS algorithm that has work efficiency comparable to the sequential algorithm. Luo et al. propose to parallelize each iteration of the while-loop in Fig. 12.6 by having multiple threads to collaboratively process the previous frontier array and assemble the current frontier array [LWH 2010]. This effectively parallelizes the outer for-loop in Fig. 12.6. We will pursue this direction in the current section. In the next section, we will examine optimization strategies to enhance the performance of kernels produced with this strategy.

A straightforward parallelization strategy to parallelize each iteration of the while-loop is to assign a section of the previous frontier array to each thread block. Fig. 12.7 shows a sketch of the changes that we need to make to the sequential BFS_sequential function so that it can properly launch a CUDA kernel to perform the main activities of each iteration of the while-loop in parallel. Basically, the function needs to allocate device global memory version of edges, dest, and label. The

```
void BFS_host(unsigned int source, unsigned int *edges, unsigned int *dest, unsigned int *label)
{
    // allocate edges_d, dest_d, label_d, and visited_d in device global memory
    // copy edges, dest, and label to device global memory
    // allocate frontier_d, c_frontier_tail_d, p_frontier_tail_d in device global memory

    unsigned int *c_frontier_d = &frontier_d[0];
    unsigned int *p_frontier_d = &frontier_d[MAX_FRONTIER_SIZE];

    // launch a simple kernel to initialize the following in the device global memory
    // initialize all visited_d elements to 0 except source to 1
    // *c_frontier_tail_d = 0;
    // p_frontier_d[0] = source;
    // *p_frontier_tail_d = 1;
    // label[source] = 0;

    p_frontier_tail = 1;

    while (p_frontier_tail > 0) {
        int num_blocks = ceil(p_frontier_tail/float(BLOCK_SIZE));

        BFS_Bqueue_kernel<<<num_blocks, BLOCK_SIZE>>>(p_frontier_d, p_frontier_tail_d,
                            c_frontier_d, c_frontier_tail_d, edges_d, dest_d, label_d, visited_d);

        // use cudaMemcpy to read the *c_frontier_tail value back to host and assign
        // it to p_frontier_tail for the while-loop condition test

        int* temp = c_frontier_d; c_frontier_d = p_frontier_d; p_frontier_d = temp; //swap the roles
        // launch a simple kernel to set *p_frontier_tail_d = *c_frontier_tail_d; *c_frontier_tail_d = 0;
    }
}
```

FIGURE 12.7

A sketch of the BFS host code function.

pointers to these device global memory versions will be called edges_d, dest_d, and label_d. The contents of these arrays also need to be copied from host to device using cudaMemcpy.

The kernel in Fig. 12.8 declares an extra array visited (compared to the sequential code) to track whether a node has participated in a frontier. The reason for using this new array is that we will be using atomic operations on the elements of the array and it is much simpler if the value of each element is limited to 0 or 1. The label array elements need to track the level information, which makes it more complicated for atomic operations. It is more convenient to separate visit marking (visited) from the level of information (label).

The host code then allocates the frontier_d array in the device global memory. Note that there is no need for host to maintain a copy of the frontier array since it will be only accessed by the device. The c_frontier_d and p_frontier_d pointers will be pointing to either the first half or the second half of frontier_d. Initially, the host code initializes c_frontier_d to point to the first half and p_frontier_d to the second half. Their roles will swap at the end of each while-loop iteration. The host needs to also allocate the tail variables in the device global memory. The pointers to these variables will be c_frontier_tail_d and p_frontier_tail_d.

The host code then needs to launch a simple kernel to initialize all visited_d elements to 0 except source to 1, the c_frontier_tail_d variable to 0, p_frontier_d[0] to source, p_frontier_tail_d variable to 1, and label[source] to 0. After all this work, the device is set up to execute the main activities of each while-loop iteration in parallel. Thus, the bulk of the code in the while-loop is replaced with a kernel

```
__global__ void BFS_Bqueue_kernel(unsigned int *p_frontier, unsigned int *p_frontier_tail, unsigned int *c_frontier,
unsigned int *c_frontier_tail, unsigned int *edges, unsigned int *dest, unsigned int *label, unsigned int*
visited) {

    __shared__ unsigned int c_frontier_s[BLOCK_QUEUE_SIZE];
    __shared__ unsigned int c_frontier_tail_s, our_c_frontier_tail;

    if(threadIdx.x == 0) c_frontier_tail_s = 0;
    __syncthreads();

    const unsigned int tid = blockIdx.x*blockDim.x + threadIdx.x;
    if(tid < *p_frontier_tail) {
        const unsigned int my_vertex = p_frontier[tid];
        for(unsigned int i = edges[my_vertex]; i < edges[my_vertex + 1]; ++i) {
            const unsigned int was_visited = atomicExch(&(visited[dest[i]]), 1);
            if(!was_visited) {
                label[dest[i]] = label[my_vertex] + 1;
                const unsigned int my_tail = atomicAdd(&c_frontier_tail_s, 1);
                if(my_tail < BLOCK_QUEUE_SIZE) {
                    c_frontier_s[my_tail] = dest[i];
                } else { // If full, add it to the global queue directly
                    c_frontier_tail_s = BLOCK_QUEUE_SIZE;
                    const unsigned int my_global_tail = atomicAdd(c_frontier_tail, 1);
                    c_frontier[my_global_tail] = dest[i];
                }
            }
        }
    }
    __syncthreads();

    if(threadIdx.x == 0) {
        our_c_frontier_tail = atomicAdd(c_frontier_tail, c_frontier_tail_s);
    }
    __syncthreads();

    for(unsigned int i = threadIdx.x; i < c_frontier_tail_s; i += blockDim.x) {
        c_frontier[our_c_frontier_tail + i] = c_frontier_s[i];
    }

}
```

FIGURE 12.8

A parallel BFS kernel based on block-level privatized queues.

launch and a call to cudaMemcpy() to read the value of the total number of vertices in the newly discovered frontier. This value will be used to determine if the current iteration has made any progress and the while-loop should be allowed to continue.

A kernel based on this strategy is shown in Fig. 12.8. The threads divide the section in an interleaved manner to enable coalesced memory access to the p_frontier array. This is shown as the statement that accesses p_frontier at the beginning of the kernel. As each thread processes a vertex in the p_frontier array, it inserts or writes the unvisited neighbors of the vertex into the c_frontier array. This is shown in the first for-loop in Fig. 12.8. Once all threads complete their processing of the p_frontier array, the c_frontier array will contain all the vertices of the new frontier and will become the p_frontier array for the next iteration of the while-loop.

The for-loop that visits each neighbor of a thread's assigned frontier vertex looks similar to the inner for-loop in Fig. 12.6. However, there is a slight but important difference in terms of their execution efficiency. Each of the outer for-loop iterations in Fig. 12.6 processes the neighbors for one frontier vertex. It is very possible that frontier vertices have common neighbors. For example, in Fig. 12.4(A), vertices 3, 4, and 6 are all in the level-2 frontier and they have a common neighbor vertex 8. The outer for-loop iterations in Fig. 12.6 are executed sequentially. In general, we are referring to the situation where two frontier vertices A and B have a common neighbor and the neighbor has not been visited so far. Let us assume that the outer `for`-loop iteration that processes A is executed first. The neighbor will be marked as visited as a result of processing A. When B is processed in a later iteration, it will find the neighbor marked as visited so it will not mark it again. In our example, during the processing of level-2 frontier of Fig. 12.4(A), assume that vertex 3 is processed first. Vertex 8 will be marked as visited (level 3) and will be inserted into the `c_frontier` array. When vertices 4 and 6 are subsequently processed, they will find vertex 8 already visited so they will not insert it into the `c_frontier`.

In the parallel kernel, the frontier vertices are processed by threads that execute in parallel. Since the global memory writes that are performed by a thread are not guaranteed to be visible by other threads until the kernel termination or memory fence, they will not see the marks made by each other. In our example, the threads that process vertices 3, 4, and 6 all execute in parallel. They may or may not be able to see the marks by each other. So, each of them will likely mark vertex 8 as level 3 and insert it into the `c_frontier`. As a result, a vertex could appear multiple times in the `c_frontier`. This is harmless in terms of correctness. The threads that process these redundant copies of the frontier vertices will take the same actions and will not affect the final execution result. However, there could be a significant number of such redundant processing for large graphs.

In order to avoid generating redundant copies of frontier vertices, we use atomic operations to mark and check the visit status of vertices in Fig. 12.8. The kernel uses a `visited` array to track whether a vertex has been visited. Each thread first uses an atomic operation to check if each destination of its current vertex still needs to be visited. Keep in mind that the atomic operations performed by one thread-block are visible to all other thread-blocks. This way, if a vertex is the destination of multiple vertices in the current frontier, only one thread will succeed in the condition and the destination vertex will only be entered into the `c_frontier` array once.

There are three important considerations with respect to writing vertices into the `c_frontier` array. First, the vertices written by a thread during the current iteration of the `while`-loop will likely need to be processed by another thread in another block during the next iteration of the `while`-loop. Recall that a write to global memory by a thread is not guaranteed to be visible to threads in other blocks without a kernel termination/relaunch or a memory fence. As a result, we will terminate the kernel at the end of each `while`-loop iteration and relaunch the kernel for the next iteration of the `while`-loop.

Second, since the threads would be simultaneously inserting vertices into the `c_frontier` array, they need to use atomic operations when they perform read-modify-write on the `c_frontier_tail` variable to ensure the integrity of updates to the variable.

Third, for each previous frontier vertex, a thread will likely write multiple vertices into the `c_frontier` array. This would likely create a global memory write pattern that cannot be coalesced. We will use a privatized buffer in the shared memory to assemble the contribution by the threads in a block, and have threads to write the contents of the shared memory buffer into the global memory in a coalesced manner at the end of the kernel. We will call this privatized buffer a *block-level queue*. We will also need to create a privatized `c_frontier_tail_s` variable in the shared memory for insertion into the block level queue.

In Fig. 12.8, the block-level queue is declared as a shared memory array `c_frontier_s`. Insertion into `c_frontier_s` is made through the shared memory variable `c_frontier_tail_s` variable. Thread 0 initializes the value of `c_frontier_tail_s` to 0 while all other threads wait for this initialization at the `__syncthreads()` barrier. In the first `for`-loop, each thread inserts a new found neighbor into the `c_frontier_s` array. This is done by performing an atomic operation on the `c_frontier_tail_s` variable and writing the neighbor into the `c_frontier_s` array location whose index is the old `c_frontier_tail_s` value returned by the atomic operation. In the case where the block-level queue overflows, the remaining entries are stored directly in the `c_frontier` array.

The total number of new frontier vertices found by all threads in the block is given by the final value of `c_frontier_tail_s`. We use the `if`-statement to identify thread 0 to reserve a section in the global `c_frontier` array by performing an atomic operation on `c_frontier_tail`. The atomic operation will return the beginning index of the reserved section. It will increase the `c_frontier_tail` value by the total number of vertices to be written into the section. Thus, the next block will start its section at the location indexed by the new `c_frontier_tail` value. This is illustrated by the bottom part of Fig. 12.9.

The second `for`-loop in Fig. 12.8 implements the coalesced writes to the global `c_frontier` array. During each iteration, each thread will write one element of the `c_frontier_s` array into `c_frontier` array. We design the indexing scheme so that adjacent threads will write adjacent locations in the `c_frontier` array. All threads will iterate until they have collectively completed writing all the contents of the `c_frontier_s` array.

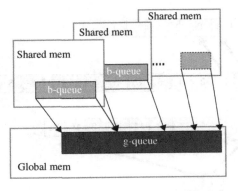

FIGURE 12.9

Block-level queue (b-queue) contents are copied into the global queue (g-queue) at the end of the kernel in a coalesced manner.

Since the block-level queue is a performance optimization scheme, falling back to the global-queue will not affect correctness. It will likely reduce performance as a reasonable tradeoff.

12.5 OPTIMIZATIONS

While we have achieved parallel execution with the BFS_Bqueue kernel in Fig. 12.8, there are several areas of improvements as far as the performance and efficiency are concerned. We will go over each area in this section [MG 2012].

MEMORY BANDWIDTH

When a thread processes its assigned frontier vertex in the kernel of Fig. 12.8, it accesses two consecutive edges array elements in the global memory in the for-loop followed by a number of consecutive dest array locations in the global memory. It then accesses a sequence of label array elements that are more or less random, indexed by the dest elements values. This means that adjacent threads are not accessing adjacent global memory locations when accessing the edges, dest, and label arrays, thus these accesses are not coalesced. One should perform these accesses through the texture memory. We will leave it as an exercise.

Fig. 12.10 illustrates the global memory access pattern for processing the level-2 frontier vertices in Fig. 12.4(B). The source of the search is vertex 2. The two level-2 frontier vertices are 0 and 8. Let us assume that threads 0 and 1 will process these vertices. The access pattern to the p_frontier array is coalesced. The accesses to the edges array are clearly not coalesced, thread 0 and thread 1 access edges[0] and edges[8] first. They are not accessing consecutive locations. They then access edges[1] and edges[9]. Again, they are not accessing consecutive locations.

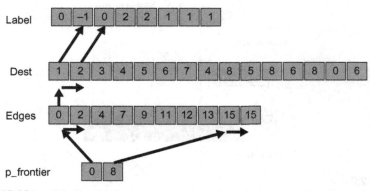

FIGURE 12.10

Memory access pattern for processing the level-2 frontier in Fig. 12.5.

Based on the `edges` element values, thread 0 will access `dest[0]` and `dest[1]` whereas thread 1 will not make any further accesses since vertex 8 does not have any outgoing edges. One can easily imagine that if vertex 8 had any outgoing edges, they would not be in consecutive locations as the ones accessed by thread 0. Thread 0 will access the `label` array based on `dest[0]` and `dest[1]` values. In this example, as shown in Fig. 12.10, it happens to access `label[1]` and `label[2]`. In general, it could access locations that are of arbitrary distance away from each other, depending on the shape of the graph and the way the vertices are numbered. Obviously, the accesses to the `label` array are not coalesced in general. Therefore, accesses to the `edges`, `dest`, and `label` arrays should go through the texture memory.

HIERARCHICAL QUEUES

The block-level queue `c_frontier_s` in Figs. 12.8 and 12.9 is an example of a hierarchical queue design. In general, when we have a queue that receives insertion requests from a large number of parallel threads, their atomic operations on the tail variable will likely cause excessive contention and therefore serialization among these threads. Giving each block its private queue significantly reduces the level of contention in queue insertion. The cost is the extra step at the end of the kernel, where the contents of the private queue need to be consolidated into the global queue.

As it turns out, even the block level queues can suffer heavy contention. This is because all threads in a warp are guaranteed to cause contention when they access their block-level queue. All threads in the same warp execute the same instruction at any point in time. So, all of them will execute the atomic operations at the same time and cause a very high level of contention. Such contention will effectively serialize the execution of the threads in a warp and drastically reduce the execution speed.

The contentions inside each warp can be addressed by adding another level of queues to the hierarchy, as shown in Fig. 12.11. We will call these warp-level queues (w-queues). The number of such warp-level queues is usually a power of two

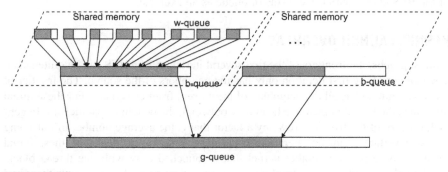

FIGURE 12.11

The design and consolidation process of w-queue, b-queue, and g-queue.

and is a parameter that can be tuned. During kernel execution, we classify threads into the same number of classes as the number of warp-level queues using the least significant bits of their `threadIdx.x` values. The rationale is that we want to evenly distribute the atomic operations executed by threads in a warp to the warp-level queues.

For example, if we have four warp-level queues, we direct all threads according to the least significant two bits of `threadIdx.x` value. All threads whose two least significant bits of the `threadIdx.x` values are 00 will access warp-level queue 0. Assume that we have 64 threads in a block, the 16 threads which are directed to the warp-level queue 0 are 0, 4, 8, 12, ..., 56, 60. In this case, there are two warps. In warp 1, 8 out of its 32 threads are directed to warp-level queue 0. These threads are 0, 4, 8, 12, 16, 20, 24, and 28. In warp 1, 8 of its 32 threads are also directed to warp-level queue 0. These threads are 32, 36, 40, 44, 48, 52, 56, and 60. The point is that whenever a warp executes an atomic operation, one fourth of its threads will be directed to warp-level queue 0. Similarly, the 16 threads which are directed to warp-level queue 1 are 1, 5, 9, 13, ..., 57, 61. Thus, one fourth of the threads of a warp will be directed to warp-level queue 1.

At the end of the kernel, we need to first consolidate the warp-level queue contents into the block-level queue, as illustrated in Fig. 12.11. Note that it may be advantageous to use a different warp to copy each warp-level queue contents into the block-level queue. This part involves significant thread index manipulation and is left as an exercise. We can then consolidate the block-level queue contents into the global queue as shown in Fig. 12.8.

By increasing the number of warp-level queues, we can decrease the level of contention to each warp-level queue. However, there is a cost of having more w-queues. As we increase the number of w-queues, the size of each w-queue becomes smaller. This increases the probability for one of the queues to overflow. The threads should check the overflow condition in a way similar to what we discussed for the block-level queue and redirect any overflowing vertices to the block-level queue. In some cases, the thread may find the block-level queue in an overflow condition and thus need to redirect the vertex to the global queue. We leave the detailed implementation of the BFS kernel with three levels of queue as an exercise.

KERNEL LAUNCH OVERHEAD

In most graphs, the frontiers of the first several iterations of a BFS can be quite small. The frontier of the first iteration only has the neighbors of the source. The frontier of the next iteration has all the neighbors of the current frontier vertices. For these initial iterations, the kernel launch overhead may outweigh the benefit of parallelism. In general, the size of the frontier grows by a factor that is the average number of out-going edges of vertices from one iteration to the next. One way to deal with these initial iterations is to prepare another kernel that is launched only with one thread block. The kernel uses only a block-level queue except for overflow. It implements the initial interations of the `while`-loop. Since the block-level queue is in the shared memory, we can use __syncthreads() to ensure that during the next iteration, other threads in the block can use the queue entries prepared by each thread in the current iteration.

Once the frontier reaches a size that overflows the block-level queue, the kernel copies the block-level queue contents to the global queue and returns to the host code. The host code will launch the regular kernel in the subsequent iterations of the while-loop. The specialized kernel eliminates the kernel launch overhead for the initial iterations. We leave the specialized kernel as an exercise.

LOAD BALANCE

The amount of work to be done by each thread depends on the connectivity of the vertex assigned to it. In some graphs, such as social network graphs, some vertices (celebrities) may have several orders of magnitude more out-going edges than others. When this happens, one or a few of the threads can take excessively long and slow down the execution of the entire thread grid. This is an extreme example of load imbalance in parallel computing. We can potentially address this by having the threads which encounter vertices that have extremely large number of out-going edges to launch a kernel and use many threads to process the problematic vertices. The mechanism that enables threads to launch new kernels without involving the host is called dynamic parallelism, which will be addressed in Chapter 13, CUDA dynamic parallelism.

12.6 SUMMARY

The graph search pattern is rich with several challenges. It is a memory bound computation. It has a significant portion of irregular memory accesses. Its input set is dynamic and depends on the data. The collection of input data for each iteration requires a well-designed hierarchy of queues that are invaluable in many real applications. Its workload varies over time and requires careful design of the kernel and even some specialized kernels.

12.7 EXERCISES

1. Extend the BFS_Bqueue kernel to check and handle the overflows when threads insert new frontier vertices in the block-level queue.

2. Extend the BFS_Bqueue kernel to use texture memory to access the edges, dest, label array.

3. Extend the BFS_Bqueue kernel to implement the warp-level queue.

4. Write a BFS_small_frontier kernel to implement the first iterations of the search until the frontier grows beyond 1024 vertices.

REFERENCES

Harish, P., & Narayanan, P. J. (2007). Accelerating large graph algorithms on the GPU using CUDA. In: *International conference on high-performance computing*. India.

Luo, L., Wong, M., & Hwu, W. (2010). An effective GPU implementation of breath-first search. In: *ACM/IEEE design automation conference (DAC)*.

Merill, D., & Garland, M. (2012). Scalable GPU graph traversal. In: *Proceedings of the 17th ACM SIGPLAN symposium on principles and practice of parallel programming (PPoPP)* (pp. 117–128).

CUDA dynamic parallelism 13

Juan Gómez-Luna and Izzat El Hajj

CHAPTER OUTLINE

Programming Massively Parallel Processors. DOI: http://dx.doi.org/10.1016/B978-0-12-811986-0.00013-3

CUDA Dynamic Parallelism is an extension to the CUDA programming model enabling a CUDA kernel to create new thread grids by launching new kernels. Dynamic parallelism is introduced with the Kepler architecture, first appearing in the GK110 chip. In previous CUDA systems, kernels can only be launched from the host code. Algorithms that involved recursion, irregular loop structures, time-space variation, or other constructs that do not fit a flat, single level of parallelism needed to be implemented with multiple kernel launches, which increase burden on the host, amount of host-device communication, and total execution time. In some cases, programmers resort to loop serialization and other awkward techniques to support these algorithmic needs at the cost of software maintainability. The dynamic parallelism support allows algorithms that dynamically discover new work to prepare and launch kernels without burdening the host or impacting software maintainability. This chapter describes the extended capabilities of the CUDA architecture which enable dynamic parallelism, including the modifications and additions to the CUDA programming model, as well as guidelines and best practices for exploiting this added capacity.

13.1 BACKGROUND

Many real-world applications employ algorithms that either have variation of work across space or dynamically varying amount of work performed over time. As we saw in Chapter 12 Parallel Patterns: Graph Search, in a graph search, the amount of work done when processing each frontier vertex can vary dramatically in graphs like social networks. For another example, Fig. 13.1 shows a turbulence simulation example where the level of required modeling details varies across both space and time. As the combustion flow moves from left to right, the level of activities and intensity increases. The level of details required to model the right side of the model is much higher than that for the left side of the model. On one hand, using a fixed fine grid would incur too much work for no gain for the left side of the model. On the other hand, using a fixed coarse grid would sacrifice too much accuracy for the right side of the model. Ideally, one should use fine grids for the parts of the model that require more details and coarse grids for those that do not.

Previous CUDA systems require all kernels to be launched from host code. The amount of work done by a thread grid is pre-determined during kernel launch. With the SPMD programming style for the kernel code, it is tedious if not extremely difficult to have thread-blocks to use different grid spacing. This limitation favors the use of fixed grid system. In order to achieve the desired accuracy, such fixed grid

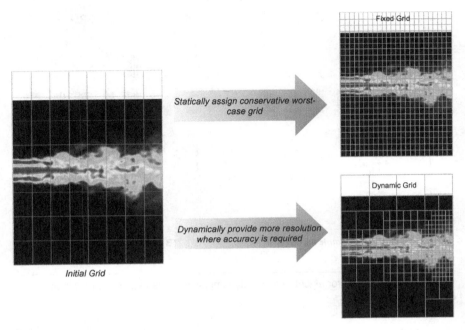

FIGURE 13.1

Fixed versus dynamic grids for a turbulence simulation model.

approach, as illustrated in the upper right portion of Fig. 13.1, typically needs to accommodate the most demanding parts of the model and perform unnecessary extra work in parts that do not require as much detail.

A more desirable approach is shown as the dynamic, variable grid in the lower right portion of Fig. 13.1. As the simulation algorithm detects fast changing simulation quantities in some areas of the model, it refines the grid in those areas to achieve desired level of accuracy. Such refinement does not need to be done for the areas that do not exhibit such intensive activity. This way, the algorithm can dynamically direct more computation work to the areas of the model that benefit from the addition work.

Fig. 13.2 shows a conceptual comparison of behavior between a system without dynamic parallelism and one with dynamic parallelism with respect to the simulation model in Fig. 13.1. Without dynamic parallelism, the host code must launch all kernels. If new work is discovered, such as refining the grid of an area of the model during the execution of a kernel, it needs to terminate itself, report back to the host code and have the host code to launch a new kernel. This is illustrated in Fig. 13.2(A), where the host launches a wave of kernels, receives information from these kernels after their termination, and launches the next level of kernels for any new work discovered by the completed kernels.

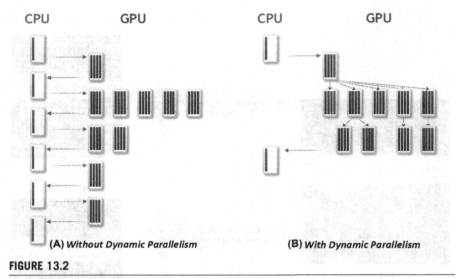

(A) *Without Dynamic Parallelism*   (B) *With Dynamic Parallelism*

FIGURE 13.2

Kernel launch patterns for algorithms with dynamic work variation, with and without dynamic parallelism.

Fig. 13.2(B) shows that with dynamic parallelism, the threads that discover new work can just go ahead and launch kernels to do the work. In our example, when a thread discovers that an area of the model needs to be refined, it can launch a kernel to perform the computation step on the refined grid area without the overhead of terminating the kernel, reporting back to the host, and having the host to launch new kernels.

13.2 DYNAMIC PARALLELISM OVERVIEW

From the perspective of programmers, dynamic parallelism means that they can write a kernel launch statement in a kernel. In Fig. 13.3, the main function (host code) launches three kernels, A, B, and C. These are kernel launches in the original CUDA model. What is different is that one of the kernels, B, launches three kernels X, Y, and Z. This would have been illegal in previous CUDA systems.

The syntax for launching a kernel from a kernel is the same as that for launching a kernel from host code:

```
kernel_name<<< Dg, Db, Ns, S >>>([kernel arguments])
```

- Dg is of type dim3 and specifies the dimensions and size of the grid.
- Db is of type dim3 and specifies the dimensions and size of each thread-block.
- Ns is of type size_t and specifies the number of bytes of shared memory that is dynamically allocated per thread-block for this call, which is in addition to the statically allocated shared memory. Ns is an optional argument that defaults to 0.

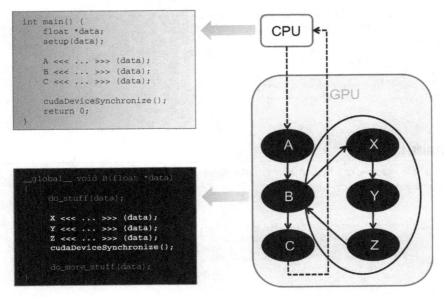

FIGURE 13.3

A simple example of a kernel (B) launching three kernels (X, Y, and Z).

- S is of type cudaStream_t and specifies the stream associated with this call. The stream must have been **allocated in the same thread-block where the call is being made**. S is an optional argument that defaults to 0. Streams are discussed in more detail in Chapter 18.

13.3 A SIMPLE EXAMPLE

In this section, we provide a simple example of coding in each of two styles – first, in the original CUDA style, and second, in the dynamic parallelism style. The example is based on a hypothetical parallel algorithm that does not compute useful results, but provides a conceptually simple computational pattern that recurs in many applications. It serves to illustrate the difference between the two styles and how one can use the dynamic parallelism style to extract more parallelism while reducing control flow divergence when the amount of work done by each thread in an algorithm can vary dynamically.

Fig. 13.4 shows a simple example kernel coded without dynamic parallelism. In this example, each thread of the kernel performs some computation (line 05) then loops over a list of data elements it is responsible for (line 07), and performs another computation for each data element (line 08).

This computation pattern recurs frequently in many applications. For example, in graph search, each thread could visit a vertex then loop over a list of neighboring

```
01    __global__ void kernel(unsigned  int* start, unsigned int* end, float* someData,
02        float* moreData) {
03
04        unsigned int i = blockIdx.x*blockDim.x + threadIdx.x;
05        doSomeWork(someData[i]);
06
07        for(unsigned int j = start[i]; j < end[i]; ++j) {
08            doMoreWork(moreData[j]);
09        }
10
11    }
```

FIGURE 13.4

A simple example of a hypothetical parallel algorithm coded in CUDA without dynamic parallelism.

```
01    __global__ void kernel_parent(unsigned int* start, unsigned int* end,
02        float* someData, float* moreData) {
03
04        unsigned int i = blockIdx.x*blockDim.x + threadIdx.x;
05        doSomeWork(someData[i]);
06
07        kernel_child <<< ceil((end[i]-start[i])/256.0) , 256 >>>
08            (start[i], end[i], moreData);
09
10    }
11
12    __global__ void kernel_child(unsigned int start, unsigned int end,
13        float* moreData) {
14
15        unsigned int j = start + blockIdx.x*blockDim.x + threadIdx.x;
16
17        if(j < end) {
18            doMoreWork(moreData[j]);
19        }
20
21    }
```

FIGURE 13.5

A revised example using CUDA dynamic parallelism.

vertices. The reader should find this kernel structure very similar to that of BFS_
Bqueue_kernel in Fig. 12.8. In sparse matrix computations, each thread could first
identify the starting location of a row of non-zero elements and loop over the nonzero values. In simulations such as the example in the beginning of the chapter, each
thread could represent a coarse grid element and loop over finer grid elements.

There are two main problems with writing applications this way. First, if the work
in the loop (lines 07-09) can be profitably performed in parallel, then we have missed
out on an opportunity to extract more parallelism from the application. Second, if the
number of iterations in the loop varies significantly between threads in the same warp,
then the resulting control divergence can degrade the performance of the program.

Fig. 13.5 shows a version of the same program that uses dynamic parallelism.
In this version, the original kernel is separated into two kernels, a parent kernel and

a child kernel. The parent kernel starts off the same as the original kernel, executed by a grid of threads referred to as the parent grid. Instead of executing the loop it launches a child kernel to continue the work (lines 07–08). The child kernel is then executed by another grid of threads called the child grid that performs the work that was originally performed inside the loop body (line 18).

Writing the program in this way addresses both problems that were mentioned about the original code. First, the loop iterations are now executed in parallel by the child kernel threads instead of serially by the original kernel thread. Thus, we have extracted more parallelism from the program. Second, each thread now executes a single loop iteration which results in better load balance and eliminates control divergence. Although these two goals could have been achieved by the programmer by rewriting the kernels differently, such manual transformations can be awkward, complicated and error prone. Dynamic parallelism provides an easy way to express such computational patterns.

13.4 MEMORY DATA VISIBILITY

In the next three sections, we will briefly explain some important details that govern the execution behavior of programs that use dynamic parallelism. It is important for a programmer to understand these details in order to use dynamic parallelism confidently. We will cover the rules for memory data visibility in this section. These rules specify how the data objects of a parent grid can be accessed by threads in a child grid. These rules are extensions to the data consistency rules between threads from the same grid vs. between threads from different grids in a non-dynamic-parallelism program. For example, the global memory data written by threads in a grid are not guaranteed to be visible to other threads until either an explicit memory fence or kernel termination. Such rules are extended in dynamic parallelism so that one can clearly understand how a parent and a child can make data values visible to each other.

GLOBAL MEMORY

A parent thread and its child grid can make their global memory data visible to each other, with weak consistency guarantees between child and parent. The memory views of the parent thread and the child grid are said to be consistent with each other if the effects of their memory operations are fully visible to each other. There are two points in the execution of a child grid when its view of memory is consistent with the parent thread:

1. When the child grid is created by a parent thread. That means that all global memory operations in the parent thread prior to invoking the child grid are visible to the child grid.
2. When the child grid completes as signaled by the completion of a synchronization API call in the parent thread. That means all memory operations of the child grid are visible to the parent after the parent has synchronized on the child grid's completion (see Section 13.6 for details about synchronization).

ZERO-COPY MEMORY

Zero-copy system memory has identical consistency guarantees as global memory, and follows the same semantics as detailed above. A kernel may not allocate or free zero-copy memory, however, but may use pointers passed in from the host code.

CONSTANT MEMORY

Constants may not be written to by a kernel, even between dynamic parallelism kernel launches. That is, the value of all __constant__ variables must be set from the host prior to launch of the first kernel. Constant memory variables are globally visible to all kernels, and so must remain constant for the lifetime of the entire dynamic parallelism launch tree invoked by the host code.

Taking the address of a constant memory object from within a thread has the same semantics as for non-dynamic-parallelism programs, and passing that pointer from parent to child or from a child to parent is fully supported.

LOCAL MEMORY

Local memory is private storage for a thread, and is not visible outside of that thread. It is illegal to pass a pointer to local memory as a launch argument when launching a child kernel. The result of dereferencing such a local memory pointer from a child is undefined. For example the following is illegal, with undefined behavior if x_array is accessed by any threads that execute the child_launch kernel:

```
int x_array[10];        // Creates x_array in parent's local memory
child_launch<<< 1, 1 >>>(x_array);
```

It is sometimes difficult for a programmer to know when a variable is placed into local memory by the compiler. As a general rule, all storage passed to a child kernel should be allocated explicitly from the global-memory heap, either with malloc() or new() or by declaring __device__ storage at global scope. For example, Fig. 13.5(A) shows a valid kernel launch where a pointer to a global memory variable is passed as an argument into the child kernel. Fig. 13.5(B) shows an invalid code where a pointer to a local memory (auto) variable is passed into the child kernel.

The NVIDIA CUDA C compiler will issue a warning if it detects that a pointer to local memory is being passed as an argument to a kernel launch. However, such detections are not guaranteed (Figure 13.6).

```
__device__ int value;              __device__ void y() {
__device__ void x() {                  int value = 5;
    value = 5;                         child<<< 1, 1 >>>(&value);
    child<<< 1, 1 >>>(&value);     }
}
    (A) Valid—"value" is global storage      (B) Invalid—"value" is local storage
```

FIGURE 13.6

Passing a pointer as an argument to a child kernel.

SHARED MEMORY

Shared memory is private storage for an executing thread-block, and data is not visible outside of that thread-block. Passing a pointer to a shared-memory variable to a child kernel either through memory or as an argument will result in undefined behavior.

TEXTURE MEMORY

Texture memory accesses (read-only) are performed on a memory region that may be aliased to the global memory region. Texture memory has identical consistency guarantees as global memory, and follows the same semantics. In particular, writes to memory prior to a child kernel launch are reflected in texture memory accesses of the child. Also, writes to memory by a child will be reflected in the texture memory accesses by a parent, after the parent synchronizes on the child's completion.

Concurrent texture memory access and writes to global memory objects which alias the texture memory objects between a parent and its children or between multiple children will result in undefined behavior.

13.5 CONFIGURATIONS AND MEMORY MANAGEMENT

Dynamic parallelism allows a CUDA thread to play the role of host code in launching kernels. There are two other types of major host code activities that support the kernel launch: configuring the device hardware and prepare the device memory for executing the kernel. A programmer also needs to understand how these activities are applied to the kernels launched by a CUDA thread.

LAUNCH ENVIRONMENT CONFIGURATION

A kernel launched with dynamic parallelism inherits all device configuration settings from its parent kernel. Such configuration settings include shared memory and L1 cache size as returned from cudaDeviceGetCacheConfig() and device execution parameter limits as returned from cudaDeviceGetLimit(). For example, if a parent kernel is configured with 16K bytes of shared memory and 48K bytes of L1 cache, then the child kernel it launches will have identical configurations. Likewise, a parent's device limits such as stack size will be passed as-is to its children.

MEMORY ALLOCATION AND LIFETIME

Dynamic parallelism makes it possible to invoke `cudaMalloc` and `cudaFree` from kernels. However they have slightly modified semantics. Within the device environment the total allocatable memory is limited to the device malloc() heap size, which may be smaller than the available unused device memory. Moreover, it is an error to invoke cudaFree from the host program on a pointer which was allocated by `cudaMalloc` on the device, or to invoke cudaFree from the device program on a pointer which was allocated by cudaMalloc on the host. These limitations may be removed in future versions of CUDA.

	`cudaMalloc() on Host`	`cudaMalloc() on Device`
`cudaFree() on Host`	Supported	Not supported
`cudaFree() on Device`	Not supported	Supported
`Allocation limit`	Free device memory	cudaLimitMallocHeapSize

NESTING DEPTH

Kernels launched with dynamic parallelism may themselves launch other kernels, which may in turn launch other kernels, and so on. Each subordinate launch is considered a new "nesting level," and the total number of levels is the "nesting depth" of the program. The maximum nesting depth is limited in hardware to 24.

In the presence of parent-child synchronization, there are additional constraints on nesting depth due to the amount of memory required by the system to store parent kernel state. These constraints will be discussed in Section 13.6 when we discuss *synchronization depth*.

PENDING LAUNCH POOL CONFIGURATION

The pending launch pool is a buffer that tracks the kernels that are executing or waiting to be executed. This pool is allocated a fixed amount of space, thereby supporting a fixed number of pending kernel launches (2048 by default). If this number is exceeded, a virtualized pool is used, but leads to significant slowdown which can be an order of magnitude or more. To avoid this slowdown, the programmer can increase the size of the fixed pool by executing the cudaDeviceSetLimit() API call from the host function to set the cudaLimitDevRuntimePendingLaunchCount configuration.

ERRORS AND LAUNCH FAILURES

Like CUDA API function calls in host code, any CUDA API function called within a kernel may return an error code. Any failed kernel launch due to reasons such as insufficient execution resources also appears to return with an error code. The last error code returned is also recorded and may be retrieved via the `cudaGetLastError()` call. Errors are recorded on a per-thread basis, so that each thread can identify the most recent error that it has generated. The error code is of type cudaError_t, which is a 32-bit integer value.[1]

---

[1] No notification of ECC errors is available to code within a CUDA kernel. ECC errors are only reported at the host side. Any ECC errors which arise during execution of a dynamic parallelism kernel will either generate an exception or continue execution (depending upon error and configuration).

13.6 SYNCHRONIZATION, STREAMS, AND EVENTS

SYNCHRONIZATION

As with kernel launches from the host, kernel launches from the device are nonblocking. If a parent thread wants to wait for a child kernel to complete before proceeding, it must perform synchronization explicitly.

One way for a parent thread to perform synchronization with its child kernels on the device is by invoking cudaDeviceSynchronize(). A thread that invokes this call will wait until **all kernels launched by any thread in the thread-block have completed**. However, this does not mean that all threads in the block will wait, so if a block-wide synchronization is desired, then cudaDeviceSynchronize() invoked by one thread in the block must also be followed by __syncthreads() invoked by all threads in the block. Synchronization can also be performed on streams within the same thread-block (which will be discussed shortly).

If a parent kernel launches other child kernels and does not explicitly synchronize on the completion of those kernels, then the runtime will perform the synchronization implicitly **before the parent kernel terminates**. This ensures that the parent and child kernels are properly nested, and that no kernel completes before its children have completed. This implicit synchronization is illustrated in Fig. 13.7.

SYNCHRONIZATION DEPTH

If a parent kernel performs explicit synchronization on a child kernel, it may be swapped out of execution while waiting for the child kernel to complete. For this

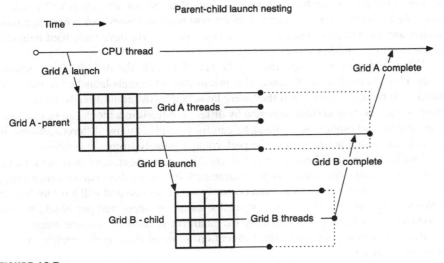

FIGURE 13.7

Completion sequence for parent and child grids.

reason, memory needs to be allocated as a backing-store for the parent kernel state. Ancestors of the synchronizing parent kernel may also be swapped out. Thus the backing store needs to be large enough to fit the state of all kernels up to the deepest nesting level at which synchronization is performed. This deepest nesting level defines the *synchronization depth*.

Conservatively, the amount of memory allocated for the backing store for each level of the synchronization depth must be large enough to support storing state for the maximum number of live threads possible on the device. On current generation devices, this amounts to ~150 MB per level, which will be unavailable for program use even if it is not all consumed. The maximum synchronization depth is thus limited by the amount of memory allocated by the software for the backing store, and is likely to be a more important constraint than the maximum nesting depth stipulated by the hardware.

The default amount of memory reserved for the backing store is sufficient for a synchronization depth of two. However, the programmer can increase this amount using the cudaDeviceSetLimit() API call from the host function to set a larger value for the cudaLimitDevRuntimeSyncDepth configuration parameter.

STREAMS

Just like host code can use streams to execute kernels concurrently, kernel threads can also use streams when launching kernels with dynamic parallelism. Both named and unnamed (NULL) streams can be used.

The scope of a stream is private to the block in which the stream was created. In other words, streams created by a thread may be used by any thread within the same thread-block, but stream handles should not be passed to other blocks or child/parent kernels. Using a stream handle within a block that did not allocate it will result in undefined behavior. Streams created on the host have undefined behavior when used within any kernel, just as streams created by a parent grid have undefined behavior if used within a child grid.

When a stream is not specified to the kernel launch, the default NULL stream in the block is used by all threads. This means that all kernels launched in the same block will be serialized even if they were launched by different threads. However, it is often the case that kernels launched by different threads in a block can be executed concurrently, so programmers must be careful to explicitly use different streams in each thread if they wish to avoid the performance penalty from serialization.

Similar to host-side launch, work launched into separate streams may run concurrently, but actual concurrency is not guaranteed. Programs that require concurrency between child kernels in order to run correctly are ill-formed and will have undefined behavior. An unlimited number of named streams are supported per block, but the maximum concurrency supported by the platform is limited. If more streams are created than can support concurrent execution, some of these may serialize or alias with each other.

The host-side NULL stream's global-synchronization semantic is not supported under dynamic parallelism. To make this difference between the stream behavior on the host-side and the device side with dynamic parallelism explicit, all streams created in a kernel must be created using the cudaStreamCreateWithFlags() API with the cudaStreamNonBlocking flag (an example is shown later in Fig. 13.10). Calls to cudaStreamCreate() from a kernel will fail with a compiler "unrecognized function call" error, so as to make clear the different stream semantic under dynamic parallelism.

The cudaStreamSynchronize() API is not available within a kernel, only cudaDeviceSynchronize() can be used to wait explicitly for launched work to complete. This is because the underlying system software implements only a block-wide synchronization call, and it is undesirable to offer an API with incomplete semantics (that is, the synchronization function guarantees that one stream synchronizes, but coincidentally provides a full barrier as a side-effect). Streams created within a thread-block are implicitly synchronized when all threads in the thread-block exit execution.

EVENTS

Only the inter-stream synchronization capabilities of CUDA events are supported in kernel functions. Events within individual streams are currently not supported in kernel functions. This means that cudaStreamWaitEvent() is supported, but cudaEventSynchronize(), timing with cudaEventElapsedTime(), and event query via cudaEventQuery() are not. *These may be supported in a future version.*[2]

Event objects may be shared between the threads within a block that created them but are local to that block and should not be passed to child/parent kernels. Using an event handle within a block that did not allocate it will result in undefined behavior.

An unlimited number of events are supported per block, but these consume device memory. Owing to resource limitations, if too many events are created (exact number is implementation-dependent), then device-launched grids may attain less concurrency than might be expected. Correct execution is guaranteed, however.

13.7 A MORE COMPLEX EXAMPLE

We now show an example that is a more interesting and useful case of adaptive subdivision of spline curves. This example illustrates a variable number of child kernel launches, according to the workload. The example is to calculate Bezier Curves [Wiki_Bezier], which are frequently used in computer graphics to draw smooth, intuitive curves that are defined by a set of *control points*, which are typically defined by a user.

---

[2]To ensure that this restriction is clearly seen by the user, dynamic parallelism cudaEvents must be created via cudaEventCreateWithFlags(), which currently only accepts the cudaEventDisableTiming flag value when called from a kernel.

Mathematically, a Bezier curve is defined by a set of control points $\mathbf{P}_0$ through $\mathbf{P}_n$, where n is called its order (n=1 for linear, 2 for quadratic, 3 for cubic, etc.). The first and last control points are always the end points of the curve; however, the intermediate control points (if any) generally do not lie on the curve.

LINEAR BEZIER CURVES

Given two control points $\mathbf{P}_0$ and $\mathbf{P}_1$, a linear Bezier curve is simply a straight line connecting between those two points. The coordinates of the points on the curve is given by the following linear interpolation formula:

$$\mathbf{B}(t) = \mathbf{P}_0 + t(\mathbf{P}_1 - \mathbf{P}_0) = (1 - t)\mathbf{P}_0 + t\mathbf{P}_1, t \in [0,1]$$

QUADRATIC BEZIER CURVES

A quadratic Bezier curve is defined by three control points $\mathbf{P}_0$, $\mathbf{P}_1$, and $\mathbf{P}_2$. The points on a quadratic curve are defined as a linear interpolation of corresponding points on the linear Bezier curves from $\mathbf{P}_0$ to $\mathbf{P}_1$ and from $\mathbf{P}_1$ to $\mathbf{P}_2$, respectively. The calculation of the coordinates of points on the curve is expressed in the following formula:

$$\mathbf{B}(t) = (1 - t)[(1 - t)\mathbf{P}_0 + t\mathbf{P}_1] + t[(1 - t)\mathbf{P}_1 + t\mathbf{P}_2], \quad t \in [0,1],$$

which can be simplified into the following formula:

$$\mathbf{B}(t) = (1 - t)^2 \mathbf{P}_0 + 2(1 - t)t\mathbf{P}_1 + t^2\mathbf{P}_2, \quad t \in [0,1].$$

BEZIER CURVE CALCULATION (WITHOUT DYNAMIC PARALLELISM)

Fig. 13.8 shows a CUDA C program that calculates the coordinates of points on a Bezier curve. The main function (line 48) initializes a set of control points to random values (line 51[3]). In a real application, these control points are most likely inputs from a user or a file. The control points are part of the bLines_h array whose element type BezierLine is declared in line 07. The storage for the bLines_h array is allocated in line 50. The host code then allocates the corresponding device memory for the bLines_d array and copies the initialized data to bLines_d (lines 54–56). It then calls the computeBezierLine() kernel to calculate the coordinates of the Bezier curve.

The computeBezierLine() kernel starting at line 13 is designed to use a thread-block to calculate the curve points for a set of three control points (of the quadratic Bezier formula). Each thread-block first computes a measure of the curvature of the curve defined by the three control points. Intuitively, the larger the curvature, the

---

[3] Function initializeBLines() can be found in Fig. A13.8 in Code Appendix at the end of the chapter.

```
01  #include <stdio.h>
02  #include <cuda.h>
03
04  #define MAX_TESS_POINTS 32
05
06  //A structure containing all parameters needed to tessellate a Bezier line
07  struct BezierLine {
08      float2 CP[3];                      //Control points for the line
09      float2 vertexPos[MAX_TESS_POINTS]; //Vertex position array to tessellate into
10      int nVertices;                     //Number of tessellated vertices
11  };
12
13  __global__ void computeBezierLines(BezierLine *bLines, int nLines) {
14      int bidx = blockIdx.x;
15      if(bidx < nLines){
16          //Compute the curvature of the line
17          float curvature = computeCurvature(bLines);
18
19          //From the curvature, compute the number of tessellation points
20          int nTessPoints = min(max((int)(curvature*16.0f),4),32);
21          bLines[bidx].nVertices = nTessPoints;
22
23          //Loop through vertices to be tessellated, incrementing by blockDim.x
24          for(int inc = 0; inc < nTessPoints; inc += blockDim.x){
25              int idx = inc + threadIdx.x;  //Compute a unique index for this point
26              if(idx < nTessPoints){
27                  float u = (float)idx/(float)(nTessPoints-1);  //Compute u from idx
28                  float omu = 1.0f - u;   //pre-compute one minus u
29                  float B3u[3]; //Compute quadratic Bezier coefficients
30                  B3u[0] = omu*omu;
31                  B3u[1] = 2.0f*u*omu;
32                  B3u[2] = u*u;
33                  float2 position = {0,0};  //Set position to zero
34                  for(int i = 0; i < 3; i++){
35                      //Add the contribution of the i'th control point to position
36                      position = position + B3u[i] * bLines[bidx].CP[i];
37                  }
38                  //Assign value of vertex position to the correct array element
39                  bLines[bidx].vertexPos[idx] = position;
40              }
41          }
42      }
43  }
44
45  #define N_LINES 256
46  #define BLOCK_DIM 32
47
48  int main( int argc, char **argv ) {
49      //Allocate and initialize array of lines in host memory
50      BezierLine *bLines_h = new BezierLine[N_LINES];
51      initializeBLines(bLines_h);
52
53      //Allocate device memory for array of Bezier lines
54      BezierLine *bLines_d;
55      cudaMalloc((void**)&bLines_d, N_LINES*sizeof(BezierLine));
56      cudaMemcpy(bLines_d,bLines_h, N_LINES*sizeof(BezierLine), cudaMemcpyHostToDevice);
57
58      //Call the kernel to tessellate the lines
59      computeBezierLines<<<N_LINES, BLOCK_DIM>>>(bLines_d, N_LINES );
60
61      cudaFree(bLines_d); //Free the array of lines in device memory
62      delete[] bLines_h;  //Free the array of lines in host memory
63  }
```

FIGURE 13.8

Bezier curve calculation without dynamic parallelism (support code in Fig. A13.8).

more the points it takes to draw a smooth quadratic Bezier curve for the three control points. This defines the amount of work to be done by each thread-block. This is reflected in lines 20 and 21, where the total number of points to be calculated by the current thread-block is proportional to the curvature value.

In the `for`-loop in line 24, all threads calculate a consecutive set of Bezier curve points in each iteration. The detailed calculation in the loop body is based on the formula we presented earlier. The key point is that the number of iterations taken by threads in a block can be very different from that taken by threads in another block. Depending on the scheduling policy, such variation of the amount of work done by each thread-block can result in decreased utilization of SMs and thus reduced performance.

BEZIER CURVE CALCULATION (WITH DYNAMIC PARALLELISM)

Fig. 13.9 shows a Bezier curve calculation code using dynamic parallelism. It breaks the `computeBezierLine()` kernel in Fig. 13.8 into two kernels. The first part, `computeBezierLine_parent()`, discovers the amount of work to be done for each control point. The second part, `computeBezierLine_child()`, performs the calculation.

With the new organization, the amount of work done for each set of control points by the `computeBezierLines_parent()` kernel is much smaller than the original `computeBezierLines()` kernel. Therefore, we use one thread to do this work in `computeBezierLines_parent()`, as opposed to using one block in `computeBezier-Lines()`. In line 58, we only need to launch one thread per set of control points. This is reflected by dividing the `N_LINES` by `BLOCK_DIM` to form the number of blocks in the kernel launch configuration.

There are two key differences between the `computeBezierLines_parent()` kernel and the `computeBezierLines()` kernel. First, the index used to access the control points is formed on a thread basis (line 08 in Fig. 13.9) rather than block basis (line 14 in Fig. 13.8). This is because the work for each control point is done by a thread rather than a block, as we mentioned above. Second, the memory for storing the calculated Bezier curve points is dynamically determined and allocated in line 15 in Fig. 13.9. This allows the code to assign just enough memory to each set of control points in the `BezierLine` type. Note that in Fig. 13.8, each `BezierLine` element is declared with the maximal possible number of points. On the other hand, the declaration in Fig. 13.9 has only a pointer to a dynamically allocated storage. Allowing a kernel to call the `cudaMalloc()` function can lead to substantial reduction of memory usage for situations where the curvature of control points vary significantly.

Once a thread of the `computeBezierLines_parent()` kernel determines the amount of work needed by its set of control points, it launches the `computeBezierLines_child()` kernel to do the work (line 19 in Fig. 13.9). In our example, every thread from the parent grid creates a new grid for its assigned set of control points. This way, the work done by each thread-block is balanced. The amount of work done by each child grid varies.

After the `computeBezierLines_parent()` kernel terminates, the main function can copy the data back and draw the curve on an output device. It also calls a kernel to free all storage allocated to the vertices in the `bLines_d` data structure in parallel (line 61). This is necessary since the vertex storage was allocated on the device by the `computeBezierLines_parent()` kernel so it has to be freed by device code (Section 13.5).

```
01   struct BezierLine {
02       float2 CP[3];      //Control points for the line
03       float2 *vertexPos; //Vertex position array to tessellate into
04       int nVertices;     //Number of tessellated vertices
05   };
06   __global__ void computeBezierLines_parent(BezierLine *bLines, int nLines) {
07       //Compute a unique index for each Bezier line
08       int lidx = threadIdx.x + blockDim.x*blockIdx.x;
09       if(lidx < nLines){
10           //Compute the curvature of the line
11           float curvature = computeCurvature(bLines);
12
13           //From the curvature, compute the number of tessellation points
14           bLines[lidx].nVertices = min(max((int)(curvature*16.0f),4),MAX_TESS_POINTS);
15           cudaMalloc((void**)&bLines[lidx].vertexPos,
16               bLines[lidx].nVertices*sizeof(float2));
17
18           //Call the child kernel to compute the tessellated points for each line
19           computeBezierLine_child<<<ceil((float)bLines[lidx].nVertices/32.0f), 32>>>
20               (lidx, bLines, bLines[lidx].nVertices);
21       }
22   }
23   __global__ void computeBezierLine_child(int lidx, BezierLine* bLines,
24       int nTessPoints) {
25       int idx = threadIdx.x + blockDim.x*blockIdx.x;//Compute idx unique to this vertex
26       if(idx < nTessPoints){
27           float u = (float)idx/(float)(nTessPoints-1);  //Compute u from idx
28           float omu = 1.0f - u;   //Pre-compute one minus u
29           float B3u[3];   //Compute quadratic Bezier coefficients
30           B3u[0] = omu*omu;
31           B3u[1] = 2.0f*u*omu;
32           B3u[2] = u*u;
33           float2 position = {0,0};  //Set position to zero
34           for(int i = 0; i < 3; i++) {
35               //Add the contribution of the i'th control point to position
36               position = position + B3u[i] * bLines[lidx].CP[i];
37           }
38           //Assign the value of the vertex position to the correct array element
39           bLines[lidx].vertexPos[idx] = position;
40       }
41   }
42   __global__ void freeVertexMem(BezierLine *bLines, int nLines) {
43       //Compute a unique index for each Bezier line
44       int lidx = threadIdx.x + blockDim.x*blockIdx.x;
45       if(lidx < nLines)
46           cudaFree(bLines[lidx].vertexPos);   //Free the vertex memory for this line
47   }
48   int main( int argc, char **argv ) {
49       //Allocate array of lines in host memory
50       BezierLine *bLines_h = new BezierLine[N_LINES];
51       initializeBLines(bLines_h);
52
53       //Allocate device memory for array of Bezier lines
54       BezierLine *bLines_d;
55       cudaMalloc((void**)&bLines_d, N_LINES*sizeof(BezierLine));
56       cudaMemcpy(bLines_d,bLines_h, N_LINES*sizeof(BezierLine),cudaMemcpyHostToDevice);
57
58       computeBezierLines_parent<<<ceil((float)N_LINES/(float)BLOCK_DIM), BLOCK_DIM>>>
59           (bLines_d, N_LINES);
60
61       freeVertexMem <<<ceil((float)N_LINES/(float)BLOCK_DIM), BLOCK_DIM>>>
62           (bLines_d, N_LINES);
63       cudaFree(bLines_d);   //Free the array of lines in device memory
64       delete[] bLines_h;    //Free the array of lines in host memory
65   }
```

FIGURE 13.9

Bezier calculation with dynamic parallelism (support code in Fig. A13.8).

LAUNCH POOL SIZE

As explained in Section 13.6, the launch pool storage may be virtualized when the fixed-pool size is full. That is, all launched grids will still be queued successfully. However, using the virtualized pool has a higher cost than using the fixed-size pool. The Bezier curve calculation with dynamic parallelism helps us to illustrate this.

Since the default size of the fixed-size pool is 2048 (it can be queried with `cudaDeviceGetLimit()`), launching more than 2048 grids will require the use of the virtualized pool, when the fixed-size pool is full. That is, if `N_LINES` (defined in Fig. 13.8, line 45) is set to 4096, half of the launches will use the virtualized pool. This will incur a significant performance penalty. However, if the fixed-size pool is set to 4096, the execution time will be reduced by an order of magnitude.

As a general recommendation, the size of the fixed-size pool should be set to the number of launched grids (if it exceeds the default size). In the case of the Bezier curves example, we would use `cudaDeviceSetLimit(cudaLimitDevRuntimePendi ngLaunchCount, N_LINES)` before launching the `computeBezierLines_parent()` kernel (line 58).

STREAMS

Named and unnamed (NULL) streams are offered by the device runtime, as mentioned in Section 13.6. One key consideration is that the default NULL stream is block-scope. This way, by default all launched grids within a thread-block will use the same stream, even if they are launched by different threads. As a consequence, these grids will execute sequentially.

The Bezier example launches as many grids as threads in the `computeBezier-Lines_parent()` kernel (line 19 in Fig. 13.9). Moreover, since `MAX_TESS_POINTS` is equal to 32 (see Fig. 13.8, line 04) and the thread-block size in `computeBezier-Lines_child()` is 32, the number of blocks per grid will be 1 for the `computeBezi-erLines_child()` kernel. If the default NULL stream is used, all these grids with one single block will be serialized. Thus, using the default NULL stream when launching the `computeBezierLines_child()` kernel can result in a drastic reduction in parallelism compared to the original, non-CDP kernel.

Given that `N_LINES` is 256 and `BLOCK_DIM` is 64, only four blocks are launched in `computeBezierLines_parent()`. Thus, only four default streams will be available for the `computeBezierLines_child()` kernel. Consequently, some streaming multiprocessors (SM) will remain unused on any GPU with more than four SMs. Since each grid in the same stream consists of only one thread-block and all grids in the same stream are serialized with respect to each other, each SM can also be underutilized.

If more concurrency is desired (with the aim of better utilizing all SM), named streams must be created and used in each thread. Fig. 13.10 shows the sequence of instructions that should replace line 19 in Fig. 13.9.

```
cudaStream_t stream;
// Create non-blocking stream
cudaStreamCreateWithFlags(&stream, cudaStreamNonBlocking);

//Call the child kernel to compute the tessellated points for each line
computeBezierLine_child<<<ceil((float)bLines[lidx].nVertices/32.0f), 32, 0, stream>>>
    (lidx, bLines, bLines[lidx].nVertices);

// Destroy stream
cudaStreamDestroy(stream);
```

FIGURE 13.10

Child kernel launch with named streams.

Using the code in Fig. 13.10, kernels launched from the same thread-block will be in different streams and can run concurrently. This will better utilize all SMs in the situation described above, leading to a considerable reduction of the execution time.

13.8 A RECURSIVE EXAMPLE

Dynamic parallelism allows programmers to implement recursive algorithms. In this section, we illustrate the use of dynamic parallelism for implementing recursion with a quadtree [Quadtree 1974]. Quadtrees partition a two-dimensional space by recursively subdividing it into four quadrants. Each quadrant is considered a node of the quadtree, and contains a number of points. If the number of points in a quadrant is greater than a fixed minimum, the quadrant will be subdivided into four more quadrants, that is, four child nodes.

Fig. 13.11 depicts an overview of how the construction of a quadtree can be implemented with dynamic parallelism. In this implementation one node (quadrant) is assigned to one thread-block. Initially (depth = 0), one thread-block is assigned the entire two-dimensional space (root node), which contains all points. It divides the space into four quadrants, and launches one thread-block for each quadrant (depth = 1). These child blocks will again subdivide their quadrants if they contain more points than a fixed minimum. In this example the minimum is two; thus, blocks 00 and 02 do not launch children. Blocks 01 and 03 launch a kernel with four blocks each.

As the flow graph in the right-hand side of Fig. 13.11 shows, a block first checks if the number of points in its quadrant is greater than the minimum required for further division and the maximum depth has not been reached. If either of the conditions fails, the work for the quadrant is complete and the block returns. Otherwise, the block computes the center of the bounding box that surrounds its quadrant. The center is in the middle of four new quadrants. The number of points in each of them is counted. A four-element scan operation is used to compute the offsets to the locations where the points will be stored. Then, the points are reordered, so that those points in the same quadrant are grouped together and placed into their section of the point storage. Finally, the block launches a child kernel with four thread-blocks, one for each of the four new quadrants.

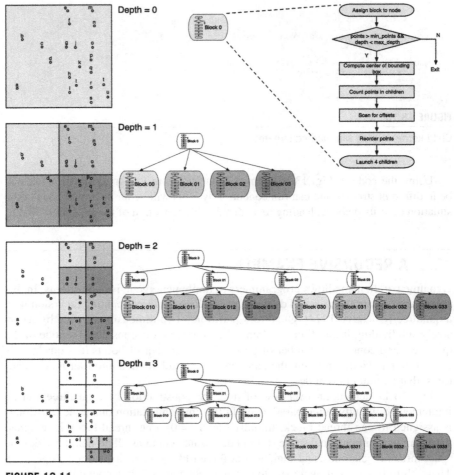

FIGURE 13.11

Quadtree example. Each thread-block is assigned to one quadrant. If the number of points in a quadrant is more than 2, the block launches 4 child blocks. Shadowed blocks are active blocks in each level of depth.

Fig. 13.12 continues the small example in Fig. 13.11 and illustrates in detail how the points are reordered at each level of depth. In this example, we assume that each quadrant must have a minimum of two points in order to be further divided. The algorithm uses two buffers to store the points and reorder them. The points should be in buffer 0 at the end of the algorithm. Thus, it might be necessary to swap the buffer contents before leaving, in case the points are in buffer 1 when the terminating condition is met.

In the initial kernel launch from the host code (for depth = 0), thread-block 0 is assigned all the points that reside in buffer 0, shown in Fig. 13.12(A). Block 0 further

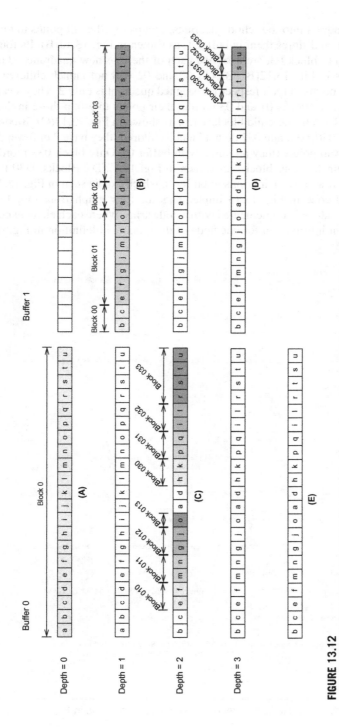

FIGURE 13.12

Quadtree example. At each level of depth, a block groups all points in the same quadrant together.

divides the quadrant into four child quadrants, groups together all points in the same child quadrant, and stores them in buffer 1, as shown in Fig. 13.12(B). Its four children, block 00 to block 03, are assigned each of the four new quadrants, shown as marked ranges in Fig. 13.12(B). Blocks 00 and 02 will not launch children, since the number of points in their respective assigned quadrant is only 2. They swap their points to buffer 0. Blocks 01 and 03 reorder their points to group those in the same quadrant, and launch four child blocks each, as shown in Fig. 13.12(C). Blocks 010, 011, 012, 013, 030, 031, and 032 do not launch children (they have 2 or fewer points) nor need to swap points (they are already in buffer 0). Only block 033 reorders its points, and launches four blocks, as shown in Fig. 13.12(D). Blocks 0330 to 0333 will exit after swapping their points to buffer 0, which can be seen in Fig. 13.12(E).

The kernel code in Fig. 13.13 implements the flow graph from Fig. 13.11 in CUDA. The quadtree is implemented with a node array, where each element contains all the pertinent information for one node of the quadtree (definition in Fig. A13.14

```
01    __global__ void build_quadtree_kernel
02              (Quadtree_node *nodes, Points *points, Parameters params) {
03        __shared__ int smem[8]; // To store the number of points in each quadrant
04
05        // The current node
06        Quadtree_node &node = nodes[blockIdx.x];
07        node.set_id(node.id() + blockIdx.x);
08        int num_points = node.num_points(); // The number of points in the node
09
10        // Check the number of points and its depth
11        bool exit = check_num_points_and_depth(node, points, num_points, params);
12        if(exit) return;
13
14        // Compute the center of the bounding box of the points
15        const Bounding_box &bbox = node.bounding_box();
16        float2 center;
17        bbox.compute_center(center);
18
19        // Range of points
20        int range_begin = node.points_begin();
21        int range_end   = node.points_end();
22        const Points &in_points = points[params.point_selector]; // Input points
23        Points &out_points = points[(params.point_selector+1) % 2]; // Output points
24
25        // Count the number of points in each child
26        count_points_in_children(in_points, smem, range_begin, range_end, center);
27
28        // Scan the quadrants' results to know the reordering offset
29        scan_for_offsets(node.points_begin(), smem);
30
31        // Move points
32        reorder_points(out_points, in_points, smem, range_begin, range_end, center);
33
34        // Launch new blocks
35        if (threadIdx.x == blockDim.x-1) {
36            // The children
37            Quadtree_node *children = &nodes[params.num_nodes_at_this_level];
38
39            // Prepare children launch
40            prepare_children(children, node, bbox, smem);
41
42            // Launch 4 children.
43            build_quadtree_kernel<<<4, blockDim.x, 8 *sizeof(int)>>>
44                          (children, points, Parameters(params, true));
45        }
46    }
```

FIGURE 13.13

Quadtree with dynamic parallelism: recursive kernel (support code in Fig. A13.13).

in Code Appendix). As the quadtree is constructed, new nodes will be created and placed into the array during the execution of the kernels. The kernel code assumes that the `node` parameter points to the next available location in the node array.

At each level of depth, every block starts by checking the number of points in its node (quadrant). Each point is a pair of floats representing `x` and `y` coordinates (definition in Fig. A13.13 in Code Appendix). If the number of points is less than or equal to the minimum or if the maximum depth is reached (line 11), the block will exit. Before exiting, the block carries out a buffer swap if necessary. This is done in the device function `check_num_points_and_depth()` shown in Fig. 13.14.

If the block doesn't exit, the center of the bounding box is computed (line 17). A bounding box is defined by its top-left and bottom-right corners. The coordinates of the center are computed as the coordinates of the middle point between these two corner points. The definition of a bounding box (including function `compute_center()`) is in Fig. A13.13 in the Code Appendix.

As the center defines the four quadrants, the number of points in each quadrant is counted (line 26). The device function `count_points_in_children()` can be found in Fig. 13.14[4]. The threads of the block collaboratively go through the range of points, and update atomically the counters in shared memory for each quadrant.

The device function `scan_for_offsets()` is called then (line 29). As can be seen in Fig. 13.14, it performs a sequential scan on the four counters in shared memory. Then, it adds the global offset of the parent quadrant to these values to derive the starting offset for each quadrant's group in the buffer.

Using the quadrants' offsets, the points are reordered with `reorder_points()` (line 32). For simplicity, this device function (Fig. 13.14) uses an atomic operation on one of the four quadrant counters to derive the location for placing each point.

Finally, the last thread of the block (line 35) determines the next available location in the node array (line 37), prepares the new node contents for the child quadrants (line 40), and launches one child kernel with four thread-blocks (line 43). The device function `prepare_children()` prepares the new node contents for the children by setting the limits of the children's bounding boxes and the range of points in each quadrant. The `prepare_children()` function can be found in Fig. 13.14.

The rest of the definitions and the main function can be found in Fig. A13.14 in the Code Appendix.

13.9 SUMMARY

CUDA dynamic parallelism extends the CUDA programming model to allow kernels to launch kernels. This allows each thread to dynamically discover work and launch new grids according to the amount of work discovered. It also supports dynamic allocation of device memory by threads. As we show in the Bezier Curve calculation example, these extensions can lead to better work balance across threads and blocks

---

[4] The device functions in Fig. 13.14 are simplified for clarity.

```
001  // Check the number of points and its depth
002  __device__ bool check_num_points_and_depth(Quadtree_node &node, Points *points,
003                                 int num_points, Parameters params){
004      if(params.depth >= params.max_depth || num_points <= params.min_points_per_node) {
005          // Stop the recursion here. Make sure points[0] contains all the points
006          if(params.point_selector == 1) {
007              int it = node.points_begin(), end = node.points_end();
008              for (it += threadIdx.x ; it < end ; it += blockDim.x)
009                  if(it < end)
010                      points[0].set_point(it, points[1].get_point(it));
011          }
012          return true;
013      }
014      return false;
015  }
016
017  // Count the number of points in each quadrant
018  __device__ void count_points_in_children(const Points &in_points, int* smem,
019      int range_begin, int range_end, float2 center) {
020      // Initialize shared memory
021      if(threadIdx.x < 4) smem[threadIdx.x] = 0;
022      __syncthreads();
023      // Compute the number of points
024      for(int iter=range_begin+threadIdx.x; iter<range_end; iter+=blockDim.x){
025          float2 p = in_points.get_point(iter); // Load the coordinates of the point
026          if(p.x < center.x && p.y >= center.y)
027              atomicAdd(&smem[0], 1); // Top-left point?
028          if(p.x >= center.x && p.y >= center.y)
029              atomicAdd(&smem[1], 1); // Top-right point?
030          if(p.x < center.x && p.y < center.y)
031              atomicAdd(&smem[2], 1); // Bottom-left point?
032          if(p.x >= center.x && p.y < center.y)
033              atomicAdd(&smem[3], 1); // Bottom-right point?
034      }
035      __syncthreads();
036  }
037
038  // Scan quadrants' results to obtain reordering offset
039  __device__ void scan_for_offsets(int node_points_begin, int* smem){
040      int* smem2 = &smem[4];
041      if(threadIdx.x == 0){
042          for(int i = 0; i < 4; i++)
043              smem2[i] = i==0 ? 0 : smem2[i-1] + smem[i-1]; // Sequential scan
044          for(int i = 0; i < 4; i++)
045              smem2[i] += node_points_begin;   // Global offset
046      }
047      __syncthreads();
048  }
049
050  // Reorder points in order to group the points in each quadrant
051  __device__ void reorder_points(
052                  Points& out_points, const Points &in_points, int* smem,
053                  int range_begin, int range_end, float2 center){
054      int* smem2 = &smem[4];
055      // Reorder points
056      for(int iter=range_begin+threadIdx.x; iter<range_end; iter+=blockDim.x){
057          int dest;
058          float2 p = in_points.get_point(iter); // Load the coordinates of the point
059          if(p.x<center.x && p.y>=center.y)
060              dest=atomicAdd(&smem2[0],1); // Top-left point?
061          if(p.x>=center.x && p.y>=center.y)
062              dest=atomicAdd(&smem2[1],1); // Top-right point?
063          if(p.x<center.x && p.y<center.y)
064              dest=atomicAdd(&smem2[2],1); // Bottom-left point?
065          if(p.x>=center.x && p.y<center.y)
066              dest=atomicAdd(&smem2[3],1); // Bottom-right point?
067          // Move point
068          out_points.set_point(dest, p);
069      }
070      __syncthreads();
071  }
```

FIGURE 13.14

Quadtree with dynamic parallelism: device functions (support code in Fig. A13.14).

```
072
073    // Prepare children launch
074    __device__ void prepare_children(Quadtree_node *children, Quadtree_node &node,
075                                    const Bounding_box &bbox, int *smem){
076        int child_offset = 4*node.id(); // The offsets of the children at their level
077
078        // Set IDs
079        children[child_offset+0].set_id(4*node.id()+ 0);
080        children[child_offset+1].set_id(4*node.id()+ 4);
081        children[child_offset+2].set_id(4*node.id()+ 8);
082        children[child_offset+3].set_id(4*node.id()+12);
083
084        // Points of the bounding-box
085        const float2 &p_min = bbox.get_min();
086        const float2 &p_max = bbox.get_max();
087
088        // Set the bounding boxes of the children
089        children[child_offset+0].set_bounding_box(
090            p_min.x , center.y, center.x, p_max.y);       // Top-left
091        children[child_offset+1].set_bounding_box(
092            center.x, center.y, p_max.x , p_max.y);       // Top-right
093        children[child_offset+2].set_bounding_box(
094            p_min.x , p_min.y , center.x, center.y);      // Bottom-left
095        children[child_offset+3].set_bounding_box(
096            center.x, p_min.y , p_max.x , center.y);      // Bottom-right
097
098        // Set the ranges of the children.
099        children[child_offset+0].set_range(node.points_begin(),   smem[4 + 0]);
100        children[child_offset+1].set_range(smem[4 + 0], smem[4 + 1]);
101        children[child_offset+2].set_range(smem[4 + 1], smem[4 + 2]);
102        children[child_offset+3].set_range(smem[4 + 2], smem[4 + 3]);
103    }
```

FIGURE 13.14

(Continued)

as well as more efficient memory usage. CUDA Dynamic Parallelism also helps programmers to implement recursive algorithms, as the quadtree example shows.

Besides ensuring better work balance, dynamic parallelism offers many advantages in terms of programmability. However, it is important to keep in mind that launching grids with a very small number of threads could lead to severe underutilization of the GPU resources. A general recommendation is launching child grids with a large number of thread-blocks, or at least thread-blocks with hundreds of threads, if the number of blocks is small.

Similarly, nested parallelism, which can be seen as a form of tree processing, will provide a higher performance when tree nodes are thick (that is, each node deploys many threads), and/or when the branch degree is large (that is, each parent node has many children). As the nesting depth is limited in hardware, only relatively shallow trees can be implemented efficiently.

13.10 EXERCISES

1. **True or False:** Parent and child grids have coherent access to global memory, with weak consistency between child and parent.

2. **True or False:** Zero-copy system memory has no coherence and consistency guarantees between parent and children.

3. **True or False:** Parent kernels can define new __constant__ variables that will be inherited by child kernels.

4. **True or False:** Child kernels can inherit parent's shared and local memories, and coherence is guaranteed.

5. Six (6) blocks of 256 threads run the following parent kernel:

```
__global__ void parent_kernel(int *output, int *input,
int *size) {
    // Thread index
    int idx = threadIdx.x + blockDim.x*blockIdx.x;
    // Number of child blocks
    int numBlocks = size[idx] / blockDim.x;
    // Launch child
    child_kernel<<< numBlocks, blockDim.x >>>(output, input,
    size);
}
```

   How many child kernels could run concurrently?
   a. 1536
   b. 256
   c. 6
   d. 1

6. Choose the right statement for the Bezier example:
   a. If N_LINES = 1024, and BLOCK_DIM = 64, the number of child kernel launches will be 16.
   b. If N_LINES = 1024, the fixed-size pool should be set to 1024 (Note: Default size is 2048).
   c. If N_LINES = 1024, BLOCK_DIM = 64, and per-thread streams are used, a total of 16 streams will be deployed.
   d. If N_LINES = 1024, BLOCK_DIM = 64, and aggregation is used, the number of child kernel launches will be 16.

7. Consider a two-dimensional organization of 64 equidistant points that is classified with a quadtree. What will be the maximum depth of the quadtree (including the root node)?
   a. 21
   b. 4
   c. 64
   d. 16

8. For the same quadtree, what will be the total number of child kernel launches?
   a. 21
   b. 4
   c. 64
   d. 16

REFERENCES

Bezier Curves. <http://en.wikipedia.org/wiki/B%C3%A9zier_curve>.

Finkel, R. A., & Bentley, J. L. (1974). Quad trees: A data structure for retrieval on composite keys. *Acta informatica*, *4*(1), 1–9.

A13.1 **CODE APPENDIX**

```
01    //Some inline vector math functions
02    __forceinline__ __device__ float2 operator+(float2 a, float2 b) {
03        float2 c;
04        c.x = a.x + b.x;    c.y = a.y + b.y;
05        return c;
06    }
07
08    __forceinline__ __device__ float2 operator -(float2 a, float2 b) {
09        float2 c;
10        c.x = a.x - b.x;    c.y = a.y - b.y;
11        return c;
12    }
13
14    __forceinline__ __device__ float2 operator*(float a, float2 b) {
15        float2 c;
16        c.x = a * b.x;    c.y = a * b.y;
17        return c;
18    }
19
20    __forceinline__ __device__ float length(float2 a) {
21        return sqrtf(a.x*a.x + a.y*a.y);
22    }
23
24    //Device function that computes the curvature of a line
25    __device__ float computeCurvature(BezierLine *bLines){
26        int bidx = blockIdx.x;
27        float curvature = length(bLines[bidx].CP[1] - 0.5f*(bLines[bidx].CP[0]
28            + bLines[bidx].CP[2]))/length(bLines[bidx].CP[2]
29            - bLines[bidx].CP[0]);
30        return curvature;
31    }
32
33    void initializeBLines(BezierLine *bLines_h) {
34        //Set initial point to zero (last is last point in the previous segment)
35        float2 last = {0,0};
36        for(int i = 0; i < N_LINES; i++){
37            //Set first point of this line to last point of previous line
38            bLines_h[i].CP[0] = last;
39            for(int j = 1; j < 3; j++) {
40                //Assign random coordinate between 0 and 1
41                bLines_h[i].CP[j].x = (float)rand()/(float)RAND_MAX;
42                //Assign random coordinate between 0 and 1
43                bLines_h[i].CP[j].y = (float)rand()/(float)RAND_MAX;
44            }
45            last = bLines_h[i].CP[2];    //keep the last point of this line
46            //Set number of tessellated vertices to zero
47            bLines_h[i].nVertices = 0;
48        }
49    }
```

FIGURE A13.8

Support code for Bezier Curve calculation without dynamic parallelism.

```
01    // A structure of 2D points
02    class Points {
03        float *m_x;
04        float *m_y;
05
06        public:
07        // Constructor
08        __host__ __device__ Points() : m_x(NULL), m_y(NULL) {}
09
10        // Constructor
11        __host__ __device__ Points(float *x, float *y) : m_x(x), m_y(y) {}
12
13        // Get a point
14        __host__ __device__ __forceinline__ float2 get_point(int idx) const {
15            return make_float2(m_x[idx], m_y[idx]);
16        }
17
18        // Set a point
19        __host__ __device__ __forceinline__ v oid set_point(int idx, const float2 &p) {
20            m_x[idx] = p.x;
21            m_y[idx] = p.y;
22        }
23
24        // Set the pointers
25        __host__ __device__ __forceinline__ void set(float *x, float *y) {
26            m_x = x;
27            m_y = y;
28        }
29    };
30
31    // A 2D bounding box
32    class Bounding_box {
33        // Extreme points of the bounding box
34        float2 m_p_min;
35        float2 m_p_max;
36
37        public:
38        // Constructor. Create a unit box
39        __host__ __device__ Bounding_box(){
40            m_p_min = make_float2(0.0f, 0.0f);
41            m_p_max = make_float2(1.0f, 1.0f);
42        }
43
44        // Compute the center of the bounding-box
45        __host__ __device__ void compute_center(float2 &center) const {
46            center.x = 0.5f * (m_p_min.x + m_p_max.x);
47            center.y = 0.5f * (m_p_min.y + m_p_max.y);
48        }
49
50        // The points of the box
51        __host__ __devic e__ __forceinline__ const float2 &get_max() const {
52            return m_p_max;
53        }
54
55        __host__ __device__ __forceinline__ const float2 &get_min() const {
56            return m_p_min;
57        }
58
59        // Does a box contain a point
60        __host__ __device__ bool contains(const float2 &p) const {
61            return p.x>=m_p_min.x && p.x<m_p_max.x && p.y>=m_p_min.y && p.y< m_p_max.y;
62        }
63
64        // Define the bounding box
65        __host__ __device__ void set(float min_x, float min_y, float max_x, float max_y){
66            m_p_min.x = min_x;
67            m_p_min.y = min_y;
68            m_p_max.x = max_x;
69            m_p_max.y = max_y;
70        }
71    };
```

FIGURE A13.13

Support code for quadtree with dynamic parallelism: definition of points and bounding box.

```
001   // A node of a quadtree
002   class Quadtree_node {
003       // The identifier of the node
004       int m_id;
005       // The bounding box of the tree
006       Bounding_box m_bounding_box;
007       // The range of points
008       int m_begin, m_end;
009
010   public:
011       // Constructor
012       __host__ __device__ Quadtree_node() : m_id(0), m_begin(0), m_end(0) {}
013
014       // The ID of a node at its level
015       __host__ __device__ int id() const {
016           return m_id;
017       }
018
019       // The ID of a node at its level
020       __host__ __device__ void set_id(int new_id) {
021           m_id = new_id;
022       }
023
024       // The bounding box
025       __host__ __device__ __forceinline__ const Bounding_box &bounding_box() const {
026           return m_bounding_box;
027       }
028
029       // Set the bounding box
030       __host__ __device__ __forceinline__ void set_bounding_box(float min_x,
031           float min_y, float max_x, float max_y) {
032           m_bounding_box.set(min_x, min_y, max_x, max_y);
033       }
034
035       // The number of points in the tree
036       __host__ __device__ __forceinline__ int num_points() const {
037           return m_end - m_begin;
038       }
039
040       // The range of points in the tree
041       __host__ __device__ __forceinline__ int points_begin() const {
042           return m_begin;
043       }
044
045       __host__ __device__ __forceinline__ int po  ints_end() const {
046           return m_end;
047       }
048
049       // Define the range for that node
050       __host__ __device__ __forceinline__ void set_range(int begin, int end) {
051           m_begin = begin;
052           m_end = end;
053       }
054   };
055
056   // Algorithm parameters
057   struct Parameters {
058       // Choose the right set of points to use as in/out
059       int point_selector;
060       // The number of nodes at a given level (2^k for level k)
061       int num_nodes_at_this_le vel;
062       // The recursion depth
063       int depth;
064       // The max value for depth
065       const int max_depth;
066       // The minimum number of points in a node to stop recursion
067       const int min_points_per_node;
068
069       // Constructor set to default values.
070       __host__ __device__ Parameters(int max_depth, int min_points_per_node) :
071           point_selector(0),
072           num_nodes_at_this_level(1),
073           depth(0),
074           max_depth(max_depth),
075           min_points_per_node(min_points_per_node) {}
076
```

FIGURE A13.14

Support code for quadtree with dynamic parallelism: definitions and main function.

```
077        // Copy constructor. Changes the values for next iteration
078        __host__ __device__ Parameters(const Parameters &params, bool) :
079            point_selector((params.point_selector+1) % 2),
080            num_nodes_at_this_level(4*params.num_nodes_at_this_level),
081            depth(params.depth+1),
082            max_depth(params.max_depth),
083            min_points_per_node(params.min_points_per_node) {}
084    };
085
086    // Main function
087    void main(int argc, char **argv) {
088
089        // Constants to control the algorithm
090        const int num_points = atoi(argv[0]);
091        const int max_depth  = atoi(argv[1]);
092        const int min_points_per_node = atoi(argv[2]);
093
094        // Allocate memory for points
095        thrust::device_vector<float> x_d0(num_points);
096        thrust::device_vector<float> x_d1(num_points);
097        thrust::device_vector<float> y_d0(num_points);
098        thrust::device_vector<float> y_d1(num_points);
099
100        // Generate random points
101        Random generator rnd;
102        thrust::generate(
103            thrust::make_zip_iterator(thrust::make_tuple(x_d0.begin(), y_d0.begin())),
104            thrust::make_zip_iterator(thrust::make_tuple(x_d0.end(), y_d0.end())),
105            rnd);
106
107        // Host structures to analyze the device ones
108        Points points_init[2];
109        points_init[0].set(thrust::raw_pointer_cast(&x_d0[0]),
110                           thrust::raw_pointer_cast(&y_d0[0]));
111        points_init[1].set(thrust::raw_pointer_cast(&x_d1[0]),
112                           thrust::raw_pointer_cast(&y_d1[0]));
113
114        // Allocate memory to store points
115        Points *points;
116        cudaMalloc((void **) &points, 2*sizeof(Points));
117        cudaMemcpy(points, points_init, 2*sizeof(Points), cudaMemcpyHostToDevice);
118
119        // We could use a close form...
120        int max_nodes = 0;
121
122        for (int i=0, num_nodes_at_level=1 ; i<max_depth ; ++i, num_nodes_at_level*=4)
123            max_nodes += num_nodes_at_level;
124
125        // Allocate memory to store the tree
126        Quadtree_node root;
127        root.set_range(0, num_points);
128        Quadtree_node *nodes;
129        cudaMalloc((void **) &nodes, max_nodes*sizeof(Quadtree_node));
130        cudaMemcpy(nodes, &root, sizeof(Quadtree_node), cudaMemcpyHostToDevice);
131
132        // We set the recursion limit for CDP to max_depth
133        cudaDeviceSetLimit(cudaLimitDevRuntimeSyncDepth, max_depth);
134
135        // Build the quadtree
136        Parameters params(max_depth, min_points_per_node);
137        const int NUM_THREADS_PER_BLOCK = 128;
138        const size_t smem_size = 8*sizeof(int);
139        build_quadtree_kernel<<<1, NUM_THREADS_PER_BLOCK, smem_size>>>
140            (nodes, points, params);
141        cudaGetLastError();
142
143        // Free memory
144        cudaFree(nodes);
145        cudaFree(points);
146
147    }
```

FIGURE A13.14

(Continued)

Application case study— non-Cartesian magnetic resonance imaging

14

An introduction to statistical estimation methods

CHAPTER OUTLINE

Application case studies teach computational thinking and practical programing techniques in a concrete manner. They also help demonstrate how the individual techniques fit into a top-to-bottom application development process. Most importantly, they help us to visualize the practical use of these techniques in solving problems. In this chapter, we start with the background and problem formulation of a relatively simple application that has traditionally been constrained by the limited capabilities of the main stream computing systems. We show that parallel execution not only speeds up the existing approaches, but also allows the applications experts to pursue an approach that has been known to provide benefit but was previously ignored due to their excessive computational requirements. *This approach represents an increasingly important class of computational methods that derive statistically optimal estimation of unknown values from a very large amount of observational data.* We use an example algorithm and its implementation source code from such an approach to illustrate how a developer can systematically determine the kernel parallelism structure, assign variables into different types of memories, steer around limitations of the hardware, validate results, and assess the impact of performance improvements.

Programming Massively Parallel Processors. DOI: http://dx.doi.org/10.1016/B978-0-12-811986-0.00014-5

14.1 BACKGROUND

Magnetic resonance imaging (MRI) is commonly used by the medical community to safely and noninvasively probe the structure and function of biological tissues in all regions of the body. Images that are generated using MRI have made profound impact in both clinical and research settings. MRI consists of two phases, acquisition (scan) and reconstruction. During the acquisition phase, the scanner samples data in the k-space domain (i.e., the spatial-frequency domain or Fourier transform domain) along a predefined trajectory. These samples are then transformed into the desired image during the reconstruction phase. Intuitively, the reconstruction phase *estimates* the shape and texture of the tissues based on the observation k-space data collected from the scanner.

The application of MRI is often limited by high noise levels, significant imaging artifacts, and/or long data acquisition times. In clinical settings, short scan times not only increase scanner throughput but also reduce patient discomfort, which tends to mitigate motion-related artifacts. High image resolution and fidelity are important because they enable early detection of pathology, leading to improved prognoses for patients. However, the goals of short scan time, high resolution, and high signal-to-noise ratio (SNR) often conflict; improvements in one metric tend to come at the expense of one or both of the others. One needs new technological breakthroughs to be able to simultaneously improve on all of three dimensions. This study presents a case where massively parallel computing provides such a breakthrough.

The reader is referred to MRI textbooks such as Liang and Lauterbur [LL 1999] for the physics principles behind MRI. For this case study, we will focus on the computational complexity in the reconstruction phase and how the complexity is affected by the k-space sampling trajectory. The k-space sampling trajectory used by the MRI scanner can significantly affect the quality of the reconstructed image, the time complexity of the reconstruction algorithm, and the time required for the scanner to acquire the samples. Eq. (14.1) shows a formulation that relates the k-space samples to the reconstructed image for a class of reconstruction methods.

$$\hat{m}(\mathbf{r}) = \sum_j W(\mathbf{k}_j) s(\mathbf{k}_j) e^{i2\pi \mathbf{k}_j \cdot \mathbf{r}} \tag{1}$$

In Eq. (14.1), $\hat{m}(\mathbf{r})$ is the reconstructed image, $s(\mathbf{k})$ is the measured k-space data, and $W(\mathbf{k})$ is the weighting function that accounts for nonuniform sampling. That is, $W(\mathbf{k})$ decreases the influence of data from k-space regions where a higher density of samples points are taken. For this class of reconstructions, $W(\mathbf{k})$ can also serve as an *apodization* filtering function that reduces the influence of noise and reduces artifacts due to finite sampling.

If data are acquired at uniformly spaced Cartesian grid points in the k-space under ideal conditions, then the $W(\mathbf{k})$ weighting function is a constant and can thus be factored out of the summation in Eq. (14.1). Furthermore, with uniformly spaced Cartesian grid samples, the exponential terms in (1) are uniformly spaced in the k-space. As a result, the reconstruction of $\hat{m}(\mathbf{r})$ becomes an inverse Fast Fourier Transform (iFFT) on $s(\mathbf{k})$, an extremely efficient computation method. A collection of data measured at such uniformly spaced Cartesian grid points is referred to as a *Cartesian scan trajectory*. Fig. 14.1A depicts a Cartesian scan trajectory. In practice, Cartesian scan trajectories allow straightforward implementation on scanners and are widely used in clinical settings today.

Although the iFFT reconstruction of Cartesian scan data is computationally efficient, non-Cartesian scan trajectories often have advantage in reduced sensitivity to patient motion, better ability to provide self-calibrating field inhomogeneity information, and reduced requirements on scanner hardware performance. As a result, non-Cartesian scan trajectories like spirals (shown in Fig. 14.1C), radial lines (also known as projection imaging) and rosettes have been proposed to reduce motion-related artifacts and address scanner hardware performance limitations. These improvements have recently allowed the reconstructed image pixel values to be used for measuring subtle phenomenon such as tissue chemical anomalies before they become anatomical pathology. Fig. 14.2 shows such an MRI reconstruction-based measurement that generates a map of sodium, a heavily regulated substance in normal human tissues. The information can be used to track to tissue health in stroke and cancer treatment processes. Because sodium is much less abundant than water molecules in human tissues, reliable measure of sodium levels requires a higher SNR through higher number of samples and thus needs to mitigate the extra scan time with non-Cartesian scan trajectories.

Image reconstruction from non-Cartesian trajectory data presents both challenges and opportunities. The main challenge arises from the fact that the exponential terms are no longer uniformly spaced; the summation does not have the form of a Fast Fourier Transform (FFT) anymore. Therefore, one can no longer perform reconstruction by directly applying an iFFT to the k-space samples. In a commonly used approach called gridding, the samples are first interpolated onto a uniform Cartesian grid and then reconstructed using the FFT (see Fig. 14.1B). For example, a convolution approach to gridding takes a k-space data point, convolves it with a gridding convolution mask, and

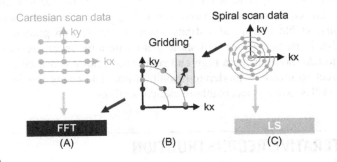

FIGURE 14.1

Scanner k-space trajectories and their associated reconstruction strategies: (A) Cartesian trajectory with FFT reconstruction, (B) Spiral (or non-Cartesian trajectory in general) followed by gridding to enable FFT reconstruction, (C) spiral (non-Cartesian) trajectory with linear solver based reconstruction. Note: *Based on Fig 1 of Lustig et al. Fast Fourier Transform for Iterative MR Image Reconstruction, IEEE Int'l Symp. on Biomedical Imaging, 2004.

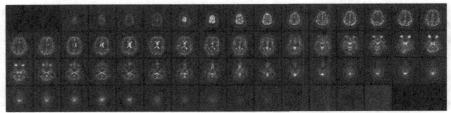

Courtesy of Keith Thulborn and Ian Atkinson, Center for MR Research, University of Illinois at Chicago

FIGURE 14.2

Non-Cartesian k-space sample trajectory and accurate linear-solver-based reconstruction enable new capabilities with exciting medical applications. The improved SNR enables reliable collection of in-vivo concentration data on chemical substance such as sodium in human tissues. The variation or shifting of sodium concentration gives early signs of disease development or tissue death. For example, the sodium map of a human brain shown in this figure can be used to give early indication of brain tumor tissue responsiveness to chemotherapy protocols, enabling individualized medicine.

accumulates the results on a Cartesian grid. As we have seen in Chapter 7, Parallel patterns: convolution, convolution is quite computationally intensive and is an important pattern for massively parallel computing. Accelerating convolution gridding computation with parallel computing facilitates the application of the current FFT approach to non-Cartesian trajectory data. Since we will be examining two convolution-style applications in the next two chapters, we will not cover the approach here.

In this chapter, we will cover an iterative, *statistically optimal* image reconstruction method which can accurately model imaging physics and bound the noise error in the resulting image pixel values. Such statistically optimal methods are gaining importance in the wake of big data analytics. However, such iterative reconstruction methods have been impractical for large-scale 3D problems due to their excessive computational requirements compared to gridding. Recently, these reconstructions have become viable in clinical settings when accelerated on graphics processing unit (GPUs). In particular, we will show that an iterative reconstruction algorithm that used to take hours using a high-end sequential central processing unit (CPUs) to reconstruct an image of moderate resolution now takes only minutes using both CPUs and GPUs, a delay acceptable in clinical settings.

14.2 ITERATIVE RECONSTRUCTION

Haldar and Liang proposed a linear-solver-based iterative reconstruction algorithm for non-Cartesian scan data, as shown in Fig. 14.1C. The algorithm allows for explicit modeling and compensation for the physics of the scanner data acquisition process, and can thus reduce the artifacts in the reconstructed image. It is, however, computationally expensive. The reconstruction time on high-end sequential CPUs has been

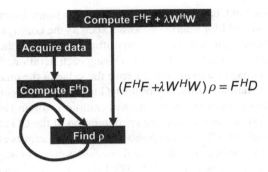

FIGURE 14.3

An iterative linear-solver-based approach to reconstructing non-Cartesian k-space sample data.

hours for moderate-resolution images and thus impractical in clinical use. We use this as an example of innovative methods that have required too much computation time to be considered practical. We will show that massive parallelism can reduce the reconstruction time to the order of a minute so that one can deploy the new imaging capabilities such as sodium imaging in clinical settings.

Fig. 14.3 shows a solution of the quasi-Bayesian estimation problem formulation of the iterative linear-solver-based reconstruction approach, where ρ is a vector containing voxel values for the reconstructed image, F is a matrix that models the physics of imaging process, D is a vector of data samples from the scanner, and W is a matrix that can incorporate prior information such as anatomical constraints. In clinical settings, the anatomical constraints represented in W are derived from one or more high resolution, high-SNR water molecule scans of the patient. These water molecule scans reveal features such as the location of anatomical structures. The matrix W is derived from these reference images. The problem is to solve for ρ given all the other matrices and vectors.

On the surface, the computational solution to the problem formulation in Fig. 14.3 should be very straightforward. It involves matrix–matrix multiplications and addition ($F^H F + \lambda W^H W$), matrix–vector multiplication ($F^H D$), matrix inversion ($F^H F + \lambda W^H W)^{-1}$, and finally matrix–matrix multiplication (($F^H F + \lambda W^H W)^{-1} * F^H D$). However, the sizes of the matrices make this straightforward approach extremely time consuming. F^H and F are 3D matrices whose dimensions are determined by the resolution of the reconstructed image ρ. Even in a modest resolution 128^3-voxel reconstruction, there are 128^3 columns in F with N elements in each column where N is the number of k-space samples used. Obviously, F is extremely large. Such massive dimensions are commonly encountered in big-data analytics, when one tries to use iterative-solver methods to estimate the major contributing factors of a massive amount of noisy observational data.

The sizes of the matrices involved are so large that the matrix operations involved in a direct solution of the equation in Fig. 14.3 using methods such as Gaussian elimination discussed in Chapter 6, Numerical considerations, are practically intractable. An iterative method for matrix inversion, such as the conjugate gradient (CG) algorithm, is therefore preferred. The CG algorithm reconstructs the image by iteratively solving the equation in Fig. 14.3 for ρ. During each iteration, the CG algorithm updates the current image estimate ρ to improve the value of the quasi-Bayesian cost function. The computational efficiency of the CG technique is largely determined by the efficiency of matrix–vector multiplication operations involving $F^H F + \lambda W^H W$ and ρ, as these operations are required during each iteration of the CG algorithm.

Fortunately, matrix W often has a sparse structure that permits efficient multiplication by $W^H W$, and matrix $F^H F$ is Toeplitz that enables efficient matrix–vector multiplication via the FFT. Stone et al. [SHT 2008] present a GPU accelerated method for calculating Q, a data structure that allows us to quickly calculate matrix–vector multiplication involving $F^H F$ without actually calculating $F^H F$ itself. The calculation of Q can take days on a high-end CPU core. It only needs to be done once for a given trajectory and can be used for multiple scans.

The matrix–vector multiply to calculate $F^H D$ takes about one order of magnitude less time than Q but can still take about three hours for a 128^3-voxel reconstruction on a high-end sequential CPU. Recall that D is the vector of data samples from the scanner. Thus, $F^H D$ needs to be computed for every image acquisition; it is desirable to reduce the computation time of $F^H D$ to minutes.[1] We will show the details of this process. As it turns out, the core computational structure of Q is identical to that of $F^H D$; Q just has much larger data structure dimensions. As a result, the same methodology can be used to accelerate the computation of both.

The "find ρ" step in Fig. 14.3 performs the actual CG based on $F^H D$. As we explained earlier, precalculation of Q makes this step much less computationally intensive than $F^H D$, accounting for only less than 1% of the execution of the reconstruction of each image on a sequential CPU. As a result, we will leave the CG solver out of the parallelization scope and focus on $F^H D$ in this chapter. We will however, revisit its status at the end of the chapter.

14.3 COMPUTING $F^H D$

Fig. 14.4 shows a sequential C implementation of the computations for the core step of computing a data structure for matrix–vector multiplications between $F^H * F$ and ρ (referred to as Q computation in Fig. 14.4A) during the iterative CG solution process without explicitly calculating $F^H F$ and that for computing $F^H D$ (Fig. 14.4B). It should be clear from a quick glance at Fig. 14.4A and Fig. 14.4B that the core step of Q and $F^H D$ have identical loop structure. Both computations start with an outer loop, which encloses an inner loop. The only differences are the particular calculation done in each loop body and the fact that the core step of Q involves a much larger m, since it implements a matrix–matrix multiplication as opposed to a matrix–vector

---

[1] Note that the FHD computation can be approximated with gridding and can run in a few seconds, with perhaps reduced quality of the final reconstructed image.

(A)
```
for (m = 0; m < M; m++) {

    phiMag[m] = rPhi[m]*rPhi[m] +
                iPhi[m]*iPhi[m];

    for (n = 0; n < N; n++) {
      expQ = 2*PI*(kx[m]*x[n] +
                   ky[m]*y[n] +
                   kz[m]*z[n]);

      rQ[n] +=phiMag[m]*cos(expQ);
      iQ[n] +=phiMag[m]*sin(expQ);
    }
}
```

(B)
```
for (m = 0; m < M; m++) {

    rMu[m] = rPhi[m]*rD[m] +
             iPhi[m]*iD[m];
    iMu[m] = rPhi[m]*iD[m] -
             iPhi[m]*rD[m];

    for (n = 0; n < N; n++) {
      expFhD = 2*PI*(kx[m]*x[n] +
                     ky[m]*y[n] +
                     kz[m]*z[n]);

      cArg = cos(expFhD);
      sArg = sin(expFhD);

      rFhD[n] +=  rMu[m]*cArg -
                  iMu[m]*sArg;
      iFhD[n] +=  iMu[m]*cArg +
                  rMu[m]*sArg;
    }
}
```

FIGURE 14.4

Computation of Q and F^{H}D. (A) Q computation, (B) F^{H}D computation.

multiplication; thus it incurs a much longer execution time. Thus it suffices to discuss one of them from the parallelization perspective. We will focus on F^{H}D, since this is the one that will need to be run for each data acquisition.

A quick glance at Fig. 14.4B shows that the C implementation of F^{H}D is an excellent candidate for acceleration because it exhibits substantial data parallelism. The algorithm first computes the real and imaginary components of Mu (rMu and iMu) at each sample point in the k-space, it then computes the real and imaginary components of F^{H}D at each voxel in the image space (M is the total number of k-space samples and N is the total number of voxels in the reconstructed image). The value of F^{H}D at any voxel depends on the values of all k-space sample points. However, no voxel elements of F^{H}D depend on any other elements of F^{H}D. Therefore, all elements of F^{H}D can be computed in parallel. Specifically, all iterations of the outer loop can be done in parallel and all iterations of the inner loop can be done in parallel. The calculations of the inner loop, however, have a dependence on the calculation done by the preceding statements in the same iteration of the outer loop.

Despite the algorithm's abundant inherent parallelism, potential performance bottlenecks are evident. First, in the loop that computes the elements of F^{H}D, the ratio of floating-point operations to memory accesses is at best 3:1 and at worst 1:1. The best case assumes that the sin and cos trigonometry operations are computed using five-element Taylor series that require 13 and 12 floating-point operations, respectively. The worst case assumes that each trigonometric operation is computed as a single operation in hardware. As we have seen in Chapter 5, Performance considerations, a floating-point to memory access ratio of 16:1 or more is needed for the kernel to be not limited by memory bandwidth. Thus, the memory accesses will clearly limit the performance of the kernel unless the ratio is drastically increased.

Second, the ratio of floating-point arithmetic to floating-point trigonometry functions is only 13:2. Thus, GPU-based implementation must tolerate or avoid stalls due to long-latency and low-throughput of `sin` and `cos` operations. Without a good way to reduce the cost of trigonometry functions, the performance will likely be dominated by the time spent in these functions.

We are now ready to take the steps in converting F^HD from sequential C code to a CUDA kernel.

STEP 1: DETERMINE THE KERNEL PARALLELISM STRUCTURE

The conversion of a loop into a CUDA kernel is conceptually straightforward. Since all iterations of the outer loop of Fig. 14.4B can be executed in parallel, we can simply convert the outer loop into a CUDA kernel by mapping its iterations to CUDA threads. Fig. 14.5 shows a kernel from such a straightforward conversion. Each thread implements an iteration of the original outer loop. That is, we use each thread to calculate the contribution of one k-space sample to all F^HD elements. The original outer loop has M iterations, and M can be in the millions. We obviously need to have a large number of thread blocks to generate enough threads to implement all these iterations.

To make performance tuning easy, we declare a constant `FHD_THREADS_PER_BLOCK` that defines the number of threads in each thread block when we invoke the `cmpFHD` kernel. Thus, we will use `M/FHD_THREADS_PER_BLOCK` for the grid size (in terms of number of blocks) and `FHD_THREADS_PER_BLOCK` for block size (in terms of number of threads) for kernel invocation. Within the kernel, each thread calculates

```
__global__ void cmpFhD(float* rPhi, iPhi, rD, iD,
    kx, ky, kz, x, y, z, rMu, iMu, rFhD, iFhD, int N) {

  int m = blockIdx.x * FHD_THREADS_PER_BLOCK + threadIdx.x;

  rMu[m] = rPhi[m]*rD[m] + iPhi[m]*iD[m];
  iMu[m] = rPhi[m]*iD[m] - iPhi[m]*rD[m];

  for (int n = 0; n < N; n++) {
    floatexpFhD = 2*PI*(kx[m]*x[n] + ky[m]*y[n] + kz[m]*z[n]);

    floatcArg = cos(expFhD);  floatsArg = sin(expFhD);

    rFhD[n] +=  rMu[m]*cArg - iMu[m]*sArg;
    iFhD[n] +=  iMu[m]*cArg + rMu[m]*sArg;
  }
}
```

FIGURE 14.5

First version of the F^HD kernel. The kernel will not execute correctly due to conflicts between threads in writing into rFhD and iFhD arrays.

the original iteration of the outer loop that it is assigned to cover using the familiar formula: `blockIdx.x * FHD_THREADS_PER_BLOCK + threadIdx.x`. For example, assume that there are 65,536 k-space samples and we decided to use 512 threads per block. The grid size at kernel innovation would be 65,536/512= 128 blocks. The block size would be 512. The calculation of m for each thread would be equivalent to `blockIdx.x*512 + threadIdx`.

While the kernel of Fig. 14.5 exploits ample parallelism, it suffers from a major problem: all threads write into all `rFhD` and `iFhD` voxel elements. This means that the kernel must use atomic operations in the global memory in the inner loop in order to keep threads from trashing each other's contributions to the voxel value. As we have seen in Chapter 9, Parallel patterns: parallel histogram computation, heavy use of atomic operation on global memory data can seriously reduce the performance of kernel. Furthermore, the size of the rFhD and iFhD arrays make privatization infeasible. We need to explore other options.

The other option is to use each thread to calculate one `FhD` value from all k-space samples. In order to do so, we need to first swap the inner loop and the outer loop so that each of the new outer loop iterations processes one `FhD` element. That is, each of the new outer loop iterations will execute the new inner loop that accumulates the contribution of all k-space samples to the `FhD` element handled by the outer loop iteration. This transformation of the loop structure is called *loop interchange*. It requires a perfectly nested loop, meaning that there is no statement between the outer `for`-loop statement and the inner `for`-loop statement. This is however, not true for the FhD code in Fig. 14.4B. We need to find a way to move the calculation of `rMu` and `iMu` elements out of the way.

From a quick inspection of Fig. 14.6A which is a replicate of Fig. 14.4B, we see that the F^{H}D calculation can be split into two separate loops, as shown in Fig. 14.6B using a technique called *loop fission* or loop splitting. This transformation takes the body of a loop and splits it into two loops. In the case of F^{H}D, the outer loop consists of two parts: the statements before the inner loop and the inner loop itself. As shown in Fig. 14.6B, we can perform loop fission on the outer loop by placing the statements before the inner loop into a loop and the inner loop into a second loop. The transformation changes the relative execution order of the two parts of the original outer loop. In the original outer loop, both parts of the first iteration execute before the second iteration. After fission, the first part of all iterations will execute; they are then followed by the second part of all iterations. The reader should be able to verify that this change of execution order does not affect the execution results for F^{H}D. This is because the execution of the first part of each iteration does not depend on the result of the second part of any preceding iterations of the original outer loop. Loop fission is a transformation often done by advanced compilers that are capable of analyzing the (lack of) dependence between statements across loop iterations.

With loop fission, the F^{H}D computation is now done in two steps. The first step is a single-level loop that calculates the `rMu` and `iMu` elements for use in the second loop. The second step corresponds to the loop that calculates the FHD elements based on the rMu and iMu elements calculated in the first step. Each step can now be

(A)
```
for (m = 0; m < M; m++) {

    rMu[m] = rPhi[m]*rD[m] +
             iPhi[m]*iD[m];
    iMu[m] = rPhi[m]*iD[m] -
             iPhi[m]*rD[m];

    for (n = 0; n < N; n++) {
      expFhD = 2*PI*(kx[m]*x[n] +
                     ky[m]*y[n] +
                     kz[m]*z[n]);

    cArg = cos(expFhD);
    sArg = sin(expFhD);

    rFhD[n] +=   rMu[m]*cArg -
                 iMu[m]*sArg;
    iFhD[n] +=   iMu[m]*cArg +
                 rMu[m]*sArg;
    }
}
```

(B)
```
for (m = 0; m < M; m++) {

    rMu[m] = rPhi[m]*rD[m] +
             iPhi[m]*iD[m];
    iMu[m] = rPhi[m]*iD[m] -
             iPhi[m]*rD[m];
}
for (m = 0; m < M; m++) {
  for (n = 0; n < N; n++) {
    expFhD = 2*PI*(kx[m]*x[n] +
                   ky[m]*y[n] +
                   kz[m]*z[n]);

    cArg = cos(expFhD);
    sArg = sin(expFhD);

    rFhD[n] +=   rMu[m]*cArg -
                 iMu[m]*sArg;
    iFhD[n] +=   iMu[m]*cArg +
                 rMu[m]*sArg;
  }
}
```

FIGURE 14.6

Loop fission on the F^HD computation. (A) F^HD computation, (B) after loop fission.

```
__global__ void cmpMu(float* rPhi, iPhi, rD, iD, rMu, iMu)
{
    int m = blockIdx.x*MU_THREAEDS_PER_BLOCK + threadIdx.x;

    rMu[m] = rPhi[m]*rD[m] + iPhi[m]*iD[m];
    iMu[m] = rPhi[m]*iD[m] - iPhi[m]*rD[m];
}
```

FIGURE 14.7

cmpMu kernel.

converted into a CUDA kernel. The two CUDA kernels will execute sequentially with respect to each other. Since the second loop needs to use the results from the first loop, separating these two loops into two kernels that execute in sequence does not sacrifice any parallelism.

The cmpMu() kernel in Fig. 14.7 implements the first loop. The conversion of the first loop from sequential C code to a CUDA kernel is straightforward: each thread implements one iteration of the original C code. Since the M value can be very big, reflecting the large number of k-space samples, such a mapping can result in a large number of threads. Since each thread block can have only 512 threads in each block, we will need to use multiple blocks to allow the large number of threads. This can be accomplished by having a number of threads in each block, specified by `MU_THREADS_PER_BLOCK` in Fig. 14.4C, and by employing `M/MU_THREADS_PER_BLOCK` blocks needed to cover all `M` iterations of the original loop. For example, if there are 65,536 k-space samples, the kernel could be invoked with a configuration of 512 threads per block and 65,536/512 = 128 blocks. This is done by defining `MU_THREADS_PER_BLOCK` as 512 and using `MU_THREADS_PER_BLOCK` as block size and `M/MU_THREADS_PER_BLOCK` as grid size during kernel innovation.

Within the kernel, each thread can identify the iteration assigned to it using its `blockIdx` and `threadIdx` values. Since the threading structure is one-dimensional, only `blockIdx.x` and `threadIdx.x` need to be used. Because each block covers a section of the original iterations, the iteration covered by a thread is `blockIdx.x*MU_THREADS_PER_BLOCK + threadIdx`. For example, assume that `MU_THREADS_PER_BLOCK=512`. The thread with `blockIdx.x=0` and `threadIdx.x=37` covers the 37th iteration of the original loop, whereas the thread with `blockIdx.x=5` and `threadIdx.x=2` covers the 2562nd (5*512 + 2) iteration of the original loop. Using this iteration number to access the Mu, Phi, and D arrays ensures that the arrays are covered by the threads in the same way they were covered by the iterations of the original loop. Because every thread writes into its own Mu element, there is no potential conflict between any of these threads.

Determining the structure of the second kernel requires a little more work. An inspection of the second loop in Fig. 14.6B shows that there are at least three options in designing the second kernel. In the first option, each thread corresponds to one iteration of the inner loop. This option creates the most number of threads and thus exploits the largest amount of parallelism. However, the number of threads would be `N*M`, with both `N` in the range of millions and `M` in the range of hundred thousands. Their product would result in too many threads in the grid.

A second option is to use each thread to implement an iteration of the outer loop. This option employs fewer threads than the first option. Instead of generating `N*M` threads, this option generates `M` threads. Since `M` corresponds to the number of k-space samples and a large number of samples, on the order of a hundred thousand, are typically used to calculate F^{H}D, this option still exploits a large amount of parallelism. However, this kernel suffers the same problem as the kernel in Fig. 14.5. That is, each thread will write into all `rFhD` and `iFhD` elements, thus creating an extremely large number of conflicts between threads. As in the case of Fig. 14.5, the code in Fig. 14.8 requires atomic operations that will significantly slow down the execution. Thus, this option does not work well.

A third option is to use each thread to compute one pair of `rFhD` and `iFhD` elements. This option requires us to interchange the inner and outer loops and then use each thread to implement an iteration of the new outer loop. The transformation is shown in Fig. 14.9. Loop interchange is necessary because the loop being implemented by the CUDA threads must be the outer loop. Loop interchange makes each of the new outer loop iteration to process a pair of `rFhD` and `iFhD` elements. Loop interchange is permissible here because all iterations of both levels of loops are

```
__global__ void cmpFhD(float* rPhi, iPhi, phimag,
        kx, ky, kz, x, y, z, rMu, imu, int N) {

    int m = blockIdx.x * FHD_THREADS_PER_BLOCK + threadIdx.x;

    for (int n = 0; n < N; n++) {
        float expFhD = 2*PI*(kx[m]*x[n]+ky[m]*y[n]+kz[m]*z[n)];

        float CArg = cos(expFhD);
        float sArg = sin(expFhD);

        atomicAdd(&rFhD[n], rMu[m]*cArg - imu[m]*sArg);
        atomicAdd(&rFhD[n], iMu[m]*cArg + imu[m]*sArg);
    }
}
```

FIGURE 14.8

Second option of the F^{H}D kernel.

(A)
```
for (m = 0; m < M; m++) {
    for (n = 0; n < N; n++) {
        expFhD = 2*PI*(kx[m]*x[n] +
                       ky[m]*y[n] +
                       kz[m]*z[n]);

        cArg = cos(expFhD);
        sArg = sin(expFhD);

        rFhD[n] +=  rMu[m]*cArg -
                    iMu[m]*sArg;
        iFhD[n] +=  iMu[m]*cArg +
                    rMu[m]*sArg;
    }
}
```

(B)
```
for (n = 0; n < N; n++) {
    for (m = 0; m < M; m++) {
        expFhD = 2*PI*(kx[m]*x[n] +
                       ky[m]*y[n] +
                       kz[m]*z[n]);

        cArg = cos(expFhD);
        sArg = sin(expFhD);

        rFhD[n] +=  rMu[m]*cArg -
                    iMu[m]*sArg;
        iFhD[n] +=  iMu[m]*cArg +
                    rMu[m]*sArg;
    }
}
```

FIGURE 14.9

Loop interchange of the F^{H}D computation. (A) Before loop interchange, (B) after loop interchange.

independent of each other. They can be executed in any order relative to one another. Loop interchange, which changes the order of the iterations, is allowed when these iterations can be executed in any order. This option generates N threads. Since N corresponds to the number of voxels in the reconstructed image, the N value can be very large for higher-resolution images. For a 128^3 image, there are $128^3=2,097,152$ threads, resulting in a large amount of parallelism. For higher resolutions, such as 512^3, we may need to invoke multiple kernels, each kernel generates the value of a subset of the voxels. Note these threads now all accumulate into their own rFhD and

```
__global__ void cmpFHd(float* rPhi, iPhi, phiMag,
         kx, ky, kz, x, y, z, rMu, iMu, int M) {

   int n = blockIdx.x * FHD_THREADS_PER_BLOCK + threadIdx.x;

   for (int m = 0; m < M; m++) {
      float expFhD = 2*PI*(kx[m]*x[n]+ky[m]*y[n]+kz[m]*z[n]);

      float cArg = cos(expFhD);
      float sArg = sin(expFhD);

      rFhD[n] +=  rMu[m]*cArg - iMu[m]*sArg;
      iFhD[n] +=  iMu[m]*cArg + rMu[m]*sArg;
   }
}
```

FIGURE 14.10

Third option of the FHD kernel.

iFhD elements since every thread has a unique n value. There is no conflict between threads. These threads can run totally in parallel. This makes the third option the best choice among the three options.

The kernel derived from the interchanged loops is shown in Fig. 14.10. The threads are organized as a two-level structure. The outer loop has been stripped away; each thread covers an iteration of the outer (n) loop, where n is equal to blockIdx.x*FHD_THREADS_PER_BLOCK + threadIdx.x. Once this iteration (n) value is identified, the thread executes the inner loop based on that n value. This kernel can be invoked with a number of threads in each block, specified by a global constant FHD_THREADS_PER_BLOCK. Assuming that N is the variable that stores the number of voxels in the reconstructed image, N/FHD_THREADS_PER_BLOCK blocks cover all N iterations of the original loop. For example, if there are 65,536 k-space samples, the kernel could be invoked with a configuration of 512 threads per block and 65,536/512 = 128 blocks. This is done by assigning 512 to FHD_THREADS_PER_BLOCK and using FHD_THREADS_PER_BLOCK as block size and N/FHD_THREADS_PER_BLOCK as grid size during kernel innovation.

STEP 2: GETTING AROUND THE MEMORY BANDWIDTH LIMITATION

The simple cmpFhD kernel in Fig. 14.10 will result in limited speedup due to memory bandwidth limitations. A quick analysis shows that the execution is limited by the low compute to memory access ratio of each thread. In the original loop, each iteration performs at least 14 memory accesses: kx[m], ky[m], kz[m], x[n], y[n], z[n], rMu[m] twice, iMu[m] twice, rFhD[n] read and write, and iFhD[n] read and write. Meanwhile, about 13 floating-point multiply, add, or trigonometry operations are performed in each iteration. Therefore, the compute to memory access ratio is approximately 1, which is too low according to our analysis in Chapter 5, Performance considerations.

We can immediately improve the compute to memory access ratio by assigning some of the array elements to automatic variables. As we discussed in Chapter 5, Performance considerations, the automatic variables will reside in registers, thus converting reads and writes to the global memory into reads and writes to on-chip registers. A quick review of the kernel in Fig. 14.10 shows that for each thread, the same x[n], y[n], and z[n] elements are used across all iterations of the for loop. This means that we can load these elements into automatic variables before the execution enters the loop. The kernel can then use the automatic variables inside the loop, thus converting global memory accesses to register accesses. Furthermore, the loop repeatedly reads from and writes into rFhD[n] and iFhD[n]. We can have the iterations read from and write into two automatic variables and only write the contents of these automatic variables into rFhD[n] and iFhD[n] after the execution exits the loop. The resulting code is shown in Fig. 14.11. By increasing the number of registers used by five for each thread, we have reduced the memory access done in each iteration from 14 to 7. Thus, we have increased the compute to memory access ratio from 13:14 to 13:7. This is a good improvement and a good use of the precious register resource.

Recall that the register usage can limit the occupancy, number of blocks that can run in an streaming multiprocessor (SM). By increasing the register usage by 5 in the kernel code, we increase the register usage of each thread block by 5*FHD_THREADS_PER_BLOCK. Assuming that we have 128 threads per block, we just increased the block register usage by 640. Since each SM can accommodate a combined register usage of 65,536 registers among all blocks assigned to it (in SM Version 3.5 or higher), we need be careful, as any further increase of register usage can begin to limit the number of blocks that can be assigned to an SM. Fortunately, the register usage is not a limiting factor to parallelism for this kernel.

We want to further improve the compute to memory access ratio to something closer to 10 by eliminating more global memory accesses in the cmpFhD kernel. The next candidates to consider are the k-space samples kx[m], ky[m], and kz[m]. These array elements are accessed differently than the x[n], y[n], and z[n] elements: different elements of kx, ky, and kz are accessed in each iteration of the loop in Fig. 14.11. This means that we cannot load a k-space element into a register and expect to access that element off a register through all the iterations. So, registers will not help here. However, we should notice that the k-space elements are not modified by the kernel. This means that we might be able to place the k-space elements into the constant memory. Perhaps the cache for the constant memory can eliminate most of the memory accesses.

An analysis of the loop in Fig. 14.11 reveals that the k-space elements are indeed excellent candidates for constant memory. The index used for accessing kx, ky, and kz is m. We know that m is independent of threadIdx, which implies that all threads in a warp will be accessing the same element of kx, ky, and kz. This is an ideal access pattern for cached constant memory: every time an element is brought into the cache, it will be used at least by all 32 threads in a warp for a current generation device. This means that for every 32 accesses to the constant memory, at least 31 of them will be served by the cache. This allows the cache to effectively eliminate 96% or more of

```
__global__ void cmpFHd(float* rPhi, iPhi, phiMag,
       kx, ky, kz, x, y, z, rMu, iMu, int M) {

  int n = blockIdx.x * FHD_THREADS_PER_BLOCK + threadIdx.x;

  float xn_r = x[n]; float yn_r = y[n]; float zn_r = z[n];
  float rFhDn_r = rFhD[n]; float iFhDn_r = iFhD[n];

  for (int m = 0; m < M; m++) {
    float expFhD = 2*PI*(kx[m]*xn_r+ky[m]*yn_r+kz[m]*zn_r);

    float cArg = cos(expFhD);
    float sArg = sin(expFhD);

    rFhDn_r +=  rMu[m]*cArg - iMu[m]*sArg;
    iFhDn_r +=  iMu[m]*cArg + rMu[m]*sArg;
  }
  rFhD[n] = rFhD_r; iFhD[n] = iFhD_r;
}
```

FIGURE 14.11

Using registers to reduce memory accesses in the F^{H}D kernel.

the accesses to the global memory. Better yet, each time when a constant is accessed from the cache, it can be broadcast to all the threads in a warp. This makes constant memory almost as efficient as registers for accessing k-space elements.[2]

There is, however, a technical issue involved in placing the k-space elements into the constant memory. Recall that constant memory has a capacity of 64 kB. However, the size of the k-space samples can be much larger, in the order of hundreds of thousands or even millions. A typical way of working around the limitation of constant memory capacity is to breakdown a large data set into chunks or 64 kB or smaller. The developer must reorganize the kernel so that the kernel will be invoked multiple times, with each invocation of the kernel consuming only a chunk of the large data set. This turns out to be quite easy for the cmpFhD kernel.

A careful examination of the loop in Fig. 14.11 reveals that all threads will sequentially march through the k-space arrays. That is, all threads in the grid access the same k-space element during each iteration. For large data sets, the loop in the kernel simply iterates more times. This means that we can divide up the loop into sections, with each section processing a chunk of the k-space elements that fit into the 64 kB capacity of the constant memory.[3] The host code now invokes the kernel

---

[2] The reason why a constant memory access is not exactly as efficient as a register access is that a memory load instruction is still needed for access the constant memory.

[3] Note not all accesses to read-only data are as favorable for constant memory as what we have here. In Chapter 12, Parallel patterns: graph search, we present a case where threads in different blocks access different elements in the same iteration. This more diverged access pattern makes it much harder to fit enough of the data into the constant memory for a kernel launch.

```
       __constant__ float  kx_c[CHUNK_SIZE],
                           ky_c[CHUNK_SIZE],
                           kz_c[CHUNK_SIZE];
   ...
   void main() {

     for (int i = 0; i < M/CHUNK_SIZE; i++);
       cudaMemcpyToSymbol(kx_c,&kx[i*CHUNK_SIZE],4*CHUNK_SIZE,
                          cudaMemCpyHostToDevice);
       cudaMemcpyToSymbol(ky_c,&ky[i*CHUNK_SIZE],4*CHUNK_SIZE,
                          cudaMemCpyHostToDevice);
       cudaMemcpyToSymbol(ky_c,&ky[i*CHUNK_SIZE],4*CHUNK_SIZE,
                          cudaMemCpyHostToDevice);

       ...
       cmpFHD<<<FHD_THREADS_PER_BLOCK, N/FHD_THREADS_PER_BLOCK>>>
           (rPhi, iPhi, phiMag, x, y, z, rMu, iMu, CHUNK_SIZE);
     }
     /* Need to call kernel one more time if M is not */
     /* perfect multiple of CHUNK SIZE */
   }
```

FIGURE 14.12

Chunking k-space data to fit into constant memory.

multiple times. Each time the host invokes the kernel, it places a new chunk into the constant memory before calling the kernel function. This is illustrated in Fig. 14.12. (For more recent devices and CUDA versions, a "const__restrict__" declaration of kernel parameters makes the corresponding input data available in the "read-only data" cache, which is a simpler way of getting the same effect as using constant memory.)

In Fig. 14.12, the cmpFhD kernel is called from a loop. The code assumes that kx, ky, and kz arrays are in the host memory. The dimension of kx, ky, and kz is given by M. At each iteration, the host code calls the cudaMemcpyToSymbol() function to transfer a chunk of the k-space data into the device constant memory. The kernel is then invoked to process the chunk. Note that when M is not a perfect multiple of CHUNK_SIZE, the host code will need to have an additional round of cudaMemcpyTo-Symbol() and one more kernel invocation to finish the remaining k-space data.

Fig. 14.13 shows a revised kernel that accesses the k-space data from constant memory. Note that pointers to kx, ky, and kz are no longer in the parameter list of the kernel function. The kx_c, ky_c, and kz_c arrays are accessed as global variables declared under __constant__ keyword as shown in Fig. 14.12. By accessing these elements from the constant cache, the kernel now has effectively only four global memory accesses to the rMu and iMu arrays. The compiler will typically recognize that the four array accesses are made to only two locations. It will only perform two global accesses, one to rMu[m] and one to iMu[m]. The values will be stored in temporary register variables for use in the other two. This makes the final number of memory accesses reduced to two. The compute to memory access ratio is up to 13:2.

```
__global__ void cmpFHd(float* rPhi, iPhi, phiMag,
       x, y, z, rMu, iMu, int M) {

   int n = blockIdx.x * FHD_THREADS_PER_BLOCK + threadIdx.x;

   float xn_r = x[n]; float yn_r = y[n]; float zn_r = z[n];
   float rFhDn_r = rFhD[n]; float iFhDn_r = iFhD[n];

   for (int m = 0; m < M; m++) {
     float expFhD =
        2*PI*(kx_c[m]*xn_r+ky_c[m]*yn_r+kz_c[m]*zn_r);

     float cArg = cos(expFhD);
     float sArg = sin(expFhD);

     rFhDn_r +=   rMu[m]*cArg - iMu[m]*sArg;
     iFhDn_r +=   iMu[m]*cArg + rMu[m]*sArg;
   }
   rFhD[n] = rFhD_r; iFhD[n] = iFhD_r;
}
```

FIGURE 14.13

Revised F^{H}D kernel to use constant memory.

This is still not quite the desired 10:1 ratio but is sufficiently high that the memory bandwidth limitation is no longer the only factor that limits performance. As we will see, we can perform a few other optimizations that make computation more efficient and further improve performance.

If we ran the code in Figs. 14.12 and 14.13, we would have found out that the performance enhancement was not as high as we expected for some devices. As it turns out, the code shown in these figures does not result in as much memory bandwidth reduction as we expected. The reason is that the constant cache does not perform very well for the code. This has to do with the design of the constant cache and the memory layout of the k-space data. As shown in Fig. 14.14A, each constant cache entry is designed to store multiple consecutive words. This design reduces the cost of constant cache hardware. When an element is brought into the cache, several elements around it are also brought into the cache. This is illustrated in shaded sections surrounding the kx[i], ky[i], and kz[i], which is shown as dark boxes in Fig. 14.14. Three cache lines in the constant cache are needed to support the efficient execution of each iteration of a warp.

In a typical execution, we will have a fairly large number of warps that are concurrently executing on an SM. Since different warps can be at very different iterations, they may require many entries altogether. For example, if we define each thread block to have 512 threads and expect to assign three blocks to execute concurrently in each SM, we will have (512/32)*3 = 48 warps executing concurrently in an SM. If each of them requires a minimal of three cache lines in the constant cache to sustain efficient execution, in the worst case, we need a total of 48*3 = 144 cache

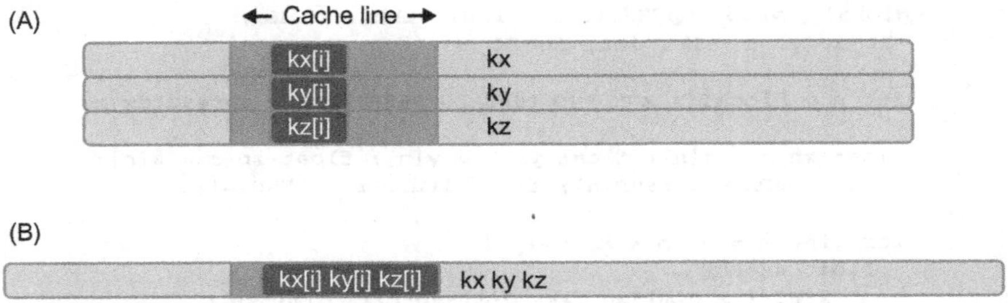

FIGURE 14.14

Effect of k-space data layout on constant cache efficiency. (A) k-space data stored in separate arrays, (B) k-space data stored in an array whose elements are structs.

lines. Even if we assume that on average, three warps will be executing at the same iteration and thus can share cache lines, we still need 48 cache lines. This is referred to as the working set of all the active warps.

Due to cost constraints, the constant caches of some devices have a small number of cache lines, say 32. When there are not enough cache lines to accommodate the entire working set, the data being accessed by different warps begin to compete with each other for the cache lines. By the time a warp moves to its next iteration, the next elements to be accessed have already been purged to make room for the elements accessed by other warps. As it turns out, the constant cache capacity in some devices indeed has insufficient number of entries to accommodate the entries for all the warps active in an SM. As a result, the constant cache fails to eliminate many of the global memory accesses.

The problem of inefficient use of cache entries has been well studied in the literature and can be solved by adjusting the memory layout of the k-space data. The solution is illustrated in Fig. 14.14B and the code based on this solution in Fig. 14.15. Rather than having the x, y, and z components of the k-space data stored in three separate arrays, the solution stores these components in an array whose elements comprise a `struct`. In the literature, this style of declaration is often referred to as *array of structs*. The declaration of the array is shown on top of Fig. 14.15. By storing the x, y, and z components in the three fields of an array element, the developer forces these components to be stored in consecutive locations of the constant memory. Therefore, all three components used by an iteration of a warp can now fit into one cache entry, reducing the number of entries needed to support the execution of all the active warps. Note that since we have only one array to hold all k-space data, we can just use one cudaMemcpy to copy the entire chunk to the device constant memory. Assuming each k-space sample is a single precision floating-point number, the size of the transfer is adjusted from `4*CHUNK_SIZE` to `12*CHUNK_SIZE` to reflect the transfer of all three components in one `cudaMemcpy-ToSymbol` call.

```
struct kdata {
    float x, float y, float z;
};

__constant__ struct kdata k_c[CHUNK_SIZE];
…

void main() {

  for (int i = 0; i < M/CHUNK_SIZE; i++){
    cudaMemcpyToSymbol(k_c,k,12*CHUNK_SIZE,cudaMemCpyHostToDevice);

    cmpFhD<<<FHD_THREADS_PER_BLOCK, N/FHD_THREADS_PER_BLOCK>>>(…);

  }
}
```

FIGURE 14.15

Adjusting k-space data layout to improve cache efficiency.

With the new data structure layout, we also need to revise the kernel so that the access is done according to the new layout. The new kernel is shown in Fig. 14.16. Note that kx[m] has become k[m].x, ky[m] has become k[m].y, and so on. This small change to the code can result in significant enhancement of its execution speed on some devices.[4]

STEP 3: USING HARDWARE TRIGONOMETRY FUNCTIONS

CUDA offers hardware implementations of mathematic functions that provide much higher throughput than their software counterparts. These functions are implemented as hardware instructions executed by the SFU (special function units). The procedure for using these functions is quite easy. In the case of the cmpFHD kernel, what we need to do is to change the calls to sin() and cos() functions into their hardware versions: __sin() and __cos() (two "_" characters in front of the function name). These are intrinsic functions that are recognized by the compiler and translated into SFU instructions. Because these functions are called in a heavily executed loop body, we expect that the change will result in a very significant performance improvement. The resulting cmpFhD kernel is shown in Fig. 14.17.

---

[4]The reader might notice that the adjustment from multiple arrays to an array of structure is opposite to what is often done to global memory data. When adjacent threads in a warp access consecutive elements of an array of structure, it is much better to store the fields of the structure into multiple arrays so that the memory accesses are coalesced. The key difference here is that all threads in a warp are accessing the same elements.

```
__global__ void cmpFhD(float* rPhi, iPhi, phiMag,
    x, y, z, rMu, iMu, int M) {

  int n = blockIdx.x * FHD_THREADS_PER_BLOCK + threadIdx.x;

  float xn_r = x[n]; float yn_r = y[n]; float zn_r = z[n];
  float rFhDn_r = rFhD[n]; float iFhDn_r = iFhD[n];

  for (int m = 0; m < M; m++) {
    float expFhD = 2*PI*(k[m].x*xn_r+k[m].y*yn_r+k[m].z*zn_r);

    float cArg = cos(expFhD);
    float sArg = sin(expFhD);

    rFhDn_r +=  rMu[m]*cArg - iMu[m]*sArg;
    iFhDn_r +=  iMu[m]*cArg + rMu[m]*sArg;
  }
  rFhD[n] = rFhD_r; iFhD[n] = iFhD_r;
}
```

FIGURE 14.16

Adjusting for the k-space data memory layout in the F^HD kernel.

```
__global__ void cmpFHd(float* rPhi, iPhi, phiMag,
    x, y, z, rMu, iMu, int M) {

  int n = blockIdx.x * FHD_THREADS_PER_BLOCK + threadIdx.x;

  float xn_r = x[n]; float yn_r = y[n]; float zn_r = z[n];
  float rFhDn_r = rFhD[n]; float iFhDn_r = iFhD[n];

  for (int m = 0; m < M; m++) {
    float expFhD = 2*PI*(k[m].x*xn_r+k[m].y*yn_r+k[m].z*zn_r);

    float cArg = __cos(expFhD);
    float sArg = __sin(expFhD);

    rFhDn_r +=  rMu[m]*cArg - iMu[m]*sArg;
    iFhDn_r +=  iMu[m]*cArg + rMu[m]*sArg;
  }
  rFhD[n] = rFhD_r; iFhD[n] = iFhD_r;
}
```

FIGURE 14.17

Using hardware __sin() and __cos() functions.

However, we need to be careful about the reduced accuracy when switching from software functions to hardware functions. As we discussed in Chapter 6, Numerical considerations, hardware implementation currently has less accuracy than software libraries (the details are available in the CUDA C Programming

$$MSE = \frac{1}{mn} \sum_i \sum_j (l(i,\,j) - l_0(i,\,j))^2$$

$$PSNR = 20 \log_{10} \left(\frac{\max(l_0(i,\,j))}{\sqrt{MSE}} \right)$$

FIGURE 14.18

Metrics used to validate the accuracy of hardware functions. I_0 is perfect image. I is reconstructed image. PSNR is peak signal-to-noise ratio.

Guide). In the case of MRI, we need to make sure that the hardware implementation passes provide enough accuracy, as defined in Fig. 14.18. The testing process involves a "perfect" image (I_0) of a fictitious object, sometimes referred to as a *phantom* object. We use a reverse process to generate a corresponding "scanned" k-space data that is synthesized. The synthesized scanned data is then processed by the proposed reconstruction system to generate a reconstructed image (I). The values of the voxels in the perfect and reconstructed images are then fed into the peak SNR (PSNR) formula in Fig. 14.18.

The criteria for passing the test depend on the application that the image is intended for. In our case, we worked with experts in clinical MRI to ensure that the PSNR changes due to hardware functions are well within the accepted limits for their applications. In applications where the images are used by physicians to form an impression of injury or evaluate a disease, one also needs to have visual inspection of the image quality. Fig. 14.19 shows the visual comparison of the original "true" image. It then shows that the PSNR achieved by CPU double precision and single precision implementation are both 27.6 dB, well above the acceptable level for the application. A visual inspection also shows that the reconstructed image indeed corresponds well with the original image.

The advantage of iterative reconstruction compared to a simple bilinear interpolation gridding/iFFT is also obvious in Fig. 14.19. The image reconstructed with the simple gridding/iFFT has a PSNR of only 16.8 dB, substantially lower than the PSNR of 27.6 dB achieved by the iterative reconstruction method. A visual inspection of the gridding/iFFT image in Fig. 14.19(2) shows that there are severe artifacts that can significantly impact the usability of the image for diagnostic purposes. These artifacts do not occur in the images from the iterative reconstruction method.

When we moved from double precision to single precision arithmetic on the CPU, there was no measurable degradation of PSNR, which remains at 27.6 dB. When we moved the trigonometry function from software library to the hardware units, we observed a negligible degradation of PSNR, from 27.6 dB to 27.5 dB. The slight loss of PSNR is within an acceptable range for the application. A visual inspection confirms that the reconstructed image does not have significant artifacts compared to the original image.

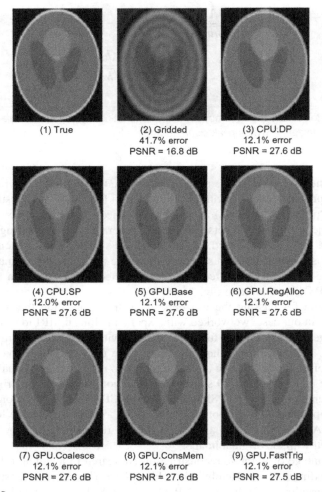

FIGURE 14.19

Validation of floating-point precision and accuracy of the different F^{H}D implementations.

STEP 4: EXPERIMENTAL PERFORMANCE TUNING

Up to this point, we have not determined the appropriate values for the configuration parameters for the kernel. For example, we need to determine the optimal number of threads for each block. On one hand, using a large number of threads in a block is needed to fully utilize the thread capacity of each SM (given that sixteen blocks can be assigned to each SM at maximum). On the other hand, having more threads in each block increases the register usage of each block and can reduce the number of blocks that can fit into an SM. Some possible values of number of threads per block are 32, 64, 128, 256, and 512. One could also consider nonpower-of-two numbers.

Another kernel configuration parameter is the number of times one should unroll the body of the for-loop. This can be set using a "#pragma unroll" followed by the number of unrolls we want the compiler to perform on a loop. On one hand, unrolling the loop can reduce the number of overhead instructions, and potentially reduce the number of clock cycles to process each k-space sample data. On the other hand, too much unrolling can potentially increase the usage of registers and reduce the number of blocks that can fit into an SM.

Note that the effects of these configurations are not isolated from each other. Increasing one parameter value can potentially use the resource that could be used to increase another parameter value. As a result, one needs to evaluate these parameters jointly in an experimental manner. That is, one may need to change the source code for each joint configuration and measure the run time. There can be a large number of source code versions to try. In the case of F^HD, the performance improves about 20% by systematically searching all the combinations and choosing the one with the best measured runtime, as compared to a heuristic tuning search effort that only explores some promising trends. Ryoo, et al. present a Pareto-Optimal-Curve-based method to screen away most of the inferior combinations using [RRS 2008].

14.4 FINAL EVALUATION

To evaluation the advantage of each alternative approach, we can use a sample data set obtained from a simulated, three-dimensional, non-Cartesian scan of a phantom image. There are 284,592 sample points in the scan data set, and the image is reconstructed for a total of 221 voxels. In the first set of experiments, the simulated data contains no noise. In the second set of experiments, we added complex white Gaussian noise to the simulated data. When determining the quality of the reconstructed images, the percent error and PSNR metrics are used. The percent error is the root-mean-square (RMS) of the voxel error divided by the RMS voxel value in the true image.

To facilitate comparison of the iterative reconstruction with a conventional reconstruction, we also evaluated a reconstruction based on bilinear interpolation gridding and iFFT. Our version of the gridded reconstruction is not optimized for speed, but it is already quite fast. For example, the total reconstruction time for the test image using bilinear interpolation gridding followed by iFFT takes less than 1 minute on a high-end sequential CPU. It is, however, obvious from Fig. 14.19(2) that the resulting image exhibits an unacceptable level of artifacts. It should be noted that the quality of the reconstruction can be improved with more sophisticated convolutional gridding methods at increased computation cost.

The actual execution time of the reconstruction steps will of course vary across devices. Therefore, we will discuss the results in approximate terms. For the preparation of the system for each patient, the sequential Q computation for our experimental input and output takes tens of hours on a high-end CPU. This time is reduced to a few minutes on the GPU with all the optimizations described in Section 14.3.

The total reconstruction of each image time using a sequential F^HD implementation on a high-end CPU requires a few hours. This time is reduced to about 3 minutes using the final version of the cmpFhD kernel on a high-end GPU. A naïve implementation of the cmpFhD would result in a reconstruction time of about 30 minutes on a high-end GPU. There is about $10 \times$ speed improvement going from the naïve version to the final version as discussed in Section 14.3.

An interesting observation is that in the end, the CG solver (the find ρ step in Fig. 14.3) can actually take more time than F^HD. This is because we have accelerated F^HD dramatically. Any further acceleration will now require acceleration of the CG solver. Before parallelization, F^HD used to account for nearly 100% of the execution time. After successful parallelization, it only accounts for about 50%. The other 50% is largely spent in the CG solver. This is a well-known phenomenon in parallelizing real applications. As some phases of the execution are accelerated by successful parallelization efforts, the execution time becomes dominated by other phases that used to account for insignificant portions of the execution.

14.5 EXERCISES

1. Loop fission splits a loop into two loops. Use the F^HD code in Fig. 14.4B and enumerate the execution order of the two parts of the outer loop body: (1) the statements before the inner loop and (2) the inner loop. (1) List the execution order of these parts from different iterations of the outer loop before fission. (2) List the execution order of these parts from the two loops after fission. Determine if the execution results will be identical. The execution results are identical if all data required by a part is properly generated and preserved for its consumption before that part executes, and the execution result of the part is not overwritten by other parts that should come after the part in the original execution order.

2. Loop interchange swaps the inner loop into the outer loop and vice versa. Use the loops from Fig. 14.9 and enumerate the execution order of the instances of loop body before and after the loop exchange. (1) List the execution order of the loop body from different iterations before loop interchange. Identify these iterations with the values of m and n. (2) List the execution order of the loop body from different iterations after loop interchange. Identify these iterations with the values of m and n. Determine if the (1) and (2) execution results will be identical. The execution results are identical if all data required by a part is properly generated and preserved for its consumption before that part executes, and the execution result of the part is not overwritten by other parts that should come after the part in the original execution order.

3. In Fig. 14.11, identify the difference between the access to x[] and kx[] in the nature of indices used. Use the difference to explain why it does not make sense to try to load kx[n] into a register for the kernel shown in Fig. 14.11.

4. During a meeting, a new graduate student told his advisor that he improved his kernel performance by using cudaMalloc() to allocate constant memory and using cudaMemcpy() to transfer read-only data from the CPU memory to the constant memory. If you were his advisor, what would be your response?

REFERENCES

Liang, Z. P., & Lauterbur, P. (1999). *Principles of magnetic resonance imaging: A signal processing perspective*. New York: John Wiley & Sons, Inc.

Ryoo, S., Ridrigues, C. I., Stone, S. S., Stratton, J. A., Ueng, Z., Baghsorkhi, S. S., et al. (2008). Program optimization carving for GPU computing. *Journal of Parallel and Distributed Computing* http://dx.doi.org/10.1016/j.jpdc.2008.05.011.

Stone, S. S., Haldar, J. P., Tsao, S. C., Hwu, W. W., Sutton, B. P., & Liang, Z. P. (2008). Accelerating advanced MRI reconstruction on GPUs. *Journal of Parallel and Distributed Computing* http://dx.doi.org/10.1016/j.jpdc.2008.05.013.

Application case study— molecular visualization and analysis

15

John Stone

CHAPTER OUTLINE

The previous case study used a statistical estimation application to illustrate the process of selecting an appropriate level of a loop nest for parallel execution, transforming the loops for reduced memory access interference, using constant memory for magnifying the memory bandwidth for read-only data, using registers to reduce the consumption of memory bandwidth, and the use of special hardware functional units to accelerate trigonometry functions. In this case study, we use a molecular dynamics application based on regular grid data structures to illustrate the use of additional practical techniques that achieve global memory access coalescing and improved computation throughput. As we did in the previous case study, we present a series of implementations of an electrostatic potential map calculation kernel, with each version improving upon the previous one. Each version adopts one or more practical techniques. Some of the techniques are in common with the previous case study but some are new: systematic reuse of computational results, thread granularity coarsening, and fast boundary condition checking. This application case study shows that the effective use of these practical techniques can significantly improve the execution throughput of the application.

Programming Massively Parallel Processors. DOI: http://dx.doi.org/10.1016/B978-0-12-811986-0.00015-7

15.1 BACKGROUND

This case study is based on VMD (Visual Molecular Dynamics) [HDS 1996], a popular software system designed for displaying, animating, and analyzing bio-molecular systems. VMD has more than 200,000 registered users. It is an important foundation for the modern "computational microscope" for biologists to observe the atomic details and dynamics of tiny life forms such as viruses that are too small for traditional microscopy techniques. While it has strong built-in support for analyzing bio-molecular systems such as calculating maps of the electrostatic field that surround a molecular system, it has also been a popular tool for displaying other large data sets such as sequencing data, quantum chemistry calculations, and volumetric data due to its versatility and user extensibility.

While VMD is designed to run on a diverse range of hardware—laptops, desktops, clusters, and supercomputers—most users use VMD as a desktop science application for interactive 3D visualization and analysis. For computation that runs too long for interactive use, VMD can also be used in a batch mode to render movies for later use. A motivation for accelerating VMD is to make batch mode jobs fast enough for interactive use. This can drastically improve the productivity of scientific investigations. With CUDA devices widely available in PCs, such acceleration can have broad impact on the VMD user community. To date, multiple aspects of VMD have been accelerated with CUDA, including electrostatic potential map calculation, ion placement (HSS 2009), calculation and display of molecular orbitals (SSHVHS 2009), molecular surfaces (KSES 2012), radial distribution histograms (LSK 2011), and electron density map quality-of-fit (SMIS 2014), and high fidelity ray tracing of large biomolecular complexes for conventional and panoramic displays (SVS 2013, Stone et al. 2016), and virtual reality headsets (SSS 2016).

The particular calculation used in this case study is the calculation of electrostatic potential maps in 3D grids with uniform spacing. This calculation is often used in placement of ions into a molecular structure for molecular dynamics simulation. Fig. 15.1 shows the placement of ions into a protein structure in preparation for molecular dynamics simulation. In this application, the electrostatic potential map is used to identify spatial locations where ions (red dots) can fit in according to physical laws. The function can also be used to calculate time-averaged potentials during molecular dynamics simulation, which is useful for the simulation process as well as the visualization/analysis of simulation results.

There are several methods for calculating electrostatic potential maps. Among them, Direct Coulomb Summation (DCS) is a highly accurate method that is particularly suitable for GPUs [SPF 2007]. The DCS method calculates the electrostatic potential value of each grid point as the sum of contributions from all atoms in the system. This is illustrated in Fig. 15.2. The contribution of atom i to a lattice point j is the charge of atom i divided by the distance from lattice point j to atom i. Since this needs to be done for all grid points and all atoms, the number of calculations is proportional to the product of the total number of atoms in the system and the total number of grid points. For a realistic molecular system, this product can be very large. Therefore, the calculation of the electrostatic potential map had been traditionally done as a batch job in VMD.

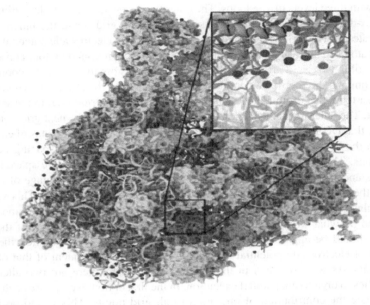

FIGURE 15.1

Electrostatic potential map is used in building stable structures for molecular dynamics simulation.

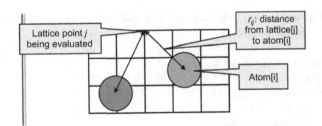

FIGURE 15.2

The contribution of atom[i] to the electrostatic potential at lattice point j (potential[j]) is atom[i] charge/r_{ij}. In the Direct Coulomb Summation method, the total potential at lattice point j is the sum of contributions from all atoms in the system.

15.2 A SIMPLE KERNEL IMPLEMENTATION

Fig. 15.3 shows the base C code of the DCS code. The function is written to process a two-dimensional (2D) slice of a three-dimensional (3D) grid. The function will be called repeatedly for all the slices of the modeled space. The structure of the function is quite simple with three levels of `for` loops. The outer two levels iterate over the y-dimension and the x-dimension of the grid point space. For each grid point, the innermost for loop iterates over all atoms, calculating the contribution of electrostatic potential energy from all atoms to the grid point. Note that each atom is represented by four consecutive elements of the `atoms[]` array. The first three elements store the x, y, and z coordinates of the atom and the fourth element the electrical charge of the atom. At the end of the innermost loop, the accumulated value of the grid point is written out to the grid data structure. The outer loops then iterate and take the execution to the next grid point.

Note that DCS function in Fig. 15.3 calculates the x and y coordinates of each grid point on the fly by multiplying the grid point index values by the spacing between grid points. This is a uniform grid method where all grid points are spaced at the same distance in all three dimensions. The function does take advantage of the fact that all the grid points in the same slice have the same z coordinate. This value is precalculated by the caller of the function and passed in as a function parameter (z).

Based on what we learned from the MRI case study, two attributes of the DCS method should be apparent. First, the computation is massively parallel: the computation of electrostatic potential for each grid point is independent of that of other grid points. As we have seen in the previous case study, there are two alternative approaches to organizing parallel execution. In the first option, we can use each thread to calculate the contribution of one atom to all grid points. This would be a poor choice since each thread would be writing to all grid points, requiring extensive use of atomic memory operations to coordinate the updates done by different threads to each

```
void cenergy(float *energygrid, dim3 grid, float gridspacing, float z, const float *atoms,
             int numatoms) {
  int i,j,n;
  int atomarrdim = numatoms * 4;
  for (j=0; j<grid.y; j++) {
    float y = gridspacing * (float) j;
    for (i=0; i<grid.x; i++) {
      float x = gridspacing * (float) i;
      float energy = 0.0f;
      for (n=0; n<atomarrdim; n+=4) {     // calculate potential contribution of each atom
        float dx = x - atoms[n   ];
        float dy = y - atoms[n+1];
        float dz = z - atoms[n+2];
        energy += atoms[n+3] / sqrtf(dx*dx + dy*dy + dz*dz);
      }
      energygrid[grid.x*grid.y*k + grid.x*j + i] = energy;
    }
  }
}
```

FIGURE 15.3

Base Coulomb potential calculation code for a 2D slice.

grid point. The second option uses each thread to calculate the accumulated contributions of all atoms to one grid point. This is a preferred approach since each thread will be writing into its own grid point and there is no need to use atomic operations.

We will form a 2D thread grid that matches the 2D potential grid point organization. In order to do so, we need to modify the two outer loops into perfectly nested loops so that we can use each thread to execute one iteration of the two-level loop. We can either perform a loop fission (as we did in the previous case study), or we move the calculation of the y coordinate into the inner loop. The former would require us to create a new array to hold all y values and result in two kernels communicating data through global memory. The latter increases the number of times that the y coordinate will be calculated. In this case, we choose to perform the latter since there is only a small amount of calculation that can be easily accommodated into the inner loop without significant increase in execution time of the inner loop. The amount of work to be absorbed into the inner loop is much smaller than that in the previous case study. The former would have added a kernel launch overhead for a kernel where threads do very little work. The selected transformation allows all i and j iterations to be executed in parallel. This is a tradeoff between the amount of calculation done and the level of parallelism achieved.

The second experience that we can apply from the MRI case study is that the electrical charge of every atom will be read by all threads. This is because every atom contributes to every grid point in the DCS method. Furthermore, the values of the atomic electrical charges are not modified during the computation. This means that the atomic charge values can be efficiently stored in the constant memory (in the GPU box in Fig. 15.4).

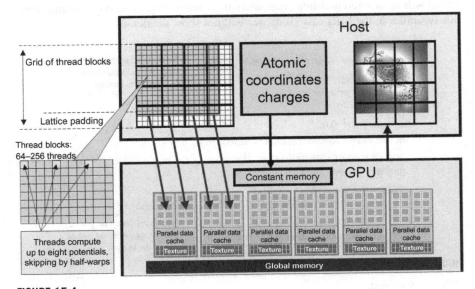

FIGURE 15.4

Overview of the DCS kernel design.

Fig. 15.4 shows an overview of the DCS kernel design. The host program (shown as the Host box) inputs and maintains the atomic charges and their coordinates in the system memory. It also maintains the grid point data structure in the system memory. The DCS kernel is designed to process a 2D slice of the electrostatic potential grid point structure (not to be confused with thread grids). The right-hand side grid in the Host box shows an example of a 2D slice. For each 2D slice, the CPU transfers its grid data to the device global memory. Similar to the *k*-space data, the atom information is divided into chunks to fit into the constant memory. For each chunk of the atom information, the CPU transfers the chunk into the device constant memory, invokes the DCS kernel to calculate the contribution of the current chunk to the current slice, and prepares to transfer the next chunk. After all chunks of the atom information have been processed for the current slice, the slice is transferred back to update the grid point data structure in the CPU system memory. The system moves on to the next slice.

Within each kernel invocation, the thread blocks are organized to calculate the electrostatic potential of tiles of the grid structure. In the simplest kernel, each thread calculates the value at one grid point. In more sophisticated kernels, each thread calculates multiple grid points and exploits the redundancy between the calculations of the grid points to improve execution speed. This is illustrated in the left-hand side portion labeled as "Thread blocks" in Fig. 15.4 and is an example of the granularity adjustment optimization discussed in Chapter 5, Performance Considerations.

Fig. 15.5 shows the resulting CUDA kernel code. We omitted some of the declarations. As was in the MRI case study, the `atominfo[]` array is declared in the constant memory by the host code. The host code divides up the atom information into chunks that fit into the constant memory for each kernel invocation. This means that kernel will be invoked multiple times when there are multiple chunks of atoms. Since this is similar to the MRI case study, we will not show the details.

```
...
float curenergy = energygrid[outaddr];        Start global memory reads
float coorx = gridspacing * xindex;           early. Kernel hides some of
float coory = gridspacing * yindex;           its own latency.
int atomid;
float energyval=0.0f;
 for (atomid=0; atomid<numatoms; atomid++) {
  float dx = coorx - atominfo[atomid].x;
  float dy = coory - atominfo[atomid].y;
  energyval += atominfo[atomid].w *
               rsqrtf(dx*dx + dy*dy + atominfo[atomid].z);
 }                                             Only dependency on global
energygrid[outaddr] = curenergy + energyval;  memory read is at the end of
                                              the kernel...
```

FIGURE 15.5

DCS kernel version 1.

The outer two levels of the loop in Fig. 15.3 have been removed from the kernel code and are replaced by the execution configuration parameters in the kernel invocation. Since this is also similar to one of the steps we took in the MRI case study, we will not show the kernel invocation but leave it as an exercise for the reader. The rest of the kernel code is straightforward and corresponds directly to the original loop body of the innermost loop.

One particular aspect of the kernel is somewhat subtle and worth mentioning. The kernel code calculates the contribution of a chunk of atoms to a grid point. The grid point must be stored in the global memory and updated by each kernel invocation. This means that the kernel needs to read the current grid point value, add the contributions by the current chunk of atoms, and write the updated value to global memory. The code attempts to hide the global memory latency by loading the grid value at the beginning of the kernel and using it at the end of the kernel. This helps to reduce the number of warps needed by the SM scheduler to hide the global memory latency.

The performance of the kernel in Fig. 15.5 is quite good. However, there is definitely room for improvement. A quick glance over the code shows that each thread does nine floating-point operations for every four memory elements accessed. On the surface, this is not a very good ratio. We need a ratio of 10 or more to avoid global memory congestion. However, all four memory accesses are done to `atominfo[]` array. These `atominfo[]` array elements for each atom are cached in a hardware cache memory in each SM and are broadcast to a large number of threads. A calculation similar to that in the MRI case study shows that the massive reuse of memory elements across threads makes the constant cache extremely effective, boosting the effective ratio of floating operations per global memory access much higher than 10. As a result, global memory bandwidth is not a limiting factor for this kernel.

15.3 THREAD GRANULARITY ADJUSTMENT

Although the kernel in Fig. 15.5 avoids global memory bottlenecks through constant caching, it still needs to execute four constant memory access instructions for every nine floating-point operations performed. These memory access instructions consume hardware resources that could be otherwise used to increase the execution throughput of floating-point instructions. More importantly, the execution of these memory access instructions consumes energy, an important limiting factor for many large scale parallel computing systems. This section shows that we can fuse several threads together so that the `atominfo[]` data can be fetched once from the constant memory, stored into registers, and used for multiple grid points.

We observe that all grid points along the same row have the same y-coordinate. Therefore, the difference between the y-coordinate of an atom and the y-coordinate of any grid point along a row has the same value. In the DCS kernel version 1 in Fig. 15.5, this calculation is redundantly done by all threads for all grid points in a row when calculating the distance between the atom and the grid points. We can eliminate this redundancy and improve the execution efficiency.

The idea is to have each thread calculate the electrostatic potential for multiple grid points. The kernel in Fig. 15.7 has each thread calculate four grid points. For each atom, the code calculates `dy`, the difference of the y-coordinates, in line 2. It then calculates the expression `dy*dy` plus the pre-calculated `dz*dz` information and saves it to the auto variable `dysqpdzsq`, which is assigned to a register. This value is the same for all four grid points. Therefore, the calculation of `energyvalx1` through `energyvalx4` can all just use the value stored in the register. Furthermore, the electrical charge information is also accessed from constant memory and stored in the automatic variable `charge`. Similarly, the x-coordinate of the atom is also read from constant memory into auto variable `x`. Altogether, this kernel eliminates three accesses to constant memory for `atominfo[atomid].y`, three accesses to constant memory for `atominfo[atomid].x`, three accesses to constant memory for `atominfo[atomid].w`, three floating-point subtraction operations, five floating-point multiply operations, and nine floating-point add operations when processing an atom for four grid points. A quick inspection of the kernel code in Fig. 15.7 shows that each iteration of the loop performs four constant memory accesses, five floating-point subtractions, nine floating-point additions, and five floating-point multiplications for four grid points.

The reader should also verify that the version of DCS kernel in Fig. 15.5 performs 16 constant memory accesses, 8 floating-point subtractions, 12 floating-point additions, and 12 floating-point multiplications, a total of 48 operations for the same four grid points. Going from Figs. 15.5 to 15.7, there is a total reduction from 48 operations down to 25 operations, a sizable reduction. This is translated into about 40% increased execution speed and about the same percentage reduction in energy consumption.

The cost of the optimization is that more registers are used by each thread. This can potentially reduce the number of threads that can be accommodated by each SM. However, as the results show, this is a good tradeoff with an excellent performance improvement.

15.4 MEMORY COALESCING

While the performance of the DCS kernel version 2 in Fig. 15.7 is quite high, a quick profiling run reveals that the threads perform memory writes inefficiently. As shown in Figs. 15.6 and 15.7, each thread calculates four neighboring grid points. This seems to be a reasonable choice. However, as we illustrate in Fig. 15.8, the write pattern of adjacent threads in each warp will result in un-coalesced global memory writes.

There are two problems that cause the un-coalesced writes in DCS kernel version 2. First, each thread calculates four adjacent neighboring grid points. Thus, for each statement that accesses the `energygrid[]` array, the threads in a warp are not accessing adjacent locations. Note that two adjacent threads access memory locations that are three elements apart. Thus, the 16 locations to be written by all the threads in warp write are spread out, with three elements in between the loaded/written locations.

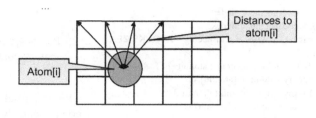

FIGURE 15.6

Reusing computation results among multiple grid points.

```
...for (atomid=0; atomid<numatoms; atomid++) {
    float dy = coory - atominfo[atomid].y;
    float dysqpdzsq = (dy * dy) + atominfo[atomid].z;
    float x = atominfo[atomid].x;
    float dx1 = coorx1 - x;
    float dx2 = coorx2 - x;
    float dx3 = coorx3 - x;
    float dx4 = coorx4 - x;
    float charge = atominfo[atomid].w;
    energyvalx1 += charge * rsqrtf(dx1*dx1 + dysqpdzsq);
    energyvalx2 += charge * rsqrtf(dx2*dx2 + dysqpdzsq);
    energyvalx3 += charge * rsqrtf(dx3*dx3 + dysqpdzsq);
    energyvalx4 += charge * rsqrtf(dx4*dx4 + dysqpdzsq);
}
```

> Compared to non-unrolled kernel: memory loads are decreased by 4x, and FLOPS per evaluation are reduced, but register use is increased...

FIGURE 15.7

Version 2 of the DCS kernel.

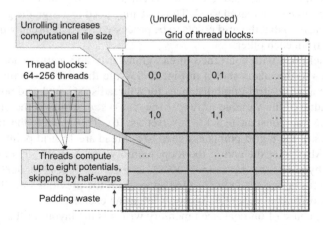

FIGURE 15.8

Organizing threads and memory layout for coalesced writes.

```
...float coory = gridspacing * yindex;
  float coorx = gridspacing * xindex;
  float gridspacing_coalesce = gridspacing * BLOCKSIZEX;
  int atomid;
  for (atomid=0; atomid<numatoms; atomid++) {
    float dy = coory - atominfo[atomid].y;
    float dyz2 = (dy * dy) + atominfo[atomid].z;
    float dx1 = coorx - atominfo[atomid].x;
[...]
    float dx8 = dx7 + gridspacing_coalesce;
    energyvalx1 += atominfo[atomid].w * rsqrtf(dx1*dx1 + dyz2);
[...]
    energyvalx8 += atominfo[atomid].w * rsqrtf(dx8*dx8 + dyz2);
  }
  energygrid[outaddr                 ] += energyvalx1;
[...]
  energygrid[outaddr+7*BLOCKSIZEX] += energyvalx7;
```

Points spaced for memory coalescing

Reuse partial distance components $dy^2 + dz^2$

Global memory ops occur only at the end of the kernel, decreases register use

FIGURE 15.9

DCS kernel version 3.

This problem can be solved by assigning adjacent grid points to adjacent threads in each half-warp. Most previous generation devices form coalesced memory accesses on a half-warp basis. Assuming that we still want to have each thread calculate four grid points, we first assign 16 consecutive grid points to the 16 threads in a half-warp. We then assign the next 16 consecutive grid points to the same 16 threads. We repeat the assignment until each thread has the number of grid points desired. This assignment is illustrated in Fig. 15.8. For more recent devices, the number of threads in a coalesced access has increased to 32. Thus, we may need to assign the grid points on a full-warp basis so that the grid points to be processed by each thread will be 32 grid points apart from each other.

The kernel code with coarsened thread granularity and warp-aware assignment of grid points to threads is shown in Fig. 15.9. Note that the x-coordinates used to calculate the atom-to-grid-point distances for a thread's assigned grid points are offset by the value of the variable gridspacing_coalesce, which is the original gridspacing times the constant BLOCKSIZEX (set as 16). This reflects the fact that the x-coordinates of the 8 grid points assigned to a thread are 16 grid points away from each other. Also, after the end of the loop, memory writes to the energygrid array are indexed by outaddr, outaddr+BLOCKSIZEX, …, outaddr+7*BLOCKSIZEX. Each of these indices is one BLOCKSIZEX (16) away from the previous one. The detailed thread block organization for this kernel is left as an exercise.

The other cause of un-coalesced memory writes is the layout of the energygrid array, which is a 3D array. If the x-dimension of the array is not a multiple of the half-warp size (16), the beginning location of the row 1, as well as those of the subsequent rows will no longer be at the 16-word boundaries. For example, if the `energygrid` array starts at location 0 and the x-dimension has 1000 elements, row 1 of the array will start at location 1000, which is not a 16-word boundary. The nearest 16-word boundaries are 992 and 1008. Therefore, starting at row 1, the accesses to the `energygrid` by threads in a half-warp will span two 16-word units in the global memory address space.

In some devices, this means that the half-warp accesses will not be coalesced, even though they write to consecutive locations. This problem can be corrected by padding each row with additional elements so that the total length of the x-dimension is a multiple of 16. This can require adding up to 15 elements, or 60 bytes to each row, as shown in Fig. 15.8. In our example, since the x-dimension has 1000 elements, we need to pad 8 elements at the end of each row so that the number of words in each row is a multiple of 16 (1008).

If we want to avoid `if`-statements for handling boundary conditions, we will need to make the x-dimension a multiple of the number of grid points processed by each thread block. Each block has 16 threads in the x-dimension. With the kernel of Fig. 15.9, the number of elements in the x-dimension needs to be a multiple of $8 \times 16 = 128$. This is because each thread actually writes eight elements in each iteration. Thus, one may need to pad up to 127 elements, or 1016 bytes to each row. In our example, the nearest multiple of 128 that we can pad from 1000 is 1024. Therefore, we will need to pad 24 elements at the end of each row to avoid adding if-statements for handling the boundary condition.

Finally, there is a potential problem with the last row of thread blocks. Each thread block is 16×16 so there are 16 threads in the y dimension. Since the number of rows grid array may not be a multiple of 16, some of the threads may end up writing outside the grid data structure without adding if-statements to handle the boundary conditions. Since the grid data structure is a 3D array, these threads will write into the next slice of grid points. As we discussed in Chapter 3, Scalable parallel execution, we can add a test in the kernel and avoid writing the array elements that are out of the known y-dimension size. However, this would have added a number of overhead instructions and incurred control divergence. An alternative solution is to pad the y-dimension of the grid structure so that it contains a multiple of tiles covered by thread blocks. This is shown in Fig. 15.8 as the bottom padding in the grid structure. In general, one may need to add up to 15 rows due to this padding.

The cost of padding can be substantial for smaller grid structures. For example, if the potential energy grid has 100×100 grid points in each 2D slice, it would be padded into a 128×112 slice. The total number of grid points increases from 10,000 to 14,336, or a 43% overhead. At such overhead, one should consider much less coarsening. On the other hand, for a 1000×1000 grid, one will need to pad it to 1024 $\times 1008 = 1,032,192$ T, or 3.2% overhead. This makes it very cost-effective to assign eight grid points to each thread. This is the reason why high-performance libraries often have multiple kernels for the same type of computation. When the user calls the library function, the interface would choose the version according to the size and shape of the actual data set.

If we had to pad the entire 3D structure, the grid points would have increased from $100 \times 100 \times 100$ (1,000,000) to $128 \times 112 \times 112$ (1,605,632), or a 60% overhead! This is part of the reason why we calculate the energy grids in 2D slices and use the host code to iterate over these 2D slices. Writing a single kernel to process the entire 3D structure would have incurred a lot more extra overhead. This type of tradeoff appears frequently in simulation models, differential equation solvers, and video processing applications. Decomposing the problem into individual 2D slices also allows multiple GPUs to be used concurrently, with each GPU computing independent slices.

The DCS version 3 kernel shown in Fig. 15.9 achieves about 535.16 GFLOPS or 72.56 billion atom evaluations per second on a Fermi GPU. On a recent GeForce GTX 680 (Kepler 1), it achieves a whopping 1267.26 GFLOPS or 171.83 billion atom evaluations per second! This measured speed of the kernel also includes a slight boost from moving the read access to the energygrid array from the beginning of the kernel to the end of the kernel. The contribution to the grid points are first calculated in the loop. The code loads the original grid point data after the loop, adds the contribution to them, and writes the updated values back. Although this movement exposes more of the global memory latency to each thread, it saves the consumption of eight registers. Since the version 3 kernel is using many registers to hold the atom data and the distances, such savings in number of registers used relieve a critical bottleneck for the kernel. This allows more thread blocks to be assigned to each SM and achieved an overall performance improvement.

15.5 SUMMARY

The relative merit of the three versions of the DCS kernel depends on the dimension lengths of the potential energy grid. However, the DCS version 3 (CUDA-Unroll8clx) will perform consistently better than all others once the grid dimension length is sufficiently large, say 300×300 or more.

A detailed comparison of between the sequential code performance on a CPU and the CPU–GPU joint performance shows a commonly observed tradeoff. Fig. 15.10 shows plot of the execution time of a medium-sized grid for varying number of atoms to be evaluated. For 400 atoms or fewer, the CPU performs better. This is because the particular GPU used has a fixed initialization overhead of 110 ms regardless of the number of atoms to be evaluated. Also, for a small number of atoms, the GPU is underutilized, thus the curve of the GPU execution time is quite flat between 100 atoms and 1000 atoms.

The plot in Fig. 15.10 reinforces a commonly held principle that GPUs perform better for large amounts of data. Once the number of atoms reaches 10,000, the GPU is fully utilized. The slope of the CPU and the CPU–GPU execution time becomes virtually identical, with the CPU–GPU execution being consistently 44 × times faster than the sequential CPU execution for all input sizes.

While DCS is a highly accurate method for calculating the electrostatic potential energy map of a molecular system, it is not a scalable method. The number of operations to be performed of the method grows proportionally with the number of

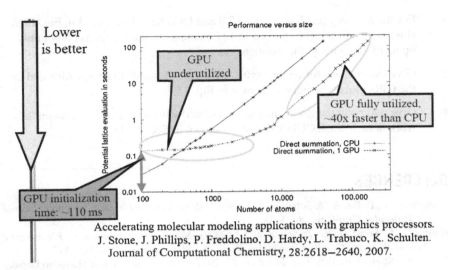

Accelerating molecular modeling applications with graphics processors.
J. Stone, J. Phillips, P. Freddolino, D. Hardy, L. Trabuco, K. Schulten.
Journal of Computational Chemistry, 28:2618–2640, 2007.

FIGURE 15.10

Single-threads CPU versus CPU–GPU comparison.

atoms and the number of grid points. When we increase the physical volume of the molecular system to be simulated, we should expect that both the number of grid points and the number of atoms to increase proportional to the physical size. As a result, the number of operations to be performed will be approximately proportional to the square of the physical volume. That is, the number of operations to be performed will grow quadratically with the volume of the system being simulated. This makes the use of DCS method not suitable for simulating realistic biological systems. Therefore, one must devise a method whose number of operations grows linearly with the volume of the biological systems being simulated. We will revisit this topic in Chapter 17, Parallel programming and computational thinking.

15.6 EXERCISES

1. Complete the implementation of the DCS kernel as outlined in Fig. 15.5. Fill in all of the missing declarations. Give the kernel launch statement with all the execution configuration parameters.

2. Compare the number of operations (memory loads, floating-point arithmetic, branches) executed in each iteration of the kernel in Fig. 15.7 compared to that in Fig. 15.5. Keep in mind that each iteration of the former corresponds to four iterations of the latter.

3. Complete the implementation of the DCS kernel version 3 in Fig. 15.9. Explain in your own words how the thread accesses are coalesced in this implementation.

4. For the memory padding in Fig. 15.8 and DCS kernel version 3 in Fig. 15.9, show why one needs to pad up to 127 elements in the x dimension but only up to 15 elements in the y dimension.

5. Give two reasons for adding extra "padding" elements to arrays allocated in the GPU global memory, as shown in Fig. 15.8.

6. Give two potential disadvantages associated with increasing the amount of work done in each CUDA thread, as shown in Section 15.3.

REFERENCES

Humphrey, W., Dalke, A., & Schulten, K. (1996). VMD—Visual molecular dyanmics. *Journal of Molecular Graphics, 14*, 33–38.

Hardy, D. J., Stone, J. E., & Schulten, K. (2009). Multilevel Summation of Electrostatic Potentials Using Graphics Processing Units. *Parallel Computing, 28*, 164–177.

Krone, M., Stone, J. E., Ertl, T., & Schulten, K. (2012). Fast Visualization of Gaussian Density Surfaces for Molecular Dynamics and Particle System Trajectories. EuroVis-Short Papers, pp. 67–71.

Levine, B. G., Stone, J. E., & Kohlmeyer, A. (2011). Fast Analysis of Molecular Dynamics Trajectories with Graphics Processing Units—Radial Distribution Function Histogramming. *Journal of Computational Physics, 230*(9), 3556–3569.

Stone, J. E., McGreevy, R., Isralewitz, B., & Schulten, K. (2014). GPU-Accelerated Analysis and Visualization of Large Structures Solved by Molecular Dynamics Flexible Fitting. *Faraday Discussions, 169*, 265–283.

Stone, J. E., Phillips, J. C., Freddolino, P. L., Hardy, D. J., Trabuco, L. G., & Schulten, K. (2007). Accelerating molecular modeling applications with graphics processors. *Journal of Computational Chemistry, 28*, 2618–2640.

Stone, J.E., Saam, J., Hardy, D.J., Vandivort, K.L., Hwu, W., & Schulten, K. (2009). High Performance Computation and Interactive Display of Molecular Orbitals on GPUs and Multi-core CPUs. In Proceedings of the 2nd Workshop on General-Purpose Processing on Graphics Processing Units, ACM International Conference Proceeding Series, *383*, 9–18.

Stone, J. E., Sener, M., Vandivort, K. L., Barragan, A., Singharoy, A., Teo, I., ... Schulten, K. (2016). Atomic Detail Visualization of Photosynthetic Membranes with GPU-Accelerated Ray Tracing. *Journal of Parallel Computing, 55*, 17–27.

Stone, J. E., Sherman, R., & Schulten, K. (2016). Immersive Molecular Visualization with Omnidirectional Stereoscopic Ray Tracing and Remote Rendering. High Performance Data Analysis and Visualization Workshop, 2016 IEEE International Parallel and Distributed Processing Symposium Workshops (IPDPSW), pp. 1048–1057.

Stone, J. E., Vandivort, K. L., & Schulten, K. (2013). GPU-Accelerated Molecular Visualization on Petascale Supercomputing Platforms. UltraVis'13: Proceedings of the 8th International Workshop on Ultrascale Visualization, pp. 6:1–6:8.

Application case study— machine learning

16

Boris Ginsburg

CHAPTER OUTLINE

In this chapter, we will describe a case study of accelerating machine learning algorithms with GPUs. Machine learning has been used in numerous applications to train or adapt the application logic in accordance with the experience gleaned from data sets. To be effective, one often needs to conduct such training with a massive amount of data. While machine learning has existed as a subject in computer science for a considerable time, it has recently gained significant practical industry acceptance because of the availability of inexpensive, massively parallel GPU computing systems that can effectively train application logic with massive data sets. We will start with a brief introduction to deep learning and then consider one of the most widely used algorithms, convolutional neural networks (ConvNets), in more detail. ConvNets are characterized by high compute-to-bandwidth ratio and high levels of parallelism, which are perfect attributes for GPU acceleration. We will first implement a ConvNet with a basic algorithm. We will then show how we can improve this basic implementation with shared memory. Finally, we will demonstrate how one can formulate the convolutional layers as matrix–matrix multiplication problems.

Programming Massively Parallel Processors. DOI: http://dx.doi.org/10.1016/B978-0-12-811986-0.00016-9

16.1 BACKGROUND

Machine learning is a field of computer science that explores algorithms whose logic can be learned directly from data rather than be explicitly programmed. Machine learning is most successful in computing tasks where designing explicit algorithms is infeasible, mostly because knowledge in the design of such explicit algorithms is inadequate. Machine learning is the foundation of automatic speech recognition, computer vision, natural language processing, and search engines.

Conventional machine learning systems require humans with considerable domain expertise to define meaningful features for transforming raw data (e.g., the pixels of an image or speech signal) into a curated representation. From this representation, machine learning algorithms could detect important patterns that can be used for training the application logic. By contrast, deep learning is a set of methods that allows a machine learning system to automatically discover the complex features needed for detection directly from raw data [LBH 2015]. This area of machine learning is described as "deep" because it is based on the idea of hierarchical, multilevel feature representation. The hierarchical features are obtained by composing simple nonlinear modules that each transforms a representation at one level (starting with the raw input) into another at a higher, slightly more abstract level. For example, in computer vision, the first layer of representation typically detects edges at particular orientations and locations in the image. The second layer typically detects the so-called "motifs" by spotting particular patterns of edges, regardless of small variations in the edge positions. The third layer assembles these motifs into larger parts. Such layered structures, as illustrated in Fig. 16.1, are often referred to as "feed forward networks" because the information flows in one direction from one layer to the next in these systems.

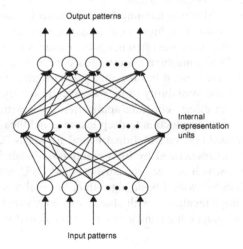

FIGURE 16.1

A multilayer feedforward network.

Deep learning procedures based on feedforward networks can learn highly complex features that can achieve more accurate pattern recognition results compared with features that are manually engineered by humans; however, this method requires that sufficient information is accessible in order to allow the system to automatically discover an adequate number of relevant patterns. One type of a deep learning procedure is based on a particular type of feedforward network called the ConvNet. These procedures are easier to train and can be generalized much better than others.

The ConvNet was invented in late 1980s [LBB 1998]. By the early 1990s, ConvNet had been successfully applied to automated speech recognition, optical character recognition, handwriting recognition, and face recognition. However, the mainstream of computer vision and that of automated speech recognition had been based on carefully engineered features until the late 1990s. The amount of labeled data was insufficient for a deep learning system to compete with recognition/classification functions crafted by human experts. The common notion was that it was computationally infeasible to automatically build hierarchical feature extractors that have enough layers to perform better than human-defined application-specific feature extractors.

Interest in deep feedforward networks was revived around 2006 by a group of researchers who introduced unsupervised learning methods that could create multilayer, hierarchical feature detectors without requiring labeled data [HOT 2006]. The first major application of this approach was in speech recognition. The breakthrough was made possible by GPUs that allowed researchers to train networks 10 times faster than traditional CPUs [RMN 2009]. This advancement, coupled with a massive amount of media data available online, drastically elevated the position of deep learning approaches. Despite their success in speech, ConvNets were largely ignored in the field of computer vision until 2012.

In 2012, a group of researchers from University of Toronto trained a large, deep ConvNet to classify 1000 different classes in the ImageNet Large Scale Visual Recognition Competition contest [KSH 2012]. The network was huge by the norms of the time: it had approximately 60 million parameters and 650,000 neurons. It was trained on 1.2 million high-resolution images from the ImageNet database. The network was trained in only one week on two GPUs, using the very efficient cuda-convnet library [Krizhevsky] written by Alex Krizhevsky. The network achieved breakthrough results with a winning top-5 test error of 15.3%. By comparison, the second place team that used the traditional computer vision algorithms achieved an error rate of 26.2%. This success triggered a revolution in computer vision, and ConvNet became a mainstream tool in computer vision, natural language processing, reinforcement learning, and many other traditional machine learning areas.

16.2 CONVOLUTIONAL NEURAL NETWORKS

To explain how ConvNets work, we will use LeNet-5, the network designed in the late 1980s for handwritten digit recognition [LBB 1998]. As shown in Fig. 16.2, LeNet-5 is composed of three types of layers: convolutional layers, subsampling layers, and full connection layers. We will consider each type of layer in the next section. The input to the network appears as a gray image with a handwritten digit represented as 2D 32 × 32 pixel array. The last layer computes the output, the vector which contains the probabilities for the original image to belong to each of the 10 classes (digits) that the network is set up to recognize.

CONVNETS: BASIC LAYERS

The computation in a convolutional network is organized as a sequence of layers. Inputs and outputs to layers will be referred to as "feature maps." In Fig. 16.2, the computation of the C1 layer is organized to generate six output feature maps from the INPUT pixel array. The computation result or output to be generated for input feature maps consists of pixels, each of which is produced by performing a convolution between a small local patch of feature map pixels of the previous layer (INPUT in the case of C1) and a set of weights (i.e., a convolution mask as defined in Chapter 7, Parallel patterns: convolution) called "filter bank."

All pixels in an input feature map are processed with the same filter bank when generating a particular output feature map. Different feature maps in a layer use different filter banks. Although not shown in Fig. 16.2, all filter banks used in LeNet-5 are 5 × 5 convolutions. They differ in the 25 weights that are present in them. If a convolution layers has n input feature maps and m output feature maps, n*m different filter banks will be used.

Recall from Chapter 7, Parallel patterns: convolution that generating a 32 × 32 convolution image from a 32 × 32 input image and a 5 × 5 convolution mask requires making assumptions regarding "ghost cells." However, instead of making such assumption, the LeNet-5 design simply uses two elements at the edge of each dimension as ghost cells. By so doing, the size of each dimension is reduced by four: two at the top, two at the bottom, two at the left, and two at the right. We see that by performing convolution with each filter bank, the 32 × 32 image results in a feature map that is a 28 × 28 image. Fig. 16.2 illustrates this computation by showing that a pixel in the C1 layer is generated from a square (5× 5 although not explicitly shown) patch of INPUT pixels.

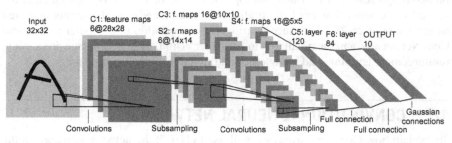

FIGURE 16.2

LeNet-5, a convolutional neural network for handwritten digit recognition.

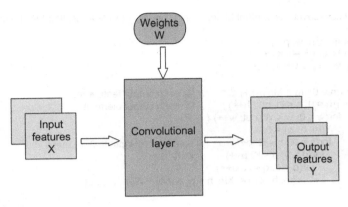

FIGURE 16.3

Overview of the forward propagation path of a convolution layer.

Fig. 16.3 provides an overview of the forward propagation path of a convolution layer. We assume that the input feature maps are stored in a 3D array X[C, H, W], where "C" is the number of input feature maps, "H" is the height of each input map image, and "W" is the width of each input map image. The highest dimension index selects one of the feature maps and the lower two dimension indexes selects one of the pixels in a feature map. To illustrate, the input feature maps for the C1 layer is stored in X[1, 32, 32] because only one input image (INPUT in Fig. 16.2) consists of 32 pixels in each of the x and y dimensions.

The output feature maps of a convolutional layer is also stored in a 3D array Y[M, H-K+1, W-K+1], where "M" is the number of output feature maps, "H" is the height of each input map image, "W" is the width of each input map image, and "K" is the height (and width) of each filter bank W[C, M, K, K]. For instance, the output feature maps for the C1 layer are stored in Y[6, 28, 28] because C1 generates six output feature maps and a 5 × 5 filter bank. Two elements are used at each edge of the image, as halo cells, when generating the convolved image. There are MxC filter banks. Filter bank W[m, c,_,_] is used for the input feature map X[c,_,_] to calculate the output feature map Y[m,_,_]. Note that each output feature map is the sum of convolutions of all input feature maps. Therefore, we can consider the forward propagation path of a convolutional layer as a set of M 3D convolutions, where each 3D convolution is specified by a 3D filter bank that is a C x K x K submatrix of W. Note that W is used for both the width of the images and the name of the filter bank matrix. In each case, the usage should be clear from the contex.

Fig. 16.4 shows a sequential implementation of the forward propagation path of a convolution layer. Each iteration of the outermost (m) for-loop generates an output feature map. Each of the next two levels (h and w) of for-loops generates one pixel of the current output feature map. The three innermost levels perform the 3D convolution between the input feature maps and the 3D filter banks.

```
void convLayer_forward(int M, int C, int H, int W, int K, float* X, float* W, float* Y)
{
  int m, c, h, w, p, q;
  int H_out = H − K + 1;
  int W_out = W − K + 1;

  for(m = 0;  m < M;  m++)          // for each output feature maps
    for(h = 0; h < H_out; h++)      // for each output element
     for(w = 0; w < W_out; w++) {
       Y[m, h, w] = 0;
       for(c = 0;  c < C; c++)      // sum over all input feature maps
        for(p = 0; p < K; p++)      // KxK  filter
          for(q = 0; q < K; q++)
            Y[m, h, w] += X[c, h + p, w + q] * W[m, c, p, q];
    }
}
```

FIGURE 16.4

A sequential implementation of the forward propagation path of a convolution layer.

The output feature maps of a convolution layer typically go through a subsampling (also known as pooling) layer. A subsampling layer reduces the size of image maps by combining pixels. For example, in Fig. 16.2, the subsampling layer S2 takes six input feature maps of size 28 × 28 and generates six feature maps of size 14x14. Each pixel in a subsampling feature map is generated from a 2x2 neighborhood in the corresponding input feature map. The values of these four pixels are averaged to form one pixel in the output feature map. The output of a subsampling layer has the same number of output feature maps as the previous layer; however, each map has half the number of rows and columns. To illustrate, the number of output feature maps (6) of the subsampling layer S2 is the same as the number of its input feature maps or the output feature maps of the convolutional layer C1.

Fig. 16.5 shows a sequential C implementation of the forward propagation path of a subsampling layer. Each iteration of the outermost (m) for-loop generates an output feature map. The next two levels (h, w) of for-loops generate individual pixels of the current output map. The two innermost for-loops sum up the pixels in the neighborhood. K is equal to 2 in our LeNet-5 example in Fig. 16.2. A bias value b[m] that is specific to each output feature map is then added to each output feature map, and the sum goes through a nonlinear function such as the tanh, sigmoid, or ReLU functions to provide the output pixel values a more desirable distribution. ReLU [JKL 2009], a very simple nonlinear filter, passes only nonnegative values, as follows:

$Y = X$, if $X \geq 0$, and 0 otherwise.

To complete our example, the convolutional layer C3 has 16 output feature maps, each of which is a 10 × 10 image. This layer contains 6 × 16 filter banks, with each filter bank having 5 × 5 weights. The output of C3 is passed through the subsampling layer S4, which generates 16 5 × 5 output feature maps. The last convolutional layer

```
void poolingLayer_forward(int M, int H, int W, int K, float* Y, float* S)
{
  int m, h, w, p, q;
   for(m = 0;  m < M;  m++)         // for each output feature maps
    for(h = 0; x < H/K; h++)        // for each output element
     for(w = 0; y < W/K; y++) {
      S[m, x, y] = 0.;
      for(p = 0; p < K; p++) {      // loop over KxK input samples
       for(q = 0; q < K; q++)
        S[m, h, w] = S[m, h, w] + Y[m, K*x + p, K*y + q]/(K*K);
      }
      // add bias and apply non-linear activation
      S[m, h, w] = sigmoid(S[m, h, w] + b[m])
     }
}
```

FIGURE 16.5

A sequential C implementation of the forward propagation path of a subsampling layer.

C5, which uses $16 \times 120 = 1920$ 5×5 filter banks to generate 120 one-pixel output features from its 16 input feature maps.

These feature maps are passed through the Fully Connected layer F6 with 84 output units, where each output is fully connected to all inputs. The output is computed as a product of a weight matrix W with an input vector X. For the F6 example, W is a 120×84 matrix. Then bias is added, and output is passed through the sigmoid function. In summary, the output is an 84-element vector $Y6 = \text{sigmoid}(W*X + b)$, assuming the implementation presented in Fig. 16.2.

The final stage is an output layer that uses Gaussian filters to generate a vector of 10 elements, which correspond to the probability that input image contains 1 of 10 digits. It also computes *loss* functions, which estimate the difference between the true label and the prediction.

CONVNETS: BACKPROPAGATION

Training of ConvNets is based on a procedure called gradient backpropagation [RHW 1986]. The training data set is labeled with the "correct answer." In the handwriting recognition example, the labels give the correct digit in the image. The label information can be used to generate the "correct" output of the last stage: the correct probability values of the 10-element vector would be all "0" except the right digit which should have probability "1".

For each training image, the final stage of the network calculates the loss function or the error as the difference between the generated output vector element values and the "correct" output vector element values. Given a sequence of training images, we can calculate the gradient of loss function with respect to the elements of the output vector. Intuitively, it gives the rate at which the loss function value changes when the values of the output vector elements change.

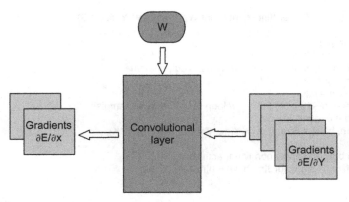

FIGURE 16.6

Convolutional layer: Backpropagation of $\partial E/\partial X$.

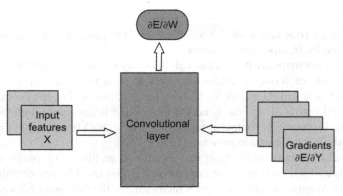

FIGURE 16.7

Convolutional layer: Backpropagation of $\partial E/\partial w$.

Backpropagation starts by calculating the gradient of loss function $\partial E/\partial Y$ for the last layer. This process then propagates the gradient from the last layer toward the first layer through all layers of the network. Each layer receives as its input $\partial E/\partial Y$—gradient with respect to its output feature maps and calculates $\partial E/\partial X$—gradient with respect to its input feature maps (Fig. 16.6).

If a layer has learned parameters ("weights") W, then the layer also calculates $\partial E/\partial W$—gradient of loss with respect to weights (Fig. 16.7).

For instance, the fully connected layer is given as $Y = W*X$. The backpropagation of gradient $\partial E/\partial Y$ is expressed by two equations:

$$\frac{\partial E}{\partial X} = W^T * \frac{\partial E}{\partial Y} \text{ and } \frac{\partial E}{\partial W} = \frac{\partial E}{\partial Y} * X^T$$

```
void convLayer_backward_xgrad(int M, int C, int H_in, int W_in, int K,
       float* dE_dY, float* W, float* dE_dX)
{
  int m, c, h, w, p, q;
  int H_out = H_in − K + 1;
  int W_out = W_in − K + 1;
  for(c = 0;  c < C; c++)
   for(h = 0; h < H_in; h++)
    for(w = 0; w < W_in; w++)
     dE_dX[c, h, w] = 0.;

  for(m = 0;  m < M;  m++)
   for(h = 0; h < H_out; h++)
    for(w = 0; w < W_out; w++)
     for(c = 0;  c < C; c++)
      for(p = 0; p < K; p++)
       for(q = 0; q < K; q++)
        dE_dX[c, h + p, w + q] += dE_dY[m, h, w] * W[m, c, p, q];
}
```

FIGURE 16.8

dE/dX calculation of the backward path of a convolution layer.

We will now describe backpropagation for a convolutional layer, starting with the calculation of $\partial E/\partial X$.

Note that the calculation of $\partial E/\partial X$ is important for propagating the gradient to the previous layer. The gradient $\partial E/\partial X$ with respect to the channel c of input X is given as the sum of "backward convolution" with corresponding $W^T(c,m)$ over all layer outputs m:

$$\frac{\partial E}{\partial X}(c,h,w) = \sum\nolimits_{m=1}^{M}\sum\nolimits_{p=1}^{k}\sum\nolimits_{q=1}^{k}\left(W(p,q) * \frac{\partial E}{\partial Y}(h-p,w-q)\right)$$

Fig. 16.8 demonstrates the calculation of the $\partial E/\partial X$ function in the form of one matrix for each input feature map. The code assumes that $\partial E/\partial Y$ has been calculated for all the output feature maps of the layer and passed with a pointer argument dE_dY. It also assumes that the space of dE_dX has been allocated in the device memory whose handle is passed as a pointer argument. The kernel will be generating the elements of dE_dX.

The algorithm for calculating $\partial E/\partial W$ for a convolution layer computation is very similar to that of $\partial E/\partial X$ and is shown in Fig. 16.9. Since each W(c,m) affects all elements of the output Y(m), we should accumulate gradients over all pixels in the corresponding output feature map:

$$\frac{\partial E}{\partial W}(c,m;p,q) = \sum\nolimits_{h=1}^{H_{out}}\sum\nolimits_{w=1}^{W_{out}}\left(X(h+p,w+q) * \frac{\partial E}{\partial Y}(h,w)\right)$$

Note that while the calculation of $\partial E/\partial X$ is important for propagating the gradient to the previous layer, the calculation of $\partial E/\partial W$ is key to the weight value adjustments of the current layer.

```
void convLayer_backward_wgrad(int M, int C, int H, int W, int K,
        float* dE_dY, float* X, float* dE_dW)
{
  int m, c, h, w, p, q;
  int H_out = H - K + 1;
  int W_out = W - K + 1;
  for(m = 0; m < M; m++)
   for(c = 0; c < C; c++)
    for(p = 0; p < K; p++)
     for(q = 0; q < K; q++)
      dE_dW[m, c, p, q] = 0.;

  for(m = 0;  m < M;  m++)
   for(h = 0; h < H_out; h++)
    for(w = 0; w < W_out; w++)
     for(c = 0;  c < C; c++)
      for(p = 0; p < K; p++)
       for(q = 0; q < K; q++)
        dE_dW[m, c, p, q] += X[c, h + p, w + q] * dE_dY[m, c, h, w];
}
```

FIGURE 16.9

dE/dW calculation of the backward path of a convolutional layer.

After the $\partial E/\partial W$ values at all positions of feature map elements are evaluated, weights are updated iteratively to minimize the expected error: $W(t + 1) = W(t) - \lambda*$ $\partial E/\partial W$, where λ is a constant called the learning rate. The initial value of λ is set empirically and reduced through the iterations in accordance with the rule defined by the user. The value of λ is reduced through the iterations to ensure the convergence to a minimal error. The negative sign of the adjustment term makes the change opposite to the direction of the gradient so that the change will likely reduce the error. Recall that the weight values of the layers determine how the input is transformed through the network. This adjustment of the weight values of all the layers adapts the behavior of the network, i.e. the network "learns" from a sequence of labeled training data and adapts its behavior by adjusting weight values at all layers.

The training data sets are usually large; thus, the training of ConvNets is typically accomplished using Stochastic Gradient Descent. Instead of performing a forward–backward step to determine $\partial E/\partial W$ for the whole training data set, one randomly selects a small subset ("mini-batch") of N images from the training data set and computes the gradient only for this subset. Subsequently, one selects another subset, and so on. If we would work by the "optimization book," we should return samples to the training set and then build a new mini-batch by randomly picking subsequent samples. In practice, we go sequentially over the entire training set. We then shuffle the entire training set and start the subsequent epoch. This procedure adds one additional dimension to all data arrays with n—the index of the sample in the mini-batch. It also adds another loop over samples.

Fig. 16.10 shows the revised forward path implementation of a convolutional layer. It generates the output feature maps for all samples of a mini-batch. During

```
void convLayer_forward(int N, int M, int C, int H, int W, int K, float* X, float* W, float* Y)
{
  int n, m, c, h, w, p, q;
  int H_out = H– K + 1;
  int W_out = W – K + 1;
  for(n = 0;  n < N;  n++)          // for each sample in the mini-batch
   for(m = 0;  m < M;  m++)         // for each output feature maps
    for(h = 0; h < H_out; h++)      // for each output element
     for(w = 0; w < W_out; w++) {
      Y[n, m, h, w] = 0;
      for (c = 0;  c < C; c++)      // sum over all input feature maps
       for (p = 0; p < K; p++)      // KxK  filter
        for (q = 0; q < K; q++)
         Y[n, m, h, w]  += X[n, c, h + p, w + q] * W[m, c, p, q];
     }
}
```

FIGURE 16.10

Forward path of a convolutional layer with mini-batch training.

backpropagation, one first computes for the average gradient of the error with respect to the weights of the last layer over all samples in a mini-batch. The gradient is then propagated backward through the layers and used to adjust all the weights. Each iteration of the weight adjustment processes one mini-batch. The training is measured in epochs, where one epoch is a sequential pass over all the samples in the training data set. The training data set is typically reshuffled between epochs.

16.3 CONVOLUTIONAL LAYER: A BASIC CUDA IMPLEMENTATION OF FORWARD PROPAGATION

The computation pattern in training a convolutional network is highly similar to matrix multiplication: compute-intensive and highly parallel. We can compute in different parallel samples in a mini-batch, different output feature maps for the same sample, and different elements for each output feature map. Fig. 16.11 presents a conceptual parallel code for the forward path of a convolutional layer. Each `parallel_for` loop indicates that all its iterations can be executed in parallel.

As shown in Fig. 16.11, the parallelism in the forward-path convolutional layer has four levels. The total number of parallel iterations is the product $N*M*H\_out*W\_out$. This high degree of available parallelism makes ConvNets an excellent candidate for GPU acceleration. To illustrate, forward path for a convolutional layer is implemented.

We will refine the high-level parallel code into a kernel by making some high-level design decisions. Assume that each thread will compute one element of one output feature map. We will use 2D thread blocks, with each thread block computing a tile of `TILE_WIDTH` x `TILE_WIDTH` elements in one output feature map. For instance,

```
void convLayer_forward(int N, int M, int C, int H, int W, int K, float* X, float* W, float* Y)
{
  int n, m, c, h, w, p, q;
  int H_out = H - K + 1;
  int W_out = W - K + 1;
  parallel_for(n = 0;  n < N;  n++)
   parallel_for (m = 0;  m < M;  m++)
    parallel_for(h = 0; h < H_out; h++)
     parallel_for(w = 0; w < W_out; w++) {
      Y[n, m, h, w] = 0;
      for (c = 0;  c < C; c++)
       for (p = 0; p < K; p++)
        for (q = 0; q < K; q++)
         Y[n, m, h, w] += X[n, c, h + p, w + q] * W[m, c, p, q];
     }
}
```

FIGURE 16.11

Parallelization of the forward path of a convolutional layer with mini-batch training.

if we set `TILE_WIDTH=16`, we would have a total of 256 threads per block. Blocks will be organized into a 3D grid:

1. The first dimension (X) of the grid corresponds to samples (N) in the batch;
2. The second dimension (Y) corresponds to the (M) output features maps; and
3. The last dimension (Z) will define the location of the output tile inside the output feature map.

The last dimension Z depends on the number of tiles in the horizontal and vertical dimensions of the output image. Assume for simplicity that `H_out` (height of the output image) and `W_out` (width of the output image) are multiples of the tile width (set to 16 below):

```
# define TILE_WIDTH 16
W_grid = W_out/TILE_WIDTH; // number of horizontal tiles per output map
H_grid = H_out/TILE_WIDTH; // number of vertical tiles per output map
Z = H_grid * W_grid;
dim3 blockDim(TILE_WIDTH, TILE_WIDTH, 1);
dim3 gridDim(N, M, Z);
ConvLayerForward_Kernel<<< gridDim, blockDim>>>(…);
```

As previously discussed, each thread block is responsible for computing one 16×16 tile in the output $Y(n, c, .. .)$, and each thread will compute one element $Y[n, m, h, w]$ where

```
n = blockIdx.x;
m = blockIdx.y;
h = blockIdx.z / W_grid + threadIdx.y;
w = blockIdx.z % W_grid + threadIdx.x;
```

```
__global__ void
ConvLayerForward_Kernel(int C, int W_grid, intK, float* X, float* W, float* Y)
{
  int n, m, h, w, c, p, q;
  n = blockId.x;
  m = blockId.y;
  h = blockId.z / W_grid + threadId.y;
  w = blockId.z % W_grid + threadId.x;
  float acc = 0.;
  for (c = 0;  c < C; c++) {        // sum over all input channels
    for (p = 0; p < K; p++)         // loop over KxK  filter
      for (q = 0; q < K; q++)
        acc = acc + X[n, c, h + p, w + q] * W[m, c, p, q];
  }
  Y[n, m, h, w] = acc;
}
```

FIGURE 16.12

Kernel for the forward path of a convolution layer.

This result is the kernel shown in Fig. 16.12. Note that in the code above, we use a multidimensional index in arrays. We leave it to the reader to translate this pseudo-code into a regular C, with the assumption that X, Y, and W must be accessed via linearized indexing based on a row-major layout (see Chapter 3: Scalable parallel execution).

The kernel in Fig. 16.12 exhibits a considerably high degree of parallelism but consumes excessive global memory bandwidth. Like in the convolution-based pattern, the execution speed of the kernel will be limited by the global memory bandwidth. We will now modify the basic kernel to reduce traffic to global memory. We can use shared memory tiling to dramatically improve the execution speed of the kernel as in Chapter 7, Parallel patterns: convolution. The kernel appears in Fig. 16.13. The basic design is stated in the comments and outlined below, as follows:

1. Load the filter W[m, c] into the shared memory.
2. All threads collaborate to copy the portion of the input X[n,c,.,.] that is required to compute the output tile into the shared memory array X_shared.
3. Compute for the partial sum of output Y_shared[n, m,.,.].
4. Move to the next input channel c.

We need to allocate shared memory for the input block X_tile_width * X_tile_width, where X_tile_width = TILE_WIDTH + K-1. We also need to allocate shared memory for K*K filter coefficients. Thus, the total amount of shared memory will be (TILE_WIDTH + K-1)* (TILE_WIDTH + K-1)+ K*K. Since we do not know K at compile time, we need to add it to the kernel definition as the third parameter.

```
    ...
    size_t shmem_size = sizeof(float) * ( (TILE_WIDTH + K-1)*(TILE_
WIDTH + K-1) + K*K );
    ConvLayerForward_Kernel<<< gridDim, blockDim, shmem_size>>>(...);
    ...
```

```
__global__ void
ConvLayerForward_Kernel(int C, int W_grid, int K, float* X, float* W, float* Y)
{
  int n, m, h0, w0, h_base, w_base, h, w;
  int X_tile_width = TILE_WIDTH + K-1;
  extern __shared__ float shmem[];
  float* X_shared = &shmem[0];
  float* W_shared = &shmem[X_tile_width * X_tile_width];
  n = blockIdx.x;
  m = blockIdx.y;
  h0 = threadIdx.x;  // h0 and w0 used as shorthand for threadIdx.x and threadIdx.y
  w0 = threadIdx.y;
  h_base = (blockIdx.z / W_grid) * TILE_SIZE; // vertical base out data index for the block
  w_base = (blockIdx.z % W_grid) * TILE_SIZE; // horizontal base out data index for the block
  h = h_base+ h0;
  w = w_base+ w0;

  float acc = 0.;
  int c, i, j, p, q;
  for (c = 0; c < C; c++) {              // sum over all input channels

    if (( h0 < K) && ( w0 < K))
      W_shared[h0, w0]= W [m, c, h0, w0]; // load weights for W [m, c,..],
      __syncthreads()                     // h0 and w0 used as shorthand for threadIdx.x
                                          // and threadIdx.y


    for (i = h; i < h_base+ X_tile_width; i += TILE_WIDTH) {
      for (j = w; j < w_base + X_tile_width; j += TILE_WIDTH)
        X_shared[i -h_base, j -w_base] = X[n, c, h, w]
    }                                     // load tile from X[n, c,...]into shared memory
    __syncthreads();
    for (p = 0; p < K; p++) {
      for (q = 0; q < K; q++)
        acc = acc + X_shared[h + p, w + q] * W_shared[p, q];
    }
    __syncthreads();
  }
  Y[n, m, h, w] = acc;
}
```

FIGURE 16.13

A kernel that uses shared memory tiling to reduce the global memory traffic of the forward path of the convolutional layer.

We will divide the shared memory between the input buffer and the filter inside the kernel. The first X_tile_width * X_tile_width entries are allocated to the input tiles, and the remaining entries are allocated to the weight values.

The use of shared memory tiling leads to a considerably high level of acceleration in the execution of the kernel. The analysis is similar to that discussed in Chapter 7, Parallel patterns: convolution, and is left as an exercise to the reader.

16.4 REDUCTION OF CONVOLUTIONAL LAYER TO MATRIX MULTIPLICATION

We can build an even faster convolutional layer by reducing it to matrix multiplication and then using highly efficient matrix multiplication, GEneral Matrix to Matrix Multiplication (GEMM), from CUDA linear algebra library (cuBLAS). This method was proposed by Chellapilla, Puri, and Simard [CPS 2006]. The central idea is unfolding and replicating the inputs to the convolutional kernel such that all elements needed to compute one output element will be stored as one sequential block. This technique will reduce the forward operation of the convolutional layer to one large matrix–matrix multiplication. See also https://petewarden.com/2015/04/20/why-gemm-is-at-the-heart-of-deep-learning/ for an elaborate explanation.

Consider a convolutional layer that takes as input C = 3 feature maps of size 3 × 3 and produces the M = 2 output features 2 × 2. It uses M*C = 6 filter banks, with each filter bank of size 2 × 2. The matrix version of this layer will be constructed as follows:

First, we will rearrange all input elements. Since the results of the convolutions are summed across input features, the input features can be concatenated into one large matrix. Each row of this matrix contains all input values necessary to compute one element of an output feature. This process means that each input element will be replicated multiple times. To illustrate, the center of each 3 × 3 input feature is used four times to compute for each element of an output feature for it to be reproduced four times. The central element on each edge is used two times so that it will be duplicated. The four elements at the corners of each input feature are used only once and will not need to be reproduced. Therefore, the total number of elements in the expanded input feature matrix is 4*1 + 2*4 + 1*4 = 16.

In general, the size of the expanded (unrolled) input feature map matrix can be derived by considering the number of input feature map elements required to generate each output feature map element. In general, the height (or the number of rows) of the expanded matrix is the number of input feature elements contributing to each output feature map element. The number is C*K*K: each output element is the convolution of K*K elements from each input feature map, and there are C input feature maps. In our example, K is two since the filter bank is 2 × 2, and there are three input feature maps. Thus, the height of the expanded matrix should be 3*2*2 = 12, which is exactly the height of the matrix in Fig. 16.14.

The width, or the number column, of the expanded matrix should be the number of elements in each output feature map. Assuming that the output feature maps are H_out x W_out matrices, the number of columns of the expanded matrix is H_out*W_out. In our example, each output feature map is a 2 × 2 matrix so that the expanded matrix consists of four columns. The number of output feature maps M does not affect the duplication as all output feature maps share the same expanded matrix.

The ratio of expansion for the input feature maps is the size of the expanded matrix over the total size of the original input feature maps. The reader should verify

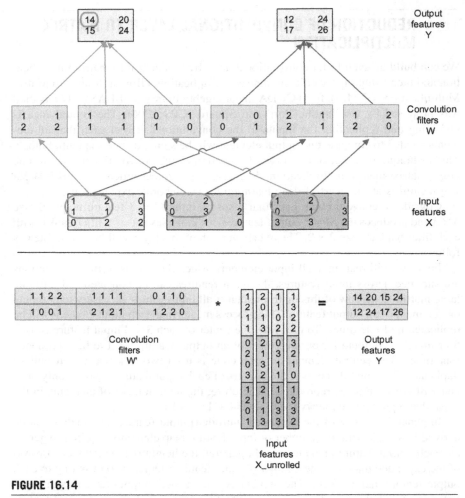

FIGURE 16.14

Reduction of a convolutional layer to GEMM.

that the expansion ratio is (K*K*H_out*W_out)/(H_in*W_in), where H_in and W_in denote the height and width of each input feature map, respectively. In our example, the ratio is (2*2*2*2)/(3*3) = 16/9. In general, if the input feature maps and output feature maps are much larger than the filter banks, the ratio will approach K*K.

The filter banks are represented as a filter-bank matrix in a fully linearized layout, where each row contains all weight values needed to produce one output feature map. The height of the filter-bank matrix is the number of output feature maps (M). The height of the filter-bank matrix allows the output feature maps to share a single expanded input matrix. Meanwhile, the width of the filter-bank matrix is the number of weight values needed to generate each output feature map element, which is C*K*K. Note that no duplication occurs when placing the weight values into the filter-banks matrix. In our example, the filter-bank matrix is simply a linearized arrangement of six filter banks.

When the filter-bank matrix **W** is multiplied by the expanded input matrix X_unrolled, the output features **Y** are computed as one large matrix of height M and width H_out*W_out.

The discussion that follows is on the method of implementing this algorithm in CUDA. We will first discuss the data layout, starting with the layout of the input and output matrices.

- We assume that the input feature map samples in a mini-batch will be supplied in the same way as that for the basic CUDA kernel. It is organized as an N x C x H x W array, where N is the number of samples in a mini-batch, C is the number of input feature maps, H is the height of each input feature map, and W is the width of each input feature map.
- As shown in Fig. 16.14, the matrix multiplication will naturally generate an output Y stored as an M x H_out*W_out array. This output is what the original basic CUDA kernel would generate.
- Since the filter-bank matrix does not involve duplication of weight values, we assume that it will be prepared as early and organized as an M x C x (K x K) array, as illustrated in Fig. 16.14.

The preparation of the expanded input feature map matrix X_unroll involves greater complexity. Since each expansion increases the size of the input by approximately up to K*K times, the expansion ratio can be very large for typical K values of 5 or larger. The memory footprint for keeping all sample input feature maps for a mini-batch can be prohibitively large. To reduce the memory footprint, we will allocate only one buffer for X_unrolled [C * K * K* H_out * W_out]. We will reuse this buffer by adding a loop over samples in the batch. During each iteration, we will convert the simple input feature map from its original form into the expanded matrix.

Fig. 16.15 shows the sequential implementation of the forward path of a convolutional layer with matrix multiplication. The code loops through all samples in the batch.

Fig. 16.16 shows a sequential function that produces the X_unroll array by gathering and duplicating the elements of an input feature map **X**. The function uses five levels of loops. The two innermost levels of the for-loop (w and h) place one element of the input feature map for each of the output feature map elements. The next two levels repeat the process for each of the K*K element of the input feature map for the filtering operations. The outermost loop repeats the process of all input feature maps. This implementation is conceptually straightforward and can be quite easily parallelized since the loops do not impose dependencies among their iterations. In addition, successive iterations of the innermost loop read from a localized tile of one of the input feature maps in X and write into sequential locations in the expanded matrix X_unrolled. This process should result in efficient usage of memory bandwidth on a CPU.

```
void convLayer_forward(int N, int M, int C, int H, int W, int K, float* X, float* W_unroll, float* Y)
{
  int W_out = W– K + 1;
  int H_out = H– K + 1;
  int W_unroll = C * K * K;
  int H_unroll = H_out * W_out;
  float* X_unrolled = malloc(W_unroll * H_unroll * sizeof(float));
  for (int n=0; n < N; n++) {
   unroll(C, H, W, K, n,X, X_unrolled);
   gemm(H_unroll, M, W_unroll, X_unrolled, W, Y[n]);
  }
}
```

FIGURE 16.15

Implementing the forward path of a convolutional layer with matrix multiplication.

```
void unroll(int C, int H, int W, int K, float* X, float* X_unroll)
{
  int c, h, w, p, q, w_base, w_unroll, h_unroll;
  int H_out = H– K + 1;
  int W_out = W– K + 1;
  for(c = 0; c < C; c++) {
   w_base = c * (K*K);
   for(p = 0; p < K; p++)
    for(q = 0; q < K; q++) {
     for(h = 0; h <  H_out; h++)
      for(w = 0; w < W_out; w++){
      w_unroll = w_base + p * K + q;
       h_unroll = h * W_out + w;
       X_unroll(h_unroll, w_unroll) = X(c, h + p, w + q);
      }
    }
  }
}
```

FIGURE 16.16

The function that generates the unrolled X matrix.

We are now ready to design a CUDA kernel that implements the input feature map unrolling. Each CUDA thread will be responsible for gathering (K*K) input elements from one input feature map for one element of an output feature map. The total number of threads will be (C * H_out * W_out). We will use one-dimensional blocks. If we assume that a maximum number of threads per block is CUDA_MAX_NUM_THREADS (e.g., 1024), the total number of blocks in the grid will be num_blocks = ceil((C*H_out*W_out) / CUDA_MAX_NUM_THREADS) (Fig. 16.17).

Fig. 16.18 illustrates an implementation of the unroll kernel. Each thread will build a K*K section of a column, shown as a shaded box in the Input Features X_Unrolled array in Fig. 16.14. Each such section contains all elements of the input

```
void unroll_gpu(int C, int H, int W, int K, float* X, float* X_unroll)
{
    int H_out = H – K + 1;
    int W_out = W– K + 1;
    int num_threads = C * H_out * W_out;
    int num_blocks = ceil((C * H_out * W_out) / CUDA MAX_NUM_THREADS);
    unroll_Kernel<<<num_blocks, CUDA MAX_NUM_THREADS>>>();
}
```

FIGURE 16.17

Host code for invoking the unroll kernel.

```
__global__ void unroll_Kernel(int C, int H, int W, int K, float* X, float* X_unroll)
{
    int c, s, h_out, w-out, h_unroll, w_base, p, q;
    int t = blockId.x * CUDA MAX_NUM_THREADS + threadId.x;
    int H_out = H– K + 1;
    int W_out = W– K + 1;
    int W_unroll = H_out * W_out;

    if (t < C * W_unroll) {
     c = t / W_unroll;
     s = t % W_unroll;
     h_out = s / W_out;
     w_out = s % W_out;
     h_unroll = h_out * W_out + w_out;
     w_base = c * K * K;
     for(p = 0; p < K; p++)
       for(q = 0; q < K; q++) {
        w_unroll = w_base + p * K + q;
        X_unroll(h_unroll, w_unroll) = X(c, h_out + p, w_out + q);
       }
     }
}
```

FIGURE 16.18

High-performance implementation of the unroll kernel.

feature map X from channel c, which is required for convolution with a corresponding filter to produce one element of output Y.

Comparison of the loop structure in Figs. 16.16 and 16.18 indicates that the two innermost loop levels in Fig. 16.16 have been exchanged into outer level loops. Having each thread collect all input feature map elements from an input feature map needed to generate an output generates a coalesced memory write pattern. As shown in Fig. 16.16, adjacent threads will be writing adjacent X_unroll elements in a row as they all move vertically to complete their sections. The read access patterns to X are similar. We leave the analysis of the read access pattern as an exercise.

An important high-level assumption is that we keep the input feature maps, filter bank weights, and output feature maps in the device memory. The filter-bank matrix is prepared once and stored in the device global memory for use by all input feature maps. For each sample in the mini-batch, we launch the `unroll_Kernel` to prepare an expanded matrix and launch a matrix multiplication kernel, as outlined in Fig. 16.15.

Implementing convolutions with matrix multiplication can be highly efficient because matrix multiplication is highly optimized on all hardware platforms. Matrix multiplication is especially fast on GPUs because it has a high ratio of floating-point operations per byte of global memory data access. This ratio increases as the matrices become larger, implying that matrix multiplication is less efficient on small matrices. Accordingly, this approach to convolution is most effective when it creates large matrices for multiplication.

As mentioned earlier, the filter-bank matrix is an `M x C*K*K` matrix and the expanded input feature map matrix is a `C*K*K x H_out*W_out` matrix. Note that except for the height of the filter-bank matrix, the sizes of all dimensions depend on the products of the parameters to the convolution, not the parameters themselves. While individual parameters can be small, their products tend to be large. The implication is that the matrices tend to be consistently large; thus, this approach can exhibit a consistent performance. For instance, C is often small in the early layers of a convolutional network, whereas `H_out` and `W_out` are large. At the end of the network, C is large, whereas `H_out` and `W_out` tend to be small. However, the product `C*H_out*W_out` is usually fairly large for all layers, so performance can be consistently good.

The disadvantage of forming the expanded input feature map matrix is that it involves duplicating the input data up to `K*K` times, which can require a prohibitively large temporary allocation. To work around this, implementations such as the one shown in Fig. 16.15 materialize the `X_unroll` matrix piece by piece, e.g. by forming the expanded input feature map matrix and calling matrix multiplication iteratively for each sample of the mini-batch. However, this process limits the parallelism in the implementation and can lead to matrix multiplication being too small to effectively use the GPU. This approach also lowers the computational intensity of the convolutions. The reason is that `X_unroll` must be written and read, in addition to X reading itself, requiring significantly more memory traffic as a more direct approach. Accordingly, the highest performance implementation involves even more complex arrangements in realizing the unrolling algorithm to both maximize GPU utilization while keeping the reading from DRAM minimal. We will return to this point when we present the cuDNN approach in the subsequent section.

16.5 CUDNN LIBRARY

cuDNN is a library of optimized routines for implementing deep learning primitives [CWVCT-2014]. It was designed to help deep learning frameworks take advantage of GPUs. The library provides a flexible, easy-to-use C-language deep learning API that integrates neatly into existing frameworks (Caffe, Tensorflow, Theano, Torch, etc.).

Table 16.1 Convolution Parameters for cuDNN

Parameter	Meaning
N	Number of images in mini-batch
C	Number of input feature maps
H	Height of input image
W	Width of input image
K	Number of output feature maps
R	Height of filter
S	Width of filter
u	Vertical stride
v	Horizontal stride
pad_h	Height of zero padding
pad_w	Width of zero padding

*Note that the cuDNN naming convention is slightly different than what we
have been using in previous sections.*

The library requires that input and output data reside in the GPU device memory, as
discussed in the previous section. This requirement is analogous to that of cuBLAS.

The library is thread-safe, and its routines can be called from different host
threads. Convolutional routines for the forward and backward paths use a common
descriptor that encapsulates the attributes of the layer. Tensors and filters are accessed
through opaque descriptors, with the flexibility to specify the tensor layout by using
arbitrary strides along each dimension. The most important computational primitive
in ConvNets is a special form of batched convolution. In this section, we describe the
forward form of this convolution. The cuDNN parameters governing this convolution
are listed in Table 16.1.

There are two inputs to convolution:

- D is a four-dimensional N x C x H x W tensor which forms the input data.
  Tensor is a mathematical term for arrays that have more than two dimensions.
  In mathematics, matrices have only two dimensions. Arrays with three or more
  dimensions are called tensors. For the purpose of this book, one can simply treat
  a T-dimensional tensor as a T-dimensional array.
- F is a four-dimensional K x C x R x S tensor, which forms the convolutional
  filters.

The input data array (tensor) D ranges over N samples in a mini-batch, C input
feature maps per sample, H rows per input feature map, and W columns per input feature map. The filters range over K output feature maps, C input feature maps, R rows
per filter bank, and S columns per filter bank. The output is also a four-dimensional
tensor O that ranges over N samples in the mini-batch, K output feature maps, P rows
per output feature map, and Q columns per output feature map, where P = f(H;R; u;
pad_h) and Q = f(W; S; v; pad_w). The height and width of the output feature maps

depend on the input feature map and filter bank height and width, along with padding and striding choices. The striding parameters u and v allow the user to reduce computational load by computing only a subset of the output pixels. The padding parameters allow users to specify the number of rows or columns of 0 entries are appended to each feature map for improved memory alignment and/or vectorized execution.

cuDNN supports multiple algorithms for implementing a convolutional layer: matrix multiplication-based (GEMM and Winograd [Lavin & Gray]), fast-Fourier-transform-based [VJM 2014], etc. The GEMM-based algorithm used to implement the convolutions with a matrix multiplication is similar to the approach presented in Section 16.4. As discussed at the end of Section 16.4 materializing the expanded input feature matrix in global memory can be costly in both the global memory space and bandwidth consumption. cuDNN prevents this problem by lazily generating and loading the expanded input feature map matrix X_unroll into on-chip memory only, rather than by gathering it into off-chip memory before calling a matrix multiplication routine. NVIDIA provides a matrix multiplication-based routine that achieves a high utilization of maximal theoretical floating-point throughput on GPUs. The algorithm for this routine is similar to that described in [TLT 2011]. Fixed-sized submatrices of the input matrices A and B are successively read into on-chip memory and are then used to compute a submatrix of the output matrix C. All indexing complexities imposed by the convolution are handled in the management of tiles in this routine. We compute on tiles of A and B while fetching the subsequent tiles of A and B from off-chip memory into on-chip caches and other memories. This technique hides the memory latency associated with the data transfer; consequently, the matrix multiplication computation is limited only by the time it takes to perform the arithmetic.

Since the tiling required for the matrix multiplication routine is independent of any parameters from the convolution, the mapping between the tile boundaries of X_unroll and the convolution problem is nontrivial. Accordingly, the cuDNN approach entails computing this mapping and using it to load the correct elements of A and B into on-chip memories. This process occurs dynamically as the computation proceeds, which allows the cuDNN convolution implementation to exploit optimized infrastructure for matrix multiplication. It requires additional indexing arithmetic compared with matrix multiplication but fully leverages the computational engine of matrix multiplication to perform the work. Once the computation is complete, cuDNN performs the required tensor transposition to store the result in the desired data layout of the user.

16.6 EXERCISES

1. Implement the forward path for the pooling layer described in Section 16.2.

2. We used an [N x C x H x W] layout for input and output features. Can we reduce the required memory bandwidth by changing it to an [N x H x W x C]? What are the potential benefits of the [C x H x W x N] layout?

3. Implement the convolutional layer employing fast Fourier transform by using the schema described in [VJM 2014].

4. Implement the backward path for the convolutional layer described in Section 16.2.

5. Analyze the read access pattern to X in `unroll_kernel` in Fig. 16.18 and determine whether the memory reads done by adjacent threads can be coalesced.

REFERENCES

Chellapilla, K., Puri, S., & Simard, P. (2006). *High performance convolutional neural networks for document processing.* <https://hal.archives-ouvertes.fr/inria-00112631/document>.

Chetlur, S., Woolley, C., Vandermersch, P., Cohen, J., & Tran, J. (2014). *cuDNN: efficient primitives for deep learning.* NVIDIA.

Hinton, G. E., Osindero, S., & Teh, Y. -W. (2006). A fast learning algorithm for deep belief nets. *Neural Comp, 18,* 1527–1554. <https://www.cs.toronto.edu/~hinton/absps/fastnc.pdf>.

Jarrett, K., Kavukcuoglu, K., & Lecun Y. (2009). *What is the best multi-stage architecture for object recognition?* In Proc. IEEE 12th ICCV, 2146–2153. <http://ieeexplore.ieee.org/document/5459469/?arnumber=5459469&tag=1>.

Krizhevsky, A. *Cuda-convnet.* <https://code.google.com/p/cuda-convnet/>.

Krizhevsky, A., Sutskever, I., & Hinton, G. (2012). ImageNet classification with deep convolutional neural networks. In *Proc. advances in NIPS 25 1090–1098.* <https://papers.nips.cc/paper/4824-imagenet-classification-with-deep-convolutional-neural-networks.pdf>.

Lavin, A., & Gray, S. *Fast algorithms for convolutional neural networks.* <http://arxiv.org/abs/1509.09308>.

LeCun, Y. et al. (1990). Handwritten digit recognition with a back-propagation network. In *Proc. advances in neural information processing systems 396–404.* <http://yann.lecun.com/exdb/publis/pdf/lecun-90c.pdf>.

LeCun, Y., Bengio, Y., & Hinton, G. E. (2015). Deep learning. *Nature, 521,* 436–444. (28 May 2015). <http://www.nature.com/nature/journal/v521/n7553/full/nature14539.html>.

LeCun, Y., Bottou, L., Bengio, Y., & Haffner, P. (1998). Gradient-based learning applied to document recognition. *Proceedings of the IEEE, 86*(11), 2278–2324. <http://yann.lecun.com/exdb/publis/pdf/lecun-01a.pdf>.

Raina, R., Madhavan, A., & Ng, A. Y. (2009). Large-scale deep unsupervised learning using graphics processors. In *Proc. 26th ICML 873–880.* <http://www.andrewng.org/portfolio/large-scale-deep-unsupervised-learning-using-graphics-processors/>.

Rumelhart, D. E., Hinton, G. E., & Wiliams, R. J. (1986). Chapter 8: Learning internal representations by error propagation. In D. E. Rumelhart & J. L. McClelland (Eds.), *Parallel distributed processing* (volume 1, pp. 319–362.). MIT Press.

Tan, G., Li, L., Treichler, S., Phillips, E., Bao, Y., & Sun, N. (2011). Fast implementation of DGEMM on Fermi GPU. In *Supercomputing 2011, SC '11.*

Vasilache, N., Johnson, J., Mathieu, M., Chintala, S., Piantino, S., & LeCun, Y. (2014). *Fast convolutional nets with fbfft: a GPU performance evaluation.* <http://arxiv.org/pdf/1412.7580v3.pdf>.

Parallel programming and computational thinking

17

We have so far concentrated on the practical experience of parallel programming, which consists of features of the CUDA programming model, performance and numerical considerations, parallel patterns, and application case studies. We will now switch gears to more abstract concepts. We will first generalize parallel programming into a computational thinking process that decomposes a domain problem into well-defined, coordinated work units that can each be realized with efficient numerical methods and well-studied algorithms. A programmer with strong computational thinking skills not only analyzes but also transforms the structure of a domain problem: which parts are inherently serial, which parts are amenable to high-performance parallel execution, and the domain-specific tradeoffs involved in moving parts from the former category to the latter. With good problem decomposition, the programmer can select and implement algorithms that achieve an appropriate compromise between parallelism, computational efficiency, and memory bandwidth consumption. A strong combination of domain knowledge and computational thinking skills is often needed for creating successful computational solutions to challenging domain problems. This chapter will give the reader more insight into parallel programming and computational thinking in general.

Programming Massively Parallel Processors. DOI: http://dx.doi.org/10.1016/B978-0-12-811986-0.00001-7

17.1 GOALS OF PARALLEL COMPUTING

Before we discuss the fundamental concepts of parallel programming, it is important for us to first review the three main reasons why people pursue parallel computing. The first goal is to solve a given problem in less time. For example, an investment firm may need to run a financial portfolio scenario risk analysis package on all its portfolios during after-trading hours. Such an analysis may require 200 hours on a sequential computer. However, the portfolio management process may require that analysis be completed in 4 hours in order to be in time for major decisions based on that information. Using parallel computing may speed up the analysis and allow it to complete within the required time window.

The second goal of using parallel computing is to solve bigger problems within a given amount of time. In our financial portfolio analysis example, the investment firm may be able to run the portfolio scenario risk analysis on its current portfolio within a given time window using sequential computing. However, the firm is planning on expanding the number of holdings in its portfolio. The enlarged problem size would cause the running time of analysis under sequential computation to exceed the time window. Parallel computing that reduces the running time of the bigger problem size can help accommodate the planned expansion to the portfolio.

The third goal of using parallel computing is to achieve better solutions for a given problem and a given amount of time. The investment firm may have been using an approximate model in its portfolio scenario risk analysis. Using a more accurate model may increase the computational complexity and increase the running time on a sequential computer beyond the allowed window. For example, a more accurate model may require consideration of interactions between more types of risk factors using a more numerically complex formula. Parallel computing that reduces the running time of the more accurate model may complete the analysis within the allowed time window.

In practice, parallel computing may be driven by a combination of these three goals.

It should be clear from our discussion that parallel computing is primarily motivated by increased speed. The first goal is achieved by increased speed in running the existing model on the current problem size. The second goal is achieved by increased speed in running the existing model on a larger problem size. The third goal is achieved by increased speed in running a more complex model on the current problem size. Obviously, the increased speed through parallel computing can be used to achieve a combination of these goals. For example, parallel computing can reduce the run time of a more complex model on a larger problem size.

It should also be clear from our discussion that applications that are good candidates for parallel computing typically involve large problem sizes and high modeling complexity. That is, these applications process a large amount of data, require a lot of computation in each iteration, and/or perform many iterations on the data, or both. Applications that do not process large problem sizes or incur high modeling complexity tend to complete within a small amount of time and do not offer much motivation for increased speed. In order for a problem to be solved with parallel computing, the problem must be formulated in such a way that the large problem can be decomposed into sub-problems that can be safely solved at the same time. Under such formulation and decomposition, the programmer writes code and organizes data to solve these sub-problems concurrently.

In Chapters 14 and 15, Application case study—non-Cartesian MRI and Application case study—molecular visualization and analysis, we presented two problems that are good candidates for parallel computing. The magnetic resonance imaging (MRI) reconstruction problem processes a large amount of k-space sample data. Each k-space sample data is also used many times for calculating its contributions to the reconstructed voxel data. For a reasonably high resolution reconstruction, each sample data is used a very large number of times. We showed that a good decomposition of the F^HD problem in MRI reconstruction forms sub-problems that each calculate the value of an F^HD element. All of these subproblems can be solved in parallel with each other. We use a massive number of CUDA threads to solve these sub-problems.

Similarly, the electrostatic potential calculation problem involves the calculation of the contribution of a large number of atoms to the potential energy of a large number of grid points. Fig. 15.10 further shows that the electrostatic potential calculation problem should be solved with a massively parallel CUDA device only if there are 400 or more atoms. In reality, this is not a very restricting requirement. A realistic molecular system model typically involves at least hundreds of thousands of atoms and millions of energy grid points. The electrostatic charge information of each atom is used many times in calculating its contributions to the energy grid points. We showed that a good decomposition of the electrostatic potential calculation problem forms sub-problems that each calculates the energy value of a grid point. All the sub-problems can be solved in parallel with each other. We use a massive number of CUDA threads to solve these sub-problems.

The process of parallel programming can typically be divided into four steps: problem decomposition, algorithm selection, implementation in a language, and performance tuning. The last two steps were the focus of previous chapters. In the next two sections, we will discuss the first two steps with more generality as well as depth.

17.2 PROBLEM DECOMPOSITION

Finding parallelism in large computational problems is often conceptually simple but can be challenging in practice. The key is to identify the work to be performed by each unit of parallel execution, which is a thread, so that the inherent parallelism of the problem is well utilized. For example, in the electrostatic potential map calculation problem, it is clear that all atoms can be processed in parallel and all energy grid points can be calculated in parallel. However, one must take care when decomposing the calculation work into units of parallel execution, which will be referred to as

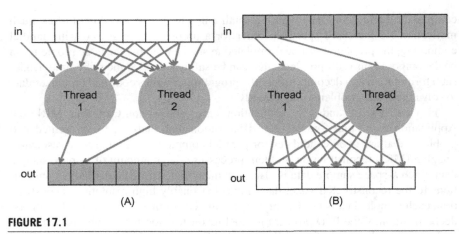

FIGURE 17.1

(A) Gather and (B) scatter based thread arrangements.

threading arrangement. As we discussed in Section 15.2, the decomposition of the electrostatic potential map calculation problem can be atom-centric or grid-centric. In an atom-centric threading arrangement, each thread is responsible for calculating the effect of one atom on all grid points. In contrast, a grid-centric threading arrangement uses each thread to calculate the effect of all atoms on a grid point.

While both threading arrangements lead to similar levels of parallel execution and same execution results, they can exhibit very different performance in a given hardware system. The grid-centric arrangement has a memory access behavior called *gather*, where each thread gathers or collects the effect of input atoms into a grid point. Fig. 17.1A illustrates the gather access behavior. Gather is a desirable thread arrangement in CUDA devices because the threads can accumulate their results in their private registers. Also, multiple threads share input atom values, and can effectively use constant memory caching or shared memory to conserve global memory bandwidth.

The atom-centric arrangement, on the other hand, exhibits a memory access behavior called *scatter*, where each thread scatters or distributes the effect of an atom into grid points. The scatter behavior is illustrated in Fig. 17.1B. This is an undesirable arrangement in CUDA devices because the multiple threads can write into the same grid point at the same time. The grid points must be stored in a memory that can be written by all the threads involved. Atomic operations must be used to prevent race conditions and loss of value during simultaneous writes to a grid point by multiple threads. These atomic operations are typically slower than the register accesses used in the atom-centric arrangement. Understanding the behavior of the threading arrangement and the limitations of hardware allows a parallel programmer to steer toward the more desired gather-based arrangement.

A real application often consists of multiple modules that work together. Fig. 17.2 shows an overview of major modules of a molecular dynamics application. For each

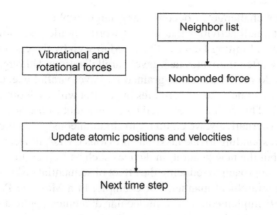

FIGURE 17.2

Major tasks of a molecular dynamics application.

atom in the system, the application needs to calculate the various forms of forces, e.g., vibrational, rotational, and nonbonded, that are exerted on the atom. Each form of force is calculated by a different method. At the high level, a programmer needs to decide how the work is organized. Note that the amount of work can vary dramatically between these modules. The nonbonded force calculation typically involves interactions among many atoms and incurs much more calculation than the vibrational and rotational forces. Therefore, these modules tend to be realized as separate passes over the force data structure.

The programmer needs to decide if each pass is worth implementing in a CUDA device. For example, he/she may decide that the vibrational and rotational force calculations do not involve sufficient amount of work to warrant execution on a device. Such a decision would lead to a CUDA program that launches a kernel that calculates nonbonded force fields for all the atoms while continuing to calculate the vibrational and rotational forces for the atoms on the host. The module that updates atomic positions and velocities may also run on the host. It first combines the vibrational and rotational forces from the host and the nonbonded forces from the device. It then uses the combined forces to calculate the new atomic positions and velocities.

The portion of work done by the device will ultimately decide the application level speedup achieved by parallelization. For example, assume that the nonbonded force calculation accounts for 95% of the original sequential execution time and it is accelerated by 100× using a CUDA device. Further assume that the rest of the application remains on the host and receives no speedup. The application level speedup is $1/(5\% + 95\%/100) = 1/(5\% + 0.95\%) = 1/(5.95\%) = 17\times$. This is a demonstration of Amdahl's Law: the application speedup due to parallel computing is limited by the sequential portion of the application. In this case, even though the sequential portion of the application is quite small (5%), it limits the application level speedup to 17× even though the nonbonded force calculation has a speedup of 100×. This example illustrates a major challenge in decomposing large applications: the accumulated execution time of small activities that are not worth parallel execution on a CUDA device can become a limiting factor in the speedup seen by the end users.

Amdahl's Law often motivates task-level parallelization. Although some of these smaller activities do not warrant fine-grained massive parallel execution, it may be desirable to execute some of these activities in parallel with each other when the data set is large enough. This could be achieved by using a multi-core host to execute such tasks in parallel. Alternatively, we could try to simultaneously execute multiple small kernels, each corresponding to one task. The previous CUDA devices did not support such parallelism but the new generation devices such as Kepler do.

An alternative approach to reducing the effect of sequential tasks is to exploit data parallelism in a hierarchical manner. For example, in a Message Passing Interface (MPI) [MPI 2009] implementation, a molecular dynamics application would typically distribute large chunks of the spatial grids and their associated atoms to nodes of a networked computing cluster. By using the host of each node to calculate the vibrational and rotational force for its chunk of atoms, we can take advantage of multiple host CPUs and achieve speedup for these lesser modules. Each node can use a CUDA device to calculate the nonbonded force at higher levels of speedup. The nodes will need to exchange data to accommodate forces that go across chunks and atoms that move across chunk boundaries. We will discuss more details of joint MPI-CUDA programming in Chapter 18, Programming a heterogeneous cluster. The main point here is that MPI and CUDA can be used in a complementary way in applications to jointly achieve a higher level of speed with large data sets.

17.3 ALGORITHM SELECTION

An algorithm is a step-by-step procedure where each step is precisely stated and can be carried out by a computer. An algorithm must exhibit three essential properties: definiteness, effective computability, and finiteness. Definiteness refers to the notion that each step is precisely stated; there is no room for ambiguity as to what is to be done. Effective computability refers to the fact that each step can be carried out by a computer. Finiteness means that the algorithm must be guaranteed to terminate.

Given a problem, we can typically come up with multiple algorithms to solve the problem. Some require fewer steps of computation than others; some allow a higher degree of parallel execution than others; some have better numerical stability than others, and some consume less memory bandwidth than others. Unfortunately, there is often not a single algorithm that is better than others in all the four aspects. Given a problem and a decomposition strategy, a parallel programmer often needs to select an algorithm that achieves the best compromise for a given hardware system.

In our matrix–matrix multiplication example, we decided to decompose the problem by having each thread compute the dot product for an output element. Given this decomposition, we presented two different algorithms. The algorithm in Section 4.2 is a straightforward algorithm where every thread simply performs an entire dot product. Although the algorithm fully utilizes the parallelism available in the decomposition, it consumes too much global memory bandwidth. In Section 4.4, we introduced tiling, an important algorithm strategy for conserving memory bandwidth. Note that the tiled algorithm partitions the dot products into phases. All threads involved in a tile must synchronize with each other so that they can collaboratively load the tile of input data into the shared memory and collectively utilize the loaded data before they move on to the next phase. As we showed in Fig. 4.16, the tiled algorithm requires each thread to execute more statements and incur more overhead in indexing the input arrays than the original algorithm. However, it runs much faster because it consumes much less global memory bandwidth. In general, tiling is one of the most important algorithm strategies for matrix applications to achieve high performance.

As we demonstrated in Sections 5.5 and 15.3, we can systematically merge threads to achieve a higher level of instruction and memory access efficiency. In Section 5.5, threads that handle the same columns of neighboring tiles are combined into a new thread. This allows the new thread to access each M element only once while calculating multiple dot products, reducing the number of address calculations and memory load instructions executed. It also further reduces the consumption of global memory bandwidth. The same technique, when applied to the DCS kernel in electrostatic potential calculation, further reduces the number of distance calculations while achieving a similar reduction in address calculations and memory load instructions.

One can often invent even more aggressive algorithm strategies. An important algorithm strategy, referred to as *cutoff binning*, can significantly improve the execution efficiency of grid or particle algorithms by sacrificing a small amount of accuracy. This is based on the observation that many grid or particle calculation problems are based on physical laws where numerical contributions from particles or samples that are far away from a grid point or particle can be collectively treated with an implicit method at much lower computational complexity. This is illustrated for the electrostatic potential calculation in Fig. 17.3. Fig. 17.3A shows the direct summation algorithms discussed in Chapter 15, Application case study—molecular visualization and analysis. Each grid point receives contributions from all atoms. While this is a very parallel approach and achieves excellent speedup over CPU-only execution for moderate-sized energy grid systems, as we showed in Section 15.5, it does not scale well to very large energy-grid systems where the number of atoms increases proportional to the volume of the system. The amount of computation increases with the square of the volume. For large volume systems, such an increase makes the computation excessively long even for massively parallel devices.

In practice, we know that each grid point needs to receive contributions from atoms that are close to it. The atoms that are far away from a grid point will have negligible contribution to the energy value at the grid point because the contribution is inversely proportional to the distance. Fig. 17.3B illustrates this observation with a circle drawn around a grid point. The contributions to the grid point energy from atoms outside the circle (*maroon* (dark gray in print versions)) are negligible. If we can devise an algorithm where each grid point only receives contributions from

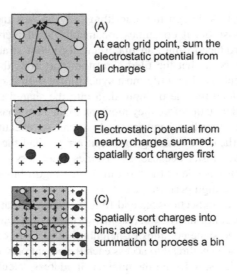

(A)
At each grid point, sum the electrostatic potential from all charges

(B)
Electrostatic potential from nearby charges summed; spatially sort charges first

(C)
Spatially sort charges into bins; adapt direct summation to process a bin

FIGURE 17.3

Cutoff summation algorithm. (A) Direct summation, (B) cutoff summation, and (C) cutoff summation using direct summation kernel.

atoms within a fixed radius of its coordinate (*green* (light gray in the print versions)), the computational complexity of the algorithm would be reduced, becoming linearly proportional to the volume of the system. This would make the computation time of algorithm linearly proportional to the volume of the system. Such algorithms have been used extensively in sequential computation.

In sequential computing, a simple cutoff algorithm handles one atom at a time. For each atom, the algorithm iterates through the grid points that fall within a radius of the atom's coordinate. This is a straightforward procedure since the grid points are in an array that can be easily indexed as a function of their coordinates. However, this simple procedure does not carry easily to parallel execution. The reason is what we discussed in Section 17.2: the atom-centric decomposition does not work well due to its scatter memory access behavior. However, as we discussed in Chapter 8, Parallel patterns – prefix-sum, it is important that a parallel algorithm matches the work efficiency of an efficient sequential algorithm.

Therefore, we need to find a cutoff binning algorithm based on the grid-centric decomposition: each thread calculates the energy value at one grid point. Fortunately, there is a well-known approach to adapting direct summation algorithm, such as the one in Fig. 15.9, into a cutoff binning algorithm. Rodrigues et al. presents such an algorithm for the electrostatic potential problem [RSH 2008].

The key idea of the algorithm is to first sort the input atoms into bins according to their coordinates. Each bin corresponds to a box in the grid space and it contains all atoms whose coordinates falls into the box. We define a "neighborhood" of bins for a grid point to be the collection of bins that contain all the atoms that can contribute to the energy value of a grid point. If we have an efficient way of managing neighborhood bins for all grid points, we can calculate the energy value for a grid point by examining the neighborhood bins for the grid point. This is illustrated in Fig. 17.3C. Although Fig. 17.3 shows only one layer (2D) of bins that immediately surround that containing a grid point as its neighborhood, a real algorithm will typically have multiple layers (3D) of bins in a grid's neighborhood. In this algorithm, all threads iterate through their own neighborhood. They use their block and thread indices to identify the appropriate bins. Note that some of the atoms in the surrounding bins may not fall into the radius. Therefore, when processing an atom, all threads need to check if the atom falls into its radius. This can cause some control divergence among threads in a warp.

The main source of improvement in work efficiency comes from the fact that each thread now examines a much smaller set of atoms in a large grid system. This, however, makes constant memory much less attractive for holding the atoms. Since thread blocks will be accessing different neighborhoods, the limited-size constant memory will unlikely be able to hold all the atoms that are needed by all active thread blocks. This motivates the use of global memory to hold a much larger set of atoms. To mitigate the bandwidth consumption, threads in a block collaborate in loading the atom information in the common neighborhood into the shared memory. All threads then examine the atoms out of shared memory. The reader is referred to Rodrigues et al. [RSH 2008] for more details of this algorithm.

One subtle issue with binning is that bins may end up with different numbers of atoms. Since the atoms are statistically distributed in space, some bins may have lots of atoms and some bins may end up with no atom at all. In order to guarantee memory coalescing, it is important that all bins are of the same size and aligned at appropriate coalescing boundaries. In order to accommodate the bins with the largest number of atoms, we would need to make the size of all other bins the same size. This would require us to fill many bins with dummy atoms whose electrical charge is 0, which causes two negative effects. First, the dummy atoms still occupy global memory and shared memory storage. They also consume data transfer bandwidth to the device. Second, the dummy atoms extend the execution time of the thread blocks whose bins have few real atoms.

A well-known solution is to set the bin size at a reasonable level, typically much smaller than the largest possible number of atoms in a bin. The binning process maintains an overflow list. When processing an atom, if the atom's home bin is full, the atom is added to the overflow list instead. After the device completes a kernel, the result grid point energy values are transferred back to the host. The host executes a sequential cutoff algorithm on the atoms in the overflow list to complete the missing contributions from these overflow atoms. As long as the overflow atoms account for only a small percentage of the atoms, the additional sequential processing time of the overflow atoms is typically shorter than that of the device execution time. One can also design the kernel so that each kernel invocation calculates the energy values for a subvolume of grid points. After each kernel completes, the host launches the next kernel and processes the overflow atoms for the completed kernel. Thus, the host will be processing the overflow atoms while the device executes the next kernel. This

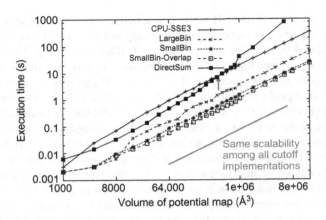

FIGURE 17.4

Scalability and performance of different algorithms for calculating electrostatic potential map.

approach can hide most, if not all, the delays in processing overflow atoms since it is done in parallel with the execution of the next kernel.

Fig. 17.4 shows a comparison of scalability and performance of the various electrostatic potential map algorithms. Note that the CPU–SSE3 curve is based on a sequential cutoff algorithm. For a map with small volumes, around 1000Å^3 the host (CPU with SSE) executes faster than the DCS kernel shown in Fig. 17.4. This is because there is not enough work to fully utilize a CUDA device for such a small volume. However, for moderate volumes, between 2000Å^3 and $500,000\text{Å}^3$, the Direct Summation kernel performs significantly better than the host due to its massive parallelism. As we anticipated, the Direct Summation kernel scales poorly when the volume size reaches about $1,000,000\text{Å}^3$, and runs longer than the sequential algorithm on the CPU! This is due to the fact that the algorithm complexity of the DCS kernel is higher than the sequential cut-off algorithm and thus the amount of work done by kernel grows much faster than that done by the sequential algorithm. For volume size larger than 1,000,000, the amount of work is so large that it swamps the hardware execution resources.

Fig. 17.4 also shows the running time of three binned cutoff algorithms. The LargeBin algorithm is a straightforward adaptation of the DCS kernel for cutoff. The kernel is designed to process a sub-volume of the grid points. Before each kernel launch, the CPU transfers all atoms that are in the combined neighborhood of all the grid points in the sub-volume. These atoms are still stored in the constant memory. All threads examine all atoms in the joint neighborhood. The advantage of the kernel is its simplicity. It is essentially the same as the Direct Summation kernel with a relatively large, pre-selected neighborhood of atoms. Note that the LargeBin approach performs reasonably well for moderate volumes and scales well for large volumes.

The `SmallBin` algorithm allows the threads running within the same kernel to process different neighborhoods of atoms. This is the algorithm that uses global memory and shared memory for storing atoms. The algorithm achieves higher efficiency than the `LargeBin` algorithm because each thread needs to examine a smaller number of atoms. For moderate volumes, around $8000\,\text{Å}^3$, the `LargeBin` algorithm slightly outperforms `SmallBin`. The reason is that the `SmallBin` algorithm does incur more instruction overhead for loading atoms from global memory into shared memory. For a moderate volume, there is limited number of atoms in the entire system. The ability to examine a smaller number of atoms does not provide sufficient advantage to overcome the additional instruction overhead. However, the difference is so small at $8000\,\text{Å}^3$ that the `SmallBin` algorithm is still a clear win across all volume sizes. The `SmallBin-Overlap` algorithm overlaps the sequential overflow atom processing with the next kernel execution. It provides a slight but noticeable improvement in running time over `SmallBin`. The `SmallBin-Overlap` algorithm achieves a 17× speedup an efficiently implemented sequential CPU–SSE cutoff algorithm and maintains the same scalability for large volumes.

17.4 COMPUTATIONAL THINKING

Computational *thinking* is arguably the most important aspect of parallel application development [Wing 2006]. We define computational thinking as the thought process of formulating domain problems in terms of computation steps and algorithms. Like any other thought processes and problem-solving skill, computational thinking is an art. As we mentioned in Chapter 1, Introduction, we believe that computational thinking is best taught with an iterative approach where students bounce back and forth between practical experience and abstract concepts.

The electrostatic potential map kernels used in Chapter 15, Application case study—molecular visualization and analysis, and this chapter serve as good examples of computational thinking. In order to develop an efficient parallel application that solves the electrostatic potential map problem, one must come up with a good high-level decomposition of the problem. As we showed in Section 17.2, one must have a clear understanding of the desirable (e.g., gather in CUDA) and undesirable (e.g., scatter in CUDA) memory access behaviors to make a wise decision.

Given a problem decomposition, parallel programmers face a potentially overwhelming task of designing algorithms to overcome major challenges in parallelism, execution efficiency, and memory bandwidth consumption. There is a very large volume of literature on a wide range of algorithm techniques that can be hard to understand. It is beyond the scope of this book to have a comprehensive coverage of the available techniques. We did discuss a substantial set of techniques that have broad applicability. While these techniques are based on CUDA, they help the readers build up the foundation for computational thinking in general. We believe that humans understand best when we learn from the bottom up. That is, we first learn the concepts in the context of a particular programming model, which provide us with solid footing before we generalize our knowledge to other programming models. An in-depth experience with the CUDA model also enables us to gain maturity, which will help us learn concepts that may not even be pertinent to the CUDA model.

There is a myriad of skills needed for a parallel programmer to be an effective computational thinker. We summarize these foundational skills as follows:

- Computer architecture: memory organization, caching and locality, memory bandwidth, Single Instruction, Multiple Thread (SIMT) vs Single Program, Multiple Data (SPMD) vs. Single Instruction, Multiple Data (SIMD) execution, and floating-point precision vs. accuracy. These concepts are critical in understanding the tradeoffs between algorithms.
- Programming models and compilers: parallel execution models, types of available memories, array data layout, and thread granularity transformation. These concepts are needed for thinking through the arrangements of data structures and loop structures to achieve better performance.
- Algorithm techniques: tiling, cutoff, scatter-gather, binning, and others. These techniques form the toolbox for designing superior parallel algorithms. Understanding of the scalability, efficiency, and memory bandwidth implications of these techniques is essential in computational thinking.
- Domain knowledge: numerical methods, precision, accuracy, and numerical stability. Understanding these ground rules allows a developer to be much more creative in applying algorithm techniques.

Our goal for this book is to provide a solid foundation for all the four areas. The reader should continue to broaden his/her knowledge in these areas after finishing this book. Most importantly, the best way of building up more computational thinking skills is to keep solving challenging problems with excellent computational solutions.

17.5 SINGLE PROGRAM, MULTIPLE DATA, SHARED MEMORY AND LOCALITY

At this point, it is worth saying a few words about some different parallel programming models, specifically Shared Memory vs. Message Passing. You may be familiar with these concepts from other studies, or you may encounter them later. We have focused on shared memory parallel programming, because this is what CUDA (and OpenMP, OpenCL) is based on. Also, most if not all future massively parallel microprocessors are expected to support shared memory at the chip level. The programming considerations of the message passing model are quite different; however, you will find similar concepts for almost every technique you learned in parallel programming.

In either case, you will need to be aware of space-time constraints. Data locality (or lack thereof) in time of access/use and data locality in access patterns can have profound effects on performance. Data sharing, whether intentional or not, can be a double-edged sword. Excessive data sharing can drastically reduce the performance advantages of parallel execution, so it is important not to overshare. Localized sharing can improve memory bandwidth efficiency without creating conflicts and contention. Efficient memory bandwidth usage can be achieved by synchronizing the execution of task groups and coordinating their usage of memory and data. Also important is efficient use of on-chip, shared storage and datapaths. Read-only sharing can usually be done at much higher efficiency than read-write sharing, which often requires more synchronization.

You can think of sharing as appearing in one of four modes: Many:Many, One:Many, Many:One, or One:One. This is true for both data sharing, and synchronization. You may think of synchronization as "control sharing." An example is barriers—barriers may cause some threads to wait until other threads catch up. This may be good in that execution is aligned, but it is also bad in that waiting is a lost opportunity for work. Atomic operations may reduce waiting, but perhaps at the cost of serialization. It is important to be aware of which work items are truly independent and not introduce false/unnecessary synchronizations into your program.

Program models and data organization drive parallel programming coding styles. One very important program model is SPMD. In this model, all PEs (processor elements) execute the same program in parallel, but program instance has its own unique data. Consequently, each PE uses a unique ID to access its portion of data, but each different PE can follow different paths through the same code. This is essentially the CUDA Grid model (also OpenCL, MPI). SIMD is a special case of SPMD where the threads move in lock-step—in CUDA execution, SIMD WARPs are used for efficiency.

SPMD programming also drives algorithm structures and coding styles. Due to the prevalence of massively parallel processors, this is currently the dominant coding style of scalable parallel computing. MPI code is mostly developed in SPMD style, so it is often used for parallel programming in multicore CPUs as well. Many OpenMP codes are also created in SPMD style, or utilize loop parallelism. This style is particularly suitable for algorithms based on task parallelism and geometric decomposition. A powerful advantage of this approach is that tasks and their interactions are visible in one piece of source code, and there is no need to correlate multiple sources and algorithm fragments to understand what is going on.

Many SPMD programs look similar, as almost all SPMD programs have the same typical program phases. These are:

1. Initialize—establish localized data structure and communication channels.
2. Uniquify—each thread acquires a unique identifier, typically ranging from 0 to N-1, where N is the number of threads. Both OpenMP and CUDA have built-in support for this.
3. Distribute data—decompose global data into chunks and localize them, or sharing/replicating major data structures using thread IDs to associate subsets of the data to threads.
4. Compute—run the core computation! Thread IDs are used to differentiate the behavior of individual threads. Use thread ID in loop index calculations to split loop iterations among threads—beware of the potential for memory/data

divergence. Use thread ID or conditions based on thread ID to branch to their specific actions—beware of the potential for instruction/execution divergence.

5. Finalize—reconcile global data structure, and prepare for the next major iteration or group of program phases.

You will see this pattern a myriad of times in your journeys through parallel programing, and it will become second nature for you to organize the solution of your problem in this fashion.

17.6 STRATEGIES FOR COMPUTATIONAL THINKING

A good goal for effective use of computing is making science better, not just faster. This requires re-examining prior assumptions and really thinking about how to apply the big hammer of massively parallel processing. Put another way, there will probably be no Nobel Prizes or Turing Awards awarded for "just recompile" or using more threads with the same computational approach! Truly important scientific discoveries will more likely come from fresh computational thinking. Consider this an exhortation to use this bonanza of computing power to solve new problems in new ways.

As a strategy for attacking computation-hungry applications, we can consider a three-step approach:

1. Tune core software for hardware architecture.
2. Innovate at the algorithm level.
3. Restructure the mathematical formulation.

This breakdown leads to three options, in increasing order of difficulty, complexity, and not surprisingly, potential for payoff. Let us call these good, better, and best! The "good" approach is simply to "accelerate" legacy program codes. The most basic approach is simply to recompile and run on a new platform or architecture, without adding any domain insight or expertise in parallelism. This approach can be improved by using optimized libraries, tools, or directives, such as CuBLAS, CuFFT, Thrust, Matlab, OpenACC, etc. This is very good and rewarding work for domain scientists—minimal Computer Science knowledge or programming skills are required. We can categorize this approach as only choosing to attack part of step 3 above.

The "better" approach involves rewriting existing codes using new parallelism skills to take advantage of new architectures, or creating new codes from scratch. We can benefit from new algorithmic techniques to increase execution efficiency. This is an opportunity for clever algorithmic thinking, and is good work for nondomain computer scientists, as minimal domain knowledge is required. We can categorize this approach as choosing only to attack part of step 2 above.

The "best" approach involves more deep and careful thought and a holistic approach involving all three steps above. We wish to not only map a known algorithm and computation to a parallel program and architecture, but also rethink the numerical methods and algorithms used in the solution. In this approach, there is the potential for the biggest performance advantage and fundamental new discoveries and capabilities. It is, however, also much more difficult. This approach is interdisciplinary and requires both Computer Science *and* domain insight, but the payoff is worth the effort. It is truly an exciting time to be a computational scientist!

The order of operations should be: Think, Understand… and then and only then, Program.

First, think deeply about the problem you are trying to solve, and truly understand the overall structure of the problem. Apply mathematical techniques to find a solution to your problem, and then map the mathematical technique to an algorithmic approach for computational solution.

Plan the structure of computation in detail. Be aware of in/dependence, interactions, and bottlenecks, and plan the work phases accordingly. Plan the organization of data, both for input and output, as well as during the computation phases. Be explicitly aware of locality, opportunities for data sharing or privatization, and minimize global data access and movement. Finally, write some code! This is the easy part ☺—all of the hard work has been done in the planning stage.

Of course this description is an oversimplification and many other techniques and considerations are left for future studies. We could explore more complex data structures, more scalable algorithms and building blocks, or more scalable or hierarchical mathematical models. We can also consider thread-aware approaches to capitalize on more available parallelism. There will also be great opportunities in locality-aware approaches, since computing is becoming bigger, and everything is becoming further away both in space and time. All of these are beyond the scope of this book, but we encourage you to pursue them.

17.7 A HYPOTHETICAL EXAMPLE: SODIUM MAP OF THE BRAIN

Let us provide a hypothetical example of rethinking a well-known and well-solved problem—MRI. We have discussed this problem in detail in previous chapters, and have described many aspects of how to use parallel computing to efficiently convert the frequency samples from the MRI device into spatial information. We will start with a worthy goal: creating 3D images of sodium in the brain, using MRI. Normally, MRI images the density of water in human tissue, as measured by the resonance of hydrogen atoms. The density of water provides imaging of anatomy—what kind of tissue exists in the 3D volume. Why is sodium imaging desirable? First, sodium is one of the most regulated substances in human tissues—any significant shift in sodium concentration signals cell death. Real-time measurement of sodium density would enable study of brain-cell viability before anatomic changes occur as a result of stroke and cancer treatment. This would provide a drastic improvement in timeliness of treatment decisions. We would be able to determine if treatment is effective within critical minutes for stroke and days for oncology, saving and improving the quality of many lives. Fig. 17.5 shows what this might look like.

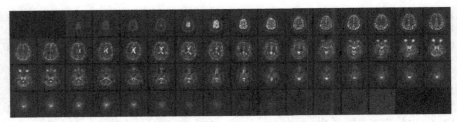

FIGURE 17.5

Sodium images of the brain. Courtesy of Keith Thulborn and Ian Atkinson, Center for MR Research, University of Illinois at Chicago.

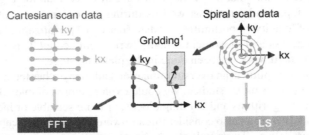

Spiral scan data + gridding + FFT:
fast scan, fast reconstruction, good images
can become realtime with about 10X speedup.

[1]Based on Fig 1 of Lustig et al. Fast Spiral Fourier Transfor for Iterative
MR Image Reconstruction, IEEE Int'l Symp. on Biomedical Imaging, 2004

FIGURE 17.6

Classical gridded MRI reconstruction from spiral scan data.

So, why is sodium imaging difficult? Unfortunately, sodium is much less abundant than water in human tissues, about 1/2000 the concentration. In addition, the magnetic resonance echo of sodium is much less strong than the echo from hydrogen/water. Thus, a very, very much larger number of samples would be required for good signal-to-noise ratio in the MRI. Another possible approach would be to choose mathematical techniques and algorithms for much higher quality signal reconstruction. This approach has been considered impractical due to the massive computation required. However, it is time to re-examine those assumptions. When MRI was first developed, computers were much slower, and MRI reconstruction required a long time on a roomful of computing equipment. Conventional MRI reconstruction is now real-time using desk-side hardware.

Non-Cartesian trajectories, such as the spiral trajectory shown here in Fig. 17.6, are becoming increasingly popular and common. These non-Cartesian scans are faster and less susceptible to artifacts than Cartesian scans. The spiral scan pattern is also a more efficient use of time on the MRI machine.

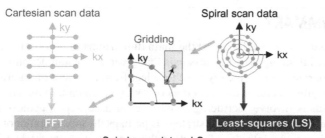

Cartesian scan data

Spiral scan data

Gridding

FFT

Least-squares (LS)

Spiral scan data + LS
Superior images at expense of significantly more computation;
several hundred times slower than gridding.
Traditionally considered impractical!

FIGURE 17.7

Least squares reconstruction of spiral scan data.

However, the FFT cannot be applied directly to the non-Cartesian scan data. One popular approach is to "grid" the data. That is, the non-Cartesian data (shown in orange (light gray in the print versions)) is interpolated onto a uniform grid (shown in blue (dark gray in the print versions)) using some sort of windowing function. The FFT can then be applied to the interpolated data. This technique introduces inaccuracies and satisfies no statistical optimality criterion, but is very fast and does produce better images than a Cartesian scan.

This is similar to the old joke about a man who has lost his keys in a dark corner of a parking lot. He is discovered looking for his keys under the streetlight. When asked why he is looking for his keys there instead of where he lost them, the reply is "because the light is better here!" While it may have been true that the gridding and FFT solution was a good choice for MRI processing at first, this is likely no longer the case.

Least-squares (LS) iterative reconstruction is a superior technique that operates directly on the nonuniform data using the LS optimality criterion. The combination of a non-Cartesian scan and the LS reconstruction produces images far superior to those obtained via Cartesian scans or gridding. Unfortunately, these superior images come at the expense of increasing the amount of computation by several orders of magnitude. For the LS reconstruction to be practical in clinical settings, it must be accelerated by a similar number of orders of magnitude.

Again, this is what we mean when we say that the GPU allows us to change the boundaries of science. The LS reconstruction algorithm isn't viable on the CPU. It's the GPU that makes the LS reconstruction practical, so that we don't have to use lossy and approximate techniques like gridding, just so that we can warp the problem into a convenient computational framework such as FFT (Fig 17.7).

Instead of simply applying brute force to the much harder problem of sodium imaging using MRI, we have achieved much more by re-examining the foundations of MRI and the related computations.

17.8 SUMMARY

In summary, we have discussed the main dimensions of algorithm selection and computational thinking. The key lesson is that given a problem decomposition decision, the programer will typically have to select from a variety of algorithms. Some of these algorithms achieve different tradeoffs while maintaining the same numerical accuracy. Others involve sacrificing some level of accuracy to achieve much more scalable running times. The cutoff strategy is perhaps the most popular of such strategies. Even though we introduced cutoff in the context of electrostatic potential map calculation, it is used in many domains including ray tracing in graphics and collision detection in games. Computational thinking skills allow an algorithm designer to work around the roadblocks and reach a good solution.

17.9 EXERCISES

1. Write a host function to perform binning of atoms. Determine the representation of the bins as arrays. Think about coalescing requirements. Make sure that every thread can easily find the bins it needs to process.

2. Write the part of the cut-off kernel function that determines if an atom is in the neighborhood of a grid point based on the coordinates of the atoms and the grid points.

3. Think about refactoring to change the organization of work. Take a scatter-gather kernel, and rewrite as scatter-scatter, or gather-gather, to improve locality. Which is better for CUDA execution?

REFERENCES

Message Passing Interface Forum. (2009). *MPI—a message passing interface standard version 2.2.* <http://www.mpi-forum.org/docs/mpi-2.2/mpi22-report.pdf> Accessed 04.09.2009.
Rodrigues, C. I., Stone, J., Hardy, D., & Hwu, W. W. (2008). GPU acceleration of cutoff-based potential summation. In: *ACM computing frontier conference 2008*, Italy, May.
Wing, J. (March 2006). Computational thinking. *Communications of the ACM, 49*(3), 33–35.

Programming a heterogeneous computing cluster

18

Isaac Gelado and Javier Cabezas

CHAPTER OUTLINE

So far, we have focused on programming a heterogeneous computing system with one host and one device. In high-performance computing (HPC), applications require the aggregate computing power of a cluster of computing nodes. Many of the HPC clusters today have one or more hosts and one or more devices in each node. Historically, these clusters have been programmed predominately with message passing interface (MPI). In this chapter, we will present an introduction to joint MPI/CUDA Programming. The reader should be able to easily extend the material to joint MPI/OpenCL, MPI/OpenACC, and so on. We will only present the MPI concepts that programmers need to understand in order to scale their heterogeneous applications to multiple nodes in a cluster environment. In particular, we will focus on domain partitioning, point-to-point communication, and collective communication in the context of scaling a CUDA kernel into multiple nodes.

Programming Massively Parallel Processors. DOI: http://dx.doi.org/10.1016/B978-0-12-811986-0.00018-2

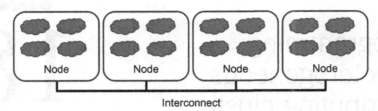

FIGURE 18.1

Programer's view of MPI processes.

18.1 BACKGROUND

While there was practically no top supercomputer using GPUs before 2009, the need for better energy efficiency has led to fast adoption of GPUs in the recent years. Many of the top supercomputers in the world today use both CPUs and GPUs in each node. The effectiveness of this approach is validated by their high rankings in the Green500 list, which reflects their high energy efficiency.

The dominating programing interface for computing clusters today is MPI [Gropp 1999], which is a set of API functions for communication between processes running in a computing cluster. MPI assumes a distributed memory model where processes exchange information by sending messages to each other. When an application uses API communication functions, it does not need to deal with the details of the interconnect network. The MPI implementation allows the processes to address each other using logical numbers, much the same way as using phone numbers in a telephone system: telephone users can dial each other using phone numbers without knowing exactly where the called person is and how the call is routed.

In a typical MPI application, data and work are partitioned among processes. As shown in Fig. 18.1, each node can contain one or more processes, shown as clouds within nodes. As these processes progress, they may need data from each other. This need is satisfied by sending and receiving messages. In some cases, the processes also need to synchronize with each other and generate collective results when collaborating on a large task. This is done with MPI's collective API functions.

18.2 A RUNNING EXAMPLE

We will use a 3D stencil computation similar to that introduced in Chapter 7, Parallel patterns: convolution, as a running example. We assume that the computation calculates heat transfer based on a finite difference method for solving a partial differential equation that describes the physical laws of heat transfer. In particular, we will use the Jacobi Iterative Method where in each iteration or time step, the value of a grid point is calculated as a weighted sum of neighbors (north, east, south, west, up, down) and

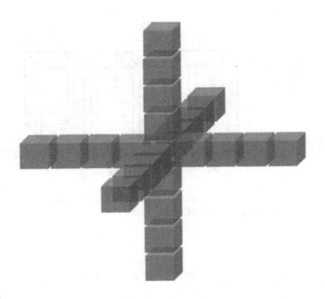

FIGURE 18.2

A 25-stencil computation example, with neighbors in the *x*, *y*, *z* directions.

its own value from the previous time step. In order to achieve high numerical stability, multiple indirect neighbors in each direction are also used in the computation of a grid point. This is referred to as a *higher order stencil* computation. For the purpose of this chapter, we assume that four points in each direction will be used.

As shown in Fig. 18.2, there are a total of 24 neighbor points for calculating the next step value of a grid point. In Fig. 18.2, each point in the grid has an x, y, and z coordinate. For a grid point where the coordinate value is $x = i$, $y = j$, and $z = k$, or (i,j,k) its 24 neighbors are $(i-4,j,k)$, $(i-3,j,k)$, $(i-2,j,k)$, $(i-1,j,k)$, $(i+1,j,k)$, $(i+2,j,k)$, $(i+3,j,k)$, $(i+4,j,k)$, $(i,j-4,k)$, $(i,j-3,k)$, $(i,j-2,k)$, $(i,j-1,k)$, $(i,j+1,k)$, $(i,j+2,k)$, $(i,j+3,k)$, $(i,j+4,k)$, $(i,j,k-4)$, $(i,j,k-3)$, $(i,j,k-2)$, $(i,j,k-1)$, $(i,j,k+1)$, $(i,j,k+2)$, $(i,j,k+3)$ and $(i,j,k+4)$. Since the data value of each grid point for the next time step is calculated based on the current data values of 25 points (24 neighbors and itself), the type of computation is often called 25-stencil computation.

We assume that the system is modeled as a structured grid, where spacing between grid points is constant within each direction. This allows us to use a 3D array where each element stores the state of a grid point. The physical distance between adjacent elements in each dimension can be represented by a spacing variable. Note that this grid data structure is similar to that used in the electrostatic potential calculation in Chapter 15, Application case study—molecular visualization and analysis. Fig. 18.3 illustrates a 3D array that represents a rectangular ventilation duct, with x and y dimensions as the cross-sections of the duct and the z dimension the direction of the heat flow along the duct.

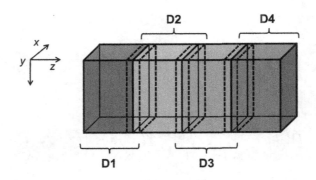

FIGURE 18.3

3D grid array for the modeling heat transfer in a duct.

D ↓	$z=0$ $y=0$	$z=0$ $y=1$	$z=1$ $y=0$	$z=1$ $y=1$	$z=2$ $y=0$	$z=2$ $y=1$	$z=3$ $y=0$	$z=3$ $y=1$
	$x=0$ $x=1$	$x=0$ $x=1$	$x=0$ $x=1$	$x=0$ $x=1$	$x=0$ $x=1$	$x=0$ $x=1$	$x=0$ $x=1$	$x=0$ $x=1$

FIGURE 18.4

A small example of memory layout for the 3D grid.

We assume that the data is laid out in the memory space so that x is the lowest dimension, y is the next, and z is the highest. That is, all elements with $y=0$ and $z=0$ will be placed in consecutive memory locations according to their x coordinate. Fig. 18.4 shows a small example of the grid data layout. This small example has only 16 data elements in the grid: two elements in the x dimension, two in the y dimension, and four in the z dimension. Both x elements with $y=0$ and $z=0$ are placed in memory first. They are followed by all elements with $y=1$ and $z=0$. The next group will be elements with $y=0$ and $z=1$. The reader should verify that this is simply a 3D generalization of the row-major layout convention of C/C++ discussed in Chapter 3, Scalable parallel execution.

When one uses a computing cluster, it is common to divide the input data into several partitions, called domain partitions, and assign each partition to a node in the cluster. In Fig. 18.3, we show that the 3D array is divided into four domain partitions: D1, D2, D3, and D4. Each of the partitions will be assigned to an MPI compute process.

The domain partitions can be further illustrated with Fig. 18.4. The first section, or slice, of four elements ($z=0$) in Fig. 18.4 are in the first partition, the second section ($z=1$) the second partition, the third section ($z=2$) the third partition, and the fourth section ($z=3$) the fourth partition. This is obviously a toy example. In a real application, there are typically hundreds or even thousands of elements in each dimension. For the rest of this chapter, it is useful to remember that all elements in a z slice are in consecutive memory locations.

18.3 MESSAGE PASSING INTERFACE BASICS

Like CUDA, MPI programs are based on the SPMD parallel execution model. All MPI processes execute the same program. The MPI system provides a set of API functions to establish communication systems that allow the processes to communicate with each other. Fig. 18.5 shows five essential MPI functions that set up and tear down the communication system for an MPI application. We will use a simple MPI program shown in Fig. 18.6 to illustrate the usage of these API functions. To launch an MPI application in a cluster, a user needs to supply the executable file of the program to the *mpirun* command or the *mpiexec* command in a cluster.

Each process starts by initializing the MPI runtime with an `MPI_Init()` call. This initializes the communication system for all the processes running the application. Once the MPI runtime is initialized, each process calls two functions to prepare for communication. The first function is `MPI_Comm_rank()` that returns a unique number to calling each process, which is called the *MPI rank* or process id for the process. The numbers received by the processes vary from 0 to the number of processes − 1. An MPI rank for a process is equivalent to the expression `blockIdx.x*blockDim.x+threadIdx.x` for a CUDA thread. It uniquely identifies the process in a communication, similar to the phone number in a telephone system.

The `MPI_Comm_rank()` function takes two parameters. The first one is an MPI built-in type `MPI_Comm` that specifies the scope of the request. Each variable of the `MPI_Comm` type is commonly referred to as a communicator. `MPI_Comm` and other MPI built-in types are defined in "`mpi.h`" header file that should be included in all C program files that use MPI. This is similar to the "`cuda.h`" header file for CUDA programs. An MPI application can create one or more *communicators* each of which is a group of MPI processes for the purpose of communication. `MPI_Comm_rank()` assigns a unique id to each process in a communicator. In Fig. 18.6, the parameter value passed is `MPI_COMM_WORLD`, which means that the communicator includes all MPI processes running the application.[1]

- int **MPI_Init** (int*argc, char***argv)
  - Initialize MPI
- int **MPI_Comm_rank** (MPI_Comm **comm**, int *rank)
  - Rank of the calling process in group of comm
- int **MPI_Comm_size** (MPI_Comm **comm**, int *size)
  - Number of processes in the group of comm
- int **MPI_Comm_abort** (MPI_Comm **comm**)
  - Terminate MPI comminication connection with an error flag
- int **MPI_Finalize** ( )
  - Ending an MPI application, close all resources

FIGURE 18.5

Five basic MPI functions for establishing and closing a communication system.

---

[1] Interested readers should refer to the MPI reference manual [Gropp 1999] for details on creating and using multiple communicators in an application, in particular the definition and use of intracommunicators and intercommunicators.

```
#include "mpi.h"

int main(int argc, char *argv[]) {
    int pad = 0, dimx = 480+pad, dimy = 480, dimz = 400, nreps = 100;
    int pid=-1, np=-1;

    MPI_Init(&argc, &argv);
    MPI_Comm_rank(MPI_COMM_WORLD, &pid);
    MPI_Comm_size(MPI_COMM_WORLD, &np);

    if(np < 3) {
        if(0 == pid) printf("Needed 3 or more processes.\n");
        MPI_Abort( MPI_COMM_WORLD, 1 ); return 1;
    }
    if(pid < np - 1)
        compute_process(dimx, dimy, dimz/ (np - 1), nreps);
    else
        data_server( dimx,dimy,dimz, nreps);

    MPI_Finalize();
    return 0;
}
```

FIGURE 18.6

A simple MPI main program.

The second parameter to the `MPI_Comm_rank()` function is a pointer to an integer variable into which the function will deposit the returned rank value. In Fig. 18.6, a variable `pid` is declared for this purpose. After the `MPI_Comm_rank()` returns, the `pid` variable will contain the unique id for the calling process.

The second API function is `MPI_Comm_size()`, which returns the total number of MPI processes running in the communicator. The `MPI_Comm_size()` function takes two parameters. The first one is of `MPI_Comm` type and gives the scope of the request. In Fig. 18.6, the parameter value passed in is `MPI_COMM_WORLD`, which means the scope of the `MPI_Comm_size()` is all the processes of the application. Since the scope is all MPI processes, the returned value is the total number of MPI processes running the application. This is a value requested by a user when the application is submitted using the mpirun command or the mpiexec command. However, the user may not have requested sufficient number of processes. Also, the system may or may not be able to create all the processes requested. Therefore, it is a good practice for an MPI application program to check the actual number of processes running.

The second parameter is a pointer to an integer variable into which the `MPI_Comm_size()` function will deposit the return value. In Fig. 18.6, a variable `np` is declared for this purpose. After the function returns, the variable `np` contains the number of MPI processes running the application. We assume that the application requires at least three MPI processes. Therefore, it checks if the number of processes is at least three. If not, it calls `MPI_Comm_abort()` function to terminate the communication connections and return with an error flag value 1.

Fig. 18.6 also shows a common pattern for reporting errors or other chores. There are multiple MPI processes but we need to report the error only once. The application code designates the process with `pid=0` to do the reporting. This is similar to the pattern in CUDA kernels where some tasks only need to be done by one of the threads in a thread-block.

As shown in Fig. 18.5, the `MPI_Comm_abort()` function takes two parameters. The first sets the scope of the request. In Fig. 18.6, the scope is set as `MPI_COMM_WORLD`, which means all MPI processes running the application. The second parameter is a code for the type of error that caused the abort. Any number other than 0 indicates that an error has happened.

If the number of processes satisfies the requirement, the application program goes on to perform the calculation. In Fig. 18.6, the application uses `np-1` processes (`pid` from 0 to `np-2`) to perform the calculation and one process (the last one whose `pid` is `np-1`) to perform I/O service for the other processes. We will refer to the process that performs the I/O services as the data server and the processes that perform the calculation as compute processes. If the `pid` of a process is within the range from 0 to `np-2`, it is a compute process and call the `compute_process()` function. If the process `pid` is `np-1`, it is the data server and calls `data_server()` function. This is similar to the pattern where threads perform different actions according to their thread ids.

After the application completes its computation, it notifies the MPI runtime with a call to the `MPI_Finalize()`, which frees all MPI communication resources allocated to the application. The application can then exit with a return value 0, which indicates that no error occurred.

18.4 MESSAGE PASSING INTERFACE POINT-TO-POINT COMMUNICATION

MPI supports two major types of communication. The first is point-to-point type, which involves one source process and one destination process. The source process calls the `MPI_Send()` function and the destination process calls the `MPI_Recv()` function. This is analogous to a caller dialing a call and a receiver answering a call in a telephone system.

Fig. 18.7 shows the syntax for using the `MPI_Send()` function. The first parameter is a pointer to the starting location of the memory area where the data to be sent can be found. The second parameter is an integer that gives that number of data elements to be sent. The third parameter is of an MPI built-in type `MPI_Datatype`. It specifies the type of each data element being sent. The `MPI_Datatype` is defined in `mpi.h` and includes `MPI_DOUBLE` (double precision floating point), `MPI_FLOAT`(single precision floating point), `MPI_INT` (integer), and `MPI_CHAR` (character). The exact sizes of these types depend on the size of the corresponding C types in the host processor. See the MPI reference manual for more sophisticated use of MPI types [Gropp 1999].

- int **MPI_Send** (void ***buf**, int **count**,
  MPI_Datatype **datatype**, int **dest**, int **tag**,
  MPI_Comm **comm)**
  - Buf: **starting address of send buffer (pointer)**
  - Count: **Number of elements in send buffer (nonnegative integer)**
  - Datatype: **Datatype of each send buffer element (MPI_Datatype)**
  - Dest: **Rank of destination (integer)**
  - Tag: **Message tag (integer)**
  - Comm: **Communicator (handle)**

FIGURE 18.7

Syntax for the MPI_Send() function.

- int **MPI_Recv** (void ***buf**, int **count**,
  MPI_Datatype **datatype**, int **source**, int **tag**,
  MPI_Comm **comm**, MPI_Status ***status)**
  - buf: **starting address of receive buffer (pointer)**
  - Count: **Maximum number of elements in receive buffer (integer)**
  - Datatype: **Datatype of each receive buffer element (MPI_Datatype)**
  - Source: **Rank of source (integer)**
  - Tag: **Message tag (integer)**
  - Comm: **Communicator (handle)**
  - Status: **Status object (Status)**

FIGURE 18.8

Syntax for the MPI_Recv() function.

The fourth parameter for MPI_Send is an integer that gives the MPI rank of the destination process. The fifth parameter gives a tag that can be used to classify the messages sent by the same process. The sixth parameter is a communicator that selects the processes to be considered in the communication.

Fig. 18.8 shows the syntax for using the MPI_Recv() function. The first parameter is a pointer to the area in memory where the received data should be deposited. The second parameter is an integer that gives the maximal number of elements that the MPI_Recv() function is allowed to receive. The third parameter is an MPI_Datatype that specifies the type (size) of each element to be received. The fourth parameter is an integer that gives the process id of the source of the message.

The fifth parameter is an integer that specifies the particular tag value expected by the destination process. If the destination process does not want to be limited to a particular tag value, it can use MPI_ANY_TAG, which means that the receiver is willing to accept messages of any tag value from the source.

We will first use the data server to illustrate the use of point-to-point communication. In a real application, the data server process would typically perform data input

```
void data_server(int dimx, int dimy, int dimz, int nreps) {
1.    int np,
      /* Set MPI Communication Size */
2.    MPI_Comm_size(MPI_COMM_WORLD, &np);

3.    num_comp_nodes = np - 1, first_node = 0, last_node = np - 2;
4.    unsigned int num_points = dimx * dimy * dimz;
5.    unsigned int num_bytes = num_points * sizeof(float);
6.    float *input=0, *output=0;
      /* Allocate input data */
7.    input = (float *)malloc(num_bytes);
8.    output = (float *)malloc(num_bytes);
9.    if(input == NULL || output == NULL) {
          printf("server couldn't allocate memory\n");
          MPI_Abort( MPI_COMM_WORLD, 1 );
      }
      /* Initialize input data */
10.   random_data(input, dimx, dimy ,dimz , 1, 10);
      /* Calculate number of shared points */
11.   int edge_num_points = dimx * dimy * ((dimz / num_comp_nodes) +
      4);
12.   int int_num_points  = dimx * dimy * ((dimz / num_comp_nodes) +
      8);
13.   float *send_address = input;
```

FIGURE 18.9

Data server process code (Part 1).

and output operations for the compute processes. However, input and output have too much system dependent complexity. Since I/O is not the focus of our discussion, we will avoid the complexity of I/O operations in a cluster environment. That is, instead of reading data from a file system, we will just have the data server to initialize the data with random numbers and distribute the data to the compute processes. The first part of the data server code is shown in Fig. 18.9.

The data server function takes four parameters. The first three parameters specify the size of the 3D grid: number of elements in the x dimension dimx, the number of elements in the y dimension dimy, and the number of elements in the z dimension dimz. The fourth parameter specifies the number of iterations that need to be done for all the data points in the grid.

In Fig. 18.9, Line 1 declares variable np that will contain the number of processes running the application. Line 2 calls MPI_Comm_size(), which will deposit the information into np. Line 3 declares and initializes several helper variables. The variable num_comp_procs contains the number of compute processes. Since we are reserving one process as data server, there are np-1 compute processes. The variable first_node gives the process id of the first compute process, which is 0. The variable last_node gives the process id of the last compute process, which is np-2. That is, Line 3 designates the first np-1 processes, 0 through np-2 as compute processes. This reflects the design decision and the process with the largest rank serves as the data server. This decision will also be reflected in the compute process code.

Line 4 declares and initializes the `num_points` variable that gives the total number of grid data points to be processed, which is simply the product of the number of elements in each dimension, or `dimx * dimy * dimz`. Line 5 declares and initializes the `num_bytes` variable that gives the total number of bytes needed to store all the grid data points. Since each grid data point is a float, this value is `num_points * sizeof(float)`.

Line 6 declares two pointer variables: `input` and `output`. These two pointers will point to the input data buffer and the output data buffer. Lines 7 and 8 allocate memory for the input and output buffers and assign their addresses to their respective pointers. Line 9 checks if the memory allocations were successful. If either of the memory allocation fails, the corresponding pointer will receive a NULL pointer from the `malloc()` function. In this case, the code aborts the application and reports an error.

Lines 11 and 12 calculate the number of grid point array elements that should be sent to each compute process. As shown in Fig. 18.3, there are two types of compute processes. The first process (Process 0) and the last process (Process 3) compute an "edge" partition that has neighbors only on one side. Partition D1 assigned to the first process has neighbor only on the right side (partition D2). Partition D4 assigned to the last process has neighbor only on the left side (partition D3). We call the compute processes that compute edge partitions the *edge processes*.

Each of the rest of the processes computes an internal partition that has neighbors on both sizes. For example, the second process (Process 1) computes a partition (partition D2) that has a left neighbor (partition D1) and a right neighbor (partition D3). We call the processes that compute internal partitions *internal processes*.

Recall that in the Jacobi Iterative Method, each calculation step for a grid point needs the values of its immediate neighbors from the previous step. This creates a need for halo cells for grid points at the left and right boundaries of a partition, shown as slices defined by dotted lines at the edge of each partition in Fig. 18.3. Note that these halo cells are similar to those in convolution pattern presented in Chapter 7, Parallel patterns: convolution. Therefore, each process also needs to receive four slices of halo cells that contains all neighbors for each side of the boundary grid points of its partition. For example, in Fig. 18.3, partition D2 needs four halo slices from D1 and four halo slices from D3. Note that a halo slice for D2 is a boundary slice for D1 or D3.

Recall that the total number of grid points is `dimx*dimy*dimz`. Since we are partitioning the grid along the z dimension, the number of grid points in each partition should be `dimx*dimy*(dimz/num_comp_procs)`. Recall that we will need four neighbor slices in each direction in order to calculate values within each slice. Because we need to send four slices of grid points for each neighbor, the number of grid points that should be sent to each internal process should be `dimx*dimy*((dimz/num_comp_procs) + 8)`. As for an edge process, there is only one neighbor. Like in the case of convolution, we assume that zero values will be used for the ghost cells and no input data needs to be sent for them. For example,

```
       /* Send data to the first compute node */
14. MPI_Send(send_address, edge_num_points, MPI_FLOAT, first_node,
              0, MPI_COMM_WORLD );

15. send_address += dimx * dimy * ((dimz / num_comp_nodes) - 4);
       /* Send data to "internal" compute nodes */
16. for(int process = 1; process < last_node; process++) {
17.     MPI_Send(send_address, int_num_points, MPI_FLOAT, process,
                0, MPI_COMM_WORLD);
18.     send_address += dimx * dimy * (dimz / num_comp_nodes);
    }

       /* Send data to the last compute node */
19. MPI_Send(send_address, edge_num_points, MPI_FLOAT, last_node,
              0, MPI_COMM_WORLD);
```

FIGURE 18.10

Data server process code (Part 2).

partition D1 only needs the neighbor slice form D2 on the right side. Therefore, the number of grid points to be sent to an edge process is `dimx*dimy*((dimz/ num_comp_procs) + 4)`. That is, each process receives four slices of halo grid points from the neighbor partition on each side.

Line 13 of Fig. 18.9 sets the `send_address` pointer to point to the beginning of the input grid point array. In order to send the appropriate partition to each process, we will need to add the appropriate offset to this beginning address for each `MPI_Send()`. We will come back to this point later.

We are now ready to complete the code for the data server, shown in Fig. 18.10. Line 14 sends Process 0 its partition. Since this is the first partition, its starting address is also the starting address of the entire grid, which was set up in Line 13. Process 0 is an edge process and it does not have a left neighbor. Therefore, the number of grid points to be sent is the value `edge_num_points`, i.e., `dimx*dimy*((dimz/ num_comp_procs) + 4)`. The third parameter specifies that the type of each element is an `MPI_FLOAT` which is C `float` (single precision, 4 bytes). The fourth parameter specifies that the value of `first_node`, i.e., 0, is the MPI rank of the destination process. The fifth parameter specifies 0 for the MPI tag. This is because we are not using tags to distinguish between messages sent from the data server. The sixth parameter specifies that the communicator to be used for sending the message should be all MPI processes for the current application.

Line 15 of Fig. 18.10 advances the `send_address` pointer to the beginning of the data to be sent to Process 1. From Fig. 18.3, there are `dimx*dimy*(dimz/num_ comp_procs)` elements in partition D1, which means D2 starts at location that is `dimx*dimy*(dimz/num_comp_procs)` elements from the starting location of `input`. Recall that we also need to send the halo cells from D1 as well. Therefore, we adjust the starting address for the `MPI_Send()` back by four slices, which results in the expression for advancing the `send_address` pointer in Line 15: `dimx*dimy*((dimz/ num_comp_procs) - 4)`.

Line 16 is a loop that sends out the MPI messages to Process 1 through Process np-3. In our small example for four compute processes, np is 5. The loop sends the MPI messages to Processes 1 and 2. These are internal processes. They need to receive halo grid points for neighbors on both sides. Therefore, the second parameter of the MPI_Send() in Line 17 uses int_num_nodes, i.e., dimx*dimy*((dimz/num_comp_procs) + 8). The rest of the parameters are similar to that for the MPI_Send() in Line 14 with the obvious exception that the destination process is specified by the loop variable process, which is incremented from 1 to np-3 (last_node is np-2).

Line 18 advances the send address for each internal process by the number of grid points in each partition: dimx*dimy*dimz/num_comp_nodes. Note that the starting locations of the halo grid points for internal processes are dimx*dimy*dimz/num_comp_procs points apart. Although we need to pull back the starting address by four slices to accommodate halo grid points, we do so for every internal process so the net distance between the starting locations remains as the number of grid points in each partition.

Line 19 sends the data to the Process np-2, the last compute process that has only one neighbor on the left. The reader should be able to reason through all the parameter values used. Note that we are not quite done with the data server code. We will come back later for the final part of the data server that collects the output values from all compute processes.

We now turn our attention to the compute processes that receive the input from the data server process. In Fig. 18.11, Lines 1 and 2 establish the process id for the

```
void compute_node_stencil(int dimx, int dimy, int dimz, int nreps )
{
      int np, pid;
1.    MPI_Comm_rank(MPI_COMM_WORLD, &pid);
2.    MPI_Comm_size(MPI_COMM_WORLD, &np);
3.    int server_process = np - 1;


4.    unsigned int num_points      = dimx * dimy * (dimz + 8);
5.    unsigned int num_bytes       = num_points * sizeof(float);
6.    unsigned int num_halo_points = 4 * dimx * dimy;
7.    unsigned int num_halo_bytes  = num_halo_points * sizeof(float);

      /* Alloc host memory */
8.    float *h_input  = (float *)malloc(num_bytes);
      /* Alloc device memory for input and output data */
9.    float *d_input = NULL;
10.   cudaMalloc((void **)&d_input,  num_bytes );
11.   float *rcv_address = h_input + num_halo_points * (0 == pid);
12.   MPI_Recv(rcv_address, num_points, MPI_FLOAT, server_process,
                MPI_ANY_TAG, MPI_COMM_WORLD, &status );
```

FIGURE 18.11

Compute process code (Part 1).

process and the total number of processes for the application. Line 3 establishes that the data server is Process `np-1`. Lines 4 and 5 calculates the number of grid points and the number of bytes that should be processed by each internal process. Lines 6 and 7 calculate the number of grid points and the number of bytes in each halo (four slices).

Lines 8–10 allocate the host memory and device memory for the input data. Although the edge processes need less halo data, they still allocate the same amount of memory for simplicity; part of the allocated memory will not be used by the edge processes. Line 11 sets the starting address of the host memory for receiving the input data from the data server. For all compute processes except Process 0, the starting receiving location is simply the starting location of the allocated memory for the input data. However, we adjust the receiving location by four slices. This is because for simplicity, we assume that the host memory for receiving the input data is arranged the same way for all compute processes: four slices of halo from the left neighbor followed by the partition, followed by four slices of halo from the right neighbor. However, we showed in Line 4 of Fig. 18.10, the data server will not send any halo data from the left neighbor to Process 0. That is, for Process 0, the MPI message from the data server only contains the partition and the halo from the right neighbor. Therefore, Line 10 adjusts the starting host memory location by four slices so that Process 0 will correctly interpret the input data from the data server.

Line 12 receives the MPI message from the data server. Most of the parameters should be familiar. The last parameter reflects any error condition that occurred when the data is received. The second parameter specifies that all compute processes will receive the full amount of data from the data server. However, the data server will send less data to Process 0 and Process `np-2`. This is not reflected in the code because `MPI_Recv()` allows the second parameter to specify a larger number of data points than what is actually received and will only place the actual number of bytes received from the sender into the receiving memory. In the case of Process 0, the input data from the data server contain only the partition and the halo from the right neighbor. The received input will be placed by skipping the first four slices of the allocated memory, which should correspond to the halo for the (non-existent) left neighbor. This effect is achieved with the term `num_halo_points*(pid==0)` in Line 11. In the case of Process `np-2`, the input data contain the halo from the left neighbor and the partition. The received input will be placed from the beginning of the allocated memory, leaving the last four slices of the allocated memory unused.

Line 13 copies the received input data to the device memory. In the case of Process 0, the left halo points are not valid. In the case of Process `np-2`, the right halo points are not valid. However, for simplicity, all compute nodes send the full size to the device memory. The assumption is that the kernels will be launched in such a way that these invalid portions will be correctly ignored. After Line 13, all the input data are in the device memory.

Fig. 18.12 shows Part 2 of the compute process code. Lines 14–16 allocate host memory and device memory for the output data. The output data buffer in the device memory will actually be used as a ping-pong buffer with the input data buffer. That

```
14. float *h_output = NULL, *d_output = NULL, *d_vsq = NULL;
15. float *h_output = (float *)malloc(num_bytes);
16. cudaMalloc((void **)&d_output, num_bytes );

17. float *h_left_boundary = NULL, *h_right_boundary = NULL;
18. float *h_left_halo = NULL, *h_right_halo = NULL;

    /* Alloc host memory for halo data */
19. cudaHostAlloc((void **)&h_left_boundary, num_halo_bytes, cudaHostAllocDefault);
20. cudaHostAlloc((void **)&h_right_boundary,num_halo_bytes, cudaHostAllocDefault);
21. cudaHostAlloc((void **)&h_left_halo,      num_halo_bytes, cudaHostAllocDefault);
22. cudaHostAlloc((void **)&h_right_halo,     num_halo_bytes, cudaHostAllocDefault);

    /* Create streams used for stencil computation */
23. cudaStream_t stream0, stream1;
24. cudaStreamCreate(&stream0);
25. cudaStreamCreate(&stream1);
```

FIGURE 18.12

Compute process code (Part 2).

is, they will switch roles in each iteration. Recall that we used a similar scheme in the BFS pattern in Chapter 12, Parallel patterns: graph search. We will return to this point later.

We are now ready to present the code that performs computation steps on the grid points.

18.5 OVERLAPPING COMPUTATION AND COMMUNICATION

A simple way to perform the computation steps is for each compute process to perform a computation step on its entire partition, exchange halo data with the left and right neighbors, and repeat. While this is a very simple strategy, it is not very effective. The reason is that this strategy forces the system to be in one of the two modes. In the first mode, all compute processes are performing computation steps. During this time, the communication network is not used. In the second mode, all compute processes exchange halo data with their left and right neighbors. During this time, the computation hardware is not well utilized. Ideally, we would like to achieve better performance by utilizing both the communication network and computation hardware all the time. This can be achieved by dividing the computation tasks of each compute process into two stages, as illustrated in Fig. 18.13.

During the first stage (Stage 1), each compute process calculates its boundary slices that will be needed as halo cells by its neighbors in the next iteration. Let's continue to assume that we use four slices of halo data. Fig. 18.13 shows that the collection of four halo slices as a dashed transparent piece and the four boundary slices as a colored piece. Note that the colored piece of Process i will be copied into the dashed piece of Process $i+1$ and vice versa during the next communication. For

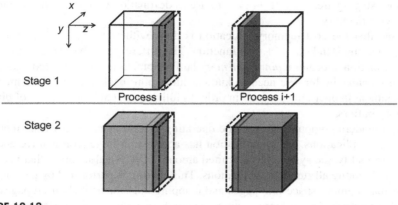

FIGURE 18.13

A two-stage strategy for overlapping computation with communication.

Process 0, the first phase calculates the right four slices of boundary data. For an internal node, it calculates the left four slices and the right four slices of its boundary data. For Process n-2, it calculates the left four pieces of its boundary data. The rationale is that these boundary slices are needed by their neighbors for the next iteration. By calculating these boundary slices first, the data can be communicated to the neighbors while the compute processes calculate the rest of its grid points.

During the second stage (Stage 2), each compute process performs two parallel activities. The first is to communicate its new boundary values to its neighbor processes. This is done by first copying the data from the device memory into the host memory, followed by sending MPI messages to the neighbors. As we will discuss later, we need to be careful that the data received from the neighbors are used in the next iteration, not the current iteration. The second activity is to calculate the rest of the data in the partition. If the communication activity takes a shorter amount of time than the calculation activity, we can hide the communication delay and fully utilize the computing hardware all the time. This is usually achieved by having enough slices in the internal part of each partition to allow each compute process to perform computation steps in between communications.

In order to support the parallel activities in Stage 2, we need to use two advanced features of the CUDA Programming model: *pinned memory allocation* and *streams*. A pinned memory allocation requests that the memory allocated will not be paged out by the operating system. This is done with the cudaHostAlloc() API call. Lines 19–22, in Fig. 18.12, allocates memory buffers for the left and right boundary slices and the left and right halo slices. The left and right boundary slices need to be sent from the device memory to the left and right neighbor processes. The buffers are used as a host memory staging area for the device to copy data into and then used as the source buffer for MPI_Send() to neighbor processes. The left and right halo slices need to be received from neighbor processes. The buffers are used as a host memory staging area for MPI_Recv() to use as destination buffer and then copied to the device memory.

Note that the host memory allocation is done with cudaHostAlloc() function rather than the standard malloc() function. The difference is that the cudaHostAlloc() function allocates a *pinned memory* buffer, sometimes also referred to as *page locked memory* buffer. We need to know a little more background on the memory management in operating systems in order to fully understand the concept of pinned memory buffers.

In a modern computer system, the operating system manages a virtual memory space for applications. Each application has access to a large, consecutive address space. In reality, the system has a limited amount of physical memory that needs to be shared among all running applications. This sharing is performed by partitioning the virtual memory space into pages and mapping only the actively used pages into physical memory. When there is much demand for memory, the operating system needs to "swap out" some of the pages from the physical memory to mass storage such as disks. Therefore, an application may have its data paged out any time during its execution.

The implementation of cudaMemcpy() uses a type of hardware called direct memory access (DMA) device. When a cudaMemcpy() function is called to copy between the host and device memories, its implementation uses a DMA to complete the task. On the host memory side, the DMA hardware operates on physical addresses. That is, the operating system needs to give a translated physical address to DMA. However, there is a chance that the data may be swapped out before the DMA operation is complete. The physical memory locations for the data may be reassigned to another virtual memory data. In this case, the DMA operation can be potentially corrupted since its data can be overwritten by the paging activity.

A common solution to this data corruption problem is for the CUDA runtime to perform the copy operation in two steps. For a host-to-device copy, the CUDA runtime first copies the source host memory data into a "pinned" memory buffer, which means the memory locations are marked so that the operating paging mechanism will not page out the data. It then uses the DMA device to copy the data from the pinned memory buffer to the device memory. For a device-to-host copy, the CUDA runtime first uses a DMA device to copy the data from the device memory into a pinned memory buffer. It then copies the data from the pinned memory to the destination host memory location. By using an extra pinned memory buffer, the DMA copy will be safe from any paging activities.

There are two problems with this approach. One is that the extra copy adds delay to the cudaMemcpy() operation. The second is that the extra complexity involved leads to a synchronous implementation of the cudaMemcpy() function. That is, the host program cannot continue to execute until the cudaMemcpy() function completes its operation and returns. This serializes all copy operations. In order to support fast copies with more parallelism, CUDA provides a cudaMemcpyAsync() function.

In order to use cudaMemcpyAsync() function, the host memory buffer must be allocated as a pinned memory buffer. This is done in Lines 19–22 for the host memory buffers of the left boundary, right boundary, left halo, and right halo slices. These buffers are allocated with the `cudaHostAlloc()` function, which ensures that the allocated memory are pinned or page locked from paging activities. Note that the `cudaHostAlloc()` function takes three parameters. The first two are the same as `cudaMalloc()`. The third specifies some options for more advanced usage. For most basic use cases, we can simply use the default value `cudaHostAllocDefault`.

The second advanced CUDA feature is *streams*, which supports managed concurrent execution of CUDA API functions. A stream is an ordered sequence of operations. When a host code calls a `cudaMemcpyAsync()` function or launches a kernel, it can specify a steam as one of its parameters. All operations in the same stream will be done sequentially. Operations from two different streams can be executed in parallel.

Line 23 of Fig. 18.12 declares two variables that are of CUDA built-in type `cudaStream_t`. Recall that the CUDA built-in types are declared in cuda.h. These variables are then used in calling the `cudaStreamCreate()` function. Each call to the `cudaStreamCreate()` creates a new stream and deposits a pointer to the stream into its parameter. After the calls in Lines 24 and 25, the host code can use either `steram0` or `stream1` in subsequent `cudaMemcpyAsync()` calls and kernel launches.

Fig. 18.14 shows Part 3 of the compute process. Lines 27 and 28 calculate the process id of the left and right neighbors of the compute process. The `left_neighbor` and `right_neighbor` variables will be used by compute processes as parameters when they send message to and receive messages from their neighbors. For Process

```
26. MPI_Status status;
27. int left_neighbor  = (pid > 0)     ? (pid - 1) : MPI_PROC_NULL;
28. int right_neighbor = (pid < np - 2) ? (pid + 1) : MPI_PROC_NULL;

    /* Upload stencil cofficients */
    upload_coefficients(coeff, 5);

29. int left_halo_offset   = 0;
30. int right_halo_offset  = dimx * dimy * (4 + dimz);
31. int left_stage1_offset = 0;
32. int right_stage1_offset = dimx * dimy * (dimz - 4);
33. int stage2_offset       = num_halo_points;

34. MPI_Barrier( MPI_COMM_WORLD );
35. for(int i=0; I < nreps; i++) {
        /* Compute boundary values needed by other nodes first */
36.     launch_kernel(d_output + left_stage1_offset,
            d_input + left_stage1_offset, dimx, dimy, 12, stream0);
37.     launch_kernel(d_output + right_stage1_offset,
            d_input + right_stage1_offset, dimx, dimy, 12, stream0);

        /* Compute the remaining points */
38.     launch_kernel(d_output + stage2_offset, d_input +
    stage2_offset,
```

FIGURE 18.14

Compute process code (Part 3).

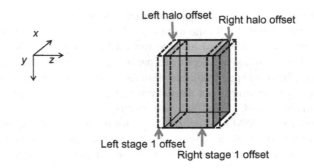

FIGURE 18.15

Device memory offsets used for data exchange with neighbor processes.

0, there is no left neighbor, so Line 27 assigns an MPI constant `MPI_PROC_NULL` to `left_neighbor` to note this fact. For Process `np-2`, there is no right neighbor, so Line 28 assigns `MPI_PROC_NULL` to `right_neighbor`. For all the internal processes, Line 27 assigns `pid-1` to `left_neighbor` and `pid+1` to `right_neighbor`.

Lines 29–33 set up several offsets that will be used to launch kernels and exchange data so that the computation and communication can be overlapped. These offsets define the regions of grid points that will need to be calculated at each stage of Fig. 18.13. They are also visualized in Fig. 18.15.

Note that the total number of slices in each device memory is four slices of left halo points (dashed white), plus four slices of left boundary points, plus `dimx*dimy*(dimz-8)` internal points, plus four slices of boundary points, and four slices of right halo points (dashed white). Variable `left_stage1_offset` defines the starting point of the slices that are needed in order to calculate the left boundary slices. This includes 12 slices of data: 4 slices of left-neighbor halo points, 4 slices of boundary points, and 4 slices of internal points. These slices are the leftmost in the partition so the offset value is set to 0 by Line 31. Variable `right_stage2_off-set` defines the starting point of the slices that are needed for calculating the right boundary slices. This also includes 12 slices: 4 slices of internal points, 4 slices of right boundary points, and 4 slices of right halo cells. The beginning point of these 12 slices can be derived by subtracting the total number of slices `dimz+8` by 12. Therefore, the starting offset for these 12 slices is `dimx*dimy*(dimz-4)`.

Line 34 is an MPI barrier synchronization, which is similar to the CUDA `__syncthreads()`. MPI barrier forces all MPI processes specified by the parameter to wait for each other. None of the processes can continue their execution beyond this point until everyone has reached this point. The reason why we want to barrier synchronization here is to ensure that all compute nodes have received their input data and are ready to perform the computation steps. Since they will be exchanging data with each other, we would like to make them all start at about the same time. This way, we will not be in a situation where a few tardy processes delay all other processes during the data exchange. `MPI_Barrier()` is a *collective communication* function. We will discuss more details about collective communication API functions in the next section.

Line 35 starts a loop that performs the computation steps. For each iteration, each compute process will perform one cycle of the two-stage process in Fig. 18.13.

Line 36 calls a function that will generate the four slices of the left boundary points in Stage 1. We assume that there is a kernel that performs one computation step on a region of grip points. The `launch_kernel()` function takes several parameters. The first parameter is a pointer to the output data area for the kernel. The second parameter is a pointer to the input data area. In both cases, we add the `left_stage1_offset` to the input and output data in the device memory. The next three parameters specify the dimensions of the portion of the grid to be processed, which is 12 slices in this case. Note that we need to have four slices on each side in order to correctly perform four computation steps for all the points in the four left boundary slices. Line 37 does the same for the right boundary points in Stage 1. Note that these kernels will be launched within `stream0` and will be executed sequentially.

Line 38 launches a kernel to generate the `dimx*dimy*(dimz-8)` internal points in Stage 2. Note that this also requires four slices of input boundary values on each side so the total number of input slices is `dimx*dimy*dimz`. The kernel is launched in `stream1` and will be executed in parallel with those launched by Lines 36 and 37.

Fig. 18.16 shows Part 4 of the compute process code. Line 39 copies the four slices of left boundary points to the host memory in preparation for data exchange with the left neighbor process. Line 40 copies the four slices of the right boundary points to the host memory in preparation for data exchange with the right neighbor process. Both are asynchronous copies in `Stream 0` and will wait for the two kernels in `Stream 0` to complete before they copy data. Line 41 is a synchronization that forces the process to wait for all operations in `Stream 0` to complete before it can continue. This makes sure that the left and right boundary points are in the host memory before the process proceeds with data exchange.

During the data exchange phase, we will have all MPI processes to send their boundary points to their left neighbors. That is, all processes will have their right neighbors sending data to them. It is therefore convenient to have an MPI function that sends data to a destination and receives data from a source. This reduces the number of MPI function calls. `MPI_Sendrecv()` function in Fig. 18.17 is such a

```
        /* Copy the data needed by other nodes to the host */
39.   cudaMemcpyAsync(h_left_boundary, d_output + num_halo_points,
                num_halo_bytes, cudaMemcpyDeviceToHost, stream0 );
40.   cudaMemcpyAsync(h_right_boundary,
                d_output + right_stage1_offset + num_halo_points,
                num_halo_bytes, cudaMemcpyDeviceToHost, stream0 );
41.   cudaStreamSynchronize(stream0);
```

FIGURE 18.16

Compute process code (Part 4).

```
int MPI_Sendrecv(void *sendbuf, int sendcount,
    MPI_Datatype sendtype, int dest, int sendtag, void
    *recvbuf, int recvcount, MPI_Datatype recvtype, int
    source, int recvtag, MPI_Comm comm, MPI_Status *status)
```
- Sendbuf: Initial address of send buffer (choice)
- Sendcount: Number of elements in send buffer (integer)
- Sendtype: Type of elements in send buffer (handle)
- Dest: Rank of destination (integer)
- Sendtag: Send tag (integer)
- Recvcount: Number of elements in receive buffer (integer)
- Recvtype: Type of elements in receive buffer (handle)
- Source: Rank of source (integer)
- Recvtag: Receive tag (integer)
- Comm: Communicator (handle)
- Recvbuf: Initial address of receive buffer (choice)
- Status: Status object (Status). This refers to the receive
  operation.

FIGURE 18.17

Syntax for the `MPI_Sendrecv()` function.

```
        /* Send data to left, get data from right */
42.    MPI_Sendrecv(h_left_boundary, num_halo_points, MPI_FLOAT,
                    left_neighbor,  i, h_right_halo,
                    num_halo_points, MPI_FLOAT, right_neighbor, i,
                    MPI_COMM_WORLD, &status );
        /* Send data to right, get data from left */
43.    MPI_Sendrecv(h_right_boundary, num_halo_points, MPI_FLOAT,
                    right_neighbor, i, h_left_halo,
                    num_halo_points, MPI_FLOAT, left_neighbor,  i,
                    MPI_COMM_WORLD, &status );

44.    cudaMemcpyAsync(d_output+left_halo_offset,  h_left_halo,
                    num_halo_bytes, cudaMemcpyHostToDevice, stream0);
45.    cudaMemcpyAsync(d_output+right_ghost_offset, h_right_ghost,
                    num_halo_bytes, cudaMemcpyHostToDevice, stream0 );
46.    cudaDeviceSynchronize();

47.    float *temp = d_output;
48.    d_output = d_input; d_input = temp;
    }
```

FIGURE 18.18

Compute process code (Part 5).

function. It is essentially a combination of `MPI_Send()` and `MPI_Recv()` so we will not further elaborate on the meaning of the parameters.

Fig. 18.18 shows Part 5 of the compute process code. Line 42 sends four slices of left boundary points to the left neighbor and receives four slices of right halo points from the right neighbors. Line 43 sends four slices of right boundary points to the right neighbor and receives four slices of left halo points from the left neighbor. In the case of Process 0, its left_neighbor has been set to MPI_PROC_NULL in Line 27 so the MPI runtime will not send out the message in Line 42 or receive the message in Line 43 for Process 0. Likewise, the MPI runtime will not receive the message in Line 42 or send out the message in Line 43 for Process np-2. Therefore, the conditional assignments in Lines 27 and 28 eliminate the need for special if-the-else statements in Lines 42 and 43.

After the MPI messages have been sent and received, Lines 44 and 45 transfer the newly received halo points to the d_output buffer of device memory. These copies are done in stream0 so they will execute in parallel with the kernel launched in Line 38.

Line 46 is a synchronize operation for all device activities. This call forces the process to wait for all device activities, including kernels and data copies to complete. When the cudaDeviceSynchronize() function returns, all d_output data from the current computation step are in place: left halo data from the left neighbor process, boundary data from the kernel launched in Line 36, internal data form the kernel launched in Line 38, right boundary data from the kernel launched in Line 37, and right halo data from the right neighbor.

Lines 47 and 48 swap the d_input and d_output pointers. This changes the output of the d_ouput data of the current computation step into the d_input data of the next computation step. The execution then proceeds to the next computation step by going to the next iteration of the loop of Line 35. This will continue until all compute processes complete the number of computations specified by the parameter nreps.

Fig. 18.19 shows Part 6, the final part of the compute process code. Line 49 is a barrier synchronization that forces all processes to wait for each other to finish

```
      /* Wait for previous communications */
49.   MPI_Barrier(MPI_COMM_WORLD);

50.   float *temp = d_output;
51.   d_output = d_input;
52.   d_input = temp;

      /* Send the output, skipping halo points */
53.   cudaMemcpy(h_output, d_output, num_bytes, cudaMemcpyDeviceToHost);
      float *send_address = h_output + num_ghost_points;
54.   MPI_Send(send_address, dimx * dimy * dimz, MPI_REAL,
               server_process, DATA_COLLECT, MPI_COMM_WORLD);
55.   MPI_Barrier(MPI_COMM_WORLD);

      /* Release resources */
56.   free(h_input); free(h_output);
57.   cudaFreeHost(h_left_ghost_own); cudaFreeHost(h_right_ghost_own);
58.   cudaFreeHost(h_left_ghost); cudaFreeHost(h_right_ghost);
59.   cudaFree( d_input ); cudaFree( d_output );
}
```

FIGURE 18.19

Compute process code (Part 6).

```
      /* Wait for nodes to compute */
20.   MPI_Barrier(MPI_COMM_WORLD);

      /* Collect output data */
21.   MPI_Status status;
22.   for(int process = 0; process < num_comp_nodes; process++)
          MPI_Recv(output + process * num_points / num_comp_nodes,
              num_points / num_comp_nodes, MPI_REAL, process,
              DATA_COLLECT, MPI_COMM_WORLD, &status );

      /* Store output data */
23.   store_output(output, dimx, dimy, dimz);

      /* Release resources */
24.   free(input);
25.   free(output);
}
```

FIGURE 18.20

Data server code (Part 3).

their computation steps. Lines 50–52 swap d_output with d_input. This is because Lines 47 and 48, in Fig. 18.18, swapped d_output with d_input in preparation for the next computation step. However, this is unnecessary for the last computation step. So, we use Lines 50–52 to undo the swap. Line 53 copies the final output to the host memory. Line 54 sends the output to the data server. Line 55 waits for all processes to complete. Lines 56–59 free all the resources before returning to the main program.

Fig. 18.20 shows Part 3, the final part of the data server code, which continues from Fig. 18.10. Line 20 is a barrier synchronization that waits for all compute nodes to complete their computation steps and send their outputs. This barrier corresponds to the barrier at Line 55 of the compute process (Fig. 18.19). Line 22 receives the output data from all the compute processes. Line 23 stores the output into an external storage. Lines 24 and 25 free resources before returning to the main program.

18.6 MESSAGE PASSING INTERFACE COLLECTIVE COMMUNICATION

The second type of MPI communication is collective communication, which involves a group of MPI processes. We have already seen an example of the second type of MPI communication API in the previous section: MPI_Barrier. The other commonly used group collective communication types are broadcast, reduction, gather, and scatter [Gropp 1999].

Barrier synchronization MPI_Barrier() is perhaps the most commonly used collective communication function. As we have seen the stencil example, barriers are used to ensure that all MPI processes are ready before they begin to interact with each other. We will not elaborate on the other types of MPI collective communication functions, but encourage the reader to read up on the details of these functions. In general, collective communication functions are highly optimized by the MPI runtime developers and system vendors. Using them usually leads to better performance as well as readability and productivity than trying to achieve the same functionality with combinations of send and receive calls.

18.7 CUDA-AWARE MESSAGE PASSING INTERFACE

Modern MPI implementations are aware of the CUDA Programming model and are designed to minimize the communication latency between GPUs. Currently, direct interaction between CUDA and MPI is supported by MVAPICH2, IBM Platform MPI, and OpenMPI.

CUDA-aware MPI implementations are capable of sending messages from the GPU memory in one node to the GPU memory in a different node. This effectively removes the need of device-to-host data transfers before sending MPI messages, and host-to-device data transfers after receiving an MPI message. This has the potential of simplifying the host code and memory data layout. Following with our stencil example, if we use a CUDA-aware MPI implementation we no longer need host-pinned memory allocations and asynchronous memory copies.

The first simplification is that we no longer need host-pinned memory buffers to transfer the halo points to the host memory. This means that we can safely remove Lines 19–22 in Fig. 18.12. However, we still need to use CUDA streams and two separate GPU kernels to start communicating across nodes as soon as the halo elements have been computed.

The second simplification is that we no longer need to asynchronously copy the halo data from the device to the host memory. As a result, we can also remove Lines 39 and 40 in Fig. 18.16. Since the MPI calls now accept device memory addresses, we need to modify the calls to MPI_SendRecv to use them. Note that these memory addresses actually correspond to the device addresses of the asynchronous memory copies in the previous versions (Fig. 18.21).

Since the CUDA-aware MPI implementations will directly update the contents of the GPU memory, we also remove Lines 44 and 45 in Fig. 18.18.

```
MPI_SendRecv(d_output + num_halo_points, num_halo_points, MPI_FLOAT,
        left_neighbor, i, d_output + left_halo_offset, num_halo_points,
        MPI_FLOAT, right_neighbor, i, MPI_COMM_WORLD, &status);
MPI_SendRecv(d_output + right_stage1_offset, num_halo_points,
        num_halo_points, MPI_FLOAT, right_neighbor, i,
        d_output + right_halo_offset, num_halo_points,
        MPI_FLOAT, left_neighbor, i, MPI_COMM_WORLD, &status);
```

FIGURE 18.21

Revised MPI SendRec calls when using CUDA-aware MPI.

Besides removing the data transfers during the halo exchange using `MPI_SendRecv()`, it would be also possible to remove the initial and final memory copies receiving/sending the input/output directly from the GPU memory.

18.8 SUMMARY

We have covered basic patterns of joint CUDA/MPI Programming for HPC clusters with heterogeneous computing nodes. All processes in an MPI application run the same program. However, each process can follow different control flow and function call paths to specialize their roles, as illustrated by the data server and the compute processes in our example. We have also presented a common pattern where compute processes exchange data. We presented the use of CUDA streams and asynchronous data transfers to enable the overlap of computation and communication. We would like to point out that while MPI is a very different Programming system, all major MPI concepts that we covered in this chapter, SPMD, MPI ranks, and barriers have counterparts in the CUDA Programming model. This confirms our belief that by teaching parallel Programming with one model well, our students can quickly pick up other Programming models easily. We would like to encourage the reader to build on the foundation from this chapter and study more advanced MPI features and other important patterns.

18.9 EXERCISES

1. For vector addition, if there are 100,000 elements in each vector and we are using three compute processes, how many elements are we sending to the last compute process?
    a. 5
    b. 300
    c. 333
    d. 334

2. If the MPI call `MPI_Send(ptr_a, 1000, MPI_FLOAT, 2000, 4, MPI_COMM_WORLD)` resulted in a data transfer of 40,000 bytes, what is the size of each data element being sent?
    a. 1 byte
    b. 2 bytes
    c. 4 bytes
    d. 8 bytes

3. Which of the following statements is true?
    a. `MPI_Send()` is blocking by default.
    b. `MPI_Recv()` is blocking by default.
    c. MPI messages must be at least 128 bytes.
    d. MPI processes can access the same variable through shared memory.

4.	Use the code base in Appendix A and examples in Chapters 3, 4, 5, and 6, Scalable parallel execution, Memory and data locality, Performance considerations, and Numerical considerations, to develop an OpenCL version of the matrix-matrix multiplication application.

5.	Modify the example code to remove the calls to `cudaMemcpy()` on the compute node code by using GPU memory addresses on `MPI_Send` and `MPI_Recv`.

REFERENCE

Gropp, William, Lusk, Ewing, & Skjellum, Anthony (1999a). *Using MPI, 2nd edition: Portable parallel programming with the message passing interface.* Cambridge, MA: MIT Press Scientific And Engineering Computation Series. ISBN 978-0-262-57132-6.

Parallel programming with OpenACC 19

Jeff Larkin

CHAPTER OUTLINE

Now that we have learned to design and express parallel algorithms in CUDA C, we are in a strong position to understand and use parallel programming interfaces to rely on the compiler to do the detailed work. OpenACC is a specification of compiler directives and API routines for writing data parallel code in C, C++, or Fortran that can be compiled to parallel architectures, such as GPUs or multicore CPUs. Rather than requiring the programmer to explicitly decompose the computation into parallel kernels, such as is required by CUDA C, the programmer annotates the existing loops and data structures in the code so that an OpenACC compiler can target the

Programming Massively Parallel Processors. DOI: http://dx.doi.org/10.1016/B978-0-12-811986-0.00019-4

code to different devices. For CUDA devices, the OpenACC compiler generates the kernels, creates the register and shared memory variables, and applies some of the performance optimizations that we have discussed in the previous chapters. The goal of OpenACC is to provide a programming model that is simple to use for domain scientists, maintains a single source code between different architectures, and is performance portable, meaning that code that performs well on one architecture will perform well on other architectures. In our experience, OpenACC also provides a convenient programming interface for highly skilled CUDA programmers to quickly parallelize large applications. The main communication channel between the user and the compiler is the set of annotations on the source code. One can think of the user being a supervisor giving directions to the compiler as employees. Just like in any other managerial scenarios, having first-hand experience in the work that an employee does helps the manager to give better advice and directions. Now that we have learned and practiced the work that the OpenACC compiler does, we are ready to learn the effective ways to annotate the code for an OpenACC compiler.

19.1 THE OPENACC EXECUTION MODEL

The OpenACC specification was initially developed by CAPS Enterprise, Cray Inc., The Portland Group (PGI), and NVIDIA with support from multiple universities and national laboratories, but has since grown to include additional vendors, universities, companies, and labs. At the time of writing, the current version of the specification is version 2.5.

OpenACC has been designed to run on modern high-performance computing (HPC) systems, which generally include multicore CPUs and frequently include distinct parallel accelerators, such as GPUs. The programming model assumes that the program execution will begin on a *host* CPU which may offload execution and data to an *accelerator device*. The accelerator may in fact be the same physical device as the host, as is the case with multicore CPUs, or may be an attached device, such as a GPU that is connected to the CPU via the PCI Express (PCIe) bus. Additionally, the programming model allows for the host and device to have physically separate memories or a shared memory. As such, the most portable way to write OpenACC code is to assume a physically distinct accelerator with physically distinct memory, as it is simpler to map these assumptions back onto machines with shared memory or shared compute resources than to do the reverse. Fig. 19.1 shows the abstract machine model assumed by the OpenACC specification.

Fig. 19.2 illustrates this offloading execution model. By default, OpenACC enforces synchronous behavior between the host and accelerator device, where execution and requisite data are migrated from the host to the device and both return to the host upon completion of the OpenACC *region*. At the end of each parallel execution on the device, the host and device performs a synchronization unless the user removes the synchronization with an explicit annotation. This is, in many ways, similar to the fork/join behavior provided by traditional threaded programming models

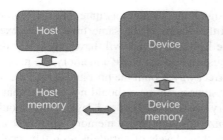

FIGURE 19.1

OpenACC abstract machine model.

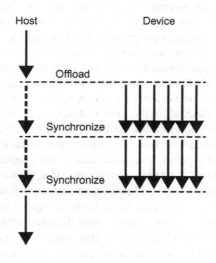

FIGURE 19.2

The OpenACC offloading execution model.

such as posix-threads, except that the forked threads may exist on a different device and the data required by those threads may need to be copied between two physical memories.

Since offloading computation may also require copying of data, which can be time consuming when the host and accelerator have physically separate memories, OpenACC also provides a means for controlling how data is moved between the host and device and how it is shared between different offloaded regions. Conceptually speaking, even though most common accelerator architecture at the time of writing has physically separate memories, OpenACC treats data as if there is always one quintessential copy of the data that lives either on the host or a device, and modifications in one place will at some point in time be reflected on the other too.

In other words, programmers cannot assume that they can modify the same data both on the host and the device at the same time, as the execution model makes no guarantees that the host and device will have physically distinct memories. On machines where the host and device share a memory, the program may behave in an unpredictable or incorrect way if both the host and device are allowed to modify the same memory. Likewise programmers should not assume that all architectures will support shared memory between the host and device; they should use the appropriate directives to synchronize host and device memory when necessary.

OpenACC exposes three levels of parallelism on the accelerator device: gangs, workers, and vectors. Gangs are fully independent execution units, where no two gangs may synchronize nor may they exchange data, except through the globally accessible memory. Since gangs work completely independently of each other, the programmer can make no assumptions about the order in which gangs will execute or how many gangs will be executed simultaneously. A CUDA C programmer should recognize the similarity between gangs and CUDA thread blocks.

Each gang contains one or more workers. Workers have access to a shared cache memory and may be synchronized by the compiler to ensure correct behavior. A CUDA C programmer should recognize the similarity between workers and CUDA threads. Workers operate on vectors of work. A vector is an operation that is computed on multiple data elements in the same instruction; the number of elements calculated in the instruction is referred to as the *vector length*. Additionally OpenACC allows loops to be run sequentially within any of these levels of parallelism.

Imagine a house that is getting its rooms painted. The painting company may send multiple groups of painters, assigning each group different rooms. Each group has its own bucket of paint, and painters within a group can easily talk to each other to plan how to paint their room, but in order for different groups to collaborate they would need to leave their rooms to discuss things with the other teams. Each painter has a roller or brush, the width of which roughly determines how much of the wall he or she can paint per stroke. In this example, the groups of painters represent OpenACC gangs, the painters represent OpenACC workers, the paint brushes or rollers represent OpenACC vectors, and the size of the brushes and rollers is the vector length. Achieving the best time to completion involves balancing the resources correctly among the levels of parallelism. Typically an OpenACC compiler will make a first, educated guess about how to balance these resources based on its knowledge of the target hardware and the information it has about the code, but the programmer is free to override these decisions to optimize the performance.

19.2 OPENACC DIRECTIVE FORMAT

The main difference between OpenACC and CUDA C is the use of compiler directives in OpenACC. OpenACC provides directives (pragmas in C and C++ or comment directives in Fortran) for offloading parallel execution, management data offloading, and optimizing loop performance. OpenACC programmers can often

```
// C or C++
#pragma acc <directive> <clauses>
{ ... }

! Fortran
!$acc <directive> <clauses>
...
!$acc end <directive>
```

FIGURE 19.3

Basic format for OpenACC directives.

start with writing a sequential version and then annotate their sequential program with OpenACC directives. They leave most of the heavy lifting to the OpenACC compiler. The details of data transfer between host and accelerator memories, data caching, kernel launching, thread scheduling, and parallelism mapping are all handled by OpenACC compiler and runtime. The entry barrier for programming accelerators becomes much lower with OpenACC.

Fig. 19.3 illustrates the basic format for the OpenACC directives. In C and C++, the *#pragma* keyword is a standardized method to provide to the compiler information that is not specified in the standard language. This mechanism is used by many directive-based language extensions including OpenACC. In C and C++, OpenACC directives start with the sentinel "acc". The use of sentinels allows each compiler to only pay attention to the directives intended for that compiler. Fig. 19.3 also shows that in Fortran, the OpenACC directives start with "!$acc" to indicate that the directive is only of interest to an OpenACC compiler.

An OpenACC directive specifies the type of directive and sometimes additional clauses to provide more information. Several OpenACC directives and clauses will be demonstrated in the sections that follow. Most OpenACC directives are applied to blocks of code, often referred to as OpenACC regions, depicted as the code surrounded by the curly brackets. Some directives, particularly data management directives, are standalone, behaving much like a function call.

By supporting the use of directives on an existing code, OpenACC provides an incremental path for moving existing code to accelerators. This is attractive because adding directives disturbs the existing code less than other approaches. Some existing scientific applications are large and their developers cannot afford to rewrite them for accelerators. OpenACC lets these developers keep their applications looking like the original C, C++, or Fortran code, and insert the directives in the code where they are needed one place at a time.

The code of an OpenACC application remains correct when a compiler ignores the directives. Because OpenACC directives are implemented in pragmas, which are treated as comments by compilers that do not support these directives, the code can be compiled by other compilers and be expected to work correctly. This allows the application code to remain as a single source that can be compiled by various compilers. The ability to maintain a single source code with and without OpenACC is frequently one of the key reasons programmers choose OpenACC. OpenACC also specifies runtime API functions that can be used for device and memory management above and beyond what is possible in directives.

19.3 OPENACC BY EXAMPLE

OpenACC is best taught by example and for that reason this chapter will present the directives by applying them to a benchmark code. The benchmark code implements a Jacobi iterative method that solves the Laplace equation for heat transfer. As we have seen in Chapter 18: Programming a heterogeneous cluster, the Jacobi iterative method is a means for iteratively calculating the solution to a differential equation by continuously refining the solution until the answer has converged upon a stable solution or some fixed number of steps have completed and the answer is either deemed good enough or unconverged. The example code represents a 2D plane of material that has been divided into a grid of equally sized cells. As heat is applied to the outer edges of this plane, the Laplace equation dictates how the heat will transfer from grid point to grid point over time. Fig. 19.4 shows the problem that the example code solves. To calculate the temperature of a given grid point for the *next* time iteration, one simply calculates the average of the temperatures of the neighboring grid points from the current iteration. Once the *next* value for each grid point is calculated, those values become the current temperature and the calculation continues. At each step the maximum temperature change across all grid points will determine if the problem has converged upon a steady state.

Fig. 19.5 shows the example code that will be used in this chapter. The example code consists of a while loop (line 53) that carries out the Jacobi iteration. This loop will end if either the maximum change reaches below a set threshold (i.e., convergence) or a fixed number of iterations have completed. All performance results in this chapter were obtained by running for 1000 iterations. The while loop contains two loop nests (lines 55 and 64), the first of which calculates the Laplace equation to determine each cell's next temperature and the second copies the next values into the working array for the next iteration. The array copy loop is frequently replaced with pointer manipulation (ping-pong buffering, Chapter 12: Parallel patterns, graph search) when implemented in production science codes, but writing it as a data copy simplifies the example code.

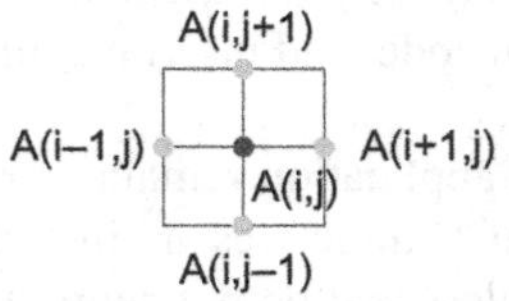

$$A_{k+1}(i,j) = \frac{A_k(i-1,j) + A_k(i+1,j) + A_k(i,j-1) + A_k(i,j+1)}{4}$$

FIGURE 19.4

A Laplace equation example.

```
53.        while ( err > tol && iter < iter_max ) {
54.          err=0.0;
55.          for( int j = 1; j < n-1; j++) {
56.            for(int i = 1; i < m-1; i++) {
57.
58.              Anew[j][i] = 0.25 * (A[j][i+1] + A[j][i-1] +
59.                                   A[j -1][i] + A[j+1][i]);
60.
61.              err = max(err, abs(Anew[j][i] - A[j][i]));
62.            }
63.          }
64.          for( int j = 1; j < n-1; j++) {
65.            for( int i = 1; i < m-1; i++ ) {
66.              A[j][i] = Anew[j][i];
67.            }
68.          }
69.          iter++;
70.        }
```

FIGURE 19.5

Jacobi Iterative Method example code.

The reader might notice that the structure of the example code is actually quite similar to that of the while-loop of the BFS_sequential function in Fig. 12.7. Indeed, the while-loop in Fig. 12.7 checks for a convergence condition. The roles of the c_frontier and p_frontier arrays are actually switched through pointer manipulation. Interested readers can apply the same idea of pointer manipulation to the current code example to make it more efficient.

THE OPENACC KERNELS DIRECTIVE

The simplest method for accelerating loops with OpenACC is the *kernels* directive. This directive informs the compiler of the programmer's desire to accelerate loops within a given region, but places the responsibility on the compiler to identify which loops can be safely parallelized and how to do so. Simply put, it instructs the compiler that the region that follows contains interesting loops that should be transformed into one or more accelerator kernels. As discussed in previous chapters, a kernel is a function that performs independent operations on different parts of the data, thus allowing these operations to be run in parallel. In a more explicit programming paradigm, such as CUDA or OpenCL, it would be the programmer's responsibility to decompose the work into parallel operations in each kernel, but OpenACC places this burden on the compiler and allows the programmer to maintain the existing loop structure.

Notice in Fig. 19.6 that a *kernels* directive is added at line 55, which informs the compiler that the code block from lines 56 to 72 contains loops that should be analyzed and considered for acceleration. The compiler will analyze this region of code,

```
53.        while ( err > tol && iter < iter_max ) {
54.            err=0.0;
55.    #pragma acc kernels
56.    {
57.        for( int j = 1; j < n-1; j++) {
58.          for(int i = 1; i < m-1; i++) {
59.
60.              Anew[j][i] = 0.25 * (A[j][i+1] + A[j][i-1] +
61.                                   A[j-1][i] + A[j+1][i]);
62.
63.              err = max(err, abs(Anew[j][i] - A[j][i]));
64.          }
65.        }
66.
67.        for( int j = 1; j < n-1; j++) {
68.          for( int i = 1; i < m-1; i++ ) {
69.            A[j][i] = Anew[j][i];
70.          }
71.        }
72.    }
73.        iter++;
74.    }
```

FIGURE 19.6

Example code with OpenACC kernels directive.

looking for loops that are free of data dependencies (one loop iteration that depends upon the results of another) to parallelize, and determining what arrays would need to be transferred if run on a device with a discrete memory. In addition to determining which loops are candidates for acceleration and how to decompose the loops into parallel kernels, it is the compiler's responsibility to identify the data used within those loops and to migrate the data to and from the accelerator device if necessary.

The code in Fig. 19.6 can be built with any OpenACC compiler, but for the purpose of this example the PGI compiler, version 16.4 will be used, targeting an NVIDIA Tesla GPU. OpenACC acceleration is enabled with the −ta = tesla compiler option, and because we would like to understand how the compiler transforms the code for the accelerator, the −Minfo =all compiler option is added. The compiler output is in Fig. 19.7.

The compiler output informs us that the compiler found parallelizable loops at lines 57, 59, 67, and 69 of the example code. Additionally it tells us that accelerator kernels were generated for the two loop nests, even showing that the loops at lines 57 and 67 were distributed to gangs and the loops at lines 59 and 69 were distributed across gangs and vectorized with a vector length of 128. Note the lack of a worker loop implies that each gang has just one worker. Lastly the output shows that at line 55 the compiler implicitly generated directives to offload the A and Anew arrays to

```
$ pgcc -fast -ta=tesla -Minfo=all laplace2d.c
main:
    40, Loop not fused: function call before adjacent loop
        Generated vector sse code for the loop
    51, Loop not vectorized/parallelized: potential early exits
    55, Generating copyout(Anew[1:4094][1:4094])
        Generating copyin(A[:][:])
        Generating copyout(A[1:4094][1:4094])
        Generating Tesla code
    57, Loop is parallelizable
    59, Loop is parallelizable
        Accelerator kernel generated
        57, #pragma acc loop gang /* blockIdx.y */
        59, #pragma acc loop gang, vector(128) /* blockIdx.x
threadIdx.x */
        63, Max reduction generated for error
    67, Loop is parallelizable
    69, Loop is parallelizable
        Accelerator kernel generated
        67, #pragma acc loop gang /* blockIdx.y */
        69, #pragma acc loop gang, vector(128) /* blockIdx.x
threadIdx.x */
```

FIGURE 19.7

Compiler output from example kernels code.

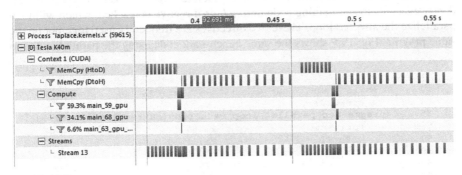

FIGURE 19.8

GPU timeline of kernels directive example code.

the device and back to the host. More information about this data offloading follows. Executing this code on a benchmark machine containing an Intel Xeon(R) CPU E5-2698 v3 CPU and NVIDIA K40 GPU, we see in Fig. 19.11 that even though our loops are now running as kernels on the GPU, the runtime benchmark actually slowed down. This is due to the compiler being overly cautious about the movement of the two arrays, something that we will correct later in this chapter. The PGProf profiler that comes with the PGI compiler can be used to generate a timeline of the program execution, which shows that at each iteration of the method our arrays are copied to and back from the GPU (MemCpy (HtoD) and Memcpy(DtoH)), requiring more time than the actual kernel execution, as shown in Fig. 19.8.

THE OPENACC PARALLEL DIRECTIVE

OpenACC provides an alternative, more programmer-driven approach to writing parallel code: the *parallel* directive. Whereas the programmer only declares a desire for loops to be accelerated when using the *kernels* directive, when the parallel directive is used the programmer declares that the compiler should generate parallelism and when combined with the *loop* directive, makes assertions about the feasibility of loops for acceleration without requiring detailed analysis by the compiler.

Compilers are still required to determine the data requirements for the loops and make decisions about how best to parallelize the loop iterations to the targeted hardware, but it is the programmer's responsibility to determine and assert that the loops are able to be parallelized; if the programmer asserts incorrectly, then it is his/her fault if wrong answers result. The parallel directive is usually paired with the loop directive, with the former indicating that the compiler should generate parallelism on the device and the latter specifying that the iterations of the loop that follow should be mapped to that parallelism.

Unlike the *kernels* directive, which encloses a region that may hold lots of loops to be accelerated, the *parallel* and *loop* directives are added to each *loop* nest that is to be accelerated. The *parallel* directive generates a parallel kernel, which redundantly executes the containing code until a *loop* directive is reached, which will then parallelize the affected loop. These two directives are frequently used together on the same pragma. Fig. 19.9 shows the same benchmark code using the parallel and loop

```
53.     while ( err > tol &&  iter < iter_max ) {
54.        err=0.0;
55.   #pragma acc parallel loop reduction(max:err) collapse(2)
56.        for( int j = 1; j < n -1; j++) {
57.          for(int i = 1; i < m -1; i++) {
58.
59.             Anew[j][i] = 0.25 * (A[j][i+1] + A[j][i-1] +
60.                                  A[j-1][i] + A[j+1][i]);
61.
62.             err = max(err, abs(Anew[j][i] - A[j][i]));
63.          }
64.        }
65.   #pragma acc parallel loop collapse(2)
66.        for( int j = 1; j < n-1; j++) {
67.          for( int i = 1; i < m-1; i++ ) {
68.            A[j][i] = Anew[j][i];
69.          }
70.        }
71.     }
72.
73.     iter++;
74.   }
```

FIGURE 19.9

Jacobi Iterative Method code using parallel directive.

directives. The directives at lines 55 and 65 generate parallelism on the accelerator, which will be turned into accelerator kernels.

Additionally, by using the *collapse* clause the programmer has declared that, not only the outer loop is free of data races and available to parallelize, but the directive should apply to the inner loop too. It should be noted that the collapse clause can only be used on tightly nested loops (nested loops with no code in between, see Chapter 14: Application case study - non-Cartesian MRI), but the loop directive can be added to individual loops to declare the independence of loop iterations when collapse cannot be used. Whenever collapse can be used, the compiler can potentially generate a multi-dimensional kernel like the one generated for the calculation of electrostatic potential energy at the 2D energy grid in Chapter 15, Application case study—molecular visualization and analysis.

The first loop nest has one small complication that needs to be addressed, however: the calculation of the maximum error. Each iteration of the loop will calculate its own error value based on the difference between the value at the current iteration and the next iteration. Not all values of error are needed, however, only the maximum of all errors is needed. This is known as a *reduction*, meaning the (n-2)*(m-2) different values for error are reduced down to one by using the max operation to choose which value to return (see Chapter 5: Performance considerations). While some compilers will detect the existence of this reduction, it is best that the user specify the reduction to be sure.

In Fig. 19.10, we once again see that the compiler has generated accelerator kernels and data motion for the code. Careful examination shows that the compiler has

```
$ pgcc -fast -ta=tesla -Minfo=all laplace2d.c
main:
     41, Loop not fused: function call before adjacent loop
         Loop not vectorized: may not be beneficial
         Unrolled inner loop 4 times
         Generated 3 prefetches in scalar loop
     52, Loop not vectorized/parallelized: potential early exits
     56, Accelerator kernel generated
         Generating Tesla code
         56, Generating reduction(max:error)
         57, #pragma acc loop gang, vector(128) collapse(2) /*
blockIdx.x threadIdx.x */
             59,   /* blockIdx.x threadIdx.x collapsed */
     56, Generating copyout(Anew[1:4094][1:4094])
         Generating copyin(A[:][:])
     67, Accelerator kernel generated
         Generating Tesla code
         68, #pragma acc loop gang, vector(128) collapse(2) /*
blockIdx.x threadIdx.x */
             70,   /* blockIdx.x threadIdx.x collapsed */
     67, Generating copyin(Anew[1:4094][1:4094])
         Generating copyout(A[1:4094][1:4094])
```

FIGURE 19.10

Compiler feedback for Jacobi Iterative Method using parallel directive.

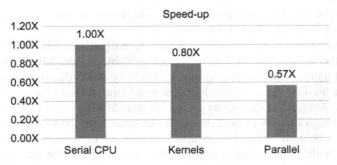

FIGURE 19.11

Performance speed-up from OpenACC kernels and parallel (higher is better).

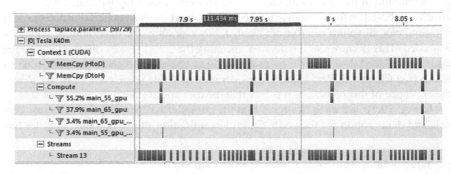

FIGURE 19.12

GPU timeline of parallel loop code.

generated data movement directives at the beginning and end of each parallel loop (lines 56 and 67), resulting in twice as much data motion as the kernels version. Fig. 19.11 shows that the performance of this version of the code is slower than the kernels version, due to the additional data transfers. Fig. 19.12 shows a portion of the GPU timeline for this run. A comparison between Figs. 19.8 and 19.12 shows additional data motion between successive kernel calls in Fig. 19.12. It is obvious that whether the kernels directive or the parallel directive is used to accelerate the loops, the programmer will need to improve the data movement of the code to obtain higher performance.

COMPARISON OF KERNELS AND PARALLEL DIRECTIVES

Some may wonder why OpenACC needs both the kernels and parallel directives, since they are so similar. The kernels directive requires a lot of work from the compiler to determine whether the contained loops are safe and profitable to parallelize. It can also be used around large blocks of codes to generate many compute kernels from the contained loops. The parallel directive, on the other hand, requires analysis by the programmer to be sure that the affected loops are both safe and profitable to accelerate. When the programmer uses the parallel directive the compiler is expected to obey, whether the programmer is correct or not. Parallel also requires the programmer to annotate each loop whose iterations should be executed in parallel by the accelerator.

The loop directive highlights the differences between the two directives fairly nicely. The loop directive has quite a few potential clauses, but two of them in particular highlight the differences between kernels and parallel: *auto* and *independent*. The *auto* clause, which is implicitly added to loop directives used in *kernels* regions, informs the compiler that the loop is interesting, but that the compiler should analyze it to automatically determine whether the loop can and should be parallelized.

The *independent* clause, which is implicitly added to loop directives used within *parallel* regions, asserts to the compiler that all iterations of the loop are independent (free of data dependencies) with regards to each other, so the compiler need not analyze them. The loop independent clause is frequently used to override compiler decisions when a compiler incorrectly thinks that a loop has data dependencies, but because it is implied or assumed on loops within parallel regions, it is the user's responsibility to ensure correct parallelization when the parallel directive is used. If the code gives wrong answers when parallelized using *kernels*, it is a compiler bug, but if it gives wrong answers with the *parallel* directive it very well may be a programmer bug.

So far, we have used the parallel and loop directives together. When the parallel directive is used by itself, one must be aware of an important detail. The statement region that follows will be executed *redundantly in parallel* except for any explicitly marked loop regions. The loops in the loop regions will not be executed redundantly; their iterations will be executed in parallel. This is the behavior when a region is annotated with both parallel and loop.

OPENACC DATA DIRECTIVES

When accelerating loops the compiler will always do what it believes will be necessary to ensure correct results based on the limited information it has, which is typically limited to what it can see in the current function or the current source file. As a general rule of thumb, this means that if a variable appears to the right of an assignment ("=") it will be copied to the accelerator, and if it appears to the left of an assignment it will be copied back. The programmer will generally have a better understanding of the big picture of an application, particularly how data is used between functions, so by providing more information to the compiler it is often possible to substantially reduce the cost of data movement compared to the compiler's choices.

In the above examples we observed that the compiler is copying the A and Anew arrays at the beginning and end of each of the OpenACC regions, since it believes that any variable that is changed on the accelerator may be needed later on the host, and any data used on the accelerator could have been changed on the host, so it must be refreshed to ensure correctness. Looking more closely at the code, the programmer should observe that A and Anew are not changed between successive iterations of the while loop, nor are they changed between the for loop nests. In fact, the only time A needs to be copied to or from the accelerator is at the beginning and end of the while loop. What may not be obvious from the abbreviated code above is that Anew is declared within the scope of this function, meaning that it is really just a temporary array that need not be copied at all; it only needs to exist on the device to be used as a temporary scratchpad. Given this, it is possible for the programmer to reduce data movement significantly by overriding the compiler's data movement with a more optimized scheme.

OpenACC's data directives and clauses enable the programmer to express the appropriate data motion to the compiler. The *data* region works much like the kernels and parallel regions, in that it identifies a block of code and augments the movement of data for the lifetime of that region. Additional information is given to the compiler through the use of *data clauses*. These clauses control the allocation and deletion of space on the accelerator and also the movement of data at the beginning and end of the region. Fig. 19.13 lists the five most common data clauses and their meanings.

It should be added that as of OpenACC 2.5 each of these data clauses first checks whether the variable is already present on the device and only does the specified action for variables that are not already on the device. The OpenACC runtime keeps a *reference count* of each variable, only performing memory actions when the reference count for the variable increases from 0 to 1 or decreases from 1 to 0. The reference count is kept for the base address of the variable, meaning that there is only one reference for an entire array. The reference count atomically increments by 1 at the beginning of data regions and decrements by 1 at the end of data regions. Copies from the host to device only occur when the count for a variable

Create	Allocate space for the listed variable on the accelerator device at the beginning of the region and delete the space at the end.
Copyin	Create the listed variables on the device, then copy the values of that variable into the device variable at the beginning of the region. The space will be deleted at the end of the region.
Copyout	Create the listed variables on the device, then copy the values of that variable from the device variable at the end of the region. The space will be deleted at the end of the region.
Copy	Behaves like a combined copyin and copyout.
Present	Declares that the variables can be assumed to already exist on the device, so no allocation, deletion, or data movement is necessary.

FIGURE 19.13

Five common data clauses and their meanings.

C/C++	`clause(start:count)`, start may be excluded if starting at 0
Fortran	`clause(start:end)`, start or end maybe excluded if they are the beginning or end of the array

FIGURE 19.14

Data clause array size notation.

```
53.    #pragma acc data create(Anew[:n][:m]) copy(A[:n][:m])
54.    while ( err > tol && iter < iter_max ) {
55.        err=0.0;
56.    #pragma acc parallel loop reduction(max:error) collapse(2)
57.        for( int j = 1; j < n-1; j++) {
58.          for(int i = 1; i < m-1; i++) {
59.
60.            Anew[j][i] = 0.25 * (A[j][i+1] + A[j][i-1]+
61.                                 A[j-1][i] + A[j+1][i]);
62.
63.            err = max(err, abs(Anew[j][i] - A[j][i]));
64.          }
65.        }
66.    #pragma acc parallel loop collapse(2)
67.      for( int j = 1; j < n-1; j++) {
68.        for( int i = 1; i < m-1; i++ ) {
69.          A[j][i] = Anew[j][i];
70.        }
71.      }
72.
73.      iter++;
74.    }
```

FIGURE 9.15

Jacobi Iterative Method with data region.

is incremented to 1 and copies from the device only occur when the count for a variable is decremented from 1 to 0. Frequently the programmer must inform the compiler of the size and shape of array variables, particular in C and C++, where arrays are simply pointers to memory. This is achieved using the syntax shown in Fig. 19.14, where start gives the beginning index of the array and count gives the number of elements in the array.

At times the compiler may be able to determine the size and shape of arrays based on the loop bounds, but it is generally a best practice to provide this information to ensure that the compiler uses the correct information. Fig. 9.15 shows the earlier parallel loop code with a data region applied to the convergence loop. With the data directives, the compiler will simply follow these directives to generate the specified data movements for A and Anew, rather than conducting its own analysis and inserting its own data movements. The same modification can be made to the kernels version, resulting in the same reduction in data movement costs.

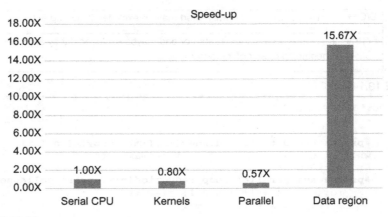

FIGURE 19.16

Speed-up with addition of data directive (higher is better).

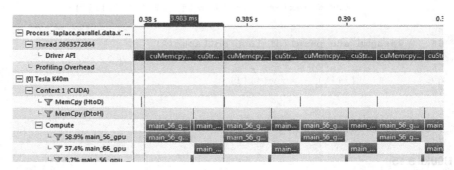

FIGURE 9.17

GPU timeline after optimizing data motion.

Rebuilding and rerunning the code with this optimization added results in the speed-up shown in Fig. 19.16. This result demonstrates the importance of using data regions in OpenACC kernel and parallel regions.

Fig. 9.17 shows the new PGProf GPU timeline, demonstrating that the A and Anew arrays are no longer copied between iterations. Note that there is still a small amount of data copy; the value for error still needs to be copied so that it can be used in evaluating for convergence.

Because data regions can only be applied to structured blocks of code, the *data* directive is not always usable, particularly in the case of C++ classes, where data is frequently allocated in a constructor, deallocated in a destructor, and used elsewhere. In these situations the unstructured *enter data* and *exit data* directives allow data to be managed anywhere in the code. Fig. 19.18 demonstrates use of *enter data* and *exit data* in a C++ class constructor and destructor, respectively.

```
1.  template <class ctype> class Data
2.  {
3.    private:
4.  /// Length of the data array
5.      int len ;
6.  /// Data array
7.      ctype *arr;
8.
9.    public:
10.       /// Class constructor
11.       Data(int length)
12.           {
13.               len = length;
14.               arr = new ctype[len];
15.       #pragma acc enter data create(arr[0:len])
16.           }
17.       /// Class destructor
18.           ~Data()
19.           {
20.       #pragma acc exit data delete(arr)
21.               delete arr;
22.               len = 0;
23.           }
24.       }
```

FIGURE 19.18

Example of unstructured data directives in C++ class.

Unstructured data directives take data clauses, like structured data regions, but due to their unstructured nature the list of available data clauses is slightly different. Fig. 19.19 shows the data clauses that can be used on each directive and their meanings. As with their structured counterparts, these data clauses implement a reference count, where the reference count for a variable is incremented by *enter data* and decremented by *exit data*. Creation of device variables and copying data to the device only occurs when a reference count is incremented from 0 to 1 and the copying data back from the device to the host and deletion of device variables only occurs when the reference count is decremented from 1 to 0. The one exception to this rule is the delete clause, as explained in Fig. 19.19.

It would be impractical to require users to create or destroy device variables each time it is necessary to perform data copies, so OpenACC also provides an *update* directive for copying data to or from the accelerator device. The update directive is used to make the device and host copies of a variable, when on machines with distinct host and device memories, coherent with each other. On machines with shared memories between the host and device the runtime is allowed to ignore update directives. The update directive is analogous to the various cudaMemcpy function calls in CUDA. To update the device memory, the *update device* clause is given, describing

Enter data	Create	Allocate space for the listed variable on the accelerator, but do not initiate any data transfer. Increments reference count.
	Copyin	Create the listed variables on the device, then copy the values of that variable into the device variable. Increments reference count.
Exit data	Copyout	Copy the values of that variable from the device variable and delete the device copy. Decrements reference count.
	Delete	Immediately set the reference count to 0 and remove the device copy of the variable without any data transfer.
	Release	Decrement the reference count for the variable and behave as a delete if the reference count is decremented to zero.

FIGURE 19.19

Data clauses for unstructured data directives.

```
1.  #pragma acc update host(u_new[offset_first_row:m-
    2],u_new[offset_last_row:m-2])
2.  MPI_Sendrecv(u_new+offset_first_row, m-2, MPI_DOUBLE,
3.              t_nb, 0, u_new+offset_bottom_boundary, m-2,
4.              MPI_DOUBLE, b_nb, 0,
5.              MPI_COMM_WORLD, MPI_STATUS_IGNORE);
6.  MPI_Sendrecv(u_new+offset_last_row, m-2, MPI_DOUBLE,
7.              b_nb, 1, u_new+offset_top_boundary, m-2,
8.              MPI_DOUBLE, t_nb, 1,
9.              MPI_COMM_WORLD, MPI_STATUS_IGNORE);
10.    #pragma acc update device(u_new[offset_top_boundary:m-
       2],u_new[offset_bottom_boundary:m-2])
```

FIGURE 19.20

Example of update directive with MPI halo exchange.

the variable or subsection of a variable that should be updated. When updating the *host* copy, the *self* clause (formerly called *host*) is used instead. Fig. 19.20 shows the use of update directives around an MPI halo exchange (see Chapter 18: Programming a heterogeneous cluster) of the top and bottom rows of a local array, where the host copies of the halo rows are first updated, then exchanged with neighboring processors, and finally the device copy is updated with the new values.

OPENACC LOOP OPTIMIZATIONS

While the OpenACC compiler will make a best effort to optimize the code for the target device, it is frequently possible for the developer to override the compiler's decisions and obtain higher performance. The OpenACC *loop* directive, which has already been discussed in the context of the *parallel* directive, enables the developer to suggest optimizations for particular loops, such as how to better decompose the loop iterations for the accelerator device. The loop *auto*, *independent*, and *collapse* clauses have been discussed previously, so they will not be discussed further in this section.

The first set of loop optimization clauses are the *gang*, *worker*, *vector*, and *seq* clauses. These clauses inform the compiler that the loop immediately following the loop directive should have the listed forms of parallelism applied to it. For instance, in Fig. 19.21, the *l* loop is distributed to gangs, the *k* loop to workers, the *j* loop is run sequentially, and the *i* loop is vectorized. In general gang loops are found at the outermost levels of loop nests and vector loops at the innermost levels, where data is accessed in a contiguous manner. Worker and vector levels are optionally used as needed in between these levels.

In addition to specifying how loops are decomposed it is sometimes useful to specify the number of gangs or workers or the vector length used. When using a *parallel* directive, these parameters are provided at the beginning of the region on the parallel directive, as shown in Fig. 19.22. When using the *kernels* directive these parameters can be provided on the loops themselves, as shown in Fig. 19.23. OpenACC 2.5 loosens these restrictions to allow either format to be used on both *parallel* and *kernels* regions. Any parameter not specified will be selected by the compiler.

```
1.  #pragma acc parallel loop gang
2.  for (int l=0; l < N; l++)
3.  #pragma acc loop worker
4.     for (int k=0; k < N; k++ )
5.  #pragma acc loop seq
6.        for (int j=0; j < N; j++ )
7.  #pragma acc loop vector
8.           for (int i=0; i < N; i++)
9.              { … }
```

FIGURE 19.21

Example of loop directive specifying levels of parallelism.

```
1.  #pragma acc parallel loop gang num_gangs(1024) num_workers(32)
    vector_length(32)
2.  for (int l=0; l < N; l++)
3.  #pragma acc loop worker
4.     for (int k=0; k < N; k++ )
5.  #pragma acc loop seq
6.        for (int j=0; j < N; j++ )
7.  #pragma acc loop vector
8.           for (int i=0; i < N; i++)
9.              { … }
```

FIGURE 19.22

Adjusting loop parameters within a parallel region.

```
1.  #pragma acc kernels loop gang(1024)
2.  for (int l=0; l < N;  l++)
3.  #pragma acc loop worker(32)
4.    for (int k=0; k < N; k++ )
5.  #pragma acc loop seq
6.      for (int j=0; j < N; j++ )
7.  #pragma acc loop vector(32)
8.        for (int i=0; i < N; i++)
9.          { … }
```

FIGURE 19.23

Adjusting loop parameters within a kernels region.

When specifying loop parameters, which are inherently device-specific, it is generally a best practice to use a device_type clause to specialize the parameters to only a particular device. For instance, to only set the vector length for NVIDIA GPUs, line 7 of Fig. 19.23 could be changed to *acc loop device_type(nvidia) vector(32)*. Using the device_type clause informs the compiler of optimizations for specific devices without making the code less portable to other devices, where the user may not have optimal values.

One more notable optimization clause for loops is the *tile* clause, which specifies the two or more tightly nested loops that follow should be broken into tiles of work to exploit the locality of their data access pattern. As we discussed in Chapter 4, Memory and data locality, tiling is a technique that involves introducing additional loops to a loop nest to change the order of loop iterations to take advantage of localized data access patterns. This transformation could be performed by the developer, but often makes the code less readable and more difficult to maintain, so it is desirable to ask the compiler to perform the transformations instead.

The Jacobi Iterative Method example belongs in the convolution parallel pattern (see Chapter 7: Parallel patterns: convolution) and is a good candidate for tiling, since each iteration accesses its neighbor values, which may already exist in cache or registers. Fig. 19.24 shows the Jacobi Iterative Method code with the two loop nests broken into 32×4 tiles on NVIDIA devices, which was experimentally determined to be the best value on the benchmark machine, giving roughly a 10% performance improvement over the previous version. Although the *parallel loop* version is shown here, the same optimization can be applied to the *kernels* version for a comparable speed-up.

OPENACC ROUTINE DIRECTIVE

Because the OpenACC compiler parallelizes loops based on the information available to it at compile time, function calls within OpenACC parallel or kernels regions can be problematic for a compiler. In fact, OpenACC 1.0 explicitly disallowed function or subroutine calls within OpenACC code regions unless the compiler was able to inline the function. OpenACC 2.0 removed this restriction, but requires that the

```
75.        while ( err > tol && iter < iter_max ) {
76.          err=0.0;
77.     #pragma acc parallel loop reduction(max:err)
        device_type(nvidia) tile(32,4)
78.
79.          for( int j = 1; j < n-1; j++) {
80.            for(int i = 1; i < m-1; i++) {
81.
82.              Anew[j][i] = 0.25 * (A[j][i+1] + A[j][i-1] +
83.                                   A[j-1][i] + A[j+1][i]);
84.
85.              err = max(err, abs(Anew[j][i] - A[j][i]));
86.            }
87.          }
88.     #pragma acc parallel loop device_type(nvidia) tile(32,4)
89.          for( int j = 1; j < n-1; j++) {
90.            for( int i = 1; i < m-1; i++ ) {
91.              A[j][i] = Anew[j][i];
92.            }
93.          }
94.      }
95.
96.        iter++;
97.      }
```

FIGURE 19.24

Jacobi Iterative Method code with loop tile clause.

```
1. #pragma acc routine seq
2. unsigned char mandelbrot(int Px, int Py);}
```

FIGURE 19.25

Example of the routine directive.

programmer update the function declaration with more information about how the function will be used.

The *routine* directive is used to essentially reserve certain levels of parallelism for loops within that function so that the compiler will know the levels of parallelism available to use on loops that call the function. The *routine* directive is placed at the function declaration, typically in a header file in C or C++ codes or module in Fortran codes, and accepts the same *gang*, *worker*, *vector*, and *seq* clauses as the loop directive. In the case of nested function calls, it is the programmer's responsibility to annotate each function in the call tree with the highest level of parallelism use in that function.

Fig. 19.25 shows the declaration for a function *mandelbrot*, which contains no parallelism, thus it is a seq function. By placing this declaration in the header file, the compiler knows when it encounters the source for the mandelbrot function that it must build a sequential version of the function for the target device, and also when it encounters the callsite for the function that it can rely on a sequential device version to be available.

ASYNCHRONOUS COMPUTATION AND DATA

All of the OpenACC directives shown thus far operate synchronously with the host, meaning that the host CPU will wait for the accelerator operation to complete before proceeding. Defaulting to synchronous behavior ensures correctness, but means that at most, one system resource (CPU, Accelerator, PCIe bus) can be busy at any given time. By opting into asynchronous behavior it is possible to concurrently use any or all of the system resources, improving overall application performance.

For instance, the earlier example saw a significant performance boost by reducing data copies to a bare minimum, but what if the time spent copying data could be reduced further by overlapping the data transfer with other, unrelated computations? Eventually data must be copied, but data copied while computation is also occurring is essentially free.

OpenACC *parallel*, *kernels*, and *update* directives accept an async clause, which informs the runtime that the operation should be sent to the accelerator, but the host CPU should continue working as soon as this has happened. This means that the CPU can either enqueue more work for the accelerator, placing the operations in an *asynchronous work queue* or even perform its own calculations on other data. When operating on an NVIDIA device, work queues directly map to CUDA streams. Before the CPU uses data that has been sent to the device asynchronously, it will need to synchronize using the *wait* directive. Fig. 19.26 shows an example using the *async* and *wait* directives.

While being able to perform work on the host and accelerator concurrently is a powerful feature, it becomes even more powerful when using multiple asynchronous work queues to overlap independent data transfers and computation on the accelerator as well. Just like when working with CUDA streams (see Chapter 18: Programming a heterogeneous cluster), work placed in the same queue is processed sequentially in the order it was enqueued, but work placed in different queues can be overlapped. On a high-end NVIDIA GPU machine, this means that the PCIe bus can be copying data in each direction while the host CPU and GPU are both performing

```
1. #pragma acc data create(A[N])
2. {
3. #pragma acc parallel loop async
4. for (int i=0; i<N; i++) A[i] = 1;
5. #pragma acc update host(A[:N]) async
6. for (int j=0; j<N; j++) B[j] = 2;
7. #pragma acc wait
8. for (int k=0; k<N; k++) C[k] = A[k] + B[k];
9. }
```

FIGURE 19.26

Example of async and wait.

```
 1. #pragma acc data create(A[WIDTH*HEIGHT])
 2. for(int block = 0; block < num_blocks; block++ ) {
 3.   int start = block * (HEIGHT/num_blocks),
 a.   end   = start + (HEIGHT/num_blocks);
 4. #pragma acc update
      device(A[block*block_size:block_size]) async(block%3)
 5. #pragma acc parallel loop async(block%3)
 6.   for(int y=start;y<end;y++) {
 a.     for(int x=0;x<WIDTH;x++) {
 b.       A[y*WIDTH+x]=x*y;
 7.     }
 8.   }
 9. #pragma acc update
      self(A[block*block_size:block_size]) async(block%3)
10.   }
11.   #pragma acc wait
```

FIGURE 19.27

Example of pipelining with async and wait.

computations. Such a process requires significant care by the developer to implement, but can result in significant performance gains.

In order to exploit different work queues, both the async and wait keywords accept an optional integer parameter to denote the queue number. If the async clause does not have a parameter, work will go into the default queue. If wait does not have a parameter, it will wait on all previously submitting asynchronous work on the current device. Fig. 19.27 demonstrates using three queues to pipeline blocks of work, thus overlapping all by the first and last data transfer.

19.4 COMPARING OPENACC AND CUDA

Since both OpenACC and CUDA can be used to accelerate applications on GPUs it is natural to wonder why both approaches are necessary. CUDA is a low-level approach to parallelizing a code for GPUs, which requires the developer to explicitly decompose the work into parallel parts and map the parallel parts to the GPU resources. OpenACC, on the other hand, is designed to express the parallelism of the code at a high enough level that compilers can parallelize the application to any parallel hardware. Each of these approaches has its own tradeoffs.

PORTABILITY

In terms of portability, OpenACC is generally considered the more portable approach to writing parallel code. CUDA is supported on only NVIDIA GPUs and thus requires maintaining both a host CPU and GPU version of the code. Any bug fixes or new capabilities need to be implemented both in the CPU and CUDA versions of the application. OpenACC on the other hand requires just one version of the code, which can be built for the CPU, GPU, or any other architecture supported by the compiler without changes. The ability to run a single source code across a wide range of architectures is OpenACC's most important feature to many HPC software developers, as it greatly reduces software development and maintenance costs and allows the code to run at any supercomputing center. Additionally, through use of the *device_type* clause, optimizations made for particular architectures do not affect portability, since they do not affect other architectures. In contrast, CUDA may require differently optimized kernels for different generations of GPUs.

PERFORMANCE

Because OpenACC is designed to run across a variety of architectures, it represents only architecture characteristics that are common everywhere. As such, there are certain optimizations that simply cannot be applied by the developer when using OpenACC. For instance, many shared memory optimizations that are commonly applied in CUDA are difficult or even impossible to express using OpenACC directives. CUDA however is a low-level approach to programming that closely follows new features in NVIDIA GPUs. Experienced programmers can achieve near assembly-level performance when writing CUDA kernels. When absolute performance on a given GPU is critical, CUDA is the more appropriate programming model of the two.

SIMPLICITY

OpenACC's primary target audience is domain scientists, many of whom have learned only enough computer programming to express their algorithms in code. Frequently these developers do not have the programming background and/or time required to explicitly parallelize their algorithms using a lower-level programming model, such as CUDA. OpenACC enables these users to maintain the familiar coding style of loops and arrays while still parallelizing the code for modern GPUs. By simplifying data management to eliminate the need for device and host arrays and transforming loops automatically into GPU kernels, OpenACC is often simpler for new users and domain scientists to learn. Nevertheless, having learned the concepts of the optimizations in CUDA often helps an OpenACC user to be much more effective.

As is always the case when choosing a programming model, it is up to the developer to choose which programming model best fits their project and skillset. Fortunately, both programming models are able to co-exist in the same application, as discussed in the next section.

When evaluating different programming models on the same hardware, developers often find it necessary to translate the concepts and terminology of each model to the other. Some concepts, such as gangs and workers, have clear 1:1 correspondence, while others, such as vectors, can be a bit murkier. Fig. 19.28 presents a commonly accepted translation between CUDA and OpenACC terminology.

CUDA	OpenACC
Grid	Gangs
Threadblock	Gang
Thread	Worker or vector lane
Warp	Vector
Threadblock size	Number of workers * vector length
Shared memory	Cache
Stream	Asynchronous work queue
CUDA memcpy	Update

FIGURE 19.28

Table of CUDA and OpenACC terminology.

19.5 INTEROPERABILITY WITH CUDA AND LIBRARIES

As noted in the previous section, choosing to use OpenACC does not preclude the use of CUDA. In fact, the most productive strategy for accelerating an application to a GPU may be to combine the use of accelerated libraries, such as cuB-LAS, CUDA, and OpenACC in the same application. This approach gives the best of all worlds, leveraging available libraries, rapid development with OpenACC, and best performance on key kernels with CUDA. For a more complete survey of ways to mix OpenACC with other programming models, refer to the following article on NVIDIA's Parallel Forall developer blog (https://devblogs.nvidia.com/parallelforall/3-versatile-openacc-interoperability-techniques/).

CALLING CUDA OR LIBRARIES WITH OPENACC ARRAYS

The most common example of OpenACC interoperating with other programming models is passing device arrays from OpenACC to CUDA libraries. This is achieved with the *host_data* region. A *host_data* region can be thought of as a reverse data region. A data region exposes arrays from the host onto the accelerator, and a *host_data* region exposes data that is already on the accelerator to the host. The *use_device* clause to the region specifies which arrays should have their device addresses exposed to the host within the region.

Take for instance the code in Fig. 19.29; the *data* region at line 1 creates device copies of the *x* and *y* arrays on the accelerator, which get populated in the *kernels* region at line 3. The *host_data* region at line 12 exposes the device addresses of

```
1.    #pragma acc data create(x[0:n]) copyout(y[0:n])
2.    {
3.      #pragma acc kernels
4.      {
5.        for( i = 0; i < n; i++)
6.        {
7.          x[i] = 1.0f;
8.          y[i] = 0.0f;
9.        }
10.   }
11.
12.     #pragma acc host_data use_device(x,y)
13.     {
14.       cublasSaxpy(n, 2.0, x, 1, y, 1);
15.     }
16.  }
```

FIGURE 19.29

Example using host_data with NVIDIA cuBLAS.

```
1. void saxpy(int n, float a, float * restrict x, float * restrict y)
2.  {
3.    #pragma acc kernels deviceptr(x,y)
4.    {
5.      for(int i=0; i<n; i++)
6.      {
7.        y[i] += a*x[i];
8.      }
9.    }
10. }
```

FIGURE 19.30

Example of deviceptr clause.

x and y to the host to be passed into the *cublasSaxpy* function, which comes from the NVIDIA cuBLAS library. This allows developers to implement the majority of their code using OpenACC, but use accelerated libraries or CUDA functions selectively for the best performance.

USING CUDA POINTERS IN OPENACC

It is also possible to expose CUDA pointers to OpenACC regions in cases where CUDA is already being used in part of the application, but OpenACC is used in another. In this case, the deviceptr data clause can be used on data, kernels, or parallel directives to inform the compiler that any time the listed variables are seen, they are device pointers. For instance, if a developer wanted to provide an OpenACC version of the same SAXPY routine as above, one could use the code in Fig. 19.30, which accepts device pointers for x and y and passes them directly to the OpenACC region.

CALLING CUDA DEVICE KERNELS FROM OPENACC

Lastly, it is even possible to use CUDA device kernels within OpenACC compute regions to hand-tune the performance for critical functions within the region. In this case the previously discussed *routine* directive can be used to inform the compiler that a copy of the declared function already exists for the device and at what level of parallelism it was built. When mixing OpenACC and CUDA in this way it is generally simplest to implement a *seq* routine, which will be called from each loop iteration. Fig. 19.31 demonstrates both the declaration of the device function, typically in a separate header file, at line 2 and the implementation of the device kernel, typically in a source file, beginning at line 6. Fig. 19.32 then shows the device kernel being called from a *parallel loop* at line 15.

```
1.    // Declaration from header file
2.    #pragma acc routine seq
3.    extern "C" float saxpy_dev(float, float, float);
4.
5.    // Implementation from source file.
6.    extern "C"
7.    __device__
8.    float saxpy_dev(float a, float x, float y)
9.    {
10.       return a * x + y;
11.    }
```

FIGURE 19.31

Example using OpenACC routine directive with CUDA device kernel.

```
1.    #pragma acc data create(x[0:n]) copyout(y[0:n])
2.    {
3.        #pragma acc kernels
4.        {
5.            for( i = 0; i < n; i++)
6.            {
7.                x[i] = 1.0f;
8.                y[i] = 0.0f;
9.            }
10.       }
11.
12.       #pragma acc parallel loop
13.           for( i = 0; i < n; i++ )
14.           {
15.               y[i] = saxpy_dev(2.0, x[i], y[i]);
16.           }
17.   }
```

FIGURE 19.32

Example calling CUDA device kernel from OpenACC.

The interoperability features of OpenACC make it a part of a much larger ecosystem of accelerated and parallel computing. There are additional interoperability features that are not shown in this chapter. As such, developers should remember when choosing a programming model that their choice isn't "OpenACC or" but rather "OpenACC and" the other available tools.

19.6 THE FUTURE OF OPENACC

OpenACC began its life as a unification of emerging and competing compiler-based solutions that existed at the time, particularly from CAPS, Cray, and PGI targeting NVIDIA GPUs. First implementations of OpenACC focused on GPUs from NVIDIA, but with an eye toward the trend of increasingly parallel processor architectures. As a result, OpenACC is frequently mistaken as a GPU programming model, when in fact it is designed as a modern parallel programming model that builds on programming models that came before it. OpenACC is not designed to address all forms of parallelism or replace all other programming models, but instead is focused on loop-level data parallelism that is commonly found in HPC applications.

The most significant challenge that the OpenACC committee is still working to solve is the representation data structures that are more complex than simple arrays, such as C++ classes, Fortran derived types, and C structures containing pointers. These data structures are a significant challenge to the compiler, since they may not fit completely in device memory, may be shared between the host and the device, and may not contain sufficient information for the compiler to understand how to manage them effectively.

So-called deep copy, that is the copying of not only the pointers contained within a structure but what they point to, remains a topic of active discussion in the OpenACC community and is considered the most important feature to be added to OpenACC 3.0. As many supercomputing centers have adopted multi-device nodes, it will also be necessary for the OpenACC community to suggest new and better ways to manage multiple devices. With these larger compute nodes also come richer and more complex memory hierarchies, yet another challenge the technical committee intends to address. With the changing landscape of computing, there will be no shortage of challenges for the OpenACC specification to address.

There are some who believe that with the addition of offloading features to the more established OpenMP specification, OpenACC is no longer necessary. Others believe that OpenACC, as the more modern specification, provides value above and beyond what is available in OpenMP. It is the author's belief that programmers are used to choosing programming models based on the needs of their project, availability of tools, and personal preference and that both specifications provide developers with value while pushing each other forward through both collaboration and competition.

19.7 **EXERCISES**

1. The code below implements a simple matrix copy routine. Parallelize these
    loops using either OpenACC kernels or parallel loop such that the inner loop
    is a vector loop with a length of 128 and the outer loop is a gang loop of 1024
    gangs.

    ```
    for( int j = 1; j < n-1; j++ ) {
      for( int i = 1; i < m-1; i++ ) {
        B[j*m+i] = A[j*m+i];
      }
    }
    ```

2. List two differences between the kernels and parallel constructs.

More on CUDA and graphics processing unit computing

20

Mark Harris and Isaac Gelado

CHAPTER OUTLINE

Our main focus has been on scalable parallel programming. CUDA C and graphics processing unit (GPU) hardware have mostly played the role of programming platform for our examples and exercises. As we have demonstrated through the later chapters, parallel programming concepts and skills learned based on CUDA C can be easily adapted into other parallel programming platforms. In Chapter 18, Programming a heterogeneous computing cluster, for instance, most key concepts of MPI, such as processes, rank, and barriers have counterparts in CUDA C. Meanwhile, as was also discussed in Chapter 18, Programming a heterogeneous computing cluster, CUDA-enabled GPUs have become widely available in HPC systems. For many readers, CUDA C will likely be an important application development and deployment platform rather than a mere learning vehicle. In this case, the reader should understand advanced CUDA C features that have been designed to support high-performance programming at the application level. To illustrate, in Chapter 18, Programming a heterogeneous computing cluster, CUDA streams enable an MPI HPC application to overlap communication with computation. Such capability can achieve whole-application performance goals. With this considered, this chapter will provide an overview of the advanced features of CUDA C and GPU computing hardware that are essential in achieving high performance and maintainability of your applications. For each feature, we will present basic concepts as well as a brief history of its evolution through different generations of GPU computing. A sufficient understanding

Programming Massively Parallel Processors. DOI: http://dx.doi.org/10.1016/B978-0-12-811986-0.00020-0

of the concepts and history of each will help clear confusion surrounding them. The goal is to help you establish a conceptual framework for more detailed studies of these features.

20.1 MODEL OF HOST/DEVICE INTERACTION

We have thus far assumed a fairly simple model of interaction between a host and a device in a heterogeneous computing system. As presented in Chapter 2, Data parallel computing, each device in this model contains a device memory (CUDA global memory) that is separate from the host memory or the system memory. The data to be processed by a kernel running on a device must be transferred from the host memory to the device memory by calling the `cudaMemcpy()` function. The data produced by the device also need to be transferred from the device memory to the host by calling the `cudaMemcpy()` function before they can be utilized by the host. While the model exhibits simplicity and is easy to understand, it leads to several problems at the application level.

First, I/O devices such as disk controllers and network interface cards are designed to operate efficiently on the host memory. Since the device memory is separate from the host memory, input data have to be transferred from the host memory to the device memory, and output data need to be transferred from the device memory to the host memory. Such additional transfers increase the I/O latency and reduces the achievable throughput of the I/O operations. For a number of applications, the ability for I/O devices to operate directly on the device memory would improve the overall application performance and simplify the application code.

Second, the host memory is where the traditional programming systems place their application data structures. Some data structures are very large. The device memory in early generations of CUDA-enabled GPUs was small compared with the host memory, compelling application developers to partition their large data structures into chunks that fit into the device memory. To illustrate, in Chapter 15, Application case study—molecular visualization and analysis, the 3D electrostatic energy grid array was partitioned into 2D slices that are transferred between the host memory and the device memory. For many applications, having the entire data structures reside in the device memory would be preferable. For some, there may not be a satisfactory way to partition the data structure into smaller chunks. For these applications, it would be best if the GPU can directly access the data in the host memory or have the CUDA runtime system software migrate the data that are actually used during kernel execution.

These limitations of the host/device interaction model were rooted in the limitations of the memory architecture of early generations of CUDA-enabled GPUs. In these early devices, the only viable host/device interaction model for applications was the simple model that was assumed in the previous chapters. As more applications adopt GPU computing, CUDA system software developers, and GPU hardware designers have been motivated to provide better solutions. Researchers have been well aware of these needs and have proposed solutions since the early days of CUDA

[GSC 2010]. The remainder of this section will discuss a brief history of advancements that address these limitations.

Zero-copy memory and unified virtual address space (UVAS). In 2009, CUDA 2.2 introduced zero-copy access to system memory. This operation enables the host code to supply a special device data pointer to host the memory to a kernel. The code running on the device can use this pointer to directly access the host memory through the system interconnect, such as the PCIe bus without calling to `cudaMemcpy()`. Zero-copy memory is pinned host memory (see chapter: Programming a heterogeneous computing cluster) and is allocated by calling `cudaHostAlloc()`, with `cudaHostAllocMapped` as the value of the flag argument. The other values of the flag argument are for more advanced usage, such as zero-copy memory allocation. The data pointer returned by `cudaHostAlloc()` cannot be directly passed to the kernel; the host code has to obtain first a valid device data pointer using `cudaHostGetDevicePointer()`and then pass the device data pointer returned by this function to the kernel. This process shows that different data pointers for host and device codes are used to access the same physical memory.

As explained in Chapter 18, Programming a heterogeneous computing cluster, the host memory pages must be pinned to prevent the operating system from accidentally paging out the data while the GPU is accessing them. Obviously, the access will suffer from the long latency and limited bandwidth of the system interconnect. The bandwidth of the system interconnect is typically less than 10% of the global memory bandwidth. As we have learned in Chapter 5, Performance considerations, the performance of a kernel is typically limited by the global memory bandwidth unless tiling techniques are used to drastically reduce the number of global memory accesses per floating-point operation. If the majority of the memory accesses of a kennel are to zero-copy memory, the execution speed of the kernel can even be more severely limited by the bandwidth of the system interconnect. Therefore, zero-copy memory should be used for application data structures that are occasionally and sparsely accessed by a kernel running on a GPU.

In 2011, CUDA 4 introduced Unified Virtual Addressing. Until this CUDA release, the host and the device had their own virtual address spaces, with each of them mapping host or device data pointers to physical host or device memory locations. These disjoint virtual address spaces imply that the same physical memory location could be accessed by different data pointers in the host and the device, which effectively happens when zero-copy memory is used. The UVAS, first introduced by the GMAC library [GSC 2010] and adopted in CUDA 4, uses a single virtual address space shared by the host and the device. The UVAS ensures that each physical memory address is only mapped to one virtual memory location. This restriction in mapping enables the CUDA runtime to determine whether a data pointer is referencing the host or device memory by merely inspecting its virtual memory address on the host. This feature eliminates the need to specify the data copy direction on `cudaMemcpy()` calls.

Notably, the UVAS in CUDA 4 does not guarantee the accessibility of the data referenced by a pointer. To illustrate, the host code cannot use a device pointer returned by `cudaMalloc()` to directly access the device memory, and vice versa.

Zero-copy memory is the exception: the host code can directly pass a pointer to zero-copy memory as a kernel launch parameter to the device. When the kernel code dereferences this zero-copy pointer, the pointer value is translated to a physical host memory location and accessed directly through the PCIe. This approach does not necessarily allow the kernel code to dereference a pointer value read from a memory location, such as following a chain of pointers while traversing a linked data structure, unless all memory has been allocated using cudaHostAlloc().

The limitations in both the types of data structures that can be supported and the bandwidth of data accesses of zero-copy memory motivate further improvements in the memory model of GPU architectures beyond UVAS.

Large virtual and physical address spaces. One fundamental limitation of early CUDA-enabled GPUs is the size of their virtual and physical addresses. These early devices support 32-bit virtual addresses and up to 32-bit physical addresses. For these devices, the size of the device memory is limited to 4 GB, the maximal amount of memory that can be addressed with 32 physical address bits. Furthermore, the CUDA kernels can only operate on data sets whose sizes are less than 4 GB, the maximal number of virtual memory locations that can be accessed through 32-bit pointers, regardless of whether the data set resides in the host memory or the device memory. Furthermore, modern CPUs are based on 64-bit virtual addresses with 48 bits actually utilized. These host virtual addresses cannot be accommodated by the 32-bit virtual addresses used by GPUs, which further restricts the types of data structures supported by zero-copy memory.

To remove this limitation, recent GPU generations, starting with the Kepler GPU architecture introduced in 2013, have adopted a modern virtual memory architecture with 64-bit virtual addresses and physical addresses of at least 40 bits. Among the obvious benefit are that that these GPUs can incorporate more than 4 GB of device memory and CUDA kernels can now operate on very large data sets. While the enlarged virtual and physical address spaces obviously enable the use of large device memories, they also allow for much improved host/device interaction models. The host and the device can now use exactly the same pointer value to access a piece of data, whether it is in the host memory or the device memory.

The large GPU physical address space allows the CUDA system software to place the device memory of different GPUs in the system into a unified physical address space. The benefit is that one GPU can directly access the memory of any other GPU attached to the same PCIe bus by simply dereferencing a data pointer mapped to the physical address of such GPU. Prior to the Kepler GPU, communication among different GPUs (e.g., halo exchange in the stencil example in see chapter: Programming a heterogeneous computing cluster) was only possible through device–to–device memory copies triggered by the host code. This resulted in extra memory consumed to store the data being copied from other GPUs and extra performance overheads because of the memory copy operations. Direct access to other device memories in the system enables merely passing the device pointer to the other GPU on the kernel launch and using it to load and/or store the data set that needs to be communicated.

Unified Memory. In 2013, CUDA 6 introduced Unified Memory, which creates a pool of managed memory shared between the CPU and GPU, thus bridging the CPU–GPU divide. Managed memory is accessible to both the CPU and GPU with the use of a single pointer. Variables in the managed memory can reside in the CPU physical memory, the GPU physical memory, or even both. The CUDA runtime software and hardware implement data migration and coherence support such as the GMAC system [GSC 2010]. The net effect is that the managed memory resembles a CPU memory to code running on the CPU and GPU memory to code running on the GPU. The application must certainly perform appropriate synchronization operations such as barriers or atomic operations to coordinate any concurrent accesses to the managed memory locations. A shared global virtual address space allows all variables in an application to have unique addresses. Such memory architecture, when exposed by programming tools and runtime system to applications, can provide major benefits.

One such benefit is the reduced amount of effort required to port a CPU code to CUDA. In Fig. 20.1, we present a simple CPU code on the right side. With Unified Memory, the code can be ported to CUDA with two simple changes. The first change is to use `cudaMallocManaged()` and `cudaFree()` instead of `malloc()` and `free()`. The second change is to launch a kernel and perform device synchronization rather than call the `qsort_char()` function. Obviously, one still needs to write or have access to a parallel qsort_char kernel. What is shown here is that the change to the host code is straightforward and easy to maintain.

However, the performance of the CUDA 6 Unified Memory was limited by the hardware capabilities of Kepler and Maxwell GPU architectures: The contents of all managed memory locations modified by the CPU had to be flushed out to the GPU device memory before any kernel launch. The CPU and GPU could not simultaneously access a managed memory allocation and the Unified Memory address space was limited to the size of the GPU physical memory. These limitations exist because these GPU architectures lacked the ability to support coherence between the host and device memories, and data migration was mostly performed by software.

In 2016, the Pascal GPU architecture added features to further simplify programming and sharing of memory between CPU and GPU, and further reduce the effort

CPU code	CUDA 6 code with unified memory
| ```
void sortfile(FILE *fp, int N) {
  char *data;
  data = (char *)malloc(N);
  fread(data, 1, N, fp);
  qsort_char(data, N, 1);


  use_data(data);
  free(data);
}
``` | ```
void sortfile(FILE *fp, int N) {
  char *data;
  cudaMallocManaged(&data, N);
  fread(data, 1, N, fp);
  qsort_char<<<...>>>(data, N, 1);
  cudaDeviceSynchronize()
  use_data(data);
  cudaFree(data);
}
``` |

FIGURE 20.1

Unified Memory simplifies porting of CPU code (left) to CUDA code (right).

required to use GPUs for significant speedups. Two main hardware features enable these improvements: support for large address spaces and handling of page faults.

The Pascal GPU architecture extends GPU addressing capabilities to 49-bit virtual addressing. Such extension can sufficiently cover the 48-bit virtual address spaces of modern CPUs, as well as GPU memory. This enhancement allows Unified Memory programs to access the full address spaces of all CPUs and GPUs in the system as a single virtual address space rather than be limited by the amount of data that can be copied to the device memory. Consequently, the CPUs and GPUs can truly share the pointer values, enabling the GPUs to traverse linked data structures in the host memory.

Memory page fault handling support in the Pascal GPU architecture is a crucial feature that provides a more seamless Unified Memory functionality. Combined with the system-wide virtual address space, the ability to handle page faults eliminates the need for the CUDA system software to synchronize (flush) all managed memory contents to the GPU before each kernel launch. The CUDA runtime can implement a coherence mechanism by allowing the host and the device to invalidate each other's copy when they modify a variable in the managed memory. Invalidation can be done using the page mapping and protection mechanisms. When launching a kernel, the CUDA system software no longer has to bring all GPU copies of the managed memory data up to date. If the kernel accesses a piece of data whose copy in the device memory has been invalidated by the host, the GPU will handle a page fault to bring the data up to date and resume execution.

If a kernel running on the GPU accesses a page that does not reside in its device memory, it also will take a page fault, allowing the page to be automatically migrated to the GPU memory on-demand. Alternatively, the page may be mapped into the GPU address space for access over the system interconnects (mapping on access can sometimes be faster than migration) if the data are to be accessed only occasionally. Unified Memory is system-wide: GPUs (and CPUs) can fault and migrate memory pages either from the CPU memory or from the memory of other GPUs in the system. If a CPU function dereferences a pointer and accesses a variable mapped to the GPU physical memory, the data access would still be serviced, although perhaps at a longer latency. Such capability allows the CUDA programs to more easily call legacy libraries that have not been ported to GPUs. In the current CUDA memory architecture, the developer must manually transfer data from the device memory to the host memory in order to use legacy library functions to process them on the CPU.

The Unified Memory with a page fault handling capability enables a much more general CPU/GPU interaction mechanism compared with zero-copy memory. It allows the GPU to traverse large data structures in the host memory. Starting with the Pascal architecture, a GPU device can traverse a linked data structure even if the data structure does not reside in zero-copy memory. The reason is that the same pointer value is used in the host and device codes to refer to the same variable. Thus, the embedded pointer values of a linked data structure built by the host can be traversed by the device, and vice versa. In some application areas such as CAD, the host physical memory system may have hundreds of gigabytes of capacity. These physical memory systems are needed because the applications require the entire data set to be "in core." With the ability to directly access very large CPU physical memories, GPUs can feasibly accelerate these applications.

20.2 KERNEL EXECUTION CONTROL

Function calls within kernel functions. Early CUDA versions did not allow function calls during kernel execution. Although the source code of kernel functions can appear to have function calls, the compiler must be able to inline all function bodies into the kernel object so that function calls are present in the kernel function at runtime. Although this function inlining model works reasonably well for performance-critical portions of various applications, it does not support the software engineering practices in more sophisticated applications. In particular, the model does not support system calls, dynamically linked library calls, recursive function calls, and virtual functions in object oriented languages such as C++.

More recent device architectures such as Kepler support function calls in kernel functions at runtime. This feature is supported in CUDA 5 and beyond. The compiler is no longer required to put inline the function bodies, but it can still do so as a performance optimization. This capability is partly enabled by cached, fast implementation of massively parallel call frame stacks for CUDA threads. It makes CUDA device code much more "composable" by allowing different authors to write different CUDA kernel components and assemble them all together without heavy re-design costs. It also allows software vendors to release device libraries without a source code for intellectual property protection.

Support for function calls at runtime allows recursion and will significantly ease the burden on programmers as they transition from legacy CPU-oriented algorithms toward GPU-tuned code for divide-and-conquer types of computation. The QuadTree example in Chapter 13, CUDA dynamic parallelism, demonstrates the benefit of recursively launching kernel functions in accordance with the data characteristics discovered at runtime. This also allows easier implementation of graph algorithms where data structure traversal often naturally involves recursion. In some cases, developers will be able to "cut and paste" a CPU code into a CUDA kernel and then obtain a reasonably performing kernel, although continued performance tuning would still be beneficial.

With the function call support, kernels can now call standard library functions such as `printf()` and `malloc()`. In our experience, the ability to call `printf()` in a kernel provides a subtle but important aid in debugging and supporting kernels in production software. Many end users are nontechnical and cannot be easily trained to run debuggers in order to provide developers with more details on what occurred before a crash. The ability to execute `printf()` in the kernel allows the developers to add a mode to the application to dump internal state so that the end users can submit meaningful bug reports.

Exception handling in kernel functions. Early CUDA systems did not support exception handling in kernel code. While not a significant limitation for performance-critical portions of many high-performance applications, it often incurs software engineering costs in production quality applications that rely on exceptions to detect and handle rare conditions without executing a code to explicitly test for such conditions.

With the availability of limited exception handling support, CUDA debuggers allow a user to perform a step-by-step execution, set breakpoints, and/or run a kernel until an invalid memory access occurs. In each case, the user can inspect the values of kernel local and global variables when the execution is suspended. In our experience, the CUDA debugger is a very helpful tool for detecting out-of-bounds memory accesses and potential race conditions.

Simultaneous execution of multiple kernels. Early CUDA systems allow only one kernel to execute on each GPU device at any point in time. Multiple kernel functions can be submitted for execution. However, they are buffered in a queue that releases the next kernel after the current one completes execution. The Fermi GPU architecture and its successors allow the simultaneous execution of multiple kernels from the same application, which reduces the pressure for the application developer to "batch" multiple kernels into a larger kernel in order to more fully utilize a device. In addition, it is at times beneficial to partition work into chunks that can execute with different levels of priority.

A typical benefit is for parallel cluster applications that segment work into "local" and "remote" partitions, where remote work is involved in interactions with other nodes and reside on the critical path of global progress (see chapter: Programming a heterogeneous computing cluster). In previous CUDA systems, kernels needed to perform a lot of work to ensure that the device is utilized efficiently, and one had to be careful not to launch local work such that global work could be blocked. This limitation meant choosing between underutilizing the device while waiting for remote work to arrive, or eagerly starting on local work to keep the device productive at the cost of increased latency for completing remote work units [PS 2009]. With multiple kernel executions, the application can use much smaller kernel sizes for launching work. Consequently, when high-priority remote work arrives, the application can start running with low latency instead of being stuck behind a large kernel of local computation.

Hardware queues and dynamic parallelism. In Kepler and CUDA 5, the multiple kernel launch facility is extended by the addition of multiple hardware queues, which allow considerably more efficient scheduling of thread blocks from multiple kernels, including kernels in multiple streams. In addition, the CUDA dynamic parallelism feature (see Chapter 13: CUDA dynamic parallelism) allows GPU work creation: GPU kernels can launch child kernels, asynchronously, dynamically, and in a data-dependent or compute load-dependent fashion. This process reduces CPU–GPU interaction and synchronization because the GPU can now manage more complex workloads independently. The CPU is, in turn, free to perform other useful computations.

Interruptible kernels. The Fermi GPU architecture allows a running kernel to be "canceled," enabling the creation of CUDA-accelerated apps that allow the user to abort a long-running calculation at any time, without requiring significant design effort on the part of the programmer. This property enables the implementation of user-level task scheduling systems that can more efficiently perform load balance between GPU nodes of a computing system and allows a smoother handling of cases where one GPU is heavily loaded and may be running more slowly than its peers [SHG 2009].

20.3 MEMORY BANDWIDTH AND COMPUTE THROUGHPUT

Double-precision speed. Early devices perform double-precision floating arithmetic with significant speed reduction (around eight times slower) compared with single precision. The floating-point arithmetic units of Fermi and its successors have been significantly strengthened to perform double-precision arithmetic at about half the speed of a single-precision arithmetic. Applications that are intensive in double-precision floating-point arithmetic benefit tremendously. Other applications that use double precision carefully and sparingly observe less performance impact.

In practice, the most significant benefit will likely be obtained by developers who are porting CPU-based numerical applications to GPUs. With improved double-precision speed, developers will have little incentive to spend the effort to evaluate whether their applications or portions of their applications can fit into single precision. The ability to use double-precision arithmetic without significant performance penalty can significantly reduce the development cost for porting CPU applications to GPUs and address a major criticism of GPUs by the high-performance computing community.

Some applications that are operating on smaller input data types (8-bit, 16-bit, or single-precision floating point) may continue to benefit from using single-precision arithmetic, because of the reduced bandwidth in using 32 vs 64-bit data. Applications such as medical imaging, remote sensing, radio astronomy, seismic analysis, and other natural data frequently fit into this category. The Pascal GPU architecture introduces a new hardware support for computing with 16-bit half-precision numbers to further improve the performance and energy efficiency of these applications.

Better control flow efficiency. Starting with the Fermi GPU architecture, CUDA systems have adopted a general compiler-driven predication technique [MHM 1995] that can more effectively handle control flow than previous CUDA systems. While this technique was moderately successful in VLIW systems, it can provide even more dramatic speed improvements in GPU warp-style SIMD execution systems. This capability broadens the range of applications that can take advantage of GPUs. In particular, major performance benefits can potentially be realized for applications that are highly data-driven, such as ray tracing, quantum chemistry visualization, and cellular automata simulation.

Configurable caching and scratchpad. The shared memory in early CUDA systems served as programmer-managed scratch memory and increased the speed of applications where key data structures have localized, predictable access patterns. Starting with the Fermi GPU architecture, the shared memory has been enhanced to a larger on-chip memory that can be configured to be partially cache memory and partially shared memory, which allows coverage of both predictable and less predictable access patterns to benefit from on-chip memory. This configurability allows programmers to apportion the resources according to the best fit for their application.

Applications in an early-stage design ported directly from the CPU code will benefit greatly from caching as the dominant part of on-chip memory. This would further smooth performance tuning by increasing the level of "easy performance" when a developer ports a CPU application to GPU.

Existing CUDA applications and those with predictable access patterns will have the ability to increase their use of fast shared memory by a factor of three while retaining the same device "occupancy" they had on previous-generation devices. For CUDA applications whose performance or capabilities are limited by the size of shared memory, the three times increase in size will be a welcome improvement. For example, in stencil computation (see chapters: Parallel patterns: convolution and Programming a heterogeneous computing cluster) such as finite difference methods for computational fluid dynamics, the state loaded into the shared memory also includes "halo" elements from neighboring areas.

The relative portion of halo decreases as the size of the stencil increases. In 3D simulation models, the halo cells can be comparable in data size as the main data for currently shared memory sizes. This can significantly reduce the effectiveness of the shared memory because of the significant portion of the memory bandwidth spent on loading halo elements. To illustrate, if the shared memory allows a thread block to load an 8^3 (=512)-cell stencil into the shared memory, with one layer of halo elements on every surface, only 6^3 (=216), or less than half of the loaded cells are the main data. The bandwidth spent on loading the halo elements is larger than that spent on the main data. A threefold increase in shared memory size allows some of these applications to have a more favorable stencil size where the halo accounts for a much smaller portion of the data in shared memory. In our example, the increased size would allow an 11^3 (=1331) tile to be loaded by each thread block. With one layer of halo elements on each surface, a total of 9^3 (=729) cells, or more than half of the loaded elements, are main data. This enhancement improves the memory bandwidth efficiency and the performance of the application.

Enhanced atomic operations. The atomic operations in the Fermi GPU architecture are much faster than those in previous CUDA systems, and the atomic operations in Kepler are still faster. In addition, the Kepler atomic operations are more general. The atomic operations over shared memory variables in the Maxwell GPU architecture are further enhanced in their throughput. Atomic operations are frequently used in random scatter computation patterns such as histograms (see Chapter 9: Parallel patterns—parallel histogram computation). Faster atomic operations reduce the need for algorithm transformations such as prefix sum (see chapter: Parallel patterns: prefix sum) [SHZ 2007] and sorting [SH 2009] to implement such random scattering computations. These transformations tend to increase the number of kernel invocations and the total number of operations required to perform the target computation. Faster atomic operations can also reduce the need to involve the host CPU in algorithms that perform collective operations or where multiple thread blocks update shared data structures, thereby reducing the data transfer pressure between CPU and GPU.

Enhanced global memory access. The speed of random memory access is much faster in Fermi and Kepler than in earlier GPU architectures. Programmers can be less concerned about memory coalescing. This improvement allows more CPU algorithms to be directly used in the GPU as an acceptable base, further smoothing the path of porting applications that access diverse data structures, such as ray tracing, and other applications that are heavily object-oriented and may be difficult to convert into perfectly tiled arrays.

The Pascal GPU architecture incorporates high-bandwidth memory version 2 3D-stacked DRAM, which provides up to thrice the memory bandwidth of previous-generation NVIDIA Maxwell architecture GPUs. Pascal is also the first architecture to support the new NVLink processor interconnect, which gives Tesla P100 up to five times the GPU–GPU and GPU–CPU communication performance of PCI Express 3.0. This new interconnect greatly improves the scalability of multi-GPU computation within a node, as well increases the efficiency of data sharing between GPUs and NVLink-capable CPUs.

20.4 PROGRAMMING ENVIRONMENT

Unified device memory space. In early CUDA devices, shared, memory, local memory, and global memory form their own separate address spaces. The developer can use pointers into the global memory but not others. Starting with the Fermi Architecture introduced in 2009, these memories are parts of a unified address space. This unified address space enables a single set of load/store instructions and pointer addresses to access any of the GPU memory spaces (global, local, or shared memory) rather than different instructions and pointers for each. This makes it easier to abstract which memory contains a particular operand, allowing the programmer to deal with this only during allocation, and making it simpler to pass CUDA data objects into other procedures and functions, irrespective of which memory area they come from.

It makes CUDA code modules much more "composable"; i.e., a CUDA device function can now accept a pointer that may point to any of these memories. To illustrate, without a unified GPU address space, a device function needs to have one implementation for each type of memory that one of its arguments can reside in. Unified GPU address space allows variables in all main types of GPU memories to be accessed similarly, thus allowing one device function to accept arguments that can reside in different types of GPU memory. The code would run faster if a function argument pointer points to a shared memory location and slower if it points to a global memory location. The programmer can still perform manual data placement and transfers as a performance optimization. This capability has significantly reduced the cost of building production-quality CUDA libraries. It also enabled full C and C++ pointer support, which was a significant advancement at the time.

Future CUDA compilers will include enhanced support for C++ templates and virtual function calls in kernel functions. Although hardware enhancements, such the runtime function calling capability, are in place, enhanced C++ language support in the compiler has been taking more time. With these enhancements, future CUDA compilers will support most mainstream C++ features. For instance, using C++ features such as new, delete, constructors, and destructors in kernel functions is already supported in recent compiler releases.

New and evolved programming interfaces will continue to improve the productivity of heterogeneous parallel programmers. As shown in Chapter 19, Parallel programming with OpenACC, OpenACC allows developers to annotate their sequential loops with compiler directives to enable a compiler to generate CUDA kernels. Appendix B shows that one can use the Thrust library of parallel type-generic functions, classes, and iterators to describe their computation and have the underlying mechanism generate and configure the kernels that implement the computation. In Appendix C, we presented CUDA FORTRAN that allows FORTRAN programmers to develop CUDA kernels in their familiar language. In particular, CUDA FORTRAN offers strong support for indexing into multidimensional arrays. Appendix D provides an overview of the C++AMP interface that allows developers to describe their kernels as parallel loops that operate on logical data structures such as multidimensional arrays in a C++ application. We fully expect that new innovations will continue to arise to further boost the productivity of developers in this exciting area.

Profiling with critical-path analysis. In heterogeneous applications that perform significant computations on both CPUs and GPUs, locating the best place to spend optimization effort presents a challenge. Ideally, when optimizing a code, one would like to target the locations in the application that will provide the highest speedup for the least effort. To this end, CUDA 7.5 introduced Program Counter (PC) sampling, providing instruction-level profiling so that the user could pinpoint specific lines of code that require the most time in his/her application.

However, a challenge facing the users of such profilers is that the longest-running kernel in an application is not always the most critical optimization target. As Fig. 20.2 shows, kernel X is the longer running kernel. However, its execution time is fully overlapped with the CPU execution activity A. Any further improvement in

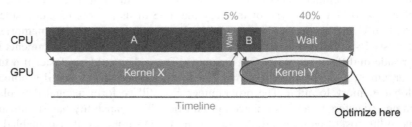

FIGURE 20.2

Importance of critical-path analysis for identifying the key kernels to optimize.

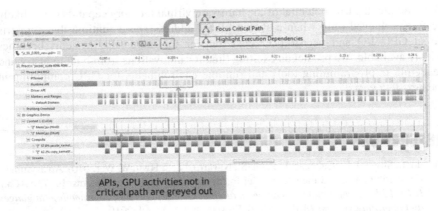

APIs, GPU activities not in
critical path are greyed out

FIGURE 20.3

Application critical-path analysis in CUDA 8 Visual Profiler.

the execution time of kernel X will unlikely improve the application performance. While the execution time of kernel Y is not as long as kernel X, it is on the critical path of the application execution. The CPU is idling while waiting for the completion of kernel Y; speeding up kernel Y will reduce the time the CPU spends waiting. Thus, it is the best optimization target.

In 2016, the Visual Profiler in CUDA 8 provides critical-path analysis between GPU kernels and CPU CUDA API calls, enhancing the precise targeting of optimization efforts. Fig. 20.3 shows critical path analysis in the CUDA 8 Visual Profiler. GPU kernels, copies, and API calls that are not on the critical path are grayed out. Only the activities on the critical path of the application execution are highlighted in color. This allows the user to easily identify the kernels and other activities to target his/her optimization efforts.

20.5 FUTURE OUTLOOK

The evolution of CUDA continues to increase its support for developer productivity and modern software engineering practices. With the new capabilities, the range of applications that will satisfactorily perform at minimal development costs will expand significantly. Developers have experienced the reduction in application development, porting, and maintenance costs compared with previous CUDA systems. The existing applications developed with Thrust and similar high-level tools that automatically generate CUDA code will also likely get an immediate boost in their performance. The benefit of hardware enhancements in memory architecture, kernel execution control, and compute core performance will be visible in the associated Software Development Kit (SDK) releases; however, the true potential of these enhancements may take years to be fully exploited in the SDKs and runtimes.

For example, the true potential of the hardware virtual memory capability will likely be fully achieved only when a shared global address space runtime that supports direct GPU I/O and peer-to-peer data transfer for multi-GPU systems becomes widely available. We predict an exciting time for innovations from both industry and academia in programming tools and runtime environments for GPU computing in the next few years.

REFERENCES

Gelado, I., Stone, J. E., Cabezas, J., Patel, S., Navarro, N., & Hwu, W. W. (2010). An asymmetric distributed shared memory model for heterogeneous parallel systems. In: *The ACM/IEEE 15th international conference on architectural support for programming languages and operating systems (ASPLOS'10)*. Pittsburgh, PA. March 2010.

Mahlke, S. A., Hank, R. E., MCormick, J. E., August, D. I., & Hwu, W. W. (1995). A comparison of full and partial predicated execution support for ILP processors. In: *Proceedings of the 22nd annual international symposium on computer architecture* (pp. 138–150). Santa Margherita Ligure, Italy. June 1995.

Phillips, J., & Stone, J. (October 2009). Probing biomolecular machines using graphics processors. *Communications of ACM*, Vol 52(No. 10), 34–41.

Satish, N., Harris, M., & Garland, M. (2009). Designing efficient sorting algorithms for many-core GPUs. In: *Proceedings of the 23rd IEEE international parallel & distributed processing symposium*. May 2009.

Sengupta, S., Harris, M., Zhang, Y., & Owens, J. D. (2007). Scan primitives for GPU computing. In: *Proceedings of the graphics hardware* (pp. 97–106). August 2007.

Stone, J. E., & Hwu, W. W. (2009). *WorkForce: A lightweight framework for managing multi-GPU computations, technical report*. Champaign, IL: IMPACT Group, University of Illinois.

Conclusion and outlook

21

CHAPTER OUTLINE

You made it! We have arrived at the finish line. In this final chapter, we will briefly review the learning goals that you have achieved through this book. Instead of drawing a conclusion, we will offer our vision for the future of massively parallel computing and how its advancements will impact the future course of science and technology.

21.1 GOALS REVISITED

As we stated in the Introduction, our primary goal is to teach you, the reader, how to program massively parallel processors. We promised that it would become easy once you develop the right intuition and go about it the right way. In particular, we promised to focus on *computational thinking* skills that would enable you to think about problems in ways that are amenable to parallel computing.

We delivered on these promises through four steps. In step one, Chapters 2–4, Data parallel computing, Scalable parallel execution, and Memory and data locality, introduces the essential concepts of parallel computing and CUDA C. Chapter 5, Performance considerations, introduces the key performance considerations in developing massively parallel code in CUDA. These chapters also introduce the pertinent computer architecture concepts needed to understand the hardware limitations that must be addressed in high-performance parallel programming. With this knowledge, developers can be confident in writing their parallel code and reason about the relative merit of alternative threading arrangements, loop structures, and coding styles.

The second step is to introduce six major parallel patterns (see chapters: Parallel patterns: convolution, Parallel patterns: prefix sum, Parallel patterns—parallel histogram computation, Parallel patterns: sparse matrix computation, Parallel patterns: merge sort, and Parallel patterns: graph search) that have been proven useful in introducing parallelism into many applications. These chapters cover the concepts behind the most useful patterns of parallel computation. Each pattern is illustrated with concrete code

Programming Massively Parallel Processors. DOI: http://dx.doi.org/10.1016/B978-0-12-811986-0.00021-2

examples. Each pattern is also used to introduce important techniques for overcoming frequently encountered performance obstacles in parallel programming.

The third step is to reinforce the knowledge with high-level thinking in parallel programming. The first part is an introduction to dynamic parallelism (see chapter 13: CUDA dynamic parallelism) that allows parallel programmers to more easily address more complex parallel algorithms with dynamically varying workload in many real-world applications. The second part consists of three detailed application case studies (see chapters 14, 15, and 16: Application case study—non-Cartesian magnetic resonance imaging, Application case study—molecular visualization and analysis, and Application case study—machine learning) that show how the parallel programming techniques presented in this book can be applied to real applications. The third part is a chapter dedicated to computational thinking skills (see chapter 17: Parallel programming and computational thinking) that help the reader to generalize the concepts learned in the previous chapters into the high-level thinking required to tackle a new problem. With these insights, high-performance parallel programming becomes a well-structured thought process, rather than a black art.

The fourth step is to expose the reader to related parallel programming activities. Chapter 18, Programming a heterogeneous computing cluster presents the basic skills required to program an HPC cluster using MPI and CUDA C. Chapter 19, Parallel programming with OpenACC is an introduction to parallel programming using OpenACC, where the compiler does most of the detailed heavy-lifting. While this approach alleviates the need for the programmer to write detailed kernel code and data transfer code, the reader is in a much better position to give the compiler good directions with all the skills covered by this book. Chapter 20, More on CUDA and GPU Computing, provides further insight, and wraps up some loose ends left from earlier in the book. To help you to branch out to other programming models, we further introduce OpenCL (Appendix A), Thrust (Appendix B), CUDA FORTRAN (Appendix C), C++AMP (Appendix D). In each case, we explain how the programming model/language relates to CUDA and how you can apply the skills you learned based on CUDA to these models/languages.

We hope that you have enjoyed the book and agree with us that you are now well equipped for programming massively parallel computing systems.

21.2 FUTURE OUTLOOK

Since the introduction of the first CUDA-enabled GPU G80 in 2007, the capability of GPUs as massively computing devices has improved at an amazing 12× in computing throughput and 8× in memory bandwidth. These advancements have stimulated tremendous progress in science, engineering, financing, and big data analytics. For example, as we have seen in Chapter 16, Application case study—machine learning, GPUs have ignited a revolution in deep learning from very large data sets, with applications in image recognition, speech recognition, and video analytics.

Since the first edition of this book in 2010, the field of parallel computing has also advanced at an amazing pace. The spectrum of problems that can be solved with scalable algorithms has broadened significantly. While the use of GPUs was initially concentrated on regular, dense matrix computation and Monte Carlo methods, their use has quickly expanded into sparse methods, graph computation, and adaptive refinement methods. In many areas, there has also been fast advancement in algorithms. Some of the algorithms presented in the parallel pattern chapters represent significant recent advancements.

It is only natural for some of us to wonder if we have reached the end of the fast advancement in parallel computing. From all indications, the answer is a definite no. We are only at the beginning of the parallel computing revolution. The amazing advancement in computing in the past three decades has triggered a paradigm shift in the industry. The major innovations used to be driven by physical instruments assisted by computing devices. They are now driven by computing assisted by physical instruments.

For example, the semiconductor industry used to rely on advancement in physical light sources assisted by computing methods that enforce design rules in their push to reduce the device feature size in the manufacturing process. Today, the advancement in physical light sources has practically stopped. The advancement in feature size reduction is primarily driven by lithography masks that are computationally designed to orchestrate the interference of light waves to result in extremely precise etching patterns on the chips.

For another example, two decades ago, GPS revolutionized the way we drive. GPS is primarily based on satellite signal sensing assisted by computing methods that determine the shortest path between two locations, using algorithms similar to the one we showed in Chapter 12, Parallel patterns—graph search. Today, the most exciting revolution in the automobile industry is self-driving cars, which is primarily based on machine-learning computing methods assisted by physical sensors.

For yet another example, MRI and PET revolutionized medicine in the past two decades. These technologies are primarily based on electromagnetic and light sensors assisted by computational image reconstruction methods. They allow doctors to see the pathology inside human bodies without surgery. Today, the field of medicine is going through the revolution of individualized medicine, which is primarily driven by computational genomics methods assisted by sequencing sensors.

The same kind of paradigm shift has been taking place in many other areas. Computing has become the primary driving force for virtually all exciting innovations in our society. This has created an insatiable demand for faster computing systems. As we discussed in Chapter 1, Introduction, parallel computing is the only viable approach to the growth of computing performance. This powerful demand will continue to motivate the industry to innovate and create more powerful parallel computing devices.

In conclusion, we are at the dawn of a golden age of computing. The industry will continue to recruit and reward highly skilled parallel programmers. Your work will make a real difference in the field of your choice.

Enjoy the ride!

An introduction to OpenCL

CHAPTER OUTLINE

In this appendix, we will give a brief overview of OpenCL for CUDA programers. The fundamental programing model of OpenCL is so similar to CUDA that there is a one-to-one correspondence for most features. With your understanding of CUDA, you will be able to start writing OpenCL programs with the material presented in this appendix. In our opinion, the best way to learn OpenCL is actually to learn CUDA first and then map the OpenCL features to their CUDA equivalents.

A.1 BACKGROUND

OpenCL is a standardized, cross-platform parallel computing API based on the C language. It is designed to enable the development of portable parallel applications for systems with heterogeneous computing devices. The development of OpenCL was motivated by the need for a standardized high-performance application development platform for the fast growing variety of parallel computing platforms. In particular, it addresses significant application portability limitations of the previous programing models for heterogeneous parallel computing system.

CPU-based parallel programing models have been typically based on standards such as OpenMP but usually do not encompass the use of special memory types or SIMD execution by high-performance programers. Joint CPU–GPU heterogeneous

461

parallel programing models such as CUDA have constructs that address complex memory hierarchies and SIMD execution but have been platform-, vendor-, or hardware-specific. These limitations make it difficult for an application developer to access the computing power of CPUs, GPUs, and other types of processing units from a single multiplatform source code base.

The development of OpenCL was initiated by Apple and managed by the Khronos Group, the same group that manages the OpenGL standard. On one hand, it draws heavily on CUDA in the areas of supporting a single code base for heterogeneous parallel computing, data parallelism, and complex memory hierarchies. This is the reason why a CUDA programer will find these aspects of OpenCL familiar once we connect the terminologies. The reader will especially appreciate the similarities between OpenCL and the low-level CUDA driver model, which was not used in this book.

On the other hand, OpenCL has a more complex platform and device management model that reflects its support for multiplatform and multivendor portability. OpenCL implementations already exist on AMD/ATI and NVIDIA GPUs, × 86 CPUs as well as some digital signal processors (DSPs) and field programable gate arrays (FPGAs). While the OpenCL standard is designed to support code portability across devices produced by different vendors, such portability does not come for free. OpenCL programs must be prepared to deal with much greater hardware diversity and thus will exhibit additional complexity. Also, many OpenCL features are optional and may not be supported on all devices. A portable OpenCL code will need to avoid using these optional features. However, some of these optional features allow applications to achieve significantly more performance in devices that support them. As a result, a portable OpenCL code may not be able to achieve its performance potential on any of the devices. Therefore, one should expect that a portable application that achieves high performance on multiple devices will employ sophisticated runtime tests and choose among multiple code paths according to the capabilities of the actual device used.

The objective of this chapter is not to provide full details on all programing features of OpenCL. Rather, the objective is to give a CUDA programer a conceptual understanding of the basic OpenCL programing model features. It also provides some basic host and kernel code patterns for jump starting an OpenCL coding project. With this foundation, the reader can immediately start to program in OpenCL and consult the OpenCL specification [KHR, 2011] and programing guides [AMD, NVIDIA] on a needs basis.

A.2 DATA PARALLELISM MODEL

OpenCL employs a data parallel execution model that has direct correspondence with CUDA. An OpenCL program consists of two parts: kernels that execute on one or more OpenCL devices, and a host program that manages the execution of kernels. Fig. A.1 summarizes the mapping of OpenCL data parallelism concepts to their CUDA equivalents. Like CUDA, the way to submit work for parallel execution in OpenCL is to launch kernel functions. We will discuss the additional kernel

OpenCL Parallelism Concept	CUDA Equivalent
Kernel	Kernel
Host program	Host program
NDRange (index space)	Grid
Work item	Thread
Work group	Block

FIGURE A.1

Mapping between OpenCL and CUDA data parallelism model concepts.

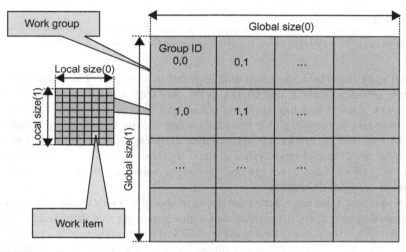

FIGURE A.2

Overview of the OpenCL parallel execution model.

preparation, device selection and management work that an OpenCL host program needs to do as compared to its CUDA counterpart in Section A.4.

When a kernel function is launched, its code is run by *work items*, which correspond to CUDA threads. An index space defines the work items and how data are mapped to the work items. That is, OpenCL work items are identified by global dimension index ranges (NDRanges). Work items form *work groups* that correspond to CUDA thread blocks. Work items in the same work group can synchronize with each other using barriers that are equivalent to __syncthreads() in CUDA. Work items in different work groups cannot synchronize with each other except by terminating the kernel function and launching a new one. As we discussed in Chapter 3, Scalable parallel execution, this limited scope of barrier synchronization enables transparent scaling.

Fig. A.2 illustrates the OpenCL data parallel execution model. The NDRange (CUDA grid) contains all work items (CUDA threads). For this example, we assume that the kernel is launched with a 2D NDRange.

OpenCL API Call	Explanation	CUDA Equivalent
`get_global_id(0)`	Global index of the work item in the x dimension	`blockIdx.x*blockDim x+threadIdx.x`
`get_local_id(0)`	Local index of the work item within the work group in the x dimension	`threadIdx.x`
`get_global_size(0)`	Size of NDRange in the x dimension	`gridDim.x*blockDim.x`
`get_local_size(0)`	Size of each work group in the x dimension	`blockDim.x`

FIGURE A.3

Mapping of OpenCL dimensions and indices to CUDA dimensions and indices.

All work items have their own unique global index values. There is a minor difference between OpenCL and CUDA in the way they manage these index values. In CUDA, each thread has `blockIdx` values and `threadIdx` values. These values are combined to form a global thread ID value for the thread. For example, if a CUDA grid and its blocks are organized as 2D arrays, the kernel code can form a unique global thread index value in the x dimension as `blockIdx.x*blockDim. x+threadIdx.x`. These `blockIdx` and `threadIdx` values are accessible in a CUDA kernel as predefined variables.

In an OpenCL kernel, a thread can get its unique global index values by calling an API function `get_global_id()` function with a parameter that identifies the dimension. See `get_global_id(0)` entry in Fig. A.3. The functions `get_global_id(0)` and `get_global_id(1)` return the global thread index values in the x dimension and the y dimension respectively. The global index value in the x dimension is equivalent to the `blockIdx.x*blockDim.x+threadIdx.x` in CUDA. See Fig. A.3 for `get_local_ id(0)` function which is equivalent to `threadIdx.x`. We did not show the parameter values in Fig. A.3 for selecting the higher dimension indices: 1 for the y dimension and 2 for the z dimension.

An OpenCL kernel can also call an API function `get_global_size()` with a parameter that identifies the dimensional sizes of its NDRanges. The calls `get_ global_size(0)` and `get_global_size(1)` return the total number of work items in the x and y dimensions of the NDRanges. Note that this is slightly different from the CUDA `gridDim` values which are in terms of blocks. The CUDA equivalent for the `get_global_size(0)` return value would be `gridDim.x * blockDim.x`.

A.3 DEVICE ARCHITECTURE

Like CUDA, OpenCL models a heterogeneous parallel computing system as a host and one or more *OpenCL devices*. The host is a traditional CPU that executes the host program. Fig. A.4 shows the conceptual architecture of an OpenCL device.

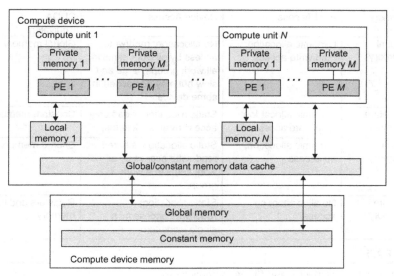

FIGURE A.4

Conceptual OpenCL device architecture. The host is not shown.

Each device consists of one or more *compute units* (CUs) that correspond to CUDA streaming multiprocessors (SMs). However, a CU can also correspond to CPU cores or other types of execution units in compute accelerators such as DSPs and FPGAs.

Each CU, in turn, consists of one or more *processing elements* (PEs), which corresponds to the streaming processors in CUDA. Computation on a device ultimately happens in individual PEs.

Like CUDA, OpenCL also exposes a hierarchy of memory types that can be used by programers. Fig. A.4 illustrates these memory types: global, constant, local, and private. Fig. A.5 summarizes the supported use of OpenCL memory types and the mapping of these memory types to CUDA memory types. The OpenCL global memory corresponds to the CUDA global memory. Like CUDA, the global memory can be dynamically allocated by the host program and supports read/write access by both host and devices.

Unlike CUDA, the constant memory can be dynamically allocated by the host. Like CUDA, the constant memory supports read/write access by the host and read-only access by devices. To support multiple platforms, OpenCL provides a device query that returns the constant memory size supported by the device.

The mapping of OpenCL local memory and private memory to CUDA memory types is more interesting. The OpenCL local memory actually corresponds to CUDA shared memory. The OpenCL local memory can be dynamically allocated by the host or statically allocated in the device code. Like the CUDA shared memory, the OpenCL local memory cannot be accessed by the host and supports shared read/write access by all work items in a work group. The private memory of OpenCL corresponds to the CUDA automatic variables.

Memory Type	Host Access	Device Access	CUDA Equivalent
Global memory	Dynamic allocation; read/write access	No allocation; read/write access by all work items in all work groups, large and slow but may be cached in some devices.	Global memory
Constant memory	Dynamic allocat ion; read/write access	Static allocation; r ead-only access by all work items.	Constant memory
Local memory	Dynamic allocation; no access	Static allocation; s hared read-write access by all work items in a work group.	Shared memory
Private memory	No alloc ation; no access	Static allocation; read/write access by a single work item.	Registers and local memory

FIGURE A.5

Mapping between OpenCL and CUDA memory types.

A.4 KERNEL FUNCTIONS

OpenCL kernels have identical basic structure as CUDA kernels. All openCL kernel declarations start with a "__kernel" keyword, which is equivalent to the "__global__" keyword in CUDA. Fig. A.6 shows a simple OpenCL kernel that performs vector addition.

The kernel takes three arguments: pointers to the two input arrays and one pointer to the output array. The "__global" declarations in the function header indicate that the input and output arrays all reside in the global memory. Note that this keyword has the same meaning in OpenCL as in CUDA, except that there are two underscore characters (__) after the global keyword in CUDA.

The body of the kernel function is instantiated once for each work item. In Fig. A.6, each work item calls the get_global_id(0) function to receive their unique global index. This index value is then used by the work item to select the array elements to work on. Once the array element index i is formed, the rest of the kernel is virtually identical to the CUDA kernel.

A.5 DEVICE MANAGEMENT AND KERNEL LAUNCH

OpenCL defines a much more complex model of device management than CUDA. The extra complexity stems from the need for OpenCL to support multiple hardware platforms. OpenCL supports runtime construction and compilation of kernels

```
__kernel void  vadd(__global const float *a,
    __global const float *b, __global float *result) {

    int i = get_global_id(0);
    result[i] = a[i] + b[i];
}
```

FIGURE A.6

A simple OpenCL kernel.

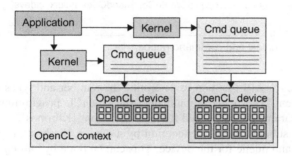

FIGURE A.7

OpenCL contexts are needed to manage devices.

to maximize an applications ability to address portability challenges across a wide range of CPUs and GPUs. Interested readers should refer to OpenCL specification for more insight into the work that went into the OpenCL specification to cover as many types of potential OpenCL devices as possible [KHR, 2011].

In OpenCL, devices are managed through *contexts*. Fig. A.7 illustrates the main concepts of device management in OpenCL. In order to manage one or more devices in the system, the OpenCL programer first creates a context that contains these devices. A context is essentially an address space that contains the accessible memory locations to the OpenCL devices in the system. This can be done by calling either clCreateContext() or clCreateContextFromType() in the OpenCL API.

Fig. A.8 shows a simple host code pattern for managing OpenCL devices. In Line 4, we use clGetContextInfo() to get the number of bytes needed (parmsz) to hold the device information, which is used in Line 5 to allocate enough memory to hold the information about all the devices available in the system. This is because the amount of memory needed to hold the information depends on the number of OpenCL devices in the system. We then call clGetContextInfo() again in Line 6 with the size of the device information and a pointer to the allocated memory for the device information so that the function can deposit information on all the devices in the system into the allocated memory. An application could also use the

```
...
1. cl_int clerr = CL_SUCCESS;

2. cl_context clctx=clCreateContextFromType(0, CL_DEVICE_TYPE_ALL,
       NULL, NULL, &clerr);

3. size_t parmsz;
4. clerr= clGetContextInfo(clctx, CL_CONTEXT_DEVICES, 0, NULL, &parmsz);

5. cl_device_id* cldevs= (cl_device_id *) malloc(parmsz);
6. clerr= clGetContextInfo(clctx, CL_CONTEXT_DEVICES, parmsz, cldevs, NULL);

7. cl_command_queue clcmdq=clCreateCommandQueue(clctx, cldevs[0], 0, &clerr);
```

FIGURE A.8

Creating OpenCL context and command queue.

clGetDeviceIDs() API function to determine the number and types of devices that exist in a system. The reader should read the OpenCL programing guide on the details of the parameters to be used for these functions [Khronos].

In order to submit work for execution by a device, the host program must first create a command queue for the device. This can be done by calling the clCreate-CommandQueue() function in the OpenCL API. Once a command queue is created for a device, the host code can perform a sequence of API function calls to insert a kernel along with its execution configuration parameters into the command queue. When the device is available for executing the next kernel, it removes the kernel at the head of the queue for execution.

Fig. A.8 shows a simple host program that creates a context for a device and submits a kernel for execution by the device. Line 2 shows a call to create a context that includes all OpenCL available devices in the system. Line 4 calls clGetContextInfo() function to inquire about the number of devices in the context. Since Line 2 asks that all OpenCL available devices be included in the context, the application does not know the number of devices actually included in the context after the context is created. The second argument of the call in Line 4 specifies that the information being requested is the list of all devices included in the context. However, the fourth argument, which is a pointer to a memory buffer where the list should be deposited, is a NULL pointer. This means that the call does not want the list itself. The reason is that the application does not know the number of devices in the context and does not know the size of the memory buffer required to hold the list.

Rather, Line 4 provides a pointer to the variable parmsz. After Line 4, the parmsz variable holds the size of the buffer needed to accommodate the list of devices in the context. The application now knows the amount of memory buffer needed to hold the list of devices in the context. It allocates the memory buffer using parmsz and assigns the address of the buffer to pointer variable cldevs at Line 5.

Line 6 calls clGetContextInfo() again with the pointer to the memory buffer in the fourth argument and the size of the buffer in the third argument. Since this is based on the information from the call at Line 4, the buffer is guaranteed to be the right size for the list of devices to be returned. The `clGetContextInfo` function now fills the device list information into the memory buffer pointed to by `cldevs`.

Line 7 creates a command queue for the first OpenCL device in the list. This is done by treating `cldevs` as an array whose elements are descriptors of OpenCL devices in the system. Line 7 passes `cldevs[0]` as the second argument into the `clCreateCommandQueue(0)` function. Therefore, the call generates a command queue for the first device in the list returned by the `clGetContextInfo()` function.

The reader may wonder why we did not see this complex sequence of API calls in our CUDA host programs. The reason is that we have been using the CUDA runtime API that hides all this type of complexity for the common case where there is only one CUDA device in the system. The kernel launch in CUDA handles all the complexities on behalf of the host code. If the developer wanted to have direct access to all CUDA devices in the system, he/she would need to use the CUDA driver API, where similar API calling sequences would be used. To date, OpenCL has not defined a higher-level API that is equivalent to the CUDA runtime API. Until such a higher-level interface is available, OpenCL will remain much more tedious to use than the CUDA runtime API. The benefit, of course, is that an OpenCL application can execute on a wide range of devices.

A.6 ELECTROSTATIC POTENTIAL MAP IN OPENCL

We now present an OpenCL case study based the DCS kernel in Fig. 15.9. This case study is designed to give a CUDA program a practical, top to bottom experience with OpenCL. The first step in porting the kernel to OpenCL is to design the organization of the NDRange, which is illustrated in Fig. A.8. The design is a straightforward mapping of CUDA threads to OpenCL work items and CUDA blocks to OpenCL work groups. As shown in Fig. A.9, each work item will calculate up to eight grid points and each work group will have 64–256 work items. All the efficiency considerations in Chapter 15, Application case study—molecular visualization and analysis also apply here.

The work groups are assigned to the CUs the same way that CUDA blocks are assigned to the SMs. Such assignment is illustrated in Fig. A.10. One can use the same methodology used in Chapters 5 and 15, Performance considerations and Application case study—molecular visualization and analysis to derive high performance OpenCL DCS kernel. Although the syntax is different, the underlying thought process involved in developing a high-performance OpenCL kernel is very similar to CUDA.

Fig. A.10 assumes the work assignment and work group organization shown in Fig. A.9. These work groups are assigned to CUs. The number of work groups that can be assigned to each CU depends on the resource requirements of each group and the resources available in each CU.

The OpenCL kernel function implementation matches closely the CUDA implementation. Fig. A.11 shows the key differences. One is the __kernel keyword in

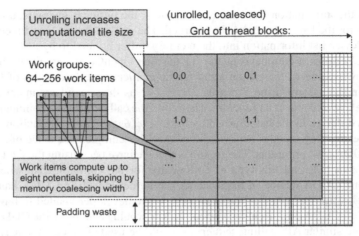

FIGURE A.9

DCS kernel version 3 NDRange configuration.

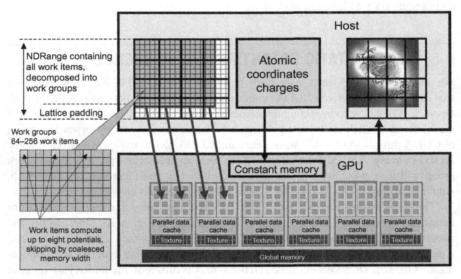

FIGURE A.10

Mapping DCS NDRange to OpenCL Device.

OpenCL vs. the __global keyword in CUDA. The main difference lies in the way the data access indices are calculated. In this case, the OpenCL get_global_id(0) function returns the equivalent of CUDA blockIdx.x*blockDim.x+threadIdx.x.

Fig. A.12 shows the inner loop of the OpenCL kernel. The reader should compare this inner loop with the CUDA code in Fig. 15.9. The only difference is that

```
Device
OpenCL:
__kernel voidclenergy(…) {
unsigned int xindex= get_global_id(0);
unsigned int yindex= get_global_id(1);
unsigned int outaddr= get_global_size(0) * UNROLLX
*yindex+xindex;

CUDA:
__global__ void cuenergy(…) {
Unsigned int xindex= blockIdx.x *blockDim.x +threadIdx.x;
unsigned int yindex= blockIdx.y *blockDim.y +threadIdx.y;
unsigned int outaddr= gridDim.x *blockDim.x *
UNROLLX*yindex+xindex
```

FIGURE A.11

Data access indexing in OpenCL and CUDA.

```
…
for (atomid=0; atomid<numatoms; atomid++) {
float dy = coory -atominfo[atomid].y;
float dyz2= (dy * dy) + atominfo[atomid].z;
float dx1 = coorx -atominfo[atomid].x;
float dx2 = dx1 + gridspacing_coalesce;
float dx3 = dx2 + gridspacing_coalesce;
float dx4 = dx3 + gridspacing_coalesce;
float charge = atominfo[atomid].w;
energyvalx1 += charge* native_rsqrt(dx1*dx1 + dyz2);
energyvalx2 += charge* native_rsqrt(dx2*dx2 + dyz2);
energyvalx3 += charge* native_rsqrt(dx3*dx3 + dyz2);
energyvalx4 += charge* native_rsqrt(dx4*dx4 + dyz2);
}
```

FIGURE A.12

Inner loop of the OpenCL DCS kernel.

__rsqrt() call has been changed to native_rsqrt() call, the OpenCL way for using the hardware implementation of math functions on a particular device.

OpenCL adopts a dynamic compilation model. Unlike CUDA, the host program can explicitly compile and create a kernel program at run time. This is illustrated in Fig. A.13 for the DCS kernel. Line 1 declares the entire OpenCL DCS kernel source code as a string. Line 3 delivers the source code string to the OpenCL runtime system by calling the clCreateProgramWith Source() function. Line 4 sets up the compiler flags for the runtime compilation process. Line 5 invokes the runtime compiler to build the program. Line 6 requests that the OpenCL runtime create the kernel and its data structures so that it can be properly launched. After Line 6, clkern points to the kernel that can be submitted to a command queue for execution.

Fig. A.14 shows the host code that launches the DCS kernel. It assumes that the host code for managing OpenCL devices in Fig. A.8 has been executed. Lines 1 and

1 const char* clenergysrc =

> OpenCL kernel source code as a big string

"__kernel __attribute__((reqd_work_group_size_hint(BLOCKSIZEX, BLOCKSIZEY, 1))) \n"

"void clenergy(__constant int numatoms, __constant float gridspacing, __global float *energy, __constant float4 *atominfo) { \n" [...etc and so forth...]

2 cl_program clpgm;

> Gives raw source code string(s) to OpenCL

3 clpgm = clCreateProgramWithSource(clctx, 1, &clenergysrc, NULL, &clerr);

char clcompileflags[4096];

4 sprintf(clcompileflags, "-DUNROLLX=%d -cl-fast-relaxed-math -cl-single-precision-constant -cl-denorms-are-zero -cl-mad-enable", UNROLLX);

5 clerr = clBuildProgram(clpgm, 0, NULL, clcompileflags, NULL, NULL);

6 cl_kernel clkern = clCreateKernel(clpgm, "clenergy", &clerr);

> Set compiler flags, compile source, and retreive a handle to the "clenergy" kernel

FIGURE A.13

Building OpenCL kernel.

```
1. doutput= clCreateBuffer(clctx, CL_MEM_READ_WRITE,volmemsz,
      NULL, NULL);
2. datominfo= clCreateBuffer(clctx, CL_MEM_READ_ONLY,
      MAXATOMS *sizeof(cl_float4), NULL, NULL);
...
3. clerr= clSetKernelArg(clkern, 0,sizeof(int), &runatoms);
4. clerr= clSetKernelArg(clkern, 1,sizeof(float), &zplane);
5. clerr= clSetKernelArg(clkern, 2,sizeof(cl_mem), &doutput);
6. clerr= clSetKernelArg(clkern, 3,sizeof(cl_mem), &datominfo);
7. cl_event event;
8. clerr= clEnqueueNDRangeKernel(clcmdq,clkern, 2, NULL,
      Gsz,Bsz, 0, NULL, &event);
9. clerr= clWaitForEvents(1, &event);
10. clerr= clReleaseEvent(event);
...
11. clEnqueueReadBuffer(clcmdq,doutput, CL_TRUE, 0,
      volmemsz, energy, 0, NULL, NULL);
12. clReleaseMemObject(doutput);
13. clReleaseMemObject(datominfo);
```

FIGURE A.14

OpenCL Host code for kernel launch and parameter passing.

2 allocate memory for the energy grid data and the atom information. The `clCreate-Buffer()` function corresponds to the `cudaMalloc()` function. The constant memory is implicitly requested by setting the mode of access to ready only for the atominfo array. Note that each memory buffer is associated with a context, which is specified by the first argument to the `clCreateBuffer()` function call.

Lines 3–6 in Fig. A.14 set up the arguments to be passed into the kernel function. In CUDA, the kernel functions are launched with C function call syntax extended with <<<>>>, which is followed by the regular list of arguments. In OpenCL, there is no explicit call to kernel functions. Therefore, one needs to use the clSetKernel-Arg() functions to set up the arguments for the kernel function.

Line 8 in Fig. A.14 submits the DCS kernel for launch. The arguments to the clEnqueueNDRangeKernel() function specify the command queue for the device that will execute the kernel, a pointer to the kernel, and the global and local sizes of the NDRange. Lines 9 and 10 check for errors if any.

Line 11 transfers the contents of the output data back into the energy array in the host memory. The OpenCL clEnqueueReadBuffer() copies data from the device memory to the host memory and corresponds to the device to host direction of the cudaMemcpy() function.

The clReleaseMemObject() function is a little more sophisticated than cudaFree(). OpenCL maintains a reference count for data objects. OpenCL host program modules can retain (clRetainMemObject()) and release (clReleaseMemObject()) data objects. Note that clCreateBuffer() also serves as a retain call. With each retain call, the reference count of the object is incremented. With each release call, the reference count is decremented. When the reference count for an object reaches 0, the object is freed. This way, a library module can "hang on" to a memory object even though the other parts of the application no longer need the object and thus have released the object.

A.7 SUMMARY

OpenCL is a standardized, cross-platform API designed to support portable parallel application development on heterogeneous computing systems. Like CUDA, OpenCL addresses complex memory hierarchies and data parallel execution. It draws heavily on the CUDA driver API experience. This is the reason why a CUDA programer finds these aspects of OpenCL familiar. We have seen this through the mappings of the OpenCL data parallelism model concepts, NDRange API calls, and memory types to their CUDA equivalents.

On the other hand, OpenCL has a more complex device management model that reflects its support for multiplatform and multivendor portability. While the OpenCL standard is designed to support code portability across devices produced by different vendors, such portability does not come for free. OpenCL programs must be prepared to deal with much greater hardware diversity and thus will exhibit more complexity. We see that the OpenCL device management model, the OpenCL kernel compilation model, and the OpenCL kernel launch are much more complex than their CUDA counterparts.

We have by no means covered all the programing features of OpenCL. The reader is encouraged to read the OpenCL specification [KHR, 2011] and tutorials [Khronos] for more OpenCL features. In particular, we recommend that the reader pay special attention to the device query, object query, and task parallelism model. Further, the reader is encouraged to learn the new featuresntroduced in OpenCL 2.0.

A.8 EXERCISES

1. Use the code base in Appendix A and examples in Chapters 2–5, Data parallel computing, Scalable parallel execution, Memory and data locality, and Performance considerations, to develop an OpenCL version of the matrix–matrix multiplication application.

2. Read the "OpenCL Platform Layer" section of the OpenCL specification. Compare the platform querying API functions with what you have learned in CUDA.

3. Read the "Memory Objects" section of the OpenCL specification. Compare the object creation and access API functions with what you have learned in CUDA.

4. Read the "Kernel Objects" section of the OpenCL specification. Compare the kernel creation and launching API functions with what you have learned in CUDA.

5. Read the "OpenCL Programing Language" section of the OpenCL specification. Compare the keywords and types with what you have learned in CUDA.

REFERENCES

AMD OpenCL Resources. <http://developer.amd.com/gpu/ATIStreamSDK/pages/Tutorial OpenCL.aspx>.
Khronos Group. (2011). The OpenCL Specification version 1.1, rev44. <http://www.khronos.org/registry/cl/specs/opencl-1.1.pdf>.
Khronos OpenCL samples, tutorials, etc. <http://www.khronos.org/developers/resources/opencl/>.
NVIDIA OpenCL Resources. <http://www.nvidia.com/object/cuda_opencl.html>.

THRUST: a productivity-oriented library for CUDA

Nathan Bell, Jared Hoberock and Chris Rodrigues

CHAPTER OUTLINE

This chapter demonstrates how to leverage the Thrust parallel template library to implement high-performance applications with minimal programming effort. Based on the C++ Standard Template Library (STL), Thrust brings a familiar high-level interface to the realm of GPU Computing while remaining fully interoperable with the rest of the CUDA software ecosystem. Thrust provides a set of type-generic parallel algorithms that can be used with user-defined data types. These parallel algorithms can significantly reduce the effort of developing parallel applications. Applications written with Thrust are concise, readable, efficient, and portable.

B.1 BACKGROUND

C++ provides a way for programmers to define generics, functions that can be invoked on any data types. In situations when a programming problem has the same solution for many different data types, the solution can be written once and for all using *generics*. For example, the two C++ functions shown below sum a `float` array and an `int` array. They are defined without using type-generics. The only difference between the first and second function is that "`float`" is changed to "`int`."

```float sum(int n, float *p) { float a = 0; for (int i=0; i <n; i++) a += p[i]; return a; }```	```int sum(int n, int *p) { int a = 0; for (int i=0; i <n; i++) a += p[i]; return a; }```

Instead of writing a different version of "sum" for each data type, the following generic "sum" function can be used with any data type. The idea is that the programmer prepares a template of sum function that can be instantiated on different types of array. The "template" keyword indicates the beginning of a type-generic definition. From this point on, we will use type-generic and generic interchangeably.

```
template<typename T>
T sum(int n, T *p) {
  T a=0;
  for (int i=0; i <n; i++) a += p[i];
  return a;
}
```

The code uses T as a placeholder where the actual type needs to be. Replacing "T" by "float" in the generic code yields one of the two definitions of "sum", while replacing "T" by "int" yields the other. "T" could also be replaced by other types, including user-defined types. A C++ compiler will make the appropriate replacement each time the "sum" function is used. Consequently, "sum" behaves much like the overloaded C++ function above, and it can be used as if it were an overloaded function. The central concept of generic programming is the use of *type parameters*, like "T" in this example that can be replaced by arbitrary types.

Thrust is a library of generic functions. By providing generic functions for each type of computation to be supported, Thrust does not need to have multiple versions of each function replicated for each eligible data type.

In reality, not all data types can be used with a generic function. Because sum uses addition and initializes "a" to 0, it requires the type T to behave (broadly speaking) like a number. Replacing T by the numeric types int or float produces a valid function definition, but replacing T by void or FILE* does not. Such requirements are called *concepts*, and when a type satisfies a requirement it is said to *model* a concept. In "sum", whatever replaces T must model the "number" concept. That is, "sum" will compute a sum provided that it's given a pointer to some type T that acts like a numeric type. Otherwise, it may produce an error or return a meaningless result. Generic libraries like Thrust rely on concepts as part of their interface.

C++ Classes can be generic as well. The idea is similar to generic functions, with the extra feature that a class's fields can depend on type parameters. Generics are commonly used to define reusable *container classes*, such as those in the STL [HB 2011]. Container classes are implementations of data structures, such as queues, linked lists, and hash tables that can be used to hold arbitrary data types. For instance, a very simple generic array container class could be defined as follows:

```
template<typename T>
class Array {
  T contents[10];
public:
  T read(int i) {return contents[i];}
  void write(int i, T x) {contents[i] = x;}
};
```

Containers for different data types can be created using this generic class. Their types are written as the generic class name followed by a type in angle brackets: `Array<int>` for an array of `int`, `Array<float *>` for an array of `float*`, and so forth. The type given in angle brackets replaces the type parameter in the class definition.

While this is not a complete description of how generics work, it conveys the essential ideas for understanding the use of generics in this chapter.

We will introduce one more background concept: iterators. In the same way that pointers are used to access arrays, *iterators* are used to access container classes. The term "iterator" refers to both a C++ concept and a value whose type is a model of this concept. An iterator represents a position within a container: it can be used to access the element at that position, used to go to neighboring position, or compared to other positions.

Pointers model the iterator concept, and they can be used to loop over an array as shown below:

```
int a[50];
for (int *i = a; i < a + 50; i++) *i = 1;
```

Iterators can be used to loop over an STL vector in a very similar way:

```
vector<int> a(50);
for (vector<int>::iterator i = a.begin(); i < a.end(); i++) *i = 1;
```

The member functions `begin()` and `end()` return iterators referencing the beginning and just past the end of the vector. The ++, <, and * operators are overloaded to act like their pointer counterparts. Because many container classes provide an iterator interface, generic C++ code using iterators can be reused to process different kinds of containers.

B.2 MOTIVATION

CUDA C allows developers to make detailed decisions about how computations are decomposed into parallel threads and executed on the device. The level of control offered by CUDA C is an important feature: it facilitates the development of high-performance algorithms for a variety of computationally demanding tasks which (1) merit significant optimization and (2) profit from low-level control of the mapping onto hardware. For this class of computational tasks CUDA C is an excellent solution.

Thrust [HB 2011] solves a complementary set of problems, namely those that are (1) implemented efficiently without a detailed mapping of work onto the target architecture or those that (2) do not merit or simply will not receive significant optimization effort by the developers. With Thrust, developers describe their computation using a collection of *high-level* algorithms and completely *delegate* the decision of how to implement the computation to the library. This abstract interface allows programmers to describe *what to compute* without placing any additional restrictions on how to carry out the computation. By capturing the programmer's intent at a high level, Thrust has the discretion to make informed decisions on behalf of the programmer and select the most efficient implementation.

The value of high-level libraries is broadly recognized in high-performance computing. For example, the widely used BLAS standard provides an abstract interface to common linear algebra operations. First conceived more than three decades ago, BLAS remains relevant today in large part because it allows valuable, platform-specific optimizations to be introduced behind a uniform interface.

Whereas BLAS is focused on numerical linear algebra, Thrust provides an abstract interface to fundamental parallel algorithms such as scan, sort, and reduction that we have introduced in this book. Thrust leverages the power of C++ templates to make these algorithms generic, enabling them to be used with arbitrary user-defined types and operators. Thrust establishes a durable interface for parallel computing with emphasis on generality, programmer productivity, and real-world performance.

B.3 BASIC THRUST FEATURES

Before going into greater details, let us consider the program in Fig. B.1, which illustrates the salient features of Thrust.

Thrust provides two vector *containers*: host_vector and device_vector. As the names suggest, host_vector is stored in host memory while device_vector lives in device memory on the GPU. Like the vector container in the C++ STL, host_vector and device_vector are generic containers (i.e., they are able to store any data type) that can be resized dynamically. As the example shows, containers automate the allocation and de-allocation of memory and simplify the process of exchanging data between the host and the device.

The program acts on the vector containers using the generate, sort, and copy algorithms. Here, we adopt the STL convention of specifying *ranges* using pairs of *iterators*. In this example, the iterators h_vec.begin() and h_vec.end() point to the first element and the element that is one past the end of the array respectively. Together the pair defines a *range* of integers of size h_vec.end()-h_vec.begin().

```
#include <thrust/host vector.h>
#include <thrust/device vector.h>
#include <thrust/generate.h>
#include <thrust/sort.h>
#include <thrust/copy.h>
#include <cstdlib>

int main(void)
{
    //   generate 16M random numbers on the host

    thrust::host vector<int> h vec(1 << 24);
    thrust::generate(h vec.begin(), h vec.end(), rand);

        //   transfer data to the device
    thrust::device vector<int> d_vec  = h vec;

    //   sort data on the device

    thrust::sort(d vec.begin(), d vec.end());

        //   transfer data back to host
    thrust::copy(d vec.begin(),  d_vec.end(),  h_vec.begin());

    return 0;
}
```

FIGURE B.1

A complete Thrust program which sorts data on the GPU.

Note that even though the computation implied by the call to the `sort` algorithm suggests one or more CUDA kernel launches, the programmer has not specified a launch configuration. Thrust's interface *abstracts* these details. The choice of performance-sensitive variables such as grid and block size of the library, the details of memory management, and even the choice of sorting algorithm are left to the discretion of the implementer.

ITERATORS AND MEMORY SPACE

Although vector iterators are similar to pointers, they carry additional information. Notice that in Fig. B.1, we did not have to instruct the `thrust::sort` function that it was operating on the elements of a `device_vector` or hint that the `copy` was from device memory to host memory. In Thrust the memory spaces of each range are automatically *inferred* from the iterator arguments and used to dispatch the appropriate implementation.

In addition to memory space, Thrust's iterators implicitly encode a wealth of information which can guide the dispatch process. For instance, our `sort` example in Fig. B.1 operates on `int`, a primitive data type with a fundamental comparison operation. In this case, Thrust dispatches a highly tuned radix sort algorithm [MG

2010] which is considerably faster than alternative comparison-based sorting algorithms such as the merge sort discussed in Chapter 11, Parallel patterns: merge sort. It is important to realize that this dispatch process incurs no performance or storage overhead: metadata encoded by iterators exists only at compile time, and dispatch strategies based on it are selected *statically*. In general, Thrust's static dispatch strategies may capitalize on any information that is derivable from the type of an iterator.

INTEROPERABILITY

Thrust is implemented entirely within CUDA C/C++ and maintains interoperability with the rest of the CUDA ecosystem. Interoperability is an important feature because no single language or library is the best tool for every problem. For example, although Thrust algorithms use CUDA features like shared memory internally, there is no mechanism for users to exploit shared memory directly through Thrust. Therefore, it is sometimes necessary for applications to access CUDA C directly to implement a certain class of specialized algorithms, as illustrated in the software stack of Fig. B.2. Interoperability between Thrust and CUDA C allows the programmer to replace a Thrust kernel with a CUDA kernel and vice versa by making a small number of changes to the surrounding code.

Interfacing Thrust to CUDA C is straightforward and analogous to the use of the C++ STL with standard C code. Data that resides in a Thrust container can be accessed by external libraries by extracting a "raw" pointer from the vector. The code example in Fig. B.3 illustrates the use of raw pointer cast to obtain an `int` pointer to the contents of a device vector.

In Fig. B.3A, the function `raw_pointer_cast()` function takes the address of element 0 of a device vector `d_vec` and return a raw C pointer `raw_ptr`. This pointer can then be used to call CUDA C API functions (`cudaMemset()` in this example) or passed as a parameter to a CUDA C kernel (`my_kernel` in this example).

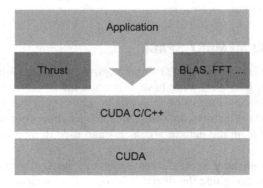

FIGURE B.2

Thrust is an abstraction layer on top of CUDA C/C++.

```
size t  N  =  1024;

// allocate Thrust container
device vector<int>  d vec(N);

// extract  raw  pointer  from
container

int raw ptr = raw pointer cast(&d
vec[0]);

// use raw ptr in non Thrustfunctions

cudaMemset(raw ptr,  0,  N
sizeof(int));

// pass raw ptr to a kernel
my kernel<<<N / 128, 128>>>(N, raw
ptr);

// memory is automatically freed
```

(A)

```
size t  N  =  1024;

// raw  pointer  to  device  memory
int raw ptr;
cudaMalloc(&raw ptr, N sizeof(int));

// wrap raw pointer with a device ptr
device ptr<int> dev ptr = device
pointer cast(raw ptr);


// use device ptr in Thrust  algorithms
sort(dev ptr, dev ptr + N);


// access device memory through device
ptr
dev ptr[0] = 1;

// free  memory
cudaFree(raw ptr);
```

(B)

FIGURE B.3

Thrust interoperates smoothly with CUDA C/C++. (A) Interfacing Thrust to CUDA and (B) Interfacing CUDA to Thrust.

Applying Thrust algorithms to raw C pointers is also straightforward. Once the raw pointer has been wrapped by a device_ptr it can be used like an ordinary Thrust iterator. In Fig. B.3B, the C pointer raw_ptr points to a piece of device memory allocated by cudaMalloc(). It can be converted or wrapped into a device pointer to a device vector by function device_pointer_cast() function. The wrapped pointer provides the memory space information Thrust needs to invoke the appropriate algorithm implementation and also allows a convenient mechanism for accessing device memory from the host. In this case, the information indicates that dev_ptr points to a vector in the device memory and the elements are of type int.

Thrust's native CUDA C interoperability ensures that Thrust always *complements* CUDA C and that a Thrust plus CUDA C combination is never worse than either Thrust or CUDA C alone. Indeed, while it may be possible to write whole parallel applications entirely with Thrust functions, it is often valuable to implement domain-specific functionality directly in CUDA C. The level of abstraction targeted by native CUDA C affords programmers fine-grained control over the precise mapping of computational resources to a particular problem. Programming at this level provides developers the flexibility to implement exotic or otherwise specialized algorithms. Interoperability also facilitates an iterative development strategy: (1) quickly prototype a parallel application entirely in Thrust, (2) identify the application's hot spots, and (3) write more specialized algorithms in CUDA C and optimize as necessary.

B.4 GENERIC PROGRAMMING

Thrust presents a style of programming emphasizing code reusability and composability. Indeed, the vast majority of Thrust's functionality is derived from four fundamental parallel algorithms: `for_each`, `reduce`, `scan`, and `sort`. For example, the `transform` algorithm is a derivative of `for each` while inner product is implemented with `reduce`.

Thrust algorithms are generic in both the type of the data to be processed and the operations to be applied to the data. For instance, the `reduce` algorithm may be employed to compute the sum of a range of integers (a `plus` reduction applied to `int` data) or the maximum of a range of floating point values (a `max` reduction applied to `float` data). This generality is implemented via C++ templates, which allow user-defined types and functions to be used in addition to built-in types such as `int` or `float` or Thrust operators such as `plus`.

Generic algorithms are extremely valuable because it is impractical to anticipate precisely which particular types and operators a user will require. Indeed, while the computational structure of an algorithm is fixed, the number of *instantiations* of the algorithm is limitless. However, it is also worth mentioning that while Thrust's interface is general, the abstraction affords implementers the opportunity to specialize for specific types and operations known to be important use cases. These opportunities may be exploited statically.

In Thrust, user-defined operations take the form of C++ function objects, or *functors* (see sidebar). Functors allow the programmer to adapt a generic algorithm to perform a specific user-defined operation. For example, the code samples in Fig. B.4 implement SAXPY, the well-known BLAS operation, using CUDA C and Thrust respectively. The CUDA C code should be very familiar and is provided for comparison.

The Thrust code in Fig. B.4 has two parts. In the first part, the code sets up a SAXPY functor that receives an input floating value a and maintains it as a state. It can then be called as an operator that performs `a*x +y` on two input values x and y. Finally, the generic `transform` algorithm is called with the user-defined `saxpy_functor func`. The iterators provided to the `transform` algorithm will apply func to each pair of the x and y elements and produce the `saxpy` results. Note that the operator defined in the `saxpy_functor` declaration can be overloaded so that different types of a, x, y can be passed into the `transform` algorithm and the correct operator will be invoked to generate the expected output values for each type of inputs. This makes it possible to create a generic SAXPY function.

C++ FUNCTION OBJECTS

A C library developer can set up a generic function by allowing the user to provide a callback function. For example, a sort function can allow the user to pass a function pointer as a parameter to perform the comparison operation for determining the order between two input values. This allows the user to pass any types of input as long as he/she can define a comparison function between two input values.

(A) global
```
void saxpy kernel(int n, float a, "float*" x, "float*" y)
{
const int i = blockDim.x * blockIdx.x + threadIdx.x;

if  (i < n)  y[i]  =  a * x[i]  +  y[i];
}


void saxpy(int n, float a, "float*" x, "float*" y)
{
// set launch configuration parameters int block size = 256;
int grid size = (n + block_size - 1) / block size;

// launch saxpy kernel

saxpy kernel<<<  grid_size, block_size>>>(n, a, x, y);
}
```

(B)
```
struct saxpy_functor
{
  const float a;

  saxpy_functor(float   _a)  :  a(_a)  {}

  __host__   __device__
  float operator() (float x, float y)
  {
   return  a * x + y;
  }
}

void saxpy(float a, device_vector <float> &x, device_vector<float>&y)
{
   // setup functor
   saxpy_functor  func(a);

   //    call  transform
   transform(x.begin(), x.end(), y.begin(), y.end(), func);
}
```

FIGURE B.4

SAXPY implementations in (A) CUDA C and (B) Thrust.

It is sometimes desirable for a callback function to maintain a state. The C++ function object, or functor, provides a convenient way to do so. A functor is really a function defined on an object which holds a state. The function that is passed as the callback function is just a member function defined in the class declaration of the object. In the case of the saxpy_functor class, a is the class data and operator is the member function defined on the data. When an instance of saxpy_functor, func(), is passed to a generic algorithm function such as transform(), the operator will be called to operate on each pair of x and y elements.

B.5 BENEFITS OF ABSTRACTION

In this section we will describe the benefits of Thrust's abstraction layer with respect to programmer productivity, robustness, and real-world performance.

PROGRAMMER PRODUCTIVITY

Thrust's high-level algorithms enhance programmer productivity by automating the mapping of computational tasks onto the GPU. Recall the two implementations of SAXPY shown in Fig. B.4. In the CUDA C implementation of SAXPY the programmer has described a specific decomposition of the parallel vector operation into a grid of blocks with 256 threads per block. In contrast, the Thrust implementation does not prescribe a launch configuration. Instead, the only specifications are the input and output ranges and a functor to apply to them. The kernel launch will be performed as part of the transform implementation. Otherwise, the two codes are roughly the same in terms of length and code complexity.

Delegating the launch configuration to Thrust has a subtle yet profound implication: the launch parameters can be automatically chosen based on a model of machine performance. Currently, Thrust targets *maximal occupancy* and will compare the resource usage of the kernel (e.g., number of registers, amount of shared memory) with the resources of the target GPU to determine a launch configuration with highest occupancy. While the maximal occupancy heuristic is not necessarily optimal, it is straightforward to compute and effective in practice. Furthermore, there is nothing to preclude the use of more sophisticated performance models. For instance, a run-time tuning system that examined hardware performance counters could be introduced behind this abstraction without altering client code.

Thrust also boosts programmer productivity by providing a rich set of algorithms for common patterns. For instance, the map-reduce pattern is conveniently implemented with Thrust's `sort by key` and `reduce by key` algorithms, which implement key-value sorting and reduction respectively.

ROBUSTNESS

Thrust's abstraction layer also enhances the robustness of CUDA applications. In the previous section we noted that by delegating the launch configuration details to Thrust we could automatically obtain maximum occupancy during execution. In addition to maximizing occupancy, the abstraction layer also ensures that algorithms "just work," even in uncommon or pathological use cases. For instance, Thrust automatically handles limits on grid dimensions (no more than 64K in current devices), works around limitations on the size of global function arguments, and accommodates large user-defined types in most algorithms. To the degree possible, Thrust circumvents such factors and ensures correct program execution across the full spectrum of CUDA-capable devices.

REAL-WORLD PERFORMANCE

In addition to enhancing programmer productivity and improving robustness, the high-level abstractions provided by Thrust can improve performance in real-world use cases. In this section we examine two instances where the discretion afforded by Thrust's high-level interface is exploited for meaningful performance gains.

To begin, consider the operation of filling an array with a particular value. In Thrust, this is implemented with the `fill` algorithm. Unfortunately, a straightforward implementation of this seemingly simple operation is subject to severe performance hazards. Early generations of GPUs such as the G80 architecture (i.e., Compute Capability 1.0 and 1.1) impose strict conditions on which memory access patterns may benefit from memory coalescing (see chapter: Performance considerations). In particular, memory accesses of sub-word granularity (i.e., less than 4 bytes) are not coalesced by these processors. This artifact is detrimental to performance when initializing arrays of `char` or `short` types.

Fortunately, the iterators passed to `fill` implicitly encode all the information necessary to intercept this case and substitute an optimized implementation. Specifically, when `fill` is dispatched for smaller types, Thrust selects a "wide" version of the algorithm that issues word-sized accesses per thread. While this optimization is straightforward to implement, users are unlikely to invest the effort of making this optimization themselves. Nevertheless, the benefit, shown in Table B.1, is worthwhile, particularly on earlier architectures. Note that with the relaxed coalescing rules on the more recent processors, the benefit of the optimization has somewhat decreased but is still significant.

Like `fill`, Thrust's sorting functionality exploits the discretion afforded by the abstract `sort` and `stable sort` functions. As long as the algorithm achieves

Table B.1 Memory Bandwidth of Two Fill Kernels

GPU	Data Type	naive `fill`	thrust::`fill`	Speedup
GeForce 8800 GTS	Char	1.2 GB/s	41.2 GB/s	34.15x
	short	2.4 GB/s	41.2 GB/s	17.35x
	int	41.2 GB/s	41.2 GB/s	1.00x
	long	40.7 GB/s	40.7 GB/s	1.00x
GeForce GTX 280	char	33.9 GB/s	75.0 GB/s	2.21x
	short	51.6 GB/s	75.0 GB/s	1.45x
	int	75.0 GB/s	75.0 GB/s	1.00x
	long	69.2 GB/s	69.2 GB/s	1.00x
GeForce GTX 480	char	74.1 GB/s	156.9 GB/s	2.12x
	short	136.6 GB/s	156.9 GB/s	1.15x
	int	146.1 GB/s	156.9 GB/s	1.07x
	long	156.9 GB/s	156.9 GB/s	1.00x

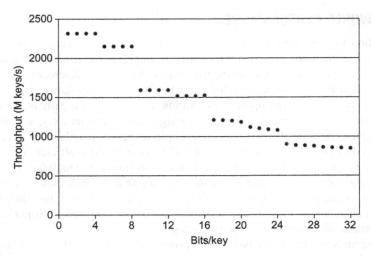

FIGURE B.5

Sorting integers on the GeForce GTX 480: Thrust's dynamic sorting optimizations improve performance by a considerable margin in common use cases where keys are less than 32 bits.

the promised result, we are free to utilize sophisticated static (compile-time) and dynamic (run-time) optimizations to implement the sorting operation in the most efficient manner.

As mentioned in Section B.3, Thrust statically selects a highly optimized radix sort algorithm [MG 2010] for sorting primitive types (e.g., char, int, float, and double) with the standard less and greater comparison operators. For all other types (e.g., user-defined data types) and comparison operators, Thrust uses a general merge sort algorithm. Because sorting primitive types with radix sort is considerably faster than merge sort, this static optimization has significant value.

Thrust also applies dynamic optimizations to improve sorting performance. Since the cost of radix sort is proportional to the number of significant key bits, we can exploit unused key bits to reduce the cost of sorting. For instance, when all integer keys are in the range (0, 16), only four bits must be sorted, and we observe a 2.71 speedup versus a full 32-bit sort. The relationship between key bits and radix sort performance is plotted in Fig. B.5.

B.6 BEST PRACTICES

In this section we highlight three high-level optimization techniques that programmers may employ to yield significant performance speedups when using Thrust.

FUSION

The balance of computational resources on modern GPUs implies that algorithms are often *bandwidth limited*. Specifically, the execution speed of kernels with low *computation intensity*, the ratio of calculations per memory access, are constrained by the available memory bandwidth and do not fully utilize the computational resources of the GPU. One technique for increasing the computational intensity of an algorithm is to *fuse* multiple pipeline stages together into a single operation. In this section we demonstrate how Thrust enables developers to exploit opportunities for kernel fusion and better utilize GPU memory bandwidth.

The simplest form of kernel fusion is scalar function composition. For example, suppose we have the functions $f(x) \rightarrow y$ and $g(y) \rightarrow z$ and would like to compute $g(f(x)) \rightarrow z$ for a range of scalar values. The most straightforward approach is to read x from memory, compute the value $y = f(x)$, write y to memory, and then do the same to compute $z = g(y)$. In Thrust this approach would be implemented with two separate calls to the `transform` algorithm, one for f and one for g. While this approach is straightforward to understand and implement, it needlessly wastes memory bandwidth, which is a scarce resource.

A better approach is to fuse the functions into a single operation $g(f(x))$ and halve the number of memory transactions. Unless f and g are computationally expensive operations, the fused implementation will run approximately twice as fast as the first approach. In general, scalar function composition is a profitable optimization and should be applied liberally.

Thrust enables developers to exploit other less obvious opportunities for fusion. For example, consider the following two Thrust implementations of the BLAS function `Snrm2` shown in Fig. B.6, which computes the Euclidean norm of a `float` vector.

Note that `Snrm2` has low arithmetic intensity: each element of the vector participates in only two floating-point operations, one multiply (to square the value) and one addition (to sum values together). Therefore, an implementation of `Snrm2` using the `transform reduce` algorithm, which fuses the `square transformation` with a `plus reduction`, should be considerably faster. Indeed this is true and `snrm2_fast` is fully 3.8 times faster than `snrm2` slow for a 16 M element vector on a Tesla C1060.

While the previous examples represent some of the more common opportunities for fusion, we have only scratched the surface. As we have seen, fusing a transformation with other algorithms is a worthwhile optimization. However, Thrust would become unwieldy if all algorithms came with a `transform` variant. For this reason Thrust provides `transform` iterator, which allows transformations to be fused with any algorithm. Indeed, `transform reduce` is simply a convenience wrapper for the appropriate combination of transform iterator and reduce. Similarly, Thrust provides `permutation iterator`, which enables gather and scatter operations to be fused with other algorithms.

```
struct square
{
    __host__ __device__
    float operator() (float x) const
    {
    return x *x;
    }
}

float snrm2_slow(const thrust::device vector<float>& x)
{
    // without fusion
    device vector<float> temp(x.size()); transform(x.begin(),
    x.end(), temp.begin(), square());

    return sqrt( reduce(temp.begin(), temp.end()) );
}
float snrm2_fast(const thrust::device vector<float>& x)
{
    // with fusion
    return sqrt( transform_reduce(x.begin(),x.end(),square(),0.0f,
    plus<float>());
}
```

FIGURE B.6

SNRM2 has low arithmetic intensity and therefore benefits greatly from fusion.

STRUCTURE OF ARRAYS

In the previous section we examined how fusion minimizes the number of off-chip memory transactions and conserves bandwidth. Another way to improve memory efficiency is to ensure that all memory accesses benefit from *coalescing*, since coalesced memory access patterns are considerably faster than non-coalesced transactions.

Perhaps the most common violation of the memory coalescing rules arises when using a so-called Array of Structures (AoS) data layout. Generally speaking, access to the elements of an array filled with C `struct` or C++ `class` variables will be uncoalesced. Only explicitly aligned structures such as the `uint2` or `float4` vector types satisfy the memory coalescing rules.

An alternative to the AoS layout is the Structure of Arrays (SoA) approach, where the components of each struct are stored in separate arrays. Fig. B.7 illustrates the AoS and SoA methods of representing a range of three-dimensional `float` vectors. The advantage of the SoA method is that regular access to the x, y, and z components of a given vector is coalesceable (because float satisfies the coalescing rules), while regular access to the `float3` structures in the AoS approach is not.

The problem with SoA is that there is nothing to logically encapsulate the members of each element into a single entity. Whereas we could immediately apply Thrust algorithms to AoS containers like `device vector<float3>`, we have no direct means

```
struct  float3                    struct  float3_soa
{
                                  {

   float  x;                         float    x[100];
   float  y;                         float    y[100];
   float  z;                         float    z[100];
}                                 }
float3  aos[100];                 float3_soa soa;
   ...                               ...
aos[0].x  =  1.0f;                soa.x[0]  =  1.0f;
```
         (A)   (B)

FIGURE B.7

Data layouts for three-dimensional float vectors. (A) Array of structures and (B) structure of arrays.

of doing the same with three separate `device_vector<float>` containers. Fortunately Thrust provides `zip iterator`, which provides encapsulation of SoA ranges.

The `zip iterator` [Boost] takes a number of iterators and *zips* them together into a virtual range of tuples. For instance, binding three `device_vector<float>` iterators together yields a range of type `tuple<float,float,float>`, which is analogous to the `float3` structure.

Consider the code sample in Fig. B.8 which uses `zip iterator` to construct a range of three-dimensional `float` vectors stored in SoA format. Each vector is transformed by a rotation matrix in the `rotate tuple` functor before being written out again. Note that `zip iterator` is used for both input and output ranges, transparently packing the underlying scalar ranges into tuples and then unpacking the tuples into the scalar ranges. On a Tesla C1060, this SoA implementation is 2.85× faster than the analogous AoS implementation (not shown).

IMPLICIT RANGES

In the previous sections we considered ways to efficiently transform ranges of values and ways to construct ad hoc tuples of values from separate ranges. In either case, there was some underlying data stored *explicitly* in memory. In this section we illustrate the use of *implicit* ranges, i.e., ranges whose values are defined programmatically and not stored anywhere in memory.

For instance, consider the problem of finding the index of the element with the smallest value in a given range. We could implement a special reduction kernel for this algorithm, which we will call `min index`, but that would be time-consuming and unnecessary. A better approach is to implement `min index` in terms of existing functionality, such as a specialized reduction over (`value, index`) tuples, to achieve the desired result. Specifically, we can zip the range of values `v[0], v[1], v[2],` ... together with a range of integer indices `0, 1, 2, :::` to form a range of tuples

```
struct rotate tuple {
   __host__ __device__
   tuple<float,float,float> operator()(tuple<float,float,float>& t) {
      float x = get<0>(t);
      float y = get<1>(t);
      float z = get<2>(t);
      float rx = 0.36f * x + 0.48f * y + 0.80f * z;
      float ry = 0.80f * x + 0.60f * y + 0.00f * z;
      float rz = 0.48f * x + 0.64f * y + 0.60f * z;
       return make_tuple(rx, ry, rz);
   }
};
device vector<float> x(N), y(N), z(N);
transform(make_zip_iterator(make_tuple(x.begin(), y.begin(), z.begin())),
     make_zip_iterator(make_tuple(x.end(), y.end(), z.end())),
     make_zip_iterator(make_tuple(x.begin(), y.begin(), z.begin())),
     rotate tuple());
```

FIGURE B.8

The zip iterator facilitates processing of data in structure of arrays format.

```
struct smaller_tuple {
   tuple<float,int> operator()(tuple<float,int> a,tuple<float,int> b) {
      // return the tuple with the smaller float value
      if (get<0>(a) < get<0>(b)) return a;
      else  return b;
   }
};

int min_index(device vector<float>& values) {
   // [begin,end) form the implicit sequence [0,1,2, ... value.size())
   counting iterator<int> begin(0);
   counting iterator<int> end(values.size());

   // initial value of the reduction
   tuple<float,int> init(values[0], 0);

   // compute the smallest tuple
   tuple<float,int> smallest =
      reduce(make_zip_iterator(make_tuple(values.begin(), begin)),
      make_zip_iterator(make_tuple(values.end(), end)),
      init, smaller_tuple());
   // return the index
   return get<1>(smallest);
}
```

FIGURE B.9

Implicit ranges improve performance by conserving memory bandwidth.

(v[0], 0), (v[1], 1), (v[2],2), … and then implement `min index` with the standard `reduce` algorithm. Unfortunately, this scheme will be much slower than a customized reduction kernel, since the index range must be created and stored explicitly in memory.

To resolve this issue Thrust provides `counting iterator` [Boost], which acts just like the explicit range of values we need to implement in `min index`, but does not carry any overhead. Specifically, when `counting iterator` is dereferenced it generates the appropriate value "on the fly" and yields that value to the caller. An efficient implementation of `min index` using `counting iterator` is shown in Fig. B.9.

B.7 EXERCISES

1.   Here `counting iterator` has allowed us to efficiently implement a special-purpose reduction algorithm without the need to write a new, special-purpose kernel. In addition to `counting iterator` Thrust provides `constant iterator`, which defines an implicit range of constant value. Note that these implicitly defined iterators can be combined with the other iterators to create more complex implicit ranges. For instance, counting iterator can be used in combination with transform iterator to produce a range of indices with nonunit stride.

Read Fig. B.9 and explain the operation of the algorithm using an s small example. In practice there is no need to implement `min index` since Thrust's `min element` algorithm provides the equivalent functionality. Nevertheless the `min index` example is instructive of best practices. Indeed, Thrust algorithms such as `min element`, `max element`, and `find if` apply the exact same strategy internally.

REFERENCES

Boost Iterator Library. <www.boost.org/doc/libs/release/libs/iterator/ > .
Hoberock, J., & Bell, N. (2011). Thrust: a parallel template library. Version 1.4.0.
Merrill, D., & Grimshaw, A. (2010). Revisiting sorting for gpgpu stream architectures, Technical report CS2010-03. Charlottesville, VA: University of Virginia, Department of Computer Science.

CUDA Fortran

Greg Ruetsch and Massimiliano Fatica

This appendix gives an introduction to CUDA Fortran, the Fortran interface to the CUDA architecture. CUDA Fortran was developed in 2009 as a joint effort between the Portland Group (PGI) and NVIDIA. CUDA Fortran shares much in common with CUDA C, as it is based on the runtime API; however there are some differences in how the CUDA concepts are expressed using Fortran 90 constructs. The first section of this appendix discusses some of the basic differences between CUDA Fortran and CUDA C at a high level, and subsequent sections use various examples to illustrate CUDA Fortran programing.

C.1 CUDA FORTRAN AND CUDA C DIFFERENCES

CUDA Fortran and CUDA C have much in common, as CUDA Fortran is based on the CUDA C runtime API. Just as CUDA C is C with a few language extensions, CUDA Fortran is Fortran with a similar set of language extensions. Before we jump into CUDA Fortran code, it is helpful to summarize some of differences between these two programing interfaces to the CUDA architecture.

493

Fortran is a strongly typed language, and this strong typing carries over into the CUDA Fortran implementation. Device data declared in CUDA Fortran host code is declared with the `device` variable attribute, unlike CUDA C where both host and device data are declared the same way. Differentiating host and device data when variables are declared can simplify several aspects of dealing with device data. Allocation of device data can occur where the variable is declared, for example:

```
real, device :: a_d(N)
```

will allocate `a_d` to contain `N` elements on device 0. Device data can also be declared as allocatable, and allocated using the Fortran 90's allocate statement:

```
real, device, allocatable :: a_d(:)
...
allocate(a_d(N))
```

where the Fortran `allocate` routine has been overloaded to allocate arrays on the current device in the same way `cudaMalloc` does in CUDA C. CUDA Fortran's strong typing also affects how data transfers between host and device can be performed. While one can use the `cudaMempy` function to perform host-to-device and device-to-host blocking transfers, it is far easier to use assignment statements:

```
real :: a(N)
real, device :: a_d(N)
...
a_d = a
```

where the Fortran array assignment kicks off a `cudaMemcpy` behind the scenes. Transfer via assignment statements applies only to blocking or synchronous transfers, for asynchronous transfers one must use the `cudaMemcpyAsync` call.

CUDA Fortran makes use of other variable attributes besides the `device` attribute. The attributes `shared`, `constant`, `pinned`, and `value` also find frequent use in CUDA Fortran. Shared memory used in device code uses the `shared` variable attribute just as CUDA C uses the `__shared__` qualifier. Constant memory must be declared in a Fortran module that contains the device code where it is used, and the module must be used in the host code where it is initialized. The initialization of constant data in host code is done via assignment statement rather than by function calls. Pinned host memory is declared using the `pinned` variable attribute, and must also be declared `allocatable`. Since Fortran passes data by reference by default and in CUDA we typically deal with separate memory spaces for the host and device, host parameters passed to a kernel via the argument list must be declared in the kernel with the `value` variable attribute.

CUDA Fortran also uses the `attributes(global)` and `attributes(device)` function attributes in the same way CUDA C uses declaration specifiers `__global__` and `__device__` to declare kernels and device functions.

Within CUDA Fortran device code the predefined variables `gridDim`, `blockDim`, `blockIdx`, and `threadIdx` are available as they are in CUDA C. Following typical

Fortran convention, the components of blockIdx and threadIdx have a unit, rather than 0, offset, so a typical index calculation would look like:

```
i = blockDim%x * (blockIdx%x - 1) + threadIdx%x
```

in contrast to CUDA C's:

```
i = blockDim.x*blockIdx.x + threadIdx.x;
```

This rounds out the major differences in the expression of CUDA concepts between CUDA C and CUDA Fortran. The CUDA Fortran notation will become clearer as we go through several examples in the following sections.

C.2 A FIRST CUDA FORTRAN PROGRAM

The SAXPY (Single-Precision A Times X Plus Y) routine has been used several times to illustrate various aspects of CUDA programing, and we continue this tradition with our first CUDA Fortran example:

```
module mathOps
contains
  attributes(global) subroutine saxpy(x, y, a)
    real :: x(:), y(:)
    real, value :: a
    integer :: i, n
    n = size(x)
    i = blockDim%x * (blockIdx%x - 1) + threadIdx%x
    if (i <= n) y(i) = y(i) + a*x(i)
  end subroutine saxpy
  end module mathOps
program testSaxpy
  use cudafor
  use mathOps
  implicit none
  integer, parameter :: N = 40000
  real :: x(N), y(N), a
  real, device :: x_d(N), y_d(N)
  type(dim3) :: grid, tBlock
  tBlock = dim3(256,1,1)
  grid = dim3(ceiling(real(N)/tBlock%x),1,1)
  x = 1.0; y = 2.0; a = 2.0
  x_d = x
  y_d = y
  call saxpy<<<grid,tBlock>>>(x_d, y_d, a)
  y = y_d
  write(*,*) 'Max error: ', maxval(abs(y-4.0))
end program testSaxpy
```

In this complete code the SAXPY kernel is defined in the Fortran module `mathOps` using the `attributes(global)` qualifier. The kernel has three arguments, the one-dimensional arrays x and y, and the scalar value a. The size of the x and y arrays does not need to be passed as a kernel argument since x and y are declared as assumed-shape arrays allowing the Fortran `size()` intrinsic to be used. Because a is defined on the host and must be passed by value, the `value` variable attribute is required in a's declaration in the kernel. The predefined `blockDim`, `blockIdx`, and `threadIdx` variables are used to calculate a global index i used to access elements of x and y. Once again note that `blockIdx` and `threadIdx` have unit offset as opposed to CUDA C's zero offset. After checking for inbound access, the SAXPY operation is performed.

The host code uses the `cudafor` module which defines CUDA runtime API routines, constants, types, such as the `type(dim3)` used to declare the execution configuration variables `grid` and `tBlock`. In the host code, both host arrays x and y are declared as well as their device counterparts, x_d and y_d, where the latter are declared with the `device` variable attribute. The thread block and grid are defined in the first executable lines of host code, where the ceiling function is used to launch enough blocks to process all array elements in case that the size of the array is not evenly divisible by the number of threads in a thread block. After the host arrays x and y, as well as the parameter a, are initialized, the assignment statements x_d=x and y_d=y are used to transfer the data from host to device. The scalar a is not passed to the device in this manner, as it is passed by value as a kernel argument. Since the transfers by assignment statement are blocking transfers, we can call the SAXPY kernel after the transfers without any synchronization. The kernel invocation specifies the execution configuration in the triple chevrons placed between the kernel name and its argument list as is done in CUDA C. Also similar to CUDA C, integer expressions can be used between the triple chevrons in place of the `type(dim3)` variables. This is followed by a device-to-host transfer of the resultant array, which is then checked for correctness.

C.3 MULTIDIMENSIONAL ARRAY IN CUDA FORTRAN

Multidimensional arrays are first-class citizens in Fortran, and the ease of dealing with multidimensional data in Fortran is extended to CUDA Fortran. We have already seen one aspect of this in array assignments used for transfers between the host and device. The ease of programing kernel code is evident from the following CUDA Fortran implementation of matrix multiply:

```
module mathOps
  integer, parameter :: TILE_WIDTH = 16
contains
  attributes(global) subroutine matrixMul(Md, Nd, Pd)
    implicit none
```

```fortran
      real, intent(in) :: Md(:,:), Nd(:,:)
      real, intent(out) :: Pd(:,:)
      real, shared :: Mds(TILE_WIDTH, TILE_WIDTH)
      real, shared :: Nds(TILE_WIDTH, TILE_WIDTH)
      integer :: i, j, k, m, tx, ty, width
      real :: Pvalue
      tx = threadIdx%x; ty = threadIdx%y
      i = (blockIdx%x-1)*TILE_WIDTH + tx
      j = (blockIdx%y-1)*TILE_WIDTH + ty
      width = size(Md,2)
      Pvalue = 0.0
      do m = 1, width, TILE_WIDTH
        Mds(tx,ty) = Md(i,m+ty-1)
        Nds(tx,ty) = Nd(m+tx-1,j)
        call syncthreads()
        do k = 1, TILE_WIDTH
          Pvalue = Pvalue + Mds(tx,k)*Nds(k,ty)
        enddo
        call syncthreads()
      enddo
      d(i,j) = Pvalue
    end subroutine matrixMul
  end module mathOps
  program testMatrixMultiply
    use cudafor
    use mathOps
    implicit none
    integer, parameter :: m=4*TILE_WIDTH, n=6*TILE_WIDTH,
  k=2*TILE_WIDTH
    real :: a(m,k), b(k,n), c(m,n), c2(m,n)
    real, device :: a_d(m,k), b_d(k,n), c_d(m,n)
    type(dim3) :: grid, tBlock
    call random_number(a); a_d = a
    call random_number(b); b_d = b
    tBlock = dim3(TILE_WIDTH, TILE_WIDTH, 1)
    grid = dim3(m/TILE_WIDTH, n/TILE_WIDTH, 1)
    call matrixMul<<<grid, tBlock>>>(a_d, b_d, c_d)
    c = c_d
    ! test against Fortran 90 matmul intrinsic
    c2 = matmul(a, b)
    write(*,*) 'max error: ', maxval(abs(c-c2))
  end program testMatrixMultiply
```

The matrixMul kernel uses shared memory tiles Mds and Nds just as in the CUDA C code, however passing in two-dimensional arrays as kernel arguments allows for a more intuitive indexing on the global arrays Md and Nd when copying to shared memory.

C.4 OVERLOADING HOST/DEVICE ROUTINES WITH GENERIC INTERFACES

In the above matrix multiplication, we used the Fortran 90 `matmul` intrinsic to check our results. Because of the distinction between host and device data in host code, it is possible to build generic interfaces that overload routines to execute either on the host or on the device depending on whether the arguments are host or device data. To illustrate how this is done, we present a generic interface to the matrix multiplication example in the previous section:

```fortran
module mathOps
  integer, parameter :: TILE_WIDTH = 16
  interface matrixMultiply
    module procedure mmCPU, mmGPU
  end interface matrixMultiply
contains
  function mmCPU(a, b) result(c)
    implicit none
    real :: a(:,:), b(:,:), c(:,:)
    c = matmul(a,b)
  end function mmCPU
  function mmGPU(a_d, b_d) result(c)
    use cudafor
    implicit none
    real, device :: a_d(:,:), b_d(:,:)
    real :: c(:,:)
    real, device, allocatable :: c_d(:,:)
    integer :: m, n
    type(dim3) :: grid, tBlock
    m = size(c,1); n = size(c,2)
    allocate(c_d(m,n))
    tBlock = dim3(TILE_WIDTH, TILE_WIDTH, 1)
    grid = dim3(m/TILE_WIDTH, n/TILE_WIDTH, 1)
    call matrixMul<<<grid, tBlock>>>(a_d, b_d, c_d)
    c = c_d
    deallocate(c_d)
  end function mmGPU
  attributes(global) subroutine matrixMul(Md, Nd, Pd)
    implicit none
    real, intent(in) :: Md(:,:), Nd(:,:)
    real, intent(out) :: Pd(:,:)
    real, shared :: Mds(TILE_WIDTH, TILE_WIDTH)
    real, shared :: Nds(TILE_WIDTH, TILE_WIDTH)
    integer :: i, j, k, m, tx, ty, width
    real :: Pvalue
    tx = threadIdx%x; ty = threadIdx%y
    i = (blockIdx%x-1)*TILE_WIDTH + tx
```

```
      j = (blockIdx%y-1)*TILE_WIDTH + ty
    width = size(Md,2)
    Pvalue = 0.0
    do m = 1, width, TILE_WIDTH
      Mds(tx,ty) = Md(i,m+ty-1)
      Nds(tx,ty) = Nd(m+tx-1,j)
      call syncthreads()
      do k = 1, TILE_WIDTH
        Pvalue = Pvalue + Mds(tx,k)*Nds(k,ty)
      enddo
      call syncthreads()
    enddo
    Pd(i,j) = Pvalue
  end subroutine matrixMul
end module mathOps
program testMatrixMultiply
  use cudafor
  use mathOps
  implicit none
  integer, parameter :: m=4*TILE_WIDTH, n=6*TILE_WIDTH,
k=2*TILE_WIDTH
  real :: a(m,k), b(k,n), c(m,n), c2(m,n)
  real, device :: a_d(m,k), b_d(k,n)
  call random_number(a); a_d = a
  call random_number(b); b_d = b
  c = matrixMultiply(a_d, b_d)
  c2 = matrixMultiply(a, b)
  write(*,*) 'max error: ', maxval(abs(c-c2))
end program testMatrixMultiply
```

The interface to matrixMultiply in this code is overloaded using two procedures defined in the module, mmCPU and mmGPU. mmCPU operates on host data and simply calls the F90 intrinsic matmul. mmGPU takes device data for the input matrices, and returns a host array with the result. (It could just have easily been defined to return a device array.) The device array used for the result in mmGPU, c_d, is a local array that is declared on the 6th line of mmGPU, and allocated on the 10th line of that routine. After this allocation, the locally defined execution configuration parameters are determined and the kernel is launched, which is followed by a device-to-host transfer and the deallocation of c_d. The actual matrix multiple kernel is not modified from the previous section. In the host code, matrixMultiply is used to access both of these routines.

C.5 CALLING CUDA C VIA ISO_C_BINDING

In the previous section we demonstrated how an interface can be used to allow a single call to perform operations on either the host or device depending on where the input data reside. An interface can also be used to call C or CUDA C functions from

CUDA Fortran using the `iso_c_binding` module introduced in Fortran 2003. Such functions can either be CUDA C routines developed by the user or library routines. In our matrix multiplication code, for example, we might wish to call the CUBLAS version of SGEMM rather than our hand-coded version. This can be done in the following manner:

```
module cublas_m
  interface cublasInit
    integer function cublasInit() bind(C,name='cublasInit')
    end function cublasInit
  end interface
  interface cublasSgemm
    subroutine cublasSgemm(cta,ctb,m,n,k,alpha,A,lda,B,ldb,beta,c,
ldc) &
        bind(C,name='cublasSgemm')
      use iso_c_binding
      character(1,c_char), value :: cta, ctb
      integer(c_int), value :: k, m, n, lda, ldb, ldc
      real(c_float), value :: alpha, beta
      real(c_float), device :: A(lda,*), B(ldb,*), C(ldc,*)
    end subroutine cublasSgemm
  end interface cublasSgemm
end module cublas_m
program sgemmDevice
  use cublas_m
  use cudafor
  implicit none
  integer, parameter :: m = 100, n = 100, k = 100
  real :: a(m,k), b(k,n), c(m,n), c2(m,n)
  real, device :: a_d(m,k), b_d(k,n), c_d(m,n)
  real, parameter :: alpha = 1.0, beta = 0.0
  integer :: lda = m, ldb = k, ldc = m
  integer :: istat
  call random_number(a); a_d = a
  call random_number(b); b_d = b
  istat = cublasInit()
  call cublasSgemm('n','n',m,n,k,alpha,a_d,lda,b_d,ldb,beta,c_d,ldc)
  c = c_d
  c2 = matmul(a,b)
  write(*,*) 'max error =', maxval(abs(c-c2))
end program sgemmDevice
```

Here the module `cublas_m` contains interfaces for the CUBLAS routines `cublasInit` and `cublasSgemm` which are bound to C functions as dictated by the `bind(C,name='...')` clause. The `iso_c_binding` module is used in the `cublasSgemm` interface as this module contains the type kind parameters used in the declarations for the function arguments.

One could manually write these interfaces for all of the CUBLAS routines, but this has already been done in the `cublas` module provided with the PGI CUDA Fortran compiler. In the above code, one can simply remove the `cublas_m` module and change the "use `cublas_m`" to "use `cublas`" in the main program. The `cublas` module also contains generic interfaces to overload the standard BLAS functions to execute the CUBLAS versions when the array arguments are device arrays. So we can further change the above program to call `sgemm` rather than `cublasSgemm`. The complete program then becomes:

```
program sgemmDevice
  use cublas
  use cudafor
  implicit none
  integer, parameter :: m = 100, n = 100, k = 100
  real :: a(m,k), b(k,n), c(m,n), c2(m,n)
  real, device :: a_d(m,k), b_d(k,n), c_d(m,n)
  real, parameter :: alpha = 1.0, beta = 0.0
  integer :: lda = m, ldb = k, ldc = m
  integer :: istat
  call random_number(a); a_d = a
  call random_number(b); b_d = b
  istat = cublasInit()
  call sgemm('n','n',m,n,k,alpha,a_d,lda,b_d,ldb,beta,c_d,ldc)
  c = c_d
  c2 = matmul(a,b)
  write(*,*) 'max error =', maxval(abs(c-c2))
end program sgemmDevice
```

C.6 KERNEL LOOP DIRECTIVES AND REDUCTION OPERATIONS

There are many occasions when one wishes to perform simple operations on device data, such as scaling or normalization of a device array. For such operations, it can be cumbersome to write separate kernels, and fortunately CUDA Fortran provides kernel loop directives, or CUF kernels. CUF kernels essentially allow the programer to inline simple kernels in host code. For example, our SAXPY code using CUF kernels becomes:

```
program testSaxpy
  use cudafor
  implicit none
  integer, parameter :: N = 40000
  real :: x(N), y(N), a
  real, device :: x_d(N), y_d(N)
```

```
    integer :: i
    x = 1.0; x_d = x
    y = 2.0; y_d = y
    a = 2.0
    !$cuf kernel do <<<*,*>>>
    do i = 1, N
      y_d(i) = y_d(i) + a*x_d(i)
    end do
    y = y_d
    write(*,*) 'Max error: ', maxval(abs(y-4.0))
end program testSaxpy
```

In this complete code, the module containing the saxpy kernel has been removed and in its place in host code is the loop which contains device arrays. The directive "!$cuf kernel do" informs the compiler to generate a kernel for the operation in the following do loop. The execution configuration can be manually specified in the "<<<...,...>>>", or asterisks can be used to have the compiler choose an execution, as is done in this case. CUF kernels can operate on nested loops, and can use nondefault streams.

One particular useful aspect of CUF kernels is their ability to perform reductions. When the left-hand side of an expression in CUF kernel loop is a host scalar variable, a reduction operation is performed on the device. This is useful because coding a well-performing reduction in CUDA is not a trivial matter. The calculation of the sum of the device array elements using compiler generated CUF kernels looks like:

```
program testReduction
  use cudafor
  implicit none
  integer, parameter :: N = 40000
  real :: x(N), xsum
  real, device :: x_d(N)
  integer :: i
  x = 1.0; x_d = x
  xsum = 0.0
  !$cuf kernel do <<<*,*>>>
  do i = 1, N
    xsum = xsum + x_d(i)
  end do
  write(*,*) 'Error: ', abs(xsum - sum(x))
end program testReduction
```

C.7 DYNAMIC SHARED MEMORY

In our matrix multiplication example we demonstrated how static shared memory is used, which is essentially analogous to how it is declared in CUDA C. For dynamic shared memory, there are several options in CUDA Fortran. If a single dynamic shared memory array is used, then once again the CUDA Fortran implementation parallels what is done in CUDA C:

```
attributes(global) subroutine dynamicReverse1(d)
  real :: d(:)
  integer :: t, tr
  real, shared :: s(*)
  t = threadIdx%x
  tr = size(d)-t+1
  s(t) = d(t)
  call syncthreads()
  d(t) = s(tr)
end subroutine dynamicReverse1
```

where the shared memory array s, used to reverse elements of a single thread block array in this kernel, is declared with as an assumed-size array. The size of this dynamic shared memory array is determined from the number of bytes of dynamic shared memory specified in the third execution configuration parameter:

```
threadBlock = dim3(n,1,1)
grid = dim3 (1,1,1)
...
call dynamicReverse1<<<grid,threadBlock,4*threadBlock%x>>>(d_d)
```

When multiple dynamic shared memory arrays are used in CUDA C, essentially one large block of memory is allocated and pointer arithmetic is used to determine offsets into this block for the various variables. In CUDA Fortran, automatic arrays are used:

```
attributes (global) subroutine dynamicReverse2(d, nSize)
  real :: d(nSize)
  integer, value :: nSize
  integer :: t, tr
  real, shared :: s(nSize)
  t = threadIdx%x
  tr = nSize-t+1
  s(t) = d(t)
  call syncthreads()
  d(t) = s(tr)
end subroutine dynamicReverse2
```

Here nSize is not known at compile time, hence s is not a static shared memory array. Any in-scope variable, such as a variable declared in the module that contains this kernel, can be used to determine the size of the automatic shared memory arrays. Multiple dynamic shared memory arrays, of different types, can be specified in this fashion. The total amount of dynamic shared memory must still be specified in the third execution configuration parameter.

C.8 ASYNCHRONOUS DATA TRANSFERS

Asynchronous data transfers are performed using the cudaMemcpy*Async() API calls as is done in CUDA C, with a couple of differences that apply not only to these asynchronous data transfer API calls but also the synchronous cudaMemcpy*() variants. The first difference is that the size of the transfer specified in the third argument is in terms of the number of elements rather than the number of bytes, and the second is that the direction of transfer is an optional argument as the direction can be inferred from the types of the first two arguments.

As with CUDA C, for asynchronous transfers the host memory must be pinned, which is accomplished through the pinned variable attribute rather than through a specific allocation function. Pinned memory in CUDA Fortran must be allocatable, and can be allocated and deallocated through the Fortran 90 allocate() and deallocate() statements.

To overlap kernel execution and data transfers, in addition to pinned host memory the data transfer and kernel must use different, nondefault streams. Nondefault streams are required for this overlap because memory copy, memory set functions, and kernel calls that use the default stream begin only after all preceding calls on the device (in any stream) have completed, and no operation on the device (in any stream) commences until they are finished. An example of overlapping kernel execution and data transfer is:

```
real, allocatable, pinned :: a(:)
...
integer (kind=cuda_stream_kind) :: stream1, stream2
...
allocate(a(nElements))
istat = cudaStreamCreate(stream1)
istat = cudaStreamCreate(stream2)
istat = cudaMemcpyAsync(a_d, a, nElements, stream1)
call kernel <<<gridSize, blockSize, 0, stream2 >>>(b_d)
```

In this example, two streams are created and used in the data transfer and kernel executions as specified in the last arguments of the cudaMemcpyAsync() call and the kernels execution configuration. We make use of two device arrays, a_d and b_d, and assign work on a_d to stream1 and b_d to stream2.

If the operations on a single data array in a kernel are independent, then data can be broken into chunks and transferred in multiple stages, multiple kernels launched to operate on each chunk as it arrives, and each chunk's results transferred back to the host when the relevant kernel completes. The following code segments demonstrate two ways of breaking up data transfers and kernel work in order to hide transfer time:

```
! baseline case - sequential transfer and execute
a = 0
istat = cudaEventRecord(startEvent, 0)
a_d = a
```

```
call kernel <<<n/blockSize, blockSize >>>(a_d, 0)
a = a_d
istat = cudaEventRecord(stopEvent, 0)
! Setup for multiple stream processing
strSize = n / nStreams
strGridSize = strSize / blocksize
i = 1, nStreams
  istat = cudaStreamCreate(stream(i))
enddo
! asynchronous version 1: loop over {copy, kernel, copy}
a = 0
istat = cudaEventRecord(startEvent, 0)
do i = 1, nStreams
  offset = (i-1)* strSize
  istat = cudaMemcpyAsync(a_d(offset+1), a(offset+1), strSize,
stream(i))
  call kernel <<<strGridSize, blockSize, 0, stream(i)>>>(a_d,
offset)
  istat = cudaMemcpyAsync(a(offset+1), a_d(offset+1), strSize,
stream(i))
enddo
istat = cudaEventRecord(stopEvent, 0)
! asynchronous version 2:
! loop over copy, loop over kernel, loop over copy
a = 0
istat = cudaEventRecord(startEvent, 0)
do i = 1, nStreams
  offset = (i-1)* strSize
  istat = cudaMemcpyAsync(a_d(offset+1), a(offset+1), strSize,
stream(i))
enddo
do i = 1, nStreams
  offset = (i-1)* strSize
  call kernel <<<strGridSize, blockSize, 0, stream(i)>>>(a_d,
offset)
enddo
do i = 1, nStreams
  offset = (i-1)* strSize
  istat = cudaMemcpyAsync(a(offset+1), a_d(offset+1), strSize,
stream(i))
enddo
istat = cudaEventRecord(stopEvent, 0)
```

The asynchronous cases are similar to the sequential case, only that there are multiple data transfers and kernel launches which are distinguished by different streams and an offset corresponding to the particular stream. In this code, we limit the number of streams to four, although for large arrays there is no reason why a larger number of streams could not be used. Note that the same kernel is used in the sequential and asynchronous cases in the code, as an offset is sent to the kernel to accommodate the data in different streams. The difference between the two asynchronous versions is the order in which the copies and kernels are executed. The first version loops over each stream and for each stream issues a host-to-device copy, kernel, and device-to-host copy. The second version issues all host-to-device copies, then all kernel launches, and then all device-to-host copies. We also make use of a third approach, which is a variant of the second where a dummy event is recorded after each kernel launch:

```
do i = 1, nStreams
  offset = (i-1)* strSize
  call kernel <<<strGridSize, blockSize, 0, stream(i)>>>(a_d,
offset)
  ! Add a dummy event
  istat = cudaEventRecord(dummyEvent, stream(i))
enddo
```

At this point you may be asking why we have three versions of the asynchronous case. The reason is that these variants perform differently on different hardware. Running this code on the NVIDIA Tesla C1060 produces:

```
Device: Tesla C1060
Time for sequential transfer and execute (ms): 12.92381
Time for asynchronous V1 transfer and execute (ms): 13.63690
Time for asynchronous V2 transfer and execute (ms): 8.845888
Time for asynchronous V3 transfer and execute (ms): 8.998560
```

and on the NVIDIA Tesla C2050 we get:

```
Device: Tesla C2050
Time for sequential transfer and execute (ms): 9.984512
Time for asynchronous V1 transfer and execute (ms): 5.735584
Time for asynchronous V2 transfer and execute (ms): 7.597984
Time for asynchronous V3 transfer and execute (ms): 5.735424
```

To decipher these results we need to understand a bit more about how devices schedule and execute various tasks. CUDA devices contain engines for various tasks, and operations are queued up in these engines as they are issued. Dependencies between tasks in different engines are maintained, but within any engine all dependence is lost, as tasks in an engine's queue are executed in the order they are issued by the host thread. For example, the C1060 has a single copy engine and a single kernel engine. For the above code, time lines for the execution on the device are schematically shown in Fig. C.1. In this schematic we have assumed that the time required for the host-to-device transfer, kernel execution, and device-to-host transfer are approximately the same, and in the code provided, a kernel was chosen in order to make these times comparable.

For the sequential kernel, there is no overlap in any of the operations as one would expect. For the first asynchronous version of our code the order of execution in the

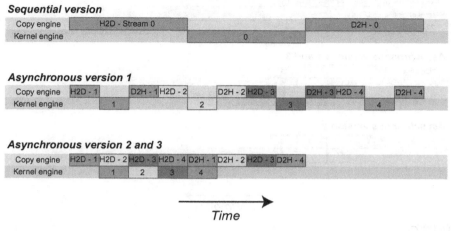

FIGURE C.1

Data transfer and kernel execution timing for the sequential and asynchronous versions when there is only one copy engine.

copy engine is: H2D `stream(1)`, D2H `stream(1)`, H2D `stream(2)`, D2H `stream(2)`, and so forth. This is why we do not see any speedup when using the first asynchronous version on the C1060: tasks were issued to the copy engine in an order that precludes any overlap of kernel execution and data transfer. For versions two and three, however, where all the host-to-device transfers are issued before any of the device-to-host transfers, overlap is possible as indicated by the lower execution time. From our schematic, we would expect the execution of versions two and three to be 8/12 of the sequential version, or 8.7 ms, which is what is observed in the timing above.

On the C2050, two features interact to cause different behavior than that observed on the C1060. The C2050 has two copy engines, one for host-to-device transfers and another for device-to-host transfers, in addition to a single kernel engine. Having two copy engines explains why the first asynchronous version achieves good speedup on the C2050: the device-to-host transfer of data in `stream(i)` does not block the host-to-device transfer of data in `stream(i+1)` as it did on the C1060 because these two operations are in different engines on the C2050, which is schematically shown in Fig. C.2:

From the schematic we would expect the execution time to be cut in half relative to the sequential version, which is roughly what is observed in the timings above. This does not explain the performance degradation observed in the second asynchronous approach, however, which is related to the C2050's support to concurrently run multiple kernels. When multiple kernels are issued back-to-back, the scheduler tries to enable concurrent execution of these kernels and as a result delays a signal

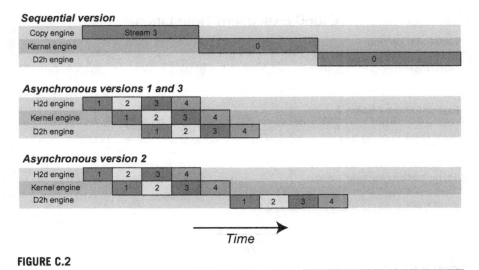

FIGURE C.2

Data transfer and kernel execution timing for the sequential and asynchronous versions when there are two copy engines.

which normally occurs after each kernel completion (and is responsible for kicking off the device-to-host transfer) until all kernels complete. So, while there is overlap between host-to-device transfers and kernel execution in the second version of our asynchronous code, there is no overlap between kernel execution and device-to-host transfers. From the figure one would expect an overall time for the second asynchronous version to be 9/12 of the time for the sequential version, or 7.5 ms which is what we observe from the timings above. This situation can be rectified by recording a dummy CUDA event between each kernel, which will inhibit concurrent kernel execution but enable overlap of data transfers and kernel execution, as is done in the third asynchronous version.

C.9 COMPILATION AND PROFILING

CUDA Fortran codes are compiled using PGI Fortran compiler. Files with the .cuf or .CUF extensions have CUDA Fortran enabled automatically, and the compiler option -Mcuda can be used when compiling file with other extensions to enable CUDA Fortran. Compilation of CUDA Fortran code can be as simple as issuing the command:

```
pgf90 saxpy.cuf
```

Behind the scenes, a multistep process takes place. The first step is a source-to-source compilation where CUDA C device code is generated by CUDA Fortran.

From here compilation is similar to compilation of CUDA C. The device code is compiled into the intermediate representation PTX, and the PTX code is then further compiled to a executable code for a particular compute capability. The host code is compiled using `pgfortran`. The final executable contains the host binary, the device binary, and the PTX. The PTX is included so that a new device binary can be created when the executable is run on a card of different compute capability than originally compiled for.

Specifics of the above compilation process can be controlled through options to `-Mcuda`. A specific compute capability can be targeted, for example `-Mcuda=cc20` generates executables for devices of compute capability 2.0. There is an emulation mode where device code is run on the host, specified by `-Mcuda=emu`. The specific version of the CUDA Toolkit can be specified, for example `-Mcuda=cuda4.0` causes compilation with the 4.0 CUDA Toolkit. CUDA has a set of fast, but less accurate, intrinsics for single precision functions like `sin()` and `cos()`, which can be enabled by the `-Mcuda=fastmath` option. Use of these functions requires no change in the CUDA Fortran source code, as the intermediate CUDA C code will be generated with the corresponding `__sinf()` and `__cosf()` functions, respectively. For finer (selective) control, the latter versions are available when the `cudadevice` module is used in device code. The option `-Mucda=maxregcount:N` can by used to limit the number of registers used per thread to `N`. And the option `-Mcuda=ptxinfo` prints information on memory usage in kernels. Multiple options to `-Mcuda` can be given in a comma-separated list, e.g., `-Mcuda=cc20,cuda4.0,ptxinfo`.

Profiling CUDA Fortran codes can be performed using the command-line profiling facility used in CUDA C. Setting the environment variable `COMPUTE_PROFILE` to 1:

```
% export COMPUTE_PROFILE=1
```

and executing the code generates a file of profiling results, by default `cuda_profile_0.log`. For use of the command-line profiler, see the documentation distributed with the CUDA Toolkit.

C.10 CALLING THRUST FROM CUDA FORTRAN

Previously we demonstrated calling external CUDA C libraries from CUDA Fortran, in particular the CUBLAS library, using the `iso_c_binding` module. In this section we demonstrate how CUDA Fortran can interface with Thrust, the standard template library for the GPU discussed in a previous appendix. Relative to calling CUDA C functions, interfacing with Thrust requires the additional step of creating C pointers that access the Thrust device containers, such as in the following code segment:

```
// allocate device vector
thrust::device_vector d_vec(4);
// obtain raw pointer to device vector's memory
int *ptr = thrust::raw_pointer_cast(&d_vec[0]);
```

The basic procedure to interface Thrust with CUDA Fortran is to create C wrapper functions that access Thrust's functions through standard C pointers, and then use the `iso_c_binding` module to access these functions through a generic interface in CUDA Fortran. For an example, we use Thrust's `sort` routine. The wrapper functions for the `int`, `float`, and `double` sort routines are:

```
// Filename: csort.cu
// nvcc -c -arch sm_20 csort.cu
#include <thrust/device_vector.h>
#include <thrust/device_vector.h>
#include <thrust/sort.h>
extern "C" {
  //Sort for integer arrays
  void sort_int_wrapper(int *data, int N)
  {
    // Wrap raw pointer with a device_ptr
    thrust::device_ptr <int> dev_ptr(data);
    // Use device_ptr in Thrust sort algorithm
    thrust::sort(dev_ptr, dev_ptr+N);
  }
  //Sort for float arrays
  void sort_float_wrapper(float *data, int N)
  {
    thrust::device_ptr <float> dev_ptr(data);
    thrust::sort(dev_ptr, dev_ptr+N);
  }
  //Sort for double arrays
  void sort_double_wrapper(double *data, int N)
  {
    thrust::device_ptr <double> dev_ptr(data);
    thrust::sort(dev_ptr, dev_ptr+N);
  }
}
```

Compiling the code using:

```
nvcc -c -arch sm_20 csort.cu
```

will generate an object file, `csort.o` that we will use later on in the linking stage of the CUDA Fortran code.

With the C wrapper functions available, we can now write a Fortran module with a generic interface to Thrust's `sort` functionality:

```
module thrust
  interface thrustsort
    subroutine sort_int(input,N) bind(C,name="sort_int_wrapper")
      use iso_c_binding
      integer(c_int),device:: input(*)
```

```
      integer(c_int),value:: N
    end subroutine sort_int
    subroutine sort_float(input,N) bind(C,name="sort_float_wrapper")
      use iso_c_binding
      real(c_float),device:: input(*)
      integer(c_int),value:: N
    end subroutine sort_float
    subroutine sort_double(input,N) bind(C,name="sort_double_wrapper")
      use iso_c_binding
      real(c_double),device:: input(*)
      integer(c_int),value:: N
    end subroutine sort_double
  end interface thrustsort
end module thrust
```

With the C wrapper functions and the Fortran module written, we can now turn to the main Fortran code that generates and transfers the data to the device, calls the sort functions, and transfers the data back to the host:

```
program testsort
  use thrust
  ! Declare two arrays, one on CPU (cpuData), one on GPU (gpuData)
  real, allocatable :: cpuData(:)
  real, allocatable, device :: gpuData(:)
  integer:: N=10
  ! Allocate the arrays using standard allocate
  allocate(cpuData(N),gpuData(N))
  ! Generate random numbers on the CPU
  do i=1,N
    cpuData(i)=random(i)
  end do
  cpuData(5)=100.
  print *,"Before sorting", cpuData
  ! Copy the data to GPU with a simple assignment
  gpuData=cpuData
  ! Call the Thrust sorting function. The generic interface will
  ! select the proper routine, in this case the one operating on
floats
  call thrustsort(gpuData,size(gpuData))
  ! Copy the data back to CPU with a simple assignment
  cpuData=gpuData
  print *,"After sorting", cpuData
  ! Deallocate the arrays using standard deallocate
  allocate(cpuData(N),gpuData(N))
end program testsort
```

If we save the module in a file mod_thrust.cuf and the program in simplesort. cuf, we are ready to compile and execute:

```
$ pgf90 -Mcuda=cc20 -O3 -o simple_sort mod_thrust.cuf simple_sort.
cuf csort.o
$ ./simple_sort
Before sorting 4.1630346E-02 0.9124327 0.7832350 0.6540373
100.0000 0.3956419 0.2664442 0.1372465
8.0488138E-03 0.8788511
After sorting 8.0488138E-03 4.1630346E-02 0.1372465 0.2664442
0.3956419 0.6540373 0.7832350 0.8788511
0.9124327 100.0000
```

We can modify the main code to evaluate the performance using the CUDA event API as follows:

```
program timesort
  use cudafor
  use thrust
  implicit none
  real, allocatable :: cpuData(:)
  real, allocatable, device :: gpuData(:)
  integer:: i,N=100000000
  ! CUDA events for elapsing time
  type (cudaEvent):: startEvent, stopEvent
  real:: time, random
  integer:: istat
  ! Create events
  istat = cudaEventCreate(startEvent)
  istat = cudaEventCreate(stopEvent)
  ! Allocate arrays
  allocate(cpuData(N),gpuData(N))
  do i=1,N
    cpuData(i)=random(i)
  end do
  print *,"Sorting array of ",N, " single precision"
  gpuData=cpuData
  istat = cudaEventRecord (startEvent, 0)
  call thrustsort(gpuData,size(gpuData))
  istat = cudaEventRecord (stopEvent, 0)
  istat = cudaEventSynchronize (stopEvent)
  istat = cudaEventElapsedTime (time, startEvent, stopEvent)
  cpuData=gpuData
  print *," Sorted array in:",time," (ms)"
  !Print the first five elements and the last five.
  print *,"After sorting", cpuData(1:5),cpuData(N-4:N)
end program timesort
```

With the CUDA events, we are timing only the execution time of the sorting kernel. We can sort a vector of 100 M elements in .222 second on a Tesla M2050 with ECC on when the data are resident in GPU memory:

```
$ pgf90 -Mcuda=cc20 -O3 -o time_sort mod_thrust.cuf time_sort.cuf
csort.o
$ ./time_sort
Sorting array of 100000000 single precision
Sorted array in: 222.1711 (ms)
After sorting 7.0585919E-09 1.0318221E-08 1.9398616E-08
3.1738640E-08
4.4078664E-08 0.9999999 0.9999999 1.000000 1.000000 1.000000
```

C.11 **EXERCISES**

1. Write a CUF kernel version of a matrix multiplication.

2. Write a CUDA Fortran code that reverses elements of a 4096-element array.

An introduction to C++ AMP

D

David Callahan

CHAPTER OUTLINE

C++ Accelerated Massive Parallelism, or C++ AMP, is a programming model for expressing data-parallel algorithms and exploiting heterogeneous computers using mainstream tools. C++ AMP was designed to offer productivity, portability and performance. Developed initially by Microsoft, C++ AMP is defined by an open specification which took input from multiple sources, including from AMD and NVIDIA. In this appendix we provide an overview of C++ AMP [C++ AMP Open].

The focus of C++ AMP is to express the important data-parallel algorithm pattern while providing minimum new language features and shielding common scenarios from the intricacies of today's GPU programming. This provides a foundation of portability for applications written in C++ AMP across a range of different hardware. This portability creates future-proofing to preserve investment as hardware continues to evolve as well as improving reusability of code across different devices and different manufacturers. At the same time, the full C++ AMP feature set includes advanced mechanisms for achieving performance when system intricacies must be addressed. In this appendix, we discuss first the most straightforward examples of C++ AMP, and then we more lightly address these advanced features.

C++ AMP is a small extension to the current C++ 11 standard and is dependent on some of the core features of that standard. In particular, we will assume the readers are familiar with modern C++ including the use of lambda expressions to build function closures, the use of templates for type-generic programming, the use of namespaces to control visibility of names, and the standard template library (STL). The common patterns are simple so a deep understanding is not a prerequisite to use C++ AMP. Unlike CUDA and OpenCL, C++ AMP allows a rich subset of C++ inside data-parallel computations as well as using C++ for the host. C++ AMP has the same base compilation model as C++ with header files for interface specification and separate compilation units combined into a single executable.

C++ AMP does rely on two extensions to the language. The first places restrictions on the C++ operations that may be used in bodies of functions and the second supports a form of limited cross-thread data sharing within data-parallel kernels. Both of these will be illustrated below. All other aspects of C++ AMP are delivered as a library accessed via a few header files.

C++ AMP shares many concepts with CUDA. In the text below we will illustrate this by showing C++ AMP equivalents for CUDA examples from earlier chapters. C++ AMP terminology differs from CUDA in small ways and we will highlight those differences as they arise.

D.1 CORE C++ AMP FEATURES

We describe the core features of C++ AMP by translating an example used in Chapter 2, Data parallel computing, from CUDA into C++ AMP. Fig. D.1 is the CUDA code for performing vector addition on host vectors using a CUDA device.

```
__global__void vecAddKernel(float* d_A, float* d_B, float* d_C, int n)
{
        int i = blockDim.x * blockIdx.x + threadIdx.x;
        if (i < n) C[i] = A[i] + B[i];
}
void vecAdd(float* A, float* B, float* C, int n)
{
        int size = n * sizeof (float); float* d_A, d_B, d_C;
        cudaMalloc((void **) &d_A, size);
        cudaMemcpy(d_A, A, size, cudaMemcpyHostToDevice);
        cudaMalloc((void **) &d_B, size);
        cudaMemcpy(d_B, B, size, cudaMemcpyHostToDevice);
        cudaMalloc((void **) &d_C, size);
        vecAddKernel<<<ceil(n/256.0), 256>>>(d_A, d_B, d_C, n);
        cudaMemcpy(C, d_C, size, cudaMemcpyDeviceToHost);
        cudaFree(d_A); cudaFree(d_B); cudaFree (d_C);
}
```

FIGURE D.1

CUDA vector addition from Chapter 2, Data parallel computing.

```
1  #include <amp.h>
2  using namespace concurrency;
3
4  void vecAdd(float* A, float* B, float* C, int n)
5  {
6      array_view<const float,1> AV(n,A), BV(n,B);
7      array_view<float,1> CV(n,C);
8      CV.discard_data();
9      parallel_for_each(CV.extent, [=](index<1> i) restrict(amp)
10     {
11         CV[i] = AV[i] + BV[i];
12     });
13     CV.synchronize();
14 }
```

FIGURE D.2

Vector addition in C++ AMP.

The corresponding C++ AMP code is shown in Fig. D.2. Line 1 includes the C++ AMP header, amp.h, which provides the declarations of the core features. The C++ AMP classes and functions are part of the concurrency namespace. The using directive on the next line makes the C++ AMP names visible in the current scope. It is optional but avoids the need to prefix C++ AMP names with a concurrency:: scope specifier.

The function vecAdd on Line 4 is functionally identical to the same function starting Fig. D.1, Line 6. This function is executed by a thread running on the host and it contains a data-parallel computation that may be accelerated. The term "host" has the same meaning in C++ AMP documentation as it is used in CUDA. While CUDA uses the term "device" to refer to the execution environment used for accelerated execution, C++ AMP uses the term *accelerator*—discussed more in Section D.3.

In C++ AMP, the primary vehicle for reading and writing large data collections is the class template array_view. An array_view provides a multidimensional reference to a rectangular collection of data locations. This is not a new copy of the data but rather a new way to access the existing memory locations. The template has two parameters: the type of the elements of the source data, and an integer that indicates the dimensionality of the array_view. Throughout C++ AMP, template parameters that indicate dimensionality are referred to as the *rank* of the type or object. In this example, we have a one-dimensional array_view (or "an array_view of rank 1") of C++ float values.

The constructor for array views of rank 1, such as CV on Line 7, takes two parameters. The first is an integer value which is the number of data elements. In general the set of per-dimension lengths is referred to as an *extent*. To represent and manipulate extents, C++ AMP provides a class template, extent, with a single integer template parameter which captures the rank. For objects with a low number of dimensions, various constructors are overloaded to allow specification of an extent as one or more integer values as is done for CV. The second parameter to the CV constructor is a pointer to the host data. In vecAdd the host data is expressed as a C-style pointer to contiguous data. An array_view may also overlay STL containers (see Section A.1) such as std::vector when they support a data method to access underlying contiguous storage.

The CUDA code explicitly allocates memory (Fig. D.1, Lines 9–13) that is accessible by the device and copies host data into it. These actions are implicit in C++ AMP by creating the association between an array_view and host data and subsequently accessing the data through the array_view on the accelerator. The method array_view::discard_data optimizes data transfers for some accelerators and is discussed below in the next section. In this example, it is used when existing data values are immaterial because they are about to be overwritten.

Line 9 illustrates the parallel_for_each construct that is the C++ AMP code pattern for a data-parallel computation. This corresponds to the kernel launch in CUDA (Fig. D.1, Line 14). In CUDA terminology (as in Fig. 3.3), the parallel_for_each creates a "grid of threads". In C++ AMP the set of elements for which a computation is performed is called the *compute domain* and is defined by an extent object. Like in CUDA, each thread will invoke the same function for every point and threads are distinguished only by their location in the domain (grid). Unlike CUDA, this domain need not be treated as an array of thread blocks (as in Fig. 3.12). The index parameter combines information needed for common cases from the separate CUDA keyword blockIdx.x, blockDim.x, and threadIdx.x.

Similar to the standard C++ STL algorithm, for_each, the parallel_for_each function template specifies a function to be applied to a collection of values. The first argument to a parallel_for_each is a C++ AMP extent object which describes the domain over which a data-parallel computation is performed. In this example, we perform an operation over every element in an array_view and so the extent passed into the parallel_for_each is the extent of the CV array view. In the example, this is accessed through the extent property of the array_view type. This is a one-dimensional extent and the domain of the computation consists of integer values $0...n-1$.

The second argument to a parallel_for_each is a C++ function object (or functor). In these examples we use the C++ 11 lambda syntax as a convenient way to build such an object. The core semantics of a parallel_for_each is to invoke the function defined by the second parameter exactly once for every element in the compute domain defined by the extent argument.

The leading [=] indicates that variables declared inside the containing function but referenced inside the lambda are "captured" and copied into data members of the function object built for the lambda. In this case this will be the three array_view objects. The function invoked has a single parameter that is initialized to the location of a thread within the compute domain. This is again represented by a class template, index, which represents a short vector of integer values. The rank of an index is the length of this vector and is the same as the rank of the extent. The index parameter conveys the same information as the explicitly computed value i in the CUDA code (Fig. D.1, Line 3). These index values can be used to select elements in an array view as illustrated on Line 11.

A key extension to C++ is shown in this example: the restrict(amp) modifier. In C++ AMP, the existing C99 keyword restrict is borrowed and allowed in a new context: it may trail the formal parameter list of a function (including lambda functions). The restrict keyword is then followed by a parenthesized list of one or more restriction specifiers. While other uses are possible, in C++ AMP there are only two such specifiers defined: amp and cpu.

The function object passed to parallel_for_each must have its call operator annotated with a restrict(amp) specification. Any function called from the body of that operator must similarly be restricted. The restrict(amp) specification is analogous to the __device__ keyword in CUDA. It identifies functions that may be invoked on a hardware accelerator. Analogously, restrict(cpu) corresponds to the CUDA __host__ keyword and indicates functions that may be invoked on the host. When no restriction is specified, the default is restrict(cpu). C++ AMP has no need for an analog to the CUDA __global__ keyword. A function may have both restrictions, restrict(cpu,amp), in which case it may be called in either host or accelerator contexts and must satisfy the restrictions of both contexts.

The restrict modifier allows a subset of C++ to be defined for use in a body of code. In the first release of C++ AMP, the restrictions reflect current common limitations of GPUs when used as accelerators of data parallel code. The set of restrictions includes:

- No reference may be made to global or static variables except when they have const type qualification and can be reduced to an integer literal value that is only used as an rvalue.
- A lambda expression used in a parallel_for_each must capture most variables by value with the exception of C++ AMP array and texture objects, each described later.
- Targets of function calls may not be virtual methods, pointers to functions, or pointer to member functions.
- Functions may not be recursively invoked and must be inlineable.
- Only bool, int, unsigned int, long, unsigned long, float, double, and void may be used as C++ primitive types.
- C++ compound user-defined types are generally permitted but may not have virtual base classes or bit fields and all data members and base classes must be 4-byte aligned.
- No use of dynamic_cast or typeid is permitted.
- No use of goto statements is permitted.
- No use of asm statements is permitted.
- No use of try, catch or throw is permitted.

These restrictions reflect a common set of limitations for the GPU-based accelerators broadly available today. Over time we expect these restrictions to be lifted and the open specification for C++ + AMP includes a possible roadmap of future versions which are less restrictive. The `restrict(cpu)` specifier of course permits all of the capabilities of C++ but, because some functions that are part of C++ AMP are accelerator-specific. they do not have `restrict(cpu)` versions and so may only be used in `restrict(amp)` code.

The restriction specifiers for a function are part of the type of the function and function names may be overloaded when they have different restrictions. Thus two functions may have identical signatures except one has `restrict(amp)` specification and the other has `restrict(cpu)` specification. This allows context-specific implementations of functions to be created. A function that has two overloads, one for each context, may be called from a `restrict(amp,cpu)` function and the appropriate overload will be invoked that corresponds to whether the function is being invoked on the host or on an accelerator. In particular, this capability is used within C++ AMP to allow context-specific implementations of mathematic operations but is also available to application and library developers.

Inside the body of the `restrict(amp)` lambda (Fig. D.2, Lines 10–12), there are references to the `array_view` objects declared in the containing scope. These are "captured" into the function object that is created to implement the lambda. Other variables from the function scope may also be captured by value. Each of these other values is made available to each invocation of the function executed on the accelerator. As for any C++ 11 nonmutable lambda, variables captured by value may not be modified in the body of the lambda. However, the elements of an `array_view` may be modified and those modifications will be reflected back to the host. In this example, any changes to `CV` made inside the `parallel_for_each` will be reflected in the host data `C` before the function `vecAdd` returns.

The final statement on Line 13 uses the `array_view::synchronize` method to insure the underlying host data structure is updated with any changes. This is also discussed in the next section. This operation is not needed if the host accesses the data through the array view `CV` but is needed to reliably access through the host pointer `C`. The central purpose of the `array_view` is to allow coherent access to data from both host and accelerator without need for explicit synchronization or data copies.

Fig. D.3 is a more complex example borrowed from Chapter 12, Parallel patterns: graph search. It performs a calculation on a slice of a three-dimensional data structure. We use it to illustrate the handing of higher-dimensional `array_view` objects and compute domains. The function interface is essentially identical to the source where the CUDA `dim3` type is replaced with a C++ AMP `extent<3>` for the `grid` parameter. The contiguous data pointed to by `energygrid` is overlaid with a three-dimensional `array_view` (named `energygrid_view`). C++ AMP follows a row-major storage layout so higher-numbered dimensions are less significant in the linear storage order. C++ AMP has mechanisms to create an `array_view` that is a section of another `array_view` and also to project down to select a lower-dimensional slice. This operation is used on Line 6 to select the portion of the data actually defined by the kernel. As above, we use the `discard_data` method to avoid copying

```
#include <amp_math.h>
void cenergy_2(float * energygrid, extent<3> grid,
               float gridspacing, float z, int k,
               const float * atoms, int numatoms) {
    array_view<float,3> energygrid_view(grid, energygrid);
    array_view<float,2> energy_slice = energygrid_view(k);
    energy_slice.discard_data();
    array_view<const float,2> atom_view(numatoms,4,atoms);
    parallel_for_each(energy_slice.extent, [=](index<2> ji)
    restrict(amp) {
        float y = gridspacing * float(ji[0]);
        float x = gridspacing * float(ji[1]);
        float energy = 0.0f;
        for(int n =0; n < numatoms; n++) {
            float dx = x - atom_view(n,0);
            float dy = y - atom_view(n,1);
            float dz = z - atom_view(n,2);
            energy + = atom_view(n,3)/
                        precise_math::sqrtf(dx*dx + dy*dy+dz*dz);
        }
        energy_slice[ji] = energy;
    });
    energy_slice.synchronize();
}
```

FIGURE D.3

Base Coulomb potential calculation.

the immaterial existing values to the GPU. We overlay the atoms data with the 2-d array_view named atom_view to simplify the expression of the accesses. This does not fundamentally change how the actual addressing arithmetic is performed but seems to model the problem more accurately.

The data-parallel computation is then over the extent of the slice where the original sequential loop indices j and i are translated into the index<2> ji. Except for the indexing of atom_view, and the indexing into energy_slice, the body of the loop is largely unchanged.

C++ AMP provides a set of basic math operations for use in restrict(amp) contexts. These functions are accessed by includingamp_math.h (which is not shown). The concurrency::fast_math and concurrency::precise_math names spaces respectively declare faster and more precise versions of functions. In the example, we chose to use precise_math::sqrtf for illustration. In restrict(cpu) code, both of these name spaces establish aliases to std:: implementations of these functions so a function that is declared restrict(cpu,amp) can still reference math functions and get the best implementation for the target.

To summarize this section, the core C++ AMP concepts include: an array_view which provides a multidimensional view into rectangular data; an extent which is the shape of such a view and also the shape of a data-parallel computation; an index which is used to select elements of an array_view or a data-parallel computation, the `parallel_for_each` which launches a data-parallel computation; and `restrict(amp)` modified functions which are evaluated at each point in that computation.

D.2 DETAILS OF THE C++ AMP EXECUTION MODEL

The core C++ AMP features above focus on expressing data-parallelism essentially as concurrent invocation of a collection of threads that access multidimensional arrays of data. Many accelerators today run in a separate memory and cannot directly access host data. Furthermore, these accelerators run concurrently with the continuing execution of host code. While minimizing the impact of these concerns, these aspects are part of the execution model of C++ AMP.

EXPLICIT AND IMPLICIT DATA COPIES

C++ AMP provides the class template `array` to allocate storage on an accelerator. Similar to an `array_view` and with a nearly identical interface, an `array` has element type and rank template parameters. The constructor includes extent information. Unlike an `array_view`, an `array` allocates new storage on an accelerator. The data elements of an array may only be accessed from that accelerator and all operations that copy data between an array and host memory are explicit.

To illustrate this, consider Fig. D.4 which rewrites Fig. D.2 to use explicit array operations. Each `array_view` is replaced with an `array` declaration of the same extent. Lines 5 and 6 show explicit copies from host data to an `array` using the C++ AMP `copy` function template. The lambda is changed slightly to capture `array` variables by reference rather than default by-value as in the other examples. C++ AMP `array` objects must be captured by reference, while `array_view` objects must be captured by value for the lambda used in a `parallel_for_each`. Line 12 specifies the data to be copied back to the host after completion of the computation.

```
1  void vecAdd(float* A, float* B, float* C, int n)
2  {
3      array<float,1> AA(n), BA(n);
4      array<float,1> CA(n);
5      copy(A,AA);
6      copy(B,BA);
7      parallel_for_each(CA.extent,
8                [&AA,&BA,&CA](index<1> i) restrict(amp)
9      {
10         CA[i] = AA[i] + BA[i];
11     });
12     copy(CA,C);
13 }
```

FIGURE D.4

Explicit memory and copy management.

On an accelerator that cannot access host memory, all of the operations in Fig. D.4 also happen for the code in Fig. D.2 but they are performed transparently either when the `parallel_for_each` is launched or when `array_view::synchronize` is called. The intended use of the explicit mechanisms is to provide more control of memory management and allow copy operations to be initiated earlier and overlapped with other computations (although overlapped copies can be achieved through other means).

When an `array_view` overlays storage on the host but is accessed on the accelerator, the data is copied to an unnamed `array` on that accelerator and the access is made to that `array`. This copy of the host data may persist for the remainder of the lifetime of the `array_view`. This allows the C++ AMP runtime to avoid redundant copies of the same data to the accelerator. C++ AMP provides operations to influence how and when data is copied between these implicit copies and the source storage. Line 8 of Fig. D.2 shows the use of `array_view::discard_data`. This method is an assertion that the values stored in the host storage are immaterial, for example because they are about to be overwritten. The effect of this assertion is that when the `array_view` is subsequently used in a `parallel_for_each`, no copy is performed from the source data to the implicit `array` created for accelerator access.

When an unnamed array is created to hold a copy of data associated with an `array_view`, and that array may be modified, the C++ AMP runtime system is permitted to copy the values back to the host storage immediately or leave them on the accelerator. If the `array_view` is destructed or an element is accessed on the host, then values will be copied promptly to make sure host accesses get the most recent definition. The method `array_view::synchronize` is available to force any such copies to be performed by a particular program point. The method `array_view::refresh` indicates to the C++ AMP runtime that all cached copies of the host data should be discarded. Generally this method would be used when the underlying host data is modified directly without accessing through the `array_view`. This coherence between implicit cached copies and the underlying host data is the responsibility of the programmer.

An `array_view` may also refer to an `array`. This allows data allocated on an accelerator to be accessed by the host. Again, where necessary, this may involve creating copies of the data that are accessible by the host. The copies of data values between the source storage on the accelerator and the copies on the host are controlled using the same mechanisms and functions as above.

ASYNCHRONOUS OPERATION

Most C++ AMP operations that initiate work on an accelerator, including operations to copy data to the accelerator are *asynchronous*. This means that the host operation returns and the host thread continues to the next statement before the work completes. We illustrate this in Fig. D.5 which shows three strands of concurrent activity where time logically flows from the top to the bottom of the figure. On the left is the sequence of host operations that initiate accelerator operations. In the middle, we indicate three copy operations that take some duration each. On the right, we show the actual data-parallel computation which begins after the two copies to the accelerator complete and finishes before the final copy back to the host begins. On the host, the final copy-out is called before the data is ready and that operation blocks until the copy completes. When it returns, the `return` statement executes and the function returns with updated host data.

To provide finer-grain notification on which operation on the accelerator complete, C++ AMP provides the `completion_future` class. This class that is analogous to `std::shared_future`, the C++ standard method for coordination with asynchronous operations. In particular it provides the `completion_future::get` method which blocks the calling thread until the asynchronous operation completes. C++ AMP has variants of methods discussed above that are nonblocking and return a `completion_future`. In particular there are `array_view::synchronize_async` and various overloads of `copy_async`. These will initiate the data transfer implied and return a synchronization object immediately rather than blocking the thread until the operation has completed. Fig. D.6 provides a simple illustration where we assume

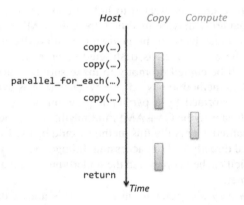

FIGURE D.5

Concurrent host/accelerator execution.

```
1 parallel_for_each(CV.extent, [=](index<1> i) restrict(amp)
2 {
3         CV[i] = AV[i] + BV[i];
4 });
5 completion_future done = CV.synchronize_async();
6 otherProcessing(A,B);
7 done.get();
```

FIGURE D.6

Overlapped accelerator and host processing.

that following the vector add computation there is some other computation involving the unmodified host data A and B. Upon completion of that other processing, the host then waits for the results from the `parallel_for_each` to be available on the host by using the `completion_future::get` call on the object returned from the `array_view::synchronize_async` method. After the `get` call returns, the host vector C will hold the results.

As discussed in Chapter 2, Data parallel computing, CUDA has an explicit notion of "global" memory which is accessible by all threads in a kernel. In C++ AMP this concept is only available by having `array` objects associated with an accelerator. C++ AMP does not provide a facility for having file-scope objects accessible by functions running on the accelerator the way CUDA interprets __device__ as a qualification on file-scope object declarations. Similarly, C++ AMP does not expose a concept of constant memory, although values captured in the top-level lambda passed to a `parallel_for_each` may be stored in constant memory. The differences between CUDA and C++ AMP represent conscience design choices for C++ AMP to simplify the programming model. Some elements of CUDA reflect specifics of current GPU architectures that are not necessarily present in other forms of accelerators or may be significantly less common in the future. C++ AMP chose to leave these as implementation details rather than part of the model.

SECTION SUMMARY

In this section we have discussed the features of C++ AMP that support a discrete accelerator that does not share memory with the host and runs concurrently with host computations. The key features are the `array` data container, explicit `copy` operations, and explicit asynchronous work mechanisms. We also indicated when and where such copies are made when the more flexible `array_view` is used when targeting discrete accelerators. We discussed the relationship of CUDA memory types with that of C++ AMP.

D.3 MANAGING ACCELERATORS

A computer system may include multiple accelerators suitable for implementing C++ AMP data-parallel computations. This includes both specialized hardware accelerators such as GPUs and simply the use of multicore CPUs with SIMD instructions. A system may also have multiple GPUs that may or may not have similar hardware characteristics. C++ AMP has mechanisms to enumerate available accelerators and to manage how work is mapped to those accelerators.

The class `accelerator` is the C++ AMP abstraction used for a specific mechanism for implementing data-parallelism. As shown in Fig. D.7, the `accelerator::get_all` static method returns a vector of available accelerators in the system. A few properties associated with each accelerator may be used to select one when special requirements are required. For example, support of double precision data types is an optional

```
1  accelerator find_accelerator() {
2      vector<accelerator> accs = accelerator::get_all();
3      auto result =
4          find_if(accs.begin(), accs.end(), [](const accelerator& acc)
5          {
6              return acc.supports_double_precision &&
7                     !acc.has_display;
8          });
9      if(result == accs.end())
10         throw std::string("No suitable accelerator found");
11     return *result;
12 }
```

FIGURE D.7

Example of finding an accelerator.

feature. For compute intensive applications, it may be desirable to avoid placing work on the GPU that is used to drive an interactive display. Other properties include the amount of memory dedicated to the accelerator (accelerator::dedicated_memory) and a std::wstring that uniquely identifies the device (accelerator::device_path). The example uses the STL std::find algorithm to capture this search.

In addition to finding a specific accelerator, a system may support multiple suitable accelerators. C++ AMP enables off-loading work from one or more host threads to multiple accelerators. All such accelerator instances are returned by the call to accelerator::get_all and they may be used concurrently by an application.

In C++ AMP, an accelerator_view is an object which refers to a specific underlying accelerator and can be used to specify that accelerator for the purpose of indicating where an array is allocated and where work for a particular parallel_for_each should be executed. Similar to a CUDA stream (cudaStream_t), various operations performed against a particular accelerator_view are performed in order but operations on different accelerator_views have no defined order.

In C++ AMP there is a default accelerator which is automatically selected by the runtime but can be explicitly set using the accelerator::set_default static method which takes a device path string parameter. Each accelerator has a default accelerator_view (accelerator::default_view). The default view of the default accelerator is used for allocating an array when none is specified. A parallel_for_each may also have an explicit accelerator_view. Fig. D.8 is a variant of the vector add sample that makes use of defaults explicit. It is not necessary to use explicit arrays to direct work using an accelerator_view. Even when all data is accessed with array_view objects that overlay host data, a parallel_for_each may have an explicit accelerator_view indicating where the work should be performed.

Fig. D.9 is another illustration of explicit use of an accelerator_view. Here we provide a modified vector add operation which is parameterized by an accelerator_view that identifies where the work should be performed. The function determines the memory available on the accelerator, converted from kilobytes to bytes and

```
1    void vecAdd (float* A, float* B, float* C, intn)
2    {
3            accelerator acc;
4            accelerator_view view(acc.default_view);
5            array<float,1> AA(n,view), BA(n,view);
6            array<float,1> CA(n,view);
7            copy(A,AA);
8            copy(B,BA);
9            parallel_for_each(view, CA.extent,
10                   [&AA,&BA,&CA](index<1> i) restrict(amp)
11           {
12               CA[i] = AA[i] + BA[i];
13           });
14           copy(CA,C);
15   }
```

FIGURE D.8

Explicit accelerator use.

```
1    using std::vector;
2    void vecAddLong(float *A, float *B, float *C, int n,
3                    accelerator_view acc)
4    {
5        int block = (acc.accelerator.dedicated_memory * 1024)
6                         /(3*sizeof(float));
7        vector<completion_future> results;
8        for(int i = 0; i < n; i += block) {
9            int m = min(n-i,block);
10           array_view<const float,1> AV(m,A+i), BV(m,B+i);
11           array_view<float,1> CV(m,C+i);
12           CV.discard_data();
13           parallel_for_each(acc, CV.extent, [=](index<1> idx) restrict(amp)
14           {
15               CV[idx] = AV[idx] + BV[idx];
16           });
17           results.push_back(CV.synchronize_async());
18       }
19       std::for_each(results.begin(), results.end(),
20                    [](completion_future f) { f.get(); });
21   }
```

FIGURE D.9

Explicit accelerator with asynchronous transfers.

used to determine the largest block size (block) where three blocks may be stored concurrently. Line 8 then loops over the input vectors in chunks of this size. For each chunk, a computation is launched as was done in Fig. D.2 but here the accelerator is explicitly specified by the first parameter, acc, to the parallel_for_each. On Line 17, we initiate an asynchronous transfer of the results back to the host data structure. The completion_future returned by this operation is moved into a vector of such results. After all operations are started, Lines 19 and 20 iterate over the `vector` of results using C++ STL methods and wait for each one to complete by calling the `get` method before the function returns to the caller.

D.4 TILED EXECUTION

This section touches on a topic important for some scenarios. We discuss a "tiled" version of data parallelism and the additional tools for optimizing memory available in that model.

As described above, a data-parallel computation has an associated computational domain defined by a C++ AMP `extent` object. A computational domain of rank 3 or less may also be blocked into regular, rectangular subdomains called *tiles*. The widths of these tiles must be compile-time constants. The threads that are associated with the same tile may share variables and participate in barrier synchronization. In CUDA, the term *block* is used to describe these groups of threads. A new storage class is also added to C++ AMP, `tile_static`, to indicate a variable that has a single instance per-tile which is shared by all threads (in CUDA this is indicated with the `__shared__` keyword). Chapter 4, Memory and data locality, discusses the motivation for using tiling and tile-shared variables to optimize memory bandwidth. Objects with this storage class may only be accessed in `restrict(amp)` code.

We illustrate tiling as was done in Chapter 4, Memory and data locality, by using matrix multiplication. Fig. 4.12 shows a CUDA kernel which we expand into a host function (Fig. D.10) containing the kernel as well assuming host pointers are used to refer to dense arrays following the interface from Chapter 4, Memory and data locality. As before, we overlay `array_view` objects on top of the host data and discard the output data that is about to be overwritten so it is not copied to the accelerator.

A `tiled_extent` is a form of `extent` that captures tile dimensions as template parameters. C++ AMP only supports tiling for 1, 2, and 3 dimensions and the rank of a `tiled_extent` object is inferred from the number of tile dimensions specified. In this case, the `tiled_extent` has rank 2 (Line 6).

The `parallel_for_each` method has an overload for `tiled_extents`. The structure is the same as before and the lambda function will be invoked once for each element in the compute domain. C++ AMP requires that the extent of the compute domain must be evenly divisible by the tile size. In this example, `Width` must be multiples of `TILE_WIDTH`. When this condition is not met a runtime exception is thrown.

In the case of a `parallel_for_each` for a `tiled_extent`, the parameter to the lambda must be a `tiled_index` instead of an `index`. The `tiled_index` is a class template where again the tile sizes are captured as template parameters. The `tiled_index` (t_idx in the figure) provides both a mapping for each thread into the compute domain (t_idx.global) as well as the relative position of a thread within its tile (t_idx.local).

```
1   void MatrixMul(float * M, float * N, float *P, int Width) {
2       extent<2> dims(Width,Width);
3       array_view<const float,2> d_M(dims,M), d_N(dims,N);
4       array_view<float,2> d_P(dims,P);
5       d_P.discard_data();
6       tiled_extent<TILE_WIDTH,TILE_WIDTH> tiled(dims);
7       parallel_for_each(tiled,
8           [=](tiled_index<TILE_WIDTH,TILE_WIDTH> t_idx) restrict(amp){
9               tile_static float Mds[TILE_WIDTH][TILE_WIDTH];
10              tile_static float Nds[TILE_WIDTH][TILE_WIDTH];
11              int tx  = t_idx.local[0],  ty  = t_idx.local[1];
12              int Row = t_idx.global[0], Col = t_idx.global[1];
13              float Pvalue = 0;
14              for (int m = 0; m < Width/TILE_WIDTH; ++m) {
15                  Mds[tx][ty] = d_M(m*TILE_WIDTH+tx, Row);
16                  Nds[tx][ty] = d_N(Col, m*TILE_WIDTH+ty);
17                  t_idx.barrier.wait();
18                  for(int k = 0; k < TILE_WIDTH; k++)
19                      Pvalue += Mds[tx][k] * Mds[k][ty];
20                  t_idx.barrier.wait();
21              }
22              d_P(Row,Col) = Pvalue;
23      });
24      d_P.synchronize();
25  }
```

FIGURE D.10

Tiled matrix multiplication.

Line 9 declares a `tile_static` array named `Mds` which is shared by all threads in a tile. It will hold a copy of the values in `M` that are needed to perform a subblock matrix multiple computation for all of the threads in the tile. Similarly Line 10 declares analogous `Nds` to hold subblocks of `N`.

As in Fig. 4.12, the loop on Fig. D.10, Line 14 multiples a block-row times a block column in tile-size chunks. The variable `Width` is used uniformly by all threads and is captured from the containing function scope for reuse in the lambda automatically. The threads in the tile cooperatively copy blocks of `M` and `N` into `tile_static` storage. Line 17 is the barrier synchronization point where all threads in the tile wait for the stores into shared variables to complete. A second barrier on Line 20 makes sure all of the reads from shared variables are completed before writes on the next iteration begin. In C++ AMP, the object of type `tile_index` includes a `tile_barrier` object as a data member and that object provides methods to perform barriers. C++ AMP provides different forms of barriers which indicate whether the barrier applies to just `tile_static` data, applies to global data, or both. Here we only need to protect `tile_static` data and so could use `wait_with_tile_static_memory_fence` but chose to use the `wait` method to match the source from Chapter 4, Memory and data locality.

Fig. D.11 illustrates some details of C++ AMP tiling. It shows a 20 by 20 compute domain as a grid of small squares and the variable e im the code fragment. Rows (dimension 0) are shown as numbered from top to bottom and columns (dimension 1) from left to right. This domain might be blocked into 8× 8 tiles. These tiles are illustrated with the larger black squares and the variable te or alternately the variable te2 which shows the extent::tile method template for creating a tiled_extent. We also illustrate the use of C++ 11 auto keyword to infer types of variables from their initializers.

Note that the tile size in this example does not evenly divide the dimensions of the compute domain. A tiled parallel_for_each requires the extent be a multiple of the tile size in each dimension and the developer must explicitly handle the boundary cases when this is not the case. The tiled_extent class template provides methods to either pad or truncate the underlying extent. In the example variable pte corresponds to the padded exetent, extent<2>(24,24), while the variable tte corresponds to the truncated extent, extent<2>(16,16).

The tiled_index parameter supports a variety of members to facilitate tiled computations. The global member is an index<2> holding the position in the underlying compute domain. The solid red square in the figure cooresponds to position (9,6) in the compute domain. The set of tiles (large squares) forms a domain, extent<2>(3,3) in this case, which is returned by the tile_extent member. The tile member is an index<2> holding the position of a point projected into this domain. The highlighted point (9,6) is in tile (1,0). The light blue square is the first element in each dimension in the same tile as point (9,6). This is available as tile_origin and in this example corresponds to the global index (8,0). Finally, the points within a tile can be thought of as a small domain and the local member returns the position in this space (1,6) formed basically by subtracting tile_origin from global.

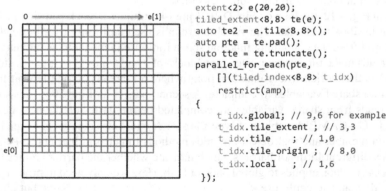

FIGURE D.11

Illustration of tiling 20× 20 compute domain.

D.5 C++ AMP GRAPHICS FEATURES

The primary motivation for C++ AMP is to support data-parallelism as an important algorithm pattern for general computing. Rendering and imaging processing are very important mainstream workloads for which C++ AMP includes some more specialized support which is discussed briefly in this section. These facilities include: normalized floating points, short vector types, textures, and—optionally on Microsoft platforms—interoperations with DirectX. Many of these features are segregated into a separate namespace, `concurrency::graphics`. Fig. D.12 illustrates some of the types defined in that namespace and discussed in this section.

C++ AMP provides two types, `norm`, and `unorm`, which provide arithmetic that is floating point in nature but of bounded range. The `norm` type holds signed values with magnitude no more than one while `unorm` type holds nonnegative values with magnitude no more than one. Common arithmetic operations are defined on these types where result values that would exceed the range are forced to the extreme value ("clamped"). These types may be mixed with C++ types and convert to `float`. They may also be used as element types for C++ AMP composite types `array`, `array_view`, and the `texture` objects described below.

Graphics programs frequently manipulate short vectors of primitive types. C++ AMP supports graphics programming by including definitions of these. For C++ AMP types, `int`, `unsigned int` (as `uint`), `float`, `double`, `norm`, and `unorm`, and for each vector length 2, 3, and 4, there exist types such as `int_2`, `unit_3`, and `float_4`. Each of these holds a number of component values that are accessed by name. The names supported are x, y, z, and w or alternately r, g, b, and w. Thus, given the

```
1  #include <amp_graphics.h>
2  using namespace graphics;
3  ...
4          norm n;           // normalized types
5          unorm u;
6          float_2 f2;
7          float_4 f4;       // short vector types;
8          int_2 i2;
9          norm_2 n2;
10         f2 = f4.xy + i2.x*f4.zw;
11         // usable in arrays, array_views
12         extent<2> e(1024,1024);
13         array<norm_2,2> an2(e);
14         // and in textures
15         texture<unorm_4,2> tu2(e, data, e.size() * 16U, 16U);
16         writeonly_texture_view<unorm_4,2> wotv(tu2);
```

FIGURE D.12

Examples of type from `concurrency::graphics`.

declarations in Fig. D.10, we might access a component `f4.z` which is a single float that can be used as either an rvalue or an lvalue. Certain compound patterns are also supported such as `f4.xy` corresponds to a short vector of suitable length, `float_2` in this case, that may be used as either rvalue or lvalue. Assignment and arithmetic on short vectors is done in a component-wise style with scalar arguments promoted to vectors with that value in each component.

A `texture` is a special form of array that allows data-parallel code to access values that are stored using reduced precision. This is common representation for image data and is the only method in the first version of C++ AMP to access partial word data types in an `restrict(amp)` context. Like an `array`, a `texture` is a class template that is parameterized by an element type and a rank. The set of allowed element types is constrained to be a subset of the `restrict(amp)` compatible primitive types and their short vector variants.

When a `texture` is constructed, in addition to the extent and a data source, a final unsigned integer argument indicates the number of bits per primitive data value used to store the value. Line 15 shows an example texture with a four-wide vector of unsigned normalized floating point values. The `16U` passed to the constructor indicates each of these values is stored with only 16-bits of information. Not all combinations of data type, vector length, and storage width are supported (details in the specification listed in the references below).

A texture is a storage container like an `array` and may be associated with a particular `accelerator_view`. A texture is also indexed like an `array` with overloads of the index operator with an `index` instance of suitable rank as a parameter. As for `array`, these operations are `restrict(amp)` and may not be used in host code. Overloads of the function template `copy` support transfers to and from host data structures.

A subset of textures may be written to directly and this is done explicitly via a `texture::set` method. For texture formats for which writing is not directly supported by hardware accelerators, C++ AMP provides the `writeonly_texture_view` class template illustrated with the variable named `wotv` (Line 16). These are analogous to `array_view` objects but only overlay `texture` data. The `set` method on this object may be used in a `restrict(amp)` context that is defining values in a texture.

Beyond support for these types, C++ AMP on Microsoft platforms includes specific features to enable interoperation with the DirectX framework. These interfaces are in the `graphics::direct3d` namespace. This includes the following capabilities:

- Treating an existing Direct3D device interface pointer as a C++ AMP `acclerator_view`.
- Treating an existing Direct3D buffer interface pointer as a C++ AMP `array`.
- Treating an existing Direct3D texture interface pointer as a C++ AMP `texture`.

These capabilities allow C++ AMP to provide a C++ language solution for GPU compute scenarios that integrates smoothly with the DirectX rendering framework.

```
1  struct Vertex2D { float_2 Pos; };
2  IUnknown * my_rotate(ID3D11Device* d3ddevice, float THETA,
3                       int num_elements, const float_2 * data)
4  {
5      // copy data into a DX buffer
6      accelerator_view acc = create_accelerator_view(d3ddevice);
7      array<Vertex2D,1> vertices(num_elements, data, acc);
8      parallel_for_each(vertices.extent,
9                        [=, &vertices] (index<1> idx) restrict(amp) {
10         // Rotate the vertex by angle THETA
11         float_2 pos = vertices[idx].Pos;
12         vertices[idx].Pos.y = pos.y * cos(THETA) - pos.x * sin(THETA);
13         vertices[idx].Pos.x = pos.y * sin(THETA) + pos.x * cos(THETA);
14      });
15     // return the DX buffer use of transformed data.
16     return get_buffer(vertices);
17 }
```

FIGURE D.13

Examples DirectX interop—rotate vertex list.

Fig. D.13 illustrates the interop features. Function `my_rotate` consumes a vector of vertex data which is located on the host. Parameter `d3ddevice` is the existing DirectX interface which is used to first construct an `accelerator_view` and then an `array`. The `parallel_for_each` performs a rotation of the vertices where the result is left on the accelerator. Since the `array` instance `vertices` is located on a particular `accelerator_view`, the `parallel_for_each` will be executed on that same `accelerator_view`. We extract the underlying buffer object (typed only as `IUnknown`) and return this to the caller for subsequent use in scene rendering.

D.6 SUMMARY

This appendix has presented an overview of C++ AMP, a small extension to C++ 11 to support hardware acceleration of data-parallel computations. The discussion is not complete but the full specification is available at the URL listed in the references. The focus of C++ AMP is to create features that integrate well into modern C++ and leverage features such as templates, lambdas, and futures to provide a highly-productive set of abstractions that compose with other aspects of C++ and parallelism. The features are layered to allow use by a very broad set of developers with limited knowledge of computer architecture, as well as providing access to the rich execution model needed for the most performance-critical scenarios. Lowering the barrier to expressing data-parallelism and ensuring portability across hardware platforms will help more applications deliver the benefits of hardware acceleration and heterogeneous computing.

D.7 EXERCISES

1. Translate the simple, untiled version of matrix multiplication into C++ AMP. The CUDA kernel is shown in Fig. 4.7. Write a host-function that applies this computation to three `array_view<float,2>` inputs. Rather than implementing C = A*B, accumulate in the output and implement C += A*B.

2. Given an array view of rank 2, X, and `index<2>` ij, and `extent<2>` e, the operation X.section(ij,e) returns a new `array_view` which overlays the same data as X. If we denote this new view as S, then for all valid indices idx of S we have S[idx] is the same location as X[idx+ij]. Assume now there are three `array_view<float,2>` objects, A, B, and C. Assume they will not fit simultaneously in the `dedicated_memory` of the `accelerator` in the system. Use the `array_view::section` method, explicit array objects, and the matrix multiply building block from the first exercise, to implement matrix multiplication for the large arrays.

3. Assume the `std::vector gpu` holds two elements of type `accelerator_view` that refer to different but similar GPUs in a system. Modify the solution to Exercise D.3 to use both accelerators to implement the work.

4. Translate the tiled version of matrix transpose from Exercise 3.2 into C++ AMP.

5. The inner loop in Fig. D.3 redundantly loads data through `atom_view` that is used in multiple threads and these references are not coalesced (see Section 5.2). Rewrite the function in Fig. D.3 to use `tile_static` memory to improve the memory efficiency for accessing the data in `atom_view`.

REFERENCE

C++ AMP Open Specification. <http://blogs.msdn.com/b/nativeconcurrency/archive/2012/02/03/c-amp-open-spec-published.aspx>.

Index

Note: Page numbers followed by "*b*", "*f*" and "*t*" refer to boxes, figures, and tables, respectively.

A

Abrupt underflow convention, 137
Abstraction, 484–486
  memory bandwidth of filling kernels, 485*t*
  programmer productivity, 484
  real-world performance, 485–486
  robustness, 484
Accelerator, 517
  device, 414
  management, 525–528, 526*f*
Accelerator, class, 525–526
Accelerator::set_default static method, 526
Accelerator_view, C++ AMP, 526
AddVecKernel function, 36, 120
Adjacency matrix, 258
  representation of simple graph, 259*f*
  sparse matrix representation of, 259*f*
Adjacent synchronization, 193
Algorithm, 153–156
  considerations, 140–142
  selection, 374–379
ALU. *See* Arithmetic and logic unit (ALU)
AMD Opteron family, 1
Amdahl's law, 10, 373–374
ANSI C code, 23, 34–36
ANSI C standard, 49
AoS. *See* Array of Structures (AoS)
APIs. *See* Application programming interfaces (APIs)
Apodization filtering function, 306
Application programming interfaces (APIs), 6, 19–20
  communication functions, 388
Applications software, 2
Arithmetic accuracy, 139–140
Arithmetic and logic unit (ALU), 78–80
Arithmetic instructions, 78–80
Array data layout
  column-major layout, 50–51
  row major layout, 50–51, 50*f*, 168*f*
Array of structs, 322
Array of Structures (AoS), 488
Array_view, 517–518, 521–523
Asynchronous, 405, 409
  async and wait, 434*f*
  computation and data, 434–435
  data transfers, 504–508

operation, 523–525, 524*f*
  pipelining with async and wait, 435*f*
Atomic operations, 202–205, 334–335
  atomic operation in cache memory, 210
  CUDA kernel for calculation histogram, 206*f*
  in Fermi GPU, 452–453
  intrinsic functions, 205*b*
  race condition, 203*f*, 204*f*
  strategy I for parallelizing histogram
    computation, 202*f*
  throughput of, 207–209
Atomic operations, enhanced, 452–453
Audio digital signal processing, 150
Auto clause, 425

B

Backward convolution, 353
Backward substitution, 143
Bank conflict, 114
Barrier synchronizations, 58, 117, 404–405,
    407–408
  execution timing of, 59*f*
  syncthreads() points, 59
Barrier__syncthreads(), 93
Basic Linear Algebra Subprograms (BLAS), 50–51,
    73
Bezier curve
  calculation, 288–290, 301*f*
  linear, 288
  quadratic, 288
BFS. *See* Breadth-first search (BFS)
Bi-directional relations, 258
Big Data, 9–10, 200–201
Binning process, 377–378
BLAS. *See* Basic Linear Algebra Subprograms
    (BLAS)
Block partitioning, 206–207
Block-level queue, 268–270, 269*f*
blockDim variable, 33–34
  blockDim.x variable, 33–36
blockDim.x, 33–36
  gridDim.x threads, 51, 207
BlockIdx variable, 34
BlockIdx.x, 34–36
Bottlenecks, 103
Boundary checks, 94–96

P

Printed in the United States
By Bookmasters